Fodo

COMPLETE GUIDE
TO AFRICAN
SAFARIS

Welcome to Your African Safari

African safaris produce unforgettable moments, whether a lion's powerful roar shakes your core, a hyena's maniacal laugh tingles your spine, or a mountain gorilla's piercing gaze freezes you in your tracks. These singular events hold you in thrall and profoundly connect you to your environment. And what environments they are: the golden plains of the Serengeti, the pristine waterways of the Okavango Delta, the star-shaped sand dunes of the Namibian desert. Africa's varied landscapes stage nature's most spectacular wonders, and a safari is your front-row seat.

TOP REASONS TO GO

★ **Accommodations:** Supremely comfortable lodges and camps surrounded by wilderness.

★ **Parks and Reserves:** Africa's protected areas are home to the most animals on earth.

★ **Village Visits:** Fascinating tours of Himba, Maasai, Zulu, and other local communities.

★ **Beaches:** Coastal towns such as Zanzibar and Mombasa have beautiful shores.

★ **Epic Landscapes:** Mt. Kilimanjaro, Victoria Falls, the Bwindi rainforest, and more.

★ **Adventure:** Walking safaris, balloon flights, and camel treks are thrilling journeys.

Contents

MAPS

Fodor's Features

EXPERIENCE AN AFRICAN SAFARI

25 ULTIMATE EXPERIENCES

African safaris offer terrific experiences that should be on every traveler's list. Here are Fodor's top picks for a memorable trip.

1 Rise over vast plains or deserts in a hot-air balloon

Take game-viewing to new heights on a hot-air balloon ride and watch the sun bathe the sky and landscapes at sunrise. The most popular rides are over Kenya's Masai Mara, Tanzania's Serengeti, and the Namib Desert in Namibia. (Ch. 3, 4, 9)

2 Trek to meet mountain gorillas in Uganda or Rwanda

Groups of habituated mountain gorillas can be visited on treks at Bwindi Impenetrable National Park, Mgahinga Gorilla National Park, and Volcanoes National Park. (Ch. 6, 7)

3 Watch the Great Migration cross the Mara River

A dramatic safari highlight during the Great Migration is when wildebeest, zebra, and smaller antelope cross the turbulent Mara River in search of fresh grazing. (Ch. 3, 4)

4 Trek to the "roof of Africa" on Mt. Kilimanjaro

The round-trip trek to the summit of Kilimanjaro, Africa's highest mountain, takes five to nine days depending on the route; it's a popular addition to any East African safari. (Ch. 4)

5 Walk on the wild side

You hear, smell, and see the little things rarely experienced from a vehicle on a walking safari. Guides point out plants, trees, insects, birds, and spoor (tracks), and encountering big game on foot is highly exciting.

6 Climb giant sand dunes in the Namib Desert

Considered Earth's oldest desert, the Namib gives rise to some of the planet's tallest dunes; the highest is Big Daddy (325 meters [1,066 feet]). Don't miss scrambling to the top to watch the sunrise. (Ch. 9)

7 Scuba dive or snorkel in the Indian Ocean

The crystal clear Indian Ocean, which flanks the gorgeous white-sand beaches of coastal Kenya and Tanzania, has excellent scuba diving and snorkeling on the fringing coral reefs. (Ch. 3, 4)

8 Drift through the Okavango Delta on a mokoro

There's no better way to explore Botswana's magical Okavango Delta than by traditional mokoro (dugout canoe), propelled gently along by a poler standing at the rear. (Ch. 8)

9 Learn from the Maasai, Samburu, and other local guides

Many guides in Kenya, and some in Tanzania, are members of local tribes, who have expert wildlife knowledge and a deep understanding and affinity with the bush. (Ch. 3, 4)

10 Ride among game on a horseback safari

This is a great way to get close to wildlife in a quiet, unobtrusive way, as antelope, giraffe, zebra, wildebeest, elephant, and buffalo, simply see horses as other four-legged creatures.

11 Be awed by Tanzania's Ngorongoro Crater

Often called Africa's Eden, the world's largest intact caldera is a highlight for safari-goers as its open grasslands, sturdy woodlands, and freshwater lakes support immense concentrations of animals. (Ch. 4)

12 Take a photographic safari

Capturing high-quality images is a must for serious photographers, and operators are providing custom-built vehicles with unobstructed, elevated views, swivel chairs, camera mounts, and charging points.

13 Spy wildlife from a swimming pool

Yes, lolling by or even in the pool as wildlife strolls by is possible as many lodges boast well-designed pools that overlook the plains or a waterhole where animals come down to drink.

14 Experience "the smoke that thunders" of Victoria Falls

This spectacular sight is best seen from the spray-drenched rainforests of Victoria Falls National Park or Zambia's Mosi-oa-Tunya National Park. (Ch. 10)

15 Find the Big Five in Greater Kruger

The vast plains and wooded river valleys of Greater Kruger are best known for relatively easy and thrilling encounters with the magnificent Big Five. (Ch. 5)

16 Follow the herds on a mobile safari

With all the comforts of a lodge—lavish tents, flush toilets, hot showers, delicious food—mobile safaris are a great way to see the Great Migration; it's also popular in Botswana and Namibia. (Ch 3, 4, 8, 9)

17 Sleep outside in a star-bed

Perched on raised wooden platforms with sweeping views, these open-air bedrooms (complete with mosquito nets) are lit with candles and lanterns at night and beautiful sunrises in the morning.

18 Join an excursion with a conservationist or biologist

A resident biologist can share insights about animal behavior, while conservation safaris offer activities like game counts or tree planting which make your safari experience all the richer.

19 Explore Stone Town's intriguing alleyways

Historical mosques, imposing cathedrals, and grand 19th-century Arab houses with giant brass-studded wooden doors line the alleys. Now they are trendy restaurants, boutiques, and hotels. (Ch. 4)

20 Spot nocturnal species on a night drive

To view wildlife rarely seen during the day, set out from camp after dinner to explore. Guides (or trackers/spotters) use a powerful spotlight to search for glittering eyes in the bush like lions on the prowl.

21 Take a scenic flight by small plane, helicopter, or microlight

There's the "Flight of Angels" over Victoria Falls; helicopter rides over Botswana's Okavango Delta or Cape Town's Table Mountain; and air safaris over Namibia's magnificent dunes. (Ch. 5, 8, 9, 10)

22 Relax on a post-safari Kenyan beach escape

Easily reached by air from the safari destinations, the Kenyan coast has a sunny climate, bone-white sands, and turquoise water, which beg for a few days of relaxation. (Ch. 3)

23 Try bird-watching, or twitching, on game drives

While not on most people's must-see safari list, Africa is fabulous for birding; one can't help but be fascinated by the diversity of species, sizes, and colors. Guides can assist with identifying them and explaining their behavior.

24 Stargaze clear southern hemisphere night skies

Most safari lodges and camps are far from the pollution and ambient light of cities, which allows for a dizzying array of stars and Southern Hemisphere constellations to appear.

25 Watch cheetah stalk in the Serengeti's golden grasses

A perfect cheetah habitat, the Serengeti features open plains dotted with kopjes (granite outcrops) and an abundance of prey. Seeing one at full sprint is a memorable safari experience. (Ch. 4)

WHAT'S WHERE

1 Kenya. Expect golden lions, red-robed warriors, snowcapped mountains, pristine white beaches, and some of the world's most famous safari destinations—Masai Mara—and world-class beach destinations like Diani Beach and Lamu.

2 Tanzania. Some of Africa's greatest tourist attractions—the Serengeti, the Great Migration, Olduvai Gorge, Ngorongoro Crater, and Kilimanjaro—are here.

3 South Africa. At the very tip of Africa, you'll find many worlds in one: modern bustling cities, ancient rock art, gorgeous beaches, fabulous game lodges, well-run national parks, mountain ranges, desert, and Winelands. Popular safari destinations include Kruger, its adjoining private reserves, and the KwaZulu-Natal parks.

4 Rwanda. Trek mountain gorillas in Volcanoes National Park, visit Akagera National Park, Central Africa's largest protected wetland, and see Nyungwe National Park, home to Africa's largest mountain rainforest.

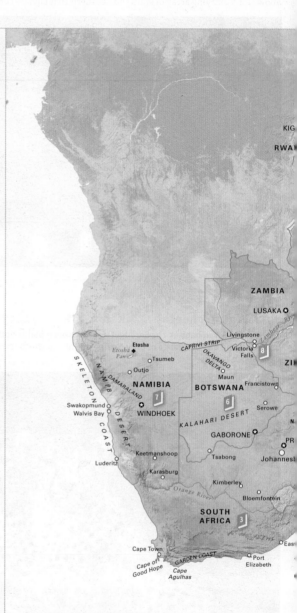

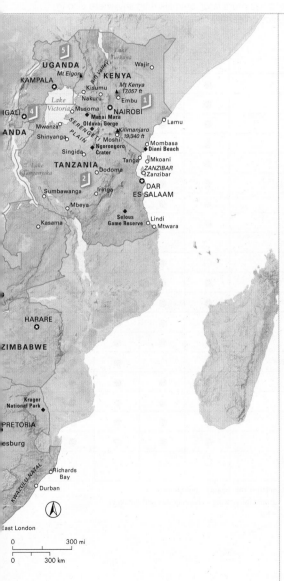

5 Uganda. Home to dense forests, snowcapped mountains, the Nile River, and 10 national parks including Bwindi Impenetrable National Park where more than half of the world's mountain gorillas live.

6 Botswana. From vast salt pans to the pristine waterways of the Okavango Delta, expect lots of game, few tourists, and stars brighter than you'll ever see.

7 Namibia. The Namib Desert, the fog-enshrouded Skeleton Coast, the great game park of Etosha, Damara-land's stark beauty: you've never been anywhere like Namibia.

8 Victoria Falls. Shared by Zambia and Zimbabwe, Vic Falls is one of the greatest natural wonders of the world. Africa's adventure center with everything from bungee jumping and white-water rafting to rappelling and jet skiing.

Finding the Big Five

The fauna that can be found on an African safari is as varied and vast as the continent's landscape. Africa has more large animals than anywhere else in the world and is the only place on earth where vast herds still roam the plains.

		African Buffalo	Elephant	Leopard	Lion	Rhino
BOTSWANA	The Okavango Delta	●	●	●	●	●
	Moremi Game Reserve	●	●	●	●	●
	Chobe Nat'l Park	●	●	●	●	●
	Kwando Reserve	●	●	●	●	○
KENYA	Masai Mara	●	●	●	●	●
	Amboseli Nat'l Park	●	●	●	●	●
	Tsavo Nat'l Park	●	●	●	●	●
	Laikipia Plateau	●	●	●	●	●
NAMIBIA	Namib-Naukluft Park*	○	○	◐	◐	○
	Damaraland	○	●	○	○	●
	Etosha Nat'l Park	●	●	●	●	●
SOUTH AFRICA	Kruger Nat'l Park	●	●	●	●	●
	Sabi Sand Game Reserve	●	●	●	●	●
	KwaZulu-Natal Parks	●	●	●	●	●
	Kgalagadi Transfrontier Park	○	○	●	●	○
TANZANIA	Serengeti Nat'l Park	●	●	●	●	●
	Ngorongoro Crater	●	●	●	●	●
	Lake Manyara Nat'l Park	●	●	●	●	○
	Selous Game Reserve	●	●	●	●	●
	Gombe Stream and Mahale Mountains Nat'l Parks**	○	○	○	○	○

*This park is noted for its stunning scenic beauty - not game
**These parks are primarily for primate viewing - chimpanzees and monkeys
KEY: ● = yes ◐ = Rarely ○ = No

Continued on page 32

There's nothing quite like the feeling of first setting eyes on one of the Big Five—buffalo, elephant, leopard, lion, and rhino—in the African bush. Being just a few feet from these majestic creatures is both terrifying and exhilarating, even for the most seasoned safari-goer.

THE BIG 5

The Big Five was originally a hunting term referring to those animals that posed the greatest risk to hunters on foot—buffalo, elephant, leopard, lion, and rhino. Today it has become one of the most important criteria used in evaluating a lodge or reserve, though it should never be your only criterion.

THE AFRICAN BUFFALO

Often referred to as the Cape buffalo, this is considered by many to be the most dangerous of the Big Five because of its unpredictability and speed. Do not confuse it with the docile Asian water buffalo, as the Cape buffalo is a more powerful and untameable beast with a massive build and short, strong legs. They have few predators other than human hunters and lions. It generally takes an entire lion pride to bring down an adult buffalo, although calves or weak and sick adults can be taken by wild dogs and spotted hyenas. Lions risk being mobbed by the herd when they do attack, and are sometimes trampled and gored.

Cape buffalo can reach up to 1,900 pounds and in the wild can live up to 15 or so years, much longer if they are in captivity. Never found very far from water, they are grazers and widespread throughout sub-Saharan Africa, especially in Kenya, Tanzania, Botswana, Zambia, Zimbabwe, and South Africa. Large, mixed herds can number up to a few hundred, and in the Serengeti, during the rains, in their thousands. You shouldn't fear a herd, but beware lone old males, which have mostly been thrown out of the herd and are now bad-tempered and volatile. Known as "Dagha Boys"—dagha is the clay mixture used for building traditional huts—they spend much of their days in mud wallows and are usually thickly coated in the stuff. While seemingly lethargic, these old boys can turn on a dime and charge like lightning. If you are charged, run for cover or climb the nearest tree.

THE ELEPHANT

The largest of the land animals, it once roamed the continent by the millions. Today, according to the World Wildlife Fund (WWF), the population is about 415,000; a quarter to a third of the population are forest elephants.

African elephants are divided into two species. Savannah elephants are the largest, at 13 feet and 7 tons, and can be found by lakes, marshes, or grasslands. Forest elephants have an average height of 10 feet and weight of 10,000 pounds. They're usually found in central and West African rainforests.

An elephant's gestation period is 22 months—the longest of any land animal. The average calf is 265 pounds. When calves are born, they are raised and protected by the entire herd—a group of about 10 females led by the oldest and largest. Males leave the herd after 15 years, often living with other males or alone.

When an elephant trumpets in a showy manner, head up and ears spread, it's a mock charge—frightening but not physically dangerous. If an elephant stomps the ground, holds its ears back and head forward, and issues a loud, high-pitched screech, this means real trouble. A charging elephant is extremely fast and surprisingly agile. If you're on foot make for the nearest big tree or embankment; elephants seldom negotiate these obstacles. If you're in a vehicle, hit the gas.

THE RHINO

There are two species of these massive primeval-looking animals in Africa: the black, or hook-lipped rhino, and the white, or square-lipped rhino. Both species have poor eyesight but excellent hearing, and because of their erratic tempers, they may sometimes charge without apparent reason.

These animals are surprisingly agile for their size. The white rhino is slighter taller (up to 60 inches at the shoulder) and heavier at over two tons, the black rhino is shorter and stockier by a few inches and can weigh up to one and a half tons. Although they share habitats, the white rhino is a grazer eating only grasses, the black, a browser, eating leaves and shrubs. The black rhino which is more aggressive than the white, prefers thick thornveld and dense vegetation, while the white sticks more to open grassland and the plains. Both love to wallow in mud. They mark their territory by means of defecating in individual middens, or dung heaps, which they make along rhino paths and territorial boundaries, regularly patrolling these 'signposts' on the look out for intruders.

The black rhino tends to be more solitary unless it is a very small mother/father/calf group; the white rhino stays together in small groups called crashes. Calves of both species stay with their mothers until they are four or five, when they leave to find a new territory.

Sadly, the survival of this incredible mammal is under serious threat from poaching, as rhino horn is traded on the black market in many Asian countries to cure a variety of ailments (an empty claim).

According to Save the Rhino, poaching increased rapidly from 2008 and hit a peak in 2015 when 1,349 were killed across the continent. Today, most rhino are protected in national parks, sanctuaries or reserves, often by heavily-armed guards, and there are major efforts by conservationists to try to stem the problem. But poaching continues in Kenya, Zimbabwe, and Namibia, and in South Africa (home to the majority of the world's rhino), 451 were lost in 2021.

THE LION

Known as the king of beasts—the Swahili word for lion, "simba," also means "king," "strong," and "aggressive"—this proud animal was once found throughout the world. Today, the majority of the estimated 20,000 lions are found in sub-Saharan Africa—a small population is also found in India—in grasslands, savannah, and dense bush.

Watching a lion stalk its prey can be one of the most exciting safari encounters. Females do most of the hunting, typically setting up a plan of attack, which is then carried out by the pride. Lionesses take turns hunting and this collective labor allows them to conserve their energy and survive longer in the bush. They are most active from dusk to dawn. A pride consists of between four and six adults but occasionally may go up to 20 or even 30. The males, identified by their gorgeous golden-red or black manes, are often brothers who behave territorially; their main task is to protect the females and the cubs. Typically, the females in the pride will give birth at approximately the same time, and the cubs will be raised together. Litters usually consist of two to three cubs that weigh about three pounds each. Sometimes, males that take over a pride will kill existing cubs so that they can sire their own with the lioness.

Lions can sleep for up to 18 hours a day. Lounging about in the grass, lions will often lick each other, rub heads, and play. But don't be fooled by their charms. When a lion moves, it can do so with awesome speed and power—a charging lion can cover 330 feet in four seconds. If you come face to face with a lion, never, ever turn your back and try to run—that is your death warrant. Your best bet is to stand as still as possible and try to outface the lion.

THE LEOPARD

Secretive, stealthy, and shrewd, the leopard is the most successful predator of all Africa's big cats. They are often difficult to spot on safari, primarily because they are nocturnal, but if you go on a night game drive your chances will increase tremendously.

Leopards can vary in appearance, their coat ranging from a light tawny hue in dry areas to darker shades in the forest. Their spots, called rosettes, are round in East Africa, but square in Southern Africa. Leopards can also be found in India, China, Siberia, and Korea. The female leopard, whose litter usually ranges from about one to three cubs, will keep her young hidden for about two months after birth, then feed and nurse them for an additional three months or so until her cubs are strong enough to roam with her. What about dad? Male leopards play no part in rearing the cubs.

In fact, the male is usually long gone by the time the female gives birth.

Most small to medium herbivores, large birds, rodents and primates, and smaller carnivores like servals and jackals, are fair game to leopards. Leopard use a combination of teeth and razor-sharp claws to kill their prey; it's not uncommon for a leopard's lunch to be taken away by lion or hyena. In order to avoid this, the leopard will often drag their larger kills up a tree where they can dine amongst the leaves in relative peace and quiet.

THE LITTLE 5

We've all heard of the Big Five, but keep a look out for the Little Five, a term given to the animals with names that include the Big Five: antlion, buffalo weaver, elephant shrew, leopard tortoise, and rhinoceros beetle.

RHINOCEROS BEETLE

The rhinoceros beetle grows up to two inches long. It has large spikes—similar in appearance to a rhino's horns—which are used in battle with other rhino beetles, or for digging, climbing, and mating.

LEOPARD TORTOISE

The largest tortoise in sub-Saharan Africa, the leopard tortoise can grow up to two feet long and weigh up to 100 pounds. It lives in the grasslands of East and Southern Africa and doesn't mate until it's at least 10 years old. Its name stems from its black and yellow-spotted shell, which resembles a leopard's coat.

ELEPHANT SHREW

These ground-dwelling mammals range in size from that of a mouse to a large rabbit. They live in lowland forests, woodlands, rocky outcrops, and deserts and eat small fruits and plants. They get their name from their long nose, which resembles a miniature elephant's trunk.

ANTLION

Also known as a "doodlebug" because of the winding patterns it leaves in the sand when building traps, the antlion makes its home on dry, sandy slopes sheltered from the wind. Essentially larva, it eventually grows into an insect akin to a dragonfly.

RED-BILLED BUFFALO WEAVERS

These black birds with red bills and legs make big sturdy communal nests out of sticks which are defended by the dominant male and nearly always face westward. Inside, the nests are separate chambers with individual tunnels leading to the outside. Their mating is unique amongst birds as it lasts up to two minutes instead of seconds as in most birds.

Animals You'll See on an African Safari

BABOON
The most adaptable of the ground-dwelling primates, baboons travel in large groups and live in all manner of habitats as long as they have water and a safe place to sleep. They have huge canine teeth and can be vicious when they feel threatened, so keep your vehicle's windows closed.

SPRINGBOK
A cinnamon-color antelope with a dark brown stripe on its flanks, a white underside, and short, slender horns, these herbivores often engage in a mysterious activity known as "pronking," a seemingly sudden spurt of high jumps into the air with its back bowed. They travel in herds that usually include a few territorial males; the young will stay with their mothers for about four months.

GIRAFFE
The biggest ruminant and tallest living animal, giraffes are found in most national parks. Social creatures that live in loose herds, it's easy to tell males from females—females have bushy tips like paintbrushes. The tops of the male's horns are bare and shiny from fighting; males fight over females using a "necking" technique, winding their necks around each other, pushing and shoving.

HIPPO
The comical nighttime sounds of this herbivorous animal snorting and chortling will be one of your safari's most memorable experiences, but remember, this is one of Africa's most dangerous animals. If you see a hippo yawn, back off, and never get between a hippo and its water as it may feel threatened.

CHEETAH
Reaching speeds of 70 mph, cheetahs are the world's fastest land animals. Found mainly in open savanna, you'll usually see one or two males—often brothers—together while females watch the cubs. With characteristic dark spots, these endangered animals generally prey on gazelles and impalas.

IMPALA

Similar in appearance to a deer, these ubiquitous antelopes are reddish-brown with white and black markings; they can be found in grasslands and wooded areas, usually near water. A typical herd has one dominant male, although bachelor herds are usually in the vicinity, with hopeful individuals awaiting their turn to oust the ruling male.

AFRICAN WILD DOG

Known as the "painted dog" or "painted wolf" because of their uniquely spotted coats, the endangered wild dog is a highly social animal that lives in small packs of about 15. Intelligent and quick, they hunt as a coordinated pack running down their prey, which varies from antelopes to zebras, until exhausted.

NILE CROCODILE

Found in sub-Saharan Africa and the Nile River, this croc averages about 16 feet and 700 pounds and is a favorite of poachers. Mainly fish eaters, they will eat almost anything, including a baby hippo or a human. Fearsome to look at and lightning quick, they're unusually sensitive with their young.

BUSH BABY

These small nocturnal primates, which make cries similar to that of a human baby, range in size from 2 ounces to 3 pounds. During the day, they stay in tree hollows and nests, but at night you'll see them leaping and bouncing from tree to tree in pursuit of night-flying insects. Their main predators are some of the larger carnivores, genets, and snakes.

HYENA

There are three species: brown, spotted, and striped. They live in groups called clans and make their homes in dens. They mark their territory with gland secretions or droppings. Cubs are nursed for about 18 months, at which point they go on hunting and scavenging sprees with their mothers. Both strategic hunters and opportunists, hyenas feed on their own kill as well as that of others.

MOUNTAIN GORILLA
The global gorilla population is about 1,000, but more than half are found in the Virunga Mountains in Uganda, Rwanda, and DRC. Since they dwell at elevations of up to 13,000 feet, their body hair is thick and long, for warmth. Like humans, females give birth at 9 months, adding to the troop which is led by an older dominant male silverback.

WILDEBEEST
This ubiquitous herbivore has a large head and front end, curved horns, and slender body and rear. Often called "the clowns of the veld" they toss their heads as they run and kick up their back legs. Calves can run within minutes of being born, keeping up with the herd after two days.

WARTHOG
A member of the pig family, warthogs have a wart-covered (actually protective bumps) flat head that's disproportionate to their body. They mostly graze, but will eat anything. They sleep and nurse in burrows abandoned by aardvarks, going in tail first and charging out at full speed in case a predator is waiting.

JACKAL
There are three species of this canine: golden, black-backed, and side-striped, all of whose habitat ranges from savannahs and grasslands to mountains. They pair up for life and together, mark their territory with urine and feces. After a gestation period of about 2 months, these omnivores birth and nurse their 4-6 pups in burrows.

CHIMPANZEE
Dwelling anywhere from tropical rainforests to grasslands in Central and West Africa, an alpha male leads the community. Grooming is an important social activity for bonding while they remove bugs and dirt. Chimps mainly eat fruit and plants but are omnivores and hunt for meat. They sleep in trees for up to 10 hours a night and build their nests from branches.

ELAND

Found in East and southern Africa, the world's largest antelope weighs up to 2,200 lbs. Good at jumping, elands can scale a 4-foot shrub with ease. Herds are highly nomadic and favor browsing over grazing; they often use their spiral horns to bring higher leaves within reach. Older males are more solitary and sedentary than females.

ZEBRA

Africa has three species: the Burchell's (or common) zebra, East Africa's Grevy's zebra, and the mountain zebra of southern and southwestern Africa. All have striped coats and strong teeth for chewing grass and often travel in large herds. A baby zebra can remember its mother's stripes. A male zebra can break a lion's jaw with one kick.

DIK DIK

Extremely shy, these small antelopes are mostly seen darting away in a zigzag pattern on twig-thin legs making a high-pitched sound like "zik zik," hence the name. Weighing no more than 13 lbs., adults mate for life; when a partner dies, the other can deliberately hand itself to a predator.

KUDU

The name comes from the Khoikhoi language indigenous to Southern and East Africa where they are largely found. When they sense danger, kudus stay very still and camouflage into the wooded savannah surroundings thanks to their skin color and thin white stripes. Bulls are bigger and have spiral horns that can grow to an impressive 2 meters (6 feet).

PANGOLIN

Despite the scales, pangolins are mammals, with eight species split halfway across Africa and Asia. They live in burrows and are nocturnal—making them notoriously hard to spot on safari—and they have long sticky tongues and claws perfect for eating ants. With a small head and no external ears, when alarmed, they curl into a ball and are easy for poachers to smuggle.

Birds You'll See on an African Safari

KORI BUSTARD
One of the world's heaviest flying birds is found in southern and East Africa. Reaching almost 30 pounds and about 3½ feet in length, the male is much larger than the female but both are gray, have crests, and gray-and-white necks. Although it does fly, the majority of its time is spent on land, where it eats insects, lizards, snakes, and seeds. One male mates with several females, which then raise the young on their own.

BATELEUR EAGLE
Black with a red back, legs, and beak, and white underneath its wings, this spectacular bird is found throughout sub-Saharan Africa. It can fly up to 322 km (200 miles) at a time in search of prey, which ranges from antelope to snakes and carrion. Mates for life, the same nest is often reused.

LAPPET-FACED VULTURE
The largest, most dominant, and most aggressive vulture, this scavenger feeds mainly on carrion and carcasses. It will also, on occasion, kill other weaker birds or attack the nests of young birds. It has a bald head and is pink in color with a wingspan of up to 8½ feet.

LILAC-BREASTED ROLLER
With a blue-and-lilac-color breast, this stunning bird is found in sub-Saharan Africa's open woodlands and savannas. Parents are extremely territorial and aggressive when it comes to defending the nest. During mating, the male flies high and then rolls over and over as it descends, making screeching cries.

PEL'S FISHING OWL
A large, monogamous, ginger-brown owl with no ears, bare legs, and dark eyes, it lives along river banks in South Africa's Kruger Park, Botswana's Okavango Delta, and Zimbabwe. One of only three fishing owls in the world, it hunts at night with its sharp talons. They communicate with each other through synchronized hooting at night as they guard their stretch of riverbank.

WATTLED CRANE

The rarest African crane is found in Ethiopia, Zambia, Botswana, Mozambique, and South Africa. A gray-and-white bird, it can reach up to 5 feet tall and, while mating, will nest in pairs along the shallow wetlands of large rivers. They're omnivorous and sometimes wander onto farmlands where they're vulnerable to poisoning by farmers.

GREY-CROWNED CRANE

They are so-called for the yellow quiff that looks like a crown on their heads. Uganda's national bird, it's found in wetland grasslands in East and Southern Africa. They live in flocks, but during the breeding season in rainy months, monogamous pairs go off to nest and lay eggs and become highly territorial.

OSTRICH

Reaching 300 lbs. and over 2 meters (6½ feet), the world's heaviest and tallest bird can't fly but it can run fast and its kick can kill. Found in savannahs and deserts, herds are led by an alpha male, who mates with the alpha female; all other hens lay in her nest, and the pair do the incubation.

GUINEA FOWL

Native to Africa, you'll spot the helmeted guinea fowl in flocks, walking around looking for insects and seeds, although they can fly short distances to roost on trees. In the wild, they stand out for their grey polka-dotted plumage and small blue head with a red beak. It is increasingly becoming domesticated, reared alongside poultry.

AFRICAN FISH EAGLE

They live near fresh water in tropical rainforests, fynbos, swamps, and grasslands across sub-Saharan Africa. The talons have rough soles and a good grip for holding slippery fish. They live in monogamous pairs and will swoop down to snatch fish out of the water and then fly it back to their perch. Their nests are made with sticks and grow quite large as they get refurbished over time.

Plants and Trees You'll See on an African Safari

FEVER TREE
Found in damp, swampy habitats throughout sub-Saharan Africa, the tree got its name because travelers often contracted malaria where fever trees grew and thus they were wrongly thought to transmit it. Bees are attracted by its clusters of yellow flowers, and birds often nest in its branches as its thorns offer extra protection against predators.

BAOBAB
Found throughout Africa, the baobab is known for storing water in its trunk and can live up to 1,000 years. The hollow trunks are large enough that they've been used as a prison and a post office.

AFRICAN MAHOGANY
Originally from West Africa, this majestic tree is found in warm humid climates; it's also found in the Florida Everglades. It requires significant rainfall in order to thrive and can reach up to 140 feet with a 6-foot trunk diameter. Its much-prized, strong, richly colored wood is used to make furniture and boats.

FIG
Found in southern and East Africa, these gigantic trees grow wherever there's water. The fruit provides nourishment for a variety of birds, bats, and other animals (who spread the seeds via their droppings), but they're most noted for their symbiotic relationship with wasps, which pollinate the flowers while reproducing.

JACKALBERRY
The large, graceful jackalberry, also known as the African ebony, is a riverine tree found all over sub-Saharan Africa. It can grow up to 80 feet tall and 16 feet wide. It bears fragrant white flowers and a fleshy yellow fruit that jackals, monkeys, baboons, and fruit-eating birds love. Its bark and leaves are used in traditional medicine with proven pharmacological benefits.

SAUSAGE TREE

This unique tree, found in southern Africa, bears sausage-like fruit that can grow up to 2 feet long and weigh as much as 15 pounds. It's also poisonous but can be made into various medicines and alcohol similar to beer. The tree grows to be about 40 feet with fragrant red flowers that bloom at night and are pollinated by bats and insects.

TRELITZIA FLOWER

Also known as Bird of Paradise or the crane flower, the trelitzia is indigenous to South Africa. It grows up to 6½ feet tall with a beautiful fan-shape crown with bright orange and bluish-purple petals that grow perpendicular to the stem, giving it the appearance of a graceful bird.

CAPE FYNBOS

A term given to the collection of plants found in South Africa's Cape, fynbos includes more than 8,600 plant species including shrubs, proteas, bulbous plants (like gladiolus), and aloe. Table Mountain alone hosts about 1,500 species of plants and 69 protea species (there are 112 worldwide).

MAGIC GUARRI

This round shrub with dark green leaves and white or cream-color flowers grows along floodplains and rivers. Its fleshy, purple fruit can be made into alcohol; the bark is used to dye baskets. The twigs have been used as toothbrushes, while the root can be used as mouthwash. The wood is said to have magical or supernatural powers and is never burned as firewood.

WELWITSCHIA MIRABILIS

With its long, wide leathery leaves creeping over the ground, this somewhat surreal-looking plant is also one of the world's oldest; it's estimated to live at least 1,500 years. Found in the Namib Desert, it consists solely of two leaves, a stem base, and roots. The leaves lie on the ground getting tattered and torn, but grow longer and longer each summer.

BEST BETS

Fodor's writers and editors have
chosen our favorites to help you plan.

THE OUT OF AFRICA EXPERIENCE
Cottar's 1920s Safari Camp, *Kenya*
Finch Hattons, *Kenya*
Governors' Il Moran Camp, *Kenya*
King's Pool, *Botswana*
Sabi Sabi Selati Camp, *South Africa*
Angama Mara, *Kenya*

TO SEE THE GREAT MIGRATION
Grumeti River Camp, *Tanzania*
Klein's Camp, *Tanzania*
Little Governors' Camp, *Kenya*
Mara Serena Safari Lodge, *Kenya*
Sayari Camp, *Tanzania*
Serengeti Under Canvas, *Tanzania*

DROP-DEAD LUXURY
Bisate Lodge, *Rwanda*
MalaMala Rattray's Camp, *South Africa*
Mombo Camp, *Botswana*
Ngorongoro Crater Lodge, *Tanzania*

ANIMAL ENCOUNTERS
Sheldrick Wildlife Trust, *Kenya*
Clouds Mountain Gorilla Lodge, *Uganda*
Desert Rhino Camp, *Namibia*
Giraffe Manor, *Kenya*
Greystoke Mahale, *Tanzania*

Varty Camp, *South Africa*
Virunga Loge, *Rwanda*

TO GET AWAY FROM THE CROWDS
Duba Plains, *Botswana*
Jack's Camp, *Botswana*
Mnemba Island Lodge, *Tanzania*
Tswalu Kalahari, *South Africa*
Ruzizi Tented Lodge, *Rwanda*
Sand Rivers Selous, *Tanzania*
!Xaus Lodge, *South Africa*

INTERACT WITH THE LOCALS
Deception Valley Lodge, *Botswana*
Forest Lodge, *Phinda, South Africa*
Il Ngwesi Eco Lodge, *Kenya*
Lake Manyara Serena Lodge, *Tanzania*
Hemingways Ol Seki Mara, *Kenya*

TO GO TO THE BEACH
Lake Kivu Serena Hotel, *Rwanda*
The Majlis, *Kenya*
Mnemba Lodge, *Tanzania*
Peponi Hotel, *Kenya*
Protea Hotel by Marriott Pelican Bay, *Namibia*
Zuri Zanzibar, *Tanzania*

TO GET OUT OF THE VEHICLE
Footsteps, *Botswana*
Lewa Wilderness, *Kenya*
Okonjima Luxury Bush Camp, *Namibia*
Porini Rhino Camp, *Kenya*
Roho ya Selous, *Tanzania*

NATURAL WONDERS
Explosion Crater Drive, *Uganda*
Great Migration, *Kenya and Tanzania*
Mt. Kilimanjaro, *Tanzania*
Namib-Naukluft Park, *Namibia*
Ngorongoro Crater, *Tanzania*
Okavango Delta, *Botswana*
Victoria Falls, *Zimbabwe and Zambia*
Virunga Mountains, *Uganda and Rwanda*

HOT AIR BALLOON RIDES
Masai Mara, *Kenya*
Serengeti, *Tanzania*
Namib Desert, *Namibia.*

GORILLA TREKS
Bwindi Impenetrable National Park, *Uganda*
Volcanoes National Park, *Rwanda*

TAKE A MOBILE SAFARI
Kenya
Tanzania
Botswana
Namibia

Safari with Kids

Most safari operators and private game reserves don't accept children under a certain age, usually under eight, but sometimes under 12. This age limit is largely for safety reasons, especially in unfenced camps where animals could be in close proximity to rooms and tents; the same goes for drives in open safari vehicles. And even though you might think your six- or seven-year-old adores all sorts of animals and bugs, you'd be surprised how overwhelmed kids can become out of the comfort of their home backyard by the size and multitude of African insects and wildlife.

Take into account, also, that when you're following a strange schedule (with jet lag) and getting in and out of small planes, safari vehicles and the like, there often is no time to deal with recalcitrant children—and fussing will, you can be guaranteed, annoy the other people in your plane or lodge, who have spent a great deal of money for what may be a once-in-a-lifetime safari trip. Finally, while smaller children may be in awe of the first elephant they see, a few hours of driving around a hot dusty reserve may result in them getting bored and restless if there's not much animal action.

One option for families with teenagers is to book one of the larger mid-range lodges which are mostly fenced and perhaps have a swimming pool and buffet meals that will suit everyone. Or if you can afford it, book a private safari

where no other people are involved and you dictate the schedule and even the menu for meals. Many private lodges will rent you the entire property for the length of your stay; this is often the only way these camps allow children under age eight on safari. Be advised that, even if you're renting the whole camp, babies and toddlers still aren't allowed out on game-viewing trips.

&Beyond has children's programs at several of its upscale camps throughout southern and East Africa. While you follow your own program, your kids pursue their own wilderness activities, and you all meet up later for meals and other activities. **Wilderness Safaris**, which also has locations throughout southern and East Africa, offers the bush buddy program at most of its camps where someone is on hand to look after the kids (either with you or in camp).

Malaria and Kids

It's best not to visit malarial areas with children under age 10. Young kidneys are especially vulnerable to both the effects of malaria and the side effects of malaria prophylactics, and you could be a long way from medical care if there are complications.

Best Lodges for Families with Kids

Here are a few places in each country that are great options for families traveling with children.

KENYA

- Angama Mara, Masai Mara

- Sanctuary Olonana, Masai Mara

- Lewa Wilderness or Lewa Safari Camp, Laikipia Plateau

TANZANIA

- Isoitok Camp, Lake Manyara National Park

- Gibbs Farm, Ngorongoro Conservation Area

- Klein's Camp, Serengeti National Park

- Selous Impala Camp, Nyerere National Park

SOUTH AFRICA

- Founders Camp or Varty Camp, Londolozi Private Game Reserve

- Mountain Lodge, Phinda Private Game Reserve

- Melton Manor or Uplands Homestead, Kwandwe Private Game Reserve

RWANDA

- Virunga Lodge, Volcanoes National Park

- Five Volcanoes Boutique Hotel, Volcanoes National Park

- Nyungwe Top View Hill Hotel, Nyungwe National Park

UGANDA

- Mihingo Lodge, Lake Mburo National Park

- Turaco Treetops Lodge, Kibale National Park

- Murchison River Lodge, Murchison Falls National Park

BOTSWANA

- Footsteps, Okavango Delta

- Kwando Lagoon or Lebala Camps, Kwando Reserve

- Tuludi, Okavango Delta

- Chitabe Lediba, Okavango Delta

NAMIBIA

- Kulala Desert Lodge, Namib-Naukluft Park

- Etosha Village, Namib-Naukluft Park

- Vingerklip Lodge, Damaraland

- Swakopmund Hotel and Entertainment Centre, Swakopmund

- Protea Hotel by Marriott Pelican Bay, Walvis Bay

VICTORIA FALLS

- Toka Leya Camp, Livingstone, Zambia

- Tongabezi Lodge, Livingstone, Zambia

- Elephant Camp, Victoria Falls, Zimbabwe

- Stanley and Livingstone, Victoria Falls, Zimbabwe

What to Read and Watch

BORN WILD

Tony Fitzjohn's memoir is much more than a story about one man's addiction to adventure. It tells the tale of his 20 years with George Adamson of *Born Free* fame, and his lifelong fight to protect African wildlife is chronicled alongside introspections about global citizenship, all in the wild man's signature storytelling style.

RUNNING WITH THE KENYANS

Adharanand Finn's story of the elite training camps of Kenya will inspire even the most devout non-runner. If you're planning ahead for your big trip, this look at Kenyan culture through the lens of the experience of running will give you a whole new way to explore the area.

IN THE HOUSE OF THE INTERPRETER

Ngugi Wa Thiong'o is a prolific Kenyan writer and political activist. His powerful two-part memoir covers a period in the 1950s when he was at a prestigious British boarding school when the Mau Mau Uprising for Independence erupted. But he eventually found himself jailed in his own subsequent fight against the colonial powers.

OUT OF AFRICA

In 1914 Danish baroness Karen Blixen went to Kenya to establish a coffee plantation at the foot of the Ngong Hills. This classic book tells her evocative stories of friendships, experiences with wildlife and her love affair with Denys Finch-Hatton. Sydney Pollock made the movie in 1985 with Meryl Streep and Robert Redford.

GORILLAS IN THE MIST

The story of Dian Fossey, an American conservationist who studied mountain gorillas in Rwanda from 1966 to her untimely murder by poachers in 1985. It chronicles both her struggles living in a remote camp and the joy of her relationships with the gorillas. Sigourney Weaver starred in the movie released in 1988.

MY LIFE WITH CHIMPANZEES

Jane Goodall is considered the world's expert on chimpanzees. She first went to Gombe Stream National park in 1960 where she made important observations of social and family behavior that have been instrumental in understanding the species. Since then she has been a leading and award-winning conservationist, environmentalist, and humanitarian.

BORN FREE

Published in 1960, this now-classic book is about Austrian-born Joy Adamson and her astonishing relationship with Elsa the orphaned lion cub in Kenya. With husband George, they successfully released Elsa into the wild where she bore cubs—the first time a lion had been fully rehabilitated. The movie premiered in 1966.

WHATEVER YOU DO DON'T RUN: THE TRUE TALES OF A BOTSWANA SAFARI GUIDE

Peter Allison's hilarious anecdotes as a top safari guide in the Okavango Delta is as much about his encounters with wildlife as it is with dealing with the ridiculous whims of wealthy guests. He fights the impulse not to run away from them as he would do a fierce pride of lions.

THE NO. 1 LADIES' DETECTIVE AGENCY

Following no-nonsense but wise detective Mma Precious Ramotswe as she solves crimes in Botswana, these charming novels are funny and entertaining and make great reading while on safari. Alexander McCall Smith has now penned a staggering 22 in the series, and the stories have also been made into TV and radio productions.

SAFARI, SO GOOD: ALL ABOUT AFRICAN WILDLIFE

Get young children (4-8 years) excited about the idea of going on safari with this delightful kids' book featuring Cat (from Cat in Hat fame) taking his friends Sally and Nick to Africa to meet and learn about the animals. The book is part of the Learning Library series inspired by Dr. Seuss's original 1957 Cat in the Hat.

THE SCRAMBLE FOR AFRICA

First published in 1990, this weighty tome by Thomas Pakenham discusses the turbulent colonial conquest of Africa from 1876 to 1912. This gripping read documents the often ruthless arrogance of the European nations in their quest for dominance of the Africans.

THE ELEPHANT WHISPERER: MY LIFE WITH THE HERD IN THE AFRICAN WILD

In 1999 the late South African conservationist Lawrence Anthony took on six destructive and traumatized 'rogue' elephants. Remarkably he managed to calm them down by simply talking to them gently until they recognized his voice and body language, and the then-placid elephants were re-released on his private reserve in KwaZulu-Natal.

AFRICA

If one documentary says "come to Africa" then this it. Sir David Attenborough narrates this epic six-episode series that took four years to film and was first aired on the BBC and Discovery Channel in 2013. It features spectacular footage of the wildlife and landscapes across the continent including the popular safari destinations.

Chapter 2

PLANNING A SAFARI

Updated by
Lizzie Williams

Know Before You Go

Do you need a visa to visit? What immunizations are required? Can you drink water from the tap? How about money? What should I wear? We've got answers and a few tips to help you make the most of your African Safari.

WHEN SHOULD I START PLANNING?

Most people start planning a safari six to nine months in advance, but it's never too soon to start. In fact, planning your trip 12 months in advance isn't unreasonable, especially if you want to travel during peak season—November through February in South Africa, July through October elsewhere—and have your heart set on a particular lodge.

WHERE CAN I SEE THE BIG FIVE?

If you're keen to see big game, particularly the Big Five, then your best bets for success will be in East Africa and South Africa. The Serengeti National Park in Tanzania is known for its plentiful game and is the stomping ground for approximately 2 million wildebeest, 250,000 zebras, and 500,000 antelopes that race more than 1,931 km (1,200 miles) May–July to find enough water and grass to survive during the Great Migration. The Masai Mara National Reserve in neighboring Kenya is probably best known for its large population of big cats, as well as hippos and the rare black rhino and spotted hyena; the Great Migration starts to arrive here in mid-July. In South Africa, Kruger National Park and the private Sabi Sand Game Reserve just outside Kruger are ideal places to observe the Big Five as well as leopards and hundreds of other species. You'll see the African elephant everywhere in the park, with lions more abundant in the central and eastern regions; rhino and buffalo make their home in the woods of southwest Kruger.

HOW DO I START PLANNING A SAFARI?

Deciding where you want to go and choosing the right safari operator are the most important things you need to do. Start planning for your safari the way you would any trip. Read travel books about the areas that most interest you. Talk to people who have been on a similar trip; word-of-mouth advice can be invaluable. Surf the 'net. Get inspired. Line up your priorities. And find someone you trust to help plan your trip.

BATHROOM BREAKS

On your game drive you'll very likely be pointed to a nearby bush (which the ranger checks out before you use it). Tissues and toilet paper are usually available in the vehicle (but you may want to make sure). Sometimes there might be a toilet—well, actually, it'll very likely be a hole in the ground below a toilet seat—called long-drop toilets. Either way, bring the paper back with you—don't bury it. If you have an emergency, ask your ranger to stop the vehicle and he or she will scout a suitable spot.

PEOPLE WITH DISABILITIES

Having a disability doesn't mean you can't go on safari. It's important, however, to plan carefully to ensure that your needs can be adequately met. South African lodges, especially the high-end private ones, are the easiest to navigate and have the fewest steps. Keep in mind that all-terrain 4x4 vehicles don't have seat belts, so you need enough muscle control to keep yourself upright while the vehicle bumps along the unpaved roads. Getting in and out of these elevated vehicles can also be challenging. MalaMala Game Reserve in South Africa is completely accessible and even has specially equipped four-wheel-drive safari vehicles with harness seat belts. Many of Kruger's camps have special accommodations. There are a number of tour operators offering wheelchair-accessible safaris, such as

Endeavour Safaris (www. endeavour-safaris.com).

NATURE IS NEITHER KIND NOR SENTIMENTAL

Don't be tempted to interfere with natural processes. The animals are going about the business of survival in a harsh environment, and you can unwittingly make this business more difficult. Don't get too close to the animals and don't try to help them cross some perceived obstacle; you have no idea what it's really trying to do or where it wants to go. If you're intrusive, you could drive animals away from feeding and, even worse, from drinking at waterholes, where they're very skittish and vulnerable to predators. That time at the waterhole may be their only opportunity to drink that day.

NEVER FEED WILD CREATURES

Not a cute monkey, not an inquisitive baboon, not a baby tree squirrel, or a young bird out of its nest. In some camps and lodges, however, animals have gotten used to being fed or steal food. The most common animals in this category are baboons and monkeys; in some places they sneak into huts, tents, and even occupied vehicles to snatch food. If you see primates around, keep all food out of sight, and keep your windows rolled up. (If a baboon manages to get into your vehicle, he will trash the interior as he searches for food and use the vehicle as a toilet.)

NEVER TRY TO POSE WITH AN ANIMAL

This is probably the biggest cause of death and injury on safaris, when visitors don't listen to or believe the warnings from their rangers or posted notices in public parks. Regardless of how cute or harmless they may look, these animals aren't tame. An herbivore hippo, giraffe, or ostrich can kill you just as easily as a lion, elephant, or buffalo can.

DO I TIP?

Yes, but the amount you tip depends on your budget and what you're comfortable with. When in doubt, it's always better to tip too much than too little; it's not unusual for a member of staff to be supporting an entire extended family on one salary and they are grateful for any help. Never tip children as it could discourage them from attending school if tourists are seen as a lucrative form of income. Hand your tip (preferably in a sealed envelope; many lodges provide them) directly to a member of staff or hand to management to distribute. However, most camps and lodges have gratuity boxes for general staff tips which are also distributed to the behind scene staff such as kitchen and laundry.

For a ranger/guide, plan about US$15-20 per person, per day, which should be handed to them directly. For the general staff, plan per day roughly $10-20 into the general tip box. In both cases families and larger groups will tip less, roughly US$60 for a family of four to the guide, and US$50 to the staff. Expect also to tip $5 per trip for a vehicle transfer (i.e. from the airport/airstrip to your hotel/lodge). Note that some safari operators, such as Micato, include tips in their price, so you don't have to worry about carrying around the correct denominations.

MALARIA CARE AND VACCINES

It's extremely important to take malaria prophylactics, but not all malaria medications are the same. Chloroquine is not an effective antimalarial drug in sub-Saharan Africa, as the mosquitoes have developed resistance, and the CDC recommends that you do not use halofantrine. The CDC's website has a comprehensive list of the different malaria medications available, and which are recommended for each country.

You must be up-to-date with all of your routine shots such as the measles/mumps/rubella vaccine, and diphtheria/pertussis/tetanus vaccine. If you're traveling to northern Kenya from December through June, don't be surprised if your doctor advises you to get inoculated against meningitis, as this part of the continent tends to see outbreaks during this time. As for yellow fever, it isn't inherent in any of the countries discussed in this book, but some countries (like Kenya) will require you to present a valid inoculation certificate if you traveled to a region infected with yellow fever before arrival.

Getting Here and Around

Air

Although there are few direct flights to Africa from the U.S., flying to the African gateway cities is fairly straightforward via Europe or the Middle East. Once there, traveling by plane is the best and most viable means of transportation to most safari destinations and saves long, arduous journeys by road.

For airline contact information and specific information for each country, see Air, in the Getting Here and Around section of each chapter.

INTERNATIONAL FLIGHTS

Comparison flight booking websites such as Kayak.com, Skyscanner.net, and eBookers.com can help you search for the best fares that meet your requirements. The best choice of flights for American travelers is by flying through Europe. Then book a flight to a regional hub like Nairobi or Johannesburg, and catch a connecting flight to your destination.

Some of Kenya's airlines like Kenya Airways (⊕ www.kenya-airways.com) and Precision Air (⊕ www.precisionairtz.com) fly from Nairobi to destinations in Tanzania. South Africa's domestic airlines like Airlink (⊕ www.flyairlink.com) fly from South Africa to Botswana, Namibia, Zambia, and Zimbabwe.

Another alternative is flying to the African cities via the Middle East—Dubai with Emirates or Doha with Qatar. You'll add extra time to your flight, but you could save big. Always book at least two months in advance, especially during the high season.

SAFARI FLIGHTS

From the gateway cities, scheduled and charter flights are a common mode of transportation when getting to safari lodges and remote destinations throughout southern and East Africa. A number of airlines serve the lodge airstrips and in some cases, like regions in the East African parks and Botswana's Okavango Delta, flying is the only option to get there. The small aircraft are well maintained and are almost always booked by your lodge or travel agent.

Scheduled flights are available with a number of airlines and seats are booked on an individual basis. They often operate on circuits and make more than one landing to drop off clients at different accommodations. Charter or on-demand flights, those made at times other than those scheduled, can be expensive for independent travelers, as they require minimum passenger loads. If it's just two passengers, you'll be charged for the vacant seats, although they may represent good value if a group is taking all the seats.

The aircraft you get depends on the number of passengers flying and can vary from a six-seat Cessna flown by bush pilots to a more spacious commuter plane seating 10-14 people. The planes have no air-conditioning and in summer can be very hot, especially in the afternoon. Bring a bottle of water with you. And go to the bathroom before flying; there are no restrooms on these planes. Most flights are short—approximately 30 minutes or so—but some can be up to an hour. Take medication if you are prone to motion sickness as flights can be bumpy and landing strips are often no more than baked earth. Those with a severe fear of small planes might want to consider road travel instead.

For information regarding airlines in each country, see the Air section in each country chapter.

LUGGAGE LIMITS

Due to the limited space and size of the aircraft, carriers observe strict luggage regulations: luggage must be soft-sided, preferably with no wheels, and usually must weigh no more than 15 kg (33 lbs); weight allowances may vary by company, so be sure to ask what the limits are before packing. Excess luggage can usually be stored with the operator or a hotel until your return. Don't just gloss over this: airlines with small planes take weight very seriously, and some will charge you for an extra ticket if you insist on bringing excess baggage.

Car

Self-drive tours are not recommended for first-time safari-goers. We repeat: Self-drive tours are not recommended for first-time safari-goers. With that said, if you are entertaining the thought, know that a 4WD vehicle is recommended. High clearance is a helpful advantage in gaining elevation over tall grass (especially after the rains in summer) and better spotting of all those animals.

■ TIP→ **Wherever you go, don't get out of your vehicle except at certain well-marked picnic sites or view sites, unless you want to make an international headline.**

INTERNATIONAL DRIVER'S LICENSE

If you're taking a self-driving safari or renting a car in countries other than South Africa and Namibia, you'll need an international driver's license. These licenses are valid for one year and are issued at any American Automobile Association (AAA) office in the United States; you must have a current U.S. driver's license. You need to bring two passport-type photographs with you for the license. A valid U.S. driver's license is acceptable in South Africa and Namibia.

RENTAL CARS

If you decide to travel on your own, it will be necessary to buy special insurance, especially if you plan to cross the border into neighboring countries. Be sure to find out exactly what is required and covered in terms of CDW and TDW (collision damage waiver and theft-damage waiver).

Game Drives

In most regions, the best time to find game is in the early morning and early evening, when the animals are most active, although old Africa hands will tell you that you can come across good game at any time of day. Stick to the philosophy "you never know what's around the next corner," and keep your eyes and ears wide open all the time. If your lodge or camp offers guided night drives on open vehicles with spotlights—go for it. You'll rarely be disappointed, seeing not only big game but also a lot of fascinating little critters that surface only at night. Book your night drive in advance or as soon as you get to camp.

Arm yourself with specialized books on mammals and birds rather than a more general one that tries to cover too much. Airports, lodges, and camp shops stock a good range, but try to bring one with you and do a bit of boning up in advance. Any bird guide by Ken Newman (Struik Publishers) and the *Sasol Guide to Birds* are recommended.

Many national parks have reception areas with charts that show the most recent sightings of wildlife in the area. To be sure you see everything you want to, stop at the nearest reception and ask about a spotting chart, or just chat with

Getting Here and Around

the other drivers, guides, and tourists you may encounter there, who can tell you what they've seen and where.

RANGERS AND TRACKERS

Game rangers are referred to as guides throughout Africa and have vast experience with and knowledge of the bush and the animals that inhabit it. Guides often work in conjunction with trackers, who spot animals, and advise the guides where to go. Often a tracker will be busy searching out animal tracks, spoor, and other clues to nearby wildlife while the guide drives (or there will be an additional driver) and discusses the animals and their environment. Guides often communicate with each other via radio when there's been a good sighting.

The quality of your bush experience depends heavily on your guide and tracker; hence why it advisable to tip. A guide wears many hats while on safari: he or she is there to entertain you, protect you, and put you as close to the wilderness as possible while serving as bush mechanic, first-aid specialist, and host. They will often eat meals with you, will explain animal habits and behavior while out in the bush, and, if you're on foot, will keep you alive in the presence of an excitable elephant, buffalo, hippo, or lion. This is no small feat, and each guide has their particular strengths. Because of the intensity of the safari experience, with its exposure to potentially dangerous animals and tricky situations, your relationship with your guide is one of trust, friendliness, and respect.

INTERACTING WITH YOUR GUIDE

Acknowledge that your guide is a professional and an expert in the field, and defer to his or her knowledge. Instead of trying to show how much you know, follow the example of the hunter, which is to walk quietly and take notice of all the little signs around you. Save social

chatter with the guide for when you're back at camp, not out on a game drive. Guides appreciate questions, which give them an idea of your range of knowledge and of how much detail to include in their animal descriptions. However, if you like to ask a lot of questions, save some for later, especially as several other people are likely to be in the safari vehicle with you. Carry a pocket notebook on game drives and jot down questions as they occur; you can then bring them up at dinner or around the campfire, when your guide has more time to talk and everyone can participate in the discussion.

Don't let your guide provide only a list of an animal's attributes. Politely ask questions and show you'd like to know more. Even the best guides may experience "bush burnout" by the end of a busy safari season with demanding clients, but any guide worthy of the title always goes out of his or her way to give you the best possible experience. If you suspect yours has a case of burnout, or just laziness, you have a right to ask for certain things. There's never any harm in asking, and you can't expect your guide to read your mind about what you like. If, for example, you have a preference for birds, insects, or whatever, ask your guide to spend time on these subjects. Given that many safari-goers concentrate on only ticking off the Big Five, you may be surprised by how happy they are to oblige.

BUSH WALKS

Guided bush walks vary, but usually a maximum of eight guests walk in single file with the armed guide up front and the tracker at the back. A bush walk is a more intimate experience than a drive and you're up close with the bush. Your guide will brief you thoroughly about where and how to walk, emergency procedures, and the like. If you're in a national park, you'll most likely have to pay an additional fee to have an armed park ranger escort you on your walk.

VEHICLES ON GAME DRIVES

Your safari transportation is determined by your destination and could range from custom-made game-viewing vehicles (full-service safari) to a combi or minivan (basic safari or self-drive). There shouldn't be more than six people per vehicle. To make sure you experience every view, suggest to your guide that visitors rotate seats for each drive.

In closed vehicles, which are used by private touring companies operating in Kruger National Park, sit as close to the driver-guide as possible so you can get in and out of the vehicle more easily and get the best views.

OPEN-SIDED LAND ROVERS

This is the most common game-viewing vehicle, especially in **South Africa, Tanzania,** and **Botswana,** and is usually a Land Rover or a Land Cruiser. Each vehicle seats six to eight people. Vehicles that have raised, stepped seating—meaning the seats in back are higher than the ones in front—are used for game drives. There are usually three rows of seats after the driver's row; the norm at a luxury lodge is to have two people per row. The more expensive the camp, the fewer people in the vehicle. Sit beside the guide/driver if you're a bit unsteady, because you won't have to climb up into the rear. In the front row you'll have the clearest conversations with the guide, but farther back you'll have a clearer, elevated view over the front of the car. The back seats tend to be bumpy, but you get great views.

POP TOPS

Used mainly in **Kenya,** because of dirt, dust, and rain (and cheetahs, who like to jump on the roof or hood of the vehicle!), these hard-topped minivans pop up so

you can stand up, get a better view, and take photos in every direction. If you're claustrophobic or very tall, this might not be the vehicle for you, but there are outfitters that have larger vehicles that can "stretch." If it gets really hot outside, you'll be happy to close up and turn on the air-conditioning. Make sure water and sodas are available.

MINIVANS

It's unlikely that you'll use one of these unless you're on a very cheap safari or a self-drive—they are, however, perfect for the **Namib Desert.** The advantage is that they sit high off the ground and provide much better views; some outfitters offer vehicles that can expand. If you're self-driving, make sure you get a van with air-conditioning and power steering. The farther north you go, check out your prospective vehicle's year and make sure it's as recent as possible.

WATERCRAFT

If your lodge is on or near a river, expect to go game viewing in a boat. In the south, options range from the big sunset safari boats with bars and bathrooms on the **Zambezi** and **Chobe rivers** to a six- or eight-seater along the **Okavango** and smaller rivers, where your amenities include a cool box of drinks and snacks but no toilet. One of the highlights of your stay in the Okavango Delta will be gliding in a *mokoro* (a canoe) poled by an expert local waterman through papyrus-fringed channels. In the north, there are a number of options in Uganda including the **Nile** in Murchison Falls National Park and at Jinja, and the **Kazinga Channel** in Queen Elizabeth National Park, which has one of Africa's largest concentrations of hippos and crocs.

Essentials

Your safari will be one of the most memorable trips you'll ever take, and it's essential that your African experience matches the one you've always imagined. Nothing should be left to chance, and that includes where you'll stay and how you'll get around.

The whos, whats, and hows still need to come into focus. If you have questions like, "Where's the best place to sit in a game-drive vehicle? Can you get near a honey badger? Where do you go to the bathroom in the bush?," then read on.

By the way, "bush" is a term used to describe the natural setting of your safari—be it in forests, plains, or on riverbanks. The expression "going to the bush" means going away from urban areas and into the wilderness.

☎ Communications

It's estimated that about half the population in Africa has a cell phone, and areas with 3G or 4G reception are widespread and can include remote areas (5G is available in parts of South Africa and Kenya, too). Generally the services are excellent, but don't count on it in remote camps and lodges. However if you urgently need to get in touch with home, all camps have a radio or satellite phone.

■ TIP→ **Leave your contact details with folks back home so they can call you if there's an emergency.**

INTERNET
Most lodges and camps have Wi-Fi, although the service can be erratic and slow. Availability and speed varies widely by location and camp; South African lodges have pretty good capability but elsewhere it can be poor, especially in remote areas of Tanzania, Botswana, and Namibia. While there will be Wi-Fi in public areas, don't always expect connectivity in your room or tent.

Telephone Country Codes

- **United States:** 1
- **Botswana:** 267
- **Kenya:** 254
- **Namibia:** 264
- **Rwanda:** 250
- **South Africa:** 27
- **Tanzania:** 255
- **Uganda:** 256
- **Zambia:** 260
- **Zimbabwe:** 263

Note: When dialing from abroad, drop the initial 0 from local area codes.

PHONES
Mobile phones work in almost all lodges and camps, although service can be patchy in remote areas. In the smaller camps, plan to charge your phone at a communal charging station in the lounge or dining area, and perhaps at certain times if the establishment is relying on a generator for power. When you don't need it, turn off your phone or switch to 'airplane mode' to save battery power. Additionally, temporarily turn off apps and Bluetooth as both can drain your battery.

If you do not want to put your phone on (potentially expensive) international roaming, you can also buy a cheap local SIM card, but remember that any phone that you take abroad must be unlocked by your company in order for it to accept a different SIM card.

If you're on a reliable high-speed connection, calling on Skype or WhatsApp generally works well from Africa. However Wi-Fi bandwidth at lodges and camps may not allow calls. If you can, text, as a text message costs a fraction of the cost of making an actual call. This is a handy option for meeting up with friends or keeping in touch with home, but for making hotel reservations, it's best to make the call.

■ TIP→ **Make sure you bring a universal adapter so you can charge your phone.**

Most people use the time on safari to "switch off" from modern life. Conducting business or making phone calls in the lodge's public areas is generally frowned upon as other guests prefer to talk to others or enjoy the views. Using your phone on a game drive is also bad form, so unless you're using your phone as a camera (and turn the volume down), leave it back at camp.

For country-specific information on phones, see the Communication section, under Planning, in each country chapter.

🌐 Customs and Duties

Visitors traveling to South Africa or other Southern Africa Customs Union (SACU) countries (Botswana, Lesotho, Namibia, and Swaziland) may bring in new or used gifts and souvenirs up to a total value of R5,000 (in South African rand, US$320 at this writing) duty-free. For additional goods (new or used) up to a value of R20,000, a fee of 20% is levied. In addition, each person may bring up to 200 cigarettes, 20 cigars, 250 grams of tobacco, 2 liters of wine, 1 liter of spirits, 50 ml of perfume, and 250 ml of eau de toilette. The tobacco and alcohol allowance applies only to people 18 and over. If you enter a SACU country from or

through another in the union, you aren't liable for any duties. You will, however, need to complete a form listing items imported.

The United States is a signatory to CITES, a wildlife protection treaty, and therefore doesn't allow the importation of living or dead endangered animals, or their body parts, such as rhino horns or ivory. If you purchase an antique that's made partly or wholly of ivory, you must obtain a CITES preconvention certificate that clearly states the item is at least 100 years old. The import of zebra skin or other tourist products also requires a CITES permit.

🍴 Dining

Meals served at lodges and camps are generally of very good quality; especially at the most exclusive where food could grace the tables of a top restaurant. While much of the produce is trucked or flown in, talented bush chefs bake fresh bread and pastries and produce soups, salads, and meat, fish, and vegetarian appetizers and entrées. Bear in mind though, that in remote places there may be set menus with a couple of choices.

Mealtimes are geared around the best game viewing times. The early morning game drive goes at dawn so coffee/tea and biscuits are provided before setting off—perhaps with a wake-up call. On return late morning, a hot and cold brunch/lunch will be waiting, and then afternoon tea with sandwiches and cakes is served before the afternoon game drive. If your guide stops for "sundowners" in the bush, there will be a cool box with drinks and snacks. Dinner is a three-course affair and depending on the venue, could be taken outside under a thatched or canvas roof where guests

Essentials

can recall the day's events on safari, often with the guides, or some lodges and camps set up intimate tables for couples in a secluded spot.

◉ Electricity

Most of southern Africa is on 220/240-volt alternating current (AC). The plug points are round. However, there are both large 15-amp three-prong sockets (with a ground connection) and smaller 5-amp two-prong sockets. Most lodges have adapter plugs, especially for recharging phones and camera batteries; check before you go, or purchase a universal plug adapter before you leave home.

Safari hotels in the Serengeti, the private reserve areas outside Kruger National Park, and the less rustic private lodges in South Africa are likely to provide you with plug points and plugs, and some offer hair dryers and electric-razor sockets as well (check this before you go). Lodges on limited generator and solar power are usually able to charge phones and cameras, as long as you have the right plug.

✚ Health and Safety

Although most countries in southern and East Africa are stable and safe, it's a good idea to do your homework and be fully aware of the areas you'll be traveling to before planning that once-in-a-lifetime trip.

Of all the horror stories and fantastic nightmares about meeting your end in the bush, the problem you're most likely to encounter will be of your own doing: dehydration. Also be wary of malaria, motion sickness, and intestinal problems. By taking

Safari Do's and Don'ts

Do observe animals silently. Talking loudly frightens animals and disturbs their activities.

Don't attempt to attract an animal's attention. Don't imitate sounds, clap hands, whistle, pound the vehicle, or throw objects.

Do respect your driver and guide's judgment. They have more knowledge and experience than you. If they say no, there's a good reason.

Drive slowly. On self-drives, stick to the speed limit and drive slowly keeping ample distance between you and the wildlife—they always have the right of way.

Don't leave your vehicle. Only get out at designated sites like picnic spots, or on a lodge game drive when your guide sees fit. Additionally, keep arms and legs within the vehicle.

Do dress in neutral tones. If everyone is wearing earth tones, the animal sees one large vegetation-color mass.

Don't litter. Any tossed item can choke or poison animals.

Don't attempt to feed or approach animals. This is especially important at lodges and campgrounds where animals are accustomed to humans.

Don't smoke. The bush ignites easily.

commonsense precautions, your safari will be uneventful from a health perspective but memorable in every other way.

The Center for Disease Control (CDC) has information on health risks associated with almost every country on the planet, as well as what precautions to take. The World Health Organization (WHO) is the health arm of the United Nations and has information by topic and by country. The International Travel and Health section of the WHO's website covers everything you need to know about staying healthy abroad.

DEHYDRATION AND OVERHEATING

The African sun is hot and the air is dry, and sweat evaporates quickly in these conditions. You might not realize how much bodily fluid you're losing as a result. Wear a hat, lightweight clothing, and sunscreen—all of which will help your body cope with high temperatures. If you're prone to low blood sugar or have a sensitive stomach, consider bringing along rehydration salts, available at pharmacies, to balance your body's fluids and keep you going when you feel listless. Alternatively drink a solution of ½ teaspoon salt and 4 tablespoons sugar dissolved in a quart of water to replace electrolytes.

Drink at least two to three quarts of water a day, and in extreme heat conditions as much as three to four quarts of water or juice. Drink more if you're exerting yourself physically. Alcohol is dehydrating, so try to limit consumption on hot or long travel days. If you do overdo it at dinner with wine or spirits, or even caffeine, you need to drink even more water to recover the fluid lost as your body processes the alcohol. Antimalarial medications are also very dehydrating, so it's important to drink water while you're taking this medicine.

Don't rely on thirst to tell you when to drink; people often don't feel thirsty until they're a little dehydrated. At the first sign of dry mouth, exhaustion, or headache, drink water, because dehydration is the likely culprit.

■ TIP→ **To test for dehydration, pinch the skin on the back of your hand and see if it stays in a peak; if it does, you're dehydrated.**

Heat cramps stem from a low salt level due to excessive sweating. These muscle pains usually occur in the abdomen, arms, or legs. When cramps occur, stop all activity and sit quietly in a cool spot and drink water. Don't do anything strenuous for a few hours after the cramps subside. If heat cramps persist for more than an hour, seek medical assistance.

INSECTS

In summer ticks may be a problem, even in open areas close to cities. If you intend to walk or hike anywhere, use a suitable insect repellent. After your walk, examine your body and clothes for ticks, looking carefully for pepper ticks, which are tiny but may cause tick-bite fever. If you're bitten, keep an eye on the bite. Most people suffer no more than an itchy bump, so don't panic. If the tick was infected, however, the bite will swell, itch, and develop a black necrotic center. This is a sure sign that you'll develop tick-bite fever, which usually hits after about eight to 12 days. Symptoms may be mild or severe, depending on the patient. This disease isn't usually life-threatening in healthy adults, but it's horribly unpleasant.

■ TIP→ **Check your boots for spiders and other crawlies and shake your clothes out before getting dressed.**

Always keep a lookout for mosquitoes. Even in nonmalarial areas they're extremely irritating. When walking anywhere in the bush, watch out for snakes. If you see

Essentials

one, give it a wide berth and you should be fine. Snakes really bite only when they're taken by surprise, so you don't want to step on a napping mamba.

INTESTINAL UPSET

Micro-fauna and-flora differ in every region of Africa, so if you drink unfiltered water, add ice to your soda, or eat fruit from a roadside stand, you might get traveler's diarrhea. All reputable hotels and lodges have filtered, clean tap water or provide sterilized drinking water, and nearly all camps and lodges have supplies of bottled water. If you're traveling outside organized safari camps in rural Africa or are unsure of local water, carry plenty of bottled water and follow the CDC's advice for fruits and vegetables: boil it, cook it, peel it, or forget it. If you're going on a mobile safari, ask about drinking water.

MALARIA

The most serious health problem facing travelers is malaria. The risk is medium at the height of the summer and very low in winter. All travelers heading into malaria-endemic regions should consult a health-care professional at least one month before departure for advice. Unfortunately, the malarial agent *Plasmodium* seems to be able to develop a hardy resistance to new prophylactic drugs quickly, so the best prevention is to avoid being bitten by mosquitoes in the first place.

After sunset, wear light-color (mosquitoes and tsetse flies are attracted to dark surfaces), loose, long-sleeve shirts, long pants, and shoes and socks, and apply mosquito repellent (containing DEET) generously. Always sleep in a mosquito-proof room or tent, and if possible, keep a fan going in your room. If you're pregnant or trying to conceive, some malaria medicines are safe to use but in general it's best to avoid malaria areas entirely.

Generally speaking, the risk is much lower in the dry season (May–October) and peaks immediately after the first rains, which are roughly from November in East and southern Africa.

If you've been bitten by an infected mosquito, you can expect to feel the effects anywhere from seven to 90 days afterward. Typically you'll feel like you have the flu, with worsening high fever, chills and sweats, headache, and muscle aches. In some cases this is accompanied by abdominal pain, diarrhea, and a cough. If it's not treated you could die. It's possible to treat malaria after you've contracted it, but this shouldn't be your long-term strategy for dealing with the disease.

■TIP→ **If you feel ill even several months after you return home, tell your doctor that you've been in a malaria-infected area.**

MEDICAL CARE AND MEDICINE

As a foreigner, you'll be expected to pay in full for any medical services and claim back on your medical travel insurance later—keep all receipts. The equipment and training in private clinics rival the best in the world, but public hospitals tend to suffer from overcrowding and underfunding and are best avoided.

OVER-THE-COUNTER REMEDIES

You can buy over-the-counter medication in pharmacies and supermarkets. For expediency, however, you should bring your own supply for your trip and rely on pharmacies just for emergency medication.

MOTION SICKNESS

If you're prone to motion sickness, be sure to examine your safari itinerary closely. Though most landing strips for chartered planes aren't paved but rather grass, earth, or gravel, landings are smooth most of the time. If you're going on safari to northern Botswana (the Okavango Delta, specifically), know that small planes and unpaved airstrips are the main means of transportation between camps; these trips can be very bumpy, hot, and a little dizzying even if you're not prone to motion sickness. If you're not sure how you'll react, take motion-sickness pills just in case. Most of the air transfers take an average of only 30 minutes and the rewards will be infinitely greater than the pains.

■TIP→ **When you fly in small planes, take a sun hat and a pair of sunglasses.**

If you sit in the front seat next to the pilot, or on the side of the sun, you'll experience harsh glare that could give you a severe headache and exacerbate motion sickness.

SWIMMING

Don't swim in lakes or streams, as many, particularly east of the watershed divide (i.e., in rivers flowing toward the Indian Ocean), are infected with *bilharzia* (schistosomiasis), a parasite carried by a small freshwater snail. The microscopic fluke enters through the skin of swimmers or waders, attaches itself to the intestines or bladder, and lays eggs. Avoid wading in still waters or in areas close to reeds. If you've been wading or swimming in dubious water, dry yourself off vigorously with a towel immediately upon exiting the water, as this may help to dislodge any flukes before they can burrow into your skin. Fast-moving water is considered safe. If you've been exposed, pop into a pharmacy and purchase a course of treatment and take it to be safe. If your trip is ending shortly after your exposure, take the medicine home and have a check-up once you get home. Bilharzia is easily diagnosed, and it's also easily treated in the early stages.

VACCINATIONS

Traveling overseas is daunting enough without having to worry about all the scary illnesses you could contract. But if you do your research and plan accordingly, there's no reason to worry.

The Centers for Disease Control, or CDC, has an extremely helpful and informative website where you can find out country by country what you'll need. Remember that the CDC is going to be extremely conservative, so it's a good idea to meet with a trusted healthcare professional to decide what you'll really need, which will be determined by your itinerary. We've also included the basic information on the countries we cover in the preceding chart.

Keep in mind that there's a time frame for vaccines. You should see your health provider four to six weeks before you leave for your trip. Also keep in mind that vaccines and prescriptions could run you from $1,000 upwards. It's important to factor this into your budget when planning, especially if your plans include a large group.

You must be up-to-date with all of your routine shots such as the measles/mumps/rubella (MMR) vaccine, and diphtheria/pertussis/tetanus (DPT) vaccine. If you're not up-to-date, usually a simple booster shot will bring you up to par. If you're traveling to northern Kenya from December through June, don't be surprised if your doctor advises you to get inoculated against meningitis, as this part of the continent tends to see an outbreak during this time.

We can't stress enough the importance of taking malaria prophylactics. But be warned that all malaria medications aren't equal. Chloroquine is *not* an effective antimalarial drug in sub-Saharan Africa, as the mosquitoes have developed

Essentials

resistance. And halofantrine (marketed as Halfan), which is widely used overseas to treat malaria, has serious heart-related side effects, including death. The CDC recommends that you do *not* use halofantrine. Their website has a comprehensive list of the different malaria medications available, and which are recommended for each country.

HEPATITIS A AND B AND OTHER BOOSTERS

Hepatitis A can be transmitted via contaminated seafood, water, or fruits and vegetables. According to the CDC, hepatitis A is the most common vaccine-preventable disease in travelers. Immunization consists of a series of two shots received six months apart. You only need to have received the first one before you travel. This should be given at least four weeks before your trip.

The CDC recommends vaccination for hepatitis B only if you might be exposed to blood (if you're a health-care worker, for example), have sexual contact with the local population, stay longer than six months, or risk exposure during medical treatment. As needed, you should receive booster shots for tetanus-diphtheria (every 10 years), measles (you're usually immunized as a child), and polio (you're usually immunized as a child).

COVID-19

COVID-19 has disrupted travel since March 2020, and travelers should expect sporadic ongoing issues. Always travel with a mask in case it's required, and keep up to date on the most recent testing and vaccination guidelines for your safari destination.

All visitors must have a valid proof of COVID-19 vaccination and/or a booster; while the need and frequency of boosters is still being discussed in the medical community, it's important to verify the

Starstruck

With vast natural open areas and little or no light pollution, you'll be awed by the brilliance of the night skies on safari, especially if you live in a city. To add romance and interest to your stargazing, study up on the Southern Hemisphere skies and bring a star guide. Also, most guides are knowledgeable about the stars, so ask questions.

most recent requirements with your physician before you travel.

YELLOW FEVER

Yellow fever isn't endemic in any of the countries discussed in this book. Some countries, however, such as Kenya, will require you to present a valid yellow-fever inoculation certificate if prior to arrival you traveled to a region infected with yellow fever.

ZIKA VIRUS

Zika virus is also spread by mosquitos and is a very low level risk in Kenya and Tanzania and most people will show no or mild symptoms. These are fever, rash, headache, joint pain, red eyes, and muscle pain but don't usually last more than a few days. All travelers should protect themselves against mosquito bites and exposure through sexual contact during their trip.

🛏 Lodging

The days are long gone when legendary 19th-century explorer Dr. David Livingstone pitched his travel-stained tent under a tree and ate his sparse rations. But whether you go simple in a basic safari tent with an adjacent bucket shower and long-drop toilet, choose ultra-comfort in a mega tent or canvas-and-thatch chalet, or go totally over the top in a glass-walled aerie-cum-penthouse with a state-of-the-art designer interior, you'll still feel very much part of the bush.

LUXURY LODGES

Some would say that using the word "luxury" with "safari lodge" is redundant, as all such lodges fall into this category. But there's luxurious, and then there's *luxurious*. Options in the latter category range from *Out of Africa*–type accommodations with antique furniture, crystal, and wrought-iron chandeliers to thatch-roofed stone chalets, Tuscan villas, and suites that wouldn't seem out of place in midtown Manhattan. In nearly all, you can expect to find air-conditioning; in many there will be a small library, a spa, a gift shop, and internet service—often in a "business center" (a computer in the main lodge) or Wi-Fi. You may even have your own plunge pool.

PERMANENT TENTED CAMPS

Think luxurious, oh-so-comfortable, and spacious … in a tent. This is no ordinary tent, though. Each has its own bathroom, usually with an outdoor shower; a wooden deck with table and chairs that overlooks the bush; carpet or wooden floors; big "windows"; and an inviting four-poster (usually) bed with puffy pillows and fluffy blankets (for those cold winter months). The public space will comprise a bar, a lounge, dining areas, viewing decks, usually a pool, and a curio shop. Some will have Wi-Fi, air-conditioning, and private plunge pools.

MOBILE TENTED CAMPS

This option varies enormously. You could have the original, roomy walk-in dome tent (complete with canvas bedrolls, crisp cotton bedding on G.I. stretchers, open-air flush toilets, and bucket showers) that's ready and waiting for you at day's end. Or you could have luxury tents (with crystal chandeliers, antique rugs, and shining silver) that stay in one place for a few months during peak seasons. They're all fully serviced (the staff travels with the tents), and you'll dine under the stars or sip coffee as the sun rises.

$ Money

Most safaris are paid in advance, so you need money only to cover personal purchases and gratuities. The cash you take should include small denominations, like US$1, US$5, and US$10, for tips, but local currency is equally accepted and if you're self-driving many places prefer to be paid in the local currency. Make sure you change money where you can; local currency information is discussed in individual chapters. MasterCard and Visa are accepted almost everywhere; American Express less so and is not accepted in Botswana. Neither Diners Club nor Discover is recognized in most African countries.

■ TIP➔ It's a good idea to notify your credit card company that you'll be traveling to Africa so that unusual-looking transactions aren't denied.

FIGURING YOUR BUDGET

Consider three things: your flight, the actual safari costs, and extras. You can have a low-budget self-catering trip in a national park or spend a great deal for a small, exclusive lodge or camp. Almost every market has high-priced options as well as some economical ones.

Besides airfare and safari costs, make sure you budget for visas, tips, medications, and other sundries such as souvenirs. You'll likely stay at a hotel in your arrival/departure city on your first and last nights in Africa. Rates range from US$75 for basic accommodations to US$750 a night in the most luxurious hotels. If

Essentials

you do splurge on your safari, but want to keep costs down elsewhere, look for special offers—sometimes South African lodges will throw in a free night's accommodation in Cape Town, for example.

Plan to spend US$20–US$25 a day per traveler on gratuities. In South Africa tips are on the higher end of this range and usually are paid in rand. Elsewhere in Africa, U.S. dollars or local currency is acceptable.

LUXURY SAFARIS

The most popular safari option is to book with a tour operator and stay in private lodges or camps, which are owned and run by an individual or company rather than a country's government. Prices at these lodges include all meals and, in some cases, alcoholic beverages, as well as two three- to five-hour-long game-viewing expeditions a day. Often high-end lodges offer extra services such as spa treatments, boat trips, bush walks, or special-occasion meals served alfresco in the bush. Prices range approximately from US$300 to US$2,000 per person per night sharing a double room. If you travel alone, expect to pay a single supplement because all safari-lodge rooms are doubles; exceptions may be made depending on the property, the size of your group, and/or the season.

MONEY SAVING TIPS

Don't let a tight budget deter you. There are many opportunities for great big-game experiences without going over the top. And, you won't have to completely abandon the idea of comfort and style either. Here are some money-saving tips that every budget can appreciate.

Stay in accommodations outside the park or in a nearby town. This cuts down on the "mark-ups" that you may experience for the convenience of staying inside a park. And if your lodgings are close to the park gates, you can go into the park on day trips even for the early morning game drive so you won't miss anything.

Book a private lodge in the off-season. Many lodges—South Africa's Sabi Sand area, for example—cost on average about US$700–$1,200 per person, per night during the high season but can drop to about US$350 a night in the very low season; on average savings can be 30%–40%. In the rainy season, however, roads may be impassable in some areas and the wildlife hard to spot, so do your research beforehand. Sometimes the high season merely correlates with the European long vacation. In South Africa, the low season is from May to September, mostly because Cape Town is cold and wet during this time. However, regions north of the country, such as Kruger, are excellent for game-viewing during this time, as the winter is the dry season and grasses are short creating excellent visibility of wildlife. Early morning and nighttime can get cold, but the daytime is usually dry and sunny. You'll also have the benefit of fewer crowds, although if you're very social, you may find the off-season too quiet. If you're a honeymooner, it's perfect.

Budget for all aspects of your trip and watch out for hidden extras. Most safaris are all-inclusive, so you don't think about the cost of your sundowner drink, snacks on your game drive, or cocktails at mealtime. However, some lodges charge extra for drinks and excursions (e.g., a visit to a Maasai village in Kenya). You can keep your costs down by going to a place where things are à la carte and pay only for the things you deem important.

■TIP→ **Local beer is usually cheap, but wines are often imported (outside of South Africa) and are quite expensive.**

When you book your trip, be clear as to whether extras such as airport transfers, use of equipment (including sleeping bags on some mobile-camping safaris), and entry fees are included in the price.

Book your trip locally, or at the last minute. Last-minute deals can offer massive discounts, as long as you're prepared to be flexible about everything to do with your trip. Alternatively, book a trip locally once you're at your destination. This is popular in Kenya and Tanzania. You can also gather a group of people at your lodging and do a group booking. This way you'll have the benefit of a guide, too, with the cost shared among a number of people. You can also save money by booking with a tour operator that is based in the country you are visiting, as you will be cutting out the commission charged by an American agent. Make sure that you thoroughly research your prospective tour operator first, however, to ensure they have a consistently good reputation.

Passports and Visas

A valid passport is a must for travel to any African country. Certain countries, such as Kenya and South Africa, require that your passport be valid for 6 months from the date you arrive.

If you don't have a passport, apply immediately, because the process takes approximately five to six weeks. For a greatly increased fee, the application process can be shortened to as little as one week, but leaving this detail to the last minute can be stressful. If you have a passport, check that you have at least two facing blank pages for visas and stamps, which is a requirement for most countries; if not you will have to renew it.

■ TIP→ **If you're planning a honeymoon safari, make sure the bride's airline ticket, passport, and visas all use the same last name.**

Any discrepancies, especially between a passport and an airline ticket, will result in your trip being grounded before you even take off. Brides may want to consider waiting to change their last name until after the honeymoon. Do be sure to let the lodge know in advance that you're on your honeymoon. You'll get lots of special goodies and extra-special pampering thrown in.

For country-specific information regarding passports and visas, see the Passports and Visas section, under Planning, in each country chapter.

Travel Insurance

Comprehensive travel insurance is essential in addition to any primary insurance you already have. It should incorporate trip cancellation; trip interruption or travel delay; loss or theft of, or damage to, baggage; baggage delay; medical expenses; emergency medical transportation; and collision damage waiver if renting a car. These are offered by most travel insurance companies in one comprehensive policy and vary in price based on both your total trip cost and your age.

It's important to note that travel insurance doesn't always include coverage for threats of a terrorist incident or for any war-related activity. It's important that you speak with your operator before you book to find out how they would handle such occurrences. For example, would you be fully refunded if your trip was canceled because of war or a threat of a terrorist incident? Would your trip be postponed at no additional cost to you?

Essentials

TIP→ **Purchase travel insurance within seven days of paying your initial trip deposit. For most policies this will not only ensure your trip deposit, but also cover you for any preexisting medical conditions.**

Many travel agents and tour operators stipulate that travel insurance offering coverage for medical emergencies and medical evacuations due to injury or illness is mandatory, as this often involves the use of jet aircraft with hospital equipment and doctors on board and can amount to many thousands of dollars.

Most travel insurance policies cover this, but also consider signing up with a medical-evacuation assistance company. A membership gets you doctor referrals, emergency evacuation or repatriation, 24-hour hotlines for medical consultation, and other assistance; International SOS, AirMed International, and MedjetAssist. In East Africa, AMREF Flying Doctors is an air and road ambulance service based in Nairobi that covers Kenya, Tanzania and Uganda and many lodges and tour operators subscribe to the service. Alternatively they offer 30-day tourist membership from $16 and evacuation is initially to hospitals in Nairobi or Johannesburg.

◉ Types of Safaris
FLY-IN SAFARIS
The mode of transportation for fly-in safaris is as central to the experience as the accommodations. In places where few roads are paved and distances make road transfers impractical, small bush planes take you from lodge to lodge. The planes stay at low altitudes over fantastic landscapes, allowing you to spot game along the way: you might see elephant and buffalo herds lined up drinking along the edges of remote waterholes, or large numbers of zebras walking across the plains. Fly-in safaris also allow you to cover more territory than other types of safaris. In Botswana, for example, the trip between the diverse game destinations of the Moremi Game Reserve in the Okavango Delta and northern Chobe National Park is 40 minutes by plane; it

Document Checklist

- Passport
- Visas (if necessary)
- Airline tickets
- Copy of travel itinerary
- Proof of yellow-fever inoculation (if necessary)
- Accommodation and transfer vouchers
- Car-rental reservation forms
- International driver's license (if needed)
- Copy of information page of your passport
- Copy of airline tickets
- Copy of medical prescriptions
- COVID vaccination certificate
- List of credit-card numbers and international contact information for each card issuer
- Copy of travel insurance and medical-emergency evacuation policies
- Travel agent's contact numbers
- Notarized letter of consent from one parent if the other parent is traveling alone with their children (if needed)

	Yellow Fever	Malaria	Hepatitis A	Hepatitis B	Typhoid	Rabies	Polio	MMR	Covid-19	Other
Kenya	◐	●	●	●	●	●	●	●	●	Cholera; Meningitis
Tanzania	◐	●	●	●	●	●	●	●	●	Cholera
South Africa	◐	●	●	●	●	●	●	●	●	
Rwanda	◐	●	●	●	●	●	●	●	●	
Uganda	●	●	●	●	●	●	●	●	●	Cholera; Meningitis
Botswana	◐	●	●	●	●	●	●	●	●	
Namibia	◐	●	●	●	●	●	●	●	●	
Zambia	◐	●	●	●	●	●	●	●	●	Cholera
Zimbabwe	◐	●	●	●	●	●	●	●	●	

KEY: ● = Necessary

● = Recommended

◐ = The government requires travelers arriving from countries where yellow fever is present to have proof that they got the vaccination

would take up to six hours by vehicle on a difficult bush road (waterlogged during the rainy season and dry and sandy in the hot summer months).

Hopping from place to place by plane is so easy and fast that many travelers make the mistake of cramming their itineraries with too many lodges. Plan your trip this way and you'll spend more time at airstrips, in planes, and shuttling to and from the airfields than tracking animals or enjoying the bush. You'll glimpse animals as you travel back and forth—sometimes you'll even see them on the airstrips—but you won't have time to stop and really take in the sights. Try to spend at least two nights at any one lodge; three nights is better.

While you can book yourself directly with the airlines, by far the best way to set up a fly-in safari is to book an all-inclusive package that includes airfares. A tour operator makes all the arrangements for flights,

transfers, and accommodations, and many offer standard trips that visit several lodges.

■TIP→ **Remember there is a weight limit for baggage on small planes of 15kg (33lb) in a soft-sided bag.**

LUXURY LODGE–BASED SAFARIS

The majority of safari-goers base their trips at luxury lodges, which pack the double punch of outstanding game-viewing and stylish, atmospheric accommodations. A lodge may be made up of stone chalets, thatch-roof huts, rondavels, or large suitelike tents. Mosquito nets and leather furnishings add to the ambiance. Dinners are served inside or in an open-air boma. All have hot-and-cold running water, flush toilets, toiletries, laundry service, electricity, and, in most cases, swimming pools. Some lodges also have air-conditioning, telephones, hair dryers, and minibars. The most lavish places also have private plunge pools.

Essentials

Make no mistake: you pay for all this pampering. Expect to spend anywhere from US$500 to US$2,000 per person per night, depending on the quality and season. All meals, beverages, house wines, game drives, and walks are included. A three-night stay is ideal, but two nights are usually sufficient to see the big game.

The time you spend at a private lodge is tightly structured. With some exceptions, the lodges offer almost identical pro-grams of events. There are usually two three- to four-hour game drives a day, one in the early morning and another in the evening. You spend a lot of time sitting and eating, and in the afternoon you can nap and relax. However, you can always opt for an after-breakfast bush walk, and many lodges now have spas and gyms. If you're tired after your night drive, ask for something to be sent to your room, but don't miss the bush *braai* (barbecue) and at least one night in the boma (if your lodge offers it).

On game drives at bigger camps, guides stay in contact with one another via radio. If one finds a rhino, for example, he relays its location to the others so they can bring their guests. The more vehicles you have in the field, the more wildlife everyone is likely to see. But don't worry, most lodges are well disciplined with their vehicles, and there are rarely more than three or four at a sighting. As your vehicle arrives, one already there will drive away. Try to go on a bush walk with an armed guide—an unforgettable experience, as the guide can point out fascinating details along the way.

All lodges arrange transfers from nearby airports, train stations, or drop-off points. In more remote areas most have their own private airstrips carved out of the bush and guests fly in on scheduled or chartered aircraft at extra cost. If you're driving yourself, the lodge will send you detailed instructions because many of the roads don't appear on maps and lack names.

MOBILE AND OVERLAND SAFARIS

Most mobile (also known as overland) safari operations are expertly run but are aimed at budget-conscious travelers. They're mostly self-sufficient camping affairs with overnights at either public or private campgrounds, depending on the safari's itinerary and price. Sometimes you stay at basic lodges along the way. Travel is often by something that looks like a 4x4 bus.

For young, hardy people, or the young at heart, mobile safaris are a great way to see the land from ground level. You taste the dust, smell the bacon cooking, stop where and when you want (within reason), and get to see some of the best places in the region. Trips usually run 14 to 21 days, although you can find shorter ones that cover fewer destinations. Prices start from around US$750 per week including food cooked by the group and climb to US$1,500 per week for trips with cooks and camp staff. Consider combining a mobile/overland safari with a lodge-based one, which gives you the best of both worlds. You could for exam-ple go on a 21-day overland trip from Cape Town to Victoria Falls via Namibia and Botswana and spend extra time in hotels and lodges at either end.

WALKING SAFARIS

Many lodges offer walks as an optional way to view game. On a walking safari, however, you spend most, if not all, of your time in the bush on foot, accompa-nied by an armed guide. Because you're trekking through big-game country, there's an element of danger. But it's the proximity to wilderness that makes this type of trip so enchanting—and exciting. Of course, you can't stop every step of the way or you'd never get very far, but you'll stop frequently to be shown something—from a native flower to spoor to animals—or to discuss some aspect of animal behavior or of tracking.

Walking treks take place on what are known as wilderness trails, which are natural tracks made by animals and are traversed only on foot, never by vehicle, to maintain their pristine condition. These trails usually lead into remote areas that you would never see on a typical safari. In some cases porters carry the supplies and bags. Accommodations are usually in remote camps or occasionally in tents.

■ TIP → **Consider your physical condition for walking safaris.**

You should be in good health and be able to walk between 6 and 16 km (3.7 and 10 miles) a day, depending on the scope of the trip. Some trips don't allow hikers under age 12 or over age 60 (but Kruger Park makes exceptions for those over 60 if you produce a doctor's certificate). Also, you shouldn't scare easily. No guide has time for people who freeze up at the sight of a beetle, spider, or something more menacing; guides need to keep their attention on the wilds around them and on the group as a whole. Guides are armed, and they take great caution to keep you away from trouble. To stay safe, always listen to your guide and follow instructions.

🗓 When to Go

The seasons in sub-Saharan Africa are opposite of those in North America. Summer is December through March, autumn is April and May, winter is June through September, and spring is October and November.

HIGH SEASON/DRY SEASON

High season, also called dry season, refers to the winter months in southern and East Africa when there's little to no rain at all. Days are sunny and bright, but the nights are cool. In the desert, temperatures can plummet to below freezing, but you'll be snug and warm in your tent wherever you stay. The landscape will be barren and dry (read: not very attractive), but vegetation is low and surface water is scarce, making it easier to spot game. This is the busiest tourist time.

The exception is South Africa, where high season is linked with the summer vacation schedules of South Africans (December–mid-January), and both the European summer vacations (July and August) and Christmas holidays (December and January).

LOW SEASON/RAINY SEASON

When we say "low season," we're saying that this is the rainy season. Although the rains are intermittent—often occurring in late afternoon—the bush and vegetation are high and it's more difficult to spot game. It can also get very hot and humid during this time. However, the upside is that there are far fewer tourists, lodge rates are much cheaper (often half price), and the bush is beautifully lush and green. Plus there are lots of baby animals, and if you're a birder all the migrant species are back from their winter habitats.

SHOULDER SEASON

The shoulder season occurs between summer and winter; it's fall in the United States. The rains are just beginning, tourist numbers are decreasing, and the vegetation is starting to die off. Lodges will offer cheaper rates.

Distances and Flying Times

UGANDA
KAMPALA
Kisumu
Lake Victoria
Musoma
KIGALI
RWANDA
Mwanza
Shinyanga
Sumbawanga
Kasama

KENYA
Wajir
Mt Kenya
Embu NAIROBI
235 kms, 30mn
SERENGETI PLAIN
Mt Kilimanjaro 430 k
Arusha Moshi 55n
665 kms, 1hr 5mn
420 kms, 50mn
480 kms, 1hr
Momba
Zanzib
DODOMA
TANZANIA
Iringa
Dar es Salaan
Lindi
Mtwara
Mbeya

Lake Turkana

Lake Tanganyika

2,900 kms, 4hr 50mn
2,245 kms 3hr 55mn

ZAMBIA
LUSAKA
CAPRIVI STRIP
Livingstone
Victoria Falls
HARARE
454 kms, 50mn
ZIMBABWE
925 kms, 1hr 30mn
945 kms, 1hr 40mn
665 kms, 1hr 45mn

Etosha Pan
Outjo Tsumeb
NAMIBIA
675 kms, 1hr 25mn
OKAVANGO DELTA
Maun
830 kms, 1hr 35mn
WINDHOEK
Swakopmund
Walvis Bay
BOTSWANA
KALAHARI DESERT
GABORONE
1,150 kms, 2hr
350 kms, 40mn
Mpumalanga
1,280 kms, 2hr 10mn
Johannesburg
275 kms, 30mn
485 kms, 50mn
Richards Bay
Luderitz
1,280 kms, 2hr 15mn
1,625 kms, 2hr 50mn
Kimberley
1,250 kms, 2hr 10mn
500 kms, 1hr
Durban
SOUTH AFRICA
Orange River
1,280 kms, 2hr
EAST CAPE
East London
Cape Town
Wilderness
Gqeberha (Port Elizabeth)
Plettenburg
Cape of Good Hope

NAMIB DESERT
ATLANTIC OCEAN
INDIAN OCEAN
Mozambique Chan

0   500 mi
0   500 km

Safari Planning Timeline

SIX MONTHS AHEAD
- Research destinations and options and make a list of sights you want to see.

- Start a safari file to keep track of information.

- Set a budget.

- Search the Internet. Post questions on bulletin boards and narrow your choices. Watch out for fake trip reviews posted by unscrupulous travel agents.

- Choose your destination and make your reservations.

- Apply for a passport, or renew yours if it's due to expire within six months of travel time. Many countries require at least two empty pages in your passport.

- Buy travel insurance.

THREE TO SIX MONTHS AHEAD
- Find out which travel documents you need.

- Confirm whether your destination requires visas and certified health documents.

- Arrange vaccinations or medical clearances.

- Research malaria precautions.

- Book excursions, tours, and side trips.

ONE TO THREE MONTHS AHEAD
- Create a packing checklist.

- Fill prescriptions for antimalarial and regular medications. Buy mosquito repellent.

- Shop for safari clothing and equipment.

- Arrange for a house and pet sitter.

ONE MONTH AHEAD
- Get copies of any prescriptions and make sure you have enough of any needed medicine to last you a few days longer than your trip.

- Confirm international flights, transfers, and lodging reservations directly with your travel agent.

- Using your packing list, start buying articles you don't have. Update the list as you go.

ONE WEEK AHEAD
- Suspend newspaper and mail delivery.

- Collect small denominations of U.S. currency ($1, $5 and $10) for tips (only the case in East Africa and Zimbabwe).

- Check antimalarial prescriptions to see whether you need to start taking medication now.

- Arrange transportation to the airport.

- Make two copies of your passport's data page. Leave one copy, and a copy of your itinerary, with someone at home; pack the other separately from your passport. Make a PDF of these pages and email them to yourself for access.

Packing for a Safari

If your itinerary states that soft bags are needed on flights between lodges, this is because storage space on light aircraft is limited and therefore luggage should be soft (e.g. a duffel bag or flexible bag made from leather, cotton or canvas) so they can be manipulated into a small hold in the plane. Weight is usually 15kg (33lb), with a maximum dimension of 25cm (10 inches) wide, 30cm (12 inches) high, and 62cm (24 inches) long—it's essential you check ahead. A personal-effects bag can go on your lap. Keep all your documents and money in this personal bag. Speak to your tour operator but in most cases other luggage is left at the airline's office at the departure airport for your safari flight. Soft bags are also recommended for mobile or overland safaris where there will be limited space for luggage in the safari 4x4 vehicle.

CLOTHING

You should need only three changes of clothing for an entire trip; almost all lodges and camps have a laundry service, although bear in mind that in remote places water maybe scarce as it is trucked in so only wash clothes when you really need to. If you're self-driving you can carry more, but washing is still easy, especially if you use drip-dry fabrics that need no ironing. On mobile safaris you can wear tops and bottoms more than once, and either bring enough underwear to last a week between lodges, or wash as you go in the bathroom sink—bring a small tube of detergent. Unless there's continual rain (unlikely), clothes dry overnight in the hot, dry African air.

TOILETRIES AND SUNDRIES

Most hotels and game lodges provide toiletries (soap, shampoo, insect repellent, etc.) so you don't need to pack these items. In the larger lodges, stores and gift shops are fairly well stocked with clothing and guidebooks; in self-drive and self-catering areas, shops also carry food and drink. Many lodges have small shops with a selection of books, clothing, and curios.

■ TIP→ **The African sun is harsh, and if you're even remotely susceptible to burning, especially coming from a northern winter, don't skimp on sunscreens and moisturizers.**

BINOCULARS

Binoculars are essential and come in many types and sizes. You get what you pay for, so avoid buying a cheap pair—the optics will be poor and the lenses usually don't stay aligned for long, especially if they get bumped, which they will on safari. Whatever strength you choose, pick the most lightweight pair, otherwise you'll be in for neck and shoulder strain. Take them with you on a night drive; you'll get great visuals of nocturnal animals and birds by the light of the tracker's spotlight. Many people find that when they start using binoculars and stop documenting each trip detail on film, they have a much better safari experience.

■ TIP→ **Many high-end camps provide binoculars, so ask before purchasing and packing them.**

PACKING CHECKLIST

Light, khaki, or neutral-color clothes are universally worn on safari and were first used in Africa as camouflage by the South African Boers, and then by the British Army that fought them during the South African War. Light colors also help to deflect the harsh sun and are less likely than dark colors to attract mosquitoes. Don't wear camouflage gear. Do wear layers of clothing that you can strip off as the sun gets hotter and put back on as the sun goes down.

- Smartphone or tablet to check emails, send texts, and store photos (also handy as an alarm clock and flashlight), plus an adapter. If electricity will be limited, you may wish to bring a portable charger.

- Three cotton T-shirts

- Two long-sleeve cotton shirts preferably with collars

- Two pairs of shorts or two skirts in summer

- Two pairs of long pants (three pairs in winter)—trousers that zip off at the knees are worth considering

- Optional: sweatshirt and sweatpants, which can double as sleepwear

- One smart-casual dinner outfit

- Underwear and socks

- Walking shoes or sneakers

- Sandals/flip-flops

- Bathing suit and sarong to use as a cover-up

- Warm padded jacket and sweater/fleece in winter

- Windbreaker or rain poncho

- Camera equipment, extra batteries or charger, and memory cards; a photographer's vest and cargo pants are great for storage

- Eyeglasses and/or contact lenses, plus extras

- Binoculars

- Small flashlight

- Personal toiletries

- Malaria tablets and prescription medication

- Sunscreen and lip balm with SPF 30 or higher

- Basic medication like antihistamine cream, eye drops, headache tablets, indigestion remedies, etc.

- Insect repellent that is at least 20% DEET and is sweat-resistant

- Tissues and/or premoistened wipes/hand sanitizer

- Warm hat, scarf, and gloves in winter

- Sun hat and sunglasses (Polaroid and UV-protected ones)

- Documents and money (cash, credit cards, etc.).

- A notebook/journal and pens

- Travel and field guide books

- A couple of large white plastic garbage bags

- Ziplock bags to keep documents dry and protect electronics from dust

- U.S. dollars in small denominations ($1, $5, $10) for tipping

Vocabulary

Mastering the basics of just two languages, Zulu (or isiZulu) and Swahili (Kiswahili), should make you well equipped for travel through much of the region and it's polite to try a few local words. Zulu is the most common of the Southern African Nguni family of languages (Zulu, Shangaan, Ndebele, Swazi, Xhosa) and is understood in South Africa and Zimbabwe. Swahili is a mixture of Arabic and Bantu and is used across East Africa. In Namibia, Botswana, and Zambia your best bet initially is to stick with English.

SAFARI SPEAK

Ablution blocks: public bathrooms

Banda: bungalow or hut

Big Five: buffalo, elephants, leopards, lions, and rhinoceroses, collectively

Boma: a fenced-in, open-air eating area, usually circular

Braai: barbecue

Bushveld: general safari area in South Africa, usually with scattered shrubs and trees and lots of game; also referred to as the bush or the veld

Camp: often with luxury tents but also used interchangeably with lodge

Campground: a place used for camping that encompasses several campsites and often includes some shared facilities

Campsite: may or may not be part of a campground

Concession: game-area lease that's granted to a safari company and gives it exclusive access to the land

Hides: small, partially camouflaged shelters from which to view game and birds; blinds

Kopje/Koppies: hills or rocky outcrops

Kraal: traditional rural settlement of huts and houses

Lodge: accommodation in rustic yet stylish tents, rondavels, or lavish suites; prices at lodges usually include all meals and game-viewing

Marula: tree from which *amarula* (the liquor) gets its name

Mobile or overland safari: usually a self-sufficient camping affair set up at a different location (public or private campgrounds) each night

Mokoro: dugout canoe; plural *mekoro*

Nocturnal: a term for animals that are active at night and can be seen by spotlight on night drives

Ranger: usually called safari guide in Africa with vast experience with and knowledge of the bush and the animals that inhabit it

Rest camp: camp in a national park

Rondavel/rondawel: a traditional round dwelling with a conical roof

Sala: outdoor covered deck

Self-catering: with some kind of kitchen facilities, so you can store food and prepare meals yourself

Self-drive safari: budget safari option in which you drive, and guide, yourself in a rented vehicle

Sundowner: cocktails at sunset

Tracker: works in conjunction with a ranger/guide, spotting animals from a special seat on the front of the 4x4 game-viewing vehicle

Vlei: wetland or marsh

SOUTH AFRICAN WORDS AND PHRASES

Abseil: rappel

Babbelas: a bad hangover

Bakkie: pickup truck (pronounced "bucky")

Berg: mountain

Boot: trunk (of a car)

Bottle store: liquor store

Bra/bru/my bra: brother (term of affection or familiarity)

Buck: antelope

Chommie: mate, chum

Djembes: drums

Dorp: village

Eish!: expression for when someone experiences surprise

Fanagalo: a mix of Zulu, English, Afrikaans, Sotho, and Xhosa languages

Highveld: the country's high interior plateau, including Johannesburg

Howzit?: literally, "How are you?" but used as a general greeting

Indaba: literally, a meeting, but also a problem, as in "That's your indaba."

Ja: yes

Jol: a party or night on the town

Kloof: river gorge

Kokerbooms: quiver trees

Lekker: nice

Lowveld: land at lower elevation, including Kruger National Park

More-ish: so good you'll want more, mouthwatering

Muthi: traditional (non-Western) medicine (pronounced "mooti")

Petrol: gasoline

Plaas: farm

Robot: traffic light

Sangoma: traditional healer or mystic

Shebeen: a place to drink, often used for taverns in townships

Sis: gross, disgusting

Sisi or usisi: sister (term of affection or respect)

Spaza shop: an informal shop, usually from a truck or container

Stoep: veranda

Takkie: sneaker (pronounced "tacky")

SWAHILI ESSENTIALS
ANIMALS

Buffalo: nyati

Cheetah: duma

Crocodile: mamba

Elephant: tembo

Giraffe: twiga

Hippo: kiboko

Impala: swala

Leopard: chui

Lion: simba

Rhino: kifalu

BASICS

Yes: ndio

No: hapana

Please: tafadhali

Excuse me: samahani

Thank you (very much): asante (sana)

Welcome: karibu

Hello: jambo

Beautiful: nzuri

Vocabulary

Good-bye: kwaheri

Cheers: kwahafya njema

FOOD AND DRINK
Food: chakula

Water: maji

Bread: mkate

Fruit(s): (ma)tunda

Vegetable: mboga

Salt: chumvi

Sugar: sukari

Coffee: kahawa

Tea: chai

Beer: pombe

USEFUL PHRASES
What's your name?: Jina lako nani?

My name is … : Jina langu ni…

How are you?: Habari?

Where are you from?: Unatoka wapi?

I come from … : Mimi ninatoka…

Do you speak English?: Una sema Kiingereza?

I don't speak Swahili.: Sisemi Kiswahili.

I don't understand.: Sifahamu.

How do you say this in Swahili?: Unasema-je kwa Kiswahili?

How much is it?: Ngapi shillings?

May I take your picture?: Mikupige picha?

Where is the bathroom?: Choo kiko wapi?

I need … : Mimi natafuta…

I want to buy … : Mimi nataka kununua…

No problem.: Hakuna matata.

ZULU ESSENTIALS
BASICS
Yes: yebo

No: cha

Please/Excuse me: uxolo

Thank you: ngiyabonga

You're welcome: nami ngiyabonga

Good morning/hello: sawubona

Good-bye: sala kahle

FOOD AND DRINK
Food: ukudla

Water: amanzi

Bread: isinkwa

Fruit: isthelo

Vegetable: uhlaza

Salt: usawoti

Sugar: ushekela

Coffee: ikhofi

Tea: itiye

Beer: utshwala

USEFUL PHRASES
What's your name?: Ubani igama lakho?

My name is … : Igama lami ngingu…

Do you speak English?: Uya khuluma isingisi?

I don't understand.: Angizwa ukuthi uthini.

How much is it?: Kuyimalini lokhu?

May I take your picture?: Mikupige picha?

Where is the bathroom?: Likuphi itholethe?

I would like … : Ngidinga…

I want to buy … : Ngicela…

Why Go With an Operator

Booking a vacation yourself online is now very much the norm, and there's a widespread perception that you'll get a more authentic and reasonably priced experience if you do it all yourself. This approach often works for American or European city visits or package beach holidays, but not as frequently for an African safari which may have complicated components such as flights, transfers, and moving between destinations. You may save money, but you could end up with hassles that outweigh the savings.

THINGS TO CONSIDER

Do you have only 12 days or less? Africa is huge and infrastructure isn't well developed outside South Africa. Flights from the United States and Europe are long and seldom direct, and if one leg is delayed you can miss your connection and derail your whole itinerary. Just getting to a lodge from an airstrip can be a time-consuming journey, too. A tour operator will know the ins and outs of local travel so you're aware of traveling times in advance, and they'll sort things out if they don't go as planned. They also know the best ways to contact lodges and airlines, which can be challenging due to time differences between countries on the continent and the United States, as well as unreliable phone and Internet.

Safety and surprises. Although the countries you're likely to visit are largely stable and safe, first-time travelers in particular can be anxious about their virgin journey into unknown terrain. Political climates can change quickly, and news can be slow to filter out through traditional news channels. Your operator has contacts on the ground who keep them up-to-date with relevant information. Natural disasters, or even heavier-than-expected rainfall, can make roads dangerous or impassable, and a tour operator can adjust your itinerary accordingly. And

they will be accountable if anything goes wrong or if you don't receive the service you paid for.

Specific requests or interests. When you plan a safari, you're presented with multiple countries and infinite options, depending on your budget, the time of year, whether you want to see animals and landscape in a vehicle, on foot, on horseback, or on a boat, and whether you want to stay in a canvas tent or a hotel. You may have dietary or health issues, or want an eco-holiday rather than a butler and private plunge pool. You might want to see three countries in 10 days or just one in a week. A good tour operator will discuss your preferences and tailor an experience that delivers exactly what you want and how you want it, saving you weeks of research. Tour operators also have the kind of overview of an area and its various options that you can't pick up from reading individual reviews of places online.

Details, big and small. Weight allowance on planes, yellow-fever certificates, visas, tipping—these are just some of the easily overlooked details that a good outfitter will tend to. You'll also receive valuable information about local culture and customs.

Choices and prices. Hotels and lodges have two sets of prices—rack rates, which are what the public pays, and a cheaper rate for tour operators. The operator will add their own markup, but you often still pay less, and you'll be aware of all the costs involved up-front, which allows you to budget better. Tour operators will also buffer you against currency fluctuations—the price you'll pay months in advance of a trip will be guaranteed. Also, many lodges don't take bookings directly from the public because they also prefer their clients to go through an

Why Go With an Operator

operator, so you'll automatically lose out on a lot of good choices.

TYPES OF SAFARI OPERATORS

African tour operator. Usually based in the United States, this type of company specializes in tours and safaris to Africa and works with a safari operator that provides support on the ground. Start dates and itineraries are set for some trips, but customized vacations can almost always be arranged. Travelers can find out the details of these trips through retail travel agents but can also deal directly with the company, usually by talking with them about their preferences on the phone and then receiving a personalized itinerary and quote via email.

African safari operator/ground operator. This type of outfitter is a company in Africa that provides logistical support to a U.S.-based tour operator by seeing to the details of your safari. An operator might charter flights, pick you up at the airport, and take you on game-viewing trips. Some operators own or manage safari lodges. In addition, a safari operator communicates changing trends and developments in the region to tour operators and serves as your on-site contact in cases of illness, injury, or other unexpected situations. For example, &Beyond is an African tour operator that uses a ground operator to handle logistics and accommodations. Micato and Wilderness Safaris on the other hand, handle every stage of your trip themselves.

Retail travel agent. In general, a travel agent sells trip packages directly to consumers. In most cases an agent doesn't have a geographical specialty. When called on to arrange a trip to Africa, the travel agent turns to an African tour operator for details.

Before you entrust your trip to tour operators or travel agents, do your best to determine the extent of their knowledge as well as the level of enthusiasm they have for the destination. There are as many travel companies claiming to specialize in Africa as there are hippos in the Zambezi, so it's especially important to determine which operators and agents are up to the challenge.

We've featured some of the best further on in this chapter.

After choosing a tour operator or travel agent, it's a good idea to discuss with him or her the logistics and details of the itinerary so you know what to expect each day. Ask questions about lodging, even if you're traveling on a group tour. A lodge that's completely open to the elements may be a highlight for some travelers and terrifying for others, particularly at night when a lion roars nearby. Also ask about the amount of time you'll spend with other travelers. If you're planning a safari honeymoon, find out if you can dine alone when you want to, and ask about honeymoon packages.

QUESTIONS TO ASK A SAFARI SPECIALIST

We recommend you withhold your deposit until you've considered your operator's answers to most of the following questions. Consider how responsive the agent is to your queries. If they take a long time to get back to you, aren't easy to get hold of on the phone, don't read your emails properly, or make mistakes with details in the beginning stages, it's not a good sign. The level of service you receive when gathering information and booking the trip is a strong indicator of the company's professionalism. Once you pay the deposit, you're liable for a penalty if you decide to cancel the arrangements for any reason.

■ **How many years have you been selling tours in Africa?**

■ How many people does your company take on safari every year?

■ Where do you have offices—do you have any in the destination itself?

■ Can you provide past traveler references?

■ To which professional organizations do you belong? For example, the American Society of Travel Agents (ASTA) or the United States Tour Operators Association (USTOA)? International Airlines Travel Agent Network (IATAN) members must have annual sales exceeding US$250,000 and carry a US$1 million liability insurance policy, which eliminates fly-by-night operators.

■ Do you have bonding insurance? (This protects you if the company goes under and your agent defaults before your trip.)

■ What is your security policy? How do you mitigate risks and stay informed of potential threats?

■ What are your cancellation policies in the event of a U.S. State Department or World Health Organization travel warning, or a natural disaster?

■ What are the payment terms? Do you offer optional trip cancellation insurance in case I need to cancel?

■ Can you handle arrangements from start to finish, including flights? Is there a 24-hour support line if needed?

■ Who will lead my trip, and what are their qualifications? Will they be with me the whole time, or will I be with different local guides at each place?

■ Do you have your own guides and vehicles? What certification and/or training is required for your guides?

■ Do you charge a fee? (Agents and operators usually make their money through commissions.)

■ What's included in the cost? For instance are permits, departure taxes, and game park fees included? What about meals and drinks? And equally, what is not included? Tips and optional excursions like balloon flights or boat trips?

■ What is the maximum and minimum size of a group? And, is the trip guaranteed to operate regardless of the number of travelers?

■ What level of fitness is required for this trip?

■ Do you operate any social and environmental responsibility programs, or support any NGOs? Can I get involved with your philanthropic efforts or learn about volunteering efforts?

■ Do you have any affiliation to a particular lodge chain, or will you refer me to lodges or camps you own yourself only? (An operator can keep costs down by doing this, but you'll benefit the most from impartial advice.)

■ Has your company won any industry or magazine awards?

■ Will you be able to arrange any add-on experiences, such as a beach break or a city stay afterward?

■ Do you accept bookings from single travelers? If so, will I have to pay a single supplement, or, are there ways around the fee, i.e. traveling at a different time of year?

GOING GREEN

How do you ensure that your operator is committed to sustainability, works with the local community, and leaves as light an impact on the landscape as possible? It can be tricky because many companies "green-wash"—they apply an eco tag to their trips or services without any real follow-through. Until an official ratings

Why Go With an Operator

system is in place, you'll have to do the research yourself—though Kenya has a reliable website with ratings. (*See box in Chapter 3*)

Conservation organizations such as The International Ecotourism Society (🌐 *www.ecotourism.org*) and the African Wildlife Foundation (🌐 *www.awf.org*) promote green tourism standards. Another excellent resource is Africa's Finest (🌐 www.africasfinest.co.za), a website started by the renowned conservationist Colin Bell and travel journalist and environmental scientist David Bristow. The team spent two years independently assessing hundreds of lodges in order to pinpoint those with truly eco credentials; although the list on their website is not exhaustive, it's a very useful resource. There's also a list of NGOs they consider worthy of support.

Private conservancies are usually able to offer a more environmentally sustainable model than national parks. Conservancies are created out of tracts of land, usually adjacent to a national park, that have been leased from the local community for the purpose of wildlife conservation. They have strict usage conditions—meaning no overcrowding—and experiences that national parks can't offer, such as night drives and walking safaris. Although lodges on conservancies can be expensive to stay in, the fees go directly toward supporting conservation and local communities.

Ask your operator the following questions to find out where they stand on the 4 C's: Commerce, Conservation, Community, and Culture.

■ Are the lodges on the itineraries solar-powered? Solar energy is inexpensive and reliable and can be used for heating water, lighting, and cooking, so there's really no excuse.

■ What are the recycling, water conservation, and waste management practices? Are environmentally friendly cleaning products used, and does the lodge purify its own water rather than bringing in hundreds of plastic water bottles?

■ Does the lodge's dining menu use local ingredients? Or, even better, are ingredients sourced on-site from local communities? Is leftover food composted?

■ Are the safari guides, rangers, and trackers employed from local ethnic groups and communities in the region in which you're traveling?

■ Do the chefs, cleaning staff, and porters hail from the surrounding area?

■ Does the company, or the lodges it uses, provide educational and economic opportunities, or promote healthcare, for local people?

■ Does the company have any philanthropic or "voluntourism" projects such as building and maintaining a school or a health clinic?

■ Does the lodge offer low-impact activities such as walking, horseback riding, cycling, or canoe excursions? The experience should be about more than just ticking off the Big Five.

■ Does the lodge support academic and scientific research, or is it involved in any programs to support or reintroduce endangered species?

Many reputable outfitters have established foundations that make donations to local peoples or wildlife, and some will arrange trips to nearby schools, orphanages, or neighborhoods. We've highlighted the philanthropic endeavors of a number of top operators in our Tour Operators list.

Tour Operators

Our list of tour operators hardly exhausts the number of reputable companies, but the following operators, sorted alphabetically, are well-established firms that offer a good selection of itineraries ranging from overland safaris to walking and fly-in safaris, under-canvas safaris, and safari lodges. They all offer fully customizable trips, too.

TOP 10 OUTFITTERS

Abercrombie & Kent. In business since 1962, this company is considered one of the best in the business and is consistently given high marks by former clients. From your first decision to go on safari to its successful conclusion, A&K offers seamless service. Their tailor-made safaris hearken back to days past when intrepid adventurers such as Teddy Roosevelt and Ernest Hemingway relied on private guides to create a safari program and escort them through the bush from start to finish. The company has a professional network of local A&K offices in all its destination countries, staffed by full-time A&K experts, and maintains its own fleet of 4X4 safari vehicles and trains its own drivers. The head office in the U.S. is in Illinois.

Destinations: Botswana, Ethiopia, Kenya, Mozambique, Madagascar, Namibia, South Africa, Tanzania, Uganda, Rwanda, Zambia, Zimbabwe.

Popular packages: Ultimate East African Safari: Kenya & Tanzania, 12 days, from $6,980.

Philanthropy: Extensive projects benefit ecosystems and wildlife, communities and cultures, and health and education. Guests can meet local people making a positive impact, and many guests build their safari around several of these projects.

What they do best: Destination knowledge—they have some of the most experienced guides on the continent. ✉ 1411 Opus Pl., Downers Grove ☎ 866/648–6751 ⊕ www.abercrombiekent.com.

Access2Tanzania. After living in Tanzania for two years as a Peace Corps volunteer, owner Brian Singer set up Access2Tanzania in 2004 with his wife Karen and Tanzanian partner Michael Musa. Brian and Karen handle all presafari planning, and Michael takes care of ground logistics. They are one of few companies in Tanzania that do not subcontract their guides; each one is a full-time employee and they all consistently receive rave reviews. They own and maintain their own air-conditioned vehicles, which have unlimited mileage and pop-up roofs to allow 360-degree views.

Destinations serviced: Rwanda, Tanzania.

Most popular packages: Tanzania's Classic North, 9 nights, from $4,235; Adventures through Northern Tanzania, 7 nights, from $2,895.

Philanthropy: The owners run a nonprofit, Project Zawadi, which supports the educational needs of orphans and other vulnerable Tanzanian children. Hundreds of children are put through school each year, and it has also built several classrooms, teacher's accommodations, and a vocational training center.

What they do best: Itineraries are custom-made and private only; the team works hard to ensure that the individual needs of each client are met. They have offices in both Tanzania and the United States, meaning service is superb before, during, and after the safari. ✉ 253 Duke St., St. Paul ☎ 718/715–1353 ⊕ www.access2tanzania.com.

Tour Operators

African Portfolio. African Portfolio's team prides themselves on discovering the best places, whether they're hidden gems, up-and-coming properties, or well-established classics. With each client, they're committed to providing a safari reminiscent of what captivates them about Africa. Their mission is to provide unique and memorable experiences through nature-based travel that educate, entertain, inspire, and provide participants with opportunities to directly contribute to conservation.

Destinations: Botswana, Kenya, Malawi, Mozambique, Namibia, Rwanda, Seychelles, South Africa, Tanzania, Uganda, Zambia, Zimbabwe.

Popular packages: Botswana and Zimbabwe Explorer: Chobe, Victoria Falls and Hwange, 11 days, from $5,300; Great Rift Valley Safari, Tanzania, 12 days, from $10,650.

Philanthropy: African Portfolio was started in Zimbabwe and they have their own charity there called Kasipiti, which supports children in need with school fees and further education opportunities. They also donate to Uthando, a charity that works to empower disadvantaged communities in Cape Town.

What they do best: Creating tailor-made safaris incorporating unique, genuine, and "off the beaten path" experiences. ✉ *146 Sound Beach Ave., Greenwich* ☎ *800/700–3677* ⊕ *www.onsafari.com.*

Deeper Africa. This small, hands-on company, based in Colorado, has built its reputation on three things: excellent service, quality guides, and amazing wildlife viewing. Owners Wil Smith and Karen Zulauf have spent nearly two decades developing unique contacts that enable privileged access for their guests. Their knowledge of wildlife migration and movement patterns means that Deeper Africa travelers are in the right places, at the right time. They highly recommend having one of their guides join guests for their entire safari, allowing for discovery of the people, culture, and politics of Africa beyond wildlife basics. They also have a number of special itineraries that can include kids from seven years old.

Destinations: Botswana, the Congo, Kenya, Rwanda, Namibia, Tanzania, Uganda, South Africa, Zambia, Zimbabwe.

Popular packages: Kenya & Tanzania Safari, 13 days, from $13,100.

Philanthropy: Deeper Africa supports conservation and community programs and creates opportunities for travelers to do the same both personally and monetarily.

What they do best: Great wildlife viewing delivered by expert guides and authentic cultural experiences that give unique insights into African culture. ✉ *5353 Manhattan Circle, Suite 202, Boulder* ☎ *303/415–2574* ⊕ *www.deeperafrica. com.*

Gamewatchers Safaris. This Nairobi-based company specializes in delivering luxury tailor-made safaris to small camps and lodges in the top game-viewing areas of East Africa with an importance put on helping protect Africa's wildlife, ecosystems, and cultures. Gamewatchers runs their own ground operations, ensuring guests are well looked after from the start of their trip to the finish. Guests often add beach trips to the end of their safaris.

Destinations: Botswana, Kenya, Mauritius, Rwanda, Seychelles, South Africa, Tanzania, Uganda, Zambia.

Popular packages: Classic Kenya & Tanzania Safari, 14 days, from $4,334; Adventure Camping Safari in Kenya, 7 days, from $2,240.

Philanthropy: Pioneers of the conservancy concept, here habitat is conserved in cooperation with local communities. They also support primary schools at Selenkay and Ol Kinyei conservancies and more than 1,000 Maasai families are direct beneficiaries of their programs that assist with water provision, sanitation, and predator protection for villages, while the Koiyaki Guiding School provides tourism training for the Maasai.

What they do best: A personal, authentic experience, as far from mass-market tourism as it's possible to get. ☎ 877/710–3014 ⊕ www.gamewatchers.com.

Micato Safaris. Family-owned and-operated, this New York–based operator offers ultraluxurious trips driven by a sustainable ethos. Safari lodges enchant with such unadulterated luxuries as private plunge pools and personal butlers. Cultured safari guides educate, instruct, and amuse, while itineraries offer an irresistible array of experiences from the sophisticated pleasures of Cape Town to the celebrated savannas of the Serengeti and the near-spiritual beauty of the Kalahari. Micato has been long praised for its ability to deliver seamless personalized "un-group-like" service and over-the-top luxury without sacrificing true immersion in the "real Africa." Stand-out inclusions on Micato programs include time-saving bush flights between lodges and an "all-included" policy that covers all gratuities, meals, alcoholic beverages, laundry, and just about anything else one could think of.

Destinations: Botswana, Kenya, Namibia, Rwanda, South Africa, Tanzania, Uganda, Zambia, Zimbabwe.

Popular packages: The Hemingway Wing Safari, Kenya, 14 days, from $18,100 per person.

Philanthropy: Their charitable endeavors are impressive, with visits to the Micato-AmericaShare Harambee Community Center, a highlight for many clients. In addition, every safari sold puts one Kenyan child in school through Micato-AmericaShare's One for One program.

What they do best: Impeccable service from start to finish alongside excellent community projects. ⊠ 15 W. 26th St., New York ☎ 212/545–7111 ⊕ www.micatosafaris.com.

Natural Habitat Adventures. Nicknamed "The Nature People," this operator is known for its focus on wildlife and conservation. Nat Hab's headquarters are in Colorado, and although they organize trips to destinations around the world they have a good reputation for arranging incredible safaris. They always choose the best destinations for viewing wildlife and focus on small groups and intimate lodges in secluded, off-the-beaten-track settings. Their online safari-building tool, iSafari.com, is a useful starting point for getting an idea of what's possible before speaking to one of the experts in their team. They can also arrange photo expeditions and family safaris.

Tour Operators

Destinations: Botswana, Kenya, Madagascar, Namibia, Rwanda, South Africa, Tanzania, Zambia, Uganda.

Popular packages: Secluded Botswana (includes Victoria Falls on the Zambia side), 12 days, from $13,995.

Philanthropy: NHA has been the official conservation partner of the World Wildlife Fund (WWF) since 2003. This unique alliance allows NHA and its guests to play a role in the WWF's mission to conserve nature and reduce threats. This is accomplished through economic support for communities visited, educational outreach, and direct financial support to the WWF.

What they do best: Sustainable ecotourism for small groups with a focus on wildlife and conservation. ✉ *833 W. South Boulder Rd., Boulder* ☎ *800/543–8917* ⊕ *www.nathab.com.*

Roy Safaris. Based in Arusha in Tanzania, and going strong since 1989, Roy Safaris maintains a mid-size operation with a clear focus on adding value at every stage of your trip. They are dependable and responsive, offering both tailor-made and small group tours, and more than 70% of their business comes from repeat customers or referrals. They can also arrange photographic safaris with specially customized vehicles, as well as add-on Mt. Kilimanjaro (and other mountain) climbs and beach breaks to Zanzibar, Pemba, and Mafia islands.

Destinations: Kenya and Tanzania.

Popular packages: Majestic Tanzania, 11 days, from $4,900; Tanzania Migration Safari, 12 days, from $5,500.

Philanthropy: Their Sasha Foundation is involved with providing education grants, building classrooms, and clean water development. Unused marketing funds from the company are allocated to the foundation, as well as parts of the proceeds of safari sales. They have also planted over 20,000 indigenous trees near the Ngorongoro Crater as part of their reforestation program.

What they do best: Excellent, personalized service, and good value. ✉ *2 Serengeti Rd., Arusha* ☎ *255/272–502–115* ⊕ *www. roysafaris.com.*

Wilderness Safaris. Founded in Botswana in 1983, Wilderness Safaris specializes in creating memorable journeys in some of Africa's most remote and pristine areas, while also helping to ensure the future of the continent's spectacular wildlife and including local communities in the process. The company operates a wide array of safari camps and lodges, from "seven star" premier accommodation to mobile safaris known as Explorations, to tailor-made itineraries and honeymoon packages. Wilderness has 40 luxury lodges and camps, all with different styles, so there is something for everyone. They have won numerous awards over the years for outstanding tourism services and for their contribution to conservation and communities in Africa.

Destinations: Botswana, Kenya, Namibia, Rwanda, Zambia, Zimbabwe.

Popular packages: Our Abundant Zimbabwe Safari, 7 days, from $10,133; Bucket List Botswana, 8 days, from $11,523.

Philanthropy: In addition to a 4C's sustainability program (Conservation, Community, Culture, and Commerce), Wilderness has also created two nonprofit programs to further its aims of helping children in Africa: Children in the Wilderness and the Wilderness Wildlife Trust.

What they do best: Incredible destinations, authentic experiences, and seamless service from start to finish. ✉ *373 Rivonia Blvd., Rivonia* ☎ *11/257–5000* ⊕ *www.wilderness-safaris.com.*

The Wild Source. Bill Given, a wildlife biologist and African big cat researcher, started taking small groups of people on private safaris in 2004 and essentially became a one-man safari operator. As his clients increased due to word of mouth, he formed The Wild Source, and the operation evolved to partnering directly with exceptional local guides to create ownership opportunities in ground operations and safari camps. Their Tanzanian guide team in particular receives rave reviews for providing "hard-core" game viewing, with all-day game drives and no mileage limits.

Destinations: Kenya, Mozambique, Namibia, Rwanda, South Africa, Tanzania, Uganda, Zambia, Zimbabwe.

Popular packages: Ultimate East Africa: Exceptional Guiding in Northern Tanzania and the Masai Mara, Tanzania, Kenya, 12 days, from $11,325; Big Five of Southern Africa, Sabi Sand in South Africa, Okavango in Botswana, and Victoria Falls in Zambia, 11 days, from $7795.

Philanthropy: The Wild Source has a wide range of programs that focus on enriching the lives of local people and conserving wildlife, including the hiring and training of local wildlife biologists, sponsoring students, and improving health clinics.

What they do best: Wild Source's belief that the direct economic empowerment of African guides through ownership is critical to establishing lasting conservation sets the company apart. ✉ *80114th St., Golden* ☎ *720/497–1250* ⊕ *www.thewildsource.com.*

HIGHLY RECOMMENDED OUTFITTERS

The Africa Adventure Company. Based in Florida, The Africa Adventure Company is renowned for arranging personalized travel with a strong focus on sustainable tourism and eco-conservation, and they only work with lodges and camps that are active in supporting local communities and the environment. Owner Mark Nolting has spent more than 35 years exploring and researching Africa and has written several guidebooks. His Zimbabwe-born partner Alison managed safari camps for many years and now works on developing new safari programs for both repeat and new clients as well as organizing volunteer programs. They also offer add-on tours, such as beach escapes and honeymoon packages. ✉ *2601 E. Oakland Blvd., Suite 600, Fort Lauderdale* ☎ *800/882–9453* ⊕ *www.africa-adventure.com.*

Tour Operators

&Beyond. One of the world's leading luxury experiential travel companies, &Beyond designs personalized high-end tours in 13 countries in Africa as well as Asia and South America. They offer some of the best accommodations in Africa—and manage 29 of their own highly regarded properties—from the Okavango Delta to remote Indian Ocean islands. The company's commitment to responsible travel, conservation, and community empowerment is combined with warm local hospitality and highly skilled guides and rangers. ⊠ *Pinmill Farm, 164 Katherine St., Sandton* ☎ *11/809–4300 in South Africa* ⊕ *www.andbeyond.com.*

Black Tomato. A luxury travel company based in London and New York City, Black Tomato specializes in tailor-made experiential travel to destinations around the world. When planning trips for their clients, the destination is taken into consideration, as are the clients' needs, passions, and interests so each trip is unique. African itineraries include Namibia's Skeleton Coast, gorilla trekking in Rwanda, and romantic safari and beach trips. ⊠ *119 W. 24th St., New York* ☎ *646/558–3644* ⊕ *www.blacktomato.com.*

Cheli & Peacock. Born in 1985 as a small Kenyan mobile safari operation, today this upmarket company is one of East Africa's leading destination-management companies and inbound tour operators. Specializing in tailor-made safaris, they have offices in Nairobi, Kenya; Arusha, Tanzania; and Kigali, Rwanda and manage all ground arrangements themselves. The variety of locations covers a broad selection of ecosystems, game, and conservation, and features small luxury camps and lodges in top national parks and reserves. Their trips are very creative—for example, horse-riding through a coffee estate adjacent to the Ngorongoro Conservation Area, or walking with camels across the Laikipia Plateau. Beach escapes can be added to safari trips. ⊠ *Peponi Plaza, Mwanza Rd., Nairobi* ☎ *727/835-402* ⊕ *www.chelipeacock.com.*

Doug Macdonald's Safaris to Africa. Founded by professional Zimbabwean walking guide Doug Macdonald, this small, hands-on company has a diverse range of clients—over 90% come from referrals—all of whom have one thing in common: a deep desire to connect with Africa in a way that resonates with them. With over 30 years of experience working in the bush, Macdonald has endless enthusiasm for Africa and is constantly looking for new and different places to introduce to his guests. This passion carries over to his team, all specialists in their own right, who pay attention to every detail of a trip and offer around-the-clock support should it be needed. ⊠ *Macorrs Bldg., Suite 3* ☎ *778/219–208* ⊕ *www.dougmacsafaris.com.*

Earthlife Expeditions. Based in Tanzania and locally owned, this small company has earned rave reviews for their knowledgeable guides and tailor-made safaris in Tanzania, Kenya, Uganda, and Rwanda for couples, families and small groups. With a focus on value for money, along with highly personalized service, Earthlife's consultants work closely with guests to arrange the perfect once-in-a-lifetime trip. They also arrange Zanzibar add-ons and Mt Kilimanjaro climbs.

✉ *Saba General Building, Namanga Rd., Arusha* ☎ *753/849–094* ⊕ *www.earthlife-expeditions.com.*

Extraordinary Journeys. Founded and operated by ex-Kenyan residents and mother-daughter team Marcia and Elizabeth Gordon who have over 60 years of combined safari knowledge, Extraordinary Journeys specializes in creating unique, custom safari experiences to southern and East Africa. Itineraries mix and match safari camps, lodges, and private villas to create a true sense of being on an exotic adventure. The Extraordinary Journeys team plans safaris that all bear the hallmarks of first-hand knowledge and personalized service, and they consciously choose sustainable, ethical, and conservation-minded properties and operators in Africa. ✉ *345 W. 58th St., New York* ☎ *212/226–7331* ⊕ *www.extraordinaryjourneys.com.*

Eyes on Africa. Whether you're a honeymooner, wildlife enthusiast, or photographer, Chicago-based Eyes on Africa will find a trip to match your budget. A wide range of interests and preferences can be catered to on customized safaris, and they have a long list of affordable camping or accommodated options too. They also cover mountainous destinations and beaches, and are well known for their occasional group photography workshop trips with a professional photographer. Eyes on Africa have expanded to a number of destinations in South and Central America and India in order to service requests from their existing customer base. ✉ *1743 W. Fletcher St., Chicago* ☎ *800/457–9575* ⊕ *www.eyesonafrica.net.*

Ker & Downey. With more than 50 years of experience in the travel industry, Ker & Downey is one of the oldest and most respected safari companies in Africa; they also have an office in Texas. The company utilizes its exclusive camps to provide luxury safari experiences and offers in-house expertise for all destinations as well as excellent on-the-ground service. They work hard to get to know their clients so they can best customize each itinerary. Ker & Downey for Africa is the philanthropic arm, which supports medical clinics and distributes mosquito nets among many other initiatives. ✉ *6703 Highway Blvd., Katy* ☎ *800/423–4236* ⊕ *www.kerdowney.com.*

Contacts

✈ Air

AIR PASS Oneworld Alliance. ⊕ *www.one-world.com.* **Star Alliance.** ⊕ *www.staralliance.com.*

INTERNATIONAL AIR-LINES British Airways. ☎ *0344/493–0747 in U.K.* ⊕ *www.britishair-ways.com.* **Emirates.** ☎ *0344/800–2777 in U.K., 0800/777–3999 in U.S.* ⊕ *www.emirates.com.* **Ethiopian Airlines.** ☎ *1753/967–980 in U.K., 352/436–1902 in U.S.* ⊕ *www.ethiopianairlines.com.* **Kenya Airways.** ☎ *0711/024–747 in Kenya* ⊕ *www.kenya-airways.com.* **KLM.** ☎ *207/660–0293 in U.K., 877/477–5134 in U.S.* ⊕ *www.klm.com.* **Lufthansa.** ☎ *371/945–9747 in U.K., 516/296–9650 in U.S.* ⊕ *www.lufthansa.com.* **Qatar Airways.** ☎ *330/912–7415 in U.K., 877/777–2827 in U.S.* ⊕ *www.qatarairways.com.* **Turkish Airlines.** ☎ *0844/800–6666 in U.K., 800/874–8875 in U.S.* ⊕ *www.turkishair-lines.com.*

▣ Customs

U.S. Customs and Border Protection. ⊕ *www.cbp.gov.* **U.S. Fish and Wildlife Service.** ⊕ *www.fws.gov.*

➕ Health and Safety

HEALTH Centers for Disease Control. (*CDC*). ☎ *800/232–4636 international travelers' health line* ⊕ *wwwnc.cdc.gov/travel.* **World Health Organization.** (*WHO*). ⊕ *www.who.int.*

MEDICAL-ASSISTANCE COMPANIES Air Med. ⊕ *www.airmed.com.* **International SOS.** ⊕ *www.inter-nationalsos.com.* **MedJet Assistance.** ⊕ *www.medjetassist.com.*

◉ Travel Insurance

Allianz Travel Insurance ⊕ *www.allianztravelinsur-ance.com.* **HTH Worldwide.** ⊕ *www.hthworldwide.com.* **International Medical Group.** ⊕ *www.imglob-al.com.* **Travel Guard.** ⊕ *www.travelguard.com.* **Wallach & Company.** ⊕ *www.wallach.com.*

◉ Visitor Information

MEDIA Africa Adventure. ⊕ *www.africa-adventure.org.* **All Africa.** ⊕ *www.allafrica.com.* **Getaway.** ⊕ *www.getawayafrica.com.* **Independent Newspa-pers.** ✉ *47 Pixley Ka Isaka Seme St., Johannesburg* ⊕ *www.iol.co.za.*

Chapter 3

KENYA

Updated by
Wendy Watta

3

WELCOME TO KENYA

TOP REASONS TO GO

★ **The Great Migration:** Millions of plains game move in an endless cycle of birth and death from Tanzania's Serengeti to Kenya's Masai Mara.

★ **Eyeball Big Game:** Visiting Kenya's legendary national parks and game reserves almost guarantees that you'll see the Big Five as well as huge herds of plains animals and hundreds of colorful birds.

★ **Africa's Fabled Tribe:** The tall and dignified red-robed Maasai have held explorers, adventurers, and writers in thrall for centuries.

★ **Beach Escapes:** Miles of white sandy beaches lined by an azure ocean and water sports galore. From diving and snorkeling to windsurfing, there's something for everyone.

★ **Turn Back the Clock:** Check out ancient history along the coast where Arab traders and Vasco da Gama once sailed. In the tiny UNESCO World Heritage town of Lamu you'll find an Arabic way of life unchanged for centuries.

Kenya lies in East Africa. It's bordered by Uganda to the west, Tanzania to the south, South Sudan and Ethiopia to the north, Somalia to the northeast, and the Indian Ocean to the southeast. It's a land of amazing diversity with extraordinary tourist attractions: great game reserves like the Masai Mara and Amboseli; the Great Rift Valley dotted with a string of lakes including Nakuru and Naivasha; fertile highlands with towering peaks such as Mt. Kenya; and a coastline and islands with long pristine sandy beaches and marine parks full of coral reefs and colorful fish. Its two largest cities couldn't be more different. Nairobi, the capital, is a bustling city where colonial buildings rub shoulders with modern skyscrapers, while steamy, coastal Mombasa retains its strong Arabic influence and history as it continues to be Kenya's largest and busiest port.

1 Masai Mara. Located in southern Kenya's Great Rift Valley, the Mara is considered to be one of the world's greatest game parks. After the Great Migration reaches here, you can see hundreds of thousands of wildebeest, zebra, and gazelle, followed by dozens of predators.

2 Amboseli National Park. Kilimanjaro's snowcapped peak, huge herds of elephants, and quintessential Kenyan landscape (open plains, acacia woodland, grasslands, bush, and marshland) greet you along the Tanzanian border.

3 Tsavo West and East National Parks. Tsavo West and Tsavo East are home to peaceful lion prides and loads of other game. Split by the Mombasa Highway, their proximity to the coast makes them a great choice for those who want to combine beach and beasts.

4 Laikipia Plateau. This region has become one of Kenya's hottest game destinations with some of its classiest camps and lodges. The nearby Samburu National Reserve boasts unusual dry-country species of animals and birds.

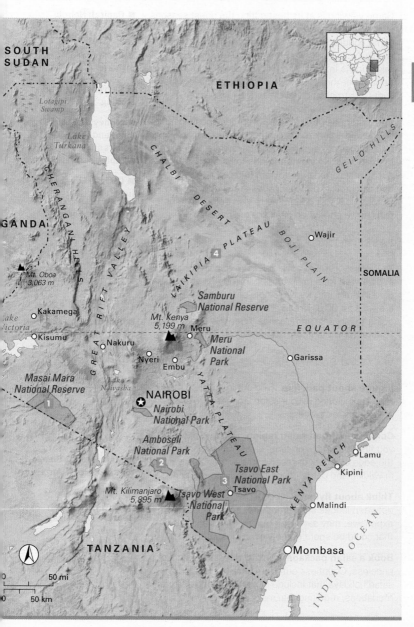

COUNTRY SNAPSHOT

WHEN TO GO

Game viewing is at its best during the driest seasons (June–September and January–February) when game congregates at water holes. Safari high season is July–November when the annual wildebeest migration is in full swing. High season at the coast is September through January and is particularly busy over Christmas and New Year. The low season coincides with the long rains of March and April and the short rains of October, November, and December because park roads can become impassable and mosquitoes are at their busiest. However, rates drop dramatically. The weather tends to be good in May but animals are harder to spot because the vegetation has grown, but again rates are far lower. Early October is also a good time to visit before the short rains arrive and when peak season has died down.

PASSPORTS AND VISAS

Your passport must have at least two blank pages and be valid for a minimum of six months after your date of entry into Kenya. Single-entry visas (US$50) are valid for 90 days and allow reentry to Kenya after going to Tanzania and Uganda. (See the Chapter Planner for more information)

WAYS TO SAVE

Inquire about park fees. Find out in advance if park fees are included in your safari lodge rate to avoid paying this fee twice.

Consider a broad safari region. Don't be put off if you find your lodge or camp is in a conservancy on the edge of a park or reserve; these are equally rich in wildlife and game drives take you into the parks.

Think about flying. While bush or safari flights between lodges and camps may at first appear expensive, they save long bumpy drives and time that could be spent game-viewing instead.

Book a safari package. Minimal stress on safari is priceless. Countless outfitters package fabulous safari holidays that include all transport and accommodations, requiring minimal planning on your part.

AT A GLANCE

- **Capital:** Nairobi
- **Population:** 56,080,350
- **Big Five** You'll find them all here.
- **Currency:** Kenyan shilling
- **Money:** ATMs in larger cities and towns; U.S. dollars and credit cards accepted at safari lodges.
- **Official Languages:** English, Swahili
- **Country Code:** 254
- **Emergencies:** 999
- **Driving:** On the left
- **Electricity:** 240v/50 cycles; plugs are UK standard three-prong
- **Time:** 7 hours ahead of New York during daylight saving time; 8 hours otherwise
- **Documents:** Entry with valid passport; visa in advance or visa on arrival
- **Mobile Phones:** GSM (900 and 1800 bands)
- **Major Mobile Companies:** Safaricom, Airtel, Telkom
- **Kenya Tourism Board:** ⊕ www.magicalkenya.com
- **Kenya Wildlife Service (KWS):** ⊕ www.kws.org

Kenya is where "going on safari" started. A hundred years or so ago, visitors from all over the world, including Teddy Roosevelt, started traveling to Africa, lured by stories of multitudes of wild animals; there were more than 3 million large mammals roving East Africa's plains at the time. Today visitors continue to flock to this East African nation each year. Although humans have made their mark, Kenya still holds onto its pristine wilderness.

Kenya's tourism industry, the main source of foreign revenue, is very susceptible to perceptions of tourist safety. Tourism declined following the 1998 terrorist bombing of the U.S. Embassies in Nairobi and Dar es Salaam in Tanzania, but visitor numbers were on the rise again before the crisis in 2007–08. Widely televised at the time, the ethnic violence that arose after disputed election results further tarnished Kenya's reputation, even though no tourists were in danger. The crisis was, however, a large contributing factor to a new constitution signed into law in 2010, aimed at limiting presidential powers and keeping corruption in check. The August 2022 general elections went on without any violence, with all disputes being settled at the supreme court rather than in the streets. As such, there's little reason to consider the country unsafe as a tourist destination.

Kenya's human history dates back at least 6 million years; the controversial Millennium Man was discovered near Lake Baringo in the northwest in 2001. Today, Kenya has more than 70 ethnic groups that range from the Maasai, Samburu, Kikuyu, Luo and Turkana tribes to the Arabs and Indians that settled on the coast and the descendants of the first white settlers. Eighty-five percent of the population identify as Christians. Islam arrived along the coast in the 8th century, followed in the 15th century by Portuguese explorers and sailors who came looking for the sea route to India. During the rule of Seyyid Said of Oman in the 1830s, German, British, and American merchants established themselves on the coast, and the notorious slave routes were created.

The British created what was then known as British East Africa in the late 1800s. After a much-publicized and often sensationalized struggle by native

Kenyans against British rule in the 1950s, known as the Mau Mau era, Kenya finally won independence in 1963.

The perennial African life-and-death drama plays out among vast populations of prey and predators in what's widely called one of the world's greatest wildlife destinations. But, Kenya isn't just about big game. It has a gorgeous tropical coastline with white sandy beaches, coral gardens, superb fishing, and snorkeling, diving, and vibey beach resorts. Traditional triangular-sailed *dhows* still ply their trade providing unforgettable seafood to the surrounding restaurants. You'll discover unique islands with ancient stone Arab buildings, where a donkey is the main mode of transport, and where time really does seem to stand still.

MAJOR REGIONS

Unfortunately, you probably won't be able to see all of Kenya in one trip. So our listings are broken down into **Must-See Parks** (Masai Mara National Reserve, Amboseli National Park, Tsavo West and East National Parks, and the Laikipia Plateau) and **If You Have Time Parks** (Nairobi National Park, Meru National Park, Samburu National Reserve, and Lakes Nakuru and Naivasha) to help you better organize your time. It's suggested, though, that you research *all* of them before you make your decision. There's also a section on **Gateway Cities,** which for Kenya is Nairobi.

Planning

Getting Here and Around

AIR

There are direct Kenya Airways flights from New York to Nairobi, and all other flight options from the United States to Kenya involve a change of planes or airlines in Europe, the Middle East, or elsewhere in Africa. Nairobi is not only the principal arrival city for Kenya, but is a hub for East Africa and has good air connections to neighboring countries such as Tanzania, Uganda, and Rwanda.

In Kenya, there are a number of domestic and regional airlines that fly from both Jomo Kenyatta International Airport and Wilson Airport in Nairobi, as well as from Moi International Airport in Mombasa. Several major towns have airports, and Kenya also has a wide network of well-maintained airstrips at the safari destinations. One airstrip will service an entire park or reserve, or in some parks like the popular Masai Mara, there are several airstrips that each serve a group of safari lodges and camps. In most cases, transfers are provided from the airstrip to your accommodations. Schedules for the safari airlines often work in circuits and drop off and pick up at a number of destinations and may often return on the same route.

AIRPORTS Jomo Kenyatta International Airport (JKIA). *(NBO) ✉ Mombasa Rd. (A104), Nairobi ✈ 16 km (10 miles) southeast of CBD ☎ 020/682–2111 ⊕ www. kaa.go.ke.* **Moi International Airport.** *(MBA) ✉ Airport Rd., Mombasa ✈ 11 km (6.6 miles) northwest of city center ☎ 0726/318–515 ⊕ www.kaa.go.ke.*

AIR TRAVEL RESOURCES IN KENYA

Kenya Airports Authority. *☎ 020/682–2111 ⊕ www.kaa.go.ke.*

INTERNATIONAL FLIGHTS

Most major international airlines fly into Jomo Kenyatta International Airport (JKIA), Kenya's largest airport and the major airline hub for East Africa. Kenya Airways offers direct flights between Nairobi and JFK–New York. There are also a number of indirect flights; British Airways via London, Ethiopian Airlines via Addis Ababa, Emirates via Dubai, KLM via Amsterdam, Lufthansa via Frankfurt, Turkish Airlines via Istanbul, and Qatar Airways via Doha. Another option is to go to Europe and continue with the national carrier Kenya Airways, which flies from London, Paris, Amsterdam, and Rome to Nairobi. Moi International Airport in Mombasa is mostly used for regional flights and seasonal air charter flights from European cities, often for package holidays that are inclusive of accommodations. Ethiopian Airlines, Lufthansa, and Turkish Airlines make scheduled stops in Mombasa as part of their Nairobi, Kilimanjaro, or Zanzibar routes. The usual connections between Nairobi and Mombasa are with Jambojet, Airkenya, Kenya Airways, or Fly540. *For airline information, see the Contacts section of Chapter 2, Planning Your Safari.*

DOMESTIC FLIGHTS

There are plenty of efficient domestic airlines offering daily flights. Kenya Airways flies between Nairobi JKIA and Eldoret, Kisumu, Malindi, and Mombasa, and several regional destinations including Entebbe in Uganda, Kigali in Rwanda, and Kilimanjaro, Dar es Salaam, and Zanzibar in Tanzania. Kenya Airway's no-frills airline, Jambojet, flies between Nairobi JKIA and Diani Beach (Ukunda), Eldoret, Kisumu, Lamu, Malindi, and Mombasa. Fly540 flies from Nairobi JKIA to Eldoret, Kisumu, Lamu, Lodwar, Malindi, and Mombasa, and Kilimanjaro and Zanzibar in Tanzania. From Nairobi's Wilson Airport, Airkenya flies to Amboseli, Diani Beach (Ukunda), Lamu, Lewa Downs, Loisaba, Malindi, the Masai Mara, Meru, Nanyuki, and Samburu, and Kilimanjaro in Tanzania. Also from Wilson Airport, Safarilink flies to Amboseli, Diani Beach (Ukunda), Lamu, Lewa Downs, Lodwar, Loisaba, the Masai Mara, Naivasha, Nanyuki, Tsavo West, Samburu, and Kilimanjaro, and from the Masai Mara to Migori, which links travelers from the Mara to the Serengeti National Park in Tanzania. Mombasa Air Safari has its hub at Moi International Airport and flies in circuits from Mombasa, Diani Beach (Ukunda), and Malindi on the coast to Amboseli, the Masai Mara, and Tsavo West.

If you want to arrange your own timetable to the safari destinations or coast, there are several air charter companies based at Nairobi's Wilson Airport such as East African Air Charters and Reliance Air Charters. Small planes like Cessnas are utilized which can seat 5–13 passengers. Although more expensive than scheduled flights, charters are convenient and are an option for families and groups.

All domestic, regional and charter flights can be booked directly with the airlines, or alternatively ask your travel agent, or local accommodation or a Kenyan tour operator, to book as part of your package. Airport departure tax is included in all scheduled flight tickets but may be additional on charter flights. Be aware that on the small planes to the airstrips in the parks, the baggage allowance is usually 15 kg (33 pounds) per person, including hand luggage and camera equipment, and bags should be soft-sided. In the event you are carrying more than this, most hotels in Nairobi will store extra luggage or ask your airline if they have facilities.

DOMESTIC AIRLINES Airkenya.
☎ 020/391–6000 ⊕ www.airkenya.com.
East African Air Charters. ☎ 0724/255–333 ⊕ eaaircharters.co.ke. **Fly540.** ☎ 0740/540–540 ⊕ www.fly540.com. **Jambojet.** ☎ 020/327–4545 ⊕ www.jambojet.com. **Mombasa Air Safari.** ☎ 0734/500–500 ⊕ www.mombasaairsafari.com. **Reliance Air Charters.** ☎ 020/600–7778 ⊕ www.relianceair.co.ke. **Safarilink.** ☎ 020/669–0000 ⊕ www.flysafarilink.com.

CAR

Self-drive safaris are an option, though it's not one we'd suggest. Poor road conditions in many places mean there can be a big difference between distance on a map and driving time (for example, it takes about five hours to drive from Nairobi to the Masai Mara, a 150-mile/240-km journey). However, if this is something you're interested in, there are a number of car rental companies that

Elephants grazing in the shadows of Mt. Kilimanjaro. Is there a more impressive sight?

specialize in 4x4s; most will also offer the services of a driver. Expect to pay from $100 a day to hire a 4x4 and $20 a day for a driver.

Communications

PHONES

Local landline and mobile calls are quite cheap, but hotels add hefty surcharges to phone calls. The need for public telephones in Kenya has fallen away given that the majority of people carry a mobile phone, so most have been decommissioned or removed. If you don't want to use your own mobile phone because of expensive international roaming fees, buy a Kenyan pay-as-you-go SIM card (from one of the service-provider stores or street vendors—there's no shortage of them) and add airtime as you need it. The local providers are Airtel, Safaricom, and Telkom (Sometimes the best way to reach customer care is through the verified pages on Twitter). Coverage is good throughout most of the country, but can

be patchy in remote places—don't expect to get a signal at an out-of-the-way safari lodge or camp.

Calling Within Kenya: City codes are (020) for Nairobi, (041) for Mombasa, (040) for Diani Beach, and (012) for Lamu; include the first 0 when you dial within the country. When making a phone call in Kenya, always use the full 10-digit number, including the area code, even if you're in the same area.

Calling Outside Kenya: When dialing out from Kenya, dial 000 before the international code. So, for example, you would dial 000 (0001) for the United States. Other country codes are 00044 for the U.K and 00027 for South Africa.

Internet: Internet is widely available in Kenya. Free Wi-Fi is available in many public places in Nairobi and Mombasa such as restaurants and coffee shops and at almost all hotels—although again, in remote places you won't be able to connect. You can top up your own phone with data on a Kenyan pay-as-you-go SIM card.

MOBILE PHONES Airtel. ☎ *100 from an Airtel number, 0733/100–100 from another number* ⊕ *www.airtelkenya.com.* **Telkom.** ☎ *100 from a Telkom number, 020/222–1000 from another number* ⊕ *www.telkom.co.ke.* **Safaricom.** ☎ *100 from Safaricom number, 0722/002–100 from another number* ⊕ *www.safaricom. co.ke.*

Customs and Duties

Each person may bring 200 cigarettes (or 50 cigars or 250 grams of tobacco), 1 liter of spirits or 2 liters of wine, and up to 568 ml of perfume. The tobacco and alcohol allowance applies only to people 18 and over.

CONTACT Kenya Revenue Authority. ☎ *020/499–9999* ⊕ *www.kra.go.ke.*

Health and Safety

Kenya is a relatively safe country, but occasional incidents of crime are a reality for residents and tourists alike; follow these basic precautions for a safe trip.

Mugging, purse snatching, and pickpocketing can occur in big towns. Leave good jewelry and watches at home, and unless you're on safari, keep cameras, camcorders, and binoculars out of sight. Always lock valuables in the hotel or lodge safe. If you must carry valuables, use a money belt under your clothes; keep some cash handy so you don't reveal your money belt in public. Don't leave belongings out on balconies or terraces or on show in a vehicle. Don't use your phone near an open window while sitting in a vehicle. If you're unfortunate to be a victim of a robbery, you will need a police report to make an insurance claim. Bring copies of all your important documents and stash them away from the originals. Carry extra passport photos in case you need new documents fast.

Always take a taxi after dark, and never take food or drinks from strangers—it could be drugged. Be on the lookout for street scams like hard-luck stories or appeals to finance a scholarship. If you're driving, be polite but firm if you're stopped by police officers charging you with an "instant fine" for a minor infraction. If you ask to go to the police station, the charges are often dismissed.

A yellow fever vaccination card is *not* needed for entry to Kenya, unless you're traveling from a country with risk of yellow fever; this does not include the United States, but does include Uganda and some other African countries. Always use sunscreen and bug repellent with DEET. The HIV infection rate is high so exercise caution. Malaria is an issue in certain areas (not in Nairobi but definitely on the coast, western Kenya and low-lying game reserves). Consult your health-provider well in advance about the best malaria prophylactics to take as most medication needs to start prior to arrival in Kenya.

You'll need full medical travel insurance that includes repatriation in the event of a medical emergency. If you're planning to dive, trek, or climb, make sure your insurance covers active pursuits. Medical bills are often paid upfront in Kenya, so keep all paperwork to make an insurance claim. The AMREF Flying Doctors service provides air evacuation and transportation between health-care facilities for medical emergencies in Kenya, Tanzania, and Uganda, or anywhere within a 1,000 km (621 miles) radius of Nairobi. The planes fly out of Nairobi's Wilson Airport 24 hours a day, 365 days a year.

EMBASSIES British High Commission. ✉ *Upper Hill Rd., Nairobi* ☎ *020/287– 3000* ⊕ *www.gov.uk.* **U.S. Embassy.** ✉ *Gigiri, Nairobi, United Nations Ave., Gigiri* ☎ *020/363–6000* ⊕ *ke.usembassy.gov.*

EMERGENCIES Kenya Police. ☎ *999* ⊕ *www.kenyapolice.go.ke.*

3

Kenya PLANNING

MEDICAL-ASSISTANCE COMPANIES
AMREF Flying Doctors. ☎ *020/699–2222 emergencies, 020/699–2000 customer service* ⊕ *www.flydoc.org.*

HOLIDAYS

If a public holiday falls on a Sunday, it'll be observed the next day, Monday. Muslim festivals are timed according to local sightings of phases of the moon; dates vary accordingly. During the lunar month of Ramadan that precedes Eid al-Fitr, Muslims fast during the day and feast at night, and normal business patterns may be interrupted. Many restaurants are closed during the day, and there may be restrictions on smoking and drinking.

Hotels and Lodges

Kenya has a broad choice of accommodations ranging from intimate tented camps and luxurious boutique hotels to midrange safari lodges and beach resorts as well as local lodgings and campsites. Hotel rates in Nairobi and other towns tend to stay the same throughout the year (although there could be midweek specials), but all room prices in the wildlife and coastal areas are seasonal. It's essential to book in advance in high season and look out for specials during the low season, while during rainy months some establishments close altogether.

There's a bewildering choice of safari lodges and tented camps in the national parks, game reserves, and wildlife conservancies. Lodges tend to be large solid structures with hotel-like rooms and restaurants. Most are family-friendly, and many have extra facilities like a swimming pool. Smaller tented camps have spacious and often luxuriously appointed walk-in tents with bathrooms, meals are taken communally in a dining tent or outside, and most are unfenced allowing for greater connection with the wildlife (as such, children aren't always permitted). Prices at lodges are almost always per person and all-inclusive, which includes accommodations, meals, and activities such as game drives and walks; find out in advance if park fees (US$40 to US$100 per day) are included. Campsites in the wildlife areas have few or no facilities and aren't really an option for a visitor with time restrictions or for first-timers, but there is the option of going on a camping safari with a tour operator.

Nairobi has hundreds of hotels and many of the international chains are represented, but there are also charming independent hotels and some older establishments with colonial ambience. Standard prices usually include a full English breakfast and other meals are available in the hotel's restaurant. All kinds of accommodations can be found on the coast, from luxurious honeymoon-hideaways to all-inclusive family beach resorts, and on Lamu, some beautifully restored historic Arabic houses have opened as hotels.

■ TIP➔ **Hotel reviews have been shortened. For full information, visit Fodors.com.**

DINING AND LODGING PRICES

What It Costs in U.S. Dollars			
$	$$	$$$	$$$$
RESTAURANTS			
under $12	$12–$20	$21–$30	over $30
HOTELS			
under $250	$250–$450	$451–$600	over $600

Money Matters

The official currency is the Kenya shilling (KSh). Available notes are 50, 100, 200, 500, and 1,000 shillings. Available coins are 1, 5, 10, 20 and 40 shillings. At this writing, the shilling exchange is about KSh116 to US$1.

Most things are priced and paid for in KSh. However many businesses in

Set in the Samburu National Reserve high above the Ewaso Nyiro River, Sasaab blends Swahili and Moroccan design.

the tourist industry like hotels, safari companies, and airlines may quote in U.S. dollars as well as shillings. If you pay with dollars, check that you're getting a fair exchange rate. Credit cards are widely accepted, but for small amounts like restaurants, shopping, taxi fares, fuel and tips, it's easiest to withdraw shillings from an ATM once you're in the country. Most ATMs dispense large denomination notes; try and break these when you can as taxi drivers and souvenir vendors often don't have change for large bills.

If you are exchanging U.S. dollars at a bank or bureau de change, bring new notes; any old, worn, or damaged bills will not be accepted.

ATMS AND BANKS

Banks open at 8:30 on weekdays and close at 4; on Saturday they open at 9 and close at noon. Banks are closed on Sundays and public holidays. Most ATMs are open 24 hours. Many banks can perform foreign-exchange services or international electronic transfers. Try to avoid banks at their busiest times—at 9 and

from noon to 2 on Friday, and at month's end—unless you're willing to arrive early and line up with the locals. Major banks are Kenya Commercial Bank (KCB), which has the largest branch network in the country, and Barclays, National Bank of Kenya, and Standard Chartered.

Major credit cards such as Visa and MasterCard are accepted at Kenyan banks and by ATMs. Most ATMs accept Cirrus, Plus, Maestro, Visa Electron, and Visa and MasterCard; the best place to withdraw cash is at an indoor ATM, preferably one at the airport, in a shopping mall, or guarded by a security officer.

CONTACTS Kenya Commercial Bank (KCB). ☎ *020/228–7000 customer care* ⊕ *ke. kcbbankgroup.com.*

TAXES

In Kenya, the value-added tax (V.A.T.) of 16% is included in the price of most goods and services, including accommodations and food. To get a V.A.T. refund on items taken out of the country such as souvenirs, foreign visitors must present receipts at the V.A.T. refund desk in the departures halls of the international airports (Nairobi and Mombasa) or at land borders. Refunds are paid by check, which can be cashed immediately at an airport bank or refunded to your credit card with a small transaction fee.

TIPPING

There isn't much of a tipping custom among Kenyans, but porters do hope for something. 10% isn't customary in restaurants... you tip what you want. Some hotels and most safari lodges and tented camps have a gratuity box for you to put a tip for all of the staff at the end of your stay. You can tip your safari driver and guide approximately US$10–US$15 per person, per day. It's not necessary to tip taxi drivers as the fare is determined before you set off.

Restaurants

Kenya prides itself on quality grilled meat, coffee, tea, organically grown vegetables, and tropical fruits (such as passion fruit, papaya, and mangoes) are excellent. The local cuisine is heavily influenced by Indian food, hence you can find chapati, curries, and stews in local menus. Sample Arabic food and seafood when you're at the coast, and most bars serve Tusker, a local beer. You'll find most cuisines, from Chinese to French to Ethiopian and Italian, in restaurants in Nairobi.

Restaurant reviews have been shortened. For full information, visit Fodors. com.

Passports and Visas

Your passport must have at least two blank pages and be valid for a minimum of six months after your date of entry into Kenya. Most nationalities require a visa, including citizens of the United States. Single-entry visas (US$50) are valid for 90 days and allow reentry to Kenya after

Keeping it Green

Ecotourism Kenya (ecotourismkenya.org) is an organization that promotes responsible practices in the Kenyan tourism industry. They provide guidelines for attaining sustainable solutions for the conservation of the environment and improving the well-being of local people, and each year they present awards to hotels, lodges, camps, and tour operators for their efforts in keeping it green.

going to Tanzania and Uganda. Children under 16 years accompanying their parent(s) *do not* require visas. Prior to travel, eVisas can be obtained online; or visas are also available in cash only (US$, euros, or UK pounds) at Nairobi's Jomo Kenyatta International Airport, Mombasa's Moi International Airport, and all land borders. To avoid queues, it's easier to get them online beforehand.

CONTACTS Kenya eVisa. ⊕ *www.evisa. go.ke.* **Kenya Embassy.** ☎ *202/387–6101 Embassy, Washington D.C., 212/421–4744 Consulate, NYC* ⊕ *www.kenyaembassy.com.*

Plan Your Time

HASSLE FACTOR

Medium. Kenya Airways launched direct flights from New York to Nairobi in October 2018; indirect flights leave from most major US cities. Once in Kenya, smaller safari planes connect remote reaches.

3 DAYS

Land in Nairobi and hop on a bush plane to reach the Masai Mara National Reserve or Laikipia Plateau. Soon you'll be immersed in wildlife country and hopefully crashing at a swanky safari lodge.

1 WEEK

You have a bit more time to hop across Kenya's interior on an extended safari. Combine the Masai Mara or Laikipia with the country's other must-see parks: Amboseli National Park and Tsavo East or West national parks.

2 WEEKS

After a week on safari, hit the coast. Enjoy the beaches and cultural richness of Diani or Lamu. Take the time to experience Nairobi for a day or two on your way home, or head west of the city to see the Rift Valley lakes like Naivasha and Nakuru.

Visitor Information

There's no official tourist office in Nairobi and the information center in Mombasa is not official or much good. Your best option is to consult the Kenya Tourist Board website before you leave home. The website for the Kenya Wildlife Service is a good source if you're going to the national parks and reserves.

VISITOR INFORMATION Kenya Tourism Board. ☎ 020/271–1262 ⊕ www.magicalkenya.com. **Kenya Tourism Federation.** ☎ 0738/617–499 tourist helpline ⊕ www.ktf.co.ke. **Kenya Wildlife Service (KWS).** ☎ 0800/597–000 ⊕ www.kws.go.ke. **National Museums of Kenya.** ⊕ www.museums.or.ke.

When to Go

Generally speaking, Kenya has one of the best climates in the world with long, sunny, dry days. The country's equator-straddling position means the length of a day hardly changes and sunrise is always 7 am–8 am and sunset 6 pm–7pm, with daytime temperatures average between 20°C (68°F) and 25°C (77°F). The coast can get hot and humid, though sea breezes cool things down, and the mountainous regions can get very cold—remember there's snow all year round on the highest peaks. Try to avoid the long rains of March and April or the short rains of October, November, and December because park roads can become impassable and mosquitoes are at their most prolific. Game-viewing is at its best during the driest seasons (May–September, January, and February) because the lack of surface water forces game to congregate at waterholes. Safari high season runs July through November when the annual wildebeest migration is in full swing, but it's much cheaper to go in the low season (April and May) when rates drop dramatically. High season at the coast is September through January (the hottest time is December and January), but avoid Christmas and New Year periods as holiday resorts are packed. If you're a birder, aim to visit between October and April when the migrant species have arrived.

FESTIVALS AND EVENTS

May or June: The annual Lewa Safari Marathon attracts runners and spectators from all over the world who cover up to 26 miles of difficult terrain through a wildlife conservancy teeming with zebras, lions and more, all to raise money for conservation and community development. ⊕ www.lewasafarimarathon.com

June: First held in 1953, WRC Safari Rally Kenya has evolved to fit the modern WRC, but still takes place on challenging dirt roads, past wildlife, and epic scenery. Spectating is just as fun, often accompanied by endless parties. ⊕ www.wrc.com

June: Rhino Charge is an annual off-road motorsport competition since 1989. The location is usually kept secret until the last minute, but is often in the wild and untamed north; it draws both campers and 4x4 enthusiasts alike. ⊕ rhinocharge.co.ke

Lion cubs out for an early-morning prowl in the Masai Mara National Reserve.

November: During the three-day Lamu Cultural Festival the town showcases Swahili culture through traditional song, dance, bridal ceremonies, and donkey racing. The annual Lamu Yoga festival held in October is also a big draw. ⊕ la-mu.go.ke

December: Jamhuri Day commemorates Kenya's formation as a republic and is filled with parades and musical performances.

Masai Mara National Reserve

The legendary Masai Mara National Reserve ranks right up there with Tanzania's Serengeti National Park and South Africa's Kruger National Park in terms of the world's finest wildlife sanctuaries.

Established in 1961, some 275 km (171 miles) southwest of Nairobi, the Mara covers an area of 1,800 square km (702 square miles) and includes part of the Serengeti ecosystem that extends from northern Tanzania into southern Kenya. This ecosystem of well-watered plains supports one of the largest populations of numerous animal groups on earth. There are more than 2 million wildebeests; 250,000 Thomson's gazelles; 250,000 zebras; 70,000 impalas; 30,000 Grant's gazelles; and a huge number of predators including lions, leopards, cheetahs, jackals, and hyenas. There are also more than 470 species of bird, including 57 species of raptor. Every January the wildebeest start to move in a time-honored clockwise movement around the Serengeti toward the new, fresh grazing in the Masai Mara. It's an unforgettable experience.

Local communities, not the Kenya Wildlife Service, manage this reserve giving the Maasai, who are pastoralists, the rights to graze their stock on the perimeters of the reserve. Although stock is lost to wild animals, the Maasai manage to coexist peacefully with the game, and rely only on their own cattle for subsistence; in Maasai communities wealth is measured by the number of cattle owned. You'll see the Maasai's *manyattas*—beehive huts made of mud and cow dung—at the entrances to the reserve. The striking appearance of the Maasai, with their red robes and ochre-dyed and braided hair, is one of the abiding images of Kenya. Many lodges offer visits to traditional Maasai villages and homes, and although inevitably these visits have become touristy, they're still well worth doing. Witnessing the dramatic *ipid,* a dance in which the *moran* (warriors) take turns leaping high into the air, will keep your camera clicking nonstop. The Maasai people named the reserve *mara,* which means "spotted," but whether mara applies to the landscape, which is spotted with vegetation, or the hundreds of thousands of wildebeest and other game that spot the landscape, is anybody's guess.

WHEN TO GO

There's no real best time to visit the Mara, but most people come in the July–October dry season, when the Great Migration is taking place and there are plenty of wildebeest and zebras for the lions, leopards, and cheetahs to prey on. There's no guarantee of seeing any epic river crossings, however. The rainy season is April and May and November, and many roads become difficult or even inaccessible.

GETTING HERE AND AROUND

Most people fly to the Mara from Nairobi's Wilson Airport, and scheduled daily air services (about 45 minutes) land at eight airstrips in the area. The cost is approximately $185 each way (some lodges include this flight and transfer in their rates). If you're a nervous flyer, note that you'll usually travel in small turbo-prop aircraft and there could be a couple of touchdowns at other airstrips, too, as the flights operate in circuits. However, tour operators can offer a driving option; the Mara is 270 km (168 miles) from

Park Ratings

Game: ★ ★ ★ ★ ★

Park Accessibility: ★ ★ ★ ★ ★

Getting Around: ★ ★ ★ ★ ★

Accommodations: ★ ★ ★ ★ ★

Scenic Beauty: ★ ★ ★ ★ ☆

Nairobi and takes approximately five hours by road. Once in the park, there are few signposts, so make sure you know exactly where you're going before you depart. The park fee is $80 per person per 24 hours, which is often included in package tours.

Hotels

All prices have been quoted at per-person, high-season rates, as most people will want to come during the migration. However, in low- and mid-season, rates can be considerably cheaper. Check for special offers before you book and what additional park and conservation fees will be added.

★ Angama Mara

$$$$ | **RESORT** | **FAMILY** | Translating to "suspended in mid-air," Angama has one of the best views in the Mara as it sits at the very top of an escarpment, with dramatic views over the valley below. **Pros:** an on-site photography studio where you can rent equipment or hire a photographer for the duration of your stay; surprise touches like Maasai dances with sundowners and starlit bush dinners; has its own organic farm where lunches can be set up. **Cons:** the main area can be windy given the elevation; phone connection can be sporadic in the rooms; night drives not permitted in this part of the Mara. $ *Rooms from: $4,300* ⊠ *Masai Mara National Reserve*

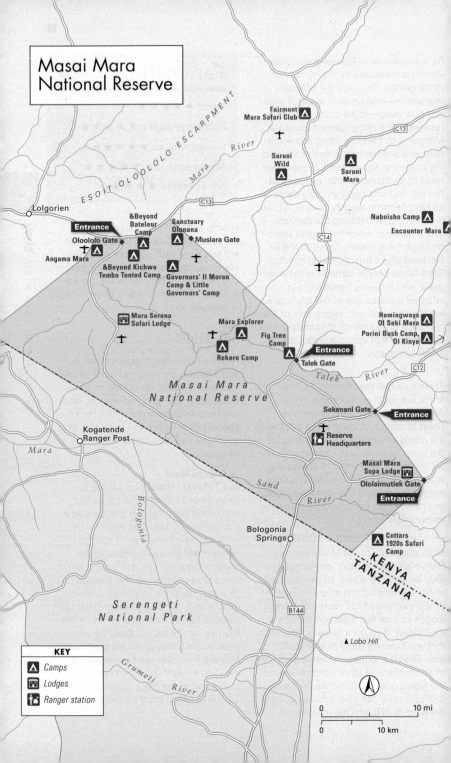

Masai Mara National Reserve

ESOIT OLOOLOLO ESCARPMENT

Mara River

Lolgorien

Fairmont Mara Safari Club

Saruni Wild

Saruni Mara

C13

Entrance

&Beyond Bateleur Camp

Sanctuary Olonana

Musiara Gate

Ol-oololo Gate

Naboisho Camp

Encounter Mara

C14

Angama Mara

&Beyond Kichwa Tembo Tented Camp

Governors' Il Moran Camp & Little Governors' Camp

Mara Serena Safari Lodge

Mara Explorer

Fig Tree Camp

Hemingways Ol Seki Mara

Porini Bush Camp, Ol Kinye

Rekero Camp

Entrance

Talek Gate

Talek River

C12

Masai Mara National Reserve

Sekenani Gate

Entrance

Kogatende Ranger Post

Reserve Headquarters

Mara

Masai Mara Sopa Lodge

Ololaimutiek Gate

Entrance

Sand River

Cottars 1920s Safari Camp

Bologonia Springs

KENYA
TANZANIA

Bologonia

Serengeti National Park

B144

▲ Lobo Hill

Grumeti River

KEY

▲	Camps
🏠	Lodges
🧍	Ranger station

0   10 mi

0   10 km

Angama Mara sits at the top of an escarpment, providing incredible views of the valley below.

☎ *0730/630–630* 🌐 *www.angama.com* 🛏 *30 suites* 🍴 *All-Inclusive.*

&Beyond Bateleur Camp

$$$$ | **RESORT** | If you're among the many who saw *Out of Africa* and began fantasizing about your own African experience, then you'll be happy to know that this totally private and very romantic world-class camp is just below the famous hill from the unforgettable final scene. **Pros:** the restaurant and public areas are never crowded; there are unexpected surprise touches along the way; knowledgeable guides, including a female guide (still a rarity in the Mara). **Cons:** monkeys are always jumping on the roof, and will likely wake you up in the morning; if you leave your door open, all sorts of insects will fly in; intermittent mobile phone and Wi-Fi reception. [$] *Rooms from: $2,470* ✉ *Masai Mara National Reserve* ☎ *11/809–4300 reservations in South Africa* 🌐 *www.andbeyond.com* 🛏 *18 tents* 🍴 *All-Inclusive.*

&Beyond Kichwa Tembo Tented Camp

$$$$ | **RESORT** | **FAMILY** | Perched on the edge of a riverine forest below the Oloololo Escarpment, Kichwa Tembo (head of the elephant in Kiswahili) lies directly in the path of the migration making it one of Kenya's most sought-after camps. **Pros:** there's an excellent curio shop; there's an organic vegetable garden where they grow their own food; infinity swimming pool. **Cons:** hair dryers in luxury tents only; a large camp, it may not be intimate enough for some; some of the rooms are a bit far from the public areas. [$] *Rooms from: $900* ✉ *Masai Mara National Reserve* ☎ *11/809–4300* 🌐 *www.andbeyond.com* 🛏 *40 tents* 🍴 *All-Inclusive.*

★ **Cottar's 1920s Safari Camp**

$$$$ | **RESORT** | **FAMILY** | If you want to turn back the clock and immerse yourself in the kind of original safari ambience that Ernest Hemingway enjoyed, this is the place to do it. **Pros:** complimentary massages; you will seldom see another game vehicle; highly trained guides. **Cons:** minimum two nights booking; conservancy

The circle of life: a cheetah chases his prey.

fees $116 per person extra; hair dryers can be used only in the office. $ *Rooms from: $2,072* ⊠ *Olderkesi Conservancy* ☎ *0733/773–377 reservations* ⊕ *www. cottars.com* ⊏⊐ *10 tents* ⦿ *All-Inclusive.*

Encounter Mara

$$$$ | **RESORT** | **FAMILY** | Tucked within a shady acacia forest on the exclusive Mara Naboisho Conservancy, the luxury tents at this comfortable and contemporary-styled camp have great views across the plains. **Pros:** a game-viewing hide experience in camp; exclusive game drives in the Mara Naboisho Conservancy; excellent Maasai guides. **Cons:** a full day is required for a game drive into the Mara; a 45-minute drive from the airstrip; the camp is fenced but bushy so parents need to supervise young children. $ *Rooms from: $1,250* ⊠ *Mara Naboisho Conservancy, Masai Mara National Reserve* ☎ *020/232–4904 in Kenya, 214/180–468 in South Africa* ⊕ *www.asiliaafrica.com* ⊙ *Closed May* ⊏⊐ *10 tents* ⦿ *All-Inclusive.*

Fairmont Mara Safari Club

$$$ | **RESORT** | **FAMILY** | Although the Fairmont's camp area has manicured lawns and flowers, it is surrounded on three sides by the croc- and hippo-filled Mara River, so you are always close to the wildlife. **Pros:** rooms have hair dryers; the views of the Mara River from the tents are excellent; good-sized pool with sun-beds and bar. **Cons:** game drives and bush walks cost extra; a large camp so can feel a little impersonal; some distance to the reserve itself or near any migration routes. $ *Rooms from: $498* ⊠ *Ol-Choro Oiroua Conservation Area, Masai Mara National Reserve* ☎ *020/226–5000 reservations* ⊕ *www. fairmont.com/masai-mara-safari* ⊏⊐ *51 tents* ⦿ *Free Breakfast.*

Fig Tree Camp

$$$ | **RESORT** | **FAMILY** | This budget option on the banks of the Talek River overlooks the plains and its location on the northeastern boundary of the reserve gives it easy access to all the game areas. **Pros:** there is a lovely pool area; there's

evening entertainment with Maasai dancers or music; 24-hour complimentary hot drinks in the lobby. **Cons:** tents are located close to each other so can be noisy; electricity limited at certain times; no fans or air-conditioning. [$] *Rooms from: $580* ✉ *Masai Mara National Reserve* ☎ *0722/202–564 reservations* 🌐 *www.madahotels.com* 🛏 *80 rooms* 🍴 *Free Breakfast.*

Governors' Il Moran Camp

$$$$ | RESORT | One of the famous Governors' Camps, Il Moran is where Kenya's first colonial governors used to twirl their handlebar mustaches and sip their gin and tonics while on safari—as you can imagine, it boasts an exclusive location that's teeming with game. **Pros:** Governors' owns its own hot air balloon company; there's a maximum of four guests per game vehicle; the tents are well-spaced along the banks of the Mara River. **Cons:** hippos and other wildlife wander into the property at night, and can be loud (there's security at all times); paths run in front of the tents' verandahs making them not very private; unfenced so no children under eight. [$] *Rooms from: $1,376* ✉ *Masai Mara National Reserve* ☎ *020/273–4000 reservations* 🌐 *www.governorscamp.com* 🛏 *10 tents* 🍴 *All-Inclusive.*

Hemingways Ol Seki Mara

$$$$ | RESORT | FAMILY | This eco-friendly camp in the middle of the exclusive Mara Naboisho Conservancy is named after the *olseki* or sandpaper tree, which is a Maasai symbol of peace, harmony, and wealth. **Pros:** positioned on an elevated ridge with great views across the plains; afternoon tea is delivered to your tent; exclusive game-driving area where you won't encounter many other vehicles. **Cons:** the bathrooms are small, although the showers are reasonably spacious; the steep wooden walkways around camp would be a problem for very young children; you'll need to enter the Mara proper to see the best migration river spots. [$] *Rooms from: $1,360* ✉ *Mara Naboisho Conservancy, Masai Mara National Reserve* ☎ *0716/613–051 reservations* 🌐 *www.hemingways-collection.com/mara* 🛏 *10 tents* 🍴 *All-Inclusive.*

Little Governors' Camp

$$$$ | RESORT | FAMILY | Getting to this camp is a mini adventure in itself—first you take a small boat that ferries you across the Mara River followed by a short, escorted walk with armed guides (so you don't become lion food) before arriving at this gorgeous little camp with elegantly furnished classic safari tents. **Pros:** the camp sits directly in the path of the wildebeest migration; bathrooms are fitted with osmosis system taps making the water safe to drink; 15-minute from the Musiara Airstrip and transfers are included. **Cons:** there are steep flights of steps on both sides of the river crossing; rooms have no safe; the tents are close together, and there is not much privacy on the verandahs. [$] *Rooms from: $1,176* ✉ *Masai Mara National Reserve* ☎ *020/273–4000 reservations* 🌐 *www.governorscamp.com* 🛏 *17 tents* 🍴 *Free Breakfast.*

Mara Explorer

$$$$ | RESORT | At this intimate camp tucked in a riverine forest on a bend on the Talek River, you'll be able to watch elephants wading, hippos snorting, and all other sorts of game from your outdoor claw-foot bathtub that overlooks the river. **Pros:** the camp is a short drive from the Mara River, where thousands of wildebeest make their perilous crossing every year between July and September; all tents overlook the Talek River; a three-minute drive from the nearest airstrip. **Cons:** Wi-Fi only in the public areas; hippos can be loud at night; hot water is available only at fixed times. [$] *Rooms from: $684* ✉ *Masai Mara National Reserve* ☎ *0732/411–105, 0722/205–894 reservations* 🌐 *www.heritage-eastafrica.com* 🛏 *10 tents* 🍴 *All-Inclusive.*

Mara Serena Safari Lodge

$$$ | RESORT | FAMILY | Perched high on a hill deep inside the Mara Triangle part of the reserve, attractive domed huts echo the style and shape of the traditional Maasai *manyattas*. **Pros:** amazing views from the bedrooms; the breakfasts at the hippo pool; has its own airstrip. **Cons:** the buffet can be uninspiring, especially if staying longer than three days; some rooms are far away and downhill from the public areas; the decor is a bit dated. [$] *Rooms from: $480* ✉ *Masai Mara National Reserve* ☎ *0732/123–333 reservations* 🌐 *www.serenahotels.com* 🛏 *74 rooms* 🍴 *Free Breakfast.*

Masai Mara Sopa Lodge

$$ | RESORT | FAMILY | On a hillside near the Ololaimutiek Gate, this well-priced family-style lodge (*sopa* means welcome in the Maasai language) is one of the most popular in the reserve. **Pros:** it's very close to the eastern entrance to the Mara; there's a bushbaby feeding table; the great pool is ideal to cool off in after a game drive. **Cons:** rondavels are located close to each other; because you're more than 6,000 feet above sea level, you'll need some warm clothes; hot water is available only at limited times. [$] *Rooms from: $347* ✉ *Masai Mara National Reserve* ☎ *020/375–0235 reservations* 🌐 *www.sopalodges.com* 🛏 *50 rondavels* 🍴 *Free Breakfast.*

★ **Naboisho Camp**

$$$$ | RESORT | FAMILY | Quite possibly the best camp in all of the Mara area, Naboisho Camp is in the 210-sq-km (82-squar-mile) Mara Naboisho Conservancy, which has exclusive use for only those guests staying at the handful of lodges there—there are no hordes of safari vehicles here. **Pros:** the guides at this camp are excellent; the conservancy is very exclusive, allowing for uninterrupted game drives; high level of personalized service. **Cons:** need to allow for a full day to do a game drive into the Mara proper; the camp is unfenced, so kids' supervision is essential at all times; Wi-Fi but mobile phone reception is poor. [$] *Rooms from: $1,790* ✉ *Mara Naboisho Conservancy, Masai Mara National Reserve* ☎ *020/232–4904 reservations* 🌐 *www.asiliaafrica.com* 🕒 *Closed April* 🛏 *9 tents* 🍴 *All-Inclusive.*

Porini Bush Camp, Ol Kinyei

$$$$ | ALL-INCLUSIVE | In the Ol Kinyei conservancy, in a picturesque valley among soaring fever and tortilis trees, this eco-friendly mobile camp has no permanent structures and when packed up, leaves no hint of ever having been there; it's visited by all sorts of game. **Pros:** the guides are fantastic and night drives are allowed; picnic lunches are included on game drives; park fees, game drives etc are included in the rate. **Cons:** Wi-Fi connection can be sporadic; pack warm clothing as evenings can be quite cold; only open from July to October. [$] *Rooms from: $790* ✉ *Ol Kinyei Conservancy, Masai Mara National Reserve* ☎ *0774/136–523* 🌐 *www.porini.com* 🕒 *Closed Nov.–June* 🛏 *8 tents* 🍴 *All-Inclusive.*

★ **Rekero Camp**

$$$$ | RESORT | Rekero is beautifully situated deep within the Masai Mara National Reserve and is tucked away in a grove of trees on a river bank near the confluence of the Talek and Mara rivers. **Pros:** each tent is tucked into the bush along the river and offers absolute privacy; excellent location next to a migration river crossing point; first-class guiding. **Cons:** the area can be busy with game-viewing vehicles from other camps; children over five are welcome, but must be carefully supervised; the access road is particularly rough. [$] *Rooms from: $1,740* ✉ *Masai Mara National Reserve* ☎ *020/232–4904 reservations* 🌐 *www.asiliaafrica.com* 🕒 *Closed Apr. and May* 🛏 *9 tents* 🍴 *All-Inclusive.*

Sanctuary Olonana

$$$$ | RESORT | FAMILY | Named after an honored Maasai chief, this attractive eco-friendly camp in game-rich country rests just outside the northwestern border of the reserve, overlooking the Mara River and the Ooloo/olo Escarpment; guests are welcomed by a Maasai man swathed in red robes playing a wooden flute. **Pros:** the honeymoon suite is beautiful and has its own private infinity pool; you can watch hippos in the Mara River from your tent; relaxing spa with a riverside deck. **Cons:** no Wi-Fi in the main areas (so guests can socialize); the farthest suites are quite a long walk from the main facilities; main pool is a little small and doesn't have any breathtaking views. $ *Rooms from: $1,750* ✉ *Masai Mara National Reserve* ☎ *1242/546–609 reservations, U.K.* ⊕ *www.sanctuaryretreats.com* ⏎ *14 suites* ♟ *All-Inclusive.*

Saruni Mara

$$$$ | **RESORT** | **FAMILY** | This exclusive eco-friendly lodge lies just outside the Masai Mara National Reserve, inside the Mara North Conservancy in a remote valley of olive and cedar trees. **Pros:** specialized guiding, such as bird-watching, is available; night drives are permitted on Mara North Conservancy; photographer's studio cottage with its old box Browning camera and prints is perfect for photography enthusiasts. **Cons:** can be a little cool at night because of the altitude; a small lodge, reservations are required well in advance; the camp is at least a 40-minute drive to the Masai Mara National Reserve. $ *Rooms from: $1,560* ✉ *Masai Mara National Reserve* ☎ *020/218–0497 reservations* ⊕ *www.sarunimara.com* ⏎ *7 cottages* ♟ *All-Inclusive.*

Saruni Wild

$$$$ | **RESORT** | **FAMILY** | You certainly won't come across another vehicle at this exclusively sited camp in the northern section of the Masai Mara ecosystem on the border between the Lemek Conservancy and the Mara North Conservancy. **Pros:** because the camp is in a conservancy, you'll hardly see another vehicle; there's a high chance

of seeing rare nocturnal species; very small with an exclusive and intimate feel. **Cons:** won't appeal to those wanting more facilities like a pool; the conservancy fee of $116 per person per night is not included in rates; it's far from the prime viewing spots during migration time. $ *Rooms from: $1,560* ✉ *Lemek Conservancy, Masai Mara National Reserve* ☎ *020/218–0497 reservations* ⊕ *www.saruniwild.com* ⏎ *3 tents* ♟ *All-Inclusive.*

Amboseli National Park

Amboseli National Park, immediately northwest of Mt. Kilimanjaro and 220 km (140 miles) southeast of Nairobi on the Tanzanian border, is certainly one of the most picturesque places in the whole of Africa to watch game. Where else could you watch a great herd of elephants on a wide empty plain dominated by Africa's highest mountain, Kilimanjaro?

At dawn, as the cloud cover breaks and the first rays of sun illuminate the snowcapped 5,895-meter (19,340-foot) peak, the sky, colored by rosy pinks and soft reds, provides the perfect backdrop for the plains below. It gets even better at dusk, when the mountain stands out in stark relief against the fiery sun.

Amboseli has a checkered history. First established as a natural reserve in 1948, it was returned to Maasai ownership and management in 1961 but soon became environmentally degraded with too many cattle and too many tourists. Some 10 years later, 392 square km (151 square miles) were designated a national park, and cattle-grazing was forbidden. This angered the pastoral Maasai, who took their revenge by killing a majority of the rhino population. Eventually peace was restored with some expedient land swapping, and today there's a responsible environmental program that controls the well-being of the game, puts limits on tourist numbers, and enforces a strict policy on off-road driving.

There are five different habitats in Amboseli: open plains, acacia woodland, thornscrub, swamps, and marshlands. To the west is the Ol Donyo Orok massif and Lake Amboseli, which is usually dry. But when the heavy rains return, the surrounding area becomes green and lush again and migratory birds flock to the park. Expect some impassable roads at these times, as well as when the lake is completely dry because the fine alkaline dust that blows up from the lake bed is hell for tires—the name "Amboseli" comes from a Maasai term that means "salty dust."

Amboseli is filled with great game: zebras, warthogs, giraffes, buffalo, hippos, impalas, wildebeest, unusual antelopes like the fringe-eared oryx, and long-necked mini giraffe-like gerenuks, and baboons galore. The park, however, is not home to rhinos and your chances of seeing predators are not quite as good as in the Masai Mara. Maasai hunters once almost killed off Amboseli's lions because they preyed on their herds of cattle, but after many years of tolerance from the local communities, populations have increased steadily and lucky visitors may spot not only lions, but hyenas, jackals, and cheetahs, too. If it's elephants you're after, then Amboseli is the place to come. Perhaps the oldest and most studied elephant population in sub-Saharan Africa lives here. There are more than 1,200 of these great pachyderms today, and because they're accustomed to visitors and vehicles you'll experience eyeball-to-knee-high close encounters.

Birdlife is also prolific, with more than 420 recorded species. There are dozens of birds of prey including more than 10 different kinds of eagles. In the swamp areas, which are fed by the melting snow of Kilimanjaro, seasonal flamingo, pelican, and more than 12 species of heron are among the profusion of water birds.

Park Ratings

Game: ★ ★ ★ ★ ★
Park Accessibility: ★ ★ ★ ★ ☆
Getting Around: ★ ★ ★ ★ ☆
Accommodations: ★ ★ ★ ★ ★
Scenic Beauty: ★ ★ ★ ★ ★

Game-viewing is best around Enkongo Narok, which means "black and benevolent." This belt of swamps in the middle of the park is home to hippos, numerous birds, beds of papyrus and waterlilies, herbivores coming to drink, and elephants taking baths. At Observation Hill, the Amboseli landmark just to the west of Lake Kioko, you are permitted to park and walk to the top for a surefire opportunity to spot game as you gaze out over the plains.

WHEN TO GO
January and February, and June through September are the best times to come here. During the rainy season (April and May) roads might become muddy and slippery, but it's a favorite time for photographers and birders to be here, when everything is green. There might also be rain in November and December.

GETTING HERE AND AROUND
Amboseli is 220 km (140 miles) from Nairobi. The best approach by road is to the gates on the southeastern side of the park via the fairly new tarred road from Emali on the Mombasa road (A109)—do not take the old route from Nairobi via the Namanga road (A104) as this is now in poor shape. There's no public transportation within the park and the roads are gravel; a 4x4 is a good idea and essential if it's wet. Amboseli's airstrip is served by scheduled flights from Nairobi's Wilson Airport as well as from Mombasa's Moi International Airport; some of which go via the Ukunda airstrip at Diani Beach.

A leopard sighting in the savannah in Tsavo East and Tsavo West National Park.

Hotels

Amboseli Serena Safari Lodge

$$ | RESORT | FAMILY | Situated beside a natural flowing spring with spectacular views of Mt. Kilimanjaro, this lodge's ochre-color guest rooms line paved walkways that weave through landscaped gardens. **Pros:** good value for money; the lodge balcony has views out onto the plains; the waterhole in front of the dining area is floodlit at night. **Cons:** not all the rooms have views; rooms don't have safes and valuables are left at reception; monkeys can be a nuisance if you're dining alfresco. ⓢ *Rooms from: $392 ✉ Amboseli National Park ☎ 0735/522–361 reservations ⊕ www.serenahotels.com ⇥ 92 rooms ⏐◯⏐ Free Breakfast.*

Amboseli Sopa Lodge

$$ | RESORT | FAMILY | When Ernest Hemingway wrote *The Snows of Kilimanjaro*, he stayed near the area on which this attractive lodge was eventually built. **Pros:** excellent early-morning views of Kilimanjaro; great pool with comfy sun loungers; plenty of wildlife around including elephants. **Cons:** hot water can be erratic; safari activities cost extra; the lodge is a 20-minute drive from Amboseli itself. ⓢ *Rooms from: $314 ✉ Amboseli National Park ☎ 0722/206–328 reservations ⊕ www.sopalodges.com ⇥ 83 rooms ⏐◯⏐ Free Breakfast.*

Ol Tukai Lodge

$$ | RESORT | FAMILY | This popular lodge is a central feature of Amboseli National Park as it's part of the fenced-off area in the middle of the park where the KWS headquarters are located, but Ol Tukai itself has only a very low electric fence which does not get in the way of the simply tremendous views across the animal-studded plains to the east. **Pros:** rooms are very spacious; the views of Kilimanjaro are fantastic; the large, fenced-in property is great for kids. **Cons:** Wi-Fi can be intermittent; the monkeys and baboons can make a racket at night; game drives, airstrip transfers, and other activities are not included. ⓢ *Rooms from: $450 ✉ Amboseli National Park*

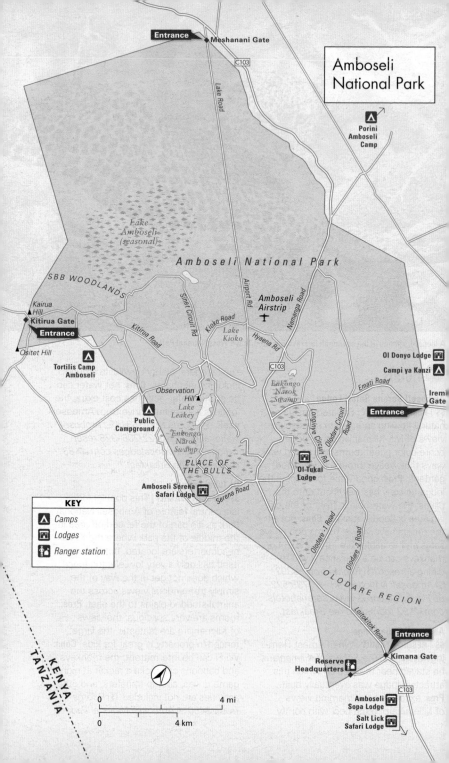

In Amboseli National Park, cheetah and wildebeest keep a watchful eye on each other.

☎ 020/444–5514 reservations ⊕ www. oltukailodge.com ⇌ 80 rooms ⦿ Free Breakfast.

Porini Amboseli Camp

$$$$ | RESORT | FAMILY | This exclusive, back-to-nature tented camp is in the remote and game-abundant 15,000-acre Selenkay Conservancy, a few miles north of Amboseli National Park. **Pros:** the camp benefits the local community and is eco-friendly; lots of activities and park/ conservancy fees covered in the rate; the curio gift shop is superb, with items from whichever village you tour. **Cons:** children under eight are not permitted, but family units recently added; no laundry facilities; as with most camps, you'll struggle to get a phone signal. $ *Rooms from: $755* ✉ *Selenkay Conservancy, Amboseli National Park* ☎ *0722/509–200, 0774/136–523 reservations* ⊕ *www. porini.com* ☉ *Closed mid-Apr.–May* ⇌ *10 tents* ⦿ *All-Inclusive.*

Tortilis Camp Amboseli

$$$$ | RESORT | FAMILY | This rustic bush camp is named after the flat-topped *Acacia tortilis* trees that surround the main thatch-roof open bar, lounge, and dining room, which also overlooks a waterhole and has superb views of Mt. Kilimanjaro and Mt. Meru in neighboring Tanzania. **Pros:** stunning views of Mt. Kilimanjaro; excellent library; lots of elephants and great birdlife. **Cons:** it's about a 45-minute drive to Amboseli's central swampy regions; accommodations are nice but lighting is insufficient; the tents are accessed by steep steps. $ *Rooms from: $1,366* ✉ *Amboseli National Park* ☎ *0730/127–000 reservations* ⊕ *www. elewanacollection.com* ⇌ *17 tents, 1 private house* ⦿ *All-Inclusive.*

Read and Watch

Out of Africa by Isak Dinesen (Blixen's pen name) is the autobiography of the Danish author Karen Blixen, who lived in Kenya for a significant portion of her life. The book was made into a romantic drama in 1985 starring Meryl Streep and Robert Redford set in the Ngong Hills outside of Nairobi.

Born Free: A Lioness of Two Worlds by Joy Adamson is the touching story of a captive lioness set free and her bonds with both the human world and the wild.

West with the Night is an autobiography about Beryl Markham, a 1920s female trailblazer in Kenya who was a pilot and racehorse trainer.

The Disney documentary *African Cats* is about the plight and family dynamics of Africa's big cats.

The Ghost and the Darkness (1996) is a film with Michael Douglas and Val Kilmer about two lions that stalk workers building the Uganda-Mombasa Railway circa late 19th century.

Based on a true story, the 2005 film *The White Masai* tells the story of a young Swiss woman who falls in love with a Maasai warrior while on holiday in Kenya, and moves to his village in the heart of Samburu, adopting his people's traditional way of life.

Near Amboseli and Tsavo West

The Chyulu Hills are a deeply green volcanic ridge of low hills between Amboseli and Tsavo West National Parks. It's a beautiful rugged wilderness and habitats include riverine bush and high mountain forests, although there are few roads and this region is fairly impenetrable unless you fly there. The altitude (up to 2,160 meters/7,087 feet above sea level) does not attract huge numbers of game, but elephant and buffalo are common and you'll find numerous antelope and more than 400 species of birds. The hills give a tremendous outlook across the broad African plains that spread out from their base and there's always a staggering view of Mount Kilimanjaro to the west. It's a good destination for hiking, bird-watching, horse-riding, or simply relaxing at the Chyulu's luxury lodges.

Hotels

★ Campi ya Kanzi
$$$$ | RESORT | FAMILY | One of Kenya's most environmentally friendly camps, this lovely spot in the Kuku Group Ranch—the natural corridor between Amboseli and Tsavo West National Parks—is owned by an Italian couple who are deeply committed to the environment and the local Maasai community. **Pros:** the tented cottages are very private; staff are from the local Maasai community; owners Luca and Antonella are superb hosts. **Cons:** not an overnight stop and 3–4 nights are needed to enjoy it; no Wi-Fi and intermittent mobile phone reception; animals are around but not in big quantities. [$] *Rooms from: $1,500* ✉ *Chyulu Hills* ☎ *0720/461–300* 🌐 *www.maasai.com* 🛏 *8 tents, 1 villa* 🍴 *All-Inclusive.*

★ Ol Donyo Lodge
$$$$ | RESORT | FAMILY | Located on the Maasai-owned Mbirikani Group Ranch on the southwestern flank of the volcanic Chyulu Hills, this stylishly romantic and

Located in the Chyulu Hills, the stylishly romantic and luxurious Ol Donyo Lodge is considered one of southern Kenya's best.

superluxurious lodge is considered one of the best in southern Kenya. **Pros:** the horizon pool has stunning views of Mt. Kilimanjaro; suites have indoor and outdoor showers as well as bathtubs; the "star beds" are an indescribable experience. **Cons:** the access road is long and rough; it's better to fly to the private airstrip; the US$120 per person conservancy fee is extra; there's less concentrated game than in Amboseli, but no other people. [$] *Rooms from: $2310* ✉ *Chyulu Hills, Mbirikani Group Ranch* ☎ *87/354–6591 reservations, South Africa* 🌐 *www.greatplainsconservation.com* 🕓 *Closed Apr.* 🛏 *10 suites, 1 house* 🍴 *All-Inclusive.*

Salt Lick Safari Lodge

$ | RESORT | This truly uniquely designed lodge is set in the Taita Hills Wildlife Sanctuary just outside Tsavo West and off the main Voi-Taveta road (A23). **Pros:** the underground viewing room; watching animals from your bed; fantastic architecture. **Cons:** the half-moon shaped rooms are small; stairs and bridges make it not suitable for small kids; no pool. [$] *Rooms from: $193* ✉ *Taita Hills Wildlife Sanctuary, Tsavo West* ✥ *40 km (25 miles) east of Voi* ☎ *078/888–8221, 011/094–3777 reservations* 🌐 *www.saltlicksafarilodge.com* 🛏 *96 rooms* 🍴 *Free Breakfast.*

Tsavo West and East National Parks

Covering almost 21,000 square km (8,108 square miles), the combined Tsavo West and Tsavo East National Parks is Kenya's largest protected game area. They are two distinct parks with different ecosystems: Tsavo West features wooded and hilly volcanic landscapes, while Tsavo East is much flatter with scattered bush on more open plains. They are administered separately, have separate entry fees and are split geographically by the Mombasa Highway—the main A109 road between Nairobi and Mombasa—as well as the railway that runs more or less alongside. Both stretch for about 130 km (80 miles) along the highway where a number of park gates provide access to the west and east. It's amazing that just a few miles away from the constant thunder of motor traffic on Kenya's busiest road is some of Kenya's best wildlife viewing.

Tsavo West

Tsavo West covers 7,065 square km (2,728 square miles), which is a little less than a third of the total area comprising all of Kenya's national parks. With its diverse habitats of riverine forest, palm thickets, rocky outcrops and ridges, mountains and plains, it's more attractive and certainly more accessible than Tsavo East. In the north, magnificent landscapes of heavily wooded hills dominate and this is where most of the lodges and game-viewing tracks are concentrated; it's generally known as the "Developed Area." The south of Tsavo West is flatter with more open plains, but access is tricky as parts of the park are disjointed and crossed by another highway between Voi and Taveta. There's evidence of volcanic activity everywhere in the park, especially where ancient lava flows absorb the rainfall. In one spectacular spot, this rainfall, having traveled underground for 40 km (25 miles) or so, gushes up in a pair of pools at Mzima Springs, in the north of the park. There's a submerged hippo blind here, but the hippos have gotten wise to tourists and often move to the far side of the pools. Because of the fertile volcanic soil and abundance of water, the park is brimming with animal, bird, and plant life. There are large numbers of elephant and you may see lion and cheetah—especially in the dry season when the grass is low—plus spotted hyena, buffalo, the beautiful Masai giraffe, and all kinds of antelope, including Thomson's and Grant's gazelle—the prettiest of the antelope. The birdlife in the park is outstanding, with more than 400 species including eight types of hornbills.

Park Ratings

Game: ★ ★ ★ ☆ ☆

Park Accessibility: ★ ★ ★ ★ ☆

Getting Around: ★ ★ ★ ★ ☆

Accommodations: ★ ★ ★ ★ ☆

Scenic Beauty: ★ ★ ★ ★ ☆

WHEN TO GO
You'll have a good experience whenever you go, but bear in mind that the long rains are from March to May, and the short rains are October to December—vegetation is dense in these wet months, making it more difficult to spot animals.

GETTING HERE AND AROUND
It's 240 km (150 miles) from Nairobi to Tsavo West's Mtito Andei Gate, which takes around five hours to drive. The park's Tsavo Gate in the southeast is approximately 200 km (125 miles) north of Mombasa and takes about four hours. You can take Kenya Railways's SGR train to Mtito Andei and Voi where there are entrance gates to Tsavo West and East, respectively, and if you drive yourself, keep an eye on the park signage (cairns at numbered junctions) or use a GPS. There are three airstrips in the park and you can fly from Nairobi's Wilson Airport, Mombasa's Moi International, and the Ukunda airstrip at Diani Beach.

CONTACTS Kenya Wildlife Service. ✉ *Tsavo West National Park* ☎ *0720/968–527 Tsavo West* ⊕ *www.kws.go.ke.* **Kenya Railways.** ⊕ *metickets.krc.co.ke/.*

Hotels

★ Finch Hattons
$$$$ | RESORT | At the turn of the 20th century, Denys Finch Hatton—if you saw the movie *Out of Africa*, then you'll have some idea, even if it's rather over-romanticized, of who he was—left his native

The elephants in Tsavo East National Park have a red tint to their skin from mud/dust bathing in the park's red soil.

England and fell in love with Kenya, cultivating a reputation for leading classy, exclusive safaris for American tycoons and British royalty, among others; his legend lives on in this superb, award-winning camp. **Pros:** you'll see an extraordinary array of wildlife right in the camp; food and service are outstanding; game drives, airstrip transfers, and sundowners are included. **Cons:** the generator is switched off at 11:30 pm; no children under six years; park fees of US$60 per night are extra. $ *Rooms from: $1,960* ✉ *Tsavo West* ☎ *0709/534–000, 020/357–7500 reservations* ⊕ *www.finchhattons.com* ➦ *17 tents* ❍ *All-Inclusive.*

Kilaguni Serena Safari Lodge
$$ | RESORT | FAMILY | This lovely old lodge was Kenya's first lodge to open in a national park (1962). **Pros:** the waterhole is floodlit at night; the airstrip is less than 1 km away; family-friendly with babysitting and kids' dining. **Cons:** room decor is a bit dated; can be full with large tour groups; not all rooms have great views. $ *Rooms from: $332* ✉ *Tsavo West*

☎ *0732/123–333, 20/284–2000* ⊕ *www.serenahotels.com* ➦ *56 rooms* ❍ *Free Breakfast.*

Severin Safari Camp
$$ | RESORT | With 27 rooms, this meticulously kept camp is large enough for you to do your own thing, yet small enough to retain its tented-camp feel with a wonderfully peaceful ambience. **Pros:** lovely, relaxing pool area, with a little spa and gym; wheelchair-friendly rooms available; sundowners at Poacher's lookout are incredible. **Cons:** water pressure can be a little low at times in the bathrooms; it's unfenced so not suitable for small children; most activities, including game drives, cost extra. $ *Rooms from: $397* ✉ *Tsavo West, Tsavo West* ☎ *0716/833–222* ⊕ *www.severinsafaricamp.com* ➦ *27 tents* ❍ *Free Breakfast.*

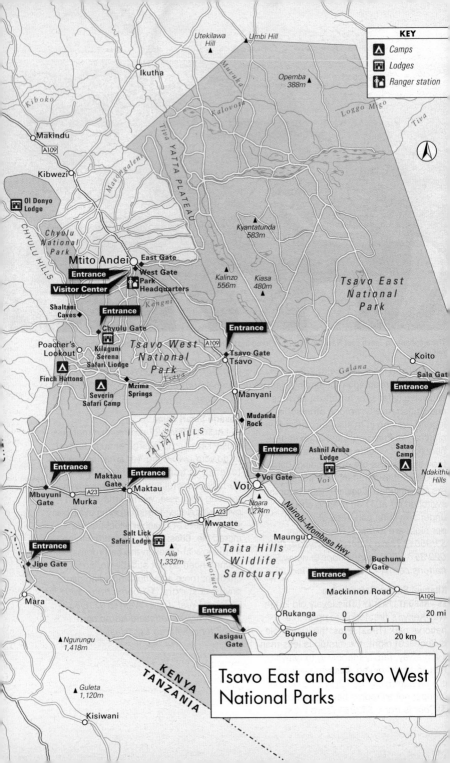

Tsavo East and Tsavo West National Parks

Tsavo East

Tsavo East—11,747 square km (4,535 square miles)—is the larger of the two Tsavos and has a fairly harsh landscape of scrubland dotted with huge baobab trees; photographers will revel in the great natural light and the vast plains stretching to the horizon. There's lots of greenery along the banks of the Voi and Galana rivers, and the big Aruba Dam, built across the Voi, attracts game and birdlife galore. The elephants here have a red tint to their skin from mud/dust bathing in the local red soil, which is one of the distinct features of the park. You'll also see herds of buffalo, waterbucks, and all kinds of animals coming to drink at the dam. The Lugard Falls, on the Galana River, is more a series of rapids than actual waterfalls; walk along the riverbank to catch a glimpse of the water-sculpted rocks. Another fascinating feature in the park is the 290-km-long (180-mile-long) Yatta Plateau, one of the world's longest lava flows. It runs parallel to the Nairobi-Mombasa Highway and is 5 to 10 km (3 to 6 miles) wide and 305 meters (1,000 feet) high. Mudanda Rock, a 1.5-km (2-mile) outcropping, is a water catchment area. You'll see plenty of wildlife coming to drink at the dam below. There's a lot of game in this park, including zebra, impala, lion, cheetah, and giraffe, and rarer animals such as the oryx, lesser kudu, and the small klipspringer antelope, which can jump nimbly from rock to rock because of the sticky suction pads under their feet. And yes, it's true: those fat and hairy marmotlike creatures you see sunning themselves on the rocks—the hyraxes—are first cousins to elephants.

The park became infamous in the late 1890s because of the "Man Eaters of Tsavo," a pride of lions that preyed on the Indian migrant laborers who were building the railway. More than 130 workers were killed; the incident was

The Legend of the Baobab

Legend has it that when the gods were planting the earth, the baobab refused many locations. In anger, the gods threw them out of heaven and they landed upside down. Take a good look. When not in leaf, they look exactly as if their roots are sticking up into the air.

retold in the 1996 thriller, *The Ghost and the Darkness,* starring Val Kilmer. In the 1970s and '80s Tsavo became notorious once again for the widespread poaching that decimated the elephant population and nearly wiped out rhinos altogether. Today, thanks to responsible management, enlightened environmental vision, and proper funding, both elephant and rhino populations are on the rise and are carefully monitored.

WHEN TO GO

Tsavo East is accessible year-round, so the peak season is actually based on demand months such as migration time in Kenya (July–October) and also vacationers getting away during the winter months—especially Europeans. That being said, March through May is the rainy season, and there are short rains in October and December. Humidity is high from December to April.

GETTING HERE AND AROUND

There are several gates to Tsavo East. Mtito Andei Gate is 233 km (148 miles) southeast of Nairobi. Voi Gate, 157 km (98 miles) northwest of Mombasa, and Buchuma Gate, 100 km (62 miles) northwest of Mombasa, are the routes often used on organized safaris from the coast. There are nine airstrips but no scheduled flights; most visitors drive up from Mombasa or charter flights are an option, but you could also take Kenya

If you fancy something extraordinary, try the Loisaba Star Beds—a wooden "platform" with a four-poster bed overlooking the Ewaso Nyiro River where guests sleep under the clear night sky.

Railways's SGR train (*see Tsavo West for contact information*) and then organize transfers from the train station with your lodge. There's no public transport within the park.

CONTACTS Kenya Wildlife Service. ✉ *Tsavo Rast National Park* 🌐 *www.kws.go.ke.*

🛏 Hotels

Ashnil Aruba Lodge

$$ | **RESORT** | **FAMILY** | This large mid-range safari lodge may not have the intimacy of a small tented camp, but its location is superb as it overlooks the Aruba Dam—one of the best places to see wildlife in the whole of Tsavo East. **Pros:** elephants can be seen from the swimming pool; hospitable and well-organized staff; easy access from Voi Gate. **Cons:** park fees and activities cost extra; Wi-Fi only in the lounge; it has a large resort feel but will suit those who like hotel rooms. [$] *Rooms from: $270* ✉ *Tsavo East* ☎ *0768/795–492, 0717/612–499 reservations* 🌐 *www.ashnilhotels.com* 🛏 *52 rooms* 🍴 *Free Breakfast.*

Satao Camp

$$ | **RESORT** | **FAMILY** | This small and friendly camp lies on a traditional migration route, so it's not short of game. **Pros:** excellent views of the waterhole; it's fully equipped for people with disabilities; up to 50% discounts for children under 12. **Cons:** rates do not include park fees or game drives; hot water for showers only in the evening; parts of the camp look onto unsightly power lines. [$] *Rooms from: $436* ✉ *Tsavo National Park East* ☎ *020/243–4610 reservations* 🌐 *www.sataocamp.com* 🛏 *20 tents* 🍴 *Free Breakfast.*

Laikipia Plateau

Stretching northwest of Mt. Kenya, the Laikipia Plateau isn't in itself a national park or reserve, but it's a broadly defined region of community group ranches and private conservancies. It has become one of Kenya's conservation successes, with many landowners turning cattle ranches into wildlife sanctuaries, too, and it is where traditional ways of pastoral life continue side by side with an abundance of free-roaming game.

This huge region covers around 9,500 square km (3,668 square miles), and the conservancies are crisscrossed by dirt roads. The Ol Pejeta Conservancy, famous for its black rhino and chimpanzee sanctuary, is open to day visitors and it's the easiest to get to from Nairobi. The Lewa Wildlife Conservancy, which was founded in the 1970s, has become a globally recognized black and white rhino conservation; it can also be reached by road from Nairobi. Some other conservancies on the fringe of Kenya's northern territory are accessible by those who stay in one of their exclusive lodges and who usually arrive by plane. This is high country, with altitudes from 1,700 meters (5,577 feet) to 2,600 meters (8,530 feet), so bring those sweaters and jackets.

Laikipia's habitats range from arid semidesert, scrubland, and sprawling open plains in the north and south, to the thick forests of cedar and olive trees in the east. The area has one of the biggest and most diverse mammal populations in Kenya—only the Masai Mara can boast more game. The Big Five are all present, and it's the only area in Kenya to have a burgeoning population of wild dogs. Many northern Kenyan animals can be spotted such as the gerenuk, Grevy's zebra, Jackson's hartebeest, and reticulated giraffe.

WHEN TO GO

Laikipia is good all year around, but the dry seasons—May to September and January to February—tend to offer the best game viewing since wildlife congregate around the waterholes and creeks and the clear air offers particularly spectacular views of the peak of Mt. Kenya in the southeast.

Park Ratings

Game: ★ ★ ★ ★ ☆

Park Accessibility: ★ ★ ★ ☆ ☆

Getting Around: ★ ★ ★ ☆ ☆

Accommodations: ★ ★ ★ ★ ★

Scenic Beauty: ★ ★ ★ ★ ☆

3

Kenya LAIKIPIA PLATEAU

GETTING HERE AND AROUND

The town of Nanyuki on the A2 road is the service center for the Laikipia Plateau and is an easy three- to four-hour drive from Nairobi. From here it's a short drive to Ol Pejeta Conservancy, and Nanyuki has an airstrip served by AirKenyaand Safarilink. In eastern Laikipia, Lewa Wildlife Conservancy is about a four-hour drive from Nairobi; Lewa Downs is the airstrip served by the same airlines. Few travelers attempt to drive to the central and far flung northern areas on their own and the many lodges will look after transport arrangements from Nairobi—the easiest option is to fly.

Hotels

★ Borana Lodge

$$$$ | RESORT | FAMILY | The traditional Borana cattle ranch—a part of Kenyan highland history—was given a whole new lease on life in 2013, when 21 highly endangered black rhinos were translocated here from Lake Nakuru National Park and from the neighboring Lewa Conservancy; they're easily viewable as you drive around. **Pros:** unique views up to the peak of Mt. Kenya; a chance to meet the Dyer family, one of Kenya's founding farming dynasties; lots of activities to experience the working ranch. **Cons:** at least one hour's drive from Lewa Downs airstrip; not fenced and steep in places so children need to be supervised at all times; people are often surprised at how chilly it can be at night

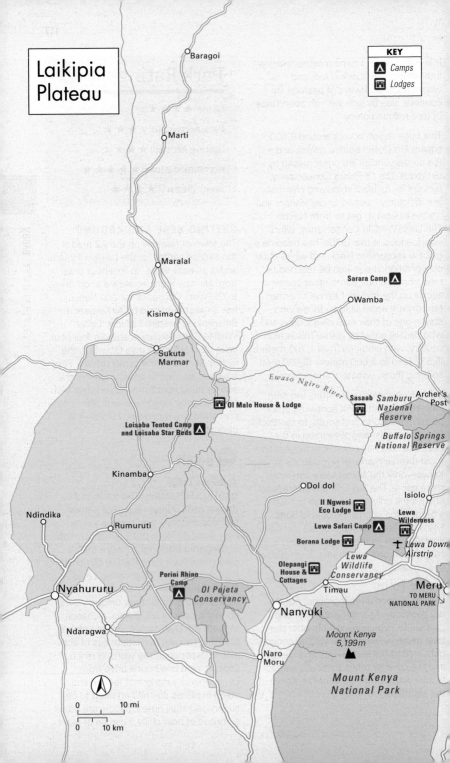

Laikipia Plateau

KEY
△ Camps
🏠 Lodges

Baragoi

Marti

Maralal

Kisima

Sukuta
Marmar

Ewaso Ngiro River

Sarara Camp △

Wamba

Kinamba

Ol Malo House & Lodge 🏠

Loisaba Tented Camp △
and Loisaba Star Beds

Sasaab 🏠 *Samburu
National
Reserve*

Archer's
Post

*Buffalo Springs
National Reserve*

Dol dol

Isiolo

Il Ngwesi
Eco Lodge 🏠

Lewa
Wilderness 🏠

Ndindika

Rumuruti

Lewa Safari Camp △

Borana Lodge 🏠

✝ Lewa Down
Airstrip

Olepangi
House &
Cottages 🏠

*Lewa
Wildlife
Conservancy*

Nyahururu

Porini Rhino
Camp △

*Ol Pejeta
Conservancy*

Timau

Meru

**TO MERU
NATIONAL PARK**

Ndaragwa

Nanyuki

*Mount Kenya
5,199m*
▲

Naro
Moru

*Mount Kenya
National Park*

0   10 mi

0   10 km

at this altitude, but hot-water bottles and romantic open fireplaces in all cottages add to the cozy atmosphere. [$] *Rooms from: $1,280* ✉ *Borana Ranch, Laikipia Plateau* ☎ *020/211–5453* 🌐 *www.borana.co.ke* 🕒 *Closed Nov.* 🛏 *8 cottages* 🍴 *All-Inclusive.*

Il Ngwesi Eco Lodge

$$$ | **RESORT** | **FAMILY** | Situated on a rocky outcrop in the Il Ngwesi Group Ranch, a community conservation and livestock region north of the Lewa Wildlife Conservancy, this intimate lodge prides itself on its successful efforts to integrate community development and sustainable environmental management. **Pros:** good children's facilities and activities; you can sleep under the stars; excellent community outreach and sustainability. **Cons:** drinks are not always cold; two-hour drive from Lewa Downs airstrip; open-air showers only. [$] *Rooms from: $600* ✉ *Il Ngwesi Group Ranch, Laikipia Plateau* ☎ *0741/770–540* 🌐 *www.ilngwesi.com* 🛏 *6 rooms* 🍴 *All-Inclusive.*

Lewa Safari Camp

$$$$ | **RESORT** | **FAMILY** | If it's rhinos you're after, then this delightful but small tented camp in the 65,000-acre Lewa Wildlife Conservancy, right where the old Rhino Sanctuary headquarters used to stand, is for you. **Pros:** tents are private and two sleep families; very few other vehicles; guides have intimate knowledge of Lewa. **Cons:** can get cold at night, but hot water bottles are provided; bathrooms are located a little close to the bed area of the tents and separated by a curtain; conservation fees excluded. [$] *Rooms from: $1,378* ✉ *Lewa Wildlife Conservancy* ☎ *0730/127–000 reservations* 🌐 *www.elewanacollection.com* 🛏 *13 tents* 🍴 *All-Inclusive.*

★ **Lewa Wilderness**

$$$$ | **RESORT** | **FAMILY** | Lewa Wildlife Conservancy is another one of Laikipia's conservation successes—there's an excellent chance of spotting both black and white rhino, the Grevy's zebra, the more elegant cousin of the regular plains zebra, and the rare aquatic sitatunga antelope. **Pros:** it's ideal for families; there's a huge range of activities available; all drinks are included from the self-service bar. **Cons:** it can get a little chilly in the evening; at least three nights are needed here to enjoy the experience; very popular and with many repeat guests, you need to book well in advance. [$] *Rooms from: $2,314* ✉ *Lewa Wildlife Conservancy, Laikipia Plateau* ☎ *0796/035–177 reservations* 🌐 *www.lewawilderness.com* 🛏 *10 rooms* 🍴 *All-Inclusive.*

Loisaba Tented Camp and Loisaba Star Beds

$$$$ | **RESORT** | **FAMILY** | The Loisaba Tented Camp sits right in the middle of the game-rich Loisaba Conservancy in the northern reaches of Laikipia and is part of the Ewaso Nyiro River ecosystem. **Pros:** small, intimate and peaceful with excellent service; good interaction with Laikipia's local people; both the tents and star beds have family options. **Cons:** Wi-Fi can be erratic; not ideal if it's windy or wet; no a/c, although the elevation means it's hardly needed. [$] *Rooms from: $960* ✉ *Loisaba Conservancy, Laikipia Plateau* ☎ *0730/127–000 reservations* 🌐 *www.elewanacollection.com* 🛏 *6 tents, 4 star beds* 🍴 *All-Inclusive.*

Olepangi House & Cottages

$$$ | **HOUSE** | **FAMILY** | This expansive 120-acre farm is set in the foothills of Mt Kenya; pad out of your four-poster bed to your cottage's wooden verandah to take in the beauty of the ever-green Lolldaigas. **Pros:** plenty of outdoor space and striking views; they grow a lot of their own food on-site; meals can be served throughout the property in a variety of settings. **Cons:** there are resident dogs, which not everyone may like; it's a bit of a climb getting to some of the shared spaces; highlands setting means it gets really cold at night. [$] *Rooms from: $550* ✉ *Timau* ☎ *0742/148–815* 🌐 *www.olepangifarm.com* 🛏 *5 cottages* 🍴 *All-Inclusive* ☞ *Minimum 2 night stay.*

Ol Malo House & Lodge

$$$$ | **RESORT** | **FAMILY** | Perched on an escarpment with views toward Mt. Kenya in the south, this lovely lodge is on a privately owned family ranch in the wild northern Laikipia Plateau. **Pros:** it's very child-friendly; the afternoon tea is excellent; a stay at the treehouse is magical. **Cons:** transfers from Loisaba airstrip cost extra; Wi-Fi has spasmodic reception; no a/c in rooms, but open walls make it airy. [$] *Rooms from: $1,800* ✉ *Laikipia Plateau* ☎ *0723/273–668 reservations* 🌐 *www.olmalo.com* 🕘 *Closed Apr., May, and Nov.* ⇨ *5 cottages (1 with 6 bedrooms)* 🍴 *All-Inclusive.*

Porini Rhino Camp

$$$$ | **RESORT** | **FAMILY** | This delightful eco-friendly tented camp is nestled among the 90,000-acre, game-rich Ol Pejeta Conservancy that lies between the snowcapped Mt. Kenya and the foothills of the Aberdares. **Pros:** the camp benefits the local community and is eco-friendly; the waterhole in front of the camp attracts a lot of wildlife; the price includes conservancy fees and a visit to the chimpanzee sanctuary. **Cons:** no Wi-Fi and limited phone reception; not recommended for children under eight; it can be cooler than reserves south of the country. [$] *Rooms from: $710* ✉ *Ol Pejeta Conservancy, Laikipia Plateau* ☎ *0774/136–523* 🌐 *www.porini.com* 🕘 *Closed mid-Apr.–May* ⇨ *8 tents* 🍴 *All-Inclusive.*

If You Have Time

Although the reviews go into great detail about the must-see parks in Kenya, there are many others to explore if you have time. Here, a few good ones are mentioned.

Nairobi National Park

The most striking thing about Nairobi National Park, Kenya's oldest national park (established in 1946), is the very fact that it exists at all. This sliver of unspoiled Africa survives on the edge of a city of more than 4 million people. Where else can you get a photo of animals in their natural habitat with skyscrapers in the background?

The park is tiny compared with Kenya's other game parks and reserves; it covers only 117 square km (44 square miles). It's characterized by open plains that slope gently from west to east and rocky ridges that are covered with rich vegetation. Seasonal streams run southeast into the Mbagathi River, which is lined with yellow-color fever and acacia trees.

Despite the urban pressures, the park contains a good variety of wildlife, even during the dry season, as there's always a source of permanent water. It's home to four of the Big Five; elephants are absent as the area isn't big enough to support them.

TIP→ If you want to see baby elephants, visit the orphanage at the Sheldrick Wildlife Trust close to the main entrance of the park.

Zebras, impalas, Grant's and Thomson's gazelles, warthogs, and ostriches are common on the open plains. Good populations of lions and cheetahs can be seen on the grasslands, Masai giraffes browse in the woodlands, black rhinos are sometimes found around the forest area, and more than 400 species of permanent and migratory birds have been recorded in the park.

Nairobi National Park has very pleasant picnic sites, a boardwalk to see a hippo pool, and a monument to Kenya's famous ivory-burning site. Both the Kenya Wildlife Service's Nairobi Safari Walk and the Animal Orphanage are near the KWS headquarters at the main gate of the park. Each has a separate entry fee and offers the opportunity to walk around for

an hour or so and get close to many of Kenya's animals that you might see on safari, all of which are kept at these facilities in spacious natural enclosures.

GETTING HERE AND AROUND

A 20-minute drive from downtown Nairobi (7 km/4 miles), the park's network of paved and all-weather dirt roads can be negotiated by regular cars; junctions are signposted and clearly marked on the official park map, which you can pick up at the gate. Most safari operators will arrange a half-day trip; otherwise hire a taxi for a few hours. Rangers keep a careful note of the movements of the larger animals, so it's worth asking at the gate where to look for lions or rhinos.

CONTACT Kenya Wildlife Service. ✉ *Langata Rd., Nairobi* ☎ *0800/597–000 KWS headquarters, 020/242–3423 Nairobi National Park* 🌐 *www.kws.go.ke.*

Hotels

Nairobi National Park is easy enough to visit on a day trip from accommodations in Nairobi. However, the lodge and a tented camp in the park are a good way to kick-start your safari. Stay here and you could be viewing lions and rhinos within an hour of stepping off your plane.

The Emakoko

$$$$ | RESORT | FAMILY | A 45-minute drive from Nairobi's Jomo Kenyatta International Airport is a luxurious paradise bush lodge in a seemingly remote and hidden valley. **Pros:** close to both of Nairobi's airports, but in a remote area; dinner by the pool is a starlit experience; log fires in the rooms turn cooler nights into sheer romance. **Cons:** the upper-level rooms are reached by steps; the access road is steep and tricky for drivers; windows and doors might have to be closed because of monkeys. [$] *Rooms from: $940* ✉ *Nairobi National Park, Nairobi* ☎ *0724/156–044* 🌐 *www.emakoko.com* 🛏 *10 rooms* 🍴 *All-Inclusive.*

Nairobi Tented Camp

$$ | RESORT | FAMILY | Insulated by a hidden glade—home to leopards, lions, and hyenas—Nairobi Tented Camp is in a secluded part of Nairobi National Park, providing an authentic bush experience within a few miles of the city center. **Pros:** short transfers from JKIA and Wilson airports; if your plane lands after dark you'll be treated to a night drive en route to the camp; lunch served under an olive tree, dinners under the sky. **Cons:** the access road is bumpy with the last 200 meters (656 feet) on foot; the tents are quite close together; Nairobi National Park entrance and camping fees are extra. [$] *Rooms from: $280* ✉ *Nairobi National Park, Nairobi* ☎ *0726/982 701* 🌐 *www.nairobitentedcamp.com* 🛏 *9 tents* 🍴 *Free Breakfast.*

Meru National Park

Situated 348 km (216 miles) northeast of Nairobi and west of Mt. Kenya, this little-visited park (1,810 square km/699 square miles) offers some of Kenya's wildest country, but was taken off the mainstream safari circuit because of the lawless poachers who wiped out a considerable amount of wildlife in the 1980s. But starting in 2000, the Kenya Wildlife Service embarked on a restoration mission and restocked the park with many large mammals—including elephant and black and white rhino—which have since thrived, and today the park is home to all of the Big Five. It's yet to attract large numbers of safari-goers, but Meru is a safe and fulfilling destination again—after all, this is the place where wildlife champions Joy and George Adamson hand-reared Elsa the lioness made famous by the 1966 film *Born Free.*

Game here includes buffalo, lion, leopard, cheetah, hippo, lesser kudu, hartebeest, Grevy's and Burchell's zebra, the gerenuk, the reticulated or Somali giraffe,

Continued on page 128

Blue wildebeest in Tanzania's Serengeti National Park

THE GREAT MIGRATION

Nothing will prepare you for the spectacle that is the Great Migration. This annual journey of more than 2 million animals is a safari-seeker's Holy Grail, the ultimate in wildlife experiences. Some say it's one of the world's greatest natural wonders.

The greater Serengeti ecosystem, which includes Kenya's Masai Mara (north) and Tanzania's Serengeti (south), is the main arena for this awesome sight. At the end of each year during the short rains—November to early December—the herds disperse into the southeast plains of Tanzania's Seronera. After calving early in the new year (wildebeests drop up to 8,000 babies a day), huge numbers of animals start the 800-km (497-mile) trek from these now bare southeast plains to lush northern pastures. On the way they will face terrible, unavoidable danger. In June and July braying columns—40 km (25 miles) long—have to cross the crocodile-infested Grumeti River. Half of the great herds that successfully survive the crossing will stay in northern Tanzania, the other half will cross over into Kenya's Masai Mara. In early October the animals begin their return journey back to Seronera and come full circle, only to begin their relentless trek once again early the following year.

WHO'S MIGRATING

What will you see during the migration?

More than **2 million** wildebeest
250,000 Thompson's gazelle
200,000 zebra
70,000 impala
30,000 Grant's gazelle

In addition, huge numbers of predators follow the herds. You're likely to see lion, leopard, cheetah, jackal, hyena, and numerous smaller predators.

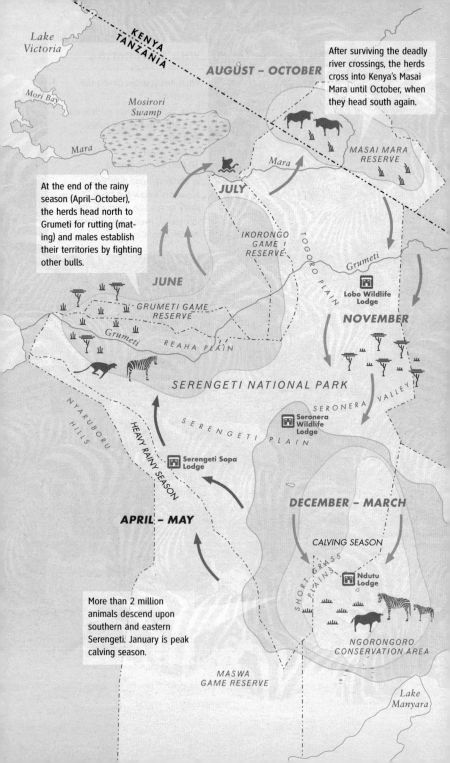

Lake
Victoria

Mori Bay

KENYA
TANZANIA

Mosirori
Swamp

Mara

AUGUST – OCTOBER

After surviving the deadly
river crossings, the herds
cross into Kenya's Masai
Mara until October, when
they head south again.

MASAI MARA
RESERVE

Mara

JULY

At the end of the rainy
season (April–October),
the herds head north to
Grumeti for rutting (mat-
ing) and males establish
their territories by fighting
other bulls.

IKORONGO
GAME
RESERVE

TOGORO PLAIN

Grumeti

Lobo Wildlife
Lodge

JUNE

GRUMETI GAME
RESERVE

Grumeti

REAHA PLAIN

NOVEMBER

SERENGETI NATIONAL PARK

SERONERA VALLEY

NYARUBORU HILLS

HEAVY RAINY SEASON

Serengeti Sopa
Lodge

SERENGETI PLAIN

Seronera
Wildlife
Lodge

SERENGETI
PLAIN

DECEMBER – MARCH

APRIL – MAY

CALVING SEASON

SHORT GRASS PLAINS

Ndutu
Lodge

More than 2 million
animals descend upon
southern and eastern
Serengeti. January is peak
calving season.

NGORONGORO
CONSERVATION
AREA

MASWA
GAME RESERVE

Lake
Manyara

DRIVEN BY DINNER

WHERE THE MAGIC HAPPENS

The Serengeti more than lives up to its awesome reputation as an amazing spot to see wildlife and it's here that the Great Migration begins and ends. The park's ecosystem supports some of the most abundant mammal populations left anywhere on earth and it covers almost 15,000 square km (9,320 square miles) of seemingly endless plains, riverine bush, forest, and scrubland roughly the size of Northern Ireland or Connecticut. It stretches between the Ngorongoro highlands, Lake Victoria, and Tanzania's northern border with Kenya. It was named a UNESCO World Heritage Site in 1978 and an International Biosphere Reserve (a UNESCO international conservation area) in 1981.

WHEN TO GO

Because rainfall patterns are unpredictable, it's difficult to anticipate timings for the migration. But usually, by the beginning of each year, the grazing on the southeast plains of Serengeti's Seronera is exhausted and the herds

STAGGERING NUMBERS

The Great Migration, as we know it, is a fairly young phenomenon, having only started in the 1960s when wildebeest numbers exploded. However, an estimated 250,000 wildebeests don't survive the annual migration.

start to move northwest into Tanzania's Western Corridor. The actual crossing of the Grumeti River, usually between June and July, when an unrivalled bloody spectacle of terrified frantic wildebeest and huge lashing crocodiles unfolds, is a gruesome, unforgettable spectacle. You'll see hundreds of thousands of animals between March and November, including predators. Seronera in March, April, and May is an ideal time for a safari because there are huge concentrations of predators preying on all the baby animals. Safaris are much cheaper between April and June, and although you may not witness the actual river crossings, you'll still be privy to prime game-viewing experiences. Plus there will be far fewer vehicles.

The Kikuyu people account for almost 25% of Kenya's population, and most live around Mt. Kenya.

waterbuck, oryx, and Grant's gazelle. The park is part of an ecosystem that includes Kora National Park and Mwingi, Rahole, and Bisanadi reserves. It straddles the equator and is home to a great variety of habitats, including scrubland dotted with baobab trees, lush green grasslands, and riverine forests. Tana, Kenya's longest river, is fed by 13 rivers that create a superb habitat for birdlife, including the Somali ostrich and raptors such as the red-necked falcon and the palm-nut vulture. You may also see that megascore on a serious birder's "life list," the Pel's fishing owl, which hides in the huge ancient trees along the rivers.

GETTING HERE AND AROUND

There's a daily flight between Nairobi's Wilson Airport and Meru National Park with AirKenya, which takes one hour. You can drive from Nairobi; the road isn't particularly bad save for the last dusty stretch past Maua leading up to the main gate, and it takes six hours. If you're already at a property in the area, say at Laikipia or Samburu, it can make sense to drive, but a 4x4 vehicle is required for driving within the park.

CONTACT Kenya Wildlife Service. ✉ *Meru National Park* ☏ *0786/348–875* ⊕ *www. kws.go.ke.*

 ## Hotels

There's a good choice of Kenya Wildlife Service accommodations at Meru if you are on a self-drive safari. Kinna Guesthouse is by the Bwatherongi River and has five one- or two-bedroom basic thatched *bandas*, as well as a spacious guesthouse with a kitchen and that can sleep up to 10, as well as a campsite with toilets and showers—all of which share a delightful swimming pool. Murera Cottages is near the gate of the same name and has four simple cottages sharing a barbecue area, as well as a guesthouse with a kitchen and it sleeps up to three. You'll need your own 4x4 vehicle, and be well equipped with drinking water and firewood.

★ Elsa's Kopje

$$$$ | RESORT | FAMILY | The best place to stay in Meru, this stylish and romantic lodge is set above George Adamson's original campsite, where he and his wife, author Joy Adamson, released their lioness Elsa (after which the lodge is named) back into the wild. **Pros:** high standard of food with homegrown vegetables; free laundry service; spectacular views across Meru. **Cons:** in some rooms, lighting is quite dim; there are quite a number of steps between the rooms and the main area; not all rooms have tubs. $ *Rooms from: $1,124* ✉ *Meru National Park* ☎ *0730/127–000 reservations* ⊕ *www. elewanacollection.com* ⤴ *10 rooms, 1 private house* ❍ *Free Breakfast.*

Lake Naivasha

One of the Rift Valley's few freshwater lakes, Lake Naivasha is a popular spot for day trips and weekends away from Nairobi. Although the lake is not part of a national park or game reserve, it has pleasant forested surroundings, which are a far cry from the congestion and noise of Nairobi and there is plentiful wildlife around. Keep an eye out for the fever trees, and the abundant populations of birds, giraffes, zebras, monkeys, and hippos. This is also Kenya's premier area for growing flowers for export—especially roses—and you'll see the farms all around the lake shore. Such an attractive location lured a group of British settlers to build their homes on its shores. Known collectively as "White Mischief," these settlers were internationally infamous for their decadent, hedonistic lifestyle. A 1987 movie of the same name, starring Greta Scacchi, was based on a notorious society murder set during this time in this very location.

There are numerous things to do around Lake Naivasha and the lodges and camps on the grassy lake shore make perfect bases for a couple of days' exploration.

Cross over by boat to Crescent Island Game Sanctuary where you can see (and walk with) giraffes, zebras, and other plains herbivores; there are no predators so it's quite safe. Visit Elsamere, the former home of George and Joy Adamson of *Born Free* fame, for afternoon tea on the lawns and a look at the small museum to learn about their lives and conservation work. Rock climb, hike, or even cycle in Hell's Gate National Park, which is named after its magnificent red sandstone cliffs and is home to numerous plains game and fantastic birdlife including plenty of raptors such as the Rüppell's vulture and Verreaux's eagle.

GETTING HERE AND AROUND

Lake Naivasha is a one- to two-hour drive from Nairobi. There are two routes—a shorter but badly potholed route along the escarpment, or a longer but better maintained road, the A104 Uplands, which leads to Naivasha town. Hotels and lodges around the lake shore will arrange pickups from Nairobi, and taxis can transport you around the area.

Sights

Crescent Island Game Sanctuary

WILDLIFE REFUGE | The only way to get here is by boat, past kingfishers and pelicans, from one of the lakeshore hotels to Crescent Island Game Sanctuary, where you can see (and walk with) giraffe, zebra, and other plains herbivores; there are no predators so it's quite safe. On the way to the crater keep your eyes open for hippos as you are on the outer rim of a volcanic crater, which is also the deepest part of the lake. ✉ *Naivasha, Naivasha* ☎ *0759/636–468* ⊕ *www.crescentisland.co* ✉ *$30.*

Hotels

Crater Lake Tented Camp

$$ | RESORT | FAMILY | About a half-hour drive from the town of Naivasha, Crater Lake Tented Camp is situated in the cauldron of a crater in the Crater Lake

Game Sanctuary, on the edge of a lovely salt-water lake, which itself lies just off the southwestern shore of Lake Naivasha. **Pros:** the views are lovely; birding is excellent with birdbaths everywhere; it's the only camp in the Crater Lake Game Sanctuary. **Cons:** the swimming pool is not always well maintained; accommodation is rustic and basic, but has charm; steep steps to access tents. [$] *Rooms from: $308* ✉ *Crater Lake Game Sanctuary, Moi North Lake Rd., Naivasha* ☎ *0720/488–392* 🌐 *www.craterlake.co.ke* 🛏 *15 rooms* 🍴 *Free Breakfast.*

Lake Naivasha Country Club
$ | **HOTEL** | **FAMILY** | This resort sits on a large lakeside property and oozes historical character as it dates back to the 1930s when it served as a staging post for a flying boat service between Durban and Ireland; today's Country Club has received a massive overhaul and now features lavish public areas, although the original rooms themselves by modern standards are very small. **Pros:** lovely lakeside setting; top-quality buffet meals; bush dinner with a bonfire can be arranged. **Cons:** property needs some renovations; can be busy with conference groups; very small bathrooms. [$] *Rooms from: $239* ✉ *Lake Naivasha, Moi South Lake Rd., Naivasha* ☎ *0703/048–000 reservations* 🌐 *www.sunafricahotels.com* 🛏 *58 rooms* 🍴 *Free Breakfast.*

Lake Naivasha Sopa Resort
$$ | **RESORT** | **FAMILY** | In lovely forested grounds with huge established trees, very large rooms and loads of facilities, the comfortable and friendly Sopa offers everything you'll need for a couple of days at Lake Naivasha. **Pros:** kid-friendly with children's pool, menu, and babysitting; lovely forest environment; has two wheelchair accessible rooms. **Cons:** not ideal for those seeking more intimate accommodations; monkeys can be a nuisance around the pools; be careful after dark as hippos graze on the lawns. [$] *Rooms from: $325* ✉ *Lake Naivasha, Moi South Lake Rd., Naivasha* ☎ *020/375–0235 reservations* 🌐 *www.sopalodges.com* 🛏 *82 rooms* 🍴 *Free Breakfast.*

Lake Nakuru National Park

This delightful and compact park covers around 188 square km (73 square miles) and completely surrounds Lake Nakuru on the floor of the Great Rift Valley. Until a few years ago it was most famous for the hundreds of thousands of flamingos that fed on the algae in the shallows. However because of rising lake levels, the water has lost much of its salinity. There are still some flamingos seen on the lake's edge but the mass flocks have gone elsewhere. Nevertheless this is still a very rewarding and easy park to visit. There are more than 400 other bird species, plus incredible game including leopard (often seen in daylight hours), good numbers of both black and white rhino, big herds of buffalo, and lots of plains game including Rothschild's giraffe, waterbuck, and eland. The beauty of game driving here is that many of the animals are used to vehicles on the small network of roads that encircle the lake, and it's possible they will allow you to get very close. The scenery is spectacular too and the lake is surrounded by escapements covered in thick acacia bush—don't miss stopping at the viewpoint at Baboon Cliffs for the expansive view down to the lake, but as the name suggests, keep an eye out for those mischievous baboons. Most people don't know about the waterfall here... ask your guide to show you.

GETTING HERE AND AROUND

Lake Nakuru National Park is 166 km (103 miles) northwest of Nairobi, and the drive takes approximately 2½ to 3 hours along the main A104 road. You can drive around the park in just three hours, and this is one of the few parks that you can get around in a normal (not 4x4) car. Many

Hippos are a common sight in Lake Naivasha.

taxi drivers in Nakuru town know the park well and can take you around, and for an extra fee you can take an expert Kenya Wildlife Service guide with you. A trip to Lake Nakuru can be arranged from Nairobi with a safari operator and is often combined with a stay at Lake Naivasha too, or is included on a longer safari to the Masai Mara.

Kenya Wildlife Service. ✉ *Nakuru National Park* ✥ *5 km (3.1 miles) south of Nakuru town* ☎ *0728/355–267* 🌐 *www.kws.go.ke.*

Hotels

Lake Nakuru Sopa Lodge
$$ | RESORT | FAMILY | If you'd like to do an overnight in Lake Nakuru National Park, then the smart mid-range Sopa lodge is a good choice thanks to its commanding position high up on a ridge in the quiet western area. **Pros:** amazing lake views from the rooms; easy game-viewing drives; wheelchair friendly. **Cons:** the swimming pool is not heated and it can be too cold to swim; the road to entrance is a bit steep; on a hill, hence the walk to the rooms and pool can be tiring.
[$] *Rooms from: $325* ✉ *Lake Nakuru National Park* ☎ *020/375–0235 reservations* 🌐 *www.sopalodges.com* 🛏 *60 rooms* 🍴 *Free Breakfast.*

Samburu National Reserve

In the far northeast of the Laikipia Plateau, north of Mt. Kenya, is the remote Samburu National Reserve. Lying in the traditional homeland of the Samburu people in hot, arid, and relatively low country on the fringes of Kenya's vast northern deserts, this reserve is highly regarded by experienced travelers and old Africa hands alike. The drive from the foothills of Mt. Kenya into the semi-desert is awesome, and from the road that follows the Ewaso Nyiro River in the reserve, you'll be treated to the unusual spectacle of riverine bush and acacia and doum palm forest that provides a slash of greenery in the sandy plains. The Ewaso Nyiro flows north from Laikipia and is a life-giving resource to this parched region. There's game galore, and you're likely to see at least lions, cheetahs, or leopards, or even all three—in addition to hippos, numerous antelope and elephants, and some dry-country species like gerenuks, Grevy's zebras, and reticulated giraffes. Look out for the particularly large Nile crocodiles in the river too. You might also see genuine traditional way of life such as the red-robed Samburu tribesmen bringing their cattle down to the river to drink. The lives of the Samburu, like the closely related Maasai, are centered round their livestock, their traditional source of wealth. Most visitors go to Samburu National Reserve itself as most of the lodges and camps are here on the north bank of the river. But Buffalo Springs National Reserve is on the south side of the river, and across the A2 highway is Shaba National Reserve—the 24-hour entrance ticket of US$70 to any one of these covers game drives in the others, too. Additionally there are private and community conservancies to the north and west of Samburu.

GETTING HERE AND AROUND
Samburu is often combined with visits to the Laikipia Plateau and/or Meru National Park as it's fairly easily accessed from the road that runs along the northern reaches of Mt. Kenya. The gates to Samburu (and Buffalo Springs and Shaba) are reached via the good tarred A2 road through Isiolo and Archer's Post, and it's approximately a five-hour drive from Nairobi. There are also daily scheduled flights to the reserve's airstrip.

 Hotels

Sarara Camp
$$$$ | RESORT | FAMILY | North of Samburu National Reserve, this small and remote tented camp lies below the peaks of the Mathews Mountains in the 850,000-acre Namunyak Wildlife Conservation Trust—a community conservancy that has been created between landowners and the local Samburu people. **Pros:** there's a wide range of activities available; staff are from the local community; wild and romantic and the only lodge in the conservancy. **Cons:** no power points in tents; Wi-Fi only in the lounge; it's off the beaten track and is best reached by air. $ *Rooms from: $1,800* ⊠ *Namunyak Wildlife Conservation Trust* ☎ *0715/145–869 satellite phone* ⊕ *www.sarara.co* ⏗ *6 tents* ⦿ *All-Inclusive.*

★ **Sasaab**
$$$$ | RESORT | FAMILY | It's not just where Sasaab is located but how it's situated that makes it a wonderful place to stay in the Samburu region. **Pros:** sumptuous, spacious tents; guided walking safaris; beautifully designed common areas. **Cons:** long, bumpy drive to and from local airstrip; about an hour's drive to Samburu National Reserve; some tents are far from the dining lodge. $ *Rooms from: $1,900* ⊠ *Westgate Community Conservancy* ☎ *0725/675–830 reservations* ⊕ *www.thesafaricollection.com* ⏗ *9 tents* ⦿ *All-Inclusive.*

Gateway Cities

The starting point for safaris since the days of Teddy Roosevelt and Ernest Hemingway, Nairobi is still the first stop for many travelers heading to the wildlife parks of East Africa. With both Jomo Kenyatta International Airport and Wilson Airport, Kenya's capital city is the main hub for visitors, and it's very likely that you'll be spending at least an overnight here between flights.

Nairobi

Nairobi's modern skyline often surprises first-time visitors, whose visions of the country are often shaped by stories of its colonial legacy or wildlife documentaries. With a population of more than 4 million people, Nairobi is now one of the

What to Eat and Drink

Nyama Choma: roasted meat, usually beef or goat

Ugali: a plain, white cornmeal of sorts served alongside meats and usually vegetables

Mukimo: a potato mash with corn, made green with pumpkin leaves

Mutura: sausages Kenyan style, with goat or cow parts and blood stuffed inside the intestines

Tusker beer: a local brew and Kenyan staple

Mandazi: fried bread that tastes somewhat like a donut, best accompanied by Kenyan chai

fastest developing cities in sub-Saharan Africa and is dominated by modern offices, shopping, and residential towers. This isn't to say the city has lost all its charm though, and some early historical architecture survives here and there—the venerable Norfolk Hotel still recalls the elegant lifestyles of the city's early settlers, while the colonial farmhouse of *Out of Africa* author Karen Blixen (who wrote under the pen name Isak Dinesen) still sits at the foot of the Ngong Hills and is a reminder of Kenya's coffee heritage.

But Nairobi has had more than its share of urban problems. This city that grew too fast has paralyzing traffic jams, with public service vehicles that flout traffic rules, corrupt policing, and no hint of emissions control. Crime can be an issue and there are occasional incidents of muggings and carjackings. In addition, there's a growing disparity between rich and poor—private estates on the edge of Nairobi feature opulent mansions with stables, tennis courts, and swimming pools, while not far away you can glimpse vast mazes of tin shacks in a slum, many with no electricity or running water.

But with booming economic growth and Nairobi being the preferred seat of many corporate institutions as well as the United Nations, Nairobi has done much to shake off its chaotic past in recent years. Neighborhoods have become more

affluent, the middle class is expanding, crime is being reduced and infrastructure improves all the time—the sleek Nairobi Expressway was completed in March 2022, for example, and is going a long way to alleviate chronic traffic congestion. For the visitor, there's an interesting cross-section of attractions, good shopping and restaurants, and many top-class hotels serving safari-bound tourists.

GETTING HERE AND AROUND

Nairobi National Park is to the south of the city, with Jomo Kenyatta International Airport (JKIA) and Wilson Airport on the park periphery. Karen, a suburb of Nairobi where there are hotels and sightseeing attractions, is southwest of the city center, while the Ngong Hills, on the edge the Great Rift Valley, is beyond that. The suburbs of Muthaiga, Gigiri, and Runda are to the north of the city center.

International airlines and some domestic services fly into JKIA, Kenya's major airport, which is 16 km (10 miles) southeast of the city center. It has modern terminals with cafés, facilities to leave excess luggage, mobile phone stores, and ATM-equipped banks and Bureaux de Change. It usually takes about 40 minutes to drive from the airport to the city center by taxi (ride-hailing apps like Uber, Bolt, and Little Cab cost US$15 at most), although it can take up to two hours in rush hour. Many hotels have comfortable shuttle

It's not unheard of for a giraffe to give a friendly and grateful lick to guests as they feed them at Nairobi's Giraffe Centre.

services in a/c vehicles from about US$35 per person; be sure to organize this when you book your room.

Wilson Airport, 5.5 km (3.4 miles) southwest of the city center off Langata Road, is Nairobi's second airport. It's used for domestic, charter, and some regional flights. It has few facilities, but some of the airlines like Airkenya and Safarilink have lounges and cafés. A regular taxi into the city center from Wilson is about $15, and again, hotels can organize shuttle services.

■ TIP→ **When you book a local flight, make sure to note which airport it departs from.**

If you're in Nairobi overnight or for a few hours, you won't need to rent a car. Take a taxi to the attractions, but remember it's compulsory to buckle up, and *always* negotiate the price before setting out. Locals travel around on *matatus* (passenger minivans carrying up to 15 passengers), but the drivers can sometimes be reckless.

EMERGENCIES

Police in general are friendly and helpful to tourists. There are two private hospitals (avoid the government hospitals) with excellent staff and facilities, which have 24-hour pharmacies. There are plenty of pharmacies all over downtown Nairobi. Consult your concierge or host.

EMERGENCY CONTACTS The Aga Khan University Hospital. ✉ *3rd Parklands Ave., Parklands* ☎ *020/366–2000* ⊕ *www. agakhanhospitals.org/nairobi.* **Central Police Station.** ✉ *University Way, Nairobi* ☎ *999 from a landline, 112 from a mobile* ⊕ *www.kenyapolice.go.ke.* **The Nairobi Hospital.** ✉ *Argwings Kodhek Rd., Nairobi* ☎ *0703/082–000* ⊕ *www.thenairobihosp. org.*

DINING AND LODGING PRICES

What It Costs in U.S. Dollars			
$	$$	$$$	$$$$
RESTAURANTS			
under $12	$12–$20	$21–$30	over $30
HOTELS			
under $150	$150–$250	$251–$350	over $350

Sights

Nairobi is more than a gateway to your dream safari destination. It's a thriving city with restaurants, shopping malls, museums, and interesting wildlife attractions. There are cooking classes, comedy shows, jewelry-making workshops, venues with live bands, cheese or coffee farms, forests and nature trails begging to be hiked, and much more. If you only have a few hours in the morning, combine the Sheldrick Wildlife Trust, where you can watch adorable baby elephants at the orphanage, and the Giraffe Centre, where you can hand feed Rothschild's giraffes from an elevated tower. If you have a bit more time, or days, check out the Big Five (minus elephants) on a game drive in the **Nairobi National Park.** It's just a 20-minute drive from downtown Nairobi (7 km/4 miles). You could also take in some history and culture at one of the museums, or go shopping for souvenirs in the many markets or curio stores—from carved wooden animals and batik art to Maasai beaded jewelry and leather sandals.

City Market
MARKET | Designed in 1930 as an aircraft hangar, this vast space between Muindi Mbingu Street and Koinange Street is a jumble of color, noise, and activity. It has dozens of stalls selling wooden and soapstone carvings, drums, shields, and Maasai jewelry and there are also fruit, vegetable, and flower sellers and butchers. Look for *kikois* and *kangas,* traditional fabrics worn by Kenyan women, which are good for wearing over a bathing suit or throwing over a picnic table; they are half the price here than in the hotel shops. ✉ *Muindi Mbingu St., CBD, Nairobi.*

★ Giraffe Centre
WILDLIFE REFUGE | FAMILY | Established by the African Fund for Endangered Wildlife (AFEW), this unique giraffe sanctuary is a wonderful excursion for children and adults alike. Located in Nairobi's western suburb of Langata, it has greatly contributed to boosting Kenya's population of rare Rothschild's giraffes—after being born and raised at this center, many have been relocated to the game parks and reserves. The original house of the founders is now the very impressive Giraffe Manor hotel. You can climb a giraffe-height tower for an eye-to-eye view and it's not unheard of for a giraffe to give a friendly and grateful lick as you feed them—great for photos. There's a café and a short nature trail where you might also spot warthogs, as well as a souvenir shop. ✉ *Duma Rd., off Koitobos Rd., Nairobi* ☎ *020/807–0804* ⊕ *www.giraffecentre.org* 💲 *KSh1500.*

Karen Blixen Museum
HISTORIC HOME | *Out of Africa* author Karen Blixen, who wrote under the pen name Isak Dinesen, lived at this estate from 1913 to 1931. This is where she threw a grand dinner party for the Prince of Wales and where she carried on a torrid relationship with aviator Denys Finch Hatton. The museum contains a few of her belongings and furniture, and outside is some of the farm machinery she used to cultivate the land for coffee and tea; guides will take you on a tour. There is a magnificent view of the Ngong Hills from her lawn, which is dominated by euphorbia, the many-armed plant widely known as the candelabra cactus. On the way to the museum you may notice a signpost reading "ndege." On this road, whose

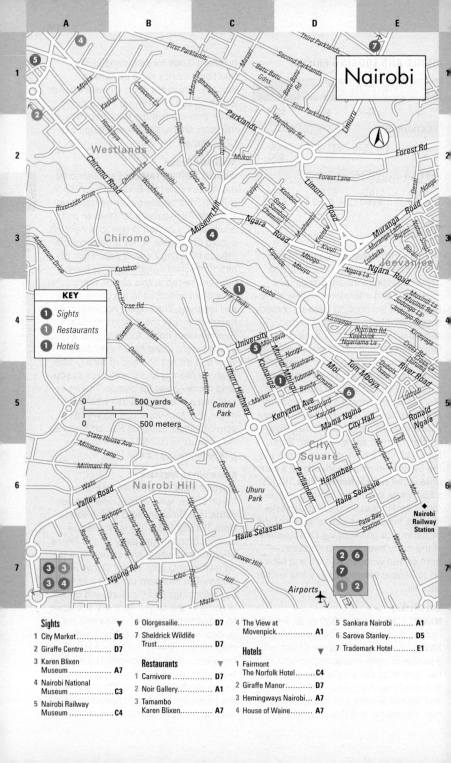

Nairobi

KEY
- 1 Sights
- 1 Restaurants
- 1 Hotels

0   500 yards
0   500 meters

Swahili name means "bird," Finch Hatton once landed his plane for his visits with Blixen. After his plane crashed in Voi, he was buried nearby in the Ngong Hills. ⊠ *Karen Rd., Nairobi* ☎ *020/800–2139* ⊕ *www.museums.or.ke* ✉ *KSh1200.*

Nairobi National Museum

SCIENCE MUSEUM | On Museum Hill just to the north of downtown Nairobi, this interesting museum has good reproduction rock art displays and excellent prehistory exhibits of the archaeological discoveries of Richard and Mary Leakey. When working near Lake Turkana in the 1960s, the Leakeys discovered the skull and bones of *Homo habilis,* believed to be the ancestor of early humankind. Their findings established the Rift Valley as the possible Cradle of Humankind, although both South Africa's Sterkfontein Caves and Ethiopia's Hadar region claim the same distinction. There are also excellent paintings by Joy Adamson, better known as the author of *Born Free,* and a good collection of Kenya's birds and butterflies. There are some good craft shops and a museum shop, and it's worthwhile wandering around the gardens to see the sculptures and perhaps visiting the small snake park. ■**TIP**→ **Nature Kenya runs guided bird walks every Wednesday morning at 8:45 from the museum (KSh200).** ⊠ *Museum Hill, off Chiromo St., Nairobi* ✛ *City Center* ☎ *020/816–4136* ⊕ *www.museums.or.ke* ✉ *KSh1200.*

Nairobi Railway Museum

TRANSPORTATION | **FAMILY** | Established to preserve relics and records of East African railways and harbors, this museum is enormous fun for rail enthusiasts and children of all ages. You can see the rhino catcher that Teddy Roosevelt rode during his 1908 safari and climb into the carriage where Charles Ryall, a British railroad builder, was dragged out a window by a hungry lion. There are great photos and posters, plus silver service from the more elegant days of the overnight train to Mombasa. You can clamber over the

British-built locomotives in the old rail yard. ⊠ *Station Rd., off Haile Sellasie Ave., Nairobi* ✛ *City Center* ☎ *0709/907– 411* ⊕ *www.krc.co.ke* ✉ *KSh500.*

Olorgesailie

HISTORIC SIGHT | **FAMILY** | Set in the eastern branch of the Great Rift Valley, Olorgesailie is one of Kenya's best-known archaeological sites. Discovered in 1919 by geologist J. W. Gregory, the area was excavated by Louis and Mary Leakey in the 1940s. They discovered tools thought to have been made by residents of the region more than a half million years ago. A small museum shows some of the axes and other tools found nearby. The journey here is unforgettable. As you drive south on Magadi Road, you'll find that past the town of Kiserian the route climbs over the southern end of the Ngong Hills, affording fine views of the entire valley. Volcanic hills rise out of the plains as the road drops into dry country where the Maasai people graze their herds. There's a campsite should you wish to spend the night, and this area boasts the largest population of migratory birds in the country. ⊠ *Nairobi* ✛ *65 km (40 miles) south of Nairobi* ⊕ *www. museums.or.ke* ✉ *KSh600.*

★ Sheldrick Wildlife Trust

WILDLIFE REFUGE | **FAMILY** | Take the morning excursion at 11 am, which you can book through your tour guide or hotel concierge, to this amazing elephant rescue center and orphanage on the edge of Nairobi National Park. It was set up by Dame Daphne Sheldrick after the death of her husband, David, who was famous for his anti-poaching activities in Tsavo East National Park. You'll be able to watch baby elephants at play or having a bath, knowing that one day when they're old enough they will be successfully reintroduced into the wild. It's an absolutely unmissable and heartwarming experience. Make a donation, however small, or go for gold and adopt your own baby elephant.

■ TIP→ The center is only open from 11 am–noon. If you miss the 11 am tour, you won't be able to visit until the following day. ✉ *Nairobi National Park, entrance at maintenance gate off Magadi Rd., Nairobi* ✣ *16 km (10 miles) southwest of the city center* ☎ *011/104–4200* 🌐 *www.sheldrick-wildlifetrust.org* 🎟 *KSh1500 or US$12.50 (cash only)* ✍ *Reservations required.*

🍴 Restaurants

Carnivore

$$$$ | BARBECUE | FAMILY | A firm fixture on the tourist trail, Carnivore became famous for serving wild game. Although this is no longer the case, you can still get crocodile and ostrich as well as beef, pork, and lamb. **Known for:** dawa cocktails; a Maasai barbecue pit; all-you-can eat meat. [$] *Average main: $45* ✉ *Carnivore Rd., off Langata Rd., Nairobi* ☎ *020/514–1300* 🌐 *www.tamarind.co.ke.*

Noir Gallery

$$$$ | AFRICAN | FAMILY | This space merges an art gallery featuring local and international artists with manicured green lawns complete with a water fountain, live music, and food. In the backyard is a coffee stand by Ethiopian brand, Tomoca coffee, and plenty of areas to sit where customers enjoy dishes like chicken satay or lamb chops with hasselback potatoes. **Known for:** art gallery showcasing local and international artists; beautiful green garden setting; live music performances. [$] *Average main: $40* ✉ *Muthangari Dr., Nairobi* ☎ *0713/286–254* 🌐 *www.noir-gallery.business.site.*

The View at Movenpick

$$$$ | MEDITERRANEAN | FAMILY | Expect breathtaking 360-degree views of the city, while you dine at this revolving restaurant on the 24th floor of the Movenpick Hotel & Residences. The Mediterranean-inspired menu features an array of seafood, pasta, and soups to choose from; try the antipasti platter for a starter, and the roast pork loin with merlot wine sauce, served with grilled red bell pepper for the main. **Known for:** panoramic views of the city; revolving restaurant; centrally located in the Westlands neighborhood. [$] *Average main: $60* ✉ *Movenpick Hotel & Residences, Mkungu Close, off Parklands Rd., Nairobi* ☎ *0709/548–180* 🌐 *www.movenpick.com* 🕒 *Closed Mon.*

🛏 Hotels

The two landmark lodgings in the capital, the Norfolk Hotel and the Sarova Stanley, have opened their doors to visitors for more than a century. Both have been renovated in recent years and now have everything from health clubs to business centers. However, newer luxury hotels such as Sankara Nairobi and Trademark Hotel are giving them a run for their money and will appeal to those wanting a more contemporary experience.

Although corporate travelers may need to stay in downtown Nairobi, those wishing to get away from the hustle and bustle can head to the distilled air of the leafy western suburbs such as Langata or Karen where several establishments offer more peaceful surroundings. Alternatively the modern suburb of Westlands is also a popular choice for hotels thanks to its good shopping, restaurants, and nightlife.

Another option, perfect to kick-start your safari, is to stay in Nairobi National Park. There are two properties—The Emakoko, a luxury lodge, and Nairobi Tented Camp, which is tucked into a forest in the park. Both offer comfortable accommodations within an hour of Nairobi's airports.

See the section on Nairobi National Park for details.

Fairmont The Norfolk Hotel

$ | HOTEL | FAMILY | This grand old colonial lady will take you back to the heady early days when settlers, adventurers, colonial officers, and their ladies arrived in the capital to make their names and their fortunes. **Pros:** the breakfast buffet is incredible; the terrace is a great place to watch the world go by; large heated swimming pool. **Cons:** can be dominated by large conferences; very good but expensive restaurants; lost a bit of its old-world charm in modern refurbishments. $ *Rooms from: $248* ⊠ *Harry Thuku Rd., Nairobi* ☎ *020/226–5000* ⊕ *www.fairmont.com* ⇆ *170 rooms* ⦿ *Free Breakfast.*

Giraffe Manor
$$$$ | HOTEL | FAMILY | One of the world's most Instagrammed hotels, yes, giraffes really do pop their heads through the windows and bat their eyelashes at you at this stately old look-alike gabled Scottish hunting lodge. **Pros:** rates are full board and include most drinks; nonguests can book a table for lunch, subject to availability; there's a vehicle available for local sightseeing tours. **Cons:** no pool; children need to be supervised in the garden because of the giraffes; you need to book ahead as it's often fully booked. $ *Rooms from: $1,240* ⊠ *Gogo Falls Rd., Nairobi* ☎ *0725/675–830 reservations* ⊕ *www.thesafaricollection.com* ⇆ *12 rooms* ⦿ *All-Inclusive.*

Hemingways Nairobi
$$ | HOTEL | Named after writer Ernest Hemingway, this airy and elegant boutique hotel is in a peaceful location in Karen with views of the Ngong Hills. **Pros:** beautifully furnished with African artwork and contemporary touches; high level of service with butlers for every room; the food is incredible. **Cons:** swimming pool is unheated; some rooms are a long walk from the main facilities; food and beverages are expensive. $ *Rooms from: $325* ⊠ *Mbagathi Ridge, Nairobi* ☎ *0711/032–204* ⊕ *www.hemingways-collection.com* ⇆ *45 suites* ⦿ *Free Breakfast.*

House of Waine
$$$$ | HOTEL | FAMILY | You'll find nostalgia, history, and romantic surroundings at this family-owned boutique hotel. **Pros:** you can choose to take your meal in your room, next to the pool, or in the dining room; the swimming pool is heated; the Karen Blixen Museum is just next door. **Cons:** the wooden floors can be noisy; the area gets really cold, although hot water bottles are provided; the dining room feels too formal. $ *Rooms from: $640* ⊠ *Masai La., off Bogani Rd., Nairobi* ☎ *020/260–1455* ⊕ *www.houseofwaine.com* ⊙ *Closed May* ⇆ *11 rooms* ⦿ *Free Breakfast.*

Sankara Nairobi
$ | HOTEL | This stylish city hotel is conveniently located in Westlands, close to a number of restaurants and malls, although you will find all you need for a relaxing stay in the hotel itself. **Pros:** varied dining options; the hotel has been beautifully designed and is an art lover's paradise; great views of Nairobi's skyline from the rooftop. **Cons:** spa treatments are expensive; children are welcome but it's more business-oriented; the pool is small. $ *Rooms from: $193* ⊠ *5 Woodvale Grove, Westlands* ☎ *020/420–8000* ⊕ *www.sankara.com* ⇆ *156 rooms* ⦿ *No Meals.*

Sarova Stanley
$ | HOTEL | The city's oldest hotel was established in 1902, but has switched owners and undergone major upgrades through the years; the Stanley was named after the journalist Henry Morton Stanley who immortalized himself by discovering a long-lost Scots explorer with one of the best sound-bites in history: "Doctor Livingstone, I presume?" A lot of history lies within these walls which have hosted African presidents, author Ernest Hemingway in the 30s, Frank Sinatra and his wife, Princess Elizabeth just before she became Britain's sovereign, and even a young Barack Obama. **Pros:** security is good; the Swahili breakfast buffet is a delight; good choice of well-priced restaurants and bars. **Cons:** there's often heavy traffic around the hotel since it sits in the CBD; service can be slow at busy times; standard rooms

are small. $ *Rooms from: $190* ✉ *Kenyatta Ave. at Kimathi St, CBD, Nairobi* ☎ *0709/111–000* ⊕ *www.sarovahotels.com* ↪ *217 rooms* ⦿| *No Meals.*

Trademark Hotel

$$ | HOTEL | This sleek and urban business hotel sits in the new wing of one of Nairobi's leading malls, The Village Market in the suburb of Gigiri, where you can find clothing and jewelry stores, two food courts, a bowling alley, art gallery, wine, cheese and chocolate shops, trampoline park, and more. **Pros:** friendly and efficient staff with a good concierge; Harvest Restaurant is one of the best in town; conveniently located within a mall, with plenty of restaurants and stores. **Cons:** a little far from the Giraffe Centre and Sheldrick's Trust in Karen; shares spa with its sister property, Tribe Hotel, which is also within the mall; the garden is small for those who would like vast outdoor space. $ *Rooms from: $350* ✉ *Village Market, Limuru Rd., Nairobi* ☎ *0730/886–000* ⊕ *www.trademark-hotel.com* ↪ *215 rooms* ⦿| *Free Breakfast.*

Beach Escapes

Intricately carved doorways studded with brass and white walls draped with bougainvillea distinguish the towns that dot Kenya's coastline. Arab traders who landed on these shores in the 9th century brought their own culture, creating a different style of dress and architecture from what you see in other parts of Kenya.

Men stroll the streets wearing traditional caps called *kofias* and billowing kaftans known as *khanzus*, while women wear black modest dresses called *bui-buis*, complete with *hijabs* (headscarves). The term "Swahili" comes from the Arabic words *sahil*, meaning "coast," and *i*, meaning "of the." The coastal communities of Lamu and Mombasa are strongholds of this language and culture

The Beach Boys

Hawkers and hustlers known as "beach boys" prowl Kenya's coastline. They sell everything from boat rides and souvenirs to drugs and sex, and their incessant pestering can ruin a beach walk (hotels employ guards to keep them off hotel grounds). You can purchase something if you so wish, otherwise, be politely firm and don't engage much.

that once dominated communities from Somalia to Mozambique.

Mombasa is the country's second-largest city and has a population of about two million. It's home to Kenya's only large seaport, and for centuries has been a hub of trade—from the early wooden dhows that crossed the Indian Ocean to the giant steel container ships that bring commodities to East Africa today. A hot, busy commercial city, the impressive Fort Jesus and atmospheric Old Town are on most visitors' itinerary.

The best-preserved Swahili town in Kenya, Lamu has streets hardly wide enough for a donkey cart. Winding alleyways are lined with houses set tight against one another. It's said that the beautifully carved doors found here are built first, then the house constructed around them.

The azure Indian Ocean waters from Lamu in the north to Wasini in the south are protected by the 240-km (150-mile) coral reef that runs parallel to the coast. The beautiful beaches are mostly white sand, are usually lined with shady coconut palms, and have calm and clear surf that hovers around 27°C (80°F).

GETTING HERE AND AROUND

Getting to the towns along the Kenyan Coast is easier than ever. Mombasa has an international airport, but you can also fly directly to Lamu, Malindi, Vipingo, or the Ukunda airstrip at Diani Beach. Traveling by car around Mombasa is fairly safe and can be a good option if you want to stay at a few places along the coast. For shorter distances, there are tuk tuks and motorbike taxis aplenty.

HOTELS

Accommodations along the Kenya Coast range from sprawling resorts with several restaurants to small beach houses with kitchens where you can prepare your own meals. Most accommodations can arrange snorkeling, windsurfing, waterskiing, and deep-sea fishing.

For an alternative to a hotel stay, there's a large variety of cottages and houses for rent along the beach. Most come with a cook and housekeeper. You provide your own food—which is easy to do as there are nearby stores and supermarkets. Check out ⊕ www.eastafricanretreats. com or ⊕ www.lamuretreats.com to start your search.

RESTAURANTS

The excellent cuisine reflects the region's rich history. Thanks to Italians, basil is everywhere, along with olive oil, garlic, and fresh lettuce. The Portuguese introduced tomatoes, corn, and cashews. Local staples include pilau and biryani, and everything is combined with pungent spices such as cardamom and ginger and the rich coconut milk often used as a cooking broth.

The Indian Ocean delivers some of the world's best fishing, so tuna, marlin, sailfish, red snapper, kingfish, and many other types of fish are on the menus. Not surprisingly, sashimi made from yellowtail tuna is favored by connoisseurs (and was listed on menus here as "fish tartare" before the rest of the world discovered Japanese cuisine). Prawns can

be gargantuan, and wild oysters are small and sweet. You'll easily find boys who are happy to deliver fresh seafood to your door, and you can even place your order for the next day.

Mombasa

The city of Mombasa (actually an island linked to the mainland by bridges and a ferry) is the second oldest trade center with Arabia and the Far East. Today it still plays an important role as the main port for Kenya. A famous landmark is the pair of intersecting tusks above Moi Avenue commemorating the 1952 visit of Britain's Queen Elizabeth II (then Princess Elizabeth). Also forming the letter "M" for Mombasa, they mark the entrance to the heart of town where visitors will find most of the banks, shops, and markets. The city is associated with the phrase *Mombasa Raha. Raha* means 'fun' in Swahili; for some that means frolicking on the beautiful beaches in Nyali, trying the local food or visiting popular attractions, and for others, it's endless parties and/or transactional sex. Still, it has a rich, fascinating history. Visit the Old Town with its narrow streets lined with tiny shops and *souks* (markets). The Old Harbour, frequented by numerous dhows, is an ideal place to arrange a short cruise on one of these local boats that have plied the oceans for centuries. Fort Jesus, designed by an Italian and built by the Portuguese in the late 16th century, is a major visitor draw and well worth a visit. In summer there's an impressive sound-and-light show. There are a lot of other family-friendly attractions too, such as Nguuni Nature Sanctuary, where you can come up close with giraffes; Bombolulu Workshops and Cultural Center, where physically disabled artisans make beautiful crafts; and Haller Park in Bamburi, which was once a wasteland but now has a game sanctuary, with different sections with crocodiles, fish, and snakes, all thriving amid beautiful green foliage.

GETTING HERE AND AROUND

Between Kenya Airways, Fly540, and Jambojet, there are several daily flights between Nairobi and Mombasa, and from Mombasa you can fly to Lamu. The airport is located 10 km (6 miles) from the city center, on the mainland. Several taxi companies operate from the airport and have fixed rates to either the center of town or the beach resorts. You can also arrange for your hotel to pick you up. Taxis in Mombasa are inexpensive. The drivers are friendly and helpful and will wait or return to collect you if you ask.

Tired of flying? There's a daily train between Nairobi and Mombasa on a line that was completed in 2017. The old overnight train on the original railway line built by the British in the late 19th century took 12–15 hours—the new service takes about 4½ hours. It departs both Nairobi and Mombasa at 8 am (makes several stops along the way), 3 pm (express) and 10 pm. To facilitate the line, a station was built at Miritini on the mainland near the airport, 11 km (6.8 miles) from downtown Mombasa. In Nairobi a station was built at Syokimau, which is about 17 km (11 miles) southeast of the city center and is also near the airport. Fares are KSh1,000 in economy and KSh3,000 in first class. Tickets can only be booked up to four days before date of travel, either from the stations, through the USSD code *639# if you have a local SIM, or through a local tour operator—ask your hotel to recommend one.

MONEY MATTERS

Most major banks have ATMs in Mombasa. If you want to change money, you can find several Forex Exchange Bureaus such as at the airport, at City Mall in Nyali, Iddi building on Nkrumah Road (there are a couple along this road), on Digo Road near the Municipal Market, and near the entrance of Fort Jesus.

SAFETY

The best way to see Mombasa is by hailing tuk tuks. If it's not too hot and humid, or far, you can walk, but be cautious at night. If you take a taxi at night, make sure it delivers you all the way to the door of your destination. Purse snatchers are all too common particularly in the Old Town after 6 pm. Beware of people who might approach you on Mombasa's Moi Avenue offering to become your guide. Tell them, "*Hapana, asante sana*" ("No, thank you"), and move on.

ESSENTIALS

EMERGENCIES Mombasa Central Police Station. ☏ *041/225–501, 999 emergencies.*

HOSPITALS The Aga Khan Hospital. ✉ *Vanga Rd., Kizingo, Mombasa* ☏ *0714/524–948* ⊕ *www.agakhanhospitals.org/mombasa.* **Pandya Memorial Hospital.** ✉ *Dedan Kimathi Ave., Mombasa* ☏ *0722/206–424.*

TAXIS Kenatco Taxis Ltd. ☏ *0709/642–000.*

VISITOR INFORMATION Kenya Coast. ⊕ *www.kenya-coast.com.*

PLANNING

Safaris to Tsavo East and Tsavo West can be arranged from any of the beach resorts between Malindi in the north and Diani Beach in the south. Alternatively book ahead with a tour operator such as Diani Tours & Safaris (⊕ *www.dianisafaris-kenya.com*), Pollman's Tours & Safaris (⊕ *www.pollmans.com*), or Southern Cross Safaris (⊕ *www.southerncrosssafaris.com*).

 Sights

To get a good insight into the daily life of downtown Mombasa, head to the narrow, cluttered streets of the Old Town north of Fort Jesus. Here ornately carved doors and balconies adorn the old buildings along the atmospheric alleys, and you can shop for souvenirs, antiques, fragrant oils and spices and stop for a glass

This pair of intersecting tusks above Mombasa's Moi Avenue is a famous landmark that commemorates the 1952 visit of Britain's Queen Elizabeth II.

of chai (tea) at one of the tiny cafés and watch the world go by. There are more than 20 historic mosques in the area, but keep your eyes peeled for the impressive Basheikh Mosque on Old Kilindini Road and the New Burhani Bohra Mosque off Ndia Kuu Road.

In the northern part of the Old Town, Biashara (Swahili for "business") Street, which is just off Digo Road, you'll find all sorts of small shops that have been around for generations—selling everything from leather to textiles, live chickens, and food. While you're here, take a wander through the fruit, vegetable, and spice market, near where Biashara Street meets Digo Road. People are friendly and hospitable but, as in most poor backstreet areas, watch your belongings.

Bombolulu Workshops & Cultural Center

ARTS CENTER | FAMILY | An array of well-priced jewelry made from recycled materials such as brass and soda cans, wood carvings, colorful fabrics, leather and canvas handbags, and more, all made by people with various physical disabilities, fill the shelves. The organization was set up to offer them employment in a society where they were traditionally stigmatized. Stop by to shop, watch the artisans work, tour the cultural center with traditional homesteads which provide great insight into the history and culture of the indigenous communities in this region, watch traditional dances, and more. Getting here shouldn't be a problem as most taxi and tuk tuk drivers will know the place. ⊠ Mombasa ☎ 0723/560–933 ⊕ www.bomboluluworkshop.co.ke 🎫 KSh 750.

Fort Jesus

HISTORIC SIGHT | Fort Jesus is a UNESCO World Heritage Site and one of Mombasa's top tourist attractions. This massive edifice was built in the late 16th century by the Portuguese, who were keen to control trade in the region. When the Omanis captured the fort at the end of the 17th century, they made some adjustments. The walls were raised to account for the improved trajectory of cannons mounted aboard attacking ships. By the end of the 18th century, turrets were erected. For water, the garrison relied on a pit cistern, which was used for bathing when the fort was a prison, between 1895 and 1958. The captain's house retains some traces of the Portuguese—note the outline of the old colonnade. The exhibits at the museum include an important display on ceramics of the coast and the remains of a Portuguese gunner, *San Antonio de Tanna,* which sank outside the fort at the end of the 17th century. Objects from the ship—shoes, glass bottles, a powder shovel, and cannon with its muzzle blown away—bring the period to life. There are also exhibits of finds from archaeological excavations at Gedi, Manda, Ungwana, and other sites. ⊠ *End of Nkrumah Rd., Mombasa* ☎ *041/222–0058* ⊕ *www. museums.or.ke* ⌨ *KSh1200.*

Mama Ngina Waterfront

PROMENADE | FAMILY | Named after Kenya's very first First Lady, this popular ocean front stretch of road popularly known as 'Mama Ngina Drive' was renovated and reopened in October 2019 to reveal landscaped grounds, paved and palm tree-lined walkways, a jetty, amphitheater, and a cultural center. Drive, jog, skate, stroll, or simply find a spot to relax and watch ships sail by. You can buy souvenirs and street snacks such as deep-fried cassava crisps, or *viazi karai* (battered and fried potatoes). There's also a nightclub and a restaurant nearby. ⊠ *Mama Ngina Dr.*

Mamba Village

ZOO | FAMILY | Explore Africa's largest crocodile farm; if you're lucky you might get to hold a baby. Stop by around 5 pm particularly on Friday when the crocs get fed to watch them chow down and marvel at how powerful their jaws are. The oldest, called Big Daddy because of its massive size, is well over 100 years old. A guide will show you around and share

more about their farming and conservation efforts. At the snake farm, you can hold or wear a python around your neck like a scarf, if you so dare. Horse riding and nature walks are also available, then, after having worked up an appetite, stop by the on-site restaurant where crocodile meat is listed on the menu. ⊠ *Beach Road, Off Links Road, Nyali, Mombasa* ☎ *0768/187–722* ⊕ *www.mambavillagecentre.co.ke* ⌨ *KSh800.*

Nguuni Nature Sanctuary

WILDLIFE REFUGE | FAMILY | Eight giraffes were first translocated here in 2004, and the population now stands at 20, and some are a cross of the Rothschild and Masai giraffe species. You can come as close as two meters away at the enclosure where the handler does the feeding. You will also find elands and tortoises, and once a haven for ostriches, the numbers have since dwindled. The giraffe enclosure is about 1.5km (about a mile) from the gate, and your taxi or tuk tuk is allowed to drop you there without an extra car charge, or you can walk. The road leading to the gate is really rough, and almost impassable when it rains. You can also hike or hire a bike and cycle through the woodlands and wetlands of what was once an uninhabitable wasteland, and spot up to 250 species of birds. ⊠ *Off Kiembeni Road, Mombasa* ☎ *00700700/337–068* ⌨ *KSh 800.*

🍴 Restaurants

Blue Room

$ | INDIAN | FAMILY | Serving the best samosas in Mombasa, this family-owned Indian restaurant has been in business for almost 70 years. It seats 140 people, making it one of the largest restaurants in the city and it's a good stop after a hot walk around the Old Town thanks to the whirring ceiling fans and clean restrooms. **Known for:** delicious, house-made ice-cream; affordable meals; Indian

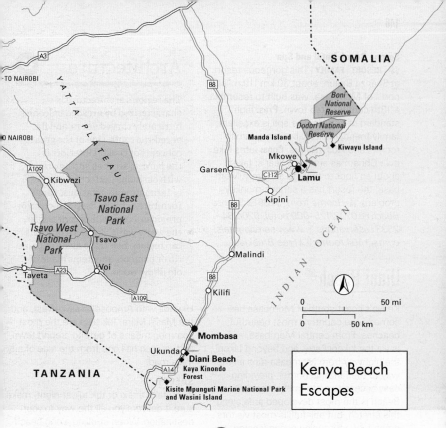

Kenya Beach
Escapes

snacks. $ *Average main: $6* ⊠ *Haile Selassie Rd. at Digo Rd., Mombasa* ☎ *0721/786–868* ⊕ *www.blueroom. co.ke.*

★ Tamarind

$$$$ | SEAFOOD | A signature house cocktail—a *dawa* made of lime, vodka, honey, and crushed ice—will introduce you to a memorable meal and unforgettable experience at the best restaurant in town. Overlooking a creek flowing into the sea, the restaurant is designed like an old Moorish palace with high arches and tiled floors, and the sunsets from here are breathtaking. **Known for:** Swahili atmosphere; good service; seafood heaven. $ *Average main: $40* ⊠ *Cement Silo Rd., Nyali* ☎ *0722/205–160, 020/513–9327* ⊕ *www.tamarind.co.ke.*

🛏 Hotels

Sarova Whitesands Beach Resort & Spa

$ | RESORT | FAMILY | It's like walking into a painting at this aptly named resort which sits on a stunning stretch of powder-white beachfront that ever so perfectly complements the Indian Ocean's turquoise blues. **Pros:** lovely stretch of beach right in front of the resort; large variety in the themed buffets every night; a kids club run by an 'animation team' that will put on lively performances and keep them occupied. **Cons:** crows can be a nuisance when eating outside; popular location for conferences; beach boys can be a nuisance. $ *Rooms from: $250* ⊠ *Off Malindi Road, Mombasa, Mombasa* ☎ *0709/111–000* ⊕ *www.sarovahotels. com* ⇥ *340 rooms* ⊚ *Free Breakfast.*

Serena Beach Hotel and Spa
$$ | **RESORT** | **FAMILY** | This gorgeous resort at Shanzu Beach, about 30 km (19 miles) north of Mombasa, was built to resemble a 13th-century Arab town. **Pros:** high standard of service; the spa is excellent; family-friendly with babysitting, family rooms, and kids' menus. **Cons:** rates hike over Christmas and New Year's; takes about an hour to drive to and from Mombasa; the resort has a serious monkey problem. [$] *Rooms from: $285* ✉ *Shanzu Beach* ☎ *0732/125–000 hotel, 020/284–2333 reservations* 🌐 *www.serenahotels.com* 🛏 *164 rooms* 🍴 *Free Breakfast.*

Architecture

The region's architecture is characterized by arcaded balconies, intricately carved doors, and flat or red-tile roofs. One of the great concepts of coastal interiors is the *baraza*, an open sitting area with cushions perfect for parties or intimate conversations. Lamu furniture, with its deep brown color, provides a compelling contrast to the white walls. Local decorations can include fish traps made of palm rib or bamboo, and items made of old dhow wood.

Diani Beach

Kenya's coast south of Mombasa has some of the country's most beautiful beaches. From central Mombasa, access is via the Likoni Ferry, and beyond Likoni, the highway from Mombasa runs all the way to the Tanzania border, providing easy access to a string of resorts. Diani Beach is the most developed area along this stretch, but still fulfills most visitors' dreams of a turquoise ocean lapping broad sun-bleached sand backed by palm trees.

GETTING HERE AND AROUND

Many people fly into Mombasa's Moi International Airport and make their way down the south coast by taxi, rental car, or hotel shuttle. You must take the Likoni Ferry, open 24 hours, to travel south of Mombasa. Two ferries run simultaneously, departing about 15 minutes apart, with fewer departures between 1 am and 4 am. The crossing takes about 10 minutes, and the drive from Likoni to Diani is 40 minutes. Vehicles are charged by length, usually about KSh150 per car. Pedestrians ride free. To avoid the ferry crossing, a number of airlines are increasingly flying to the Ukunda airstrip at Diani Beach. Airkenya, Jambojet, and Safarilink offer services to Ukunda from Nairobi, while Mombasa Air Safari connects Ukunda with Amboseli, Tsavo West, and the Masai Mara. Tuk tuks are the most common means of getting around town, and you can hail one from the side of any main road.

SAFETY

If you take a taxi or tuk tuk at night, make sure it delivers you all the way to your destination. When strolling along beaches, you'll often meet other residents and tourists walking or jogging particularly early in the morning or evening. The beach boys can also be persistent in trying to sell you souvenirs or boat tours. Don't tempt fate by bringing jewelry, cameras, or cash.

Drink plenty of bottled water and wear sunscreen. It's a good idea to wear a thick T-shirt to protect your back from sunburn when snorkeling.

Sights

Kaya Kinondo Forest
FOREST | If you're in the Diani Beach area, be sure to spend an hour or two exploring the Kaya Kinondo Forest. This UNESCO World Heritage Site has been sacred territory for the Digo people for centuries. You'll need to walk with a

guide, who will tell you about the beliefs and ceremonies held here, as well as the medicinal and culinary uses of the plants growing in the forest which, although only 75 acres, is said to boast 187 species of trees. You'll also see black-and-white colobus and Sykes monkeys, as well as baboons. A walk here is highly recommended. If you have time, ask your guide to show you around the local Digo village, or even to introduce you to the spiritual healer. ✉ *Diani Beach* ✛ *4 km (2½ miles) south from the end of the tarmac at Diani Beach* ☎ *0791/663–325, 0722/446–916* 💰 *KSh1000.*

Kisite Mpunguti Marine National Park and Wasini Island

NATIONAL PARK | FAMILY | Located on the south coast off Shimoni, and south of Wasini Island, this marine reserve is known for its beautiful coral gardens. More than 250 species of fish can be spotted feeding around the reef including barracuda, groupers, emperors, angel-fish, parrotfish, lionfish, moray eels, and stingrays. Green and hawksbill turtles and humpback, bottlenose and spin-ner dolphins are a common sight. The shallow water can be easily reached by boat arranged from the jetty at Shimoni. However the easiest way to visit is on the popular Wasini Island day trip that can be organized at any of the south coast resorts—from US$135 including park fees. The day typically includes a transfer to Shimoni where you board a dhow to explore Kisite Mpunguti and go snorkeling. This is followed by a seafood lunch at one of the restaurants on the tiny Wasini Island with time to explore before the return dhow trip. Near Wasini village you'll find the ruins of 18th- and 19th-century houses and a Muslim pillar tomb inset with Chinese porcelain. ✉ *Shimoni* ✛ *40 km (25 miles) from Ukunda* ☎ *0723/929–766 Park warden, 0722/674–183* 💰 *$17.*

Beaches

★ Diani Beach

BEACH | FAMILY | This 20-km (12-mile) stretch of picture-postcard-perfect white sand backed by coconut palms is 30 km (19 miles) south of Mombasa. It is the most developed part of the southern coast and where most holidaymakers head. Apart from the gorgeous location and climate, one reason that it's so pop-ular is that the coral reef filters out the seaweed, so the beach is truly pristine, and it protects the swimming areas from offshore swells. There are numerous resorts, but fortunately most have been built sensitively in traditional style with low buildings and thatched roofs and are hidden in clumps of coastal forest. Much of this forest is home to vervet monkeys, troops of baboons, and endan-gered Angolan black-and-white colobus monkeys, as well as butterflies and birds. Diani Beach Road runs behind the beach and is dotted with good restaurants and shops, and if you stay in one of the private cottages, local fishermen will take your order and deliver lobsters and other delicacies of the deep to your door. All along Diani is a busy lineup of water sports on offer, such as windsurfing, parasailing, snorkeling, and scuba diving for some fun in the sun, or you could simply kick back with your feet in the sand at one of the beach bars. **Best for:** snorkeling, sunrise, walking, windsurfing. **Amenities:** food and drink, water sports. ✉ *Mombasa* ⊕ *www.dianibeach.com.*

🍽 Restaurants

★ Ali Barbour's Cave Restaurant

$$$$ | SEAFOOD | Considered the best res-taurant at Diani Beach, this unique venue is in a naturally formed coral cave deep underground lit by candles and lanterns; it's definitely worth the splurge for the experience and ambience. Seafood is the main cuisine; you can't go wrong with the coconut salad with prawns, crab,

Kenya's beautiful beaches are a great place to relax after a safari.

and calamari, but you can also dine on French food such as steak with béarnaise sauce or roast duck. **Known for:** unusual and romantic setting; superb food and service. $ *Average main: $50* ⊠ *Ali Barbour's Rd., off Diani Beach Rd., Diani Beach* ☎ *0735/331–002, 0714/456–131* ⊕ *www.alibarbours.co* ⊗ *No lunch* ⋔ *Smart casual; no shorts or hats.*

Nomad Beach Bar & Restaurant

$$$ | **MODERN EUROPEAN** | **FAMILY** | The perfect place to spend a few relaxing hours on a low-slung cushioned sofa with a tropical cocktail, Nomad is a luxurious beach bar that overlooks the white sands of Diani. Open all day from breakfast right through to dinner, the menu features the usual popular snacks, sandwiches, pizzas, and pastas, but also has some dishes based on traditional Swahili cooking, plenty of seafood, and even Indian curries and Japanese sushi—there's something for everyone. **Known for:** Sushi and wood-fired Italian pizza; great ocean views; Sunday lunch buffet. $ *Average main: $30* ⊠ *The Sands at Nomad, Diani Beach Rd., Diani Beach* ☎ *0738/333–888* ⊕ *www.nomadbeachbar.com.*

Hotels

Most of the hotels and resorts are on one or two roads running parallel to the beach. Often the properties aren't numbered, so landmarks are used to guide people instead. Everyone knows where all the places are, so you don't need to instruct a tuktuk driver with specific details.

Alfajiri Villas

$$$$ | **RESORT** | **FAMILY** | Built of stone and thatch, these luxurious double-story villas are elegantly furnished; you can choose between the Garden Villa, the Cliff Villa, or the Beach Villa (book months in advance for the latter), each with its own unique architecture and interiors. **Pros:** daily menus are tailored to your preferences; villas have private pools; ideal for large families. **Cons:** you may find you don't use all the included activities, such as golf, gym, and yoga; even if there

are only two of you, you need to book the entire villa; the beach next to the hotel is not great for swimming. $ Rooms from: $1,600 ⊠ Diani Beach Rd., Diani Beach ☎ 20/269–7234 ⊕ www.alfajirivillas.com ⇨ 3 villas ⦿ Free Breakfast.

Diani Reef Beach Resort & Spa

$ | RESORT | FAMILY | This mid-range resort will make sure you get the best out of your beach break. **Pros:** the staff are extremely friendly; organized activities are excellent; good value family option. **Cons:** resident monkeys can be annoying; room decor is a little dated; the buffet food is a little bland, but there are other restaurants. $ Rooms from: $162 ⊠ Diani Beach Rd., Diani Beach ☎ 0709/481–000 ⊕ www.dianireef.com ⇨ 143 rooms ⦿ Free Breakfast.

Kinondo Kwetu

$$$$ | RESORT | Owned by a Swedish family, the delightful Kinondo Kwetu was built in an idyllic location in a section of sacred forest on Galu Beach. **Pros:** dinner is served in a variety of romantically secluded locations; there's a good choice of activities; very professional and welcoming staff. **Cons:** no children under five; Wi-Fi only in reception; the beach is only swimmable at high tide. $ Rooms from: $950 ⊠ Diani Beach Rd., Galu Beach, Kinondo ☎ 0710/898–030 ⊕ www.kinondo-kwetu.com ☽ Closed May–June ⇨ 11 rooms ⦿ All-Inclusive.

★ The Maji Beach Boutique Hotel

$$$ | RESORT | One of the finest boutique resorts in Kenya, Maji means "water" in Swahili and the first thing you'll notice on arrival is the "lazy river" swimming pool that winds in a semi-circle across the main building, wrapping itself through palm trees and lounge areas, all in view of the beach. **Pros:** stunning design and architecture; easy access to Ukunda airstrip; superb gourmet food and impeccable service. **Cons:** restaurant only open to resident guests; no children under 12; beach boys can be a nuisance. $ Rooms from: $520 ⊠ Diani Beach Rd., Diani

Beach ☎ 0773/178–874, 0773/178–873 ⊕ www.the-maji.com ⇨ 15 rooms ⦿ Free Breakfast.

The Sands at Chale Island

$$ | RESORT | FAMILY | Right at the southern end of Diani Beach Road, you'll find the access point to the only resort in Kenya that stands alone on an island—Chale lies 600 meters off the mainland and is reached by boat at high tide, and quite delightfully by tractor at low tide. **Pros:** unique island location and fun to get to; stunning beach protected by a coral reef; daily program of water sports and other activities. **Cons:** it's a long drive from both Ukunda and Mombasa; the rooms are simply furnished but comfortable; the buffet food can be a little uninspiring. $ Rooms from: $282 ⊠ Diani Beach Rd., Diani Beach ☎ 0725/546–879 ⊕ www.thesandsatchaleisland.com ⇨ 45 rooms ⦿ Free Breakfast.

Searenity Beach Villa

$$ | HOTEL | Nestled right by a postcard-ready beach in a neatly manicured green garden fringed by towering palm trees, this is one huge mansion with six en suite double rooms, a rooftop bar, and an intimate restaurant that sits just 35. **Pros:** only 3 minutes away from the airstrip; located right on the beach; only place in Diani with a seaside cinema. **Cons:** beach boys will show up as soon as you step out; monkeys could sneak into rooms if food is left unattended; no children under 12. $ Rooms from: $400 ⊠ Kivulini Beach, Diani ☎ 0708/903–732 ⊕ www.searenityvilla.com ⇨ 6 suites ⦿ Free Breakfast.

🍸 Nightlife

Tandoori Club

DANCE CLUBS | If you want to let loose and dance 'til you drop, this is the spot to go. You might be forgiven for thinking that it's quiet judging by the few patrons drinking on the outdoor area which faces Diani Beach Road, but all the action is indoors.

Step through the looking glass to a DJ blasting Kenyan music and afrobeats, and patrons that actually come to dance. Drinks are cheap with beers going for a little over $3—make sure it's opened in front of you and that you're mindful of your drink. As with most nightclubs in town, you'll find escorts trying to vie for your attention; be mindful of who you get into conversations with and what their expectations are. The clubbing scene here doesn't kick off until after 11 pm, so plan to have dinner here first before you bar hop. ⊠ *Beach Rd., Diani Beach* ⊹ *Opposite Diani Sea Lodge.*

Lamu

Designated a UNESCO World Heritage Site in 2001, Lamu Old Town is the oldest and best-preserved Swahili settlement in East Africa. Some 260 km (162 miles) north of Mombasa—and just two degrees below the equator—Lamu is separated from the mainland by a narrow channel that's fringed with thick mangroves protected from the sea by coral reefs and huge sand dunes. Winding narrow alleyways lead past the ornate carved doorways and coral walls of magnificent merchant houses to the bustling waterfront. Life goes on much as it did when Lamu was a thriving port town in the 8th century; there are no cars (most heavy lifting is by donkey), and more than 1,000 years of East African, Omani, Yemeni, Indian, and Portuguese influences have resulted in a unique mix of cultures, reflected in the faces of its inhabitants as well as in its architecture and cuisine. A stronghold of Islam for many centuries, you'll see men in *kofias* (traditional caps that Muslims wear) and *khanzus* (white caftanlike robes) and women in *bui-buis* (black veils). Some merchant houses have been converted into gorgeous boutique hotels, and rooftop restaurants offer abundant, fresh seafood for very little.

The Lamu archipelago is roughly divided into two parts: Lamu Town, in the south, and Shela, a smaller, quieter village in the north and next to the beach. Some visitors split their holiday between staying on both sides of the island, or you could opt to stay on Manda Island or in farther-flung hotels on the far northern or southern edges. You can walk between Lamu Town and Shela in about 45 minutes; a popular option is to walk one way and take a boat back. The beach offers 13 km (8 miles) of unspoiled coastline.

It's very easy to relax into the *pole-pole* ("slowly" in Swahili) pace of life in Lamu, spending hours on the beach or on your hotel terrace reading a book and sipping a delicious fresh fruit juice. There's also plenty for the energetic to do here—windsurfing, kayaking, fishing, and snorkeling. You can also take a dhow cruise to visit ruins on Pate and Manda islands.

Tourism hasn't made much of an impact on Lamu, and that's what makes it so special. In the last few years, though, motorbike taxis locally known as *boda boda* have found their way into Lamu Old Town in growing numbers, even when they look ever so out of place.

GETTING HERE AND AROUND

There are plenty of flights from Nairobi, some of which run in circuits to Malindi, too. Fly540 and Jambojet fly from Jomo Kenyatta International Airport, while East African and Safarilink fly from Wilson Airport. Flights land on Manda Island, and a speedboat from the jetty takes about 10 minutes to get to Lamu (boat taxis meet the flights or your hotel will pick you up). Getting to Lamu by road north from Malindi is not recommended; there were security issues years ago and although there are now several police checkpoints it's not recommended.

Lamu Town is easy to get around because it's so small. The cobbled streets are laid out in a grid fashion with the main street—Harambee

Donkeys are the main source of transportation of goods in the island town of Lamu.

Avenue—running parallel to the waterfront. Most hotels can arrange for a trip by dhow between Lamu Town and Shela. Find out the going price from your accommodation and confirm with the captain before setting out.

FESTIVALS AND SEASONAL EVENTS

The Maulidi festival, marking the birth of Muhammad, has been celebrated on Lamu for more than a century. Dhow races, poetry readings, and other events take place around the town's main mosques. Maulidi, which takes place in the spring, attracts pilgrims from all over Kenya. The three-day Lamu Cultural Festival takes place each November and offers a unique insight into island life. The event showcases traditional dance, handcraft displays, and music and theater performances from both local and visiting artists. The Lamu Yoga Festival hosted by Banana House & Wellness center attracts up to 400 students from around the world, with classes and workshops spread across the island throughout the day, coupled with Swahili dinners,

dhow sunset cruises and an epic bonfire party. The festival typically takes place in March, and sometimes in October.

⊙ Sights

Ask at your lodging for a local guide. Agree on a price before you head out, and then let him introduce you to the history of this remarkable little town on a leisurely walking tour.

Donkey Sanctuary

WILDLIFE REFUGE | Donkeys are the main transport in Lamu. The sanctuary was started in 1987 by Elisabeth Svendsen, a British doctor who founded The Donkey Sanctuary in the UK. Its main function is to protect and look after the working donkeys, and it's managed by the Kenyan branch of the charity. There's a treatment clinic where locals can get their donkeys wormed, a training center, and a resting place for a few of the old animals that can no longer work. The staff will show you around in the mornings, otherwise you can eyeball a few donkeys over the low wall in front of the yard. An annual prize is given to the Lamu donkey in the best physical condition. ✉ *Waterfront, Mkomani Location* ✉ *Donations accepted.*

Kiwayu Island

ISLAND | This strip of sand known as Kiwayu Island is 50 km (31 miles) northeast of Lamu. Its main attraction is its proximity to Kiunga Marine National Reserve, a marine park encompassing Kiwayu Bay. The confluence of two major ocean currents creates unique ecological conditions that nurture three marine habitats—mangroves, sea-grass beds, and coral reefs. Here you have a chance of catching a glimpse of the most endangered mammal in Kenya, the manatee; because of its tasty flesh, this gentle giant has been hunted to near extinction all along Africa's eastern coast.

Your lodge or hotel can arrange a trip for you; it's 90 minutes by speedboat and about $100. Stop by the laid-back, charming, owner-run Mike's Camp Kiwayu for a delicious lunch and even better cocktails. Ask Mike for the best spot to harvest and shuck rock oysters, or to find mud crabs in the mangrove. ✉ *Kiwayu Island, Lamu* ☎ *0714/333–916 Mike's Camp* ⚓ *Reservation required.*

Lamu Fort

MILITARY SIGHT | This imposing edifice, which was completed in 1821, is set one street away from the seafront. It was used as a prison from 1910 to 1984, when it became part of the country's museum system. Today, it is a central part of the town as it hosts conferences, exhibitions, and theater productions. If you have a few moments during your walking tour, climb up to the battlements for some great views of Lamu, and pop into the vegetable and meat markets, which are just to the left of the fort. If you see a man pressing sugarcane, limes, and ginger to make juice, buy a glass—it's delicious. The entrance fee is a package and includes entry to Takwa,

Pate, and Siyu Ruins, as well as Lamu Museum, Swahili House and the German Post Office. The latter was established in 1888 by the Germans and is now also a small museum on local history and is just across the street from the fort. ✉ *Harambee Ave., Lamu* ☎ *042/633–073* ⊕ *www. museums.or.ke* ✉ *KSh500.*

Lamu Museum

HISTORY MUSEUM | You enter this delightful museum through a brass-studded door that was imported from Zanzibar. Inside there are archaeological displays showing the Takwa Ruins excavations, some wonderful photos of Lamu taken by a French photographer from 1846 to 1849 (you'll be amazed at how little has changed in Lamu), some intricately carved Lamu headboards and throne chairs, and a library. In the Balcony Room upstairs is a fascinating display of musical instruments including the famed Siwa Horn, which is made of brass and resembles elephant tusks; the Pate Siwa horn, made of ivory, is now in the Nairobi National Museum. Dating from the 17th century, they're reputed to be the oldest surviving musical instruments in sub-Saharan Africa. ✉ *Waterfront, Lamu* ☎ *042/633–402* ⊕ *www.museums.or.ke* ✉ *KSh500.*

Manda Island

RUINS | Just across the channel from Shela, the mostly uninhabited Manda Island once held one of the area's largest cities. The once-thriving community of Takwa was abandoned in the 17th century, and archaeologists have yet to discover why. The ruins can be explored and the Friday Mosque with a large pillar on top is among the most notable features. Reached by taking a dhow up a baobab tree-lined creek, this is a popular day trip from Lamu and Shela, perhaps with a picnic. ✉ *Lamu* ✚ *30 mins by boat from Lamu* ⊕ *www.museums.or.ke* ✉ *KSh500.*

wahili House Museum

ISTORY MUSEUM | This beautifully restored 8th-century Swahili merchant's house ias original period furniture, and is a jreat depiction of a traditional Swahili iouse, and gives insight into how people ived back then. Notice the traditional »eds with woven bases of rope, and the inely carved Kalinda screen in the main oom. There's a garden full of flower-ng tropical shrubs and trees and the riginal well. ✉ *Off Harambee Ave., Lamu* ☎ *20/816-4134* 🌐 *www.museums.or.ke* 🎟 *KSh500.*

🍴 Restaurants

Most of the bigger restaurants and hotels n Lamu town are along the waterfront r the road parallel to it, called Harambee Avenue, while smaller holiday houses and villas lie in the maze of narrow streets. In Shela, the best restaurants are n hotels, and some require hopping on speedboat to get to. Being a Muslim own, only a handful of places serve alcohol.

iamond Beach Village

$$ | PIZZA | FAMILY | Opened in 2000, this eco-lodge is the type of spot where you kick off your shoes when you arrive and don't remember where you left them at the end. The menu has seafood and Swahili bbq, but the delicious wood-fired hin crust pizzas are where it's really t. **Known for:** great spot to meet new people; excellent pizzas; epic full moon parties and concerts. [$] *Average main: $30* ✉ *Ras Kitau, Manda, Kipungani* ☎ *0720/915–001* 🌐 *www.diamondbeach-village.com.*

loating Bar

| AFRICAN | Floating about a mile off-shore, this traditional wooden dhow is aid back and rustic, with simple wooden urniture and woven floor mats, and it's he spot where you'll find locals and ourists downing cocktails and beers and dancing after hours. If you plan to go for lunch, the go-to meals here are fish/seafood and chips, but you can also find a few Kenyan staples, reflecting the owner's heritage. **Known for:** only public bar of its kind in Lamu; food and beers are generally affordable; crowd is always lively. [$] *Average main: $15* ✉ *Kenyatta Rd.* ☎ *0721/510–852.*

Whispers Coffee Shop

$ | CAFÉ | Located in Lamu Town in the same building as the Baraka Gallery (which has a wonderful collection of African art, jewelry, and souvenirs for sale), this upscale café has a pretty, palm-fringed quiet courtyard where you can relax over a cappuccino. There's also a lunch and dinner menu, focusing on salads, pastas, and deli items, or you can order a packed lunch to take away. **Known for:** courtyard setting; excellent art gallery and shop; delicious ice-cold watermelon and mint juice. [$] *Average main: KSh800* ✉ *Harambee Ave., Lamu* ☎ *0701/481–468* 💳 *No credit cards* 🕒 *Closed May and June.*

🛏 Hotels

Fatuma's Tower

$ | HOTEL | FAMILY | Set against the dunes in Shela village, Fatuma's Tower is a beautiful, cool, calm escape. **Pros:** there's a cook who can do your food shopping and preparation of all meals; it's extremely peaceful and there's total serenity beyond the sound of motorboat engines; refreshing plunge pool in the garden. **Cons:** it's about a 10-minute walk through Shela to the beach; no air-conditioning but there are fans; mosquitoes can occasionally be a nuisance. [$] *Rooms from: $125* ✉ *Shela* ☎ *0716/572–370* 🌐 *www.fatumastower.com* 🛏 *10 rooms* 🍴 *Free Breakfast.*

Kijani Hotel

$ | HOTEL | FAMILY | Located right on the waterfront in Shela, Kijani Hotel offers rooms in three converted Arab merchant houses grouped around a pretty central garden (kijani is Swahili for green) with swimming pool. **Pros:** rooms look out onto the waterfront; has its own dhow for cruises, with meals aboard; one of the few places that has a bar. **Cons:** must preorder lunch and dinner; need to be appropriately dressed in Shela village on the way to and from the beach; can get hot at night. $ *Rooms from: $188* ✉ *Shela* ☎ *0780/001–741, 0733/545–264* ⊕ *www.kijani-lamu.com* ⊙ *Closed May and June* ⇨ *11 rooms* ⓘ *Free Breakfast.*

Lamu House

$ | **HOTEL** | **FAMILY** | The rooms in this boutique hotel, located next to the Donkey Sanctuary on Lamu's waterfront, are all different, but each one is superbly decorated in traditional Swahili style and has a separate dressing room and a terrace looking out either onto the water or the town. **Pros:** each room has a fridge; there are free boats to shuttle you to Shela Beach; breakfast is available all day. **Cons:** some staircases are narrow and steep; rooms downstairs are a little dark; it can be noisy as it's in the center of town. $ *Rooms from: $145* ✉ *Waterfront, Lamu* ☎ *0792/469–577* ⊕ *www. lamuhouse.com* ⇨ *10 rooms* ⓘ *Free Breakfast.*

★ The Majlis

$$ | **RESORT** | **FAMILY** | The rooms in this spectacular hotel are in three villas, and as each has a sitting room with white couches, antique Swahili furniture, and African paintings and sculptures, you'll feel as though you're staying in an ultra-stylish private beach house. **Pros:** popular restaurant, open to non-guests; an excellent beach; beautiful interiors and architecture, perfect for photos. **Cons:** alcohol isn't included in the full-board option; not all rooms face the ocean; trips to Lamu aren't included. $ *Rooms from: $420* ✉ *Ras Kitau Bay, Lamu* ☎ *0773/777–066, 0720/330–088 Reservations* ⊕ *www.themajlisresorts.com* ⇨ *38 rooms* ⓘ *All-Inclusive.*

Manda Bay

$$$$ | **RESORT** | At high tide, you can dive right off your verandah into the ocean; at low tide, a lovely strand of beach appears in front of your room. **Pros:** truly a private island getaway; boutique-hotel amenities with laid-back feel; fantastic for both honeymooners and families. **Cons:** It's a little out of the way hence farther to get to from Shela and Lamu Town; Wi-Fi limited in the rooms; music from the bar can be heard in cottages near the main area. $ *Rooms from: $700* ✉ *Manda Island, Lamu* ☎ *0716/579–999 reservations* ⊕ *www.mandabay.com* ⊙ *Closed in May* ⇨ *22 rooms* ⓘ *Free Breakfast.*

★ Peponi Hotel

$$ | **HOTEL** | **FAMILY** | Peponi is well-known for its beachfront location in Shela, lovely accommodations, and superb food. **Pros:** only hotel guests get seating on the outside balcony at dinner; you can sleep with the sea-facing windows and doors open (guards are on duty all night); well-stocked gift shop sells items by local designers. **Cons:** the beach disappears at high tide; beach boys can be a nuisance; drinks are not included in the full-board option. $ *Rooms from: $270* ✉ *Waterfront, Shela* ☎ *0722/203–082* ⊕ *www. peponihotel.com* ⊙ *Closed May and June* ⇨ *29 rooms* ⓘ *Free Breakfast.*

The Red Pepper House

$$ | **RESORT** | Guests here are practically doted on from the moment they cross the threshold of this architecturally stunning beachfront property. **Pros:** flexible scheduling of meals and activities; impeccable personalized service; extensive outdoor and indoor space in each room. **Cons:** no children under five; there are nicer beaches in the area, but the staff is willing to take you to the best spots at any time; gift shop is small. $ *Rooms from: $360* ✉ *Coconut Beach* ☎ *0721/230–521* ⊕ *www.theredpepperhouse.com* ⇨ *9 rooms* ⓘ *Free Breakfast.*

Chapter 4

TANZANIA

Updated By
Linda Markovina

WELCOME TO TANZANIA

TOP REASONS TO GO

★ **The Great Migration:** This annual movement is one of the great natural wonders of the world.

★ **Big Game Adventures:** Get the season right and this varied and unique landscape will dazzle you. You'll be amazed at how close up and familiar you get not only with the Big Five, but with thousands of other animals as well.

★ **Sea, Sand, and Sun:** Tanzania's sun-spoiled beaches are lapped by the turquoise waters of the Indian Ocean. Swim, snorkel, scuba dive, sail, fish, or just chill on soft white sands under waving palm trees.

★ **Ancient Cultures:** From the traditional red-robed, bead-bedecked nomadic Maasai in the north to the exotic heady mix of Arab and African influences in Zanzibar, Pemba, and Mafia, you'll encounter friendly people and unique cultures just about everywhere you go.

★ **Bird-Watching:** Stay glued to your binoculars in one of the finest bird-watching destinations in the world.

Tanzania is about twice the size of the state of California and is bordered by the Indian Ocean in the east, Kenya to the north, and Mozambique to the south. It's home to some of the world's most coveted tourist destinations.

1 Serengeti National Park. Endless plains of golden grass, teeming herds of game, stalking predators—you won't be disappointed.

2 Ngorongoro Conservation Area. The floor of the Ngorongoro Crater is home to the biggest concentration of predators on earth.

3 Lake Manyara National Park. This park is home to lions, baboons, giraffes, hippos, birds, ancient forest, lakeside plains, and towering cliffs.

4 Nyerere National Park. Escape the crowds in the world's second-largest conservation area where you can view game on foot, by boat, or from your vehicle.

5 Gombe Stream and Mahale Mountains National Parks. Follow in the footsteps of world-famous primatologist Jane Goodall and come face-to-face with wild chimpanzees.

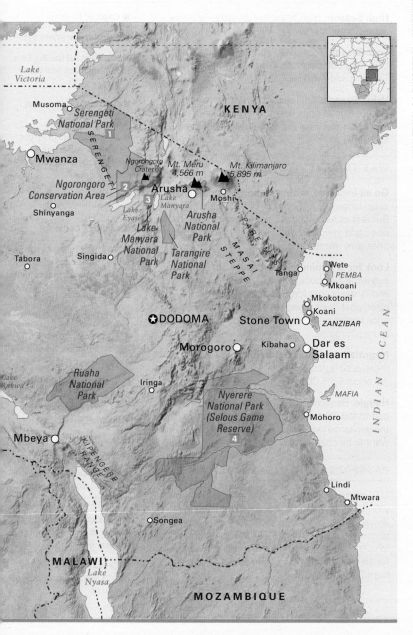

Lake Victoria

Musoma

Serengeti National Park **1**

KENYA

Mwanza

Ngorongoro Crater

Mt. Meru 4,566 m

Mt. Kilimanjaro 5,895 m

SERENGETI

Ngorongoro Conservation Area **2**

Arusha

Moshi

Shinyanga

3 Lake Manyara

Lake Eyasi

Arusha National Park

PARE MTS

Tabora

Singida

Lake Manyara National Park

Tarangire National Park

MASAI STEPPE

Tanga

Wete

PEMBA

Mkoani

Mkokotoni

Koani

ZANZIBAR

⊛DODOMA

Stone Town

INDIAN OCEAN

Morogoro

Kibaha

Dar es Salaam

Ruaha National Park

Iringa

Nyerere National Park (Selous Game Reserve) **4**

MAFIA

Mohoro

Lake Rukwa

Mbeya

KIPENGERE RANGE

Lindi

Mtwara

Songea

MALAWI

Lake Nyasa

MOZAMBIQUE

COUNTRY SNAPSHOT

WHEN TO GO

High Season: High season is January–February and June–September.

Low Season: From late February to early May, the long rains coincide with low season across mainland Tanzania and Zanzibar.

Value Season: Approaching the short rains in October, hotel rates begin to dip. The land is parched from a dry summer and wildlife sightings are excellent.

WAY TO SAVE

Go all-inclusive, within reason At some remote safari lodges its not even an option, it/s a requisite. But rest assured, you will eat and drink well. In the cities and towns try out the myriad restaurants on offer, they are worth it.

Look for last minute safari deals Get online and scour the Facebook pages of different companies and Tanzania chat forums, as lodges and hotels will often post deals, specials, or last minute drop-in-price bookings that could make your holiday much more affordable.

Negotiate taxi fares beforehand. Taxis don't have meters, so agree on the fare before getting in. Fares run about Tsh5,000 within cities.

Haggle. Bargaining, especially at marketplaces, is part of the shopping experience. Always be aware of the exchange rate and pay appropriately. You don't want to be charged exorbitant "tourist" prices.

PASSPORTS AND VISAS

U.S. citizens need a visa ($100) to enter Tanzania; it's valid for three months. A visa can be purchased upon arrival, but you'll need cash and at least two passport pictures. It's best to get a visa ahead of time to avoid long lines and headaches. Passports must be valid for six months after your planned departure date from Tanzania.

AT A GLANCE

- **Capital:** Dodoma
- **Population:** 57,091,392
- **Big Five:** All the Big Five, including black and white rhinos.
- **Currency:** Tanzanian shilling (Tsh)
- **Money:** ATMs in larger cities; U.S. dollars and credit cards accepted at safari lodges.
- **Language:** Kiswahili, English
- **Country Code:** 255
- **VAT:** 18% on everything and often not included in prices, so check beforehand
- **Emergencies:** 112
- **Driving:** On the left
- **Electricity:** 230v/50 cycles; plugs are UK standard three-prong
- **Time:** 7 hours ahead of New York during daylight saving time; 8 hours otherwise
- **Mobile Phones:** GSM (900 and 1800 bands)
- **Major Mobile Companies:** Vodacom, Airtel, MTN, ZANTEL
- **Tanzanian Tourist Board:** ⊕ www.tanzania-tourism.go.tz
- **Tanzania Tourism:** ⊕ www.tanzaniatourism.go.tz

Tanzania is the quintessential, definitive Africa of your dreams. And who wouldn't want to visit a place where the names of its legendary travel destinations roll off the tongue: Zanzibar, Serengeti, Mt. Kilimanjaro, Lake Tanganyika, Lake Victoria, the Rift Valley, the Ngorongoro Crater, and Olduvai Gorge (known as "the Cradle of Humankind").

The 945,203-square-km (364,898-square-miles) country is home to the great plains that abound with legions of game, snowcapped mountains that soar above dusty valleys, rain forests that teem with monkeys and birds, beaches that are covered in sand as soft and white as talcum powder, and coral reefs that host myriads of jewel-like tropical fish. Although Tanzania's economy—one of the poorest in the world—depends heavily on agriculture, which accounts for almost half of its GDP, it has more land (more than 25%) devoted to national parks and game reserves than any other wildlife destination in the world. Everything from coral reefs to the Crater Highlands, remote game reserves, and the famous national parks are protected by government law and placed in trust for future generations.

There are two circuits you can follow in Tanzania: the conventional northern tourist circuit, which includes the Serengeti and Ngorongoro Crater, or the lesser-traveled southern tourist circuit of Nyerere National Park (formerly Selous Game Reserve) and Ruaha, Mahale, and Gombe national parks among others. You'll be amply rewarded for the often lengthy travel times to these southern locations by having the places much more to yourself.

Serengeti *is* all it's cracked up to be with endless plains of golden grass (Serengeti means "endless plain" in the Maasai language), teeming game, abundant bird life, and an awe-inspiring sense of space and timelessness. Ngorongoro Crater justly deserves its reputation as one of the natural wonders of the world. The ride down onto the crater floor is memorable enough as you pass through misty primeval forest with wild orchids, swinging vines, and chattering monkeys, but once on the floor you could well be in the middle of a *National Geographic* special.

You can follow in the footsteps of legendary hunters and explorers when you visit Nyerere National Park in the south. Although it's the second-largest conservation area in the world after Greenland National Park, only a small part of Nyerere's northern section is open to tourists; but don't worry, you'll see all the game and birds you could wish for with the advantage of seeing it by boat and on foot.

If it's chimpanzees you're after, then Gombe Stream and Mahale Mountains national parks are the places to head for. A lot of traveling (much of it by boat) is required, but the experience is well worth the effort, and you'll join only a small community of other privileged visitors who have had the unique experience of coming face-to-face with wild chimpanzees.

The animals aren't the only wonders Tanzania has to offer. There are the islands of Zanzibar, Pemba, and Mafia, as well as Mt. Kilimanjaro, Mt. Meru, and the three great lakes of Victoria, Tanganyika, and Malawi. Wherever you go, you're guaranteed travel experiences that you'll remember for the rest of your life.

MAJOR REGIONS

With 15 national parks and too many private reserves to count, you probably won't be able to see all of Tanzania in one trip, so we've broken it down by **Must-See Parks** (Serengeti National Park, Ngorongoro Conservation Area, Lake Manyara National Park, Mount Kilimanjaro, Nyerere National Park, and Gombe Stream and Mahale Mountains National Parks) and **If You Have Time Parks** (Arusha National Park, Tarangire National Park, and Ruaha National Park) to help you better organize your time. We suggest, though, that you read about all of them and then choose for yourself.

There are also sections on **Gateway Cities** (Dar es Salaam and Arusha) and **Beach Destinations** (Zanzibar, Mafia, and Pemba Islands).

Planning

Getting Here and Around

AIR

Tanzania has three major airports: Julius Nyerere International Airport (DAR) in Dar es Salaam, Abeid Amani Karume International Airport (ZNZ) in Zanzibar, and Kilimanjaro International Airport (JRO). Most travelers arrive in Tanzania through Julius Nyerere International Airport as few airlines fly direct from Europe and the continent of Africa.

Abeid Amani Karume International Airport has direct flights from East Africa, Europe, and the Middle East, while Kilimanjaro International Airport accepts international flights with certain airlines like KLM and Qatar Airways.

Though the list is subject to change, the following airlines fly to Tanzania: Kenya Airways, Turkish Airlines, Fly Dubai, Emirates, Qatar Airways, Ethiopian Airlines, Oman Air, Egypt Air, LAM, Uganda Airlines (through Qatar), Airlink, Rwanda Air, Air Madagascar, Precision Air, Air Tanzania, Regional Air, and KLM. Always be sure to check before booking your tickets and be aware of long layover times.

AIRLINES Air Tanzania. ⊠ ATC House, Ohio St., 2nd fl., Dar es Salaam ☎ 0800/110–045 ⊕ www.airtanzania. co.tz. **Emirates.** ⊠ Haidry Plaza Complex, Ali Hassan Mwinyi Rd., Dar es Salaam ☎ 22/211–6100 ⊕ www.emirates.com. **Ethiopian Airlines.** ⊠ T.D.F.L Bldg., Upanga St., Dar es Salaam ☎ 22/211–7063 ⊕ www.ethiopianairlines.com. **Fast Jet.** ⊠ Samora Tower, Samora Ave., ground fl. Shop 1, Dar es Salaam ☎ 784/108–900 ⊕ www.fastjet.com. **Kenya Airways.** ⊠ Viva Towers, Ali Hassan Mwinyi Rd., 1st fl. Dar es Salaam ☎ 22/216–3917 ⊕ www. kenya-airways.com. **KLM.** ⊠ Viva Towers, Ali Hassan Mwinyi Rd., 1st fl., Dar es Salaam ☎ 22/216–3914 ⊕ www.klm.com. **Mango Airlines.** ⊠ OR Tambo International Airport, Johannesburg ☎ 086/101–0217 South African contact ⊕ www.flymango.com. **Oman Air.** ⊠ Serena Hotel, 12 Ohio St., Dar es Salaam ☎ 22/211–9426 ⊕ www.omanair.com. **Qatar Airways.** ⊠ Diamond Plaza, 4th fl., Dar es Salaam ☎ 22/219–8301 ⊕ www.qatarairways. com/tz. **South Africa Airways.** ⊠ Raha Towers Bldg., Bibititi St. at Maktaba St.,

Dar es Salaam ☎ *22/211–7045–7* ⊕ *www. flysaa.com.* **Swiss Air.** ✉ *Acacia Estate, 84 Kinondoni Rd., Dar es Salaam* ☎ *22/551– 0020* ⊕ *www.swiss.com.* **Turkish Airlines.** ✉ *Maktaba Sq., Azikiwe St., Business Park, 4th fl., Dar es Salaam* ☎ *22/211– 6681* ⊕ *www.turkishairlines.com.*

AIRPORTS AND TRANSFERS

Julius Nyerere International Airport is about 13 km (8 miles) from the city center. There are a plethora of white-color taxis available at the airport that will cost you about Tsh40,000 (US$18) to the city center. There is a board detailing the standard rates, but this will be more expensive if you have not organized your own taxi; drivers often will take the price as high as they can, so agree before you get in. Most hotels will send drivers to meet your plane, if arranged in advance, although this will cost more. Taxis to Msasani Peninsula, a bay to the north of the city where many of the hotels listed in this guide are located, cost about Tsh50,000 (US$23). Prices can be, but are not usually, negotiated. Traffic into the city is notorious, especially during rush hours.

AIRPORTS Arusha Airport. *(ARK)* ✉ *Dodoma Rd., Arusha* ☎ *272727/250–5920* ⊕ *www.taa.go.tz.*

CHARTER FLIGHTS

Affectionately known as the "sky donkeys" (due to the fact that they are the workhorses of the sky), there are a host of small charter companies that run daily flights from Dar es Salaam, Zanzibar, Pemba, and Mafia to all the popular tourism destinations, such as the Serengeti. From Cessna prop planes (a lucky person often gets to sit in the copilot's seat) to a slightly larger commuter plane, this is how most travelers move domestically across Tanzania. It's quick, fun, and makes for interesting photographs if you're lucky to be by the window. Low season has better prices

■ TIP→ **Those with a severe fear of small planes might consider road travel instead, although distances are far and the roads can be very bumpy.**

Due to the limited space and size of the aircraft, charter carriers observe strict luggage regulations: luggage must be soft-sided and weigh between 15 and 20 kg (33 to 44 pounds) depending on the plane.

■ TIP→ **Seats can not be booked in advance on the prop planes.**

CONTACTS Auric Air. ✉ *Viva Towers, Ali Hassan Mwinyi Rd., 2nd fl., Dar es Salaam* ☎ *746/986–123* ⊕ *www.auricair. com.* **Coastal Air.** ✉ *Slipway, Masaki* ☎ *222/699–999–999* ⊕ *www.coastal. co.tz.* **Precision Air.** ✉ *Diamond Plaza, Mirambo St. at Samora Ave, 1st fl., Dar es Salaam* ☎ *746/984–100* ⊕ *www. precisionairtz.com.* **Regional Air Tanzania.** ✉ *Sable Square, Arusha* ⊕ *www.regional-tanzania.com.*

Communications

PHONES

Calling within Tanzania: The "0" in the regional code is used only for calls placed from other areas within the country.

Calling Tanzania from abroad: To call from abroad, dial the international access number 00, then the country code 255, then the area code, (e.g., 22 for Dar es Salaam), and then the telephone number, which should have six or seven digits.

Mobile Phones: Vodacom, Airtel Tanzania, and Zantel are the main service providers in Tanzania, but Airtel and Vodacom have the best reception coverage. The best option is to bring your own phone (if it's not locked to a particular network) or rent a phone and buy a SIM card on arrival. The starter packs for pay-as-you-go cell phones are very reasonable. You'll have to buy data or call credit for your phone, but this is

Read and Watch

Read This

Through a Window: My Thirty Years with the Chimpanzees of Gombe, Jane Goodall. The world's foremost great ape conservationist recounts three decades of struggling to protect Tanzania's wild chimpanzees.

The Shadow of Kilimanjaro: On Foot Across East Africa, Rick Ridgeway. This travelogue follows a travel writer on his trek from Mount Kilimanjaro to the Indian Ocean.

The Worlds of a Maasai Warrior, Tepilit Ole Saitoti. An autobiographical memoir of the author's coming of age in the Maasailand and his journey through Africa and Europe.

Admiring Silence, Abdulrazak Gurnah. A boy who leaves Zanzibar during the revolution returns to delve into the political and sociological world of Zanzibar between 1964 and the 1990s.

Sea Level: A Portrait of Zanzibar and *Street Level: Drawing and Creative Writings Inspired by the Culture and Heritage of Dar es Salaam*, Sarah Markes. Gorgeous sketches capture the real detailed and nuanced life in Tanzania.

The Book of Secrets, M.G. Vassanji. The discovery of an early-20th-century diary leads a schoolteacher on a quest for the truth.

Watch This

Siri ya Mtungi. You can find this series on YouTube and other online forums; it tracks the fictional life happenings of a series of colorful characters from Dar Es Salaam to Bagamoyo.

Serengeti. A two-part series, narrated by Lupita Nyong'o, that provides a front-row seat to the animal dramas played out in a unique corner of the world.

National Geographic: Great Migrations. Get a sense of the scale and beauty of one of the greatest shows on earth in the Serengeti.

---

easily done at shops or roadside vendors. Most places have free Wi-Fi.

CONTACTS Airtel. ⊕ *www.africa.airtel. com.* **Tigo.** ⊠ *MIC Tanzania LTD, New Bagamoyo Rd.* ⊕ *www.tigo.co.tz.* **Zantel.** ⊠ *Zanzibar Telecom Limited, Mwai Kibaki Rd. at Old Bagamoyo Rd., Dar es Salaam* ⊕ *www.zantel.co.tz.*

Customs and Duties

You can bring in a liter of spirits or wine and 200 cigarettes duty-fee. The import of zebra skin or other tourist products requires a CITES (Convention of International Trade in Endangered Species of Wild Fauna and Flora) permit. Although you can buy curios made from animal products in Tanzania, your home country may confiscate them on arrival. Don't buy shells. It is illegal to export elephant ivory, wildlife skins, and sea turtle products without permits.

■ **TIP** → **As of 2017 there are strict rules to abide if you plan on bringing a drone into Tanzania and Zanzibar and flying it either commercial or recreational purposes.**

A permit and license from the Tanzanian Civil Aviation Authority is required, without which your drone potentially could be impounded on arrival at the airport. Drones are not allowed to be flown in National Parks at all (due to concerns over poaching) and if the rangers catch you it will be a hefty fine. Visit the

More than 1 million wildebeest take part in the annual Great Migration and some 250,000 die during the journey.

Tanzania Civil Aviation Authority website for up-to-date details.

CONTACTS Tanzania Civil Aviation Authority. (TCAA) ✉ *Tanzania Civil Aviation Authority, Nyerere Rd., Kitunda Rd. junction, Dar es Salaam* ⊕ *Aviation house* ⊕ *www.tcaa.go.tz.*

Health and Safety

Malaria is the biggest health threat in Tanzania, so be vigilant about taking antimalarials and applying bug spray. Consult with your doctor or travel clinic before leaving home for up-to-date antimalarial medication. At time of writing HIV/AIDS is less a risk than in some other African countries, but the golden rule is *never* have sex with a stranger. It's imperative to use strong sunscreen: remember you're just below the equator, where the sun is at its hottest. Stick to bottled water and ensure that the bottle seal is unbroken. Put your personal medications in your carry-on and bring copies of prescriptions.

SHOTS AND MEDICATIONS

Be up-to-date on yellow fever, polio, tetanus, typhoid, meningococcus, rabies, and Hepatitis A. It's not necessary to have a cholera jab, but if you're visiting Zanzibar it's sensible to get a cholera exception form from your GP or travel clinic. Visit a travel clinic 8 to 10 weeks before you travel to find out your requirements. If you're coming to Tanzania for a safari, chances are you're heading to a malarial game reserve. Millions of travelers take oral prophylactic drugs before, during, and after their safaris. It's up to you to weigh the risks and benefits of the type of antimalarial drug you choose to take. If you're pregnant or traveling with small children, consider a nonmalarial region for your safari.

EMBASSIES U.S. Embassy. ✉ *686 Old Bagamoyo Rd., Msasani, Msasani* ☎ *22/229–4122* ⊕ *tz.usembassy.gov.*

EMERGENCIES Police Hotline. ☎ *112, 22/211–7362.*

MEDICAL-ASSISTANCE COMPANIES The Flying Doctors Service. ✉ *Summit Center,*

Sokoine Rd., West Wing, Block A, 2nd fl., Arusha ☎ 20/699–2299 emergency, 71/988–1887 in Arusha ⊕ www.flydoc.org.

Hotels and Lodges

You'll find the ultimate in luxury at many of the safari camps, lodges, and coastal resorts and hotels. It's highly recommended that you opt for a private camp or lodge if possible, because everything is usually included—lodging, transport to and from the lodge, meals, beverages (including excellent house wines), game drives, and other activities. Note that prices are usually per person, per night. Check in advance whether park fees are included in your rate, as these can get very expensive if you have to pay them daily. The southern safari circuit is cheaper in general, but you'll need to factor in the cost of transport and that can be quite pricey. Many lodges and hotels offer low-season rates. If you're opting for a private game lodge, find out whether they accept children (many specify only kids over 12), and stay a minimum of two nights, three if you can. If you're traveling to the more remote parks, allow for more time.

▪TIP➜ **Most lodges offer a laundry service and will launder everything except underwear (it's against African culture). Remember to pack plenty of pairs or make sure you bring quick-dry ones so you can wash as you go. Most lodges will provide laundry detergent in your tent for this very purpose.**

National park accommodations are few and very basic. Unless you're a hard-core camper, it's advised that you stick with another type of accommodation. It's essential to note that more often than not, there won't be an elevator in your lodge—which are usually one story—and because of the rustic locations, accommodations aren't wheelchair-friendly.

⊕ For information on plugging in while on safari, see Electricity, in the Planning

Your Safari chapter. Restaurant and hotel reviews have been shortened. For full information, visit Fodors.com.

What It Costs In U.S. Dollars			
$	$$	$$$	$$$$
RESTAURANTS			
under $12	$12–$20	$21–$30	over $30
HOTELS			
under $250	$250–$450	$451–$600	over $600

Money Matters

The regulated currency is the Tanzanian shilling (Tsh). Notes are 500, 1,000, 2,000, 5,000, and 10,000. At this writing, the exchange rate was about Tsh2,330 to US$1. The V.A.T. in Tanzania is 18% and is added to everything, except for restaurant and activity bills. Be sure to ask for the V.A.T. to be included in the price or your bill could add up unexpectedly.

To avoid administrative hassles, keep all foreign-exchange receipts until you leave the region, as you may need them as proof when changing any unspent local currency back into your own currency at the airport when you leave. Don't leave yourself with any shillings—you won't be able to change them outside of Tanzania unless you are traveling onward to other East African countries.

Bargaining, especially at marketplaces, is part of the shopping experience. But always be aware of the exchange rate and pay appropriately—you don't want to underpay, but you also don't want to be charged exorbitant "tourist" prices.

Most large hotels accept U.S. dollars and Tanzanian shillings and take all major credit cards but do be aware that using a credit card can in some instances come with a surcharge of 3%–8% (sometimes

Serengeti Highway and the Maasai

Since 2014 there has been a continual battle for and against the construction of a paved and commercial highway through the Serengeti National Park. It is contended that the highway would cause irreparable damage to the Serengeti itself and increase wildlife poaching, and this was weighed up against the very real economic need for an improved transport system connecting Arusha to Musoma. As of this writing the highway construction inside the park is on hold; roads outside the park have been paved and those inside kept as gravel.

There is currently a struggle between the Maasai and the government when it comes to demarcating the Loliondo ward of Ngorongoro: A human-wildlife conflict of land classification and indigenous preservation alongside conservation and tourism that is ongoing.

as high as 10%). All budget hotels will accept Tanzanian shillings.

ATMS AND BANKS

There are banks and ATMs in all major cities; you can draw cash directly from an ATM in Dar es Salaam, Arusha, Mwanza, Stone Town in Zanzibar, and Chake Chake on Pemba island; there is one ATM on Mafia island. Most ATMs accept Maestro, Visa Electron, Visa, and MasterCard. The best place to withdraw cash is at an indoor ATM, preferably one guarded by a security officer. Most machines won't let you withdraw more than the equivalent of about $300 at a time. Don't leave withdrawing money to the last minute or late on Friday when everyone gets paid their salaries.

TIPPING

For a two- or three-night stay at a lodge or hotel, tip a couple of dollars for small services and US$5–US$8 per day for room steward and waiter. A good guide should get a tip of US$15–US$25 per day per person; if he's gone out of his way for you, then you may wish to give him more. It's a good idea to carry a number of small-denomination bills. U.S. dollars are acceptable almost everywhere, but if you're planning to go to more remote places, then shillings are preferred.

Restaurants and Food

Food in the lodges is plentiful and tasty, and if you head to the coast, you'll dine on superb seafood and fish with lots of fresh fruit and vegetables. Most places now cater to all food tastes and dietary requirements.

Visitor Information

The Tanzanian Tourist Board (TTB) has offices in Dar es Salaam and Arusha. The tourist board's website is a great online source for pre-trip planning. A great source of inspiration is also online at the various lodges' social media pages.

CONTACTS Tanzania National Parks.
☎ 272/970–408 ⊕ www.tanzaniaparks. go.tz. **Tanzanian Tourist Board.** ✉ Utalii House, Laibon St. at Ali Hassan Mwinyi Rd., near French Embassy, Dar es Salaam ☎ 22/266–4878/9 ⊕ www.tanzaniatourism.go.tz.

When to Go

High season is January through the end of September. Prices are much higher during this time and predator sightings in the parks are best July–September. The warmest and clearest trekking days for Kilimanjaro are from mid-December–February and June–October. This is also the best time to visit Zanzibar, with a 79ºF average temp.

The low season across mainland Tanzania and Zanzibar coincides with two rainy seasons: the short rains (*mvuli*) November through mid-January and the long rains (*masika*) from late February to early May. Given the influence of global warming, these rains aren't as regular or as intense as they once were, but it's best to avoid the heaviest rainy season as many roads become impassable. Some lodges close in April and May. In Kilimanjaro, November–December can be very wet; April and the start of May bring some snow.

Ngorongoro Crater is open all year, but the roads become extremely muddy and difficult to navigate during the wet seasons. There is also the risk of heavy fog that only dissipates in the afternoons.

Make sure you find out in advance when the lodge or destination of your choice is closed as many are open only during the dry season. The coast is always pretty hot and humid, particularly during the rains, but is cooler and more pleasant the rest of the year. The hottest time is December just before the long rains. In high-altitude areas such as Ngorongoro Highlands and Mt. Kilimanjaro, temperatures can fall below freezing.

Serengeti National Park

The very name Serengeti is guaranteed to bring a glint to even the most jaded traveler's eye. It's up there in that wish list of legendary destinations alongside Machu Picchu, Angkor Wat, Kakadu, Killarney, and the Great Pyramid of Giza. But what distinguishes Serengeti from all its competitors is its sheer natural beauty.

Park Ratings

Game: ★ ★ ★ ★ ★

Park Accessibility: ★ ★ ★ ★ ★

Getting Around: ★ ★ ★ ★ ★

Accommodations: ★ ★ ★ ★ ★

Scenic Beauty: ★ ★ ★ ★ ☆

It's 15,000 square km (5,791 square miles) of pristine wilderness and that's it. Its Maasai name *Serenget* means "Endless Plain." A primeval Eden par excellence, named a UNESCO World Heritage Site in 1978 and an International Biosphere Reserve in 1981, the Serengeti is incredibly popular and filled to the brim in high season. Despite its crowds, it's one of those iconic places in the world that manages to inspire a wild sense of adventure.

This ecosystem supports some of the most plentiful mammal populations left anywhere on earth, and the animals here seem bigger, stockier, stronger, and sturdier than elsewhere in Africa. Even the scrub hares are bigger than their southern neighbors, loping rather than scampering over the tussocks and grassy mounds. Hyenas are everywhere and raptors are in perpetual motion—tawny eagles, kestrels, harriers, kites, buzzards, and vultures. Expect to see at least one baby wildebeest that has fallen by the wayside lying alone encircled by patient, voracious vultures or prowling hyenas.

But let's put you right in the picture. You'll probably land at a busy landing strip, maybe near Ntuti, where a dozen open-sided vehicles wait to pick up the new arrivals. In your few days driving around the Serengeti you'll certainly see other vehicles, especially if there's a river crossing occurring (i.e. part of the migration). As you leave the airstrip, your vehicle will weave its way through herds of

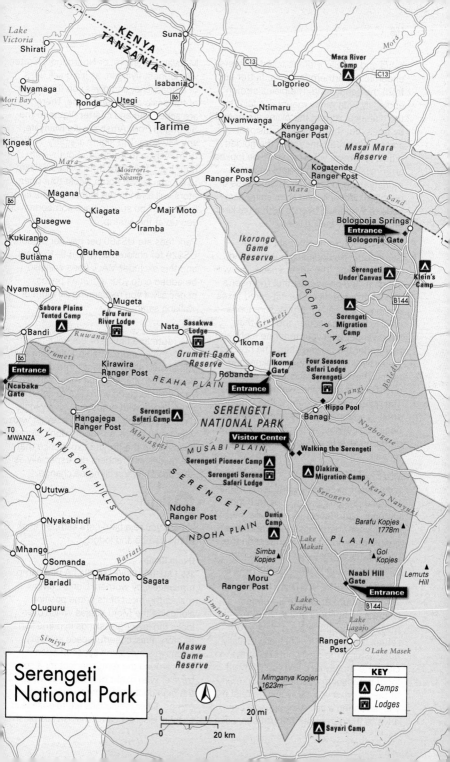

zebra and gazelle. Rufous-tailed weavers, endemic to northern Tanzania, flutter up from the sandy road. The plains stretch endlessly with misty mountains faint in the distance. At first the plains are ringed by trees, but then only an occasional and solitary tree punctuates the golden grass. Wherever you stay, you'll be looked after royally, with comfortable accommodations, good food, a dawn chorus of bubbling birdsong, and an evening serenade of whooping hyenas with a backing group of softly calling lions.

What will you remember about the Serengeti? The unending horizons and limitless plains. The sheer space. The wildebeest. The oh-so-beautiful Thomson's and Grant's gazelles. The bat-eared foxes playing in the early morning sun. Lions galore, and in particular, the one that may wander past your tent one night and roar under the blazing stars. The hosts of water birds by the streams, lakes, and rivers. The flat-top acacia trees, ancient guardians of this windswept wilderness. The quiet. The Big Country. Knowing how small is your place in the interconnectedness of all things. And how privileged you are to be able to experience the wonder of it all.

WHEN TO GO
If you want to see the wildebeest migration and predators, visit June through October. Herd Tacker (⊕ www.discoverafrica.com/herdtracker) is a real-time google map updated by rangers on the ground. It's a great way to monitor the goings-on of the larger migratory herds.

GETTING HERE AND AROUND
The drive from Arusha to Serengeti is about eight hours or 325 km (202 miles). Although there are places to refuel, breakdown facilities are virtually nonexistent. The roads outside of the cities are mostly dirt, and you'll have a lot of potholes to contend with on many of them; a 4x4 vehicle would be best if you're renting a car. Although you can drive to the Serengeti from Arusha, Lake

Manyara, Tarangire, or Ngorongoro Crater, we suggest flying in, as it's quick, less of a headache, and gives you the sense of the scale of the landscape. There are scheduled and charter flights to the Serengeti from Arusha, Lake Manyara, and Mwanza. The flights are daily. A flight from Arusha to Serengeti South is an hour long, the flight from Dar es Salaam to Arusha is two hours. Most tour operators will arrange the flights for you, and lodges will be sure to have someone pick you up at the airstrip.

Park fees are US$60 per day per person, US$20 for children between 5–15 years and this excludes V.A.T. Fees will also be added onto your activities prices, especially if you're planning on night or walking safaris.

TIMING
The route and timing of the wildebeest migration is unpredictable. With that said, you should allow at least three days to be assured of seeing the migration on your visit, longer if you'd like to see more interactions with predators. Always talk directly with the lodges and not just with your travel agent, as agents don't always have the on-the-ground experience that the guides and rangers do, especially as seasons shift and climates change.

Hotels

Unless you're a hard-core camper, stick to the camps and lodges.

Dunia Camp
$$$ | ALL-INCLUSIVE | FAMILY | A rare camp run entirely by women, Dunia Camp makes the most of its prime position alongside the Moru Kopjes which overlooks the lower grasslands in prime lion territory. **Pros:** cheerful space and very attentive service; the sense of openness around the tents; perfect for a solo traveler who might be concerned with the high double occupancy fees of other camps. **Cons:** tsetse flies are relentless in season; discreet camp that isn't as plush

as others (but that's also its appeal); not the traditional safari tent that some might expect. [$] *Rooms from: $938* ✉ *Serengeti National Park* ☎ *21/418–0468* 🌐 *www.asiliaafrica.com* 🛏 *8 tents* 🍴 *All-Inclusive.*

Faru Faru River Lodge

$$$$ | RESORT | Sprawling but intimate, Faru Faru is built in a contemporary style with lots of stone, wood, and sand emphasizing the natural surroundings. **Pros:** the service and personal attention are outstanding; modern and earthy bush decor; relaxing in one of the two horizon swimming pools. **Cons:** no mobile phone service; there can be a bit of a smell at the height of migration when, unfortunately, some animals perish in the river; flights to Grumeti are on the more expensive side. [$] *Rooms from: $2,650* ✉ *Grumeti Reserve, Serengeti National Park* ☎ *21/683–3424* 🌐 *www.singita.com* 🛏 *9 tented suites* 🍴 *All-Inclusive.*

Four Seasons Safari Lodge Serengeti

$$$$ | RESORT | FAMILY | Far from the traditional safari experience, at Four Seasons you'll find five-star amenities uncommon in the bush, such as white-glove service, multiple gourmet dining options, a fitness center, flat-screen TVs, rain showers, Internet, and air-conditioning. **Pros:** breathtaking setting; good option for families and large groups; watch herds of elephants right from the pool. **Cons:** views vary depending on room; this is a Four Seasons safari experience, which works for those who expect just that; not for those wanting intimate, traditional safari luxury. [$] *Rooms from: $1,850* ✉ *Serengeti National Park* ☎ *768/981–981* 🌐 *www.fourseasons.com* 🛏 *77 rooms* 🍴 *Free Breakfast.*

Klein's Camp

$$$$ | RESORT | Built on the crest of the Kuka Hills with 360-degree panoramic views over the Grumeti River valley, this lovely intimate camp prides itself on good service and quality game-viewing along the river. **Pros:** great service and attention to detail; stunning views from your cottage verandah; a more private and intimate atmosphere. **Cons:** time the migration, which is tricky, if you want to see it from the concession; airstrip is an hour's drive, but some may love the additional "safari"; Northern Serengeti is a good three hours' drive away. [$] *Rooms from: $850* ✉ *Serengeti National Park* ☎ *11/809–4300 South Africa* 🌐 *www.andbeyond.com* 🛏 *10 cottages* 🍴 *All-Inclusive.*

Mara River Camp

$$$$ | RESORT | Considered one of the top properties in the Northern Serengeti, the luxurious Mara River Camp has spectacular views over its namesake river and a funky, bohemian, and oh-so-chic style. **Pros:** modern, African-inspired natural beauty of the camp; exquisite views; great food and fantastic, attentive service. **Cons:** when the migration is in full swing there can be quite a smell emanating from the river due to the massive amounts of wildebeest in the area; not a traditional safari experience, but that's the allure for some; the price tag might deter anyone but the most discerning. [$] *Rooms from: $2,650* ✉ *Singita Lami, Serengeti National Park* ☎ *21/683–3424* 🌐 *www.singita.com* 🕒 *Closed Mar. and Apr.* 🛏 *8 tents* 🍴 *All-Inclusive.*

Olakira Migration Camp

$$$$ | RESORT | Light, delicate linens, fantastic dining, and touches of romantic Africa scattered all around the campsite make Olakira one of the finest mobile camps in the Serengeti. **Pros:** open-sided vehicles with exceptional guides; fantastic locations, including one near the river for crossings; spacious and stylish tents. **Cons:** no credit card payments in the south camp; group dinners might not be for everyone; there might be an odor when the migration crossing is at its peak. [$] *Rooms from: $842* ✉ *Serengeti National Park* ☎ *21/418–0468 South Africa* 🌐 *www.asiliaafrica.com* 🕒 *Closed Apr.–May* 🛏 *9 tents* 🍴 *All-Inclusive.*

Sabora Plains Tented Camp

$$$$ | RESORT | It's not often that you'll stay in a marquee-shaped tent elegantly furnished with silk curtains, antique furniture, stylish African artifacts, and a/c, but that's what you'll get at this ultra luxurious camp set among green lawns adjacent to the Great Migration route. **Pros:** wide, open spaces; gorgeous details in the tent furnishings; the little "guest deli" inside the rooms. **Cons:** modern amenities, like a gym tent, which might deter those wanting only a bush experience; not suited for families with children under 12. $ *Rooms from: $2,500* ✉ *Grumeti Game Reserve, Serengeti National Park* ☎ *21/683–3432* ⊕ *www.singita.com* ⊷ *9 tents* ❙⊙❙ *All-Inclusive.*

Sasakwa Lodge

$$$$ | RESORT | Located in the Grumeti Reserve, a 350,000-acre concession in Serengeti's western corridor, this superlative lodge is built in the style of a glamorous 1920s East African farm ranch. **Pros:** wonderful views of the Serengeti plains; your every need will be taken care of; being on a private reserve there are fewer crowds. **Cons:** luxury and privacy comes with a hefty price tag; equestrian center isn't always open; the lodge is quite formal, but many may think that is a pro. $ *Rooms from: $2,900* ✉ *Grumeti Reserves* ☎ *21/683–3424 South Africa* ⊕ *www.singita.com* ⊷ *9 suites, 1 villa* ❙⊙❙ *All-Inclusive* ☞ *wildlife, park, concession tourism development fees will added to your final bill.*

Sayari Camp

$$$$ | RESORT | Overlooking the Mara River in Serengeti's northwest, where the park borders Kenya's Masai Mara National Park, this mid-size tented camp is perfectly poised for watching the river crossing when in season—hundreds of thousands of wildebeest plunge into the crocodile-infested water on their relentless journey north. **Pros:** great location near the famous Lamai wedge; off-road driving is allowed on game drives

in certain areas; indulge in Tanzania's first mobile micro brewery after a day out. **Cons:** be prepared to fend off tsetse flies; it gets quite crowded in the area during peak season; as there are few trees on the plains you can see the other tents from your own. $ *Rooms from: $1,470* ✉ *Serengeti National Park* ☎ *21/418–0468 South Africa* ⊕ *www.asiliaafrica.com* ⊙ *Closed Apr.–May* ⊷ *15 tents* ❙⊙❙ *Free Breakfast.*

Serengeti Migration Camp

$$$$ | RESORT | Found in northeast Serengeti among the rocky Ndasiata Hills, it's hard to believe that the accommodation is actually tented because it looks so luxurious. **Pros:** 360-degree wooden deck veranda; walks along the Grumeti River; professional and attentive service. **Cons:** lots of steps may be a problem for people with mobility issues; slightly larger than other camps; camp is about a three-hour trip from central Serengeti. $ *Rooms from: $1,548* ✉ *Serengeti National Park* ☎ *730/127–000* ⊕ *www.elewanacollection.com* ⊷ *20 tented rooms* ❙⊙❙ *Free Breakfast* ☞ *min two night stay in high season.*

Serengeti Pioneer Camp

$$$ | ALL-INCLUSIVE | Perched like a crow nest up in the hills overlooking the Moru Kopjes, the plush lodge showcases the expansive grasslands of the Serengeti, while the tents are generously dotted throughout a tranquil forest along the hillside; a large family tent option caters to those looking for a special family safari experience. **Pros:** small plunge pools to cool off in after a dusty day adventuring; exquisite food and guiding; camp location is intimate and romantically inviting. **Cons:** wildlife (big cats) will be close, so steel your nerves at night; game vehicles are not the traditional open sides (but it helps with the tsetse flies); steep steps to get to the main lounge area. $ *Rooms from: $1,349* ✉ *Serengeti National Park* ☎ *784/250–630* ⊕ *www.elewanacollection.com* ⊷ *12 tents* ❙⊙❙ *All-Inclusive.*

The lake in the Ngorongoro Crater is a meeting place for flamingos, zebras, and wildebeests.

Serengeti Safari Camp
$$$$ | **ALL-INCLUSIVE** | This Nomad camp delivers a classic mobile safari camp experience that does not compromise on comfort and quality. **Pros:** the ethos of sustainable tourism drives their staffs work ethic and it shows in the best way; evenings spent fireside surrounded by the grass plains; off the beaten track so you won't be running into other vehicles. **Cons:** very remote locations; timing the migration is important to avoid disappointment; tents can get rather hot in summer (there are no fans or a/c). [$] *Rooms from: $1,042* ✉ *Grumeti Reserves* ☎ *787/595–908* 🌐 *www.nomad-tanzania.com* 🛏 *6 tents* 🍴 *All-Inclusive.*

Serengeti Serena Safari Lodge
$$$ | **RESORT** | Situated high on a hill with superb views over the central Serengeti, the two-story thatch cottages are shaped like Maasai huts and are set among indigenous trees. **Pros:** there are great views of the Serengeti from the lodge; the expanse of open plains make it ideal for hot air ballooning; wildlife often wanders around the lodge. **Cons:** all food is buffet-style so when the hotel is full you may have to wait in line; beware of tsetse flies; larger hotel style and rooms are dated. [$] *Rooms from: $421* ✉ *Serengeti National Park* ☎ *272/545–555* 🌐 *www.serenahotels.com* 🛏 *66 rooms* 🍴 *Free Breakfast.*

★ **Serengeti Under Canvas**
$$$$ | **RESORT** | This mobile camp, in the southern part of the Serengeti, follows the migration (usually in March) from an acacia-covered bluff that overlooks a small river. **Pros:** an authentic, luxury safari experience; up close wildlife experiences; friendly, attentive guides and staff. **Cons:** "mobile" means no guarantee being in the thick of the migration; the proximity to wildlife might unnerve some people, especially at night; bucket showers might not be to everyone's taste, but it is part of the experience. [$] *Rooms from: $845* ✉ *Serengeti National Park* ☎ *11/809–4300* 🌐 *www.andbeyond.com* 💳 *No credit cards* 🛏 *9 tents* 🍴 *All-Inclusive.*

Ngorongoro Conservation Area

Game: ★ ★ ★ ★ ★

Park Accessibility: ★ ★ ★ ★ ★

Getting Around: ★ ★ ★ ☆ ☆

Accommodations: ★ ★ ★ ★ ★

Scenic Beauty: ★ ★ ★ ★ ☆

Ngorongoro Crater ranks right up there among Africa's must-visit wildlife destinations: Serengeti, Masai Mara, Etosha, Kruger Park, and the Okavango Delta. One of only three UNESCO World Heritage Sites in Tanzania (together with the Serengeti and the Nyerere National Park), the Crater is often called the Eighth Wonder of the World.

It lies in the Biosphere Reserve of the Ngorongoro Conservation Area, which covers 8,300 square km (3,204 square miles) in northern Tanzania. This reserve was specifically planned to accommodate both the traditional Maasai communities and tourists. You'll see Maasai villagers grazing their sheep and cattle all over.

The Ngorongoro Crater lies in a cluster of other volcanoes (sometimes seen rather ominously smoking) that borders the Serengeti National Park to the north and west. It's actually a collapsed volcano or caldera. The original volcano, which may have been higher than Kilimanjaro, collapsed in on itself over time and now forms a perfect basin. Once inside you'll feel like you're at the bottom of a deep soup bowl with very steep sides. The basin, measuring 18 km (11 miles) in diameter, lies 500 meters (1,640 feet) below the rim, which towers above it at about 2,200 meters (7,217 feet) above sea level.

Believed to have formed some 2 million years ago, the Crater harbors an astonishing variety of landscapes—forests, peaks, craters, valleys, rivers, lakes, and plains—including the world-famous Olduvai Gorge, where some of our earliest human ancestors once hunted and gathered.

The very steep and bumpy drive into the Crater begins high up in the forest. The only downside you might face is the sheer number of safari vehicles that all clamber into the Crater at opening hours, creating often dusty drives through the Crater itself. But once you have left the masses behind, the charm of this site slowly leaves you in awe. Although this lush highland forest looks exactly like a rain forest, it's not. It's a *mist* forest, which depends on a regular and abundant amount of mist and drizzle. If you look closely enough, you'll see particles of mist swirling like raindrops among the ancient trees. The aptly named pillarwood trees stand sentinel over the strangler figs, the croton trees, the highland *bersama* (a local evergreen), and purple wild tobacco flowers. The tree trunks and branches are home to thousands of epiphytes—specialized plants such as arboreal orchids and ferns—which cling to their hosts and absorb moisture with their own aerial roots. Look for the orchids among the curtains of Old Man's Beard, or hanging tree moss.

Monkeys, bushbuck, bush pigs, and elephants frequent the forest, although it's unlikely you'll see them. What you'll see if you're staying in one of the Crater lodges are well-mown lawns, which aren't the result of hardworking gardeners but that of zebras and buffaloes, which after dark seek sanctuary from predators here. It's not dogs you hear barking after sundown but the warning calls of vigilant zebras and baboons. The Crater floor, dominated by a huge flamingo-filled alkaline lake, holds the highest concentration of predators in the world—lions, hyenas, jackals,

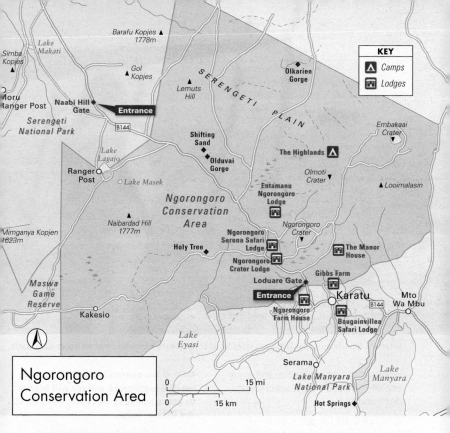

Ngorongoro
Conservation Area

and leopards. Cheetahs can occasionally be seen but fall prey to lions and hyenas, which the nervous and fragile cheetah is no match for. Big herds of plains game such as Thomson's and Grant's gazelles, impalas, giraffes, zebras, and wildebeests are easy meat for the thoroughly spoiled predators that need to expend very little energy to score a megameal. You'll probably see at least one pride of bloated lions lying on their backs, paws in air, stuffed and totally damaging their noble image as the King of Beasts. Make sure to ask your guide to point out a black or white rhino if he spots one. This is also a great place to take a boat safari down one of the hippo-dense rivers.

Birdlife is also spectacular, with some endemic species: the Rufous-tailed weaver, Schalow's wheatear, and large flocks of the incredibly beautiful crowned cranes. Because this is a continuous killing ground, you'll quickly become a vulture expert. If you're a birder, ask for a guide who knows his birds well, because not all the guides do.

WHEN TO GO

Avoid April and May as these months are particularly wet in the Crater. Because there's no restriction on the number of vehicles, there can be far more than a hundred at one time in the high season (January to the end of September). It's amazing to have a close-up encounter with some of Africa's finest game, but not if you're surrounded by other vehicles and often very noisy, boisterous tourists. It's best to go down as early as possible (the gates open at 6 am) but be aware that many others might have the same plan. Regardless, the Crater is a once-in-a-lifetime experience so grit your teeth,

Entamanu Ngorongoro Lodge is the only lodge found on the remote northwest rim of the Ngorongoro Crater.

ignore all the other tourists, and enjoy one of the world's most spectacular destinations.

GETTING HERE AND AROUND

Ngorongoro is about 180 km (112 miles) from Arusha by road. You can also fly into the Crater rim airstrip or Ndutu Lodge airstrip. Tour operators can arrange your transfer in advance.

VISITOR INFORMATION

Entrance fees are US$60 per person, and US$250 for a car per 24-hour period, excluding V.A.T., to enter the Ngorongoro Conservation Area. These fees, as well as fees for activities inside the Crater—meals, walking safaris, etc.—should be included with your group tour or accommodation-arranged safari. If you're doing a self-drive, you'll need to pay for everything at either the tourism office in Ngorongoro, Lodare gate entrance, or at the tourism board office in Arusha. You will receive a Ngorongoro card, which you present as you enter the crater entrance.

TIP→ You can pay in both USD and Tsh, but USD is preferred, and you will need to be accompanied by a licensed guide for this and Olduvai Gorge.

When packing, plan ahead for thick early-morning mist all year round, which makes it quite chilly. Be sure to pack warm clothes.

Hotels on the Crater Rim

★ Entamanu Ngorongoro Lodge

$$$$ | ALL-INCLUSIVE | Nestled high on the northwest rim of the Ngorongoro Crater, the Entamanu Lodge is found under a shady canopy of Acacia trees; it's the only lodge found on this more remote corner of the crater rim. **Pros:** massive tents with expansive, private views of the highlands; unbelievably comfortable beds and linens; food and service is of a high standard. **Cons:** a bit windy in season (you get use to it); a long drive to the lodge from the entrance (consider it a bonus safari); tsetse flies can be a bother in summer season. [$] *Rooms from: $650*

The Cradle of Humankind

If you have a great interest in evolution and human origins, Olduvai Gorge, a UNESCO World Heritage Site, is a definite must. It's about a 90-minute drive from the Ngorongoro Crater. The gorge, about 48 km (30 miles) long, is part of the Great Rift Valley, which stretches along East Africa. It has played a key role in palaeoanthropologists' understanding of the history of humanity by providing clues dating from about 2.5 million years ago. There's a museum and a fabulous lookout point with lots of information about the area.

Locals actually call Olduvai "Oldupai," which is the Maasai name for a sisal plant, *Sansevieria ehrenbergii*, which grows all over the area. The view overlooking the gorge is spectacular, but be aware that visitors aren't allowed to visit the gorge itself. If you're short on time, it may not be worth your while as it is a bit of a drive outside of the park. However, if you can get there, it will be worth it.

Archaeological rock stars like the Leakey family have made some of these important discoveries:

- *Paranthropus boisei* dates back 2.5 million years. These hominids had massive jaws and large, thickly enameled molars suitable for crushing tough vegetation. Their bite was several times more powerful than that of modern humans.

- The first specimens of *Homo habilis* lived about 2 million to 1.6 million years ago. This is the earliest known named species of the Homo genus. Scientists believe that *Homo habilis* was one of the first hominid species that could make and use stone tools, enhancing our ancestors' adaptability and chances of long-term survival.

- The world's oldest stone tools date about 2 million years old and are very primitive—basically just crude tools fashioned from pebbles.

✉ *Ngorongoro Crater* ☎ *787/595–908* 🌐 *www.nomad-tanzania.com* 🛏 *6 tents* 🍴 *All-Inclusive.*

★ **Ngorongoro Crater Lodge**

$$$$ | **RESORT** | Imagine walking into a Hollywood film set where the spectacular setting is literally "Great Zimbabwe ruins meets RMS *Titanic* baroque." Clusters of stilted rooms with woven conical banana-leaf domes and fancifully carved stone chimneys cling to the Crater's rim and somehow blend in with the natural surroundings. **Pros:** spectacular views over the Crater; unique rooms with views in every direction; expensive but service is exceptional. **Cons:** high altitude means it's not easy to walk uphill; it gets incredibly cold here in the mornings, bring warm clothes; Crater can be jam-packed with vehicles in peak season. [$] *Rooms from: $1,950* ✉ *Ngorongoro Crater* ☎ *11/809–4300 in South Africa* 🌐 *www.andbeyond.com* 🛏 *30 suites* 🍴 *All-Inclusive.*

Ngorongoro Serena Safari Lodge

$$$$ | **RESORT** | **FAMILY** | Emerging from the natural surroundings and indigenous vines of the western rim of the Ngorongoro Crater, the Serena Safari Lodge is home to one of the most famous views this side of the Mara River. **Pros:** amazing views of the Crater rim from each room; close to Crater entrance; romantic fireplace nooks to cozy up and admire the views. **Cons:** outdoor lounge areas can feel a bit dated; there are a lot of stairs across the lodge; common areas can get crowded when the lodge is full. $ *Rooms from: $602* ✉ *Ngorongoro Crater* ☎ *272/545–555* ⊕ *www.serenahotels. com* ➴ *75 rooms* ❍❘ *Free Breakfast.*

Hotels in the Ngorongoro Conservation Area

Bougainvillea Safari Lodge

$ | RESORT | As a budget-friendly option either at the start or end of your safari, the Bougainvillea, halfway between Ngrorongoro Crater and Lake Manyana, is a great option. **Pros:** fantastic budget option; big swimming pool; food is decent and plentiful. **Cons:** Wi-Fi is spotty; service can be slow, glacial even; main bar and restaurant can be a bit dark. $ *Rooms from: $235* ✉ *342 karatu, Karatu Town, Ngorongoro Conservation* ☎ *27/253–4083* ⊕ *www.bougainvillea-group.com* ➴ *32 cottages* ❍❘ *No Meals.*

Gibbs Farm

$$$$ | RESORT | With the feel of an English country house, this working organic coffee farm sits midway between Lake Manyara and the Ngorongoro Crater. **Pros:** the farm tour and campfire story evenings are a must; rooms are spacious and uniquely decorated; the horizon swimming pool is exceptional. **Cons:** food can be a bit lackluster considering the location; it's a working farm, so bear in mind there are farm smells around some of the rooms; a rather bumpy hour-long ride out to the Crater. $ *Rooms from: $1103* ✉ *Ngorongoro Crater* ☎ *272/970–436* ⊕ *www.gibbsfarm.com* ➴ *20 cottages* ❍❘ *All-Inclusive.*

★ The Highlands

$$$$ | ALL-INCLUSIVE | North of the Ngorongoro Crater, situated along the forested slopes of the Olmoti volcano, sits The Highlands, a low-impact high-luxury camp that overlooks the valley below. **Pros:** breathtaking views in a unique, remote setting; rooms unlike anything on the safari circuit; the guides and camp staff

go above and beyond. **Cons:** lower suites are a problem for those with mobility issues; 45-minute drive from the Crater; rooms can get quite chilly in the early morning if the fire goes out. $ *Rooms from: $846* ✉ *Ngorongoro Conservation* ☎ *736/500–515* ⊕ *www.asiliaafrica.com* ➴ *8 suites* ❍❘ *All-Inclusive.*

The Manor House

$$$$ | RESORT | FAMILY | A charming mix of Afro-European Architecture from a bygone era greets you after a bumpy, dusty drive from the Crater. **Pros:** bliss for families, friends and groups; glorious vegetables served up from the lodge farm; plenty of activities like horse riding, billiards, a movie theater, and hiking trails. **Cons:** chilly in the evenings, bring something warm; space and luxury comes at a price; 90-minute drive from the Crater on winding, bumpy roads. $ *Rooms from: $1,314* ✉ *Ngorongoro Crater* ☎ *784/250–630* ⊕ *www.elewan-acollection.com* ➴ *20 cottages* ❍❘ *Free Breakfast.*

Ngorongoro Farm House

$$ | HOTEL | Scattered through the winding pathways of a 750-acre coffee plantation that was once owned by a 19th-century German settler are a series of thatched cottages nestled around a generous main farmhouse. **Pros:** working farm with walking tours and coffee-making experience; garden-fresh produce used in the cooking; beautiful, rustic setting with plenty of activities. **Cons:** slightly large and impersonal dining and lounge areas; some rooms are far distances from main lodge for those with mobility issues; rooms can be very dim and dark. $ *Rooms from: $420* ✉ *Oljoro Road, Ngorongoro Crater* ☎ *785/069–944* ⊕ *www.twctanzania.com* ➴ *52 chalets* ❍❘ *Free Breakfast.*

A working organic coffee farm, Gibbs Farm is reminiscent of an English country house.

Lake Manyara National Park

In the Great Rift Valley south of Serengeti and the Ngorongoro Crater lies the Cinderella of Tanzania's parks—the once overlooked and underrated Lake Manyara National Park. When Ernest Hemingway faced the rust-red rocks of the almost 2,000-foot-high rift valley escarpment that dominates the park, he called it "the loveliest place I have seen in Africa."

Lake Manyara National Park stretches some 330 square km (127 square miles) along the base of the escarpment with two-thirds of its surface taken up by shallow, alkaline Lake Manyara. This serene lake is one of the so-called Rift Lakes, which stretch like jewels along the floor of the Rift Valley.

The park may be small, but what it lacks in size it makes up for in diversity. Its range of ecosystems at different elevations makes for dramatic differences in

scenery. At one moment you're traveling through a fairy-tale forest of tumbling, crystal-clear streams, waterfalls, rivers, and ancient trees; the next you're bumping over flat, grassy plains that edge the usually unruffled lake, pink with hundreds of flamingos. Situated near the park gate, Tanzania's first Tree Top Walkway ($20) opened in 2017. The 1,312-foot walkway takes guests through a series of suspension bridges that weave their way through the forest canopy (60 feet in the air) giving guests a bird's-eye view of the area's fauna and flora.

In the deep forest where old tuskers still roam, blue monkeys swing among huge fig and tamarind trees, giant baobabs, and mahoganies, using their long tail as an extra limb. They've got orange eyes, roman noses, and wistful expressions. In the evenings as motes of dusty sunlight dance in the setting sun, there's an excellent chance of spotting troops of more than 300 olive baboons (better looking and furrier than their chacma cousins) sitting in the road, grooming each other, chatting, and dozing, while dozens of naughty babies play around them and old granddaddies look on with knowing eyes.

The thick, tangled evergreen forest eventually gives way to woodlands with tall, flat-top acacias and fever trees, and finally to open plains where hundreds of elephants, buffalo, and antelope roam, accompanied by Masai giraffes so dark they look as if they've been dipped in chocolate. This is a great place to see hippos at close hand as they lie on the banks of the lake, or as they begin to forage as dusk approaches. The park is known for its tree-climbing lions, which are rare to see, but you can be sure if one vehicle glimpses them then the "bush telegraph" (ranger walkie-talkie chatter) will quickly reach your truck, too. No one really knows why they climb and roost in trees, but it's been suggested by one former warden of the park that this unusual behavior probably started during a fly epidemic when the cats climbed high to escape the swarms of biting flies on the ground. He suggests that the present ongoing behavior is now part of their collective memory.

If you're a birder then put this park on your must-visit list. Because of the great variety of habitats, there's a great variety of birds; more than 400 species have been recorded. As you drive through the forest you'll hear the silvery-cheeked hornbills long before you see them flapping noisily in small groups among the massive trees, braying loudly as they fly. The edges of the lake as well as its placid surface attract all manner of water birds large and small. Along the reed-fringed lakeshore you'll see huge pink clouds drifting to and fro. These "clouds" are flocks of flamingos. White-backed pelicans paddle through the water as the ubiquitous African fish eagles soar overhead. Other water birds of all kinds congregate—waders, ducks, geese, storks, spoonbills, egrets, and herons. In the thickets at the base of the red

Park Ratings

Game: ★ ★ ★ ☆ ☆
Park Accessibility: ★ ★ ★ ★ ★
Getting Around: ★ ★ ★ ☆ ☆
Accommodations: ★ ★ ★ ☆ ☆
Scenic Beauty: ★ ★ ★ ★ ☆

escarpment overlooking the lake, which angles up dramatically at 90 degrees, watch out for Nubian woodpeckers, the very pretty and aptly named silver birds (flycatchers), superb, ashy, and Hildebrand's starlings, yellow wagtails, trilling cisticolas, red-cheeked cordon bleus, Peter's twinspots, bluenecked mousebirds, and every cuckoo imaginable. The red-and-yellow barbet is known as the "bed-and-breakfast bird" for its habit of living where it eats—in termite mounds. The park is also a raptor's paradise, where you can spot up to 51 daytime species, including dozens of augur buzzards, small hawks, and harriers. Deep in the forest you might be lucky enough to see Africa's most powerful eagle, the crowned eagle, which is strong enough to carry off young antelope, unwary baboons, and monkeys. At night listen for up to six different kinds of owls, including the giant eagle owl and the diminutive but very vocal African Scops owl.

WHEN TO GO
During the dry season (June–October), it's easier to see the larger mammals and track their movements because there's less foliage. The wet season (November–April) is a great time for bird-watching, glimpsing amazing waterfalls, and canoeing.

GETTING HERE AND AROUND
You can get here by road, charter, or scheduled flights from Arusha, or en route to Serengeti and Ngorongoro Crater. The entrance gate to Lake Manyara

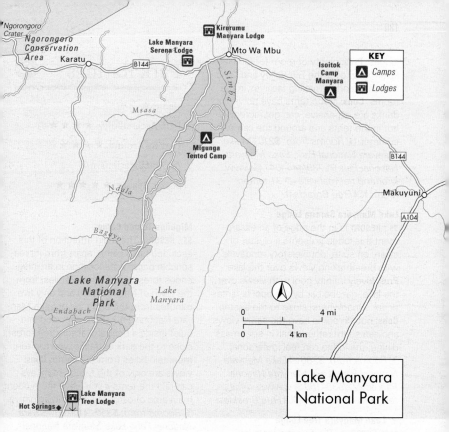

KEY

▲	Camps
🏨	Lodges

Lake Manyara National Park

National Park lies 2 hours or 126 km (80 miles) west of Arusha along a good tar road. There are daily flights that are 20 minutes from Arusha. Your safari operator or lodge can help you organize your transfers.

VISITOR INFORMATION

Entry fees for Lake Manyara National Park are US$50 per person. You can get a decent map and a bird checklist at the park's headquarters at the gate as you drive in from Mto wa Mbu.

📷 **TIP→ You can pay in both USD and Tsh, but USD is preferred.**

🏨 Hotels

★ Isoitok Camp Manyara

$ | RESORT | FAMILY | In the morning when the Maasai head out of their bomas along the Losimingorti mountain range, you'll hear the gentle clanking of their cattle's bells from your accommodations at this very authentic camp. **Pros:** staff are wonderful and food is plentiful and excellent; well-positioned camp with beautiful views towards the Rift Valley; great community and ecologically sensitive camp policy. **Cons:** keep the tent zipped to avoid evening mosquitoes; an ever-so-slightly-bumpy ride from the main road; rustic tents positioned at the back of the camp have partial views. 💲 *Rooms from: $215 ✉ Lake Manyara National Park, Lake Manyara National Park ☎ 739/503–700 ⊕ www.isoitok.com ⊟ No credit cards ⬌ 8 tents ⦿ All-Inclusive.*

Kirurumu Manyara Lodge

$ | RESORT | This intimate camp is set among indigenous bush high on the escarpment and will make you feel much closer to Africa than some of the bigger lodges. **Pros:** plenty of room for families; lovely view over the Rift Valley and Lake Manyara; coffee-making facilities in the rooms. **Cons:** some tents have no views; drinks are expensive; can get incredibly hot in the tents and around the camp in summer. [$] *Rooms from: $210* ✉ *Lake Manyara National Park, Lake Manyara National Park* ☎ *739/444–041* 🌐 *www.kirurumu.net/manyara* 🛏 *31 tented rooms* 🍴 *Free Breakfast.*

Lake Manyara Serena Lodge
$$ | **RESORT** | On the edge of an escarpment this lodge presents a cluster of clean, en suite, double-story rondavels with breathtaking views over the lake. **Pros:** lovely infinity pool with views over the lake; gazebo bar by the pool is fantastic for sundowners; close to the airstrip. **Cons:** not all rooms have the same views and can seem rather small in size; mass dining; the lodge can feel impersonal. [$] *Rooms from: $260* ✉ *Lake Manyara National Park, Lake Manyara National Park* ☎ *272/539–160* 🌐 *www.serenahotels.com* 🛏 *67 rooms* 🍴 *Free Breakfast.*

★ **Lake Manyara Tree Lodge**
$$$$ | **RESORT** | The forest-floor-level entrance is flanked by an array of upturned wooden canoes that guests pass before climbing up to the main areas built under ancient branches heavy with flowers. **Pros:** charming, luxury rooms high in the trees; undisturbed, quiet southern location; the ride from (and to) the airstrip is treated as a game drive so keep your eyes open. **Cons:** rooms do not have views over the lake; not good for people with mobility issues; located 35 km (22 miles) into the park, which requires a drive on very bumpy and dusty roads. [$] *Rooms from: $1,395* ✉ *Lake Manyara National Park* ☎ *11/809-4300 in South Africa* 🌐 *www.andbeyond.com* 🕓 *Closed Apr.* 🛏 *10 suites* 🍴 *All-Inclusive.*

Park Ratings

Game: ★☆☆☆☆

Park Accessibility: ★★★★☆

Getting Around: ★★★★☆

Accommodations: n/a

Scenic Beauty: ★★★★★

Migunga Tented Camp
$$ | **RESORT** | The main attraction of this secluded bush camp, apart from its reasonable price, is its location in an indigenous forest just 2 km (1.2 miles) from the town of Mto wa Mbu and only five minutes from the entrance of Lake Manyara National Park. **Pros:** secluded and quiet inside a beautiful acacia tree forest; close to the park entrance; you can rent mountain bikes from the camp. **Cons:** views are only of the forest; monkeys can raid the tents if you leave them open; main area of camp is a bit unimaginative. [$] *Rooms from: $350* ✉ *Lake Manyara National Park, Lake Manyara National Park* ☎ *754/324–193* 🌐 *www.moivaro.com* 🛏 *21 tents* 🍴 *Free Breakfast.*

Mount Kilimanjaro

Kilimanjaro, a dormant volcano on the roof of Africa, is one of the closest points in the world to the sun (Chimborazo in the Andes is the closest). It's also the highest peak on the continent and the tallest freestanding mountain in the world. So great is her global attraction that approximately 35,000 people from around the world attempt to reach her mighty summit each year; only 2/3 of those make it to the top.

Kili is also home to a variety of unique species found only along its slopes. Unfortunately, this biodiversity is under

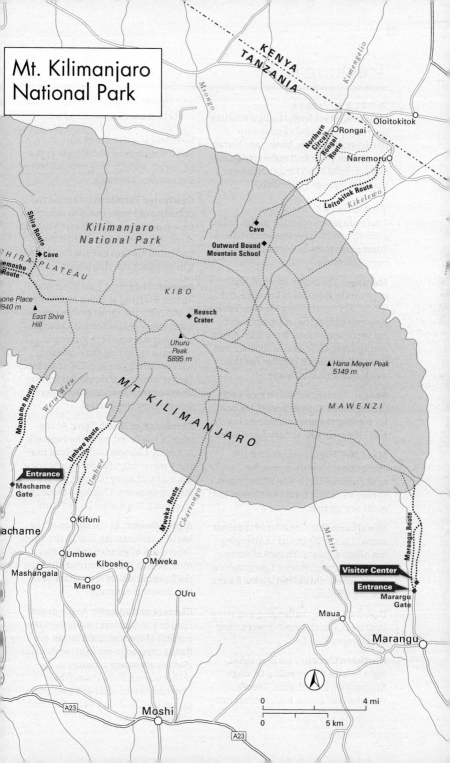

Mt. Kilimanjaro National Park

KENYA
TANZANIA

Msongo

Kimengelio

Oloitokitok

Northern Circuit

Rongai Route

○ Rongai

Naremoru ○

Loitokitok Route

Kikelewo

Kilimanjaro National Park

◆ Cave

Shira Route

CHIRA PLATEAU

◆ Cave

emosho Route

◆ Outward Bound Mountain School

one Place 940 m

▲ East Shire Hill

K I B O

◆ Reusch Crater

▲ Uhuru Peak 5895 m

▲ Hana Meyer Peak 5149 m

M A W E N Z I

M T   K I L I M A N J A R O

Weru Weru

Machame Route

Umbwe Route

Umbwe

Mweka Route

Charrongo

Mshiri

Marangu Route

▶ Entrance
◆ Machame Gate

Machame

○ Kifuni

○ Umbwe

Kibosho

○ Mweka

Mashangala

○ Mango

○ Uru

▶ Visitor Center
▶ Entrance
◆ Marargu Gate

Maua ○

Marangu ○

N

A23

Moshi ○

A23

0   4 mi

0   5 km

Trekking Kili

Where to Start

Most treks start from Moshi, a bustling town at the mountain's base with tourist stalls, tailors, banks, and restaurants. Here you'll find registered guides and accredited trekking companies that will arrange your climb.

The Routes

There are seven common routes to the summit and all have long-drop toilets. Some companies will organize private portable toilets.

Marangu: The oldest, shortest, and most established trek is known as the "Coca-Cola" route due to food and beverages available at the only permanent hut accommodations. Bunk beds, public dining areas, solar-heated showers, and flush toilets make it popular, but the quick ascent trips up many.

Rongai: This easier, but remote, route is close to the Kenyan border. It's best for birding; the drier climate makes the trekking available almost year-round.

Machame: Highly popular for the exceptional views, but best for experienced hikers. The route passes through the rain forest and below the southern ice field.

Shira/Lemosho: Considered the most scenic, this route can be challenging but offers a greater chance of success. It heads through distinct geographical zones: forest, shrubland, alpine desert, and snowfields.

Umbwe: Highly challenging and steep, Umbwe is also the most direct ascent to the summit.

Northern Circuit: This hike takes eight or nine days passing through Kilimanjaro's highlights. There's varied wilderness, a high success rate, and little foot traffic. It's also the only route to cross the northern face.

Geology and Terrain

You'll encounter five different types of terrain while trying to reach Mount Kilimanjaro's summit.

Cultivated Farmlands: Around the outskirts of Moshi near the mountain base mountain are endless subsistence plantations of maize and bananas, and small villages line the routes up to Kili's various starting points.

Forests: The forest zone is hot and humid. Starting at about 1,798 meters (5,900 feet), the forest reaches up to 2,800 meters (9,186 feet). It's home to numerous small creatures and primates, including the black-and-white colobus monkey. Tall trees reach for the sunlight and colorful flowers like the rare *impatiens kilimanjari* flower cover the ground.

Shrubland or Heath Zone: At the edge of the forest zone, the vegetation suddenly changes to shrubland like the 6-meter-high (20-foot-high) *Erica arborea* and daisy bushes that grow as big as pompoms. This zone extends up to about 3,800 meters (12,467 feet).

Alpine Desert: As the shrubs of the heath zone diminish in size, the alpine desert, full of gnarled volcanic lava rock, begins. Small burrows shelter the hyrax and field mice that live in this desert moonscape.

Glaciers and Summit: As the desert rises to 5,000 meters (16,404 feet), the summit of the mountain looms, her flanks covered in ashen scree. Ancient glaciers are slowly receding as the planet warms. Here among these towering blocks of ice at 5,895 meters (19,340 feet), is Uhuru Peak, the summit of Kilimanjaro.

Kilimanjaro Tips

• Choose an operator that's registered, has registered guides, has porters' interests at heart, and an environmental policy.

• Communicate any health problems to your tour operator when you book.

• Choose your route according to what you want: scenery, challenge, type of accommodation, and size of group.

• Train before you leave—this also helps to "train your brain" that you're heading off for a challenge. Squats, lunges, and lots of hill walking with a pack are essential.

• Read up on altitude sickness and symptoms and take the necessary medication with you. Add a day to get acclimated if possible or consider climbing Mt. Meru first.

• Drink 3–5 liters of water a day. The rule is 1 liter per 1,000 meters (3,280 feet) ascent.

• Take only photos; leave only footprints.

threat as the effects of climate change lead to the disappearance of the infamous snowcapped peaks, which scientists estimate could be gone by 2050.

Rising to an incredible height of 5,895 meters (19,336 feet) above sea level, Mt. Kilimanjaro is a continental icon. She towers over the surrounding Amboseli plains and covers an area of about 750 square km (290 square miles). On a clear day, she can be seen from 150 km (93 miles) away. Thousands attempt to reach Kilimanjaro's highest peak, but only about 64% will officially make the summit, known as Uhuru Peak. Many reach the lower Stella Point at 5,745 meters (18,848 feet) or Gilmans' Point, at 5,681 meters (18,638 feet), which earns them a certificate from the Kilimanjaro Parks Authority.

The origin of the name Kilimanjaro has varying interpretations. Some say it means "Mountain of Greatness," while others believe it to mean "Mountain of Caravans." There's a word in Swahili, *kilima,* which means "top of the hill." An additional claim is that it comes from the word *kilemakyaro,* which, in the Chagga language, means "impossible journey."

Whatever the meaning, the visual image of Kilimanjaro is of a majestic peak.

GETTING HERE
KLM, Ethiopian Air, Rwanda Air and Qatar Airlines fly to Kilimanjaro Airport (JRO); Kenya Airways (often through Precision Air), has daily flights from Nairobi. Local airlines have daily flights from Dar es Salaam. You can also fly direct to Zanzibar from here. Kilimanjaro Airport is located 45 km (28 miles) from Moshi and 50 km (31 miles) from Arusha, and it may be cheaper to fly to Arusha instead, so check before you book. Traveling overland is even cheaper but involves long journeys: a shuttle bus from Nairobi takes five or six hours, and from Dar es Salaam to Arusha or Moshi is seven to eight hours.

HEALTH AND SAFETY
Kilimanjaro is one of the few high peaks in the world that can be climbed without technical gear. Most climbers head up her flanks with the aid of trekking poles, while others abandon their poles for a camera and a zoom lens. However, don't be fooled by the absence of technical gear. Oxygen levels near the summit decrease to about 60% of levels at the

Lions cubs in Nyerere National Park, Tanzania's largest national park.

coast. The simple act of rolling up a sleeping bag can wear you out. Walking and ascending slowly will help your body adapt to the diminished oxygen levels.

TOURS

Nomadic Adventure

ADVENTURE TOURS | Offering great personal service, the Nomadic Adventure crew has climbed the mountain many times themselves and gets involved in the big Kilimanjaro Cleanup, a project that hauls thousands of pounds of waste off the mountain each year. ☏ 31/767–3373 ⊕ www.nomadicadventures.com.

VISITOR INFORMATION

Park fees will cost around US$70 per person per day, with an additional US$20 rescue fee, excluding V.A.T. Make sure these fees are included in your tour company's trekking fees.

WHEN TO GO

The warmest, clearest trekking days run mid-December through February or September and October. June, July, and August are superb trekking months, too,

but evening temperatures tend to be colder. The wettest months are November, early December, and March to the beginning of June, which brings some snow. Daytime temperatures range from 28°C (85°F) to 38°C (100°F) in the forest, but plummet to a frigid −2°C (28°F) to −16°C (3°F) at the summit. Generally, with every 200 meters ascended, the temperature drops one degree.

Nyerere National Park

A true untamed wilderness that covers 50,000 square km (19,305 square miles)—less than 5% of Tanzania—this area is one of Tanzania's seven UNESCO World Heritage Sites. It's also Africa's largest national park and the second-largest in the world. Only Greenland National Park at 972,000 square km (375,398 square miles), which is larger than England and France combined, beats this park.

As of 2022 the portion of the reserve north of the Rufiji River that was open to

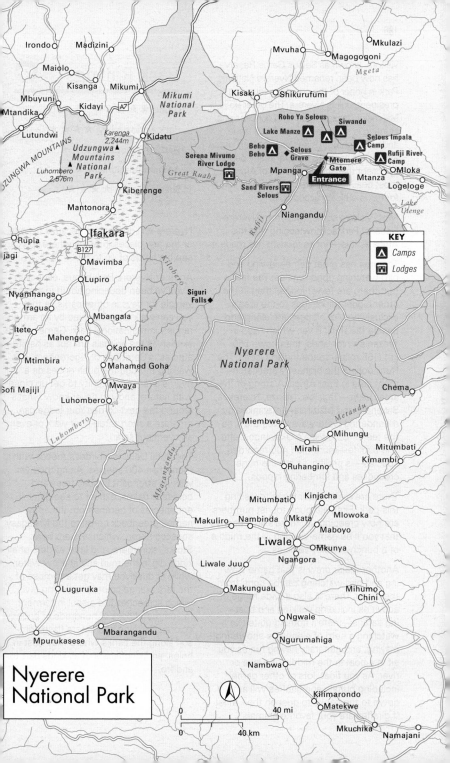

Nyerere
National Park

KEY
Camps
Lodges

Irondo
Madizini
Mkulazi
Maiolo
Mvuha
Magogogoni
Kisanga
Mikumi
Mbuyuni
Kidayi
A7
Kisaki
Shikurufumi
Mtandika
Mikumi
National
Park
Lutundwi
Karenga
2,244m
Kidatu
Roho Ya Selous
Siwandu
Lake Manze
Selous Impala
Camp
Udzungwa
Mountains
National
Park
Luhombero
2,576m
Beho
Beho
Selous
Grave
Rufiji River
Camp
Serena Mivumo
River Lodge
Mtemere
Gate
Mpanga
OMloka
Kiberenge
Great Ruaha
Entrance
Mtanza
Logeloge
Mantonora
Sand Rivers
Selous
Lake
Utenge
Ifakara
Niangandu
Rupia
B127
jagi
Mavimba
Lupiro
Siguri
Falls
Nyamhanga
Iraguao
Nyerere
National Park
Itete
Mbangala
Mahenge
Mtimbira
Kaporoina
Mahamed Goha
Chema
Sofi Majiji
Mwaya
Metandu
Luhombero
Miembwe
Mihungu
Mitumbati
Mirahi
Kimambi
Ruhangino
Mitumbati
Kinjacha
Makuliro
Nambinda
Mkata
Mlowoka
Liwale
Maboyo
Liwale Juu
Mkunya
Ngangora
Luguruka
Makunguau
Mihumo
Chini
Ngwale
Mbarangandu
Ngurumahiga
Mpurukasese
Nambwa
Kilimarondo
Matekwe
Mkuchika
Namajani

0   40 mi
0   40 km

visitors, known as Selous Game Reserve, has now been renamed Nyerere National Park in honor of the countries founding president, Julius Nyerere. The other 95% is still mainly leased to hunting concessions. Hunting is still a very contentious issue, and although both sides passionately argue a plausible case, it's hard for many people to accept that shooting some of Africa's most beautiful and precious animals just for fun is ethically acceptable.

Most visitors come away from Nyerere National Park acknowledging that this is Africa as it is—not as tourism has made it.

The area has great game-viewing and bird-watching opportunities. The fact that there are fewer lodges than in the other bigger parks adds to the area's exclusivity. Most lodges are along and beside the Rufiji River, which rises in Tanzania's highlands, then flows 250 km (155 miles) to the Indian Ocean. The Rufiji boasts the highest water-catchment area in East Africa. A string of five small lakes—Tagalala, Manze, Nzerekea, Siwando, and Mzizimia—interlinked by meandering waterways, gives the area the feel of Botswana's Okavango Delta. The birdlife—more than 400 recorded species—is prolific, as are the huge crocodiles and lumbering hippos.

There are major advantages to visiting this park. First, although tourist numbers are now creeping up, there's little chance that you'll be game-viewing in the middle of a bunch of noisy vehicles.

Another major draw is that game-viewing and bird-watching can be done from the water. There is also a wide range of activities including walking and boating safaris—there's nothing quite like watching a herd of elephants showering, playing, and generally having fun as you sit in a boat in the middle of a lake or river. As you float, lots of other game including buffalo and giraffes will amble down to the banks to quench their thirst. If giraffes are your favorite animals,

Park Ratings

Game: ★★★☆☆

Park Accessibility: ★★★★☆

Getting Around: ★★★★☆

Accommodations: ★★★☆☆

Scenic Beauty: ★★★★☆

Nyerere will delight you because it's one of the few places in Africa where you can see big herds of up to 50.

Another Nyerere Park bonus, especially if you've been bouncing about in a game vehicle for days in other parks, is that you can walk (accompanied by an armed ranger) in the national park. Game can be skittish as the animals are not as habituated as in Serengeti or Ngorongoro, but walking through the bush or beside a river is a rare opportunity to get up close with nature, and you never know what's around the next corner. Your lodge can organize a short three-hour walk or even an overnight safari.

The Rufiji Delta is a birder's mecca with more than 400 species. Along the river with its attendant baobab trees and borassus palms, expect to see different species of herons from the aptly named greenback heron to the Malagasy squacco heron, which winters here. Storks, skimmers, and little waders of all kinds dig in the mud and shallow water, while at dusk you may get a glimpse of the rare orange-color Pel's fishing owl, which screeches like a soul in torment. In summer, flocks of hundreds of brightly colored Carmine bee-eaters flash crimson along the banks where they nest in holes, and kingfishers of all kinds dart to and fro.

Beho Beho in Nyerere National Park is considered by many to be one of East Africa's best safari lodges.

WHEN TO GO

June to October is the best time to visit, as it's the driest. During the long rains from February to May, most of the camps aren't accessible, and many roads are impassable.

There's a good chance of spotting the endangered African wild dog from June to August when the dogs are denning and stay put for a few months north of the Rufiji. The park estimates that it has up to 2000 dogs in several wide-ranging packs (double that of any other African reserve).

GETTING HERE AND AROUND

Driving from Dar es Salaam is possible (the trip takes about four-and-a-half hours), but the best way to get to Nyerere National Park is by charter or scheduled flight from Dar es Salaam or Arusha. Arusha to Nyerere is a three-hour flight, Dar es Salaam to Arusha is a two-hour flight. Your operator or lodge should be able to help you arrange your transportation. ■ TIP→ **Avoid driving between February and April as the road conditions can become very bad because of the rainy season.**

VISITOR INFORMATION

Permits cost US$88.50 per person per day; it's one of the most expensive parks in Tanzania in terms of daily fees (flying or driving) so be aware as this can add up. You can also hire a guide for about US$20 per day if one isn't already provided for you.

■ TIP→ **You can pay in both USD and Tsh, but payment needs to be made to the Tanzanian Parks Authority before you arrive at the gates or you will be turned away.**

Hotels

★ Beho Beho

$$$$ | RESORT | Many safari aficionados consider Beho Beho to be one of the best accommodations in East Africa. **Pros:** private waterhole where wildlife abounds; elegant accommodations and fantastic service; breathtaking elevated and expansive views. **Cons:** vehicles have to be back in the camp at dusk;

The Future of Nyerere National Park

The future of Nyerere National Park is a bit uncertain since the introduction of the Rufiji Hydropower Project, a large industrial complex constructed in the midst of upper Nyerere to divert the Rufiji River. While the greater Nyerere National Park is the only natural World Heritage Site in southern Tanzania and it is on UNESCO'S list of World Heritage Sites, its status as such is under threat as the landscape of the park changes.

Rampant poaching has decimated the elephant and rhino populations with numbers dropping by as much as 90% since 1982. The increase in road traffic due to the dam construction coupled with extensive logging and flooding of 125,00 hectares (308,881 acres) in the reserve has also added to this.

Conservation efforts in Nyerere are desperately trying to stem the tide of poaching. There are also ongoing projects to try to protect and bolster the rhino population inside the park, which is numbering around 2000.

no riverbank or lake views; privacy and exclusivity comes at a cost. $ *Rooms from: $1250* ✉ *Selous Game Reserve* ☎ *01/1932–260–618 in the U.K.* 🌐 *www.behobeho.com* ⏲ *Closed mid-Mar.–June* 🛏 *8 chalets, 1 tree house* 🍴 *All-Inclusive* ☞ *no children under 12; minimum stay 3 nights.*

Lake Manze

$$$$ | RESORT | Manze camp is found in the far eastern section of the reserve in a bountiful game-viewing area—just follow the well-worn elephant trail from the river to a large thatch roof spreading out over the sand floor. **Pros:** great lake-side location; tents are spacious and positioned to make the most of the cooling breeze; boat cruises on the lake are a must. **Cons:** you have to pay for extras with cash; no electricity in the tents, but that is part of the eco charm; not a luxury camp. $ *Rooms from: $675* ✉ *Selous Game Reserve* ☎ *222/601–747* 🌐 *www.ed.co.tz* ⏲ *Closed Apr.–May* 🛏 *12 tents* 🍴 *Free Breakfast.*

★ **Roho Ya Selous**

$$$$ | ALL-INCLUSIVE | Part of the high-end tented camps in the national park, Roho ya Selous is a modern space with minimalist luxury. **Pros:** boating and walking safaris are a must; game viewing is great and there are plenty of activities; large swimming pool with views over the waterways. **Cons:** unique luxury comes at a cost; very open, which takes some getting use to. $ *Rooms from: $1552* ✉ *Selous Game Reserve* ☎ *736/21–418–0468 in South Africa* 🌐 *www.asiliaafrica.com* ⏲ *Closed mid Mar.–May* 🛏 *8 rooms* 🍴 *All-Inclusive.*

Rufiji River Camp

$$$ | RESORT | This camp—the oldest in the reserve—has a great location on a wide bend on the Rufiji at the end of the eastern sector of the reserve. **Pros:** family units have their own private plunge pool and deck; variety of game-viewing options gives you a different perspective of the wildlife and allows you to see a wide variety of animals, large and small; great views from the front of the lodge. **Cons:** simpler style than other camps in the area; activities are at set times; monkeys can be a problem in camp as they try to steal food from tables—don't feed them. $ *Rooms from: $465* ✉ *Selous Game Reserve* ☎ *078/7519–630–007 in the U.K.* 🌐 *www.rufijirivercamp.com* ⏲ *Closed Apr.–May* 🛏 *14 tents*

🍴 *All-Inclusive* ☞ *rates don't include park fees or the concession fee.*

Sand Rivers Selous

$$$$ | **RESORT** | Deep in the southwest corner of Nyerere National Park, this lodge is just about as isolated and exclusive as you can get, but the attentive service and home-away-from-home atmosphere is unlike any other lodge in the park. **Pros:** some of the most comfortable rooms and beds in Nyerere; beautiful riverside views from the decks around the lodge; fly camping is a must here. **Cons:** limited mobile phone reception; the very open rooms might make some nervous, but it's very safe; mischievous monkeys have been known to raid the rooms, so put your belongings safely away. [$] *Rooms from: $1,125* ✉ *Selous Game Reserve* ☎ *763/787–595–908* 🌐 *www.nomad-tanzania.com* 🛏 *8 chalets, 1 family house* 🍴 *Free Breakfast.*

Selous Impala Camp

$$$$ | **RESORT** | **FAMILY** | This attractive camp on Lake Mzizimia's shores nestles among borassus palms and riverine bush with views over the Rufiji. **Pros:** river cruises and the game and prolific birdlife you will see; the staff are delightful and very knowledgeable; the overwhelming "secret surprise sunset". **Cons:** no system for credit card payment as yet; animal sightings are not as prolific as in the north. [$] *Rooms from: $720* ✉ *Selous Game Reserve* ☎ *753/115–908* 🌐 *www.selousimpala.net* 💳 *No credit cards* 🛏 *8 tents* 🍴 *All-Inclusive.*

Serena Mivumo River Lodge

$$$$ | **RESORT** | Set high on a bluff above Tanzania's biggest river, the mighty Rufiji, Mivumo lodge hosts a beautiful location with relaxing river views. **Pros:** fantastic amenities combined with authentic bush experience; boat trips down Rufiji River; incredible location with views. **Cons:** very rough, bumpy roads; abundant game but it does require quite a drive; not the traditional luxury safari tent experience. [$] *Rooms from: $671* ✉ *Selous Game Reserve* ☎ *27/786–999–060* 🌐 *www.serenahotels.com* 🛏 *12 rooms* 🍴 *Free Breakfast.*

★ **Siwandu**

$$$$ | **RESORT** | In the middle of the riverine bush on the banks of Lake Nzerakera, this luxuriously appointed camp has become a real gem in the park. **Pros:** service goes above and beyond and the details make it a standout; beautifully appointed lounges with viewing decks to relax and take in the surroundings; divine boating safari and gourmet lunch on the river. **Cons:** the park is incredibly hot during the summer months; constant animal traffic to the water source can be noisy; the boat trip up the Rufiji River is not available all year round. [$] *Rooms from: $795* ✉ *Selous Game Reserve* ☎ *022/212–8485* 🌐 *www.selous.com* ⏲ *Closed end of Mar.–early June* 🛏 *13 rooms* 🍴 *Free Breakfast.*

Gombe Stream National Park

Bordering Burundi to the west, Tanzania's smallest national park—only 52 square km (20 square miles)—is easily one of the country's loveliest and wildest. It's tucked away on the shores of Africa's longest and deepest lake, Lake Tanganyika, 676 km (420 miles) long and 48 km (30 miles) wide. The lake is a veritable inland sea, the second deepest lake in the world after Russia's Lake Baikal. This small wonderland of a park 3½ km (2 miles) wide and only 15 km (9½ miles) long stretches from the white sandy beaches of the blue lake up into the thick forest and the mountains of the rift escarpment behind.

Though the area is famous for its primates, don't expect Tarzan-like rain forest because the area is mainly covered with thick Brachystegia woodland. There are also strips of riverine bush alongside

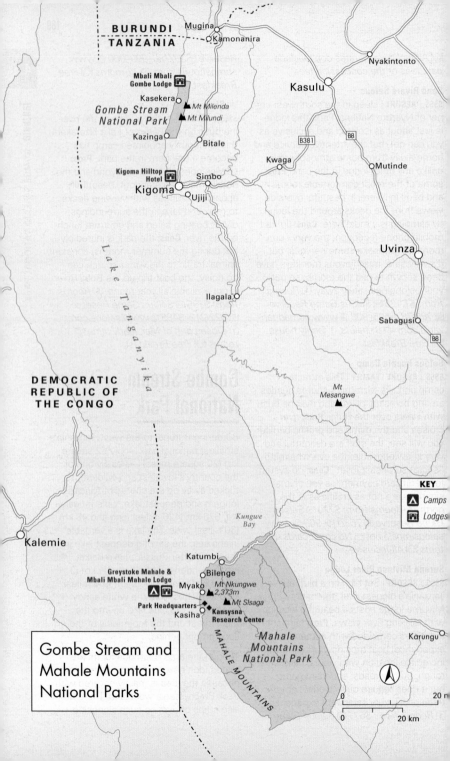

BURUNDI
TANZANIA

Mugina

Kamonanira

Nyakintonto

Mbali Mbali
Gombe Lodge

Kasekera

▲ Mt Milenda
▲ Mt Milundi

*Gombe Stream
National Park*

Kasulu

Kazinga

Bitale

B381

B8

Kwaga

Mutinde

Kigoma Hilltop
Hotel

Simbo

Kigoma

Ujiji

Lake Tanganyika

Uvinza

DEMOCRATIC
REPUBLIC OF
THE CONGO

Ilagala

Sabagusi

B8

▲ *Mt
Mesangwe*

Kalemie

*Kungwe
Bay*

Katumbi

Greystoke Mahale &
Mbali Mbali Mahale Lodge

Bilenge

Myako

▲ *Mt Nkungwe
2,373m*

Park Headquarters

▲ Mt Sisaga

Kasiha

Kansysna
Research Center

*Mahale
Mountains
National Park*

Karungu

MAHALE
MOUNTAINS

Gombe Stream and
Mahale Mountains
National Parks

0   20 m

0   20 km

KEY

▲ Camps

Lodges

the many streams that gouge out steep valleys as they make their way from the highlands to flow down into the lake.

Gombe isn't as easy to get to as other parks, and it's going to cost you, but you'll be amply rewarded with one of the most excitingly close animal encounters still possible on our planet. You'll hear the chimps long before you see them. A series of hoots and shrieks rising to a crescendo of piercing whoops sounds like a major primate battle is about to begin. But it's only the members of the clan identifying one another, recognizing one another, and finally greeting one another.

Gombe became famous when Jane Goodall came to the area in 1960 to study the chimpanzee population. At the time she wasn't known or recognized as the world-renowned primatologist she would later become. Sponsored by the legendary paleontologist Louis Leakey of Olduvai Gorge, Goodall came to Gombe as an eager but unqualified student of chimpanzees. At first many of her amazing unique studies of chimp behavior were discounted because she was a young, unknown scientist. How could a chimpanzee be a hunter and meat-eater? How could a chimpanzee possibly use grass stalks and sticks as tools? Whoever had heard of inter-troop warfare? Today her groundbreaking work is universally acknowledged. Read more about her and her experiences at Gombe in her best-selling book *In the Shadow of Man*. You'll also be able to meet descendants of those chimpanzees she studied and made famous. Fifi, who was only three when Goodall arrived at Gombe in 1960, survived until 2004. Her youngest surviving son, Ferdinand, was alpha male in 2010.

But be warned—to follow in Jane or Fifi's footsteps you need to be fairly fit. Keeping up with a group of feeding and moving chimpanzees as they climb hills and forage in deep valleys can be very strenuous work. But the effort will be worth it—there's nothing on earth quite

Park Ratings

Game: ★ ★ ☆ ☆ ☆

Park Accessibility: ★ ★ ☆ ☆ ☆

Getting Around: ★ ☆ ☆ ☆ ☆

Accommodations: ★ ★ ☆ ☆ ☆

Scenic Beauty: ★ ★ ★ ★ ★

like coming face-to-face with a chimpanzee or accompanying a group as they make their way through the forest.

WHEN TO GO

Trekking can be done throughout the year, but the dry season (May–November) is the best time to see the chimps as they spend more time on the ground. Wet season (October–May) does allow for better photography and usually better vantage points, but can be slippery trekking. No matter the season, there's never a guarantee that you'll spot the chimps. ■TIP→ **Don't go trekking if you have a cold, flu, or any other infectious disease as chimps are highly susceptible to human diseases.**

GETTING HERE AND AROUND

Kigoma is connected to Dar es Salaam, Mwanza, and Arusha by scheduled flights, and to Mwanza, Dar es Salaam, Arusha and Mbeya by rough dirt roads. Kigoma to Dar es Salaam is a three-hour flight; from Kigoma to Arusha is roughly a two-hour flight. The drive from Kigoma to Mwanza is roughly 575 km (357 miles), and the roads are bad. If you go by bus it'll take two days. To get into the park from Kigoma you can arrange a boat transfer (1–2 hours), which can be done with your lodge or with the parks authority; local taxi transfer is possible but it can be a three-hour adventure. The lodge can arrange your travel to and from your destination; talk to your safari operator about getting to and from the camps.

TIMING

Strict rules are in place to safeguard you and the chimps. Allow at least two days to see them—they're in a wild state, so there are no guarantees where they'll be each day. Trekking is done between 6 am and 6:30 pm.

VISITOR INFORMATION

Entry fees for Gombe are US$100 per person per day for a 24-hour period, the highest of any park in Tanzania. Guided walks on Lake Tanganyika will cost US$20 per person. Your guide will cost an additional US$20 per day for both activities.

TIP→ You can pay in both USD and Tsh, but USD is preferred.

Kids under seven aren't permitted to enter either park. Because of the traveling time, it's suggested that you spend at least two nights in either or both of the parks to get the most out of the experience. You can purchase a 24-entry permit with a guide, but it's best to spend a few days.

Hotels

Mbali Mbali Gombe Lodge

$$$$ | RESORT | The only accommodation inside Gombe National Park, the cozy and intimate Forest Lodge sits amid the mopane trees as a series of stand-alone canvas tents raised off the ground on wooden platforms. **Pros:** being in the midst of the park at night; right on the lake shore, this is a birder's paradise; beach-side campfires after a day of chimp trekking. **Cons:** you need to be fit to do any activities in this lodge; property is rustic; it will cost you. [$] *Rooms from: $650* ✉ *Gombe National Park, Mahale Mountains National Park* ☎ *692–700–600* 🌐 *www.mbalimbali.com* 💳 *No credit cards* 🛏 *7 tents* 🍴 *Free Breakfast.*

Kigoma Hilltop Hotel

$$ | HOTEL | On a hill overlooking the lake about 2 km (1.2 miles) from Kigoma's town center, this hotel makes an ideal base for your chimpanzee trekking. **Pros:** lovely view of Lake Tanganyika; a large pool to cool off after trekking; day trips to the park from the hotel. **Cons:** bathrooms are a little dated; boat hire to Gombe Island will be more expensive here than if you go to the Tanap office directly; only the suites have the best views so plan accordingly. [$] *Rooms from: $140* ✉ *Kigoma* ☎ *737/6926–326–59* 🌐 *www.kigomahilltop.com* 🛏 *30 cottages* 🍴 *Free Breakfast.*

Mahale Mountains National Park

Just south of Gombe on the shores of Lake Tanganyika lies Tanzania's most remote, and most astonishingly beautiful, national park. Thirty times bigger than Gombe, Mahale is a stunningly beautiful park with crystal clear streams, soaring forested mountains, and deserted, white sandy beaches. Mt. Nkungwe at 2,460 meters (8,070 feet) dominates the landscape. This is the premier place to spot chimpanzees, with hundreds living in the area; they are more accessible and more regularly seen here than at Gombe.

In 1965 the University of Kyoto in Japan established a permanent chimpanzee research station in Mahale at Kisoge, about a kilometer from the beach. It's still going strong and remains highly respected.

There are no roads in Gombe or Mahale: all your game-viewing and chimpanzee tracking is done on foot. If you're a couch potato, stick with the National Geographic TV channel. What will you see other than chimpanzees? You'll almost certainly see olive baboons, vervet monkeys, red- and blue-tailed colobus monkeys, and some exciting birds. More than 230 bird species have been recorded here, so look out for crowned eagles, the noisy trumpeter hornbills, and the "rasta" birds (the crested guinea fowls with their black punk hairdos). Don't expect to see big game, but do expect to be surrounded by some spectacular scenery and a plethora of activities such as trekking to the peak of Mount Nkungwe or kayaking along the shores of Lake Tanganyika.

WHEN TO GO

The dry season, June through October, is best for spotting the chimps up close, while the wetter months (March to May) make for some muddy trekking. Sightings are almost guaranteed, as chimps are usually spotted within two days of trekking. ■TIP➔ **If you have a cold, flu, or any other infectious disease, strongly consider postponing your trip as chimps are highly susceptible to human diseases, and run the risk of getting very sick**.

VISITOR INFORMATION

Conservation fee for the park is US$80 per person per day (excluding V.A.T.) and ranger fees are US$20 per group.

GETTING HERE AND AROUND

Arrange a charter flight from Arusha, Dar es Salaam, or Kigoma. Flights are around four hours from Arusha; there are two scheduled flights from Arusha every week (no flights in March, April, or the beginning of May). The flight from Dar es Salaam to Arusha is two hours. There's also the National Park motorboat from Kigoma, which will take three to four hours.

 Hotels

★ **Greystoke Mahale**

$$$$ | RESORT | It's difficult to imagine almost anywhere on earth that's as wildly beautiful and remote as this exotic camp on the eastern shore of Lake Tanganyika. **Pros:** the camp gives you the opportunity to watch wild chimpanzees up close and personal; immersed in the very secluded Mahale mountains; relaxing on the shores by the beach bar as the sun sets. **Cons:** long journey to get there;

Park Ratings 👁

Game: ★ ★ ★ ★ ☆

Park Accessibility: ★ ★ ☆ ☆ ☆

Getting Around: ★ ★ ☆ ☆ ☆

Accommodations: ★ ★ ★ ★ ☆

Scenic Beauty: ★ ★ ★ ★ ★

this kind of experience does not come cheap; trekking after the chimps is physically demanding. 💲 *Rooms from: $1,365 ✉ Mahale Mountains National Park, Mahale Mountains National Park ☎ 787/595–908 ⊕ www.nomad-tanzania. com ▭ No credit cards ⊗ Closed April– May ⇆ 6 bandas ⊚ Free Breakfast.*

Mbali Mbali Mahale Lodge

$$$$ | RESORT | On the same stretch of the lakeshore as Greystoke, this lodge is the only other alternative for chimp trekking in Mahale Park. **Pros:** spacious luxury bandas; fantastic lake views from your deck; electrical points in the bandas. **Cons:** watch out for the odd hippo swimming past; cost to get here and stay is high; long travel distances. 💲 *Rooms from: $1,000 ✉ Mahale Mountains National Park, Mahale Mountains National Park ☎ 692/700–600 ⊕ www.mbalimbali. com ▭ No credit cards ⇆ 10 bandas ⊚ All-Inclusive.*

If You Have Time

If you still have time after you've explored our picks for Must-See Parks, put the following national parks on your list, too: Arusha, Tarangire, and Ruaha.

Arusha National Park

Don't overlook the tiny Arusha National Park. Though it covers only 137 square km (58 square miles), it has more to see

Greystoke Mahale is located on the eastern shore of Lake Tanganyika in Mahale Mountains National Park.

than many much larger reserves. You'll find three distinct areas within the park: the forests that surround the Ngurdoto Crater, the brightly colored pools of the Momella Lakes, and the soaring peaks of Mt. Meru. And with the city of Arusha only a 32-km (20-mile) drive to the northeast, it's easy to see the park in a day.

Established in 1960, the park was originally called Ngurdoto Crater National Park, but after the mountain was annexed in 1967 it became known as Mt. Meru National Park. Today it's named for the Warusha people who once lived in this area. The Maasai also lived here, which is why many of the names for sights within the park are Swahili.

WHEN TO GO

To climb Mt. Meru, the best time is between June and February, although it may rain in November. The climb can take up to four days but count on three. The best views of Kilimanjaro are from December through February.

GETTING HERE AND AROUND

Arusha National Park/Mt. Meru/Ngurdoto Crater is a 40-minute drive from Kilimanjaro International Airport. The lakes, forest, and Ngurdoto Crater can all be visited in the course of a half-day visit.

VISITOR INFORMATION

Park fees are US$45, per person, per day.

There are some charming accommodations if you want to spend the night, including the homey Kiota Nest, the quirky and stylish Hatari Lodge, and for something truly unique, the Bedouin-styled camps with a Swahili out-of-Africa twist at Shu'mata Camp.

 Sights

Momella Lakes

OTHER ATTRACTION | Northeast of the Ngurdoto Crater, this series of seven lakes was formed by lava flow from the nearby Mt. Meru. Each body of water has its own distinct color thanks to varying mineral content, which attracts different types of birds—more than 400 species of birds have been spotted in the area. Reedbuck and waterbuck are also common sights near the dirt road and there are numerous observation points along the way for getting a closer look at the flora and fauna. You can also arrange through your safari company to go on a canoe around the smaller portion of the lake. Keep an eye out for the thousands of flamingos that feed on the algae that cover the lake in a pink hue at certain times of the year. ⊠ *Arusha National Park, Momella Lakes, Arusha.*

Mt. Meru

MOUNTAIN | Because it is not as well-known, the slopes of Mt. Meru are blissfully uncrowded.

⚠ **Although Meru looks diminutive along-side Kilimanjaro, do not underestimate what it takes to climb to the top. You must be in good shape, and you need to allow time to acclimatize.**

Climbing Mt. Meru itself takes at least four days when it is dry; during the wet season the tracks can be very slippery and it can take more than four days. Huts along the way sleep 24–48 people, but inquire beforehand whether beds are available. You can arrange for no-frills journeys up the mountain through the park service, or book a luxury package through a travel company that includes porters to carry all your supplies. Either way you'll be accompanied by an armed guard to protect you from unfriendly encounters with elephant or buffalo. The rim of Meru Crater has a breathtaking view of the sheer cliffs rising to the summit. Keep an eye out for a diminutive antelope called the klipspringer. ⊠ *Mt. Meru, Arusha.*

Ngurdoto Forest and Crater

FOREST | After entering the park through the Ngurdoto Gate, you'll pass through the fig, olive, and wild mango trees of the Ngurdoto Forest. Farther along is the Ngurdoto Crater, which is actually a caldera, or collapsed crater. Unlike the nearby Ngorongoro Crater, this caldera

appears to have had two cones. There are no roads into the crater itself, so the buffalo and other animals that make their homes in the swampy habitat remain protected. You can do a day safari around the rim, where you'll find a misty landscape covered with date palms, orchids, and lichens. The grasslands to the west are known as Serengeti Ndogo ("Little Serengeti") and boast a herd of Burchell's zebras, thriving because there are no lions nearby.

■ **TIP →** **Expect traffic during peak season.**

⊠ *Arusha National Park, Arusha.*

🍴 Restaurants

Arusha might just be a stopover city for some, but there is a lot of great food on offer in the town that goes beyond packed safari lunchboxes. For restaurant reviews, see the dining section in Arusha below.

Tarangire National Park

Although this lovely 2,600-square-km (1,004-square-mile) park is an easy drive from Arusha—just 118 km (71 miles) southwest—and adjacent to Lake Manyara, it's continued to be something of a well-kept secret. During the dry season it's part of the migratory movement and is second only to Ngorongoro Crater in concentration of wildlife. Not only does it have the highest concentration of elephants in Tanzania, as well as some of the more spectacular places to photograph baobab trees, but it's also home to the Big Five. The best time to visit is July through October, when thousands of parched animals flock to the waterholes and thousands more make their long way to the permanent water of the Tarangire River.

Staying within the park is quite an experience, especially in the plush safari-chic surrounds of Sanctuary Swala Camp or in the authentically styled Oliver Camp. Views from Maramboi Tented camp over the rift escarpment can't be beat and Chem Chem boasts a memorable stay, but at the top of the pack is by far the treetop experience of Tarangire Treetops, with its expansive rooms and wraparound balconies with views of the park.

Visit the UNESCO World Heritage Site of Kondo, near Kolo, just south of the park. From the last Stone Age, the illustrations of hunting scenes painted on the cave walls have been suggested to date back some 29,000 years and are still considered to have ritual associations with the local Hadza and Sandawe peoples who live nearby.

WHEN TO GO

You can visit year-round, but the dry season (June–October) is the best for its sheer number of animals.

GETTING HERE AND AROUND

It's an easy drive from Arusha or Lake Manyara following a surfaced road to within 7 km (4 miles) of the main entrance gate. Charter flights from Arusha and the Serengeti are also possible. The flight from Arusha to southern Serengeti is roughly 1½ hours; the drive is 335 km (208 miles), which will take around eight hours.

VISITOR INFORMATION

Park fees are around US$50 per person, per day and rare night game drives will cost US$50.

GAME-VIEWING

During the dry season, huge herds of elephant, eland, oryx, zebra, buffalo, wildebeest, giraffe, and impala roam the park. Hippos are plentiful and pythons can sometimes be seen in trees near the swamps. If you want to spot waterbuck or the gerenuk, head for the Mkungero Pools. Tarangire is much more densely wooded than Serengeti with acacia, mixed woodland, and the ubiquitous baobab trees, although you'll find grasslands

on the southern plains where cheetahs hunt.

There are more than 500 species of birds in Tarangire National Park, including martial and bateleur eagles. Especially good bird-watching can be done along the wetlands of the Silale Swamp and around the Tarangire River. Yellow-collared lovebirds, hammerkops, helmeted guinea fowl, long-toed lapwings, brown parrots, white-bellied go-away birds, and a variety of kingfishers, weavers, owls, plovers, and sandpipers make their homes here. A shallow alkaline lake attracts flamingos and pelicans in the rainy season. Raptors are plentiful, including the palm-nut vulture and lots of eagles. You may hear a cry that sounds quite similar to the American bald eagle but is in fact its look-alike cousin, the African fish eagle.

Ruaha National Park

Remote and rarely visited, Ruaha is Tanzania's second-largest park—10,300 square km (3,980 square miles). Oddly enough, it attracts only a fraction of the visitors that go to Serengeti, which could be because it's less well-known and difficult to access. But East Africa safari aficionados claim it to be the country's best-kept secret. There are huge concentrations of buffalos, spotted hyenas, elephants, lions, cheetah, antelope, and more than 400 bird species including the critically endangered vulture.

Classified as a national park in 1964, it was once part of the Sabia River Game Reserve, which the German colonial government established in 1911. Ruaha is derived from the word "great" in the Hehe language and refers to the mighty Ruaha River, which flows around the park's borders, and it's only around the river that the park is developed for tourism with a 400-km (249-mile) road circuit. The main portion of the park sits on top of a 1,800-meter (5,900-foot) plateau with spectacular views of valleys, hills, and plains—a wonderful backdrop for game-viewing. Habitats include riverine forest, savanna, swamps, and acacia woodland.

WHEN TO GO
The best time to visit is May through November because, although even in the wet season the all-weather roads are passable, it's incredibly difficult to spot game at that time because of the lush, tall vegetation. If you're into bird-watching, lush scenery, and wildflowers, you'll like the wet season (December–March).

GETTING HERE AND AROUND
Most visitors arrive by charter flight from Dar es Salaam, Nyerere National Park, the Serengeti, or Arusha. The flight is 2½ hours to Ruaha from Arusha or Dar es Salaam, and one hour from Nyerere National Park. It's possible to drive to Ruaha but it takes longer. Visitors often drive from Dar es Salaam, but not many drive from Arusha. The drive to Ruaha from Dar es Salaam is roughly 10 hours through Iringa. The roads do get a bit bumpy as you near the park. Safari companies will arrange road transfers if you so wish. If time is of the essence, fly; if it's interaction and experience (atmosphere) of the various places en route to Ruaha you'd like, drive.

VISITOR INFORMATION
There's a conservation fee of US$30 per person (excluding V.A.T.), per 24-hour visit and $US40 per vehicle (if you're driving).

■ TIP➜ You can pay in both USD and Tsh.

Ask at your lodge for a copy of the Ruaha booklet, which has maps, checklists, and hints on where to look for particular species.

TIMING
Three to four nights will give you the chance to fully experience the varied areas of the park and make the most of your visit.

Poaching

Poaching continues to be an issue throughout the Ruaha-Rungwa ecosystem due to it being part game reserves, part wildlife management areas, and part village land. Ruaha holds some of the largest elephant populations on record in East Africa as well as around a tenth of the world's lion population. This has made it an unfortunate poaching hotspot in recent years.

GAME-VIEWING
There are elephant, buffalo, lion, spotted hyena, gazelle, zebra, greater and lesser kudu, and giraffe roaming this park. If you're lucky, you might even see roan and sable antelope or witness a cheetah hunt on the open plains in the Lundu area. Lion are well habituated to vehicles, so you'd be very unlucky not to spot at least one pride, and if you've set your heart on seeing wild dogs, then try to come in June or July when they're denning; this makes them easier to spot than at other times because they stay in one place for a couple of months. There are also lots of crocs and hippos in the river areas. Bird "specials" include the lovely little Eleonora's falcon (December through January is the best time to spot one), Pel's fishing owl, and the pale-billed hornbill.

Hotels

★ Jabali Ridge
$$$$ | ALL-INCLUSIVE | Contemporary in style among the rocky outcrops, Jabali blends seamlessly into the impressive natural beauty at the heart of Ruaha. **Pros:** incredible views from all areas; expert safari guides; day, night, and walking safaris. **Cons:** Ruaha, in peak summer, is incredibly hot; not the traditional tented camp experience; you are right

among the wildlife, so be prepared for close encounters. $ *Rooms from: $914* ✉ *Ruaha National Park* ☎ *736/500–515* ⊕ *www.asiliaafrica.com* ⊘ *Closed Mid Mar.–May* ⇥ *8 rooms* |⊙| *All-Inclusive.*

★ Jongomero Tented Camp

$$$$ | RESORT | The only camp in the southwest corner of Ruaha National Park, Jongomero exudes a laid-back bush atmosphere with stellar service amid luxurious trimmings. **Pros:** enthusiastic staff and excellent food; fly camping is a must; the special little surprises and deft, thoughtful touches make this a unique experience. **Cons:** rhinos, sadly due to poaching, are a very rare sight; thicker bush during wet seasons make it harder to spot certain animals; tsetse flies are in the area and around the camp. $ *Rooms from: $705* ✉ *Ruaha National Park, Ruaha National Park* ☎ *22/0782–069–421* ⊕ *www.selous.com* ⊘ *Closed Apr.–May* ⇥ *11 tents* |⊙| *All-Inclusive.*

Kigelia Camp

$$$$ | RESORT | Set in a forest of baobabs and sausage trees along the Ifaguru sand river, Kigelia has a prime location in Ruaha. **Pros:** classic tented safari camp feel with a few modern twists; watching the fire under the stars at night; wildlife frequently move through the camp itself. **Cons:** the heat in summer during the day means there might not be much respite (no pool or a/c); time the weather to avoid the rainier seasons; the camp is an hour's drive from the airstrip. $ *Rooms from: $765* ✉ *Ruaha National Park, Ruaha National Park* ☎ *784/787–595–908* ⊕ *www.nomad-tanzania.com* ▭ *No credit cards* ⊘ *Closed Apr.–May* ⇥ *6 tents* |⊙| *Free Breakfast.*

Mwagusi Safari Camp

$$$ | RESORT | This well-established camp is situated on the shady banks of the Mwagusi River, giving it a prime position in Ruaha for game-viewing. **Pros:** delicious food; excellent guides and bush knowledge; superb location for wildlife viewing. **Cons:** bandas are close together;

you are in the midst of wildlife so be prepared for some close camp encounters; camp is rustic-looking from the outside. $ *Rooms from: $565* ✉ *Ruaha National Park* ☎ *7525–170–940 in U.K.* ⊕ *www. mwagusicamp.com* ▭ *No credit cards* ⊘ *Closed Apr.–May* ⇥ *13 bandas* |⊙| *Free Breakfast.*

Tandala Camp

$ | RESORT | Because Tandala is in a private conservancy 5 km (3 miles) outside the entrance gate, guests can take early morning game walks and game drives, engage in bird-viewing, or experience authentic cultural visits to the Maasai bomas, local village, and market. **Pros:** great views from your tent's raised deck; elephants often frequent the nearby waterhole; children of all ages welcome. **Cons:** outside of the main park; rustic and simple tents; very bumpy road to the Ruaha park entrance (10 minutes). $ *Rooms from: $165* ✉ *Ruaha National Park, Ruaha National Park* ☎ *755/680– 220* ⊕ *www.tandalacamp.com* ▭ *No credit cards* ⊘ *Closed Mar.* ⇥ *11 tents* |⊙| *All-Inclusive.*

Gateway Cities

Many visitors to Tanzania will find themselves with a layover in Dar es Salaam or Arusha before or after their safari. Dar es Salaam is often dismissed as a mere transition point, but it's a city on the rise and a wonderful expression of the changing landscape of modern Tanzania beyond the beach and safaris. For some ideas and suggestions to help determine where you should stay, eat, and, if you have time, sightsee, read on.

Dar es Salaam

Graceful triangular-sail dhows share the harbor with mammoth tankers, as the once sleepy village of Dar es Salaam, which means "haven of peace" in Arabic, has been transformed into one of East Africa's busiest ports and cities. The country's major commercial center, Dar es Salaam has also become its largest city, home to more than 4.3 million inhabitants. The city also serves as the seat of government during the very slow move to Dodoma, which was named the official capital in 1973. The legislature resides in Dodoma, but most government offices are still found in Dar es Salaam.

In the early 1860s, Sultan Seyyid Majid of Zanzibar visited what was then the isolated fishing village of Mzizima on the Tanzanian coast. Eager to have a protected port on the mainland, Majid began constructing a palace here in 1865. The city, poised to compete with neighboring ports such as Bagamoyo and Kilwa, suffered a setback after the sultan died in 1870. His successor, his half-brother Seyyid Barghash, had little interest in the city, and its royal buildings fell into ruins. Only the Old Boma, which once housed royal guests, still survives.

The city remained a small port until Germany moved its colonial capital here in 1891 and began constructing roads, offices, and many of the public buildings still in use today. The Treaty of Versailles granted Great Britain control of the region in 1919, but that country added comparatively little to the city's infrastructure during its 45-year rule.

Tanzania gained its independence in 1961. During the years that followed, President Julius Nyerere, who focused on issues such as education and health care, allowed the capital city to fall into a decline that lasted into the 1980s. When Benjamin William Mkapa took office in 1985, his market-oriented reforms helped to revitalize the city, which continues to evolve in 2022. The soaring 670 meter (2,198 feet) Tanzanite Bridge dominates the Coco Beach coastline, alleviating some of the city's more notorious traffic jams. There are a few sights to entertain visitors, but the only one really worth

Did You Know?

Tanzania is one of the world's largest producers of cashews, exporting more than 200,000 tons of raw nuts each year, a big source of income for small-scale farmers.

a visit is the National Museum, which contains the famous fossil discoveries by Richard and Mary Leakey, including the 1.7-million-year-old hominid skull discovered by Mary Leakey in the Olduvai Gorge in 1959. What Dar es Salaam has in blossoming abundance are lively restaurants, modern hotels, and some of the most enjoyable nightlife around.

GETTING HERE AND AROUND

To find your way around central Dar es Salaam, use the Askari Monument, at the intersection of Samora Avenue and Azikiwe Street, as a compass. Most sights are within walking distance. Four blocks northeast on Samora Avenue you'll find the National Museum and Botanical Gardens; about seven blocks southwest stands the Clock Tower, another good landmark. One block southeast is Sokoine Drive, which empties into Kivukoni Front as it follows the harbor. Farther along, Kivukoni Front becomes Ocean Road.

Along Samora Avenue and Sokoine Drive you'll find banks, pharmacies, grocery stores, and shops selling everything from clothing to curios. Northwest of Samora Avenue, around India, Jamhuri, and Libya streets, is the busy Swahili neighborhood where merchants sell all kinds of items, including Tanzania's best *kangas* (sarongs or wraps). Further west you'll find the large Kariakoo Market.

■ TIP→ **Don't buy tickets for transport, especially on ferries, trains, or buses, from anyone other than an accredited ticket seller.**

Julius Nyerere International Airport is about 13 km (8 miles) from the city center. Plenty of white-color taxis are available at the airport and cost about Tsh40,000 (US$18) to the city center. This is not often negotiable as the airport taxi drivers are notorious for taking advantage of tourists. Most hotels will send drivers to meet your plane if arranged in advance, although this will cost more.

Ferries depart to Zanzibar daily, starting at 7 am from the Zanzibar Ferry Terminal. The two-hour journey costs between Tsh35,000–Tsh60,000 (US$15–US$26) one way. Although thousands of locals and tourists use the service every year, two ferries capsized in 2011 and 2012 due to overcrowding (note that this was not Azam, which has not had an incident to date). If you prefer to fly to Zanzibar the cost, on average, is between US$40 and US$80 depending on the time and day of the week. Flights run every 40 minutes between the island and the mainland.

■TIP→ **Tourists aren't thought to be at risk from pirates from Somalia.**

The Nyerere Bridge connects Dar es Salaam to Kigamboni and the southern beaches.

By far, Azam is the safest and best ferry operator to Zanzibar. Tickets are booked and paid (in dollars) online and reserved up to 48 hours before you depart. You can also pay for and receive the tickets at the terminal or at the Azam office (cash only and they advise only US$) in Dar es Salaam or Zanzibar.

Taxis are the most efficient way to get around town. During the day they're easy to find outside hotels and at major intersections, but at night they're often scarce. Ask someone to call one for you. Taxis don't have meters, so you must agree on the fare before getting in. Fares run about Tsh5,000 within the city and Tsh20,000 from the city to Msisani Peninsula. While bajajis are generally not allowed around the city center, on the peninsula they are a quick and cheap alternative for getting around.

MONEY MATTERS
You can pay for most things in both USD and Tsh. There are many ATMs around the city that accept Visa and MasterCard.

SAFETY
Dar es Salaam is fine to wander around by yourself during the day, but after dark it's best to take a taxi. The area with the most street crime is along the harbor, especially Kivukoni Front and Ocean Road.

Foreign women tend to feel safe in Dar es Salaam. But remember, local women in Dar es Salaam never wear clothing that exposes their shoulders or legs. You should do the same. You'll feel more comfortable in modest dress.

VISITOR INFORMATION
The Tanzania Tourist Board's head office is in Dar es Salaam. It has maps and information on travel to dozens of points of interest around Tanzania and is very helpful. The staff will discuss hotel options with you and assist you in making reservations.

See Health and Safety in the chapter's Planning section for information on the U.S. Embassy.

ESSENTIALS
FERRIES Kigamboni Ferry. ⊠ *Kivukoni Rd., Dar es Salaam* ⌖ *The mainland port is located at Magogoni near the main fish market past the Park Hyatt Dar Es Salaam* ☎. **Zanzibar Ferry Terminal.** ⊠ *Sokoine Dr., Dar es Salaam.*

VISITOR INFORMATION Tanzania Tourist Board. *(TTB)* ⊠ *Utalii House, Laibon St. at Ali Hassan Mwinyi Rd., opposite French Embassy, Dar es Salaam* ☎ *022/266–4873 tourism services, 022/266–4878/9 general* ⊕ *www.tanzaniatouristboard. go.tz.*

Dar es Salaam

KEY
- 1 Sights
- 1 Restaurants
- 1 Quick Bites
- 1 Hotels

Sights ▼

1. Askari Monument........C4
2. Botanical Gardens......D3
3. Kivukoni
   Fish Market...............E5
4. Tanzania National
   Museum and
   House of Culture........D3

Restaurants ▼

1. Addis in Dar..............B1
2. Akemi......................C4
3. Crafty Dee's..............B1
4. George and the
   Dragon...................B1
5. Karambezi Cafe.........B1
6. Kind Earth Eatery and
   Kingston 8...............B1
7. Level 8 at the
   Park Hyatt...............D4
8. Mamboz
   Corner BBQ.............B4
9. Shooters Grill............B1
10. Thai Kani.................B1
11. 305 Karafuu.............B1
12. Veranda Tapas Bar.....B1

Quick Bites ▼

1. The Tribe.................B1

Hotels ▼

1. Coral Beach Hotel......B1
2. Courtyard Hotel..........C1
3. Dar es Salaam
   Serena Hotel.............C3
4. Hotel Slipway...........B1
5. Hyatt Regency
   Dar es Salaam,
   The Kilimanjaro.........D4
6. Peninsula Hotel.........B1
7. Sea Cliff Hotel...........B1

Sights

Askari Monument

MONUMENT | This bronze statue was erected by the British in 1927 in memory of African troops who died during World War I; the word *askari* means "soldier" in Swahili. It stands on the site of a monument erected by Germany to celebrate its victory here in 1888. That monument stood only five years before being demolished in 1916. ✉ *Samora Ave. at Azikiwe St., Dar es Salaam.*

Botanical Gardens

CITY PARK | If you are heading to the National Museum it's well worth a quiet stroll through the indigenous plants in the botanical gardens. It provides respite from the city underneath purple bougainvilleas and blue jacarandas. ✉ *Samora Ave., Dar es Salaam* 💲 *Free.*

Kivukoni Fish Market

MARKET | If you are feeling brave and interested in experiencing Dar's fish market at its nosiest and fishiest then wake up early and head down to Kivukoni. There is no charge to walk around. Be prepared for quite a smell, but the sight of hundreds of weathered fishermen hauling in their catch and the thrumming sounds of commerce—bargaining and haggling, prepping the seafood—is a fun experience. Please don't purchase any of the seashells or turtle products on sale.

■ TIP→ **If you prefer to be accompanied by a guide, take part in a city tour, which will include a stop at the market.** ✉ *Barak Obama Dr., Dar es Salaam* 💲 *Free.*

Tanzania National Museum and House of Culture

HISTORY MUSEUM | Apart from the Leakey fossil discoveries, which are some of the most important in the world, there are galleries that detail the history of Tanzania from occupation to independence. A contemporary art gallery and pleasant outdoor exhibits of an iron dinosaur, past presidential cars and a tribute to

If You Have Time

Travel 70 km (43 miles) north from Dar es Salaam to the historically fascinating and arty town of Bagamoyo, where old buildings such as the Catholic Museum, on the grounds of the Holy Ghost Mission, and the Old Fort are worth a visit—book a tour to get the most out of your day trip. Once an Arab trader's slave prison, you can see the Old Fort's underground tunnel along which slaves were herded to waiting dhows; the damp walls bore witness to the most terrible human suffering.

the US embassy bombing makes for a good morning outing. This is also a spot to learn about Tanzania's tribal heritage and the impact of the slave trade. ✉ *5 Shaaban Robert St., near Botanical Gardens, Dar es Salaam* ☎ *022222/122–030* ⊕ *www.nmt.co.za* 💲 *US$6.*

Beaches

The islands may have some exquisite beaches, but don't discount the sandy shores a few hours' drive around Dar es Salaam. North is Mbezi beach, right across the bay from Hotel Slipway and the small harbor where you can find boat trips to the infamous sandbank parties. Day trips to Mbuja and Sinda islands are well worth it. Kigamboni, in the south, is a wonderful stretch of beach ideal for families and anyone seeking respite from the city. You can stay at the simple but pleasant Marriott Amani Beach Hotel.

■ TIP→ **Roads are very good south, while north has more potholed terrain, but it's nothing a little rental car won't get through.**

Restaurants

Recent years have seen a flourish of imaginative and exciting restaurants opening up across Dar es Salaam. From rooftop bars to hearty vegan and Tanzania's first craft brewery, the city has something for everyone and every taste. You can spend as much or as little as you like, just bring your appetite, because if it's local street food fare or high-end Continental, the portion sizes are not for the picky. One thing is guaranteed, you are going to want to get out of your hotel and explore as much as you can. Be sure to watch out for the ever-present happy hour from 5 pm that runs across most restaurants and bars; the specials help with those looking to keep the budget amenable. Typical *chakula* (food) for an East African meal includes *wali* (rice) or *ugali* (a damp mound of breadlike ground corn) served with a meat, fish, or vegetable stew. A common side dish found on most menus is *kachumbari,* a fresh mixture of chopped tomatoes, onions, and cucumbers. Street-side snacks not to miss are chicken and beef kebabs, roast corn on the cob, and samosas. Breakfast isn't the same without trying the doughnut-like *mandazi.* Wash it all down with a local beer—Kilimanjaro, Tusker, or Safari—or with a fragrant and delicious hot chai.

Most tourists frequent the more well-known restaurants, which can be quite expensive; entrées can set you back $10 to $15. Even at the smallest of restaurants, reservations are rarely required. Restaurants in hotels generally are open until at least 10:30 pm, even on Sunday, although hours of local restaurants vary.

★ Addis in Dar

$$$ | ETHIOPIAN | It might look unassuming from the outside, but as soon as you climb the stairs of this Ethiopian family-run institution, you'll be welcomed into a space that has been a long-standing go-to in the city. Food is eaten communally and with the hands—traditional Ethiopian style—and you'll scoop delicious stews and sauces from the plate with the traditional *injera* bread; there are good options for vegetarians. **Known for:** atmospheric patio dining under the stars; delicious Tej (traditional honey wine); as authentically Ethiopian as you can get. [$] *Average main: $24* ✉ *35 Ursino St., Regent Estate, Dar es Salaam* ☎ *713/266–299* 🌐 *www.addisindar.com* 🕒 *Closed Sun.*

Akemi

$$ | ASIAN FUSION | On the rooftop of one of the tallest buildings in downtown Dar es Salaam, Akemi is a popular dining establishment for the well-heeled for special occasions and functions. With spectacular 360-degree views of the city and harbor, the cuisine is of a standard Continental fare with a menu that features a mix of Indian influences and Asian fusion cuisine like beef fillet with vegetables, though the fish platters tend to be the most popular. **Known for:** a decent happy hour special at the bar; the romantic city views at night; Tanzania's only revolving restaurant. [$] *Average main: $12* ✉ *Golden Jubilee Towers, Ohio St., 21st fl., Dar es Salaam* ✥ *Next to PPF Bldg.* ☎ *753/360–360* 🌐 *www.akemidining.com.*

★ Crafty Dee's

$ | CONTEMPORARY | An unassuming entrance leads you into the heart of a hip gastro pub that showcases micro brewing in all its shiny steel glory. Winning bronze at the African Beer Cup 2022 for their Belgian Ale, Crafty Dee's is quickly becoming the talk of the town when it comes to looking beyond the country's beer staples of Kilimanjaro and Safari lager; its beer and food pairings are the perfect way to start your night out. **Known for:** hand-crafted beer in Dar es Salaam; the lager and food pairings; great pre-drinks or dinner spot. [$] *Average main: Tsh15,000* ✉ *43 Chole Rd., Msasani*

What to Eat 🍴

Mishikaki: marinated skewers of meat grilled over charcoals

Chapatti: tasty and soft Indian-style flatbread used to pick up vegetables or meat

Zanzibar Pizza: Not really a pizza, more of a spicy omelette pancake hybrid made popular by tourists but now a staple

Nyama Choma: roasted meat, usually beef or goat

Chipsi Mayai: a delicious savoury comfort food of eggs and chips in a fried omelette

Ugali: a plain, white cornmeal of sorts served alongside meats and vegetables. Be sure to order it if it's fried.

Wali wa Nazi: a rich, coconut rice that accompanies most curries

Mandazi: snack food of choice best eaten with tea or coffee

Sukuma Wiki: a green, leafy vegetable similar to kale and often paired with ugali and curry

Peninsula ☎ *774/144–144 WhatsApp* 🌐 *www.dees.co.tz* 🕓 *Closed Tues.*

George and the Dragon

$ | **AMERICAN** | Known locally as The George, sports fans and those seeking a good old-fashioned burger and fries head to this classic British pub. Big screen TVs, buckets of icy cold beers, an expansive barbecue list, and a dedicated area called the sports arena keep punters, expats, and locals satisfied and jovial. **Known for:** huge sports area with pool and pub games galore; a lively outdoor beer garden with a resident DJ; large, juicy cheeseburgers with plenty of fries. [$] *Average main: $10* ✉ *Haile Selassie Rd., Kinondoni* ☎ *717/800–002* 🕓 *Closed Mon.*

Karambezi Cafe

$$ | **CONTEMPORARY** | This popular double-story open-air restaurant in the Sea Cliff Hotel is right next to the crashing sea, providing the best views in town. The café-style restaurant features a decent array of foods like battered fish-and-chips, hamburgers, and juicy steaks, while the breakfast and lunch buffet has a wonderful spread. **Known for:** live entertainment on weekends; homemade pastry and cakes for teatime treats; 180-degree views over the Indian Ocean. [$] *Average main: $15* ✉ *Sea Cliff Hotel, Toure Dr., Dar es Salaam* ☎ *784/342–500* 🌐 *www.karambezicafe.com.*

Kind Earth Eatery and Kingston 8

$$ | **VEGETARIAN** | With creative and delicious food combinations that utilize fresh, local ingredients, owner and chef Betty Delfosse-Ingleton has created a real standout vegan and vegetarian dining option in Dar. Jamaican influences are found in the raw, vegan, and vegetarian haute cuisine that's served in the little outside courtyard decorated with bright art murals, but there is a menu for those who can't quite abandon their meat thanks to the amalgamation with Kingston 8 restaurant—the jerk chicken being a real standout. **Known for:** very generous portions; delicious all-natural-ingredient cocktails; fresh and vibrant flavor combinations. [$] *Average main: $15* ✉ *11 Kahama Rd., Dar es Salaam* ✣ *Opposite Tuk Tuk Thai* ☎ *763/391–456* 🕓 *Closed Sun.*

★ Level 8 at the Park Hyatt

$$ | INTERNATIONAL | The Park Hyatt's Brasserie and Oriental restaurants are both equally fantastic, but by far the hotel's real gem is the spectacular rooftop bar, Level 8. Commanding views of both the city and the working port extend out on either side of the striking, sweeping architecture and high glass walls. **Known for:** wonderful views over the city; Friday sunset live acoustic music and cocktails; delicious snacks and light meals. [$] *Average main: $12* ✉ *24 Kivukoni Rd., Dar es Salaam* ☎ *764/701–234* 🌐 *hyattrestaurants.com.*

★ Mamboz Corner BBQ

$ | INDIAN | Nearly every major African city has a local joint where you can mingle, chat, eat hearty grilled street food, and absorb the city life. Mamboz is just this kind of place for Dar es Salaam; they fire up their street-side barbecues as the evening light fades (they open at 6 pm). **Known for:** takeaway available; simple, but filled with local atmosphere; very spicy, but mouthwatering, Gajjar Spicy chicken. [$] *Average main: $10* ✉ *Morongoro Rd. at Lybia St., Kinondoni* ☎ *784/243–735* 🌐 *www.facebook.com/MambozCornerBbq/* ⏲ *Closed Tues.*

Shooters Grill

$$ | INTERNATIONAL | A steak house and wine bar high atop Oyster Plaza where the near-constant night breeze cools down patrons indulging in a sundowner special. Arrive ready to enjoy some seriously well-cooked premium steak cuts along with the unbeatable views over the peninsula at sunset; weekends are for live music and wine tastings with food pairings. **Known for:** steaks, steaks, and more steaks; weekend seafood platters are well priced for the sheer volume; locals and visitors alike love it. [$] *Average main: Tsh18* ✉ *1196 Haile Selassie Rd., 6th floor, Dar es Salaam* ☎ *754/880–160.*

Thai Kani

$ | ASIAN | Overlooking Slipway Beach, this may be the priciest Thai food in town, but Thai Kani still has a reputation for being tasty and deliciously authentic. The outside patio views, accompanied by one of their Champagne and sushi platter specials, is a very atmospheric way to while away the evening. **Known for:** delicious and well-made sushi; great views over the bay with happy hour specials; vibrant Thai-style salads. [$] *Average main: $11* ✉ *Slipway Beach, Yacht Club Rd., Msasani Peninsula* ☎ *764/160–378* 🌐 *www.thaikani.com.*

305 Karafuu

$$ | CONTEMPORARY | Tucked away in a back street neighborhood with contemporary art adorning the walls, this family-run small-scale spot serves up some exceptionally tasty food. Light jazz wafts through the restaurant and walls adorned with tasteful local art make for the perfect atmosphere to tuck into some lovingly prepared meat and seafood dishes that are plentiful and delicious. **Known for:** the must-try chef's special steak; local neighborhood vibe; cozy and relaxed atmosphere. [$] *Average main: $13* ✉ *Plot 305, Karafuu St., Kwa Manyana, Kinondoni* ☎ *754/277–188* 🌐 *www.305karafuu.co.tz* ⏲ *Closed Mon.*

Veranda Tapas Bar

$$ | FUSION | A multiethnic fusion restaurant in every sense of the word, Veranda serves up divine morsels—perfectly sized for sharing—that range from Indian to Asian to Swahili cuisine. The intimate courtyard is draped in bright bougainvillea and quirky decor decorates the space. **Known for:** great frozen margaritas; romantic outdoor courtyard atmosphere; perfect bite-size portions that don't break the bank. [$] *Average main: $12* ✉ *Kahama Rd., Dar es Salaam* ↔ *Next to Tuk Tuk Thai* ☎ *763/491–212* 🌐 *www.veranda-tz.com* ⏲ *Closed Mon.*

Coffee and Quick Bites

The Tribe

$ | **FUSION** | What could be more refreshing and delicious than an iced coffee in the midst of the humid city? This unassuming cafe-style pit stop is the perfect spot for the weary traveler looking for something beyond burgers and buns as they serve up tasty, quick bites that mix distinct Tanzanian flavors with Mexican fusion foods and style-it-yourself burritos and tacos. **Known for:** fresh juice combinations; Tanzania spice in a burrito bowl; easy location for a quick pick up take away before heading out. [$] *Average main: Tsh6* ✉ *Haile Selaasie Rd., Oyster Bay* ✣ *next to Vodacom office* 🌐 *www.thetribe.co.tz.*

Hotels

Coral Beach Hotel

$ | **HOTEL** | **FAMILY** | When it comes to seafront views at a price that won't break the bank, the Coral Beach Hotel is the place to head. **Pros:** splurge for a junior suite with balcony and views; friendly and efficient service; executive and king rooms have balconies. **Cons:** cheaper first floor rooms are small and not worth the price; very busy on weekends or when events are hosted; pool area has limited seating space. [$] *Rooms from: $170* ✉ *Coral La., Msasani Peninsula* ☎ *222/601–934* 🌐 *www.coralbeach-tz.com* 🛏 *40 rooms* 🍴 *Free Breakfast.*

Protea Hotel Dar es Salaam Courtyard

$ | **HOTEL** | With traditional Arabic wooden balconies, glass-stained windows, and a lush courtyard, this welcoming hotel is the perfect place to escape the hustle and bustle of the city. **Pros:** beautiful architecture and more intimate than the larger chain hotels; a quiet, leafy courtyard away from the busy street; general manager who is attentive to your every need. **Cons:** no views outside; pool is central and not very private; food can be a bit hit and miss and is buffet style. [$] *Rooms from: $120* ✉ *Seaview Ocean Rd., Oyster Bay* ☎ *22/213–0130* 🌐 *www.marriott.com* 🛏 *41 rooms* 🍴 *Free Breakfast.*

Dar Es Salaam Serena Hotel

$$ | **HOTEL** | A towering feature of the cityscape for many years, the Serena stands in the center of Dar es Salaam with all the amenities one would expect from a luxury hotel, including a business center, a variety of restaurants, a large pool with outside gazebo bar, and a rather spectacular Arabic-style fitness center with sauna and steam rooms. **Pros:** surrounded by large, pleasant gardens; an expansive pool with outdoor gazebo; central location in the city. **Cons:** slightly dated decor; bathrooms in need of an overhaul; very large and caters to big groups and conferences. [$] *Rooms from: $290* ✉ *Ohio St., Dar es Salaam* ☎ *22/221–2500* 🌐 *www.serenahotels.com* 🛏 *230 rooms* 🍴 *Free Breakfast.*

Hotel Slipway

$ | **HOTEL** | Located in the Slipway, a shopping-and-leisure complex in a converted boatyard, this hotel of the same name is a great place for an overnight or home base in Dar. The large, modern block rises three stories above the shopping complex providing views of Msasani Bay. The simple, but comfortable rooms—a welcome respite from the craziness of the city in calming shades of blue and white—have balconies, free Wi-Fi, satellite TV, and air-conditioning. **Pros:** convenient for restaurants and shopping; bright and modern sea-facing rooms; suites have ample space and an extra lounge area. **Cons:** restaurant and pool seperated from main rooms; older rooms facing the street are dated; occasional loud pool parties can change the atmosphere. [$] *Rooms from: $150* ✉ *The Slipway, Chole Rd., Msasani Peninsula* ☎ *22/260–0893* 🌐 *www.hotelslipway.com* 🛏 *61 rooms* 🍴 *Free Breakfast.*

Vervet monkeys are found throughout East and Southern Africa.

★ Hyatt Regency Dar es Salaam, The Kilimanjaro

$ | HOTEL | Known as the Kilimanjaro, this hotel has carved out a niche for itself as the premier hotel in Dar es Salaam in both unique style and service; even the Obamas stayed here in 2013. **Pros:** beautiful design and charming outside bistro under a giant tree; relaxing spa and pool on the upper floors; incredibly well-equipped gym. **Cons:** every now and then you get noise from the nearby rooftop clubs; some distance from popular restaurants in Dar; traffic jams can be quite intense during rush hours around the hotel. Ⓢ *Rooms from: $220* ✉ *24 Kivukoni Rd., Dar es Salaam* ✛ *On the way to the ferry terminal* ☎ *764/701–234* ⊕ *www.hyatt.com* ↪ *180 rooms* ☩ *Free Breakfast.*

Peninsula Hotel

$ | HOTEL | Formerly known as the Best Western Plus and renamed the Peninsula, this hotel is an excellent value with friendly staff and a decent on-site restaurant. **Pros:** free Wi-Fi; clean, spacious rooms; solid amenities. **Cons:** big nightclub next door; first floor are all smoking rooms; business atmosphere. Ⓢ *Rooms from: $130* ✉ *4–6 Haille Selassie Rd., Oyster Bay* ☎ *22/266–4591* ⊕ *www.peninsula-tz.com* ↪ *45 rooms* ☩ *Free Breakfast.*

Sea Cliff Hotel

$$ | HOTEL | Only 15 minutes from downtown on the edge of the Msasani Peninsula, this classy hotel has commanding views of the sea and good-size, comfortable rooms (insist on one with a sea view). **Pros:** views over the sea; on-site ATM and good facilities; the popular resturant, Karambezi, is on your doorstep. **Cons:** city facing rooms on the lower floor have no views; can feel large and more business-travel oriented; pool area is a bit worn. Ⓢ *Rooms from: $217* ✉ *10 Toure Dr., Msasani Peninsula* ☎ *764/700–600* ⊕ *www.hotelseacliff.com* ↪ *114 rooms* ☩ *Free Breakfast.*

Shopping

You might want to pick up some amazing Tanzanian fabric, especially the colorful kanga, kitenge, and batik material. Vendors inside the Kariakoo cloth market (Congo Street) or the Slipway Shopping complex are some of your best spots to find material and cloth. Sometimes the prices are set, sometimes it's possible to haggle.

If you're looking to take home hand-crafted items like bowls, Tinga Tinga paintings, wooden carvings, jewelry, and antique masks, the Mwenge Craft Market (Sam Nujoma Rd.) is the place to find treasures of varying shapes and sizes and watch the local artists at work. Just down the road, the Mwenge Woodcarvers Market has more crafts to check out.

If it feels a bit daunting to explore the markets on your own, look into taking a tour of the city that includes the craft markets.

Arusha

Arusha may be the gateway to all of the Serengeti but on a clear day, you can see Mt. Meru, Africa's fifth highest mountain at 4,556 meters (14,947 feet), looming in the distance. There are some wonderful accommodation options on the outskirts of Arusha that are well worth a day or two pre- or post-safari, just to recharge, relax, and be pampered while experiencing some Northern Tanzanian hospitality.

The town is bisected by the Nauru River. The more modern part is to the east of the river where most of the hotels, safari companies, and banks are located; west of the river are the bus station and main market. Most people spend an overnight here either coming or going.

GETTING HERE AND AROUND

There are no direct flights from the United States to Arusha. Generally you need to connect through a city on the mainland, the easiest being Dar es Salaam.

You'll be approached immediately after you land by taxi drivers. Be sure to agree on a price before getting in, as taxis don't have meters. The fare to downtown Arusha is approximately US$30.

SAFETY

It's unlikely that you'd want to explore Arusha at night, but if you do, take a taxi. As in any city, muggings and purse-snatching are common.

VISITOR INFORMATION

The Tanzanian Tourist Board (TTB) has an Arusha office where you can pick up maps and brochures for the area, as well as book cultural excursions. Most of the lodges and hotels offer concierge services that are more than sufficient.

CONTACTS

AIRPORTS Arusha Airport. (ARK) ✉ A 104, Arusha ⊕ www.taa.go.tz.

HOSPITALS Arusha Lutheran Medical Centre. ✉ Fr. Babu Rd., block 54, Levolosi, Arusha ☎ 272/548–030 ⊕ www.almc.or.tz.

VISITOR INFORMATION Tanzania Tourist Board. (TTB) ✉ E 47 Bldg., Boma Rd., Arusha ☎ 22/266–4878 ⊕ www.tanzania-tourism.go.tz.

Restaurants

Arusha might just be a stopover city for some, but there's a lot of great food on offer in the town that goes beyond packed safari lunchboxes.

★ Blue Heron

$ | **ITALIAN** | A popular hangout for the ex-pat community, the Blue Heron has long been the go-to spot for alfresco dining in Arusha with authentic Italian pizza, local wines and beers, generous salads, and an all-you-can-eat Sunday brunch. The quirky and unique atmosphere of dining under an umbrella of twisted beach wood leads out to expansive lawns and views of Mount Meru. **Known for:** wood-fired pizzas and spit barbecue; beautiful grounds to relax with the family; bespoke outdoor eating experiences can be arranged. [$] *Average main: $10* ✉ *Arusha* ✥ *past the airport towards Olerai lodge* ☎ *78/388–5833* 🌐 *www.blueheron.co.tz* ⏲ *Closed Mon.–Wed.*

Fifi´s Restaurant & Café

$ | **INTERNATIONAL** | If you're looking for a quick meal in between flights or safaris, Fifi's is a firm favorite for those looking for simple fare in a relaxed, casual dining atmosphere. The menu is a lovely fusion of Tanzanian favorites—*mishkaki* (spicy cubes of grilled beef) and *mtori* soup (aka banana soup)—and international fare like burgers and homemade pancakes. **Known for:** the friendly staff and laid-back atmosphere; milkshakes and pizza; freshly brewed coffee and tea. [$] *Average main: $8* ✉ *Themi Rd., Arusha* ✥ *Off Sokoine Road* ☎ *789/666–518* 🌐 *fifi-s-restaurant-cafe.business.site.*

The Grill Room

$$ | **INTERNATIONAL** | If you're looking for fresh and well-prepared dishes in a fine dining setting, Arusha Coffee Lodge's Grill Room is a star in the local fine-dining scene. The eclectic and modern à la carte menu features dishes like grilled steaks with Swahili spices and Tanzania Chips Mayai (a French fry omelet) alongside fresh curries. **Known for:** an extensive, quality wine list; three choices of dining areas: formal, pub, and fireside; picturesque and luxuriously homey main dining area. [$] *Average main: $12* ✉ *Arusha Coffee Lodge, A 104, Arusha* ✥ *five minutes from the Arusha Airport* ☎ *754/250–630* 🌐 *www.elewanacollection.com.*

A Real Gem

Looking for that one-of-a-kind gift or keepsake? How about jewelry with tanzanite in it? Given by Maasai fathers to mothers upon the birth of their child, this deep-blue stone, discovered in 1967, is unique to Tanzania. And though you can purchase the gems just about anywhere these days, you can't beat the prices or the bargaining you'll find in the shops of Arusha and Dar es Salaam—you'll be able to purchase loose stones, existing pieces, or customize your own design. ■ TIP→ **Don't buy any tanzanite from street vendors as nine times out of 10 it'll be fake stone.**

★ **Machweo**

$$ | **FUSION** | A fusion of French and Swahili cuisine, the hallmark of one of Arusha's top restaurants is its inventive daily changing signature menu as well as lunches that feature dishes like Swahili-style red snapper *en papillote* (cooked in a paper wrapper), mixed grilled skewers with Belgium fries, and garden green pea soup. The outdoor dining terrace has magnificent views over the valley towards Arusha town, making it a popular spot for those seeking some quiet and comfort in classic style. **Known for:** Chef Axel's salads; seasonal, local produce-inspired lunch menu with Swahili influences; the fantastic views at sunset. [$] *Average main: $15* ✉ *Onsea Guest House, Arusha* ☎ *689/103–552* 🌐 *www.onseahouse.com/machweo.*

Restaurants ▼

1 Blue Heron........ A4
2 Fifi's Restaurant & Café....... C3
3 The Grill Room........ A4
4 Machweo... D1

Hotels ▼

1 The African Tulip D4
2 Arusha Coffee Lodge......... A4
3 Four Points by Sheraton: The Arusha Hotel......... C3
4 Ngare Sero Mountain Lodge Conservancy.... C3
5 Onsea House and Machweo Retreat...... D1

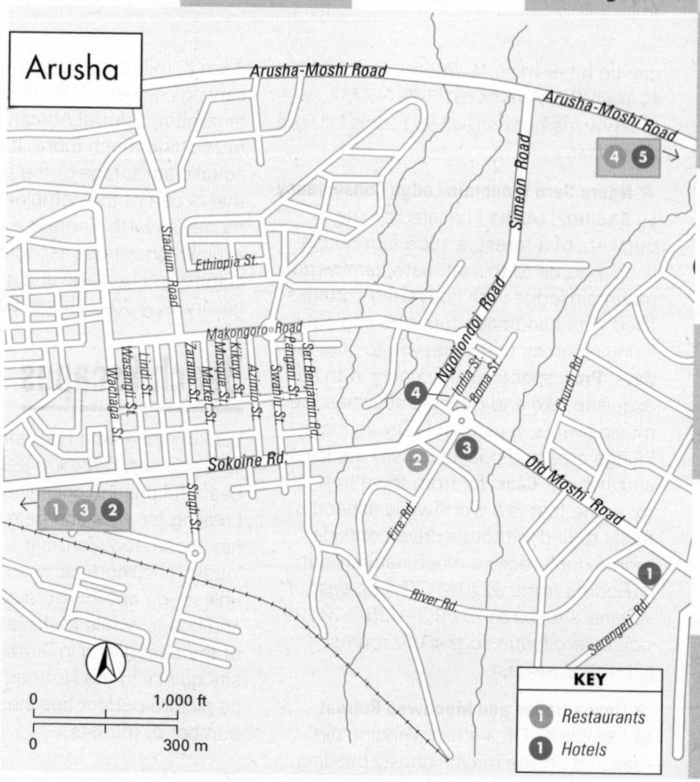

Hotels

The African Tulip

$ | **HOTEL** | If you are in need of a short stay with some modern hotel amenities before heading off into the savanna, the safari-themed Tulip is a good option outside the bustle of Arusha. **Pros:** an intimate hotel outside of the main city; great family room options; service is stellar. **Cons:** communal lounge areas is fairly small if there is a large group booked in; not all rooms have balconies; no elevator. [$] *Rooms from: $220* ✉ *4 Serengeti Rd., Arusha* ☎ *699/799–871 mobile* 🌐 *www.theafricantulip.co.tz* 🛏 *29 rooms* 🍴 *Free Breakfast.*

Arusha Coffee Lodge

$$$$ | **HOTEL** | Just 5 km (3 miles) from town, and five minutes from Arusha Airport, the lodge is a great option for pre- or post-safari layovers. **Pros:** beautiful setting; easy access to the airport; large comfortable rooms. **Cons:** many non–hotel guests at the restaurants; some room views are directly into neighbors patios; near the highway so you can hear traffic. [$] *Rooms from: $623* ✉ *Serengeti Rd., Arusha* ✈ *five minutes from Arusha Airport* ☎ *754/250–630* 🌐 *www.elewanacollection.com* 🛏 *30 rooms* 🍴 *Free Breakfast.*

Four Points by Sheraton: The Arusha Hotel

$ | **HOTEL** | Bang in the middle of town, opposite the clock tower, this historic hotel was built in 1894. **Pros:** close to banks and shops; spacious rooms; lovely historic feel to the Hatari bar area. **Cons:** location means traffic can take a while to get to airport; large conference hotel which can get very crowded with business meetings and socializing; food can be hit or miss. $ *Rooms from: $230* ✉ *Main Rd., Arusha* ☎ *27/297–7777* ⊕ *www.marriot.com* 🛏 *86 rooms* ❏ *Free Breakfast.*

★ Ngare Sero Mountain Lodge Conservancy

$ | B&B/INN | FAMILY | Located on the outskirts of a forest, a 1905 farmhouse is now home to this intimate, family-run mountain lodge with converted cottages filled with handmade furniture and public lounging areas that invite you to stay for days. **Pros:** spectacular scenery with an exquisite lake and multiple activities like music events; a peaceful retreat; main lounge area and pool hideaway are lovely and inviting. **Cons:** far from town but for some that is a worthwhile aspect; tricky to find without a driver; outside rooms don't receive much natural light. $ *Rooms from: $210* ✉ *Off A23, east of Arusha, Arusha* ☎ *764/305–435* ⊕ *www. ngare-sero-lodge.co.tz* 🛏 *14 rooms* ❏ *Free Breakfast.*

★ Onsea House and Machweo Retreat

$$ | B&B/INN | On a small, winding dirt road just off the main highway heading toward Moshi sits conjoined properties with some of the most spectacular views in the area, overlooking Arusha and Mt. Merua. **Pros:** spectacular location; beautiful outdoor deck and pool; excellent food. **Cons:** you are amid village life so you might be woken early by chickens and cattle; many stairs, so not ideal for people with mobility issues; the guest cottage is not as luxurious as the other options in Onsea. $ *Rooms from: $280* ✉ *Onsea Moivaro Rd., Arusha* ☎ *689/103–552* ⊕ *www.onseahouse.com* 🛏 *16 suites* ❏ *Free Breakfast.*

🛍 Shopping

Cultural Heritage Centre

ARTS CENTER | If you haven't yet picked up your gifts and curios, then stop by Arusha's Cultural Heritage Centre. Designed to resemble the Uhuru peak of Kilimanjaro, it's a monolith of a curio shop only

3 km (2 miles) out of town. You can buy carvings, jewelry (including the gemstone tanzanite), colorful African clothing, local music, and much more. It's a bit pricey so take advantage of the free museum that is part of the complex to get your money's worth. There are also detailed exhibits on various aspects of Tanzania's culture and heritage and an extensive art gallery. ✉ *A 104, Arusha* 🎟 *free.*

Beach Escapes

Looking for a little R&R after your safari? Tanzania has 1,424 km (883 miles) of beautiful pristine coastline to explore. Looking for an island getaway? Tanzania has those, too. Zanzibar is the larger, louder, and more party-oriented island, unless you opt for more secluded resorts and hotels, while Mafia is home to some of the best diving in Tanzania and Pemba sits quietly in the Northern corners with its picture-perfect beaches and limited number of tourists.

Zanzibar

This ancient isle once ruled by sultans and slave traders served as the stepping stone into the African continent for missionaries and explorers. Once known as the Spice Island for its export of cloves, Zanzibar—the name Zanzibar also includes the islands of Unguja (the main island) and Pemba—has become one of the most exotic flavors in travel. Today, this tiny archipelago attracts many visitors intent on discovering sandy beaches, rain forests, or blue water snorkeling; it's the perfect post-safari spot.

This tiny archipelago in the Indian Ocean was the launching base for a romantic era of expeditions into Africa. Sir Richard Burton and John Hanning Speke used it as their base when searching for the source of the Nile. It was in Zanzibar where journalist Henry Morton Stanley, perched in an upstairs room overlooking the Stone Town harbor, began his search for David Livingstone. The first ships to enter the archipelago's harbors are believed to have sailed in around 600 BC. Since then, every great navy in the eastern hemisphere has dropped anchor here at one time or another. But it was Arab traders who left an indelible mark.

The first Europeans who arrived here were the Portuguese in the 15th century, and thus began a reign of exploitation. As far inland as Lake Tanganyika, slave traders captured the residents or bartered for them from their own chiefs, then forced the newly enslaved to march toward the Indian Ocean carrying loads of ivory tusks. Once at the shore they were shackled together while waiting for dhows to collect them at Bagamoyo, a place whose name means "here I leave my heart." Although it's estimated that 50,000 slaves passed through the Zanzibar slave market each year during the 19th century, many more died en route.

Tanganyika and Zanzibar merged in 1964 to create Tanzania, but the honeymoon was brief. Zanzibar's relationship with the mainland remains uncertain as calls for independence continue. "Bismillah, will you let him go," a reference to a lyric from Queen's "Bohemian Rhapsody," has become a rebel chant for Zanzibar to break from Tanzania.

The main island of Unguja may have become a tourist beachside mecca, but the nearby islands of Pemba and Mnemba offer retreats that are still remote escapes. For many years Arabs referred to Pemba as Al Khudra, or the Green Island, and indeed it still is, with forests of king palms, mangos, and banana trees. The 65-km-long (40-mile-long) island is less famous than Unguja except among scuba divers, who enjoy the coral gardens with colorful sponges and huge fans. Archaeology buffs are also discovering Pemba, where sites from the 9th to the 15th century have been unearthed.

At Mtambwe Mkuu coins bearing the heads of sultans were discovered. Ruins along the coast include ancient mosques and tombs. In the 1930s Pemba was famous for its sorcerers, attracting disciples of the black arts from as far away as Haiti. Witchcraft is still practiced, and, oddly, so is bullfighting. Introduced by the Portuguese in the 17th century, the sport has been improved by locals, who rewrote the ending. After enduring the ritual teasing by the matador's cape, the bull is draped with flowers and paraded around the village.

WHEN TO GO

June through October is the best time to visit Zanzibar because the temperature averages 26°C (79°F); it's also high season. Spice tours are best during harvest time, July and October, when cloves (unopened flower buds) are picked and laid out to dry. Zanzibar experiences a short rainy season in November, but heavy rains can fall from February until May. Temperatures and humidity soars during this period, often reaching over 30°C (90°F). Most travelers come between June and August and from mid-November to early January. During these periods many hotels add a surcharge.

Zanzibar observes Ramadan for a month every year. During this period Muslims are forbidden to eat, drink, or smoke between sunrise and sunset. Although hotels catering to tourists aren't affected, many small shops and restaurants are closed during the day. If you plan to arrive during Ramadan, aim for the end, when a huge feast called the Eid al-Fitr (which means "end of the fast") brings everyone out to the streets.

GETTING HERE AND AROUND

There are no direct flights from the United States (though it's been talked about for years). International flights connect via Air Tanzania, Edelweiss Air, Qatar Airways, Oman Air, Fly Dubai, Neos Air, Ethiopian Air, Precision Air, and Turkish

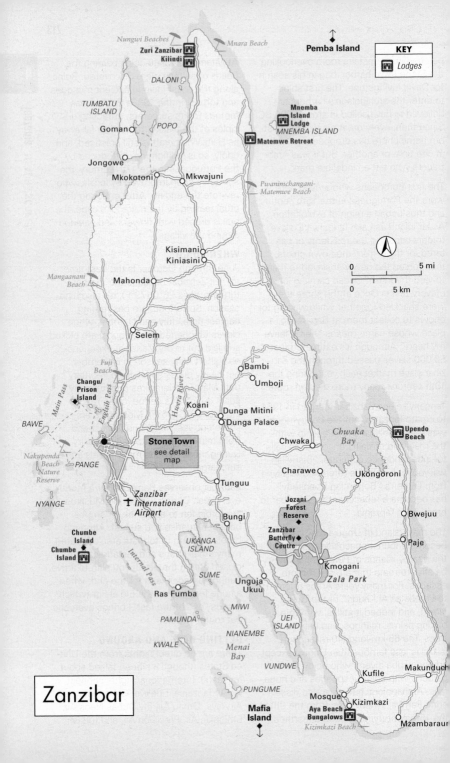

Airlines. There is now immigration and visa (and payment) on arrival, but check that you qualify before you fly.

From Dar es Salaam to Stone Town, there are regular flights in small twin-engine aircraft operated by numerous companies including Precision Air, Auric Air, and Coastal Aviation. The flight takes around 20 minutes. From Nairobi and Mombasa, you can fly to Stone Town on Kenya Airways. At this writing, the airport is undergoing some major renovations so you may have to be bused across the runways.

Visitors from the United States and Europe require visas to enter Tanzania. Zanzibar is a semiautonomous state within Tanzania, so you don't need a separate visa to visit, but you do need to show your passport, fill in an arrival form, and go through the baggage scanners.

Bikes can be rented from shops near Darajani Market. Mopeds and motorcycles are another great way to get about the island, although nothing is signposted so you could get lost frequently.

Hydrofoil ferries travel between Dar es Salaam and Stone Town. The trip takes about two hours on catamarans owned by Azam Marine, the most reliable operator. Departures leave from Dar es Salaam at 7 am, 9:30 am, 12:30 pm, and 3:45 pm. Tickets can be purchased online or at their offices—next to the port in Dar es Salaam or in their Zanzibar offices a short walk from the ferry terminal. Timetables and prices are displayed on boards outside each office. Tickets for nonresidents range from $40 (Tsh90,000) for business class to $35 (Tsh78,224) for economy. The harbor is quite busy so keep an eye on your possessions. And if you don't want help from a porter, be firm. Note that two ferries sank in 2011 and 2012, thought to be due to overcrowding, but they were the local goods and transport ferries, which may be the cheapest way to get to Zanzibar, but by

far not the safest. Whether you arrive by plane or ferry, you'll be approached by taxi drivers. Be sure to agree on a price before getting in, as taxis don't have meters. The fare to Stone Town should be around Tsh30,000 (around $15–$20). Your driver may let you out several blocks before you reach your hotel because the streets are too narrow. Ask the driver to walk you to the hotel. Alternately arrange to be picked up by your accommodation, as they will guide you into Stone Town without much fuss. Be sure to tip anyone that carries your luggage.

AIRLINES Coastal Aviation. ✉ *Bwejuu* ☎ *699/999–999* ⊕ *www.coastal.co.tz.* **Kenya Airways.** ✉ *Peugeot House, Upanga Rd., Dar es Salaam* ☎ *866/536–9224* ⊕ *www.kenya-airways.com.* **Precision Air.** ✉ *Diamond Plaza, Mirambo St., 1st fl., Dar es Salaam* ⊕ *www.precisionairtz. com.* **ZanAir.** ✉ *Muzammil Center, Stone Town* ☎ *242/233–768* ⊕ *www.zanair.com.*

AIRPORTS Abeid Amani Karume International Airport. ✉ *Abeid Amani Karume International Airport, Bwejuu* ⊕ *www. zaa.go.tz.*

FERRIES Azam Marine. ✉ *Zanzibar Terminal, Bwejuu* ☎ *22/212–3324 in Dar es Salaam, 24/223–1655 in Zanzibar* ⊕ *www.azammarine.com.*

HEALTH AND SAFETY
Visitors to Zanzibar are required to have a yellow-fever vaccination certificate; some websites also recommend polio, hepatitis A, and typhoid vaccinations. You should also talk with your doctor about a malaria prophylactic. The best way to avoid malaria is to avoid being bitten by mosquitoes, so make sure your arms and legs are covered and that you wear plenty of mosquito repellent, especially after dusk. Antihistamine cream is also quite useful to stop the itch of mosquito bites. Always sleep under a mosquito net; most hotels and guesthouses provide them. The sun can be very strong here, so make sure to slather yourself

with sunscreen as well. Drink bottled water, and plenty of it—it'll help you avoid dehydration. Avoid raw fruits and vegetables that may have been washed in untreated water.

Although the best way to experience Stone Town is to wander around its labyrinthine streets, you should always be on your guard. Don't wear jewelry or watches that might attract attention, and keep a firm grasp on purses and camera bags. Leave valuables in the safe at your hotel.

Muggings have been reported at Nungwi and other coastal resorts, so never carry valuables onto the beach or in side alleys. Nungwi is known as the party side of Zanzibar; if you want a quiet retreat free from beach boys and loud beach parties then head elsewhere.

As Zanzibar is a largely conservative Muslim state, it's advisable for everyone to dress and act modestly. This means no walking around in just swimsuits outside of the beach. Uncovered shoulders and heads are fine, but never cleavage or torsos. Many tourists often ignore this advice, and although locals are too polite to say anything, it's not appreciated and it does not put tourists in good standing among locals. It does not take much effort to cover up. There are beautiful local materials that will protect you from the heat and humidity and double up as exquisite take-home pieces. Tip: if it is really humid, a light kanga can be dipped in water and act as a homemade cooling pad if worn around the neck. Try to adhere to basic social customs, even if you might not feel like it. Holding hands is fine, but overly intimate displays of affection should be avoided.

■TIP→ **Always ask permission before taking photographs, and be prepared to pay a small tip in return, particularly to the Maasai.**

CONTACTS Zanaid Clinic. ✉ *Chukwani, Mbweni, Stone Town* ✛ *close to the airport* ☎ *777/777–122* ⊕ *www.zanaid. org.* **Zanzibar Tourist Corporation.** ✉ *Aamani, Bwejuu* ☎ *24/24–223–3485* ⊕ *www. zanzibartourism.go.tz.* **Wajamama.** ✉ *Matrekta Rd., Mjini Magharibi Region* ☎ *758/648–885* ⊕ *www.wajamama.com.*

MONEY MATTERS
Stone Town is dotted with ATMs that accept Visa and MasterCard. Make sure you don't try to withdraw money on paydays (lines can be long and ATMs empty fast) and always be cautious as you would in any city.

There are handy currency exchange booths in Stone Town that offer good rates. Most people will accept U.S. dollars, but be aware of the exchange rate and make sure you're not being overcharged.

TELEPHONES
The regional code for Zanzibar is 255 followed by the local number.

■TIP→ **Telephone numbers seem to lack consistency, so they're listed as they appear in promotional materials.**

TOURS
Spice tours are a popular way to see Zanzibar. Guides take you to farms in Kizimbani or Kindaichi and teach you to identify plants that produce cinnamon, turmeric, nutmeg, and vanilla. A curry luncheon will undoubtedly use some of the local spices. Any tour company can arrange a spice tour, with the average price for a spice tour ranging from $20 to $50, depending on the number of people, including lunch. Most depart around 9 am from Stone Town.

Various tour operators and most hotels offer tour options that include visits to Prison Island, Jozani Forest, and the Zanzibar Butterfly Centre. Unwind at Kholle House Spa with some of their signature massages or take a yoga or meditation class with Uzima Space on Kaunda Road.

Amo Zanzibar Tours

GUIDED TOURS | A family-owned tour company based in Stone Town. Options include snorkeling in Mnemba, canoeing through the mangroves, or visiting Jozani forest, the Zanzibar Butterfly Center, or a Swahili village. ✉ *Mkunazini St., Stone Town* ☎ *744/590–020* ⊕ *www.amozanzibartours.com.*

Zanzibar Dive Centre, One Ocean

ADVENTURE TOURS | Since 1993, One Ocean has been taking visitors snorkeling and scuba diving and offers scuba diving courses. ✉ *Kenyatta Rd., Stone Town* ✛ *opposite the NBC bank outside of the tunnel* ☎ *774/310–003* ⊕ *www.zanzibaroneocean.com.*

Zanzibar Different Tours

CULTURAL TOURS | Based in Zanzibar, this tour company offers more than just your standard spice and island tour. Choose from walking tours of Stone Town that focus on its history or personal wellness (think seaweed wraps). You can take a sunset dhow (traditional boat) cruise or visit an organic farm for a home-cooked lunch or participate in a tea ceremony. They even offer kid-friendly versions of their tours, and, their efforts support the local community by encouraging guests to buy local and explore the real Swahili coast. ✉ *Soko Muhogo St., Stone Town* ☎ *24/223–0004* ⊕ *www.zanzibardifferent.com.*

VISITOR INFORMATION

The free tourist magazines *Swahili Coast* and *Dar Life* can be found in hotels, shops, and on most flights. They list cultural events, as well as tide tables that are very useful.

There's a tourist information center north of Stone Town. Also, pay attention to local restaurant and hotel social media pages as they will be up to date on events and occasions happening month to month.

STONE TOWN

Stone Town, the archipelago's major metropolis, is a maze of narrow streets lined with houses featuring magnificently carved doors studded with brass. There are 51 mosques, six Hindu temples, and two Christian churches. Minarets punctuate the town's skyline, where more than 90% of the residents are Muslim. In the harbor you'll see dhows, the Arabian boats with triangular sails. Islamic women covered by black boubou veils scurry down alleyways so narrow their outstretched arms could touch buildings on both sides.

It's also regarded as a mini fashion mecca for East Africa. Don't miss visiting the famous Doreen Mashinka or the delightful Upendo Means Love and Mago for unique fashion items.

◉ Sights

The sights in Stone Town are all minutes from one another so you'll see them all as you walk. However, the old part of town is very compact and maze-like and can be a bit disconcerting. Hiring a guide is a great way to see the city without stress, and a guide can provide information about the sights you'll see. Many tour operators offer a guided walking tour for approximately US$20–US$25. Ask your hotel for guide suggestions. That said, getting lost is part of the experience of Stone Town; it is a small, compact area and you can easily ask a vendor to point you in the general direction of the Fort, an easy landmark. Take your time around the streets, don't panic if you don't know exactly where you are—the joy of traveling is chatting to people and discovering quiet corners, intimate exchanges of daily life and, yes, the shopping.

House of Wonders

NOTABLE BUILDING | Known as the House of Wonders, Beit el-Ajaib was the first building in Zanzibar to use electric lights, and this four-story palace is still one of

Stone Town's colorful alleyways are great to explore with a guide.

the largest buildings in the city. Built in the late 1800s for Sultan Barghash, it was bombarded by the British in 1886, forcing the sultan to abdicate his throne. Due to a partial collapse in 2020, the palace is closed to the public though restoration efforts are underway. However, the building is still worth checking out for its architectural elements and historical significance. ⊠ *Zanzibar* ✛ *North of Old Fort.*

Christ Church Cathedral and Slave Museum

HISTORY MUSEUM | A must-see in Stone town, this was the first Anglican cathedral in East Africa and its crucifix was carved from the tree under which explorer David Livingstone's heart was buried in the village of Chitambo. Built in 1887 to mark the end of the slave trade, the cathedral's high altar was constructed on the site of a whipping post. The moving and contemplative slave memorial and slave trade exhibit are sobering reminders of the ravages of slavery across East Africa and on the island. Nearby are underground chambers in which slaves

were forced to crouch on stone shelves less than 2 feet high. It is recommended to take a guide with you as with such a poignant space you would want to get as much information as possible. ⊠ *Off Creek Rd., Zanzibar* 💷 *Tsh12,000 (US$5).*

Darajani Bazaar

NOTABLE BUILDING | This gable-roofed structure, built in 1904 and also known as Estella Market, houses a sprawling fruit, fish, meat, and vegetable market. Goods of all sorts—colorful fabrics, wooden chests, and all types of jewelry—are sold in the shops that line the surrounding streets. To the east of the main building you'll find spices laid out in colorful displays of beige, yellow, and red. On Wednesday and Saturday there's an antiques fair. The market is most active in the morning between 9 and 11. ⊠ *Creek Rd., north of New Mkunazini St., Zanzibar* 💷 *Free.*

Forodhani Gardens

GARDEN | This pleasant waterfront park is a favorite spot for an evening stroll both for locals and tourists. Dozens of vendors

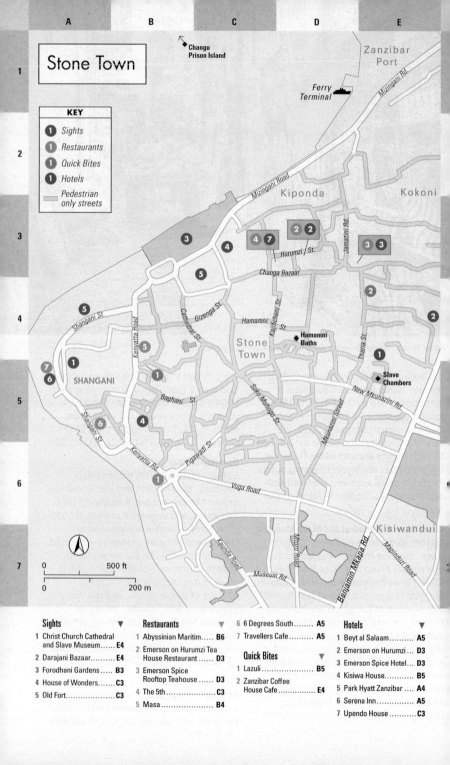

Stone Town

KEY
- Sights
- Restaurants
- Quick Bites
- Hotels
- Pedestrian only streets

Sights ▼
1. Christ Church Cathedral and Slave Museum...... **E4**
2. Darajani Bazaar.......... **E4**
3. Forodhani Gardens **B3**
4. House of Wonders....... **C3**
5. Old Fort.................. **C3**

Restaurants ▼
1. Abyssinian Maritim..... **B6**
2. Emerson on Hurumzi Tea House Restaurant **D3**
3. Emerson Spice Rooftop Teahouse **D3**
4. The 5th **C3**
5. Masa **B4**
6. 6 Degrees South......... **A5**
7. Travellers Cafe **A5**

Quick Bites ▼
1. Lazuli **B5**
2. Zanzibar Coffee House Cafe **E4**

Hotels ▼
1. Beyt al Salaam.......... **A5**
2. Emerson on Hurumzi ... **D3**
3. Emerson Spice Hotel... **D3**
4. Kisiwa House........... **B5**
5. Park Hyatt Zanzibar **A4**
6. Serena Inn.............. **A5**
7. Upendo House **C3**

sell grilled fish under the light of gas lanterns—not all the food is great, but the atmosphere is fantastic for a visit, especially during the evening hours.

■ TIP→ **Always try to smell the seafood before you eat it as some of it can be old, and don't be pressured by any of the vendors. You should look at everything before making your decisions.** ✉ *Mizingani St., Zanzibar.*

Old Fort

MILITARY SIGHT | Built by the Portuguese in 1560, this bastioned fortress is the oldest structure in Stone Town. It withstood an attack from Arabs in 1754 and was later used as a jail; prisoners who were sentenced to death met their ends here. It has undergone extensive renovation and today is headquarters for many cultural organizations, including the famous Sauti za Busara and Mashariki Jazz and Folk music festival. There is also a craft market inside. Performances of traditional dance and music are sometimes staged during the week. Check the office and posters outside for details. ✉ *Creek Rd. at Malawi Rd., Zanzibar* 🎫 *Free.*

🍴 Restaurants

Zanzibar was the legendary Spice Island, so it's no surprise the cuisine here is flavored with lemongrass, cumin, and garlic. Cinnamon enlivens tea and coffee, while ginger flavors a refreshing soft drink called Tangawizi. More than 20 types of mangos, as well as bananas, papayas, pineapples, and passion fruit grow on the island. When it comes to dinner, seafood reigns supreme. Try the prawn kebabs, roasted peanuts, and corn on the cob at the outdoor market at Forodhani Gardens (but not if you have a sensitive tummy). Try the vegetarian Zanzibar pizza for breakfast; it's more like an omelet. There is the Cape Town fish market which has opened on the pier. It's pleasant, but don't expect anything distinctly Zanzibari beyond the cocktails and views.

Gratuities are often included in the bill, so ask the staff before adding the usual 10% tip. Credit cards are widely accepted, but there is no harm in making sure you have enough cash. Lunch hours are generally 12:30 to 2:30, dinner 7 to 10:30. Dress is casual for all but upscale restaurants, where you should avoid T-shirts, shorts, and sneakers.

Abyssinian Maritim

$$ | ETHIOPIAN | The only fully traditional Ethiopian restaurant in Zanzibar, Abyssinian has all the staples—*kitfo* (beef tartare) in *mitmita* (chili powder marinade), *injera* (sourdough bread), *doro wat* (fragrant chicken stew), and of course, *Tej* (honey wine) and coffee; it's a simple but tasty menu that's perfect for sharing with groups and friends. Tucked along the edges of the busy Vuga traffic roundabout on the edge of Stone Town, inside a charming and cozy courtyard, this is truly an authentic Ethiopian dining experience. **Known for:** a traditional Ethiopian coffee ceremony; very buggy, especially if its humid (bring mosquito repellent); large portions. [$] *Average main: $20* ✉ *Stone Town* ✣ *Vuga roundabout on the edge of Stone Town next to High Court* ☎ *772/940–556* 🌐 *www.facebook.com/abyssinianmaritim* 🕒 *Closed Tues.*

★ **Emerson on Hurumzi Tea House Restaurant**

$$$$ | AFRICAN | With stunning views past the city's minarets to the harbor where dhows are setting out to sea, this rooftop restaurant is a wonderful homage to Stone Towns' rich and varied past. Dining is done at low wooden tables with plush patterned cushions, billowing fabric, and hanging lanterns, and traditional etiquette and customs are observed as you enjoy a journey back in time through the history of the region using storytelling, delicious food, and music. **Known for:** traditional Persian and Tanzanian dishes; sunset serenading by the talented Dhow Music

Academy; stunning views in a luxuriant and atmospheric setting. $ *Average main: $40* ✉ *236 Hurumzi St., Stone Town* ☎ *779/854–225* ⊕ *www.emerson-zanzibar.com* ⊘ *Closed Mon.*

Emerson Spice Rooftop Teahouse

$$$$ | SEAFOOD | One of those dining experiences that seems to be a rite of passage for visitors to Stone Town, guests ascend a mammoth series of stairs that leads to the rooftop dining area and an expansive view over Stone Town. A seasonal five-course degustation menu of tasty Swahili-inspired seafood cuisine ranges from prawns and grilled fish to slivers of seared beef in traditional spices. **Known for:** dietary adjustments possible; a downstairs secret garden filled with atmosphere that is well worth the visit for lunch; upmarket dining with popular rooftop views. $ *Average main: $40* ✉ *Emerson Spice Hotel, Tharia St., Kiponda* ☎ *779/854–225* ⊕ *www.emersonspice.com* ⊘ *Closed Thurs.*

★ The 5th

$$ | ECLECTIC | Ascend up the winding staircase past the eclectic collection of artwork to a bright and sunny sun-deck with an infinity pool overlooking downtown Stone Town. This is the spot for sunset cocktails, vibey DJ music, and delicious nibbles—the menu is a fusion of Indian, Mediterranean, and Swahili flavors like tuna and compressed watermelon and ponzu or pan seared octopus and chorizo with a chimichurri chased down with a spiced mango daiquiri. **Known for:** brunch on Saturday and Sunday; drinks come at a premium so splurge on something you really want; beautiful views over downtown Stone Town. $ *Average main: $12* ✉ *Upendo House, 213/14 Hurumzi St., Stone Town* ☎ *772/389–002* ⊕ *www.upendozanzibar.com* ☞ *3% surcharge on credit cards.*

Masa

$ | JAPANESE | Sitting on a small terrace that overlooks the colorful and lively streets of downtown Stone Town, this Japanese restaurant—the only one on the island—offers up small share plates of Asian-inspired fusion food. The wide selection of freshly prepared seafood dishes and good service make this a good bet for any occasion. **Known for:** tasty sushi and tempura; open until 11 pm nightly; a larger vegetarian menu than other restaurants; great views of the passing nightlife. $ *Average main: $5* ✉ *Shangani Post Office, 1st fl., Stone Town* ⊕ *Entrance is behind the building; follow the signs to "Tapas Bar," up some flights of stairs* ☎ *624/161–393* ⊕ *www.masazanzibar.com.*

★ 6 Degrees South

$$ | CONTEMPORARY | If you're looking for a sunset cocktail with views of the Zanzibar ocean, then head on over to 6 Degrees on Shangani Street. Fresh, modern Afro-Continental cuisine such as generously sized burgers and steaks grilled on the flame are served in a relaxed, breezy atmosphere under a large double-story terrace that's decked out with modern, white loungers. **Known for:** floor-to-ceiling wine vault offers the perfect chilled glass of vino; incredibly delicious Chips Masala; great views from the upper floor. $ *Average main: $12* ✉ *Shangani St., Zanzibar* ⊕ *near the Park Hyatt* ☎ *62/064–4611* ⊕ *www.6degreessouth.co.tz.*

Travellers Cafe

$ | BURGER | Locals and expats in the know have this as their go-to stop for a good, hearty meal with a cold beer and a charming atmosphere undisturbed by the tourist trail. Expect a full plate—burgers, grilled chicken, and chips—and a good beer at a decent price with an unassuming local atmosphere; this is not the place for cocktails and wine. **Known for:**

great vantage point for watching beach life at sunset; good service and good prices; rustic comfort and charm. $ *Average main: Tsh8* ⊠ *Shangani St., Stone Town* ⊕ *past the Serena on the right; look for the sign board on the street* ☎ *774/506–618.*

☕ Coffee and Quick Bites

Lazuli
$ | **INTERNATIONAL** | A tiny blue-lined door frame and the fine printed "Lazuli" sign are all that let you know that you have found this little street-side cafe. The large wraps and fruit smoothies are prepared with fresh, local ingredients. **Known for:** fresh juices; wonderfully well priced for the great quality; some of the best and most generously sized smoothies in town. $ *Average main: $2* ⊠ *Stone Town* ⊕ *Head past all the main tourist shops, look out for the bank on the corner—it's right there.*

Zanzibar Coffee House Cafe
$ | **CAFÉ** | If there is one place to get a good cup of locally brewed African coffee it's the unassuming Zanzibar Coffee house, a sweet paradise tucked in amid the houses to the alleyways. There might not be any Wi-Fi in the back thanks to the thick walls common in a traditional Arabic house, but it is a cool and deliciously simple café. **Known for:** lovely rooftop coffee experience; a small, cozy space; coffee and cakes. $ *Average main: $9* ⊠ *Mkunazini St., Stone Town* ⊕ *head toward Emerson Spice Hotel and then keep going a few meters* ☎ *24/223–9319* ⊕ *www.zanzibarcoffeehouse.com* ⊘ *Closed May.*

🛏 Hotels

Beyt al Salaam
$ | **B&B/INN** | This former teahouse is now an intimate hotel with a whole lot of character and great service. **Pros:** a traditional Zanzibar house; excellent location just outside of the main town; beautiful

resturant dining area that oozes old-world Zanzibar charm. **Cons:** plenty of stairs for those with mobility issues; some rooms are small, so if you need space get the deluxe rooms; rooms are dated and bathrooms could use a refurbishment. $ *Rooms from: $100* ⊠ *Kele Square, Kilele Square* ☎ *773/000–086* ⊕ *www.beytalsalaam.com* ⇆ *11 rooms* ⏸ *Free Breakfast.*

★ Emerson on Hurumzi
$ | **B&B/INN** | Tucked away in Stone Town, this small hotel, once the home of one of the richest men in Zanzibar, was the brainchild of two New Yorkers. **Pros:** unique room designs in keeping with the Emerson Spice brand; historic ambience; wonderfully authentic rooftop teahouse is a must (booking essential). **Cons:** some rooms have no sea views or a/c; some rooms have showers and toilets not separate from the room; lots and lots of wooden stairs. $ *Rooms from: $185* ⊠ *236 Hurumzi St., Stone Town* ☎ *779/854–225* ⊕ *www.emersonzanzibar.com* ⇆ *10 rooms* ⏸ *Free Breakfast.*

Emerson Spice Hotel
$ | **B&B/INN** | Located right in the center of the maze of alleyways that make up Stone Town, this historic building has been converted into a hotel with wonderfully whimsical rooms, each with a different theme. **Pros:** delightful teahouse on the roof; lunch at the Secret Garden Restaurant; authentic, quirky ambience—bring your camera!. **Cons:** rooms and general decor is slightly worn; rooms facing into other buildings might be a bit dark; lots and lots of stairs. $ *Rooms from: $225* ⊠ *Tharia St., Kipondo, Kiponda* ☎ *779/854–225* ⊕ *www.emersonspice.com* ⇆ *10 suites* ⏸ *Free Breakfast.*

★ Kisiwa House
$$ | **HOTEL** | This stylish boutique hotel, housed in a beautifully restored 19th-century Zanzibari town house, manages to combine old-fashioned authenticity—steep wooden staircases, high ceilings, an inner courtyard, and pretty rooftop

restaurant—with modern touches, such as the contemporary art on the walls, flat-screen TVs, and large, modern, luxurious bathrooms that have bathtubs as well as showers. **Pros:** rates are very reasonable considering the amenities; great location; rooms are incredibly large. **Cons:** no views from the rooms; sparse lounge areas outside the rooms; lots of steep stairs. [$] *Rooms from: $270* ✉ *572 Baghani St., Stone Town* ☎ *24/223–0685* 🌐 *www.kisiwahouse.com* 🛏 *10 rooms* 🍴 *Free Breakfast.*

Park Hyatt Zanzibar
$$ | **HOTEL** | Once the home of a 17th-century businessman, the Park Hyatt occupies the desirable beachside location near the winding streets of central Stone Town. **Pros:** high-end, classy luxury in an exquisite setting; attention to detail indoors pays homage to the building's history; views of the sunset from the beautiful outdoor areas. **Cons:** modern luxury comes at a price; outside areas are a bit lacking in personality considering the overall finishes of the hotel; a very small pool area can get crowded during peak season. [$] *Rooms from: $400* ✉ *Shangani St.* ☎ *24/550–1234* 🌐 *www.hyatt.com* 🛏 *67 rooms* 🍴 *Free Breakfast.*

★ **Upendo House**
$$ | **HOTEL** | The city hotel to its sister beach hotel in Mchumvi, Upendo House has fast become the cool kid on the winding Stone Town alleyways. **Pros:** service here is both thoughtful and attentive; fabulous sundeck with infinity pool on the rooftop; the delicious food is some of the best in Stone Town. **Cons:** standard rooms are on the slightly small size; surcharge on credit card use can make the bill add up; seating space at the sundeck is limited. [$] *Rooms from: $430* ✉ *213/4 Hurumzi St., Stone Town* ☎ *772/389–002* 🌐 *www.upendozanzibar.com* 🛏 *8 rooms* 🍴 *Free Breakfast.*

Serena Inn
$$ | **HOTEL** | On one side of Shangani Square, on the fringe of Stone Town, this beautiful hotel is the result of the restoration of two of Zanzibar's historic buildings: the old Telekoms building, an original colonial-era building, and the Chinese doctors' residence. **Pros:** location on the outside of town with beach views; spacious swimming pool area; modern rooms on upper floors have large balconies with views. **Cons:** no elevator for the upper floors; cheaper-priced rooms are quite small; rather large hotel, where service suffers in peak season. [$] *Rooms from: $319* ✉ *Shangani St., Stone Town* ☎ *732/124–000* 🌐 *www.serenahotels.com/zanzibar* 🛏 *51 rooms* 🍴 *Free Breakfast.*

BEYOND STONE TOWN

Zanzibar Island, locally known as Unguja, has amazing beaches and resorts, warm-water diving, and acres of spice plantations. Much of the western part of the larger island is a slumbering paradise where cloves, as well as rice and coconuts, still grow.

Smaller islands in the Zanzibar Archipelago range from mere sandbanks to Chumbe Island, the country's first marine national park; Mnemba, a private retreat for guests who pay hundreds of dollars per day to get away from it all; and Changu: once a prison island, it's now home to the giant Aldabra tortoise.

👁 Sights

Changuu/Prison Island (*Prison Island*)
BEACH | This tiny island, just a 20-minute boat ride from Stone Town, was once a prison and a quarantine location, hence its more well-known name of Prison Island. Now it's a tropical paradise that's home to the giant Aldabra tortoise (you can visit the tortoises for a small fee), the duiker antelope, and a variety of birds and butterflies. There's also decent swimming and snorkeling and arranged beach

barbecues by tour operators. Note that 70% of the island is private property and thus inaccessible.

■ TIP→ **You can visit Changuu Island on a tour, or arrange transport with the myriad of little boats that line the beach outside Archipelago Waterfront Cafe. There's no entry fee for the island itself.** ⊠ *Zanzibar* ✛ *5.6 km (3.5 miles) northwest of the main island of Zanzibar* ⌸ *US$23 for a boat ride.*

★ **Chumbe Island**

ISLAND | Between the Tanzanian coast and the islands of Zanzibar, Chumbe Island is the country's first marine national park and has some of the better snorkeling around. It's home to 400 species of coral and 200 species of fish. There's scuba diving, snorkeling, island hikes, and outrigger boat rides.

■ TIP→ **The island can only be visited on an organized day trip. Price includes boat transfers, lunch, snorkeling, forest walk, and V.A.T.** ⊠ *Chumbe Island, Zanzibar* ☏ *777/413–232* ⊕ *www.chumbeisland. com* ⌸ *$90.*

Jozani Forest Reserve

FOREST | Jozani Chakwa Bay National Park, Zanzibar's only national park, is home to this reserve where you'll find the rare Kirk's red colobus monkey, which is named after Sir John Kirk, the British consul in Zanzibar from 1866 to 1887. The species is known for its white whiskers and rusty coat. Many of the other animals that call this reserve home— including the blue duiker, a diminutive antelope whose coat is a dusty bluish-gray—are endangered because 95% of the original forests of the archipelago have been destroyed. There are also more than 50 species of butterfly and 40 bird species. The entry fee includes entrance to the forest and a circular boardwalk walk through mangrove swamps, plus the services of a guide (tip him if he's good).

■ TIP→ **Early morning and evenings are the best time to visit.** ⊠ *Zanzibar* ✛ *38 km (27 miles) southeast of Stone Town* ⌸ *US$7.*

Zanzibar Butterfly Centre

OTHER ATTRACTION | This well-worn center is worth a stop if you're traveling with kids. It's a community development project, and your entry fee pays for local farmers to bring in cocoons (most of which are sent to museums overseas) and helps preserve the forest. Guided tours end in a visit to an enclosure filled with hundreds of colorful butterflies and some chameleons. ⊠ *1 km (½ mile) from Jozani Forest, Zanzibar* ⊕ *www. facebook.com/ZanzibarButterflyCenter/* ⌸ *Tsh 12,000 (US$5).*

Beaches

Although Zanzibar offers quintessential powdery white sand and calm, warm turquoise waters, traveling from one beach to another by taxi can get quite expensive (and local taxis, or *daladalas,* are uncomfortable and dangerous). Most tourists opt instead to enjoy the beach in front of their resort. Doing so offers you a measure of protection from "beach boys," or touts, who frequent the beaches looking for customers. Young backpackers and those wanting some hedonistic nightlife usually head to Nungwi, or Kendwa on the north coast, which have good beaches that aren't greatly affected by the tides; it's near impossible to swim during low tide. Paje and Kizmikazi are on the more subdued side of the island. Even with the varying tide, you can always take the opportunity to explore rock pools. Just be sure to wear reef shoes—sea urchins are painful to step on.

Nakupenda Beach Nature Reserve

BEACH | Grab some snacks and plenty of bottled water and head to this charming sandbank that's about a 30-minute boat ride from Stone Town. A lovely, sandy beach and place to snorkel make it a great day trip. You can hire a boat from the harbor to take you there on a negotiated fee for a few hours or, if you prefer to be fully catered to, go with a tour company who will provide the shade and the beach picnic with seafood and drinks as part of their price. Be warned it will get crowded in high season. ■ **TIP→ There is no shade on the island, so make sure you bring a hat and umbrella.** **Amenities:** none. **Best for:** snorkeling; swimming; walking. *🎫 general cost is around $40 , but price decreases vastly with group bookings*

Hotels

Aya Beach Bungalows

$ | B&B/INN | While there are many small lodges that dot this part of the coastline, Aya Bungalows is a small boutique hotel that's intimate in space and style. **Pros:** beautiful dining area with attentive staff; family villa is the same price as the others, but with a private lounge area with views; intimate and perfect for families. **Cons:** not really a swimming beach; Kizimkazi side is remote; back rooms have limited views and are very small. *[$] Rooms from: $120 ✉ Kizimkazi ☎ 622/764–104 🛏 12 bungalows 🍴 Free Breakfast.*

★ Chumbe Island

$$$ | RESORT | The island's ecotourism concept was the brainstorm of a German conservationist who, since the early 1990s, has succeeded in developing it as one of the world's foremost marine sanctuaries. **Pros:** some of the best snorkeling in Zanzibar; excellent food and involved staff; quaint stretch of beach that is pure magic. **Cons:** it's expensive for the level of rusticity but some will like this; low tide means exposed coral on the beach; the boat trip from Stone Town takes 45 minutes, and there's only one departure a day (later departures cost extra). *[$] Rooms from: $540 ✉ Chumbe Island, Zanzibar ☎ 777/413–232 🌐 www.chumbeisland.com ⏲ Closed April and May 🛏 7 bungalows 🍴 All-Inclusive.*

Kilindi

$$$$ | RESORT | Kilindi whisks you away to a private, luxury resort on the northernmost part of the island with a combination of barefoot luxury and excellent service. **Pros:** wonderfully romantic on-site spa; your own butler to cater to your needs; remote location with a beautiful beach. **Cons:** the rooms are open, which means insects are possible; bathrooms are separate from rooms; location might be too remote for some. *[$] Rooms from: $1,300 ✉ Kendwa, Zanzibar ☎ 730/127–000 🌐 www.elewanacollection.com 🛏 15 suites 🍴 Free Breakfast ☞ Couples only; 2-night minimum.*

★ Matemwe Retreat

$$$$ | ALL-INCLUSIVE | Overlooking Mnemba Atoll on the more secluded stretch of Matemwe beach in Northern Zanzibar, the four self-contained double-story villas of Matemwe retreat are nestled amid the island palms. **Pros:** a quiet stretch of beach, away from the crowds of the north; plenty of on-site ocean activities worth venturing out of your villa for; an on-site spa for extra pampering. **Cons:** tides on the beach are very shallow for swimming; main areas are quite a walk from the villas; not the place if you want to party. *[$] Rooms from: $605 ✉ Matemwe ☎ 21/418–0468 in South Africa 🌐 www.asiliaafrica.com 🛏 4 villas 🍴 All-Inclusive ☞ 2-night minimum.*

Mnemba Island Lodge

$$$$ | HOTEL | For the ultimate beach escape where time stands still, where sand, sea, and horizon melt into each other, where there's exclusivity, total relaxation, and impeccable food and service, it would be hard to find anywhere in the world as alluring as Mnemba Island Lodge. **Pros:** an on-site PADI diver center caters to all water lovers; evenings on the beach on a private island watching the sunset are pure heaven; gorgeous communal lounge and dining spaces on the sand. **Cons:** be aware that your luxury banda is not traditionally enclosed; hordes of divers and tourists arrive twice a day even though the island is private (there is a hefty fine); large flocks of doves that come over from mainland can be noisy. $ *Rooms from: $1,320* ✉ *Mnemba Island, Mnemba Island* ☎ *11/809–4300 in South Africa* ⊕ *www.andbeyond.com* ⤳ *11 bungalows* ❍❙ *All-Inclusive.*

Upendo Beach

$$$$ | B&B/INN | Upendo in Swahili translates to "love", and guests will certainly fall in love with this small boutique beach hotel. **Pros:** outside beach lounge area has exceptional views; mobile spa and yoga experiences; the food and cocktails are delicious. **Cons:** main social areas can get busy on weekends; most villas are adults only; this level of luxury and attention is expensive. $ *Rooms from: $1530* ✉ *Michumvi* ☎ *777/770–667* ⊕ *www. upendozanzibar.com/upendobeach* ⤳ *7 suites* ❍❙ *Free Breakfast* ⌸ *2-night minimum.*

★ Zuri Zanzibar

$$$$ | ALL-INCLUSIVE | Zuri translates to "beautiful" in Swahili and they have taken that term to heart at this lodge. **Pros:** oceanfront villas are the next level in luxury; attention to detail is paramount from service to style; DJ'd sundowners on the beach. **Cons:** a behemoth of a hotel is being constructed nearby which could increase beach traffic; some views from the suites are more of jungle than water; lots of stairs for those with serious mobility issues. $ *Rooms from: $820* ✉ *Kendwa, Nungwi* ✛ *Just a little way south of Nungwi main* ☎ *778/157–041* ⊕ *www.zurizanzibar.com* ⤳ *56 suites* ❍❙ *All-Inclusive.*

Mafia Island

Just 160 km (99 miles) south of Zanzibar is an archipelago of inland bays and lagoons, towering palm groves dotted with ancient 8th-century ruins, and one of the most interesting marine ecosystems and coral reefs in Tanzania. With a population of only 50,000 people, what was once a safe haven for ships searching for supplies now offers up a far more intimate island escape with a bounty of wildlife above and below the waters without the hordes of tourists that descend on Zanzibar. The Marine Park was one of the first established in Tanzania, spanning 821 km (510 miles) and bordered by a barrier reef teeming with marine life. Whale sharks are the big attraction here and they normally frequent the waters around Mafia from November to February. Choose your operator carefully as some are only out to make a buck and put the animals' lives at risk. Walk through the ancient ruins at Kisimani Mafia, Kanga, Kua on Juani Island, and Chole Island, visit some of the most famous boat builders in East Africa, or join a sunset cruise to spot the giant flying fox (pteropus).

GETTING HERE AND AROUND

There are daily flights from Dar es Salaam and Zanzibar to Mafia Island via the many local airlines. Generally there are taxis at the airport, but it is best to arrange transport with your accommodation. If you are feeling brave you can take a bajaj (a tiny vehicle with three wheels), which will cost around Tsh20,000, but make sure you don't have a lot of luggage in tow. All snorkeling and diving activities inside Chole Bay are tide-dependent. It's better to book your diving as you arrive on the island and not through tour operators, unless you are an experienced diver. Take advantage of any good offers, but do so through the dive centers directly.

The entry fee into the marine park is US$23 per day, to be paid in cash at the offices on the way into the park. There is one international ATM on the island and you can change foreign currency at the bank in Kilondoni.

Hotels

Options for budget accommodations on Mafia Island are fairly limited, and most of them will be either outside the Marine Park or buried deep in the villages and in varying degrees of maintenance.

Big Blue Divers

$ | **RESORT** | If you are in Mafia to dive but also are watching the wallet then Big Blue is a great option, with a selection of affordable tents and bungalows. **Pros:** budget friendly; great for diving and snorkeling; lovely location near the water. **Cons:** tents can be hot during peak summer; Mafia island prices in general are quite expensive; rather Spartan accommodation, but worth it if coupled with diving packages. [$] *Rooms from: $120* ✉ *Utende Beach, Mafia Island* ☎ *787/474–108* 🌐 *www.bigblumafia.com* 🛏 *7 bungalows, 7 tents* 🍴 *No Meals.*

Butiama Beach

$ | **RESORT** | **FAMILY** | Butiama Group runs three types of properties across Mafia Island including Bustani, an intimate 10-room lodge on a hillside with a large pool and gardens outside of the marine park. **Pros:** best place for fishing or water sports and whale shark sightings; large, open dining and relaxation spaces with a swimming pool; a clean and tidy budget option. **Cons:** next to the main port area so beach is not always private; some bungalows have limited sea views; outside the Marine Park so you travel some distance to get to dive sites. [$] *Rooms from: $160* ✉ *Butiama Beach, Mafia Island* ☎ *787/474–484* 🌐 *www.butiamamafiaisland.com* 🛏 *15 bungalows* 🍴 *All-Inclusive.*

★ **Chole Mjini**

$$ | **RESORT** | Climbing up the winding steps rotating around the trunk of a baobab tree, the tree houses of Chole Mjini will satisfy anyone with an island castaway fantasy. **Pros:** sleeping in one of East Africa's unique settings; dinner by candlelight in an ancient ruin; the best place to see whale sharks in an ethical manner. **Cons:** no swimming beach; open tree house means there will be a few night critters; no toilets in the tree house, so you have to walk down stairs to get to the bathroom at night. [$] *Rooms from: $404* ✉ *Chole Island, Mafia Island* ☎ *787/712–427* 🌐 *www.cholemjini.com* 🕒 *Closed mid Mar.–mid June* 🛏 *7 treehouses* 🍴 *All-Inclusive.*

★ **Pole Pole Bungalows**

$$ | **RESORT** | In Swahili, *pole pole* means to go slowly, and at this intimate little resort this is very much encouraged. **Pros:** barefoot luxury and seclusion; lovely swimming pool; complimentary sunset cruises in traditional dhows. **Cons:** dive shop is only accessible at low tide; beach is tidal; there is no air-conditioning, but the bungalows are constructed to direct the breeze inside. [$] *Rooms from: $295* ✉ *Mafia Island, Utende* 🌐 *www.polepole.com* 🕒 *Closed late Apr.–mid-May* 🛏 *9 bungalows* 🍴 *All-Inclusive.*

Pemba Island

With a population of about 406,800 and only a small amount of visitors every year, this relatively pristine island is dotted with mangroves and ancient forests, lush lagoons, spectacular diving, delicate white-sand beaches, and a coastline that is rugged, with large stretches relatively untouched by mass tourism activities. Out here the monsoons set the pace of life, and the only constant that has survived Portuguese occupation, Omani Arab rule, and British administration are the Arab dhows that sail in and out through the lagoons bound by the old trade winds and the rising and ebbing tides. Pemba draws its name for the Arabic for "Green Island" and it produces about 70% of the world's cloves. The population here is a mix of Arab and original Swahili inhabitants, and because it has not been open to tourists until recently, it is a completely different experience from Zanzibar and Mafia. It is advised to be culturally sensitive and respect local customs and beliefs by dressing and acting accordingly: no shorts or mini dresses in villages. This is an island that might be one of the best-kept secrets in Tanzania. The people of the island are some of the friendliest and most welcoming around, curious without any pretense. The still slightly limited amount of tourism development enables it to maintain a spectacular diving and island culture.

GETTING HERE AND AROUND

The best way to get to Pemba is to use one of the local domestic flight companies like Coastal Air or Auric Air that have daily flights out of Zanzibar and Dar es Salaam. Most resorts will arrange a boat transfer. Because distances are similar no matter which resort you choose, it's roughly between US$50 to US$60 for a taxi and boat ride from Chake Chake airport to your accommodations on the north and south sides. Moving around the island can be expensive, and local buses do take a while and will not be able to get you directly to the lodges, so best to arrange transportation with your accommodations beforehand. There are ATMs in Chake Chake only; if you need money withdraw it before you get to your lodge as driving distances can be from 40 to 50 minutes.

Hotels

★ Fundu Lagoon

$$$$ | **RESORT** | Fundu is the type of place that begs you to just kick off your shoes and indulge in some restful jungle lounging—but from the balcony of your private luxury tent. **Pros:** jungle setting is exquisite and unique; the jetty bar is the perfect sundowner spot for romantics; superior rooms are on another level and have their own private plunge pools. **Cons:** a 15-minute boat ride to the nearest bathing beach; not all drinks are included; mosquitoes are in abundance. [$] *Rooms from: $1406* ✉ *Fundu Lagoon, Pemba Island* ☎ *87/073–5184* 🌐 *www.fundulagoon.com* 🛏 *18 bungalows* 🍴 *All-Inclusive* ☞ *2-night minimum.*

★ The Manta Resort

$$$$ | **ALL-INCLUSIVE** | Hidden in the ancient Ngezi Forest, home to the endemic Pemba Flying Fox, Manta Resort sits on a hillside that rolls down to tranquil turquoise waters with a breathtaking 180-degree sea-view open dining area. **Pros:** friendly, attentive staff, who go above and beyond; great diving and snorkeling is easily accessible; spectacular beach with large swimming pool above. **Cons:** standard garden rooms are quite pricey for the size; no Wi-Fi in the rooms (could be a bonus); the drive to get there is an hour and a half with bumpy terrain at the end. [$] *Rooms from: $720* ✉ *Pemba Island* ☎ *776/141–429* 🌐 *www.themantaresort.com* 🛏 *18 rooms* 🍴 *All-Inclusive.*

Pemba Eco Lodge
$$$ | **RESORT** | On the more remote Shaminiani Island, a short boat ride from a small village, a series of bandas are built facing out over a bay. **Pros:** intimate resort; neat and impeccably clean rooms; lovely beach with just you and the local fishermen. **Cons:** food is going to be of a basic but good standard; compost toilet might not be to everyone's taste; remote locales means lack of other dining options. [$] *Rooms from: $480* ✉ *Shamiani Island, Pemba Island* ☎ *655/417–070* 🌐 *www.pembalodge.com* 🛏 *5 bungalows* 🍴 *All-Inclusive.*

Chapter 5

SOUTH AFRICA

Updated by
Kate Turkington

WELCOME TO SOUTH AFRICA

TOP REASONS TO GO

★ **Big Game.** You're guaranteed to see big game—including the Big Five—both in national parks and at many private lodges.

★ **Escape the Crowds.** South Africa's game parks are rarely crowded. You'll see more game with fewer other visitors than almost anywhere else in Africa.

★ **Luxury Escapes.** Few other sub-Saharan countries can offer South Africa's high standards of accommodation, service, and food amid gorgeous surroundings of bush, beach, mountains, and desert.

★ **Take the Family.** All the national parks accept children (choose a malaria-free one if your kids are small), and many private lodges have fantastic children's programs.

★ **Beyond the Parks.** Visit Cape Town, one of the most beautiful and stylish cities in the world; the nearby stunning Winelands; the inspiring scenery of the Garden Route; and glorious, soft white-sand beaches.

1 Kruger National Park. A visit to Kruger, one of the world's great game parks, may rank among the best experiences of your life.

2 Sabi Sand Game Reserve. The most famous and exclusive of South Africa's private reserves, this 153,000-acre park is home to dozens of private lodges, including the world-famous MalaMala and Londolozi.

3 KwaZulu-Natal Parks. Zululand's Hluhluwe-iMfolozi is tiny—less than 6% of Kruger's size—but delivers the Big Five plus all the plains game. If you're looking for the ultimate in luxury, stay at Phinda or Thanda private reserves.

4 Kgalagadi Transfrontier Park. Together with its neighbor, Botswana's Gemsbok National Park, this park covers more than 38,000 square km (14,670 square miles)—one of very few conservation areas of this magnitude left in the world.

5 Madikwe Game Reserve. Bordering Botswana, this 765-square-km (475-square-mile) reserve is teeming with game including the Big Five and the endangered painted wolves and cheetah. It's also malaria-free.

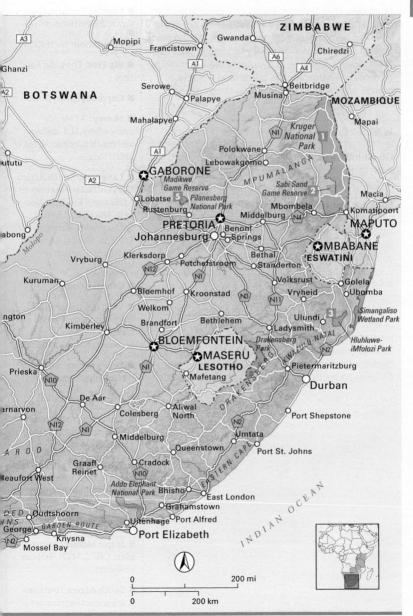

COUNTRY SNAPSHOT

WHEN TO GO

November through February is often considered the best time to visit. Though the bush is very hot in the southern hemisphere's summer season, it's the best time to see young animals. May through August has unpredictable weather, but winter is the best time to go on safari—vegetation is sparse and water is scarce, so it's easier to spot game congregating around water holes.

WAYS TO SAVE

Go all-inclusive. You will eat and drink well and everything will be taken care of including transfers and game drives.

Look for last-minute safari deals. Go online and scour the Facebook pages of different companies, as lodges and hotels will often post deals, specials, or last-minute drop-in-price bookings that could make your holiday much more affordable.

PASSPORTS AND VISAS

U.S. citizens who are visiting South Africa for 90 days or less for tourism do not need visas as long as they are traveling with a valid passport. Passports must be valid at least 30 days after the intended date of departure and must have at least two blank pages. Children under 18 must carry a birth certificate.

AT A GLANCE

- **Capital:** Pretoria, Cape Town, Bloemfontein

- **Population:** 60,266,150

- **Big Five:** The gang's all here

- **Currency:** Rand (ZAR)

- **Money:** ATMs are everywhere; U.S. dollars and credit cards accepted at safari lodges.

- **Language:** South Africa has 11 official languages: Afrikaans, English, Ndebele, North and South Sotho, Swati, Tsonga, Tswana, Venda, Xhosa, and Zulu. English is widely spoken.

- **Country Code:** 27

- **VAT:** 15% (included in the price of most goods and services, including hotel accommodations and food)

- **Emergencies:** 10111; 10177; 112 (cell phone emergency)

- **Driving:** On the left

- **Electricity:** 230v/50 cycles; plugs are UK standard three-prong

- **Time:** GMT +2 (7 hours ahead of New York, 6 hours during daylight saving time)

- **Mobile Phones:** GSM (900 and 1800 bands)

- **Major Mobile Companies:** Cell C, MTN, Telkom, Vodacom

- **South Africa Tourism:** ⊕ www.southafrica.net

Since 1994, when Nelson Mandela spearheaded its peaceful transition to democracy, South Africa has been one of the greatest tourist destinations in the world. The country is stable and affordable, with an excellent infrastructure; friendly, interesting, amazingly diverse people; and enough stunning sights, sounds, scenery, and attractions to make even the most jaded traveler sit up and take notice. And nearly everybody speaks English—a huge bonus for international visitors.

South Africa has always teemed with game. That's what drew the early European explorers, who aimed to bring something exotic home with them. After all, as Pliny the Elder, one of Africa's earliest explorers, wrote almost 2,000 years ago, "*ex Africa semper aliquid novi*" (translated, "Out of Africa always comes something new"). Sometimes it was a giraffe, a rhinoceros, a strange bird, or an unheard-of plant.

In the latter half of the 19th century, Dr. Livingstone, Scotland's most famous Christian missionary, opened up much of the interior on his evangelizing expeditions, as did the piratical Englishman Cecil John Rhodes, who famously made his fortune on the Kimberley diamond mines and planned an unsuccessful Cape-to-Cairo railway line. About the same time, lured by the rumors of gold and instant fortunes, hundreds of hunters came to the lowveld to lay their hands on much-sought-after skins, horns, and ivory. Trophy hunters followed, vying with one another to see how many animals they could shoot in one day—often more than 100 each.

Paul Kruger, president of the Transvaal Republic (a 19th-century Boer country that occupied a portion of present-day South Africa), took the unprecedented visionary step of establishing a protected area for the wildlife in the lowveld region; in 1898 Kruger National Park was born.

South Africa has 19 national parks covering deserts, wetland and marine areas, forests, mountains, scrub, and savanna. Hunting safaris are still popular but are strictly controlled by the government, and licenses are compulsory. Although hunting is a controversial issue, the revenue is substantial and can be ploughed into sustainable conservation, and the impact on the environment is minimal. Increasingly, wildlife conservation is linked with community development; many conservation areas have integrated local communities, the wildlife, and the environment, with benefits for all. Londolozi, MalaMala, and Phinda are internationally acclaimed role models for linking tourism with community-development projects.

MAJOR REGIONS

We've broken the chapter down into **Must-See Parks** (Kruger National Park, Sabi Sand Game Reserve, KwaZulu-Natal Parks, Kgalagadi Transfrontier Park, Madikwe Game Reserve) and **If You Have Time Parks** (Tswalu Kalahari Reserve, Kwandwe, Addo Elephant Park, Pilanesberg Game Reserve) to help you better organize your time. There is also a section on **Gateway Cities**, which for South Africa is Johannesburg and Cape Town.

Planning

When to Go

In the north, summers are sunny and hot (never humid), with short afternoon thunderstorms. Winter days are bright and sunny, but nights can be frosty. Although November through January is Cape Town's most popular time, with glorious sunshine and long, light evenings, the best weather is in February and March. Cape winters (May–August) are unpredictable with cold, windy, rainy days interspersed with glorious sun. The coastal areas of KwaZulu-Natal are warm year-round, but summers are steamy and hot. The ocean water is warmest in February, but it seldom dips below 17°C (65°F).

Getting Here and Around

Countless cities, towns, streets, parks, and more have gotten or will get new monikers, both to rid the country of names that recall the apartheid era and to honor the previously unsung. The names in this book were accurate at time of writing but may still change.

AIR

If you're arriving from abroad, you'll probably touch down at Johannesburg's OR Tambo International Airport. From here you can catch flights to other major cities and to many far-flung destinations like game lodges.

There are fairly long distances between gates and terminals at the airport, particularly between the international and domestic terminals, so clear security before stopping for a snack or shopping, as you don't want to scramble for your flight. ■TIP→ **Allow 10–15 minutes' walking time between international and domestic terminals.**

If you're visiting a game lodge deep in the bush, you will be arriving on a small plane and will be restricted in how much you can bring. Excess luggage can usually be stored with the operator until your return. Don't just gloss over this: charter operators take weight very seriously, and some will charge you for an extra ticket if you insist on bringing excess baggage. (see Charter Flights)

Airfares with budget airlines, such as Lift, FlySafair, and Airlink, are more expensive than bus fares, but traveling by plane is much more efficient and comfortable because the distances in South Africa can be vast. Be sure to book as far in advance as you can if you are going to fly or go by bus, as tickets can get more expensive as you approach the date of travel, and during peak holiday times (especially over Easter in April and December/January) tickets can sell out.

AIRPORT

Johannesburg's OR Tambo International Airport (JNB), sometimes abbreviated O.R.T.I.A. by safari companies, is 19 km (12 miles) from the city. The airport has a tourist information desk, a V.A.T. refund office, several ATMs, and a computerized accommodations service. Porters, who wear a bright-orange-and-navy-blue uniform, work exclusively for tips of about R10 a bag. The international terminal (Terminal A) and the domestic terminal (Terminal B) are connected by a busy and fairly long walkway.

The country's other major airports are in Cape Town and Durban, but international flights departing from Cape Town often stop in Johannesburg. Cape Town International (CPT) is 19 km (12 miles) southeast of the city, and Durban's King Shaka International Airport (DUR) is 35 km (22 miles) north of the city.

If you are traveling to or from the airport at Johannesburg or Cape Town (and, to a lesser extent, Durban) be aware of the time of day. Traffic can be horrendous between 7 and 9 in the morning and between about 3:30 and 6 in the evening.

Just 40 km (25 miles) outside Johannesburg's city center in the northern suburbs, Lanseria International Airport (HLA) handles domestic scheduled flights to and from Cape Town and some charter flights to safari camps. It has a 24-hour customs and immigration counter, a café, and a high-end flight store. It's a popular alternative for visiting VIPs.

The other major cities are served by small airports that are easy to navigate. Chief David Stuurman (Gqeberha/Port Elizabeth) and King Phalo (East London) are the main airports for the Eastern Cape, and Goringhaikona (George) serves the Garden Route. Skukuza is the only airport located in Kruger National Park and is serviced by scheduled daily nonstop flights from Johannesburg and Cape

Town. The next closest airports to Kruger National Park are Kruger Mpumalanga International Airport in Mbombela (Nelspruit) and the small airports at Hoedspruit and Phalaborwa. Most airports are managed by the Airports Company of South Africa.

INTERNATIONAL AIRPORTS Cape Town International Airport. (*CPT*) ⊠ *Matroosfontein, Cape Town* ☎ *021/937–1200* ⊕ *www.capetown-airport.com.* **King Shaka International Airport.** (*DUR*) ⊠ *King Shaka Dr., La Mercy* ☎ *032/436–6000* ⊕ *www.kingshakainternational.co.za.* **Lanseria International Airport.** (*HLA*) ⊠ *Airport Rd., Lanseria, Johannesburg* ☎ *011/367–0300* ⊕ *www.lanseria.co.za.* **OR Tambo International Airport.** (*JNB*) ⊠ *OR Tambo Airport Rd., Johannesburg* ☎ *011/921–6262* ⊕ *www.acsa.co.za.*

INTERNATIONAL FLIGHTS

South Africa's international airline is South African Airways (SAA). It offers nonstop service between Johannesburg and New York–JFK (JFK) and Washington–Dulles (IAD), though some flights from Dulles make a stopover in Dakar, Senegal. Delta also offers nonstop service from the U.S. to South Africa.

European airlines serving South Africa include Austrian Airlines, Air France, British Airways, KLM, Lufthansa, Swiss, Turkish Airlines, and Virgin Atlantic.

Some South Africa–bound flights from U.S. cities have refueling stops en route, and sometimes those stops can be delayed. Don't plan anything on the ground right after arriving; leave yourself a cushion for a connecting flight to a game lodge.

If you are returning home with souvenirs, leave time for a V.A.T. (Value-Added Tax) inspection before you check in for your international flight check-in. And it's always a good idea to check what items you can and cannot carry onto the plane.

DOMESTIC FLIGHTS

South African Airlines has flights connecting South Africa's principal airports, but recent years have seen an explosion of low-cost carriers serving popular domestic routes in South Africa with regularly scheduled flights. Lift, FlySafair, and Airlink (among others) provide reasonably priced domestic air tickets if you book in advance.

In the summer peak season (December to February) and during school holidays, give yourself at least an extra half hour at the airport for domestic flights, as the check-in lines can be endless.

DOMESTIC AIRLINES Airlink. ☎ *011/451–7300 in South Africa* ⊕ *www.flyairlink.com.* **Flysafair.** ⊕ *www.flysafair.co.za.* **LIFT Airline.** ⊕ *www.lift.co.za.*

CHARTER FLIGHTS

Charter companies are a common mode of transportation when getting to safari lodges and remote destinations throughout southern Africa. These aircraft are well maintained and are almost always booked by your lodge or travel agent.

The major charter companies run daily shuttles from OR Tambo to popular tourist destinations like Kruger National Park. Keep in mind that you probably won't get to choose the charter company you fly with. The aircraft you get depends on the number of passengers flying and can vary from very small (you will sit in the copilot's seat) to a much more comfortable commuter plane.

Because of the limited space and size of the aircraft, charter carriers observe strict luggage regulations: luggage must be soft-sided and weigh no more than 44 pounds and often less; on many charter flights the weight cannot exceed 33 pounds.

Based at Johannesburg's OR Tambo International Airport, Federal Air (Fedair) is the largest charter air company in South Africa. Its efficient terminal has a gift shop and a unique, thatched-roof outdoor lounge. It also has hubs in Durban and Kruger Mpumalanga International Airport in Mbombela (Nelspruit). Wilderness Air is a Botswana-based charter company that will take you anywhere there's a landing strip from its base in Johannesburg's Lanseria Airport.

CHARTER COMPANIES Federal Airlines. ☎ *011/395–9000* ⊕ *www.fedair.com.* **Wilderness Air.** ⊕ *www.wilderness-air.com.*

CAR

South Africa has a superb network of multilane roads and highways. Distances are vast, so guard against fatigue (a definite factor for jet-lagged drivers), which is an even bigger killer than alcohol. Toll roads, often the main routes, charge anything from R10 to R100 at 'plazas' along the way and do not accept foreign cards. Check with your hire company if your vehicle has a 'transponder' that allows prepaid access, or pay cash.

You can drive in South Africa for up to six months on any English-language license. South Africa's Automobile Association publishes a range of maps, atlases, and travel guides, available for purchase on its website (⊕ www.aa.co.za). The commercial website Drive South Africa (⊕ www.drivesouthafrica.co.za) has everything you need to know about driving in the country, including road safety and driving distances.

■ **TIP→ Carjackings can and do occur with such frequency that certain high-risk areas are marked by permanent carjacking signs.**

RENTAL CARS

Rates are similar to those in the United States. Some companies charge more on weekends, so it's best to get a range of quotes before booking your car.

For a car with automatic transmission and air-conditioning, you'll pay slightly less for a car that doesn't have unlimited mileage. When comparing prices, make sure you're getting the same thing.

Some companies quote prices without insurance, some include 80% or 90% coverage, and some quote with 100% protection. Get all terms in writing before you leave on your trip.

There's no need to rent a 4x4 vehicle, as all roads are paved, including many in Kruger National Park, although if you are going to national parks a high-clearance vehicle will allow you better game-viewing.

You can often save some money by booking a car through a broker, who will access the car from one of the main agencies. Smaller, local agencies often give a much better price, but the car must be returned in the same city. This is pretty popular in Cape Town but not so much in other centers.

To rent a car you need to be 23 years or older and have held a driver's license for three years. Younger international drivers can rent from some companies but will pay a penalty. You need to get special permission to take rental cars into neighboring countries (including Lesotho and Swaziland). Most companies allow additional drivers, but some charge.

GASOLINE
Service stations (open 24 hours) are positioned at regular intervals along all major highways in South Africa. There are no self-service stations. In return, tip the attendant R5 (more if you get tires checked and windscreens washed). South Africa has a choice of unleaded or leaded gasoline, and many vehicles operate on diesel—be sure you get the right fuel. Gasoline is measured in liters, and the cost is higher than in the United States. When driving long distances, check your routes carefully, as the distances between towns—and hence gas stations—can be more than 100 miles.

PARKING
In the countryside, parking is mostly free, but you will almost certainly need to pay for parking in cities, which will probably run you about R5–R8 per hour. Many towns have an official attendant (who should be wearing a vest of some sort) who will log the number of the spot you park in; you're asked to pay up front for the amount of time you expect to park. If the guard is unofficial, acknowledge them on arrival, ask them to look after your car, and pay a few rand when you return (they depend on these tips). At pay-and-display parking lots you pay in advance; other garages expect payment at the exit. Many (such as those at shopping malls and airports) require that you pay for your parking before you return to your car (at kiosks near the exits to the parking areas). Your receipt ticket allows you to exit. Just read the signs carefully.

CAR-RENTAL INSURANCE
In South Africa it's necessary to buy special insurance if you plan to cross borders into neighboring countries, but CDW and TDW (collision-damage waiver and theft-damage waiver) are optional on domestic rentals. Any time you are considering crossing a border with your rental vehicle, you must inform the rental company ahead of time to fulfill any paperwork requirements and pay additional fees.

EMERGENCY SERVICES Emergency numbers. ☎ *112 from mobile phone, 10111 from landline, 107 in Cape Town.*

Communications

INTERNET
Most hotels have Wi-Fi. Stores such as Woolworths, restaurants such as Wimpy, and most airports offer a countrywide Wi-Fi service called AlwaysOn (⊕ www.alwayson.co.za) that allows you 30 minutes of free Wi-Fi per day. If you need more time, you can pay for it.

PHONES
The country code for South Africa is 27. When dialing from abroad, drop the initial 0 from local area codes.

A Fodor's Choice property, Mdluli Safari Lodge is located in Kruger National Park's southern section.

CALLING WITHIN SOUTH AFRICA

When making a phone call in South Africa, always use the full 10-digit number, including the area code, even if you're in the same area. For directory assistance, call 1023. For operator-assisted national long-distance calls, call 1025. For international operator assistance, dial 10903#. These numbers are free if dialed from a Telkom (landline) phone but are charged at normal cell phone rates from a mobile—and they're busy call centers. Directory inquiry numbers are different for each cell phone network. Vodacom is 111, MTN is 200, and Cell C is 146. These calls are charged at normal rates, but the call is timed only from when it is actually answered.

CALLING OUTSIDE SOUTH AFRICA

When dialing out from South Africa, dial 00 before the international code. So, for example, you would dial 001 for the United States, since the country code for the United States is 1.

Internet calling like Skype also works well from the United States, but it's not always functional in South Africa, unless you're on a reliable high-speed Internet connection, which isn't available everywhere. However, if you have a South African "free" cell phone (meaning you can receive calls for free; all phones using an SA SIM card do this), someone in the United States can call you from their Skype account, for reasonable per-minute charges, and you won't be charged.

MOBILE PHONES

Cell (mobile) phones are ubiquitous and have quite extensive coverage. There are four cell-phone service providers in South Africa—Cell C, MTN, Virgin Mobile, and Vodacom—and you can buy these SIM cards, as well as airtime, in supermarkets for as little as R10 for the SIM card. (If you purchase SIM cards at the airport, you will be charged much more.) Bear in mind that your U.S. cell phone may not work with the local GSM system and/or that your phone may be blocked from using SIM cards outside of your plan if your phone is not unlocked. Basic but functional GSM cell phones start at

R100, and are available at the mobile carrier shops as well as major department stores like Woolworths.

Cellular Abroad rents and sells GMS phones and sells SIM cards that work in many countries, but they cost a lot more than local solutions. Mobal rents mobiles and sells GSM phones (starting at $49) that will operate in 150 countries. Per-call rates vary throughout the world. Vodacom is the country's leading cellular network.

The least complicated way to make and receive phone calls is to obtain international roaming service from your cell-phone service provider before you leave home, but this can be expensive. Any phone that you take abroad must be unlocked by your company for you to be able to use it.

Emergencies

The general emergency numbers are 10111 from a landline and 112 from a mobile phone. If you intend to scuba dive in South Africa, make sure you have DAN membership, which will be honored by Divers Alert Network South Africa (DANSA).

Health and Safety

South Africa is a modern country, but Africa still poses certain health risks even in the most developed areas.

These days everyone is sun-sensitive (and sun can be a big issue in South Africa), so pack plenty of your favorite sunblock and use it generously. Drink plenty of water to avoid dehydration.

The drinking water in South Africa is treated and, except in rural areas, is absolutely safe to drink. You can eat fresh fruits and salads and have ice in your drinks.

It is always wise for travelers to have medical insurance that includes emergency evacuation. Most safari operators require emergency evacuation coverage and may ask you to pay for it along with your tour. If you don't want general travel insurance, many companies offer medical-only policies.

COVID-19

COVID-19 brought travel to a virtual standstill from 2020 to 2022, but vaccinations have made travel possible again. However, each destination may have its own requirements. Travelers may have to wear a mask in some places and obey any other rules. Given how abruptly travel was curtailed at the onset of the pandemic, it's smart to purchase a travel insurance policy that will reimburse you for cancellations related to COVID-19. Not all travel insurance policies protect against pandemic-related cancellations, so always read the fine print.

MALARIA

In South Africa, the most serious health problem facing travelers is malaria, which is present in the prime game-viewing areas of Mpumalanga, Limpopo Province, and northern KwaZulu-Natal. The risk is moderate at the height of the summer and very low in winter. All travelers heading into malaria-prone regions should consult a healthcare professional at least a month before departure for advice. Nowadays malaria medication is safe and easy to use but still try to avoid being bitten by mosquitoes in the first place. After sunset, wear loose, light-colored, long-sleeve shirts, long pants, and shoes and socks. Apply mosquito repellent generously. Always sleep in a mosquito-proof room or tent, and, if possible, keep a fan going in your room. If you are pregnant or trying to conceive, avoid malaria areas entirely.

Generally speaking, the risk is much lower in the dry season (May–October) and peaks immediately after the first rains, which should be in November, but El Niño has made that a lot less predictable.

BILHARZIA

Many lakes and streams, particularly east of the watershed divide, are infected with *bilharzia* (schistosomiasis), a disease carried by parasitic worms. The microscopic fluke enters through the skin and lays eggs in blood vessels. Fast-moving water is considered safe, but still or slow-moving water is hazardous. If you've been wading or swimming in doubtful water, dry yourself off vigorously with a towel immediately upon exiting the water, as this may help to dislodge any flukes before they can burrow into your skin. If you have been exposed, purchase a course of treatment from a pharmacy. Have a checkup once you get home. Bilharzia is easily diagnosed, and it's also easily treated in the early stages.

HIV

Be aware of the dangers of becoming infected with HIV (a big problem in Africa) or hepatitis. Make sure you use a condom during a sexual encounter. They're sold in supermarkets, pharmacies, and most convenience stores. If you feel there's a possibility you've been exposed to the virus, you can get antiretroviral treatment (called post-exposure prophylaxis or PEP) from private hospitals, but you must do so within 48 hours of exposure.

RABIES

Rabies is extremely rare in domesticated animals in South Africa, but is more common in wild animals. If you are bitten by a monkey or other wild animal, seek medical attention immediately. The chance of contracting rabies is extremely small, but the consequences are so horrible that you really don't want to gamble on this one.

INSECTS AND OTHER PESTS

In the summer ticks may be a problem, even in open areas close to cities. If you intend to walk or hike anywhere, use a suitable insect repellent. After your walk, examine your body and clothes for ticks, looking carefully for pepper ticks, which are tiny but may cause tick-bite fever. If you find a tick has bitten you, do not pull it off. If you do, you may pull the body off but leave the head embedded in your skin, causing an infection. Smother the area with petroleum jelly and the tick will eventually let go, as it will be unable to breathe. You can then scrape it off with a fingernail. If you are bitten, don't panic. Most people who are bitten by ticks suffer no more than an itchy bump. If the tick was infected, the bite will swell, itch, and develop a black center. This is a sign of tick-bite fever, which usually hits after about 8 to 12 days. Symptoms may be mild or severe, depending on the patient. This disease is not usually life-threatening in healthy adults, but it's unpleasant.

As always, avoid mosquitoes. Even in non-malarial areas they are extremely irritating. When walking anywhere in the bush, keep a lookout for snakes. Most will slither away when they feel you coming, but keep your eyes peeled. If you see one, give it a wide berth and you should be fine. Snakes usually bite only when they are taken by surprise, so you don't want to step on a napping puff adder.

■ TIP➜ **When camping, check your boots and shake out your clothes for spiders and other crawlies before getting dressed.**

OVER-THE-COUNTER REMEDIES

You can buy over-the-counter medication in pharmacies and supermarkets, and you will find more general remedies in chain stores selling beauty products. Your body may not react the same way to the South African version of a product, even something as simple as a headache tablet. Bring your own supply and rely on pharmacies for emergency medication.

SHOTS AND MEDICATIONS

South Africa does not require any inoculations for entry. Travelers arriving within six days of leaving a country infected with yellow fever require a vaccination certificate. The U.S. Centers for Disease Control and Prevention (CDC) recommends that you be vaccinated against hepatitis A and B if you intend to travel to more isolated areas. Discuss cholera vaccines with your doctor.

If you are coming to South Africa for a safari, chances are you are heading to a malarial area. Only a handful of game reserves are non-malarial. Millions of travelers take oral prophylactic drugs before, during, and after their safaris. If you're pregnant or traveling with small children, consider a non-malarial region for your safari.

The CDC provides up-to-date information on health risks and recommended vaccinations and medications for travelers to southern Africa. In most of South Africa you need not worry about any of these, but if you plan to visit remote regions, check with the CDC's traveler's health line.

MEDICAL CARE

South African doctors are generally excellent. The equipment and training in private clinics rivals the best in the world, but public hospitals tend to suffer from overcrowding and underfunding. If you need medical treatment, ask your hotel or safari operator to recommend a hospital. In South Africa, foreigners are expected to pay in full for any medical services, so check your existing health plan to see whether you're covered while abroad, and supplement it if necessary.

On returning home, if you experience any unusual symptoms—including fever, painful eyes, backache, diarrhea, severe headache, general lassitude, or blood in urine or stool—be sure to tell your doctor where you have been. These symptoms may indicate malaria, tick-bite fever, bilharzia, or—if you've been traveling north of South Africa's borders—some other tropical malady.

Hotels and Lodges

Be warned that lodging terminology in South Africa can be misleading. The term *lodge* is a particularly tricky one. A guest lodge or a game lodge is almost always an upmarket, full-service facility with loads of extra attractions. But the term *lodge* when applied to city hotels often indicates a minimum-service hotel, like the City and Town Lodges and Holiday Inn Garden Courts. A backpacker lodge, however, is essentially a hostel.

A *rondavel* can be a small cabin, often in a rounded shape, and its cousin, the *banda,* can be anything from a basic stand-alone structure to a luxury chalet. Be sure you understand the hotel's cancellation policy. Some places allow you to cancel without any kind of penalty—even if you prepaid to secure a discounted rate—if you cancel at least 24 hours in advance. Others require you to cancel a week in advance or penalize you the cost of one night. Small inns and B&Bs are most likely to require you to cancel far in advance. Always have written confirmation of your booking when you check in.

■ TIP→ **Most hotels allow children under a certain age to stay in their parents' room at no extra charge, but others charge for them as extra adults, and some don't allow children under 12 at all.**

Ask about the policy on children before checking in, and make sure you find out the cutoff age for discounts.

In South Africa, most accommodations from hotels to guesthouses do include breakfast in the rate. Most game lodges include all meals, or they may be all-inclusive (including alcohol as well). All hotels listed have private bath unless otherwise noted.

■ TIP→ **Restaurant and hotel reviews have been shortened. For full information, visit Fodors.com.**

What It Costs in South African Rand

	$	$$	$$$	$$$$
RESTAURANTS				
	under R100	R100– R150	R151– R200	over R200
HOTELS				
	under R1,500	R1,500– R2,500	R2,501– R3,500	over R3,500

Money Matters

Rand is the South African currency: 100 cents equal 1 rand. Dollar/rand exchange rate varies from day to day, averaging a trading rate of US$1 to R15. Credit cards are widely accepted in shops, restaurants, and hotels, and there are numerous ATMs at banks, service stations, and shopping malls.

Restaurants

South Africa's cities and towns are full of dining options, from chain restaurants like the popular Nando's to chic cafés. Indian food and Cape Malay dishes are regional favorites in Cape Town, while traditional smoked meats and sausages are available countrywide. In South Africa dinner is eaten at night and lunch at midday. Restaurants serve breakfast until about 11:30; a few serve breakfast all day. If you're staying at a game lodge, your mealtimes will revolve around the game drives—usually coffee and *rusks* (similar to biscotti) early in the morning, more coffee and probably muffins on the morning game drive, either a huge brunch in the late morning or lunch at midday, tea and something sweet in the late afternoon before the evening game drive, cocktails and snacks on the drive, and a substantial supper, or dinner, at about 8 or 8:30.

Many restaurants accustomed to serving tourists accept credit cards, usually Visa and American Express, with MasterCard increasingly accepted.

Most restaurants welcome casual dress, including jeans and sneakers, but draw the line at shorts and a halter top at dinner, except for restaurants on the beach.

Visitor Info

The official South Africa Tourism website is full of general country information.

For Cape Town and Johannesburg visitor information, see Visitor Info in each city's section below.

VISITOR INFO South African Tourism.
⊕ *www.southafrica.net.*

Kruger National Park

Your visit to Kruger is likely to be one of the greatest experiences of your life, truly providing ultimate "Wow!" moments. You'll be amazed at the diversity of life forms—the tallest (the giraffe), the biggest (the elephant), the funkiest (the dung beetle), the toothiest (the crocodile), and the glitziest (the lilac-breasted roller).

Kruger lies in the hot lowveld, a subtropical section of Mpumalanga and Limpopo provinces that abuts Mozambique. The park cuts a swath 80 km (50 miles) wide and 320 km (200 miles) long from Zimbabwe and the Limpopo River in the north to the Crocodile River in the south. It's divided into 16 macro eco-zones, each supporting a great variety of plants, birds, and animals, including 147 mammal species and 500 species of birds, some of which are not found elsewhere in South Africa. In 2002 a treaty was signed between South Africa, Zimbabwe, and Mozambique to form a giant conservation area, the Great Limpopo Transfrontier Park. It's a complex ongoing process, but once all the fences between Kruger, the Gonarezhou National Park in

Read and Watch

To get a sense of South Africa of colonial yore, *Jock of the Bushveld*, by Sir James Percy Fitzpatrick, was published in 1907. It's the tale of a man and his dog exploring the present-day Transvaal in the 1880s.

A slew of books provide insight into the long and twisty road of apartheid. Alan Paton's *Cry, the Beloved Country* (1948) is the compelling and lyrical story of a Black man's country under white man's law in pre-apartheid South Africa. There have also been two film adaptations. Trevor Noah's *Born a Crime* recounts the author's childhood under apartheid. His crime? Being biracial. And *Long Walk to Freedom* (1995) is Nelson Mandela's moving autobiography detailing his extraordinary life fighting against racism.

As far as movies go, *Shaka Zulu* (1986) showcases the life of Zulu King Shaka, while *Zulu* (1964) provides insight into the battle at Rorke's Drift between Zulu warriors and British soldiers.

Released in 1987, *Cry Freedom* tells the story of South African journalist Donald Woods, played by Kevin Kline, who flees the country after investigating the death of his friend, the Black activist Steve Biko, played by Denzel Washington.

Invictus (2009) stars Morgan Freeman and Matt Damon and directed by Clint Eastwood, showcases the true tale of Nelson Mandela using rugby to unite a race-divided nation.

Available on Netflix, *Blood and Water*, a popular South African TV show follows a young woman searching for her missing sister who was kidnapped at birth by human traffickers. Also available on Netflix, *Tjovitjo* (2017) is a dance drama centering on an impoverished community that strives to do better through dance.

Netflix has curated a collection of over 80 South African films, series, documentaries, and reality shows called Made in South Africa, which showcase some of the country's most prodigious talent.

"History of South Africa" is a podcast that deep-dives into the country's history, while "Lesser Known Somebodies" features conversations with fascinating South Africans. Both can be found at the Apple Podcasts app.

Mozambique, and the Limpopo National Park in Zimbabwe are finally removed, the Peace Park will be the largest conservation area in the world.

But it's not all about game on safari. If you're into ancient human history, there are also major archaeological sites and fascinating San (Bushman) rock paintings—there is ample evidence that prehistoric humans (*Homo erectus*) roamed the area between 500,000 and 100,000 years ago. This park is a place to safari at your own pace, choosing between upscale private camps or simple campsites.

WHEN TO GO
Kruger National Park is hellishly hot in midsummer (November–March), but the bush is green, the animals are sleek and glossy, and the birdlife is prolific, even though high grass and dense foliage make spotting animals more difficult. Winter (May–September) is the high season. The bush is at its dullest, driest, and most colorless, but the game is much easier to spot, as many trees are bare,

the grass is low, and animals congregate around the few available permanent water sources. However, temperatures can drop to almost freezing at night and in the very early morning. The shoulder months of April and October are also good, and less crowded. Always book as far in advance as possible.

GETTING HERE AND AROUND

You can fly to Kruger Mpumalanga International Airport (KMIA), at Mbombela (Nelspruit); Skukuza Airport in Kruger itself; Hoedspruit Airport, close to Kruger's Orpen Gate; or Phalaborwa Airport (if you're going to the north of Kruger) from either Johannesburg or Cape Town. You can also drive to Kruger from Johannesburg in about six hours (not including comfort/food stops); if you drive, a 4x4 isn't necessary since all roads are paved.

AIRPORTS Hoedspruit Airport. (*HDS*) ⊠ *Eastgate Airport, Hoedspruit* ☎ *015/793–3681* ⊕ *www.eastgateairport. co.za.* **Kruger Mpumalanga International Airport (KMIA).** ☎ *013/753–7500* ⊕ *www. kmiairport.co.za.* **Skukuza Airport.** (*SZK*) ⊠ *Skukuza* ☎ *013/735–5074* ⊕ *www. skukuzaairport.com.*

MONEY MATTERS

Kruger accepts credit cards, which are also useful for big purchases, but you should always have some small change for staff tips (tip your cleaning person at least R30 per hut per day) and for drinks and snacks at the camp shops, although camp shops also accept credit cards.

PLANNING YOUR TIME

How and where you tackle Kruger will depend on your time frame. With excellent roads and accommodations, it's a great place to drive yourself. If you don't feel up to driving or self-catering, you can choose a private lodge in Kruger itself or just outside the park and take the guided drives—although it's not quite the same as lying in bed and hearing the hyenas prowling around the camp fence or a lion roaring under the stars.

Park Ratings

Game: ★★★★★
Park Accessibility: ★★★★★
Getting Around: ★★★★★
Accommodations: ★★★★★
Scenic Beauty: ★★★★☆

If you can spend a week here, start in the north at the very top of the park at the Punda Maria Camp, then make your way leisurely south to the very bottom at Crocodile Bridge Gate or Malelane Gate. With only three days or fewer, reserve one of the southern camps such as Berg-en-Dal or Lower Sabie and just plan to explore these areas. No matter where you go in Kruger, be sure to plan your route and accommodations (advance booking is essential). Game-viewing isn't an exact science: you might see all the Big Five plus hundreds of other animals, but you could see much less. Try to plan your route to include waterholes and rivers, which afford your best opportunity to see game. Old Africa hands claim that the very early morning, when the camp gates open, is the best time for game-viewing, but it's all quite random—you could see a leopard drinking at noon, a breeding herd of elephants midmorning, or a lion pride dozing under a tree in the middle of the afternoon. You could also head out at dawn and find very little wildlife. Be sure to take at least one guided sunset drive; you won't likely forget the thrill of catching a nocturnal animal in the spotlight.

VISITOR INFORMATION South African National Parks. ☎ *012/428–9111* ⊕ *www. sanparks.org.*

You might have to compete for your breakfast at Phinda Private Game Reserve.

Hotels

It's impossible to recommend just one camp in Kruger. One person might prefer the intimacy of Kruger's oldest camp, Punda Maria, with its whitewashed thatch cottages; another might favor big, bustling Skukuza. A great way to experience the park is to stay in as many of the camps as possible, but distances are long and you don't want to spend all your time travelling. The SANParks website (🌐 *www.sanparks.org*) has a comprehensive overview of the different camps. The bushveld camps are more expensive than the regular camps, but offer much more privacy and exclusivity—but no shops, restaurants, or pools. If you seek the ultimate in luxury, stay at one of the private luxury lodges in the concession areas, some of which also have walking trails.

Reservations for park-operated accommodations should be made through **South African National Parks.** If air-conditioning is a must for you, be sure to check the website to confirm its availability in the accommodation of your choice.

TIP→ Book your guided game drives and walks when you check in. Opt for the sunset drive. You'll get to see the animals coming to drink plus a thrilling night drive.

★ Jock Safari Lodge

$$$$ | RESORT | This lodge, one of South Africa's loveliest, is set among 14,826 acres of private concession in southwest Kruger—the park's first with game-rich traversing rights as a result—with twelve comfortable, spacious suites, each with a plunge pool and stunning views over the Biyamiti River. **Pros:** authentic safari experience; riverfront location with private viewing deck. **Cons:** no tracker to assist the field guide (as is the case at other private lodges outside Kruger); busy in season. [$] *Rooms from: R20,930* ✉ *Jock Safari Lodge, Kruger National Park* ☎ *013/010-0019, 041/509–3000 reservations* 🌐 *www.jocksafarilodge.com* 🛏 *12 rooms* 🍴 *All-Inclusive.*

Walking Kruger

If you've the time and want to get really close to nature, Kruger has ten wilderness trails in different areas of the park accommodating eight hikers each: Bushman, Lonely Bull, Mphongolo, Metsi Metsi, Napi, Nyalaland, Olifants River, Olifants, Sweni and Wolhuter. On three-day, two-night hikes, led by an armed ranger and local tracker, you walk in the mornings and evenings, with an afternoon siesta. You can generally get closer to animals in a vehicle, but many hikers can recount face-to-face encounters with everything from rhinos to lions. Be prepared to walk up to 19 km (12 miles) a day although your individual group will decide the distance and pace. No one under 12 is allowed; those over 60 must have a doctor's certificate. Hikers sleep in rustic two-bed huts and share a reed-wall bathroom (flush toilets, bucket showers). Meals are simple (stews and barbecues); you bring your own drinks. In summer, walking is uncomfortably hot (and trails are cheaper); in winter, nights can be freezing—bring warm clothes and an extra blanket. Reserve 13 months ahead, when bookings open. The cost is about R3,430 per person per trail.

★ Kruger Shalati: Train on a Bridge

$$$$ | **ALL-INCLUSIVE** | If you're looking for safari lodging that's the opposite of typical khaki trappings, the swanky suites at the Kruger Shalati sit aboard an ingeniously upcycled (and stationary) train that's been converted from 1950s coaches painstakingly collected from scrapyards across South Africa and suspended 15 meters (49 feet) above the sightings-rich Sabie River. **Pros:** excellent food options; breathtaking views; design-savvy interiors highlight South African talent. **Cons:** not for those with vertigo; the train doesn't move. [$] *Rooms from: R15,900* ✉ *Skukuza, Skukuza* ☎ *013/591–6000* 🌐 *www.krugershalati.com* 🛏 *24 suites* 🍴 *All-Inclusive.*

★ Mdluli Safari Lodge

$$$$ | **HOTEL** | Set in the fertile south of the Kruger National Park (near the Numbi Gate), this deluxe tented camp—think enormous infinity pool overlooking a water hole—has partnered with the local Mdluli Community (some 45,000 people that live adjacent to the Park) to help them earn back 2,100 acres of land inside the borders of the iconic Kruger that was seized by the government in 1967. **Pros:** family-friendly resort and safe to walk the grounds; underpriced relative to other exclusive lodges; community-empowerment and lovely lodge-style ambience. **Cons:** some tents are close together; can be noisy if a wedding party or big function is happening; it's big and can sleep 100 guests. [$] *Rooms from: R9,720* ✉ *Mdluli Safari Lodge, Kruger National Park* ☎ *078/687–2546 reception, 087/980–0431 lodge* 🌐 *www.mdlulisafarilodge.co.za* 🛏 *50 suites* 🍴 *All-Inclusive.*

Kruger Gate Hotel

$$$$ | **HOTEL** | **FAMILY** | Overlooking the Sabie River with quick access to the Kruger National Park, this sprawling hotel is large and somewhat impersonal but offers good-value accommodation in a prime location when checking into the right room. **Pros:** air-conditioning, Wi-Fi, room service and other hotel creature comforts; on-site spa that's easy on the pocket; easy and affordable proximity to Kruger. **Cons:** game drives can be generic and not catered to individual interests; not all rooms renovated. [$] *Rooms from:*

If a female elephant feels threatened, she will charge, like this one in Kruger National Park.

R5,900 ✉ *Kruger Gate Hotel, Skukuza* ☎ *13/735–5671* 🌐 *krugergatehotel.com* 🛏 *145 rooms* 🍴 *Free Breakfast* ☞ *includes buffet dinner, but game drives cost extra.*

★ **RETURN Africa Pafuri Tented Camp**

$$$$ | **ALL-INCLUSIVE** | While the southern section of Kruger is prone to overtourism, this luxurious tented camp lies in the underrated and remote northern realm of the Kruger National Park and stretches for more than a kilometer along the banks of the winding Luvuvhu River. **Pros:** culturally rich safari activities; community-empowerment initiatives; terrific biodiversity. **Cons:** quite a big camp (can sleep 100 people when full); accessible by road, but it's a long drive to get there. [$] *Rooms from: R14,500* ✉ *Kruger National Park* ☎ *011/646–1391* 🌐 *www.returnafrica.com/escapes/pafuri-tented-camp/* 🛏 *20 tents* 🍴 *All-Inclusive.*

Singita Lebombo Lodge

$$$$ | **RESORT** | Named for the nearby Lebombo mountain range, the breathtakingly beautiful Singita Lebombo—winner of numerous international accolades and eco-driven in concept—hangs on the edge of a cliff (inspired by eagle nests) with wooden walkways that connect the aptly named "lofts" (suites) seamlessly fusing the outdoor and indoor areas. **Pros:** cooking classes where community members train; good curio shop and spa; central long bar is a great gathering place; stunning avant-garde architecture and youthful feel. **Cons:** avoid if you prefer a traditional safari lodge; very pricey (rate excludes tourism and carbon offset levy). [$] *Rooms from: R69,120* ✉ *Kruger National Park* ☎ *021/683–3424 reservations* 🌐 *www.singita.co.za* 🛏 *15 rooms* 🍴 *All-Inclusive.*

Singita Sweni Lodge

$$$$ | **RESORT** | More intimate than its sister camp, Lebombo, but still smack in the middle of the 'Land of Lions', Sweni is built on wooden stilts with six huge river-facing suites glassed on three sides, wooden on the other. **Pros:** outdoor day beds transform to stargazing loungers; tiny and intimate; great location. **Cons:**

all of Singita's properties are situated in malaria-risk areas; dim lighting. $ *Rooms from: R69,120* ✉ *Kruger National Park* ☎ *021/683–3424 reservations* ⊕ *www. singita.co.za* ⟿ *7 rooms* ⦿ *All-Inclusive.*

Sabi Sand

This is the most famous and exclusive of South Africa's private reserves. Collectively-owned and managed, the 153,000-acre reserve near Kruger is home to dozens of private lodges, including the world-famous MalaMala and Londolozi. Sabi Sand fully deserves its exalted reputation, boasting perhaps the highest game density of any private reserve in southern Africa.

Although not all lodges own vast tracts of land, the majority have traversing rights over most of the reserve. With an average of 20 vehicles watching for game and communicating by radio, you're bound to see an enormous amount of game and almost certainly the Big Five, and since only three vehicles are allowed at a sighting at a time, you can be assured of a grandstand seat. Sabi Sand is the best area for leopard sightings. It's a memorable experience to see this beautiful, powerful, and often elusive cat padding purposefully through the bush at night, illuminated in your ranger's spotlight. There are many lion prides, and occasionally the increasingly rare African wild dogs (painted wolves) will migrate from Kruger to den in Sabi Sand. You'll also see white and black rhinos, zebras, giraffes, wildebeests, and most of the antelope species, plus birds galore.

The daily program at each lodge rarely deviates from a pattern, starting with tea, coffee, and muffins or rusks before an early-morning game drive (usually starting at dawn, later in winter). You return to the lodge around 10 am, at which point you dine on an extensive hot breakfast or brunch. You can then choose to go

Park Ratings 👁

Game: ★ ★ ★ ★ ★

Park Accessibility: ★ ★ ★ ★ ★

Getting Around: ★ ★ ★ ★ ★

Accommodations: ★ ★ ★ ★ ★

Scenic Beauty: ★ ★ ★ ☆ ☆

on a bush walk with an armed ranger, where you learn about some of the minutiae of the bush (including the Little Five), although you could also happen on giraffes, antelopes, or any one of the Big Five. But don't worry—you'll be well briefed in advance on what you should do if you come face-to-face with, say, a lion. The rest of the day, until the late-afternoon game drive, is spent at leisure—reading up on the bush in the camp library, snoozing, swimming, or having a spa treatment. A sumptuous afternoon tea is served at 3:30 or 4 before you head back into the bush for your night drive. During the drive, your ranger will find a peaceful spot for sundowners, and you can sip the drink of your choice and nibble snacks as you watch one of Africa's spectacular sunsets. As darkness falls, your ranger will switch on the spotlight so you can spy nocturnal animals: lions, leopards, jackals, porcupines, servals (small spotted cats like bonsai leopards), civets, and the enchanting little bush babies. You'll return to the lodge around 7:30, in time to freshen up before a three- or five-course dinner, with at least one dinner in a *boma* (open-air dining area) around a blazing fire. Often the camp staff entertains after dinner with local songs and dances—an unforgettable experience. Children under 12 aren't allowed at some of the camps; others have great kids' programs.

Sabi Sand Game Reserve

Hoedspruit Airstrip

Sand River

Dulini Private Game Reserve
Dulini Leadwood Lodge
Dulini Moya Lodge
◆ Dulini River Lodge

Silvan Safari

Leopard Hills Private Game Reserve
Singita ◆
Singita Ebony Lodge

Singita Boulders Lodge

Tree Camp

MalaMala Game Reserve
▲ MalaMala Main Camp
▲ MalaMala Sable Camp

Pioneer Camp
Londolozi Reserve ◆
Founders Camp

Varty Camp

MalaMala Rattray's Camp

KRUGER NATIONAL PARK

KEY

🏠 Lodges
⛺ Camps

Sabi Sand Game Reserve ◆

Newington ○

Sand River

Sabi Sabi Little Bush Camp
Sabi Sabi Selati Camp

Sabi Sabi Private Game Reserve ◆
Sabi Sabi Bush Lodge

&Beyond Tengile River Lodge

Sabi Sabi Earth Lodge
Lion Sands Private Game Reserve

&Beyond Kirkman's Kamp

Kruger Mpumalanga Airport

Lion Sands Ivory Lodge & Lion Sands River Lodge

H1-2

Skukuza Airport

Sabi River

Entrance
Paul Kruger Gate

○ Skukuza

N
0   5 mi
0   5 km

GETTING HERE AND AROUND

Kruger Mpumalanga International Airport (KMIA), at Nelspruit, and Hoedspruit airport, close to Kruger's Orpen Gate, serve Sabi Sand Reserve. You can also drive yourself to the reserve and park at your lodge.

AIRPORTS Hoedspruit Airport. (*HDS*)
✉ *Eastgate Airport, Hoedspruit*
☎ *015/793–3681* ⊕ *www.eastgateairport. co.za.* **Kruger Mpumalanga International Airport (KMIA).** ☎ *013/753–7500* ⊕ *www. kmiairport.co.za.*

VISITOR INFO Sabi Sand Game Reserve.
✉ *Sabi Sand Game Reserve* ☎ *013/735–5102* ⊕ *www.sabisand.co.za.*

Dulini Private Game Reserve

500 km (310 miles) from Johannesburg.

Established in 1937, Dulini (formerly called Exeter), at 160,600 acres, was an original part of Sabi Sand when it was incorporated in the 1960s.

GETTING HERE AND AROUND

Dulini is about a six-hour drive from Johannesburg (minus food and comfort stops). Charter flights from Johannesburg land at the Ulusaba Airstrip, which is near the reserve's lodges. Transfers can also be arranged from other nearby airports with regular flights. The lodges generally arrange your transportation.

Hotels

★ **Dulini Leadwood Lodge**

$$$$ | ALL-INCLUSIVE | Leadwood is the smallest lodge of the Dulini collection with just four stunning suites generously spaced across the confluence of the Mabrak and Sand Rivers with views among the best in Sabi Sand. **Pros:** location, location, location; impressively attentive, friendly service; small and intimate. **Cons:** no rails on your deck so don't wander about after a strong nightcap. [$] *Rooms from: R39,900* ✉ *Dulini, Dulini* ☎ *011/792–4927* 🌐 *www.dulini.com* 🛏 *4 suites* 🍴 *All-Inclusive.*

Dulini Moya Lodge

$$$$ | ALL-INCLUSIVE | Dulini Moya Lodge comprises six stone bungalows catering to a maximum of just 12 guests in prime game-viewing territory. **Pros:** light, fresh and imaginative meals; great game watching from the deck; rewarding experience even for safari regulars. **Cons:** children are welcome, but the adult elegance is not kid-friendly. [$] *Rooms from: R39,900* ✉ *Dulini* ☎ *011/792–4927 reservations* 🌐 *www.dulini.com* 🛏 *6 rooms* 🍴 *All-Inclusive.*

Dulini River Lodge

$$$$ | RESORT | One of Sabi Sand's oldest lodges, Dulini River Lodge scores 10 out of 10 for its gorgeous location—one of the best in the whole reserve—with lush green lawns sweeping down to the Sand River. **Pros:** genuine African-bush ambience and unbeatable setting; on-site gym for fitness plus fresh and healthy cuisine; seriously spacious suites. **Cons:** shares traversing rights with other lodges; situated in a more crowded part of Sabi Sand. [$] *Rooms from: R39,900* ✉ *Dulini* ☎ *013/735–2000 lodge, 011/792–4927 reservations* 🌐 *www.dulini.com* 🛏 *6 rooms* 🍴 *All-Inclusive.*

Sabi Sand Game Reserve

Hotels

&Beyond Kirkman's Kamp

$$$$ | RESORT | FAMILY | You'll feel as if you've stepped back in time at this camp because rooms are strategically clustered around the original 1920s homestead, which, with its colonial furniture, historic memorabilia, and wraparound verandah, makes you feel like a family guest the moment you arrive. **Pros:** character-filled with unique artifacts; family-friendly; superb game-viewing. **Cons:** rooms close together (some share a patio with a divider); gets tour groups. [$] *Rooms from: R31,700* ✉ *Kirkman's Kamp, Dulini* ☎ *011/809–4300 reservations* 🌐 *www.andbeyond.com* 🛏 *12 rooms* 🍴 *All-Inclusive.*

★ **&Beyond Tengile River Lodge**

$$$$ | ALL-INCLUSIVE | Set along the predator-dense Sand River, this exceptional lodge takes a refreshing step away from safari stereotypes—in lieu of khaki drapes and colonial heritage, Tengile embraces the riverine shadows and tones for its interior inspiration, prioritizes the luxury of space, and refines attention to detail. **Pros:** palatial riverfront suites; faultless service; complimentary Swarovski binoculars on drives. **Cons:** darker, contemporary interiors might not be to everyone's taste; pricey. [$] *Rooms from: R63,250* ✉ *Tengile River Lodge, Sabi Sand Game Reserve* ☎ *011/809–4300* 🌐 *www.andbeyond.com* 🛏 *9 suites* 🍴 *All-Inclusive.*

Silvan Safari

$$$$ | ALL-INCLUSIVE | Possibly the most exquisitely elegant lodge in the reserve, six spacious stylish suites themed around indigenous trees are clustered on the banks of the (mostly dry) Manyeleti river. **Pros:** superb, unforgettable suites; minibar stocked with all kinds of luxurious goodies; privacy guaranteed. **Cons:** game not as abundant as in south of

A leopard gets a drink at a waterhole in Sabie Sand Nature Reserve.

reserve; no handrails on suite steps; dim lighting at night. $ *Rooms from: R39,000* ✉ *Sabi Sand Game Reserve* ☎ *021/001–5880* ⊕ *www.silvansafari.com* ↗ *6 suites* ⑩ *All-Inclusive.*

Lion Sands Private Game Reserve

Situated along the Sabie River, this reserve has one of the best locations in the Sabi Sand Game Reserve. All of the lodges overlook the river, which is a magnet for all kinds of game. You'll be able to peer into Kruger Park, on the other side of the river, and watch game meander along the riverbanks among big riverine trees. You may never want to leave your personal deck, or the big viewing decks even for an exciting game drive or guided walk, because you're bound to spot animals, birds, and crocs from camp.

 Sights

★ **Lion Sands Private Game Reserve**
NATURE SIGHT | All of the lodges overlook the river, which is a magnet for all kinds of game. You'll be able to peer into Kruger National Park, on the other side of the river, and watch game meander along the riverbanks among big riverine trees. You may never want to leave your personal deck, or the big viewing decks. But when you do decide to leave your perch, you have all kinds of options for activities, including game drives and walking safaris, spa treatments, and yoga beneath the African sun. ✉ *Lion Sands Private Game Reserve* ☎ *010/109–4900* ⊕ *www.more.co.za/lionsands.*

 Hotels

★ **Lion Sands Ivory Lodge**
$$$$ | RESORT | Ivory Lodge offers the ultimate in luxury, privacy, and relaxation. **Pros:** great views; brilliant game-viewing; exclusivity. **Cons:** the temptation of abundant great food—it's so decadent,

you might forget to leave. $ *Rooms from: R67,040* ✉ *Lion Sands Private Game Reserve* ☎ *031/735–5000 lodge, 010/109–4900 head office and reservations* ⊕ *www.more.co.za/lionsands/ivory-lodge* ⇲ *9 rooms* ⦿ *All-Inclusive* ⇲ *No children under 10 years old.*

Lion Sands River Lodge

$$$$ | **RESORT** | Set on one of the longest and best stretches of river frontage in Sabi Sand, you can watch the passing animal and bird show from your deck or from the huge, tree-shaded, wooden viewing area that juts out over the riverbank facing Kruger National Park. **Pros:** fabulous river frontage; game-viewing from your personal deck; combinable rooms for families. **Cons:** some chalets quite close together so not much privacy. $ *Rooms from: R3,620* ✉ *Lion Sands Private Game Reserve* ☎ *013/735–5000 lodge, 010/109–4900 head office and reservations* ⊕ *www.more.co.za/lionsands/ river-lodge* ⇲ *21 rooms* ⦿ *All-Inclusive* ⇲ *No children under 10 years old.*

Londolozi Reserve

Since its inception in 1974 (it was a family farm and retreat before that), Londolozi has become synonymous with South Africa's finest game lodges and game experiences. (*Londolozi* is the Zulu word for "protector of all living things.") Brother-and-sister Bronwyn and Boyd Varty, the third generation of the Varty family, are now in charge with a mission to reconnect the human spirit with the wilderness and to carry on their family's quest to honor the animal kingdom. The Big Five are all here, as are the world-famous leopards of Londolozi. (You are guaranteed to see at least one.) There are five camps, each representing a different element in nature: Pioneer Camp (water), Tree Camp (wood), Granite Suites (rock), Varty Camp (fire), and Founders Camp (earth). Each is totally private, hidden in dense riverine forest on the banks of

the Sand River. The Varty family live on the property, and their friendliness and personal attention, along with the many staff who have been here for decades, will make you feel part of the family immediately. The central reception and curio shop are at Varty Camp.

◉ Sights

★ Londolozi Game Reserve

NATURE PRESERVE | Each of the five camps offers unprecedented access to 34,000 acres of Africa's best Big Five game-viewing, led by renowned rangers and trackers. The camp is most famous for its leopards, with which its rangers and trackers have forged an intimate relationship over the decades. Leopard sightings are frequent. ✉ *Londolozi Reserve* ☎ *010/109–2968 reservations, 013/735–5653 lodge* ⊕ *www.londolozi. com.*

Hotels

Founders Camp

$$$$ | **RESORT** | **FAMILY** | This inviting camp has 10 stone-and-thatch suites in individual chalets set amid thick riverine bush; some chalets are linked by interconnecting skywalks, which is great for families or groups traveling together (children six years and older are welcome). **Pros:** quick, safe access between family rooms; children over four welcome. **Cons:** lodges are in quite close proximity to one another. $ *Rooms from: R43,890* ✉ *Londolozi Reserve* ☎ *010/109-2968 reservations, 013/735–5653 lodge* ⊕ *www.londolozi.com* ⇲ *10 rooms* ⦿ *All-Inclusive.*

Pioneer Camp

$$$$ | **RESORT** | The most secluded of all of Londolozi's camps, Pioneer's three private suites overlook the river and are perfect for getting away from others. **Pros:** only three suites; most private of all Londolozi lodgings; authentic romantic-safari atmosphere. **Cons:** with only

three suites hope for compatible neighbors. $ *Rooms from: R63250* ⊠ *Londolozi Reserve* ☎ *010/109–2968 reservations, 013/735–5653 lodge* ⊕ *www.londolozi. com* ⌨ *3 rooms* ¶◎¶ *All-Inclusive* ⌔ *No children under 6 years old.*

★ Tree Camp

$$$$ | RESORT | The first Relais & Chateaux game lodge in the world, this gorgeous camp (think leopards, lanterns, leadwoods, and leopard orchids) is tucked into the riverbank overlooking indigenous forest. **Pros:** the viewing deck; state-of-the-art designer interiors. **Cons:** stylishness nudges out coziness. $ *Rooms from: R63,250* ⊠ *Londolozi Reserve* ☎ *010/109–2968 reservations, 013/735–5653 lodge* ⊕ *www.londolozi.com* ⌨ *6 rooms* ¶◎¶ *All-Inclusive* ⌔ *Children under 16 not allowed.*

Varty Camp

$$$$ | RESORT | FAMILY | Londolozi's largest camp, centered on a thatch A-frame lodge that houses a dining room, sitting areas, and lounge, has been around for more than nine decades and is the very soul and center of Londolozi. **Pros:** great game; friendly atmosphere; gym, photographic studio and healing house on-site. **Cons:** lots of kids might not be for you. $ *Rooms from: R37,290* ⊠ *Londolozi Reserve* ☎ *010/109–2968 reservations, 013/735–5653 lodge* ⊕ *www.londolozi. com* ⌨ *10 rooms* ¶◎¶ *All-Inclusive.*

MalaMala Game Reserve

This legendary game reserve (designated as such in 1929) is tops in its field. The first and only community-owned game reserve in Sabi Sand, it continues to be managed by the legendary Rattray family in partnership with the N'wandlamharhi Community. It's the largest privately owned Big Five game area in South Africa, and includes an unfenced 30-km (19-mile) boundary with Kruger National Park, across which game cross continuously. The variety of habitats range from riverine bush, favorite hiding place of the leopard, to open grasslands, where cheetahs hunt.

You'll be delighted with incomparable personal service, superb food, and discreetly elegant, comfortable accommodations, where you'll rub shoulders with statesmen and stateswomen, aristocrats, celebrities, and returning visitors alike. Mike Rattray, a legend in his own time in South Africa's game-lodge industry, describes MalaMala as "a camp in the bush," but it's certainly more than that, although it still retains that genuine bushveld feel of bygone days. Both the outstanding hospitality and the game-viewing experience keep guests coming back.

◉ Sights

★ MalaMala Private Game Reserve

NATURE PRESERVE | MalaMala's animal-viewing statistics are unbelievable: the Big Five are spotted almost every day, along with plenty of other amazing viewings. At one moment your ranger will fascinate you with the description of the sex life of a dung beetle, as you watch the sturdy male battling his way along the road pushing his perfectly round ball of dung with wife-to-be perched perilously on top; at another, your adrenaline will flow as you follow a leopard stalking impala in the gathering gloom. The rangers are top-class and will ensure that your game experience is unforgettable. ⊠ *MalaMala Game Reserve* ☎ *011/442–2267 reservations* ⊕ *www.malamala.com.*

🏨 Hotels

★ MalaMala Main Camp

$$$$ | RESORT | Stone and thatch air-conditioned rondavels with two bathrooms and an outside shower are decorated in creams and browns and luxuriously furnished with natural finishes like copper

Did you know? Rhinos have poor eyesight, but excellent hearing.

and wood, colorful handwoven tapestries and rugs, terra-cotta floors, and original artwork. **Pros:** sweeping wilderness views; amazing game-viewing; authentic. **Cons:** rondavels are a bit old-fashioned, but that goes with the ambience. [$] *Rooms from: R32,000* ✉ *MalaMala Game Reserve* ☎ *011/442–2267 reservations, 013/735–9200 MalaMala Main Camp* 🌐 *www.malamala.com* 🛏 *17 rooms* 🍴 *All-Inclusive.*

MalaMala Rattray's Camp

$$$$ | RESORT | The breathtakingly beautiful Rattray's Camp merges original bushveld style with contemporary African luxury. **Pros:** tantalizing views over the river; an exclusive feel; superb game-viewing. **Cons:** though this may be a pro for some, no children under 16; some might find the villas overly opulent. [$] *Rooms from: R43,000* ✉ *MalaMala Game Reserve* ☎ *011/442–2267 reservations, 013/735–3000 Rattray's Camp* 🌐 *www.malamala.com* 🛏 *8 rooms* 🍴 *All-Inclusive.*

MalaMala Sable Camp

$$$$ | ALL-INCLUSIVE | If you're looking for a truly exclusive experience, this lovely camp set high on stilts overlooking the Sand River at the southern end of the main MalaMala Camp fits the bill. **Pros:** whole camp can be booked; only a maximum of 6 guests per vehicle; each suite with river or waterhole view. **Cons:** no children under 12 unless whole camp is reserved; only 7 suites so hope for compatible neighbors. [$] *Rooms from: R37,000* ✉ *Sabi Sand Game Reserve* ☎ *01111/442–2267* 🌐 *malamala.com* 🛏 *7 suites* 🍴 *All-Inclusive* ☞ *whole camp can be booked.*

Sabi Sabi Private Game Reserve

Founded in 1978 at the southern end of Sabi Sand, the multi-award-winning Sabi Sabi Private Game Reserve was one of the first reserves to offer photo safaris and to link ecotourism, conservation, and community. Superb accommodations and abundant game lure guests back to Sabi Sabi in large numbers.

 ## Sights

★ Sabi Sabi Private Game Reserve

NATURE PRESERVE | Daily game drives take place in the early morning and late afternoon. There's a strong emphasis on ecology at Sabi Sabi: guests are encouraged to look beyond the Big Five and to become aware of the birds and smaller mammals of the bush. You can also take a walking safari or a specialist birding or photo safari. There's also the Amani Spa, as well as stargazing in the evenings. ⊠ *Sabi Sand Game Reserve* ☎ *011/447–7172 reservations* ⊕ *www. sabisabi.com.*

 ## Hotels

Sabi Sabi Bush Lodge

$$$$ | RESORT | FAMILY | Bush Lodge overlooks a busy waterhole (lions are frequent visitors) and the dry course of the Msuthlu River. **Pros:** always prolific game around the lodge; roomy chalets. **Cons:** big and busy might not be your idea of a relaxing getaway. $ *Rooms from: R32,000* ⊠ *Sabi Sand Game Reserve* ☎ *013/735–5656 reservations, 013/110– 0134 lodge* ⊕ *www.sabisabi.com* 🛏 *25 rooms* ❙◯❙ *All-Inclusive.*

Sabi Sabi Earth Lodge

$$$$ | RESORT | This avant-garde, eco-friendly lodge was the first to break away from the traditional safari style and strive for a contemporary theme. **Pros:** stunning architecture and design. **Cons:** if you favor traditonal safari accommodations, this is not for you. $ *Rooms from: R48,000* ⊠ *Sabi Sand Game Reserve* ☎ *013/735–5261 lodge, 011/447–7172 reservations* ⊕ *www.sabisabi.com* 🛏 *13 rooms* ❙◯❙ *All-Inclusive.*

Sabi Sabi Little Bush Camp

$$$$ | RESORT | FAMILY | Sabi Sabi's delightful little camp is tucked away in the bushveld on the banks of the Msuthlu River and combines spaciousness with a sense of intimacy. **Pros:** perfect for families; private viewing deck and heated spa bath; solo travellers don't suffer single supplement fees. **Cons:** there may be other families. $ *Rooms from: R34,000* ⊠ *Sabi Sand Game Reserve* ☎ *011/447–7172 reservations, 013/735– 5080 lodge* ⊕ *www.sabisabi.com* 🛏 *6 rooms* ❙◯❙ *All-Inclusive.*

★ Sabi Sabi Selati Camp

$$$$ | RESORT | For an *Out of Africa* experience and great game, you can't beat Selati, an intimate, stylish, colonial-style camp that was formerly the private hunting lodge of a famous South African opera singer. **Pros:** Ivory Presidential Suite superb value for money; secluded and intimate; unique atmosphere. **Cons:** some old-timers preferred the camp when it was just lantern-lit with no electricity. $ *Rooms from: R34,000* ⊠ *Sabi Sand Game Reserve* ☎ *011/447–7172 reservations, 013/735–5771 lodge* ⊕ *www. sabisabi.com* 🛏 *8 rooms* ❙◯❙ *All-Inclusive.*

Singita

Although Singita (Shangaan for "the miracle") offers much the same thrilling Sabi Sand bush and game experiences as the other lodges its superb service is truly memorable.

 ## Sights

★ Singita Sabi Sand

NATURE PRESERVE | This is among the crème de la crème of the Sabi Sands (although you pay for it) lodges. At Singita, you'll head out during the day on your choice of game drives, then prepare to be pampered. Whether you fancy a starlit private supper or just chilling alone in your mega-suite, you've only to ask.

Forget the usual lodge curio shop and take a ride to the on-site boutique and art gallery where objets d'art, handmade jewelry, classy bush gear, and artifacts from all over Africa are clustered together in a series of adjoining rooms that seem more like a curator's home than a shop. ✉ *Singita Sabi Sand* ☎ *021/683–3424 reservations* 🌐 *www.singita.co.za.*

Hotels

★ Singita Boulders Lodge

$$$$ | RESORT | Overlooking the beautiful Sand River, Singita Boulders Lodge intermingles the wildness of its setting among boulders with traditional Africa decor at its most luxurious. **Pros:** spacious accommodations; superb food. **Cons:** a bit of a walk from some suites to the main lodge although walkway is flat. [$] *Rooms from: R65,900* ✉ *Singita Sabi Sand* ☎ *021/683–3424 reservations* 🌐 *www.singita.co.za* 🛏 *12 rooms* 🍴 *All-Inclusive.*

Singita Ebony Lodge

$$$$ | RESORT | FAMILY | If Ernest Hemingway had built his ideal home in the African bush, this would be it. **Pros:** the mother lodge of all the Singita properties; cozy library; children of all ages are welcome. **Cons:** the beds are very high off the ground—if you have short legs or creak a bit, ask for a stool. [$] *Rooms from: R69,120* ✉ *Singita Sabi Sand* ☎ *021/683–3424 reservations* 🌐 *www.singita.co.za* 🛏 *12 rooms* 🍴 *All-Inclusive.*

KwaZulu-Natal Parks

The province of KwaZulu-Natal is a premier vacation destination for South Africans, with some of the finest game reserves in the country, including the Hluhluwe-iMfolozi Game Reserve. The reserve is small compared to Kruger, but here you'll see the Big Five and plenty of plains game, plus an incredibly biologically diverse mix of plants and trees. The nearby uMkuze game reserve is even smaller but is still worth a visit for the numerous bird species and game.

KwaZulu-Natal's best private lodges lie in northern Zululand and Maputaland, a remote region close to Mozambique. These lodges are sufficiently close to one another and Hluhluwe-iMfolozi Game Reserve to allow you to put together a bush experience that delivers the Big Five and a great deal more, including superb bird-watching opportunities and an unrivaled beach paradise.

Park Ratings

Game: ★★★★☆

Park Accessibility: ★★★★★

Getting Around: ★★★★★

Accommodations: ★★★★★

Scenic Beauty: ★★★★☆

WHEN TO GO

Summers are hot, hot, hot. If you can't take heat and humidity, then autumn, winter, and early summer are probably the best times to visit.

GETTING HERE AND AROUND

The Richards Bay airport is the closest to the Hluhluwe-iMfolozi area—about 100 km (60 miles) south of Hluhluwe-iMfolozi and about 224 km (140 miles) south of Ithala.

There are daily flights from Johannesburg to Richards Bay; flight time is about an hour. Private lodges will arrange your transfers for you.

If you're traveling to Hluhluwe-iMfolozi from Durban, drive north on the N2 to Mtubatuba, then cut west on the R618 to Mambeni Gate. Otherwise, continue up the N2 to the Hluhluwe exit and follow the signs to the park and Memorial Gate.

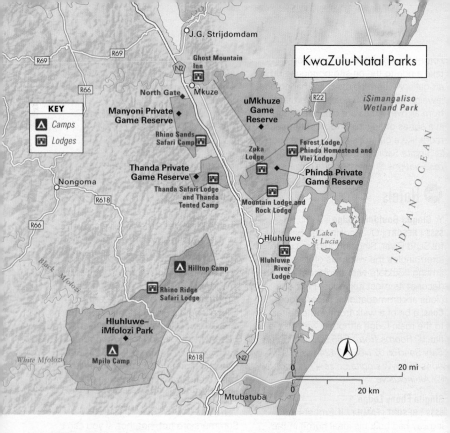

The whole trip takes about three hours, but watch out for potholes.

AIRPORT Richards Bay Airport. ✉ *30 Fish Eagle Flight, Birdswood, Richards Bay* ☎ *035/789–9630* ⊕ *www.richardsbayairport.co.za.*

Hluhluwe–iMfolozi Park

Renowned for its conservation successes—most notably with white rhinos—this park is a wonderful place to view the Big Five and many other species. Until 1989 it consisted of two separate reserves, Hluhluwe in the north and iMfolozi in the south, separated by a fenced corridor. Although a road (R618) still runs through this corridor, the fences have been removed, and the reserves—now known as Hluhluwe-iMfolozi Park or HIP—operate as a single entity.

GETTING HERE AND AROUND

If you're traveling to Hluhluwe-iMfolozi from Durban, drive north on the N2 to Mtubatuba, then cut west on the R618 to Mambeni Gate. Otherwise, continue up the N2 to the Hluhluwe exit and follow the signs to the park and Memorial Gate. The whole trip takes about three hours (without food or comfort stops) and the roads can be bad so watch out for potholes.

TIMING

Compared to Kruger, Hluhluwe-iMfolozi is tiny—less than 6% of Kruger's size—but such comparisons can be misleading. You can spend days driving around this park and still not see everything, or feel like you're going in circles. Probably the biggest advantage Hluhluwe has over Kruger is that game-viewing is good year-round, whereas Kruger has seasonal peaks and valleys. Another bonus is its proximity to uMkuze Game Reserve and the spectacular coastal reserves of iSimangaliso Greater St. Lucia Wetland Park. The park is also close enough to Durban to make it a worthwhile one- or two-day excursion.

Sights

Hluhluwe-iMfolozi Park

WILDLIFE REFUGE | FAMILY | Reputedly King Shaka's favorite hunting ground, Zululand's Hluhluwe-iMfolozi (pronounced shloo- *shloo*-ee im-fuh- *low*-zee) incorporates two of Africa's oldest reserves: Hluhluwe and iMfolozi, both founded in 1895. These days the reserves are abbreviated as HIP. In an area of just 906 square km (350 square miles), Hluhluwe-iMfolozi delivers the Big Five plus all the plains game and species like nyala and red duiker that are rare in other parts of the country. Equally important, it encompasses one of the most biologically diverse habitats on the planet, with a unique mix of forest, woodland, savanna, and grassland. You'll find about 1,250 species of plants and trees here—more than in some entire countries.

The park is administered by Ezemvelo KZN Wildlife, the province's official conservation organization, which looks after all the large game reserves and parks as well as many nature reserves. Thanks to its conservation efforts and those of its predecessor, the highly regarded Natal Parks Board, the park can take credit for saving the white rhino from extinction. So successful was the park at increasing white rhino numbers that in 1960 it established its now famous Rhino Capture Unit to relocate rhinos to other reserves in Africa. The park is currently trying to do for the black rhino what it did for its white cousins. Poaching in the past nearly decimated Africa's black rhino population, but as a result of the park's remarkable conservation program, Africa's black rhinos safely roam this reserve—and you'll get a great opportunity of seeing them in the wild here. ✉ *Hluhluwe iMfolozi* ☎ *035/562–0848* 🌐 *www.kznwildlife.com* 🎟 *R260 international guests, R125 South Africans.*

Hotels

Hluhluwe-iMfolozi offers a range of accommodations in government-run rest camps, with an emphasis on self-catering (only Hilltop has a restaurant). The park also has secluded bush lodges and camps, but most foreign visitors can't avail themselves of these lodgings, as each must be reserved in a block, and the smallest accommodates at least eight people. Conservation levies are R80 per person.

Hilltop Camp

$$ | RESORT | FAMILY | Located in the Hluhluwe half of the park, the camp's self-contained chalets have high thatch ceilings, rattan furniture, and small verandahs. **Pros:** floodlit waterhole; warm, friendly staff; incredible views. **Cons:** outdoor grill area not covered and is dimly lit at night; bathrooms can smell a little moldy; watch out for marauding monkeys. [$] *Rooms from: R1,850* ✉ *Hluhluwe* ☎ *033/845–1000 reservations, 035/562–0848 Hilltop Camp* 🌐 *www.kznwildlife.com/Hilltop.html* 🛏 *70 rooms* 🍴 *Free Breakfast.*

Hluhluwe River Lodge

$$$ | HOTEL | FAMILY | Overlooking False Bay lake and the Hluhluwe River floodplain—follow signs from Hluhluwe village—this fantastic-value, family-owned lodge is the ideal base for visiting the game reserves and the iSimangaliso Wetland Park. **Pros:** only 25 minutes from Hluhluwe-iMfolozi; great for families; excellent food. **Cons:** 35-minute drive to the park; four-wheel drive recommended; lots of kids in holiday times and activities cost extra. [$] *Rooms from: R3,500* ✉ *Hluhluwe* ☎ *035/562–0246* 🌐 *www.hluhluwe.co.za* 🛏 *13 rooms* 🍴 *All-Inclusive.*

Mpila Camp

$ | **RESORT** | **FAMILY** | In the central iMfolozi section of the park, Mpila is reminiscent of some of Kruger's older camps with lodging options that range from basic but fully equipped one-room chalets with en suite bathroom, kitchenette, and deck, to three-bedroom cottages (these come with a cook who will prepare the food you've brought with you), self-catering chalets, and the Safari Tented camp, with two- and four-bed self-catering tents with en suite bathrooms. **Pros:** free-roaming game; lovely location; good value for money compared to other parks up north. **Cons:** watch out for hyenas stealing your braai meat; little privacy; a bit tired-looking. ⓢ *Rooms from: R1,150* ✉ *Hluhluwe iMfolozi* ☎ *033/845–1000 reservations* ⊕ *www.kznwildlife.com/ Mpila.html* ⌘ *40 rooms* ❑ *No Meals.*

★ Rhino Ridge Safari Lodge

$$$$ | **ALL-INCLUSIVE** | Perched upon a hillside, the park's only 4-star private lodge commands breathtaking views across the park with each airy abode featuring glass sliding doors that enjoy those expansive views; the luxury bush villas offer the best value with private plunge pools, a romantic bath big enough for two, and cozy fireplaces for when that moody Zululand mist rolls in. **Pros:** shared community ownership of the lodge; legendary walking safaris; authentic Zulu homestay activity available. **Cons:** rates exclude bush walks; can get noisy with family groups. ⓢ *Rooms from: R8,120* ✉ *Rhino Ridge Safari Lodge, Hluhluwe iMfolozi* ☎ *035/474–1473* ⊕ *www.rhinoridge.co.za* ⌘ *18 suites* ❑ *All-Inclusive.*

🏃 Activities

BUSH WALKS

Armed rangers lead groups of eight on two- to three-hour bush walks departing from Hilltop or Mpila Camp. You may not spot much game on these walks, but you do see plenty of birds, and you learn a great deal about the area's ecology and tips on how to recognize the signs of the bush, including animal spoor. Walks depart daily at 5:30 am and 3:30 pm (6 and 3 in winter) and cost R315. Reserve a few days in advance at **Hilltop Camp** reception (035/562–0848).

GAME DRIVES

A great way to see the park is on game drives led by rangers. These drives (R385 per person) hold several advantages over driving through the park yourself: you sit high up in an open-air vehicle with a good view and the wind in your face, a ranger explains the finer points of animal behavior and ecology, and your guide has a good idea where to find animals like leopards, cheetahs, and lions. Game drives leave daily at 5:30 am in summer, 6:30 am in winter. The park also offers three-hour night drives, during which you search with powerful spotlights for nocturnal animals. These three-hour drives depart at 7, and you should make advance reservations at **Hilltop Camp** reception (035/562–0848).

WILDERNESS TRAILS

The park's **Wilderness Trails** are every bit as popular as Kruger's, but they tend to be tougher and more rustic. You should be fit enough to walk up to 16 km (10 miles) a day for a period of three days and four nights. An armed ranger leads the hikes, and all equipment, food, and baggage are carried by donkeys. The first and last nights are spent at Mndindini, a permanent tented camp. The other two are spent under canvas in the bush. While in the bush, hikers bathe in the Imfolozi River or have a hot bucket shower; toilet facilities consist of a spade and toilet-paper roll. Trails, open March through October, are limited to eight people and should be reserved a year in advance (R3,981 per person per trail).

Fully catered two- or three-night **Short Wilderness Trails** (R2,920 per person) involve stays at a satellite camp in the wilderness area. You'll sleep in a dome

You'll see all sorts of animals in uMkhuze Game Reserve, including mongoose.

tent, and although there's hot water from a bucket shower, your toilet is a spade.

If that sounds too easy, you can always opt for the four-night **Primitive Trail.** On this trek hikers carry their own packs and sleep out under the stars, although there are lightweight tents for inclement weather. A campfire burns all night to scare off animals, and each participant is expected to sit a 90-minute watch. A ranger acts as guide. The cost is R3,465 per person.

A less rugged wilderness experience can be had on the **Base Camp Trail,** based out of the tented Mndindini camp, where you're guaranteed a bed and some creature comforts. The idea behind these trails is to instill in the participants an appreciation for the beauty of the untamed bush. You can also join the Mpila night drive if you wish. Participation is limited to eight people and costs about R4,800 per person.

The **Explorer Trail,** two nights and three days, combines the most comfortable

Base Camp trail with the Primitive Trail. On this trail you sleep out under the stars at a different spot each night. The cost is R3,750 per person.

uMkhuze KZN Park

Wildlife—and amazing birdlife—abounds in this 400-square-km (154-square-mile) reserve in the shadow of the Ubombo Mountains. Lying between the uMkhuze and Msunduzi rivers, it makes up the northwestern spur of the iSimangaliso Wetland Park, a UNESCO World Heritage Site. It has been a protected area since 1912. ■TIP→ **There are variant spellings of Mkuze in the area; you may also see Mkhuze, Mkuzi, or Mkhuzi.**

 Sights

uMkhuze Game Reserve
NATIONAL PARK | Wildlife—and amazing birdlife—abounds in this 400-square-km (154-square-mile) reserve in the shadow of the Ubombo Mountains. Lying

between the uMkhuze and Msunduzi rivers, it makes up the northwestern spur of the iSimangaliso Wetland Park, a World Heritage Site. It has been a protected area since 1912.

If you're a birder, then you'll find yourself in seventh heaven: more than 420 bird species have been spotted here, including myriad waterfowl drawn to the park's shallow pans in summer. Several blinds, particularly those overlooking Nsumo Pan, offer superb views. Don't miss out on the amazing 3-km (2-mile) walk through a spectacular rare forest of towering, ancient fig trees. This is a good place to spot rhinos and elephants, although lions, cheetah, and leopards are much harder to find. However, there's is plenty of other game, including hippos, zebras, giraffes, kudus, and nyalas. ✉ *Off N2, uMkhuze* ✣ *48 km (30 miles) northeast of Hluhluwe-iMfolozi.* ☎ *035/573–9004* 🌐 *www.isimangaliso.com* 🎫 *R61 per vehicle plus R56 per person.*

Hotels

Ghost Mountain Inn

$$ | **B&B/INN** | **FAMILY** | Swaths of scarlet bougainvillea run riot in the lush gardens of this family-owned country inn with tastefully furnished rooms that each have a small verandah (the newest Mountain Rooms have the best interiors). **Pros:** good value for money and generous buffet; strategic location for bush excursions; spa on-site. **Cons:** can get noisy in peak season; hotel-like atmosphere; tour buses overnight here. [$] *Rooms from: R2,120* ✉ *Fish Eagle Rd., uMkhuze* ☎ *035/573–1025* 🌐 *www.ghostmountaininn.co.za* 🛏 *74 rooms* 🍴 *Free Breakfast.*

Phinda Private Game Reserve

Where Phinda excels is in the superb quality of its rangers, who can provide fascinating commentary on everything from local birds to frogs. It's amazing just how enthralling the love life of a dung beetle can be! There are also Phinda adventures (optional extras) down the Mzinene River for a close-up look at crocodiles, hippos, and birds; big-game fishing or scuba diving off the deserted, wildly beautiful Maputaland coast; and sightseeing flights over Phinda and the highest vegetated dunes in the world.

GETTING HERE AND AROUND

Phinda is 300 km (186 miles) from Durban by road with a journey time of just over four hours (minus food and comfort stops). Before you decide to drive, bear in mind that you won't use your vehicle after you arrive at Phinda—all transportation is provided by open game-viewing vehicles. There are scheduled flights daily from Johannesburg to King Shaka International Airport and to Richards Bay Airport as well as regular direct flights to Phinda's own airstrip (check with the lodge for latest schedules). Phinda will also arrange road transfers from the airports.

Sights

★ **Phinda Private Game Reserve**

NATURE PRESERVE | **FAMILY** | This eco-award-winning flagship &Beyond reserve, established in 1991, is a heartening example of tourism serving the environment with panache. *Phinda* (*pin*-da) is Zulu for "return," referring to the restoration of 220 square km (85 square miles) of overgrazed ranchland in northern Zululand to bushveld. It's a triumph. Today Phinda has a stunning variety of seven healthy ecosystems including the rare sand forest (which grows on the fossil dunes of an earlier coastline), savanna, bushveld, open woodland, mountain bush, and verdant wetlands. The Big Five are all here, plus cheetahs, spotted hyenas, hippos, giraffes, impalas, and the rare, elusive, tiny Suni antelope. Birdlife is prolific and extraordinary, with some special Zululand finds: the pink-throated twinspot, the crested guineafowl, the African broadbill, and the crowned eagle. The reserve is a little more than a two-hour drive from Richards Bay or four hours by road from Durban. ✉ *Phinda Game Reserve* ☎ *011/809–4300 central reservations* 🌐 *www.andbeyond.com.*

Hotels

★ Forest Lodge

$$$$ | RESORT | Hidden in a rare sand forest, this fabulous lodge overlooks a small waterhole where nyalas, warthogs, and baboons frequently come to drink. **Pros:** magical feeling of oneness with Africa's last remaining dry sand forest; stylish luxury; lovely views from the pool. **Cons:** rooms are set apart, but when guests gather it's not the most intimate stay; ; staying in a glass box may feel a bit intimidating. [$] *Rooms from: R20,700* ✉ *Phinda Game Reserve* ☎ *011/809–4300 reservations* 🌐 *www.andbeyond.com* 🛏 *16 rooms* 🍴 *All-Inclusive.*

Mountain Lodge

$$$$ | RESORT | FAMILY | This attractive thatch lodge (the first built at Phinda) sits on a rocky hill overlooking miles of bushveld plains and the Ubombo Mountains. **Pros:** superior mountain views; very family-friendly; outstanding menu variety and exceptional dining. **Cons:** pricey if you take the kids (pricey even if you don't); not the best choice if you're seeking solitude; a bigger, less discreet lodge. [$] *Rooms from: R19,000* ✉ *Phinda Game Reserve, off R22, Hluhluwe* ☎ *011/809–4300 reservations* 🌐 *www.andbeyond.com* 🛏 *25 rooms* 🍴 *All-Inclusive.*

Phinda Homestead

$$$$ | ALL-INCLUSIVE | FAMILY | Complete with a dedicated butler, chef, ranger, and tracker, this property is the only sole-use safari villa on the reserve and the most contemporary designer-chic of all the stays. **Pros:** outdoor boma overlooks the busy water hole; state-of-the-art gym; flexibility. **Cons:** eclectic design not for everyone; must rent the whole villa. [$] *Rooms from: R120,750* ✉ *Phinda Game Reserve* ☎ *011/809–4300* 🌐 *www.andbeyond.com* 🛏 *4 suites.*

Rock Lodge

$$$$ | RESORT | Ideal for honeymooners or romantic solitude, this turreted lodge feels like it's dropped from a Moroccan movie set. **Pros:** personal plunge pools and tranquility; amazing views; luxurious sitting rooms. **Cons:** not suitable for families (also, no kids under 12 allowed); not the place for a lively atmosphere; stay away if you suffer from vertigo. [$] *Rooms from: R25,800* ✉ *Phinda Game Reserve* ☎ *011/809–4300 reservations* 🌐 *www.andbeyond.com* 🛏 *6 rooms* 🍴 *All-Inclusive.*

★ Vlei Lodge

$$$$ | RESORT | Made of thatch, teak, and glass, with a distinctly Asian feel, your suite, tucked into the shade of a sand forest overlooking a marshland on the edge of an inviting woodland, is so private you'll find it hard to believe there are other guests. **Pros:** Wi-Fi en suite; superb views over the floodplains; intimate. **Cons:** no children under 12; lots of mosquitoes and other flying insects. [$] *Rooms from: R25,800* ✉ *Phinda Game Reserve* ☎ *011/809–4300* 🌐 *www.andbeyond.com* 🛏 *6 rooms* 🍴 *All-Inclusive.*

Zuka Lodge

$$$$ | RESORT | FAMILY | Designed as an exclusive, single-use lodge for a family or small group of friends, Zuka (*zuka* means "sixpence" in Zulu) is a couple of miles from the bigger lodges and can now be booked per room. **Pros:** it's like having your own private holiday retreat;

gives you the feeling of immediate celebrity status; exclusivity (that's more affordable than bigger lodges). **Cons:** entire property is best rented as a whole. $ *Rooms from: R19,700* ✉ *Phinda Game Reserve* ☎ *011/809–4300 reservations* ⊕ *www.andbeyond.com* ⇄ *4 rooms* ⊙ *All-Inclusive.*

Thanda Private Game Reserve

Thanda offers a more intimate nature experience than some of KwaZulu-Natal's game reserves. Game may sometimes be elusive, but the highly experienced and enthusiastic rangers work hard to find the Big Five and other wildlife. Enjoyable cultural interactions with local people are a highlight of any visit.

GETTING HERE AND AROUND

Road transfers from Richards Bay and Durban airports can be arranged with the reserve.

Sights

Thanda Private Game Reserve

NATURE PRESERVE | FAMILY | In wild, beautiful northern Zululand, the multi-award-winning 150-square-km (60-square-mile) Thanda reserve continues to restore former farmlands and hunting grounds to their previous pristine state, thanks to a joint venture with local communities and the king of the Zulus, Goodwill Zweletini, who donated some of his royal hunting grounds to the project. Game that used to roam this wilderness centuries ago has been reestablished, including the Big Five. *Thanda* (*tan*-da) is Zulu for "love," and its philosophy echoes just that: "for the love of nature, wildlife, and dear ones." There's a main lodge, a private villa, and a small tented camp and opportunities to interact with the local people. ✉ *D242, off N2,*

Hluhluwe ☎ *032/586–0149 reservations* ⊕ *www.thandasafari.co.za.*

Hotels

Thanda Safari Lodge

$$$$ | RESORT | FAMILY | This exquisite lodge blends elements of royal Zulu with an eclectic pan-African feel evident in the thatched, turreted dwellings perched on the side of rolling hills that overlook mountains and bushveld. **Pros:** luxurious with a generous mini bar included; private plunge pool and boma area; loads of space. **Cons:** spa treatments excluded; children three and up permitted and can disrupt romantic atmosphere; some might say it's Hollywood in the bush. $ *Rooms from: R17,330* ✉ *Off N2 and D242, Hluhluwe* ☎ *032/586–0149 reservations* ⊕ *www.thanda.com* ⇄ *9 rooms* ⊙ *All-Inclusive.*

Thanda Tented Camp

$$$$ | RESORT | FAMILY | Perfect for a family or friends' reunion (although it's great for individual travelers, too), this intimate and luxurious eco-forward camp deep in the bush brings you into close contact with your surroundings. **Pros:** eco-friendly; five-star luxury. **Cons:** no children under eight; no air-conditioning; not for the nervous type. $ *Rooms from: R4,990* ✉ *Off N2 and D242, Hluhluwe* ☎ *032/586–0149 reservations* ⊕ *www.thanda.co.za* ⇄ *15 rooms* ⊙ *All-Inclusive.*

Manyoni Private Game Reserve

50 km (31 miles) northeast of Hluhluwe; 300 km (186 miles) north of Durban.

One of KwaZulu-Natal's newest game reserves, Manyoni Game Reserve mirrors the story of nearby Phinda and also boasts incredible game viewing. There may be more lodges spread across this reserve, but a deeply-caring conservation team and some innovative activities plus affordable stays make this a wildly underrated Big Five destination.

GETTING HERE AND AROUND

Manyoni Private Game Reserve is 300 km (186 miles) from Durban by road, with a journey time of 3½ hours. Take the N2 north from Durban past the Hluhluwe turn off and take a left onto the D646 dirt road. From here, the Manyoni Private Game Reserve is plainly signposted. There are scheduled flights daily from Johannesburg to King Shaka International Airport and to Richards Bay Airport. Most lodges will also arrange road transfers from the airports.

Sights

Manyoni Private Game Reserve

NATURE PRESERVE | In 2004, 17 private properties in the northern Zululand area dropped their fences to create the Manyoni Private Game Reserve. Formerly known as the Zululand Rhino Reserve, the marriage and restoration of these properties (a mish-mash of old tomato farms, cotton fields, and seasonal cattle grazing) has created a 23,000-hectare game-rich private reserve. The terrain varies from bushveld to riverine woodland and open savanna thornveld that animals, such as wildebeest, zebras, and cheetahs love. The reserve has over 70 mammal species and an exceptional diversity of birdlife including sought-out endemics such as the pink-throated twinspot and elusive African broadbill. Apt then, that the name means the "place of birds" in isiZulu. However, this sanctuary is all the more special because it's been chosen as a safe space to rehabilitate rescued pangolins. This species is particularly susceptible to illness and takes ages to recover from the hardships of trafficking (they often suffer dehydration and malnutrition). If there is a pangolin in residence, you can join the conservation team on the ground as they walk with them to ensure they are eating, picking up weight, and getting strong enough to roam freely again. There's no touching or petting. ✉ *Manyoni Game Reserve* ✥ *50 km (31 miles) northeast of Hluhluwe* 🌐 *www.manyoni.co.za.*

Hotels

★ **Rhino Sands Safari Camp**

$$$$ | ALL-INCLUSIVE | This intimate and traditional safari camp enjoys a sublime forested setting aflutter with birdsong inside the southern stretch of the Manyoni Game Reserve. **Pros:** small and deeply personal; hands-on team; exceptional food and menu variety. **Cons:** nearby tents could mean noisy neighbors; no air-conditioning. [$] *Rooms from: R15,000* ✉ *Rhino Sands Safari Camp* ✥ *Access via East Gate and D464 dirt road* ☎ *087/004–4027 Reservations, 082/655–0927 Safari Camp* 🌐 *www.rhinosands.com* 🛏 *4 suites* 🍴 *All-Inclusive.*

Kgalagadi Transfrontier Park

If you're looking for true wilderness, remoteness, and stark, almost surreal landscapes and you're not averse to forgoing luxury and getting sand in your hair, then this uniquely beautiful park within the Kalahari Desert is for you.

In an odd little finger of the country jutting north between Botswana in the east and Namibia in the west lies South Africa's second-largest park after Kruger. The "reborn" Kgalagadi was officially launched in 2000 as the first transfrontier, or "peace park," in southern Africa by merging South Africa's vast Kalahari Gemsbok National Park with the even larger Gemsbok National Park in Botswana. The name Kgalagadi (pronounced "kala- *hardy*") is derived from the San language and means "place of thirst." It's now one of the largest protected wilderness areas in the world—an area of more than 38,000 square km (14,670 square miles). Of this awesome area, 9,600 square km (3,700 square miles) fall in South Africa, and the rest fall in Botswana.

Passing through the Twee Rivieren Gate, you'll encounter a vast desert under enormous, usually cloudless skies and a sense of space and openness that few other places can offer. With the rest camp to the left, just a little farther down the dirt road to the right is the dry Nossob River, lined by camel-thorn trees, which winds its way to Botswana, into which the park continues.

The Kgalagadi Transfrontier is less commercialized and developed than Kruger. The roads aren't paved, and you'll come across far fewer people and cars. There's less game on the whole than in Kruger, but because there's also less vegetation, the animals are much more visible. Also, because the game and large carnivores are concentrated in two riverbeds (the route that two roads follow), the park offers unsurpassed game-viewing and photographic opportunities. Perhaps the key to really appreciating this barren place is in understanding how its creatures have adapted to their harsh surroundings to survive—like the gemsbok, which has a sophisticated cooling system allowing it to tolerate extreme changes in body temperature. There are also insects in the park that inhale only every half hour or so to preserve the moisture that breathing expends.

The landscape—endless dunes punctuated with blond grass and the odd thorn tree—is dominated by two *wadis* (dry riverbeds): the Nossob (which forms the border between South Africa and Botswana) and its tributary, the Auob. The Nossob flows only a few times a century, and the Auob flows only once every couple of decades or so. A single road runs beside each riverbed, along which windmills pump water into man-made waterholes, which help the animals to survive and provide good viewing stations for visitors. There are 82 waterholes, 49 of which are along tourist roads. Park management struggles to keep up their maintenance; it's a constant battle against the elements, with the elements often winning. Similarly, the park constantly maintains and improves tourist roads, but again it's a never-ending struggle. A third road traverses the park's interior to join the other two. The scenery and vegetation on this road change dramatically from two river valleys dominated by sandy banks to a grassy escarpment. Two more dune roads have been added, and several 4x4 routes have been developed. From Nossob camp a road leads to Union's End, the country's northernmost tip, where South Africa, Namibia, and Botswana meet. Allow a full day for the long and dusty drive, which is 124 km (77 miles) one way. It's possible to enter Botswana from the South African side, but you'll need a 4x4. The park infrastructure in Botswana is very basic, with just three campsites and mostly 4x4 terrain.

The park is famous for its gemsbok, the desert-adapted springbok, and its legendary, huge, black-maned Kalahari lions. It also has leopards, cheetahs, eland, blue wildebeests, jackals, and giraffes, as well as meerkats and mongooses. Rarer desert species, such as the elusive aardvark and the pretty Cape fox, also make their home here. Among birders, the park is known as one of Africa's raptor meccas; it's filled with bateleurs, lappet-faced vultures, pygmy falcons, and the cooperatively hunting red-necked falcons and gabar goshawks.

The park's legendary night drives (approximately R300 per person) depart most evenings around 5:30 in summer, earlier in winter (check when you get to your camp), from Twee Rivieren Camp and Nossob. The drives set out just as the park gate closes to everyone else. You'll have a chance to see rare nocturnal animals like the brown hyena and the bat-eared fox by spotlight. The guided morning walks—during which you see the sun rise over the Kalahari and could bump into a lion—are also a must. Reservations are essential and can be made when you book your accommodations. All guided drives and walks are subject to availability.

WHEN TO GO

The park can be superhot in summer and freezing at night in winter (literally, with frost on the ground). Autumn—from late February to mid-April—is perhaps the best time to visit. It's cool after the rains, and many of the migratory birds are still around. The winter months of June and July are also a good time. It's best to make reservations as far in advance as possible, even up to 11 months if you want to visit at Easter or in June or July, when there are school vacations.

GETTING HERE AND AROUND

Upington International Airport is 260 km (162 miles) south of Kgalagadi Transfrontier Park; many lodgings provide shuttle service, or you can rent a car at the airport. If you reserve a car through an agency in Upington, you can pick it up from the Twee Rivieren Camp. If you drive from Johannesburg, you have a choice of two routes: either via Upington (with the last stretch a 60-km [37-mile] gravel road) or via Kuruman, Hotazel, and Vanzylrus (with about 340 km [211 miles] of gravel road). The gravel sections on both routes are badly corrugated, so don't speed.

AIRPORT INFORMATION Upington International Airport. ✉ *Diedricks St., Upington* ☎ *054/337–7900.*

VISITOR INFORMATION

There's a daily conservation fee, but Wild Cards, available at the gates or online, are more economical for stays of more than a few days. Reservations for all accommodations, bush drives, wilderness trails,

Park Ratings

Game: ★★★★☆
Park Accessibility: ★★★☆☆
Getting Around: ★★★★★
Accommodations: ★★★★☆
Scenic Beauty: ★★★★★

and other park activities must be made through South African National Parks.

South African National Parks

It's usually safest and quickest to book through the central booking office in Tshwane, although oftentimes when that office says "full," the camp itself has vacancies. ☎ *012/428–9111* ⊕ *www.sanparks.org.*

◉ Sights

Kalahari Trails Meerkat Sanctuary

WILDLIFE REFUGE | FAMILY | About 30 minutes from the Twee Rivieren entry gate to Kgalagadi Transfrontier Park, this private nature reserve was established by the late zoology professor Anna Rasa who wanted to focus on the region's smaller creatures. Her son, Richard, now oversees the 9-acre property, where activities include up-close looks at meerkats being nursed back to health; walks to see animals you wouldn't necessarily spot on drives in the Transfrontier Park; sundowner and nighttime drives, where a spotlight makes it easier to see nocturnal creatures such as aardvarks; and nighttime scorpion "hunts" using flashlights to look for these arachnids, which are collected for identification and then later released (except for the few that are fed to the meerkats).

The main treat, though, is the chance to observe the resident meerkat family in its natural environment, walking with them as they move out into the landscape,

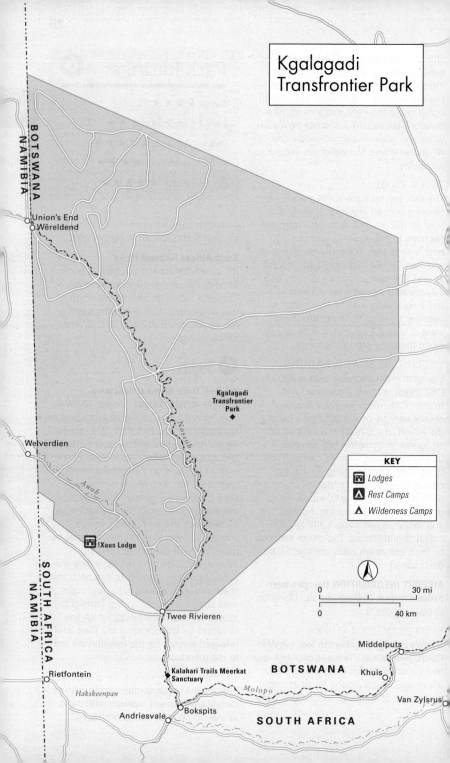

Kgalagadi
Transfrontier Park

BOTSWANA
NAMIBIA

Union's End
Wêreldend

Welverdien

Kgalagadi
Transfrontier
Park ◆

Nossob

Auob

🏠 !Xaus Lodge

SOUTH AFRICA
NAMIBIA

KEY
🏠 *Lodges*
▲ *Rest Camps*
▲ *Wilderness Camps*

0 ———— 30 mi
0 ———— 40 km

Twee Rivieren

Middelputs

Rietfontein

★ Kalahari Trails Meerkat
Sanctuary

BOTSWANA

Khuis

Hakskeenpan

Molopo

Van Zylsrus

Andriesvale ○ Bokspits

SOUTH AFRICA

Giraffes are the world's tallest mammals and can grow to be 18 feet tall!

foraging as they go. There are also some basic rooms (some with en suite bathrooms) and bush-camp accommodations if you don't mind roughing it; overnight guests are able to explore the property on foot. ✉ R360, Bokspits, Kgalagadi Transfrontier Park ⊹ 37 km (23 miles) south of the Twee Rivieren entrance to the Kgalagadi Transfrontier Park ☏ 073/963–8577, 063/087–7732 ⊕ www.kalahari-trails. co.za ✉ Daytime dune game drive R200; nighttime game drive R250; guided walks R150; scorpion hunt R100.

★ Kgalagadi Transfrontier Park

WILDLIFE REFUGE | Called Kalahari Gemsbok National Park when it was first incorporated in 1931, Kgalagadi was combined with Botswana's Gemsbok National Park to create this internationally protected area of nearly 9 million acres. Unlike Kruger, South Africa's other mammoth national park, this is a desert park, with sparse vegetation and sand dunes. The game seen here is mostly concentrated around two roads that follow the park's two (mostly) dry riverbeds. These are dotted with man-made watering holes.

Black-maned Kalahari lions, springbok, oryx, pygmy falcons, and martial eagles are among the star animal attractions. You will not find the broad range of large mammals that you see in Kruger, but because of the sparse vegetation and limited grazing areas, animals are more visible here. Among the noteworthy plant species are plenty of beautiful camel-thorn acacia trees; you will also spot many of the large communal nests of sociable weavers that are something of a visual signature all across the Kalahari.

The park has several lodges and rustic rest camps, and while its isolation means that it's never as crowded as Kruger, the pandemic saw a marked increase in South African visitors. According to SANParks reports, the rest and wilderness camps here are almost always full, so don't delay in making reservations. ✉ Twee Rivieren Rest Camp, R360, Kgalagadi Transfrontier Park ☏ 054/561–2000

🌐 *www.sanparks.co.za* 🎫 *R416 per person per day.*

Hotels

Accommodations within the park are in three traditional rest camps and several highly sought-after wilderness camps (try to reserve these if possible) that are spread around the park. All of the traditional rest camps have shops selling food, curios, and some basic equipment, but Twee Rivieren has the best variety of fresh fruit, vegetables, milk, and meat, and is the only camp with a restaurant. Twee Rivieren is also the only camp with telephone and cell-phone reception (although cell-phone reception quickly disappears as you head into the dunes) and 24-hour electricity; the other camps have gas and electricity, but the electricity runs only part of the day, at different times in each camp.

For all national park accommodations, contact South African National Parks, or you can reserve directly through the park if you happen to be there and would like to stay a night or add another night onto your stay.

For a private luxury lodge, !Xaus, owned by the ‡Khomani San community, is deep in the west of the park. Because it's roughly 50 km (32 miles) in from the gate, guests are met by a vehicle at the Kumqwa rest area, where they park their car. From there it is exactly 91 dunes to the lodge in a 4x4—and well worth it.

A limited number of campsites are available at Nossob (20) and Twee Rivieren (24). All campsites have a *braai* and access to electricity and water, and there are communal bathroom facilities and a basic communal kitchen. Before you arrive, be sure to arm yourself with the "blue camping plug"—available from any camping–RV shop—to plug into the electrical system and a long extension cord. Try to find a shady spot.

★ **!Xaus Lodge**

$$$$ | RESORT | To experience one of South Africa's most beautiful and isolated parks and gain insight into an ancient culture, stay at this simple but comfortable lodge, owned by the ‡Khomani San and Mier communities and located deep in the desert, 32 km (20 miles) along a track across the red dunes of the Kalahari. **Pros:** unique wilderness setting; only private lodge within the transfrontier park; opportunities to interact with the indigenous people. **Cons:** very rustic; it will not suit you if you need lots of creature comforts; the chalets could do with some TLC. [$] *Rooms from: R10,750* ✉ *91st Dune, off the Auob River Road, Kgalagadi Transfrontier Park* ☎ *021/701–7860* 🌐 *www.xauslodge.co.za* 🛏 *12 units* 🍴 *All-Inclusive.*

Madikwe Game Reserve

Just as leopards and Sabi Sand Game Reserve are synonymous, think of Madikwe Game Reserve and wild dogs in the same way. This is probably your best chance in South Africa to have an almost guaranteed sighting of the "painted wolves."

In 1991, the 765-square-km (475-square-mile) area bordering Botswana was a wasteland of over-grazed cattle farms, overgrown bush, and rusting fences. A brilliant and unique collaboration between the North West Parks Board, private enterprise, and local communities changed all that when Operation Phoenix—one of the most ambitious game relocation programs in the world—relocated more than 8,000 animals of 27 different species to Madikwe. Soon after, it became one of the fastest-growing safari destinations in South Africa.

Madikwe today is teeming with game. Spot the Big Five, plus resident breeding packs of the endangered painted wolves—the wild dogs of Africa, and another endangered predator, the cheetah. On your morning or evening game drive, you also might spot lions, elephants, and buffalo, but you'll certainly see zebras, wildebeests, and several kinds of antelope (South Africans refer to all antelope generically as "buck," whether they're male or female). Birders can look out for more than 350 bird species that occur here. Be dazzled by the crimson-breasted shrike, the lilac-breasted roller, yellow-billed and red-billed hornbills, blue waxbills, and many more.

Madikwe can't claim the great rivers, giant riverine trees, and range of habitats of Kruger or the Sabi Sand, but it has a diverse landscape including wide plains, thick bushveld, an area steeped in history, and a background of low, purple mountains. The reserve also has a host of advantages over many of the others: it's only 4 hours from Johannesburg on good roads, it's malaria-free, it doesn't allow day visitors or self-drives making sightings more controlled and intimate, and most of its lodges are 5-star, meaning pretty much anywhere you choose to stay is likely to be of a high standard. Choose among over 20 top-class commercial lodges, get your binoculars ready, and off you go.

GETTING HERE AND AROUND

Air travel is possible, but the best advice is to ask your potential lodge to arrange flights. Flying time is about 45 mins. However, Madikwe is an easy 4-hour drive on good roads from Johannesburg. It's such an easy journey by road that by the time you've changed airports from OR Tambo to Grand Central and faced traffic, you'd be a third of the way there by road.

If you're driving yourself, head to Sun City via Hartbeespoort Dam and follow the signs to Madikwe, which is about an hour's drive from Sun City (though your trip could be an hour longer if your lodge is in the north of the park); your lodge should provide detailed

Park Ratings

Game: ★ ★ ★ ★ ☆
Park Accessibility: ★ ★ ★ ★ ☆
Getting Around: ★ ★ ★ ★ ★
Accommodations: ★ ★ ★ ★ ★
Scenic Beauty: ★ ★ ★ ★ ★

instructions. Once you're through one of the main gates, the roads to the lodges are either gravel or tar and may be as long as 10–30 km (6–18.6 miles). Drive slowly and carefully and although you won't need a 4x4, a sedan with very low clearance (such as a sports car) is not a good idea.

Within the park, you'll be driven around in an open game vehicle by your lodge's experienced ranger; guided bush walks are also available. No day visitors are allowed.

WHEN TO GO

Madikwe is malaria-free, so any time is a good time to visit although, as with all South Africa's game reserves, winter is best for game-viewing because of low vegetation and the game's necessity to visit waterholes.

◉ Sights

Madikwe Game Reserve

NATURE PRESERVE | FAMILY | This 187,500-acre game reserve in the North West Province (about 4 hours from Johannesburg and Pretoria) close to the Botswana border is open only to overnight visitors, who can choose from over 20 luxury lodges to stay. The reserve is famous for its wild dog population, but is also known for cheetahs, the Big Five, and its general game, such as zebras, wildebeest, giraffes, and impalas. It was established in 1991 and is fast becoming one of the most popular private reserves in the

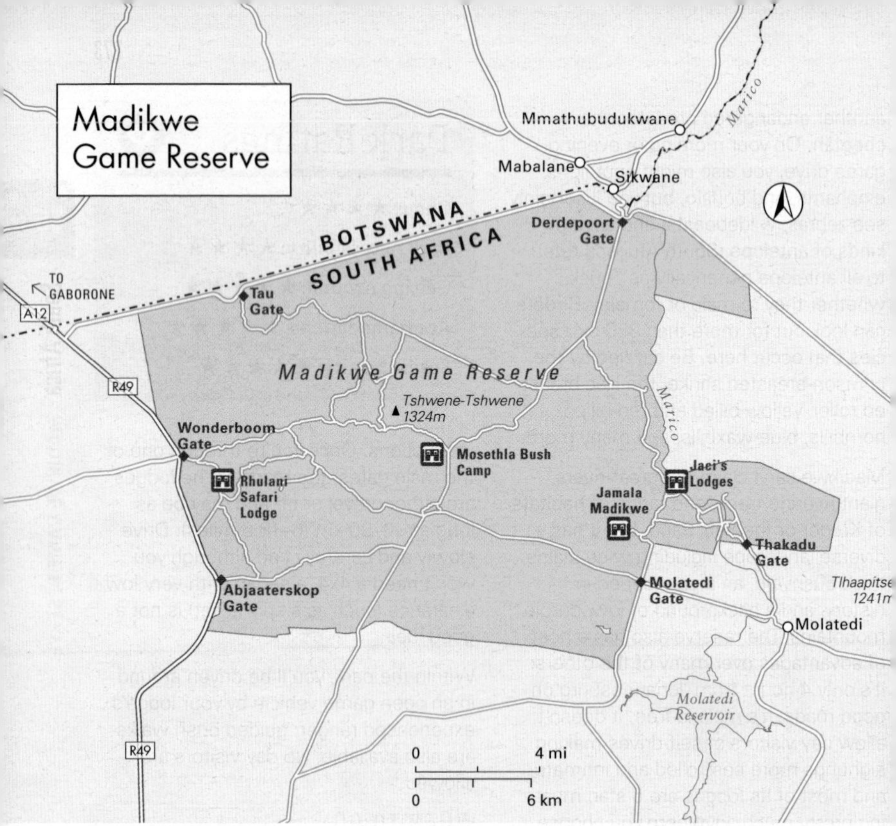

country, because of its size, abundance of game, proximity to Johannesburg, and the fact that it is malaria-free (so is very safe for children). ✉ *Madikwe Game Reserve* 🌐 *www.madikwegamereserve.co.za* 🎟 *R180 gate fee.*

Hotels

Choose between the ultra-luxurious Jamala Madikwe Lodge with its fine dining and lavish décor or quite the opposite, the Mosethla Bush Camp and Eco-Lodge, with its simple pine cabins and old-fashioned donkey boiler to make hot water. Other options include either of Jaci's Lodges, which is particularly child-friendly, and Rhulani, located in the hills in the west of the reserve, and which has an air of relaxed luxury.

Always check for special offers at any of the Madikwe lodges. You can often get very affordable rates, especially off-season or if you can leave your booking to the last minute (phone any of the lodges and ask them for their last-minute rates).

Jaci's Lodges (Jaci's Safari Lodge and Jaci's Tree Lodge)

$$$$ | **ALL-INCLUSIVE** | **FAMILY** | The two lodges that make up Jaci's Lodges are family-owned and have a longstanding reputation for friendliness, superb game drives, and comfortable accommodations. **Pros:** friendly, welcoming atmosphere; children welcome; great game-viewing. **Cons:** food is tasty, but don't expect fine dining; pricey; if children aren't your thing, stay away from Jaci's Safari Lodge. [$] *Rooms from: R22,800* ✉ *Madikwe Game Reserve* ✥ *Accessed through Molatedi Gate* ☎ *083/700–2071*

Madikwe Game Reserve is probably your best chance in South Africa to have an almost guaranteed sighting of the "painted wolves."

reservations, 083/303–0885 Jaci's Safari Lodge manager, 083/276–2387 Jaci's Tree Lodge manager ⊕ www.jacislodges. co.za ⤳ 18 suites ⦿ All-Inclusive.

Jamala Madikwe

$$$$ | **HOTEL** | This intimate lodge, with only five suites, is the ultimate in luxury, with its marble floors, elaborate chandeliers, and plush furnishings. **Pros:** memorable food; superb accommodations; excellent game-viewing. **Cons:** some rooms have better views than others; more formal than some of the other lodges; pricey. ⓢ *Rooms from: R26,310 ⊠ Madikwe Game Reserve ⊕ Accessed via Molatedi Gate* ☎ 082/929–3190, 082/927–3129 ⊕ www.jamalamadikwe. com ⤳ 5 suites ⦿ All-Inclusive.*

★ Mosethla Bush Camp

$$$$ | **RESORT** | If you're genuinely eco-conscious and seeking an authentic wilderness experience, then choose this unique bush camp set plumb in the middle of Madikwe's best game-viewing areas. **Pros:** genuine commitment to the local communities and to conservation;

most competitive prices in Madikwe; superb local guides. **Cons:** no pool; low lighting at night; basic, rustic accommodation and very cold in winter. ⓢ *Rooms from: R7,590 ⊠ Madikwe Game Reserve ⊕ Accessed through Molatedi Gate* ☎ 011/444–9345 reservations, 083/305–7809 emergencies ⊕ www.thebush-camp.com ⤳ 10 rooms ⦿ All-Inclusive.*

Rhulani Safari Lodge

$$$$ | **ALL-INCLUSIVE** | **FAMILY** | Located in the west of Madikwe, Rhulani is a multi-award-winning lodge with nine private rooms, located around an attractive communal lounge and pool area, and overlooking a waterhole frequented by elephants and other animals. **Pros:** excellent, friendly service; privacy; waterhole and hide at the lodge. **Cons:** Wi-Fi intermittent; can be cold in winter; Rhulani's position makes it slightly less accessible than some of the lodges in the center and north of Madikwe (about 30- 45 minutes longer to drive from Johannesburg). ⓢ *Rooms from: R17,200 ⊠ Madikwe Game Reserve ⊕ Accessed through*

Wonderboom Gate ☎ 014/553–3981 inquiries and reservations, 082/907–9628 inquiries and reservations ⊕ www.rhulani.com ⊃ 9 suites �| All-Inclusive.

If You Have Time

Although this chapter goes into great detail about the must-see parks in South Africa, there are many others to explore if you have time. Here are a few good ones to consider.

Tswalu Kalahari Reserve

250 km (155 miles) southeast of Kgalagadi Transfrontier Park; 262 km (163 miles) northeast of Upington; 145 km (90 miles) northwest of Kuruman.

Near the Kgalagadi Transfrontier Park is the malaria-free Tswalu Kalahari Reserve, at 1,000 square km (386 square miles) Africa's largest privately owned game reserve and the perfect place to photograph an oryx against a red dune and big blue sky. Initially founded as a conservation project by the late millionaire Stephen Boler (how he made his money is a story in itself), primarily to protect and breed the endangered desert rhino, he left it to the Oppenheimer (of De Beers diamonds fame) family in his will. Today, it spreads over endless Kalahari dunes covered with tufts of golden veld as well as much of the Northern Cape's Korannaberg mountain range.

Its initial population of 7,000 animals has grown, and it's now home to lions, cheetahs, buffalos, giraffes, and a range of antelope species—including rare roan and sable antelope, black wildebeest, and mountain zebra. Because a farm road cuts through the reserve, fences separate the reserve's two precincts, with the lion population currently only in one part. The benefit of this is that the reserve's main Tarkuni lodge is unfenced and as family-friendly as possible, and some of

the antelope (notably the sable) remain off the lions' dinner menu. That said, there are plans to construct a third lodge and possibly introduce a lion pride in the currently lion-free area. Also in the pipeline is having the road delisted so that the dividing fences can be taken down. As with most conservation endeavors, Tswalu is ever-changing, so only time will tell how it will evolve.

True to the region's aridity (annual rainfall is only about 9¾ inches), the land has a lower carrying capacity than is found in areas around Kruger National Park, for example, and therefore there's less game. But the lack of vegetation makes animal sightings spectacular. You'll definitely spot meerkats, and roan and sable might stride right past your lodge.

The reserve is also home to several significant research projects, not least of which is an ongoing study of pangolins (scaly anteaters), the world's most heavily trafficked mammal, hunted as much for their scales as for their meat. Although sightings are not guaranteed, seeing one of these mysterious nocturnal creatures will be a highlight of your trip. Other after-dark creatures here include aardvark and aardwolf, and you will almost certainly spot bat-eared foxes, a real delight with their pretty faces. Regardless, Tswalu's vast, surreal landscape is pure magic in and of itself.

GETTING HERE AND AROUND

Direct, scheduled, daily flights operate from Johannesburg (1 pm) and from Cape Town (7:30 am) to Tswalu, and seats on these small, private airplanes should be booked directly through the reserve. It's also easy enough to catch a commercial flight to Kimberley or Upington and be picked up from there by the lodge; private road transfers can similarly be arranged from just about anywhere.

It is also totally feasible to drive yourself to the reserve; you'll be provided very clear driving instructions that get you and

Although pangolin sightings are rare, it is possible in Tswalu Kalahari Reserve.

your vehicle (an ordinary sedan is fine) to the gate, where you'll be met and escorted to your lodge. If you are driving yourself, consider breaking up the trip with an overnight stay en route (somewhere like Kathu, Kuruman, or even Hotazel), so that you arrive fresh and ready to absorb the reserve's majesty.

 Sights

★ Tswalu Kalahari Reserve
WILDLIFE REFUGE | FAMILY | This game reserve northeast of Upington is one of the most child friendly in southern Africa, and children are not only welcomed but also well accommodated. The dedication of the rangers and attentiveness of the staff also allows for flexibility and special opportunities, from sleeping under the stars on the "Malori" open deck to enjoying an in-room Champagne breakfast in lieu of going out on a game drive. In addition, every group of guests is guaranteed its own game-viewing vehicle with a dedicated ranger and a tracker who knows the terrain and the animals intimately.

The reserve plays a very important conservation role. Backed by funds from the De Beers family, its desert black rhino population represents one-third of South Africa's remaining animals. In addition to rhino sightings, the on-foot experience with a colony of meerkats is a highlight, as are visits to 380,000-year-old rock engravings from the earliest residents of these phenomenal landscapes.

If you wish to see a pangolin, consider prearranging a visit with the reserve's specialist researcher. A few hours with Dr. Wendy Panaino will improve your odds of spotting one of these elusive, shy, adorable creatures. You can also explore parts of the reserve on horseback. Two stables welcome riders of all skill levels to participate in anything from short, gentle outings to adventurous outrides that offer utterly unique views of the reserve and its wild creatures.

Your stay will include a meal at the memorable Klein JAN restaurant, a true original in the culinary universe. Other meals will also be fabulous, too, with breakfast and lunch served whenever you please and, perhaps, a surprise dinner on the dunes. ✉ *Farm Korannaberg 296, Van Zylsrus, Tswalu Kalahari Reserve* ☎ *053/781–9331 for reservations, 053/781–9211 for inquiries* 🌐 *www.tswalu.com.*

🍴 Restaurants

★ Klein JAN

$$$$ | SOUTH AFRICAN | Guests at either of Tswalu Kalahari Reserve's lodges are treated to a dinner at Klein JAN, the first restaurant in the country by Jan Hendrik van der Westhuizen (South Africa's only Michelin star–awarded chef), though others do drive (or fly) in when the eight-course lunch with wine-pairings is offered. The setting is a century-old farmhouse, and meals are experiential and immersive—eye-opening introductions to the produce, culinary traditions, and flavors of the Northern Cape, with every morsel or sip seemingly designed to surprise as well as satisfy you, to fire up not only all your senses but also your imagination. **Known for:** breathtaking inventiveness; food that truly captures the specialness of the Northern Cape and its produce; setting and experience unlike anything else—anywhere. [$] *Average main: R2,500* ✉ *Boscia House, Tswalu, Farm Korannaberg 296, Van Zylsrus, Tswalu Kalahari Reserve* ☎ *053/781–9441* 🌐 *www.janonline.com/restaurantkleinjan* ☞ *Prix-fixe for multiple courses, wine pairings, and other drinks.*

🛏 Hotels

★ The Motse

$$$$ | RESORT | FAMILY | Antelope often wander by Tswalu's exquisite main lodge, where the communal area features a series of terraced indoor and outdoor lounges that spill down to a pair of pools and a floodlit watering hole and where guest quarters consist of beautiful, freestanding, thatch-and-stone suites, known as "legae." The decor is minimalist and infinitely stylish, echoing the landscape in color and texture and incorporating local stone and wood, interesting art and artifacts, and unique light fixtures. **Pros:** gorgeous, bespoke room decor; you feel immersed in the surroundings from the moment you arrive; special children's room and babysitting services and nannies available. **Cons:** hard to leave your cosseting quarters for game drives (worth it, though); you will need very, very deep pockets for a stay at this once-in-a-lifetime lodge; as it's child friendly, you might want to request a room away from the communal areas. [$] *Rooms from: R61,000* ✉ *Tswalu, Farm Korannaberg 296, Van Zylsrus, Tswalu Kalahari Reserve* ☎ *053/781–9211, 053/781–9331 for reservations* 🌐 *www.tswalu.com* 🛏 *9 suites* 🍴 *All-Inclusive.*

Tswalu Tarkuni Lodge

$$$$ | HOUSE | FAMILY | In a private section of Tswalu, this exclusive, self-contained homestead—decorated similarly to the reserve's Motse lodge and offering much the same level of luxury—is perfect for families and other small groups since it sleeps up to 10 people in 5 suites and comes with its own chef, game vehicle, and tracker. **Pros:** immaculate design that echoes the landscape; ultimate exclusivity; exceptional service. **Cons:** prohibitively expensive; you may miss the presence of other travelers; unless you're used to having a staff entirely dedicated to your needs, the attention might be overwhelming. [$] *Rooms from: R124,800* ✉ *Tswalu, Farm Korannaberg 296, Van Zylsrus, Tswalu Kalahari Reserve* ☎ *053/781–9317, 053/781–9331* 🌐 *www.tswalu.com* 🛏 *5 suites* 🍴 *All-Inclusive* ☞ *Rate, which is for up to 4 people, rises with each additional couple, up to R223000 if you use all 5 suites.*

Addo Elephant National Park

At just under 445,000 acres, Addo Elephant National Park is home to elephants, buffalo, black rhino, leopards, spotted hyena, hundreds of kudu and other antelopes, and lions.

GETTING HERE AND AROUND

The closest airport to Addo Elephant Park is Chief Dawid Stuurman International Airport (PLZ) in Gqeberha. Flights arrive daily from all of South Africa's main cities via British Airways, SA Airlink, and the budget airline FlySafair. Flights from Cape Town take roughly 1 hour and from Johannesburg 1½ hours.

Traveling by car is the easiest and best way to tour this area, as public transport is limited and unreliable. Some roads are unpaved and their conditions are highly variable. Most lodges will organize airport transfers for their guests.

For information on airlines, see Air in Travel Smart.

TOURS
Schotia Safaris

SPECIAL-INTEREST TOURS | FAMILY | If you're short on time or budget, Schotia offers a good value, family-run, no-frills safari experience in a privately owned wildlife reserve bordering the eastern side of Addo; situated just 45 minutes from Gqeberha, it's incredibly convenient. Because of its small size (4,200 acres) and the fact that it's very densely stocked (more than 2,000 animals and 40 species) you're almost guaranteed to see a wide variety of wildlife—lions, giraffes, hippos, white rhinos, crocodiles, zebras, elephants, and all kinds of buck. The popular six-hour Tooth and Claw safari starts at 2:30 pm and includes a game drive and a tasty, generous buffet dinner served in an attractive open-air area with roaring fires. After dinner you're taken on a short night drive back to the reception area—keep your eyes peeled for rarely-spotted nocturnal animals. Other options are to combine an Addo game drive, with lunch, and the Tooth and Claw safari, or a very long (and thrilling) day out that includes a boat safari to see Algoa Bay's marine wildlife. A half-day Sea Safari is also possible, commencing from Gqeberha's harbour. Basic accommodation is also available on the reserve. Transfers from your Gqeberha or Addo accommodation are included in all tours, apart from the half-day Sea Safari which commences from the harbor in Gqeberha. ✉ *Orlando Farm, Paterson, Addo Elephant National Park* ☎ *083/654–8511, 042/235–1436* ⊕ *www. schotiasafaris.com* ⊠ *From R133.*

⊙ Sights

Addo Elephant National Park

WILDLIFE REFUGE | FAMILY | Smack in the middle of a citrus-growing and horse-breeding area, Addo Elephant National Park is home to more than 600 elephants, not to mention plenty of buffalo (around 400 of them), black rhino, leopards, spotted hyena, hundreds of kudu and other antelopes, and lions. At present the park has just under 445,000 acres, including two islands, St Croix and Bird, which can be visited as part of tours out of Gqeberha. The most accessible parts of the park are the original, main section and the Colchester, Kabouga, Woody Cape, and Zuurberg sections.

The original section of Addo still holds most of the game and is served by Addo Main Camp. The Colchester section, in the south, which has one SANParks camp, is contiguous with the main area. The scenic Nyathi section is separated from the main section by a road and railway line. Just north of Nyathi is the mountainous Zuurberg section, which doesn't have a large variety of game but is particularly scenic, with fabulous hiking trails and horse trails, and it's where you might glimpse Cape mountain zebra, mountain reedbuck, blue duiker, red rock rabbits, and—if you are extremely fortunate—aardwolf. There are also hippos in the Sundays River, at the base of the Zuurberg range.

You can explore the park in your own vehicle, in which case you need to heed the road signs that claim "dung beetles have right of way." Addo is home to the almost-endemic and extremely rare flightless dung beetle, which can often be seen rolling its unusual incubator across the roads. Watch out for them (they're only about 2 inches long), and watch them: they're fascinating. Instead of driving you could take a night or day game drive with a park ranger in an open vehicle from the main camp. A more adventurous option is to ride a horse among the elephants. Warning: no citrus fruit may be brought into the park, as elephants find it irresistible and can smell it for miles. ✉ *Addo Elephant National Park* ☎ *042/233–8600* 🌐 *www.addoelephantpark.com* 🎫 *R360.*

Hotels

Camp Figtree Mountain Safari Lodge
$$$$ | **B&B/INN** | It's not within Addo Elephant National Park, but this lodge's perch on the top of a high ridge in the Zuurberg mountain range—the altitude, coupled with the vastness of the views that drop away in front of you—adds something sensational to your stay. **Pros:** unpretentious, warm hospitality; gorgeous drop-away mountain views from an incredible high-up location; wonderful meals prepared by an imaginative chef. **Cons:** younger children are not allowed to stay in the luxury tents; not for you if suffer from any height-related phobias; it's a bit of a drive to reach Addo (but worth it). [$] *Rooms from: R4,490* ✉ *Addo Elephant National Park* ☎ *042/007–0239, 082/611–3603* 🌐 *www.campfigtree.com* 🛏 *13 rooms* 🍴 *Free Breakfast.*

★ **Elephant House**
$$$ | **B&B/INN** | It's hard to believe that what looks and feels like a 150-year-old farmstead was, in fact, purpose-built from scratch in 1998—its deep verandahs, roughly whitewashed walls, thatch roofs, and a mixture of heirlooms and old prints and sepia photographs, Persian rugs, and deep, cushy sofas, are all carefully assembled to make it feel like it's a generations-old family home surrounded by a magnificent jungle-garden. **Pros:** intimate and homely environment with hosts who treat you like guests in their own home—staying here feels more like an experience than simply a standardized, functional hotel stay; excellent proximity to the national park; the owners are genuinely involved in community uplift and care about their environmental impact. **Cons:** if you prefer the anonymity of a hotel, this may not be your cup of tea; while you're near the reserve, you're not inside it so still need to drive to see animals; also not for you if you need everything spic 'n' span and the gardens manicured. [$] *Rooms from: R2,860* ✉ *Just off the R335, near Addo village, Addo Elephant National Park* ✥ *8 km (5 miles) from Addo's main entrance* ☎ *042/233–2462* 🌐 *elephanthouse.co.za* 🛏 *8 rooms, 6 cottages* 🍴 *Free Breakfast.*

★ **Gorah Elephant Camp**
$$$$ | **RESORT** | On a private concession within the main section of Addo, this picturesque colonial-themed camp has accommodations in spacious, luxurious safari tents with thick thatch canopies and interiors furnished in fine antiques from the colonial era. **Pros:** the food and service are top-notch; tents are oriented to maximize privacy; you get to watch animals going about their business directly from your private deck and from the main lodge. **Cons:** the tents can get very cold at night in winter; colonial theme not to everyone's taste; the tents don't have bathtubs. [$] *Rooms from: R17,290* ✉ *Addo Elephant National Park*

☎ *044/501–1111* 🌐 *gorah.hunterhotels.com* 🛏 *11 rooms* 🍴 *All-Inclusive.*

RiverBend Collection
$$$$ | **ALL-INCLUSIVE** | **FAMILY** | Situated on a 34,594-acre private concession within the Nyathi section of Addo Elephant National Park, River Bend consists of two exclusive-use houses—Peppergrove House and Long Hope Villa—and River-Bend Lodge, which has eight superb villas. **Pros:** children are welcome; the food is excellent, and there's a great little spa; you can see animals without even going on game drive. **Cons:** if you want a private plunge pool, you'll need to reserve the honeymoon suite; you're never quite rid of the sight of vehicles on roads in the distance; the English country decor in the public areas may not be your cup of tea. [$] *Rooms from: R21,480* ✉ *Addo Elephant National Park* ☎ *042/233–8000* 🌐 *www.riverbendcollection.co.za* 🛏 *8 rooms, 2 houses* 🍴 *All-Inclusive.*

Shamwari Game Reserve

72 km (45 miles) from Gqeberha.

Once barren farmland, the 62,000-acre Shamwari Private Game Reserve is a conservation triumph, home to an abundant wildlife population as well as indigenous plants.

GETTING HERE AND AROUND

The closest airport to Shamwari Game Reserve is Chief Dawid Stuurman International Airport (PLZ) in Gqeberha, about 72 km (45 miles) away.

For information on airlines, see Air in Travel Smart. For information on car rentals, see Car in Travel Smart.

Sights

Born Free Shamwari Big Cat Sanctuary
WILDLIFE REFUGE | Within Shamwari are two Born Free big cat sanctuaries, which guests have the option of visiting, usually as part of one of their games drives. Here African leopards and lions rescued from zoos, circuses, and even nightclubs around the world are allowed to roam in large enclosures for the rest of their lives, as they cannot safely be returned to the wild. Although these are interesting tourist attractions, the main purpose is educational, and about 500 local schoolchildren tour the centers every month. Their other purpose is to incentivize visitors to contribute financially; seeing the animals cut off from the wilderness they're meant to live in is quite depressing, and if you're sensitive to the plight of animals abused by humans, you might want to give the sanctuaries a skip. ✉ *Shamwari Game Reserve* 🌐 *www.bornfree.org.uk.*

★ **Shamwari Private Game Reserve**
WILDLIFE REFUGE | An easy 1½-hour drive from Gqeberha, Shamwari is, in every sense of the word, a conservation triumph. Unprofitable farmland has been turned into a successful tourist destination, wild animals have been reintroduced, and alien vegetation has been eradicated. The reserve, which officially opened in 1992, is constantly being expanded and now stands at about 62,000 acres. Its mandate is to conserve not only the big impressive animals (which are abundant), but everything else: indiginous plants, buildings, history, and the culture of the area. The reserve's seven lodges are all top notch, each with a unique flavor. During the summer months (October to April), you can also enjoy a unique walking safari experience at Shamwari's Explorer Camp. ✉ *Shamwari Game Reserve* ☎ *042/203–1111* 🌐 *www.shamwari.com.*

Once barren farmland, the 62,000-acre Shamwari Game Reserve is working to restore the property to its natural state complete with flora and fauna.

Shamwari Wildlife Rehabilitation Centre

WILDLIFE REFUGE | Unlike the Born Free sanctuaries at Shamwari where the big cats you see are destined never to return to the wild, the animals being nurtured back to health at this center that opened at the end of 2019 will have a brighter future. Animals found in the large enclosures here have been injured or orphaned and are being prepared for a return to the wild. Some, like meerkats, might have been born in captivity and yet will ultimately be able to fend for themselves and find a home on the reserve. The center's reception room features incredibly detailed information panels about a variety of ongoing conservation struggles and there are plenty of reminders of the epidemic of species extinction that is a direct result of human activity. As with visits to the Born Free centers, you can ask to tour the rehab center during one of your game drives. ⊠ *Shamwari Game Reserve* ⊕ *www.shamwari.com.*

 Hotels

Bayethe Tented Lodge

$$$$ | RESORT | If you're yearning for the atmosphere afforded by canvas in the bush but still prefer unbridled luxury, then these air-conditioned safari "blended canvas" suites under thatch roofs are ideal. **Pros:** each tent has an amazing outside shower and deck; tents have fabulous bathrooms; the king-size beds have comfortable 400-thread-count sheets. **Cons:** if you don't like showering outside, you'll need to specifically request one of three tents that have an indoor shower; children under 12 aren't permitted; it's slightly more rustic than the other Shamwari lodges. $ *Rooms from: R17,670* ⊠ *Shamwari Game Reserve* ☎ *042/203–1111* ⊕ *www.shamwari.com* ⇥ *12 rooms* ⦿ *All-Inclusive.*

★ **Eagles Crag**

$$$$ | RESORT | This gorgeous lodge, designed to take full advantage of its lofty views, has a charming contemporary sleekness that's very different from the other Shamwari properties. **Pros:** the rooms are enormous; the food and service are excellent; a carefully selected choice of top local wines and spirits is included. **Cons:** there's always a chance that the impressive design will steal your attention from the surroundings. $ *Rooms from: R21,500* ✉ *Shamwari Game Reserve* ☎ *042/203–1111* ⊕ *www.shamwari.com* ➦ *9 rooms* ⦿ *All-Inclusive*.

★ **Long Lee Manor**

$$$$ | **RESORT** | Originally built in 1910 as the manor house of one of the private farms that would later be incorporated into Shamwari, this studiously designed and richly furnished Edwardian property continues to evoke the colonial era and all the opulence that went with it, albeit now with a more contemporary twist. **Pros:** slick service from beginning to end; has an innovative boma and the food is exceptional; the whole place exudes considerable elegance. **Cons:** noise from adjacent rooms can sometimes be overheard; it's quite hotel-like, so may not be for you if you want something that feels more like a lodge or safari camp; it's one of the bigger lodges at Shamwari, so not the most intimate. $ *Rooms from: R17,850* ✉ *Shamwari Game Reserve* ☎ *042/203–1111* ⊕ *www.shamwari.com* ➦ *18 rooms* ⦿ *All-Inclusive*.

Riverdene Family Lodge

$$$$ | **ALL-INCLUSIVE** | **FAMILY** | Riverdene combines the great food and service of Shamwari's other lodges with a much more child-friendly atmosphere and a rather unprecedented number of facilities designed to keep youngsters engaged and entertained, making it the ultimate safari lodgings for younger families. **Pros:** children will remember this safari for years to come; rooms even have microwaves so you can warm baby's meals and milk; extremely friendly atmosphere. **Cons:** not the place for privacy or romance; some may

not appreciate the more contemporary aesthetic; all those children means it can get noisy. $ *Rooms from: R17,010* ✉ *Shamwari Game Reserve* ☎ *042/203–1111* ⊕ *www.shamwari.com* ➦ *9 rooms* ⦿ *All-Inclusive*.

Sarili

$$$$ | **ALL-INCLUSIVE** | **FAMILY** | Named for a Xhosa chief and in fact pronounced *sag-ee-leh*, this five-bedroom private villa puts guests in the heart of a marvelous wilderness area where you have the run of magnificent grounds with exquisite views onto a thrilling—and vast—landscape populated by animals that regularly make an appearance. **Pros:** impeccably stylish; exquisite views; suitable for the entire family (it's also entirely fenced, so safe for children). **Cons:** if you're traveling with friends, there may be some "debate" over who gets the best rooms; not for you if having a private staff feels intrusive; no chance for interaction with other travelers. $ *Rooms from: R96,000* ✉ *Shamwari Game Reserve* ☎ *042/203–1111* ⊕ *www.shamwari.com* ➦ *5 rooms* ⦿ *All-Inclusive*.

★ **Sindile**

$$$$ | **ALL-INCLUSIVE** | The view from Shamwari's flagship lodge will take your breath away: Built in a more contemporary style than the older Shamwari lodges, and situated in what might just be the reserve's most perfect-for-a-lodge location, the eye is constantly drawn across the ravine, over the rolling plains, to a water hole where animals gather, and on towards distant hills marching across the horizon. **Pros:** the views are exquisite; being fenced, you can walk to your room unescorted at night; it's a smaller and more intimate lodge with an emphasis on privacy. **Cons:** for parents the drawback is that children under 16 aren't permitted; some might find the pathways to the rooms tricky; for some, being fenced might be a drawback. $ *Rooms from: R23,650* ✉ *Shamwari Game Reserve* ☎ *042/203–1111* ⊕ *www.shamwari.com* ➦ *9 rooms* ⦿ *All-Inclusive*.

Kwandwe Private Game Reserve

The more than 55,000-acre Kwandwe Private Game Reserve is a conservation triumph as it's reintroduced native vegetation (eradicating alien plants) and is now home to more than 7,000 mammals, including the Big Five.

GETTING HERE AND AROUND
Kwandwe is a 30-minute drive from Makhanda, and air and road shuttles are available from Gqeberha, which is a 2-hour drive.

Sights

★ **Kwandwe Private Game Reserve**
WILDLIFE REFUGE | Tucked away in the Eastern Cape, near the historic university "city" of Makhanda (formerly known as Grahamstown, and now increasingly run down), Kwandwe is a conservation triumph as more than 55,000 acres of various vegetation types and scenic diversity, including rocky outcrops, great plains, thorn thickets, forests, desert scrub, and the Great Fish River were just ravaged farmland and goat-ridden semidesert two decades ago. Today it's home to more than 7,000 mammals, including the Big Five and the elusive black rhino, and it's likely you'll see fauna you don't always see elsewhere, such as black wildebeest, bat-eared foxes, and the endangered blue crane (*Kwandwe* means "place of the blue crane" in isiXhosa). If you spend more than a couple of nights here, you'll likely see a huge and impressive array of animals, including leopards, lions, and herds of elephants marching across the terrain. If you come in winter, you'll see one of nature's finest floral displays, when thousands of scarlet, orange, and fiery-red aloes are in bloom, attended by colorful sunbirds. The reserve also has a strong focus on community development, as evinced by the Community Centre and village within the reserve, both of which are worth a visit. ✉ *Kwandwe Private Game Reserve, Makhanda* ☎ *046/603–3400* 🌐 *www.kwandwe.com.*

Hotels

Aside from the four exclusive-use villas within the reserve, visitors can choose between two lodges—the classic colonial-with-an-African-twist Great Fish River Lodge or the modern-chic Ecca Lodge. Both are gorgeous, but offer very different experience thanks to their unique locations. No matter where you stay, you'll be cosseted, pampered, well fed, and taken on hugely memorable wildlife adventures. All the lodges listed here have cable TV in a communal area and massages available upon request. The child-friendly lodges have movies and games.

A R400 conservation fee per person per night also applies to most safari lodges.

Ecca Lodge
$$$$ | **RESORT** | **FAMILY** | Velvet cushions and rugs that echo the African sky at dawn, rough-hewn rock walls that recall the hills that dot the reserve, and decor that includes handwoven baskets, animal hides, and neutral shades offset by pale greens and blues, create the fresh, contemporary aesthetic of this intimate, classy lodge that caters to families with young children. **Pros:** superb food and an extensive self-service bar; fresh room design, with colorful, cheerful accents under a white ceiling; magnificent showers, outside and indoors. **Cons:** service can be up and down; because it's family-friendly, the sounds of children may freak you out; the modern design may have you longing for a more traditional aesthetic. [$] *Rooms from: R20,740* ✉ *Kwandwe Private Game Reserve* ☎ *046/603–3400* 🌐 *www.kwandwe.com* 🛏 *6 suites* 🍴 *Free Breakfast.*

Fort House

$$$$ | HOUSE | FAMILY | Previously used exclusively by Kwandwe's owners, this well-stocked and handsomely decorated 4-bedroom house is available to rent for exclusive use by a family or group. **Pros:** you can create your own schedule; exclusive use of the 4-bedroom mansion; good chance of spotting animals from the deck, garden, or pool. **Cons:** you might feel a bit isolated; the house lacks elevation; the study's collection of wall-mounted hunting rifles might be a turn-off for some. $ *Rooms from: R70,800* ✉ *Heatherton Towers, Fort Brown District, Kwandwe Private Game Reserve* ☎ *046/603–3400* ⊕ *www. kwandwe.com* ⇆ *4 rooms* ❄ *All-Inclusive* ☞ *A R400 conservation fee per person per night also applies.*

★ Great Fish River Lodge

$$$$ | RESORT | Public areas—dining room, cozy lounges, library, and a long terrace—sprawl along one bank of the Great Fish River (one of the few rivers in the region flowing continuously, despite a prolonged drought) with floor-to-ceiling windows that bathe the interior stone walls, Persian rugs, fireplaces, deep armchairs, bookcases, and collection of old prints and photographs in clear light. **Pros:** spectacular river and cliff views from every room; there's an effort to serve interesting food at every meal; ultrafriendly staffers go out of their way to satisfy your personal needs. **Cons:** avoid if an unfenced camp makes you nervous; does not accommodate children under 12; some rooms are a distance from the main lodge (request a nearby room if need be). $ *Rooms from: R20,740* ✉ *Heatherton Towers, Fort Brown District, Kwandwe Private Game Reserve* ☎ *046/603–3400* ⊕ *www.kwandwe.com* ⇆ *9 rooms* ❄ *All-Inclusive.*

Melton Manor

$$$$ | RESORT | FAMILY | Slightly bigger than Uplands Homestead, the Manor accommodates up to eight guests and offers the same superb service and exclusivity. **Pros:** lovely service; you feel surrounded by wilderness; creative food. **Cons:** it's not quite as opulent as Fort House; as you're in your own group you miss out on the opportunity to meet other travelers. $ *Rooms from: R54,180* ✉ *Heatherton Towers, Fort Brown District, Kwandwe Private Game Reserve* ☎ *046/603–3400* ⊕ *www.kwandwe.com* ⇆ *4 rooms* ❄ *Free Breakfast.*

Uplands Homestead

$$$$ | RESORT | FAMILY | If you're a small family or a bunch of friends and want to have a genuine, very exclusive, out-of-Africa experience, then stay at this restored 1905 colonial farmhouse. **Pros:** great food and service; perfect for that special family occasion or friends' reunion; steeped in history. **Cons:** the colonial nostalgia might be a little overwhelming for some; not a good option if you want to meet other guests; can only be booked for families or parties of up to six. $ *Rooms from: R44,330* ✉ *Heatherton Towers, Fort Brown District, Kwandwe Private Game Reserve* ☎ *046/603–3400* ⊕ *www. kwandwe.com* ⊗ *Closed June* ⇆ *3 rooms* ❄ *Free Breakfast.*

Samara Private Game Reserve

The 67,000-acre, malaria-free Samara Private Game Reserve encompasses 11 former farms and is home to a variety of reintroduced species, including cheetah, lion, Cape mountain zebra, white rhino, and giraffe.

GETTING HERE AND AROUND

If you're driving directly from Gqeberha to the reserve, travel toward Graaff-Reinet for 258 km (160 miles), and then turn right onto the R63 toward Pearston/Somerset East for 7 km (4 miles). Turn left onto the Petersburg gravel road and drive 23 km (14 miles) to reach Karoo Lodge.

Air charters to Samara (gravel airstrip) can be arranged on request; the lodge will also arrange transfer from Gqeberha's airport, or from Addo lodges.

R315 conservation fee per person per night is added to many lodges.

Sights

★ **Samara Private Game Reserve**

WILDLIFE REFUGE | FAMILY | Surrounded by the melancholic beauty of the Great Karoo with its scattered *koppies* and ridges of flat-topped mountains, Samara is a 67,000-acre private game reserve tucked beneath the Sneeuberg mountain range in the fabled plains of Camdeboo National Park some 45 minutes from the historic town of Graaff-Reinet. Owners Sarah and Mark Tompkins opened the reserve in 2005 with a promise to return former farmland to its natural state—the malaria-free reserve encompasses 11 former farms and is home to a variety of reintroduced species, including cheetah, lion, Cape mountain zebra, white rhino and desert-adapted black rhino, giraffe, black wildebeest, and a variety of antelope; there are also meerkats and aardvarks. By day, it's a build-your-own-adventure of game drives, picnics atop the lofty heights of Mount Kondoa, and exploring the reserve's topographical diversity at a civilized pace. Due to the lower density of predators and the sparseness of vegetation, rangers stop the game-viewers often so that guests can experience some of their safari on foot. One of its signature experiences is the opportunity to track a telemetry-collared rehabilitated cheetah and her family, and then get within whispering distance of them. The relatively low density of dangerous game also means this reserve is well-suited to families with children. ✉ *Petersburg Rd., off the R63 to Pearston, Graaff-Reinet* ☎ *031/262–0324, 049/940–0059* 🌐 *www.samara.co.za.*

Hotels

★ **Karoo Lodge**

$$$$ | ALL-INCLUSIVE | FAMILY | From the moment you reach this lovingly restored, 19th-century, green-roofed farmhouse set among purple mountains, 800-year-old trees, and rolling plains where cheetahs, rhinos, and giraffes roam, you'll forget another more stressful world even existed. **Pros:** the setting possesses a mesmerizing beauty; wonderfully exclusive and yet full of personality; great for families. **Cons:** farmstead rooms don't provide quite such a magical experience as the free-standing cottages; the colonial nostalgia might not suit everyone; not for you if you're fearful of being surrounded by vast empty space. [$] *Rooms from: R13,650* ✉ *Samara Private Game Reserve, Petersburg Rd., off the R63 to Pearston, Graaff-Reinet* ☎ *049/940–0059, 031/262–0324 for reservations* 🌐 *www.samara.co.za* 🛏 *9 rooms* 🍴 *All-Inclusive.*

The Manor

$$$$ | ALL-INCLUSIVE | If you're looking for the perfect place to share a safari with a group of people, this is a fabulous option—although suites can also be rented individually. **Pros:** brings a contemporary, Afro-chic design twist to the safari lodge design game; staff are extremely attentive; exquisite meals, served either in the villa, or occasionally out in the bush. **Cons:** although more exclusive, there's less chance to hear the game-viewing experiences of others guests; the contemporary decor touches may not be to your taste; you miss out on the more sociable atmosphere of Karoo Lodge. [$] *Rooms from: R16,800*

✉ *Samara Private Game Reserve, Petersburg Rd., off the R63 to Pearston, Graaff-Reinet* ☎ *049/940–0059, 031/262–0324 for reservations* 🌐 *www.samara.co.za* 🛏 *4 rooms* 🍴 *All-Inclusive.*

Pilanesberg Game Reserve

Often called the Pilanesberg National Park, this 150,000-acre game reserve is centered on the caldera of an extinct volcano dating back 1.3 billion years that may well have once been Africa's highest peak. Open grassland, rocky crags, and densely forested gorges provide ideal habitats for a wide range of plains and woodland game, including rare brown hyenas, cheetahs, wildebeests, and zebras. Since the introduction of lions in 1993, Pilanesberg (pronounced pee-*luns*-berg) can boast the Big Five. One of the best places in the country to see rhinos, it's also a birdwatcher's paradise, with a vast range of grassland species, waterbirds, and birds of prey. It's also malaria-free and an excellent choice for game-viewing if you're short on time and can't make it all the way to Kruger National Park, for instance. You can drive around the park in your own vehicle or join a guided safari. The entertainment and resort complex of Sun City is nearby.

GETTING HERE AND AROUND

To get to the Pilanesberg from Johannesburg, get on the N4 highway to Krugersdorp and take the R556 off-ramp and follow the signs. The drive is about 2½ to 3 hours. There is a shuttle from Johannesburg to Sun City, just outside the park, otherwise you'll need to rent a car, hire a transfer company, or take a guided tour from Johannesburg.

TOURS

Several major tour operators in Johannesburg offer trips to Pilanesberg, including Springbok Atlas Tours & Safaris and JMT Tours and Safaris *(see Tours in Planning)*. Booking these tours ahead of time is essential.

Sights

Pilanesberg Game Reserve

NATURE PRESERVE | The 150,000-acre Pilanesberg Game Reserve is centered on the caldera of an extinct volcano. Concentric rings of mountains surround a lake filled with crocodiles and hippos. Open grassland, rocky crags, and forested gorges provide ideal habitats for a wide range of plains and woodland game, especially wildebeests and zebras, which are plentiful here. The Pilanesberg (pronounced pee- *luns*-berg) can boast the Big Five (you have a great chance of seeing elephants and rhinos here on almost any single drive) and is malaria-free. It's a bird-watcher's paradise, with a vast range of grassland species, waterbirds, and birds of prey. The entertainment and resort complex of Sun City is nearby. ✉ *Pilanesberg Game Reserve, Sun City* ☎ *014/555–1600, 018/397–1500 North West Parks Board* 🌐 *www.pilanesbergnationalpark.org* 🎟 *R40 per vehicle, R80 per person.*

Hotels

Bakubung Bush Lodge

$$$$ | **HOTEL** | **FAMILY** | Abutting Pilanesberg, this lodge sits at the head of a long valley with terrific views of a hippo pool that forms the lodge's central attraction—it's not unusual to have hippos grazing 100 feet from the terrace restaurant. **Pros:** malaria-free; short drive to a big dam that attracts abundant game and birds; cheerful atmosphere. **Cons:** always crowded; feels vaguely institutional; close to a main gate. [$] *Rooms from: R5,360* ✉ *Bakubung, Pilanesberg Game Reserve* ☎ *014/552–6314* 🌐 *www.legacyhotels.co.za* 🛏 *100 rooms* 🍴 *Free Breakfast.*

Kwa Maritane Bush Lodge

$$$$ | **HOTEL** | **FAMILY** | The greatest asset of this hotel, primarily a time-share resort, is its location: in a bowl of rocky hills on the edge of the game reserve. **Pros:** malaria-free; you've got the best of both worlds—bushveld on your doorstep and Sun City 20 minutes away by shuttle at an additional cost; lovely swimming pools. **Cons:** busy during school holidays; it gets noisy around reception, pool, and dining areas; you can't get away from the hotel feel. [$] *Rooms from: R5,360* ✉ *Kwa Maritane, Pilanesberg Game Reserve* ☎ *014/552–5300* 🌐 *www.legacyhotels.co.za* ➪ *90 rooms* 🍴 *Free Breakfast.*

Tshukudu Bush Lodge

$$$$ | **HOTEL** | The five-star Tshukudu Bush Lodge offers a fully-inclusive experience that includes brunch, high tea, a 5-course dinner, local beverages, as well as two daily game drives. **Pros:** malaria-free; luxurious and secluded accommodations; high on a hill with panoramic views. **Cons:** game good, but not as abundant as Kruger; no children under 12 permitted; it's a 132-step climb to the main lodge from the parking area, so not suitable for guests with disabilities or who get winded easily. [$] *Rooms from: R13,120* ✉ *Tshukudu, Pilanesberg Game Reserve* ☎ *014/552–6255* 🌐 *www.legacyhotels.co.za* ➪ *10 rooms* 🍴 *All-Inclusive.*

Gateway Cities

South Africa's two hub cities are Johannesburg and Cape Town. It's almost certain that you'll arrive and leave the country from one of these two cities. Make the most of your time in transit—there's a lot you can do in 24 hours.

Johannesburg

Johannesburg, Jo'burg, Egoli ("City of Gold"), or Jozi, as it is affectionately known by locals, is the commercial heart of South Africa and the primary gateway for international visitors. Historically, it is where money is made and fortunes are found. The city has an unfair reputation for being an ugly, dangerous place you ought to avoid on any trip to South Africa. On the contrary, much of Johannesburg is quite pretty, largely because of the millions of trees that cover it (it has, purportedly, one of the largest human-planted forests in the world), and statistically speaking it is less dangerous than the Western Cape.

The city also epitomizes South Africa's paradoxical makeup—it's rich, poor, innovative, and historic all rolled into one. And it seems, at times, as though no one actually comes *from* Johannesburg. The city is full of immigrants: Italians, Portuguese, Poles, Chinese, Hindus, Swazis, English, Zimbabweans, Nigerians. The streets are full of merchants. Traders hawk *skop* (boiled sheep's head, split open and eaten off newspaper) in front of polished glass buildings as taxis jockey for position in rush hour. *Sangomas* (traditional healers) lay out herbs and roots next to roadside barbers' tents, and you never seem to be far from women selling *vetkoek* (dollops of deep-fried dough) beneath billboards advertising investment banks or cell phones.

Johannesburg is well worth a stopover of at least two or three days en route to other parts of the country. There's plenty to see here, including Constitution Hill in the city, not to mention the nearby city of Soweto, and the Cradle of Humankind World Heritage Site about 90 minutes away. Areas like Sandton, Rosebank, Greenside, and Parkhurst—as well as the day trips—are perfectly safe to visit on your own, though we recommend a tour guide to explore Soweto and the inner city.

WHEN TO GO

Jo'burgers boast that they enjoy the best climate in the world: not too hot in spring and summer (mid-September–mid-April), not too cold in autumn and winter (mid-April–mid-September), and not prone to sudden temperature changes. Summer (especially between October and January) may have the edge, though: it's when the gardens and open spaces are at their most beautiful. October and November are possibly the best time of year to visit as the jacaranda trees are in full bloom.

GETTING HERE AND AROUND

It's difficult but not impossible to see the Johannesburg area without a car. However, your best bet is to rent a car and a GPS navigator (or use Google Maps or the Waze app on your mobile phone). If you're reluctant to drive yourself, book a couple of full-day and half-day tours that will pick you up from your hotel or a central landmark. The City Sightseeing bus can give you an excellent overview of the city along its two routes, and it allows you to hop on and off at most of Johannesburg's attractions. Spend at least a full day doing this, and pair it with their two-hour guided tour of Soweto, if you want to go farther afield.

OR Tambo International Airport is about 19 km (12 miles) from the Johannesburg city center and is linked to the city by a fast highway, which is always busy but especially before 9 am and between 4 and 7 pm.

The most affordable, fastest, and safest way to travel to and from the airport is via the Gautrain, a high-speed train that connects Sandton, Rosebank, Midrand, downtown Johannesburg, and Pretoria directly with OR Tambo. It takes about 14 minutes to travel from the airport to Sandton and costs R181 one way, plus the cost of a Gautrain card (R19). The train runs from between 5 or 5:30 am and 9 or 9:30 pm every day, depending on the station. Gautrain also runs an extensive bus service that stops at various stations. Use the Gautrain website or app to plan your route, as well as departure and arrival times.

If your hotel or guesthouse does not have a shuttle, ask a staff member to arrange transportation for you with a reliable taxi or transfer company. Most lodgings have a regular service they use, so you should have no problem arranging this in advance.

Prices vary, depending on where you are staying, but plan on R400–R500 for a ride from your hotel or guesthouse in Sandton, Rosebank, or the city center to the airport. Some companies charge per head, whereas others charge per trip, so be sure to check that in advance. Most guesthouses or hotels will be able to drop you at the closest Gautrain station or Gautrain bus stop.

Alternatively, Magic Bus offers private transfers to all major Sandton hotels (R675 per vehicle for one or two people, R740 for three people, R780 for four to seven people). The journey takes 30 minutes to an hour.

Airport Link will ferry you anywhere in the central Johannesburg area for R580 for one person, plus R55 per additional person up to seven people (R635 for two people, R690 for three people).

In addition, scores of licensed taxis line up outside the airport terminal. By law, they must have a working meter. Expect to pay about R500 for a trip to Sandton. If, for whatever reason, the meter is not working, be sure to negotiate a price before you get into the taxi, and write the amount down on a piece of paper as confirmation.

Lines at the airport can be long: plan to arrive three hours before an international departure and at least an hour and a half

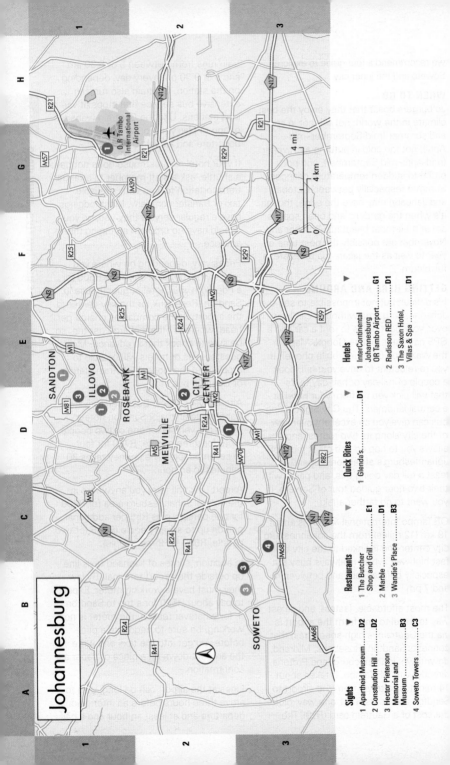

Johannesburg

Sights

1. Apartheid Museum..............D2
2. Constitution Hill................D2
3. Hector Pieterson
   Memorial and
   Museum.............................B3
4. Soweto Towers..................C3

Restaurants

1. The Butcher
   Shop and Grill..................E1
2. Marble...............................D1
3. Wandie's Place.................B3

Quick Bites

1. Glenda's...........................D1

Hotels

1. InterContinental
   Johannesburg
   OR Tambo Airport...........G1
2. Radisson RED....................D1
3. The Saxon Hotel,
   Villas & Spa.....................D1

before domestic departures. While the airport has its own police station, luggage theft has been a problem in recent years. Keep your belongings close to you at all times.

AIRPORT CONTACTS OR Tambo International Airport. ✉ Johannesburg ☎ 086/727-7888, 011/921-6262 information desk ⊕ www.acsa.co.za.

AIRPORT TRANSFERS Airport Link.
☎ 011/794-8300, 083/625-5090 ⊕ www. airportlink.co.za. **Gautrain.** ✉ Johannesburg ☎ 0800/428-87246 ⊕ www. gautrain.co.za. **Magic Transfers.** ✉ Johannesburg ☎ 011/548-0800 ⊕ www. magictransfers.co.za/us.

Traveling by car is the easiest way to get around Johannesburg, as the city's public transportation is not that reliable or extensive, though this is changing (the Gautrain, for example, is incredibly reliable). The general speed limit for city streets is 60 kph (37 mph); for rural streets, it's 80 km (50 mph); and for highways, it's 100–120 kph (62 mph). Be warned that Johannesburg drivers are known as the most aggressive in the country, and minibus taxis are infamous for ignoring the rules of the road, often stopping for passengers in undesignated areas with little or no warning. Most city roads and main countryside roads are in good condition, with plenty of signage. City street names are sometimes visible only on the curb, however. Avoid driving in rush hours, 7 to 9 am and 4 to 6:30 pm, as the main roads become terribly congested.

Gas stations are plentiful in most areas. (Don't pump your own gas, though; stations employ operators to do that for you and it's seen as a courtesy to tip them anything from R5.) And remember, South Africans drive on the left side of the road, so you will need an International Driving Permit. Almost everywhere there are security guards who look after parked cars. It's customary to give these guards a small tip (R5) when you return to your car. Most big shopping centers have parking garages (starting at R8–R10).

If you plan to drive yourself around hire a vehicle with a GPS, or rent a GPS (available at the airport and all reputable car-rental agencies), use Google Maps or the Waze mobile phone app. MapStudio also prints excellent complete street guides, available at bookstores and many gas stations and convenience stores. Be aware that smash-and-grabs are common, particularly at traffic lights and stop streets—keep your doors and windows closed, and place all valuables in the car trunk, even while driving.

Major car rental agencies have offices in the northern suburbs of the city and at the airport.

Minibus taxis form the backbone of Jo'burg's transportation for ordinary commuters, but you should avoid using them since they're often not roadworthy, drivers can be irresponsible, and it's difficult to know where they're going without consulting a local. Car taxis, though more expensive, are easier to use. They have stands at the airport and the train stations, but otherwise you must phone for one (be sure to ask how long it will take the taxi to get to you). Taxis should be licensed and have a working meter. Meters usually start at R50 (includes first 3 km [2 miles]) and are about R13 per kilometer (½ mile) thereafter. Expect to pay about R500 to the airport from town or Sandton and about R300 to the city center from Sandton.

Uber is the most entrenched e-hailing service in South Africa, with DiDi being the most recent entrant into the on-demand ride market as of mid-2021. There have been some instances of crime, particularly directed towards women, as well as driver fraud on the Bolt ride-hailing app, despite the fact that there is a 'women only' feature, which often struggles to meet demand. It's recommended to wait inside your hotel or restaurant until your vehicle arrives, as there have been cases of snatch-and-grabs of mobile phones.

CONTACTS Rose Taxis. ⊠ *Johannesburg* ☎ *083/255–0933, 011/403–0000* ⊕ *www. rosetaxis.com.* **Uber.** ⊠ *Johannesburg* ☎ ⊕ *www.uber.com/cities/johannesburg.*

TIMING

If you have only one day in Jo'burg, take a tour of Soweto and visit the Apartheid Museum, then stop by Constitution Hill if you have a chance. Spend the evening having dinner at an African-style restaurant, such as Moyo. If you have a second day, focus on what interests you most: perhaps a trip to the Cradle of Humankind, where you can explore the sites of some of the world's most significant paleontological discoveries; a trip to Cullinan, where you can visit a working diamond mine; or a fun day or two at Sun City.

TOURS

Township tours (to Soweto in particular) are offered by a number of local operators. One of the best options, if your time is limited, is to take the add-on tour with the City Sightseeing bus, where resident Soweto guides give tours. JMT Tours and Safaris, and Springbok Atlas Tours & Safaris offer half-day and full-day tours of Johannesburg and Soweto. For more recommendations of reputable tour operators, inquire at Johannesburg Tourism.

City Sightseeing Bus

BUS TOURS | FAMILY | The red, double-decker City Sightseeing bus is a hop-on, hop-off bus operator that offers a very safe and affordable way to see the city and its key attractions, particularly if you don't have a car rental. There are two routes to choose from: Johannesburg city center (Red Route) and the suburbs (Green Route). The bus departs from 12 locations every 30 minutes from 9 to 5 every day, but the best places to catch it are either at The Zone @ Rosebank (stop

1) or Gold Reef City (stop 13). Adults and kids alike will love the experience; there's a special children's soundtrack, and the adult commentary is available in 15 languages. The Red Route takes about 1½ hours if you don't get off—though you should consider at least getting off at Constitution Hill. This is also where you can jump onto the Green Route for a further hour-long drive across Jo'burg's luscious suburbs and a lookout point—you'll want to sit on the open-top level for that. There is also an option to pair either tour with a 2½-hour guided Soweto tour in a City Sightseeing shuttle bus, also highly recommended. Buy your tickets at The Zone @ Rosebank (stop 1) or on any City Sightseeing bus, but there's a discount when purchasing them online, where you can also choose from combo deals and a one- or two-day pass. ⊠ *The Zone @ Rosebank, Oxford Road, Rosebank* ☎ *0861/733–287* ⊕ *www.citysightseeing. co.za* ⊠ *From R245.*

JMT Tours and Safaris

SPECIAL-INTEREST TOURS | JMT Tours and Safaris can arrange tailor-made trips for small groups to a number of destinations. Prices will vary according to where you want to go and how many people are in your group. JMT Tours and Safaris specializes in tours of Soweto but also does the Cradle of Humankind and can take you farther afield. ☎ *027/233–0073* ⊕ *jmttours.com* ⊠ *From R690.*

Johannesburg Heritage Foundation

SPECIAL-INTEREST TOURS | Interested in checking out hundreds of heritage buildings and sights? Most are closed to the public, but the Johannesburg Heritage Foundation organizes walking tours of the houses and gardens, which will give you a glimpse of turn-of-the-20th-century grandeur. Prearranged tours looking at different aspects of Johannesburg's history are arranged for most weekends and take about two to three hours. It's also possible to arrange a private tour during the week, if you can do it far enough in advance, or join one of their virtual tours. ■TIP→ **Departure points vary by the tour.** ✉ *Johannesburg* ☎ *060/813–3377* ⊕ *www.joburgheritage.org.za* ✉ *From R100 (virtual); from R200 (walking tours).*

★ **Past Experiences**

SPECIAL-INTEREST TOURS | Specialist guide and owner of Past Experiences, Jo Buitendach has a passion for the inner city and the heritage value of graffiti and street art. Her walking tours weave through the inner city, where she greets the locals by name. Tours can be tailored based on your interests from shopping tours where you can buy Shweshwe fabric to following in the footsteps of Joburg's mining history, and eating beef tibs at the Ethiopian Quarter downtown. ✉ *Johannesburg* ☎ *083/701–3046* ⊕ *www.pastexperiences.co.za* ✉ *From R2150 for a private tour.*

SAFETY

Johannesburg is notorious for being a dangerous city—it's common to hear about serious crimes such as armed robbery and murder. That said, it's safe for visitors who avoid dangerous areas and take reasonable precautions. Do not leave bags or valuables visible in a car (put them into the car trunk), and keep the doors locked and windows up, even while driving (to minimize the risk of smash-and-grab robberies or carjackings, which mostly happen at traffic lights, intersections, or stop streets); don't wear flashy jewelry or carry large wads of cash or expensive equipment. It's also advisable to keep your valuables and handbags on your person when eating at restaurants, as there have been cases of snatch-and-grabs at restaurants with street-side seating. ■TIP→ **Don't visit a township or informal settlement on your own. Explore the inner city (Maboneng Precinct) with a guide.**

Unemployment is rife, and foreigners are easy pickings. If you wish to see a township or explore the inner city, check with reputable companies, which run

excellent guided tours and know which areas to avoid. Constitution Hill within the city, Victoria Yards, and the various day-trip destinations—such as The Cradle of Humankind, Magaliesburg, and Pilanesberg—are perfectly safe to visit on your own. ■TIP→ **If you drive yourself around the city, it's safest to keep your doors locked and windows up, and to not leave valuables such as bags, cameras, or phones on the seat or visible.**

That said, it is safe to drive yourself around Johannesburg. If you prefer, though, you could order a car service or transportation from your hotel for trips in and around the city.

VISITOR INFORMATION

The helpful Gauteng Tourism Authority has information on the whole province, but more detailed information is often available from local tourism associations. Joburg Tourism has a good website, with information about Johannesburg and up-to-date listings of events happening around the city, as does the Johannesburg In Your Pocket website.

CONTACTS Joburg Tourism. ☎ *011/883–3525* ⊕ *www.joburg.org.za.* **Soweto. co.za.** ☎ *083/535–4553, 071/204–5594* ⊕ *www.soweto.co.za.* **City of Johannesburg.** ⊕ *www.joburg.org.za.* **Johannesburg In Your Pocket.** ✉ *Johannesburg* ⊕ *www. inyourpocket.com/johannesburg.*

◉ Sights

The Greater Johannesburg metropolitan area is massive—more than 1,600 square km (618 square miles)—incorporating the large municipalities of Randburg and Sandton to the north. Most of the sights are just north of the city center, which degenerated badly in the 1990s but is now being revamped.

To the south, in Ormonde, are the Apartheid Museum and Gold Reef City; the sprawling township of Soweto is just a little farther to the southwest.

Johannesburg's northern suburbs are its most affluent. On the way to the shopping meccas of Rosebank and Sandton, you can find the superb Johannesburg Zoo and the South African Museum of Military History, in the leafy suburb of Saxonwold.

★ Apartheid Museum

HISTORY MUSEUM | The Apartheid Museum, in Ormonde, takes you on a journey through South African apartheid history—from the entrance, where you pass through a turnstile according to your assigned skin color (Black or white), to the myriad historical, brutally honest, and sometimes shocking photographs, video displays, films, documents, and other exhibits. It's an emotional, multi-layered journey. As you walk chronologically through the apartheid years and eventually reach the country's first steps to freedom, with democratic elections in 1994, you experience a taste of the pain and suffering with which so many South Africans had to live. A room with 121 ropes with hangman's knots hanging from the ceiling—one rope for each political prisoner executed in the apartheid era—is especially chilling. ⊠ *Northern Pkwy. at Gold Reef Rd., Ormonde* ☏ *011/309–4700* ⊕ *www.apartheidmuseum.org* ☎ *R150* ⊙ *Closed Mon. and Tues.*

★ Constitution Hill

HISTORIC SIGHT | Overlooking Jo'burg's inner city, Constitution Hill houses the Constitutional Court, which sits on the most important human rights cases, much like the United State's Supreme Court. The slanting columns represent the trees under which African villagers met to discuss important matters and each of the 11 chairs of the justices are covered in Nguni cowhide, representing their individuality. If not in session, you can view it and its artworks.

This is also where you will find the austere Old Fort Prison Complex (also called Number Four), where thousands of political prisoners were incarcerated, including Nobel Peace Prize laureates Albert Luthuli and Nelson Mandela, and iconic Indian leader Mahatma Gandhi. There is no fee to explore the prison ramparts (built in the 1890s) but there is an hour-long highlights tour (R120) of the Old Fort Prison Complex every hour on the hour from 9 am to 4 pm, while the two-hour full site tour (R180) takes place at 10 am and 1 pm. Both tours visit the Women's Jail. Food I Love You, in the refurbished prison kitchen, serves breakfast, lunch, and grab-and-go bites with local flavor, while Motherland Coffee has a coffee truck on-site. ⊠ *11 Kotze St., entrance on Joubert St., Braamfontein* ☏ *011/381–3100* ⊕ *www.constitutionhill.org.za* ☎ *Court free; Constitution Hill tours from R120 (tickets can only be bought via Webtickets; link found on website).*

Hector Pieterson Memorial and Museum

MUSEUM VILLAGE | **FAMILY** | Opposite Holy Cross Church, a stone's throw from the former homes of Nelson Mandela and Archbishop Desmond Tutu on Vilakazi Street, the Hector Pieterson Memorial and Museum is a crucial landmark. Pieterson, a 12-year-old student, was one of the first victims of police fire on June 16, 1976, when schoolchildren rose up to protest their second-rate Bantu (Black) education system. The memorial is a paved area with benches for reflection beneath trees that have been planted by visiting dignitaries, an inscribed stone, and water feature. Inside the museum, multimedia displays of grainy photographs and archival footage bring that fateful day to life and put it into the context of the broader apartheid struggle. The museum courtyard has 562 small granite blocks as a tribute to the children who died in the Soweto uprisings. Suggested visiting time is at least 30 minutes. You can also hire an on-site tour guide to take you around (recommended donation is minimum R100). ⊠ *Khumalo St. at Phela St., Orlando West* ☏ *011/536–0611* ⊕ *www.joburg.org.za* ☎ *R52* ⊙ *Closed Mon.*

Cradle of Humankind

Even though this UNESCO World Heritage Site sits 72 km (45 miles) northwest of Johannesburg on good roads, the Cradle of Humankind (🌐 www.maropeng.co.za) is worth a visit as it has the most complete fossil record of human evolution anywhere on earth and it has produced more hominid fossils than anywhere else. The area covers about 470 square km (181 square miles), with about 300 caves. Inside these caves, paleoanthropologists have discovered thousands of fossils of hominids and other animals, dating back some 4 million years. The most famous of these fossils are Mrs. Ples, a skull more than 2 million years old, and Little Foot, a skeleton more than 3 million years old.

Not all the fossil sites in the Cradle are open to the public, but a tour of the Sterkfontein Caves and a visit to the Maropeng Visitor Centre visitor center provide an excellent overview of the paleontological work in progress.

Soweto Towers

VIEWPOINT | Originally a coal-fired power station, the brightly painted cooling towers are now a well-known Johannesburg landmark that's been transformed into an adrenaline junkie's paradise, where you can do bungee jumping and a scad freefall from the top of the 33-story structure, as well as rock climbing and paintballing. The viewing deck offers 360-degree views of Soweto below. Afterward, you can relax at Chaf-Pozi, the popular restaurant located on the premises that serves authentic South African cuisine. ✉ *corner of Sheffield Rd. and Chris Hani Rd., Orlando* ☎ *071/674–4343* 🌐 *sowetotowers.co.za* 🎟 *R630 (bungee jumping)* ⏲ *Closed Mon.–Wed.*

🍴 Restaurants

Jo'burgers love eating out, and there are hundreds of restaurants throughout the city to satisfy them. Some notable destinations for food include Melrose Arch, Parkhurst, Sandton, and Greenside. Smart-casual dress is a good bet. Many establishments are closed on Sunday night and Monday.

There's no way to do justice to the sheer scope and variety of Johannesburg's restaurants in a few examples. What follows is a (necessarily subjective) list of some of the best. Try asking locals what they recommend; eating out is the most popular form of entertainment in Johannesburg, and everyone has a list of favorite spots, which changes often.

The Butcher Shop and Grill

$$$$ | **STEAKHOUSE** | This is a good place for hungry meat lovers, specializing in prime South African meat (as well as Wagyu and Argentinian beef) that have been aged to perfection by Alan Pick, the butcher-owner. Kudu, springbok, ostrich, and other game are staples on the menu, and only the most tender cuts are served, but there's also chicken or line fish options. **Known for:** interactive butchery for in-house and take-home orders; excellent South African wine cellar; prime location at Nelson Mandela Square. [$] *Average main: R250* ✉ *Nelson Mandela Sq., Shop 30, Sandton* ☎ *011/784–8676* 🌐 *www.thebutchershop.co.za.*

Marble

$$$$ | **SOUTH AFRICAN** | Famed for award-winning chef and co-owner David Higgs (whose cookbook, *Mile 8*, can be purchased on-site), Marble plates epicurean meals that can be expertly paired with wine. The open-plan kitchen is the restaurant's focal point, where the chef's table presents an intimate look into how Higgs and his team prepare food over a live wood fire in a quintessentially South African manner. **Known for:** premium flame-grilled meat; interior design shaped by four local artists and artisans; multiple awards since it opened. $ *Average main: R350* ⊠ *Trumpet on Keyes, corner Keyes and Jellicoe Aves., Rosebank* ☎ *010/594–5550 Landline, 064/439–2030 WhatsApp* ⊕ *www.marble.restaurant.*

★ Wandie's Place

$$ | AFRICAN | Smartly dressed waiters in ties serve truly African food—meat stews, sweet potatoes, beans, a stiff corn porridge, traditionally cooked pumpkin, chicken, and tripe laid out in a buffet of pots and containers—to a steady stream of hungry patrons. The food is hot, the drinks are cold, and the conversation flows, especially if you happen to meet Wandie, who frequently still runs operations. **Known for:** eclectic decor; tour groups; best-known township restaurant in Soweto. $ *Average main: R150* ⊠ *618 Makhalamele St., Dube* ☎ *081/420–6051.*

☕ Coffee and Quick Bites

Glenda's

$$ | EUROPEAN | This cozy, atmospheric restaurant is always busy because of the quality of its food and the gorgeous bucolic murals on its walls that complement the retro design elements, making it oh-so Instagram-worthy. The all-day menu serves breakfast, light lunches, high tea coupled with its in-house baked goods and treats, and dinner. **Known for:** takeaway patisserie counter; being an any-time-of-day kind of place; trendy cocktails, craft brews and local wines. $ *Average main: R120* ⊠ *Hyde Square, Corner Jan Smuts Ave. and North Rd., Rosebank* ☎ *011/268–6369* ⊕ *www.glendas.co.*

Hotels

Most, if not all, of the good hotels are in the northern suburbs. Many of them are linked to nearby malls and are well policed. Boutique hotels have sprung up everywhere, as have bed-and-breakfasts from Melville to Soweto. Hotels are quieter in December and January, when many locals take their annual vacations and rates are often cheaper. But beware: if there's a major conference, some of the smaller hotels can be booked months in advance.

All the hotels we list offer no-smoking rooms, and many have no-smoking floors.

InterContinental Johannesburg OR Tambo Airport

$$$$ | HOTEL | A few paces from international arrivals and adjacent to the car-rental companies and bus terminal, this is a good choice for those who have a one-night layover. **Pros:** free meet-and-greet service with escort to the hotel; ideal for those who don't need to go into Johannesburg or who have a layover before a connecting flight; free Wi-Fi. **Cons:** you won't see much of Johannesburg without leaving the hotel; large and impersonal. $ *Rooms from: R3,850* ⊠ *OR Tambo International Airport, Kempton Park* ☎ *011/961–5400, 877/859–5095* ⊕ *www.ihg.com* ⇌ *140 rooms* ⍟ *Free Breakfast.*

Radisson RED

$$ | HOTEL | The newly-built Radisson RED wows guests with its rotating collection of African prints, as well as its contemporary decor and design elements that make its open spaces and rooms pop with color. **Pros:** walking distance to The Zone @ Rosebank Mall and Keyes Art Mile; grab 'n go food station in the lobby; free shuttle to Gautrain station (650 feet away). **Cons:** the decor and atmosphere will appeal more to younger travelers; the rooftop bar and terrace can get quite lively on weekends; alongside a busy road (rooms are soundproof). $ *Rooms from: R1,800* ⊠ *4 Parks Blvd., Oxford Parks, Rosebank* ☎ *010/023–3580* ⊕ *www.radissonhotels.com* ⤵ *222 rooms* ⦿ *Free Breakfast.*

The Saxon Hotel, Villas & Spa

$$$$ | **HOTEL** | In the exclusive suburb of Sandhurst, this luxurious and impeccably designed Saxon Hotel, Villas & Spa has repeatedly received awards for its excellence. **Pros:** exclusive tranquility; exceptional spa on-site; good for business travelers or high-profile folk. **Cons:** no fine-dining option; very pricey; the atmosphere can be quite snooty. $ *Rooms from: R10,250* ⊠ *36 Saxon Rd., Sandhurst* ☎ *011/292–6000* ⊕ *www.saxon.co.za* ⤵ *53 rooms* ⦿ *Free Breakfast.*

🛍 Shopping

Whether you're after designer clothes, high-quality African art, or glamorous gifts, Johannesburg offers outstanding shopping opportunities. At the city's several markets, bargaining can get you a great price.

44 Stanley

SHOPPING CENTER | The dappled sunshine courtyards of this 1930s industrial block are lined with ateliers, galleries, family-owned cafés and restaurants, as well as one-of-a-kind stores. On the border of Melville, 44 Stanley is the kind of place where you can easily spend half the day—getting a custom T-shirt printed or a dress tailored, flipping through vinyls, picking out a limited edition print, choosing a holiday memento, or simply window shopping. It's also the newfound home of a few businesses that have relocated from Maboneng, such as the independent Bioscope cinema that screens independent documentaries and film festivals, and hosts live music performances as well as stand-up comedy. While there are many options to choose from for a bite to eat at 44 Stanley, the much-loved Little Addis Café is a must

if you want to give authentic Ethiopian cuisine a try. There is free street-side parking with car guards directly outside this leafy lifestyle complex, an off-street parking lot (R10) on Owl Street, or in the underground parking lot at Stanley Studios vis-a-vis. ⊠ *44 Stanley Ave., Emmarentia* ⊕ *www.44stanley.co.za.*

Rosebank Art and Craft Market

CRAFTS | The Rosebank Art and Craft Market, between the Rosebank Mall and The Zone, has a huge variety of African crafts from Cape to Cairo, all displayed to the background beat of traditional African music. Drive a hard bargain here—the vendors expect you to! If you want to save your shopping until the end of your trip, then this should be your destination. It's the best place in Jo'burg to buy African crafts, and it's an entertaining place to visit as well. ⊠ *Mall of Rosebank, Cradock Ave., Rosebank* ✛ *Next to Europa* ☎ *011/568–0850* ⊕ *www.rosebankartandcraftmarket.co.za.*

Cape Town and the Winelands

A favorite South African topic of debate is whether Cape Town really is part of Africa. That's how different it is, both from the rest of the country and the rest of the continent. And therein lies its attraction. South Africa's most urbane, sophisticated city sits in stark contrast to the South Africa north of the Hex River Valley. Here, the traffic lights work pretty much consistently and good restaurants are commonplace. In fact, dining establishments in the so-called Mother City always dominate the country's "best of" lists.

What also distinguishes this city is its deep sense of history. Nowhere else in the country (other than the 14th-century ancient kingdom of Mapungubwe on South Africa's northern border) will you find structures dating back to the 17th century. South Africa as it is known today began here.

A visit to Cape Town is synonymous with a visit to the peninsula south of the city, and for good reason. With pristine white-sand beaches, hundreds of mountain trails, and numerous activities from surfing to paragliding to mountain biking, the accessibility, variety, and pure beauty of the great outdoors will keep nature lovers and outdoor adventurers occupied for hours, if not days. A week exploring just the city and peninsula is barely enough.

Often likened to San Francisco, Cape Town has two things that the former doesn't: Table Mountain and Africa. The mountain, or tabletop, is vital to Cape Town's identity. It dominates the city in a way that's difficult to comprehend until you visit. In the afternoon, when creeping fingers of clouds spill over Table Mountain and reach toward the city, the whole town seems to hold its breath—because in summer it brings frequent strong southeasterly winds. Meanwhile, for all of its bon-vivant European vibe, Cape Town also reflects the diversity, vitality, and spirit of Africa, with many West and Central Africans and Zimbabweans—many of them having fled from conflicts elsewhere—calling this city home.

While parts of the Winelands—Stellenbosch, Franschhoek, and Paarl—are an easy drive from Cape Town's city center, the Cape Winelands region is so vast that you can trek to the fringes of the Karoo Desert, in the northeast, and still find a grape. There are around 18 wine routes in the Western Cape, ranging from the Olifants River, in the north, to the coastal mountains of the Overberg and beyond. There's also a well-established Winelands brandy route, and an annual port festival is held in Calitzdorp, in the Little Karoo.

The secret to touring the Cape Winelands is not to hurry. Dally over lunch on a vine-shaded veranda at a 300-year-old estate, enjoy an afternoon nap under a spreading oak, or sip wine while savoring the impossible views. Of the scores of wineries and estates in the Cape Winelands, the ones listed here are chosen for their great wine, their beauty, or their historic significance. It would be a mistake to try to cover them all in less than a week. You have nothing to gain from hightailing it around the Cape Winelands other than a headache. If your interest is more aesthetic and cultural than wine-driven, you would do well to focus on the historic estates of Stellenbosch and Franschhoek. Most Paarl wineries stand out more for the quality of their wine than for their beauty.

WHEN TO GO

Whatever activities you hope to accomplish in Cape Town, head up Table Mountain as soon as the wind isn't blowing. Cape Town wind is notorious, and the mountain can be shut for days on end when there are gales. Summer (October–March) is the windiest time of the year, and from December to April winds can reach 60 km (37 miles) an hour. But they will often happen in the winter months, too—just less frequently. If you're planning to visit Robben Island during peak season, it's also wise to book well in advance. One of the best months to visit is April, when the heat and wind have abated and the Cape is bathed in warm autumnal hues. Winter rains can put off visitors, but this time of the year holds its own surprises: the countryside is a brilliant green, and without fail the best sunny and temperate days come between the rainy spells. Whales are seen in False Bay in spring (late August to early September), when wildflowers are also in bloom.

GETTING HERE AND AROUND

Cape Town International Airport is about 19 km (12 miles) from the city center. It should take about 20 minutes to get from the airport to the city; during rush hour it can easily be double that. Private airport-transfer operators abound, and there is now public bus service to and from the airport. All major car-rental companies have counters at Cape Town

Maropeng is the official visitor center at the Cradle of Humankind, which is one of eight World Heritage Sites in South Africa.

International, and driving to the City Bowl or V&A Waterfront is straightforward in daylight. If your flight arrives after dark, consider prearranging transportation through your hotel. There are tourist information desks in both the domestic and international terminals.

CONTACTS Cape Town International Airport. ✉ *Matroosfontein, Cape Town* ☎ *021/937–1200, 086/727–7888 flight information* ⊕ *capetown-airport.co.za.*

Metered taxis and shuttle services (usually minivans) are based inside the domestic baggage hall and outside the international and domestic terminals and can also be phoned for airport drop-offs. Rates vary depending on the operator, number of passengers, destination, and time of arrival. The fare for one person to the city center is R300 in a metered taxi; a group of up to four will usually pay the same rate. A surcharge of up to R50 is sometimes levied from 10 pm until early morning, and some services charge more for arrivals than for departures to cover waiting time. For single travelers,

a prearranged shared shuttle is the most economical, costing about R150–R180 per person; however, there may be numerous drop-offs, so this can be slow. MyCiti, a public bus, also serves the airport, and for R90 it's the cheapest way to or from the airport and City Centre.

▮**TIP→ Reports of overcharging are common, so discuss the fare before entering any taxi.**

Rikkis provides inexpensive, unmetered fares (R220 to City Centre, for example) from the airport.

Recommended shared-van services include Legend Tours and Transfers or Magic Bus Airport. Citi Hopper provides both shared-van transfers and private-car transfers.

AIRPORT TRANSFERS Citi Hopper. ☎ *021/936–3460/1, 082/773–7678* ⊕ *www.citihopper.co.za.* **Legend Tours and Transfers.** ✉ *Cape Town* ☎ *021/704–9140* ⊕ *www.legendtours.co.za.* **Magic Bus Airport Transfers.** ✉ *Cape Town* ☎ *021/505–6300* ⊕ *www.magicbus.co.za.*

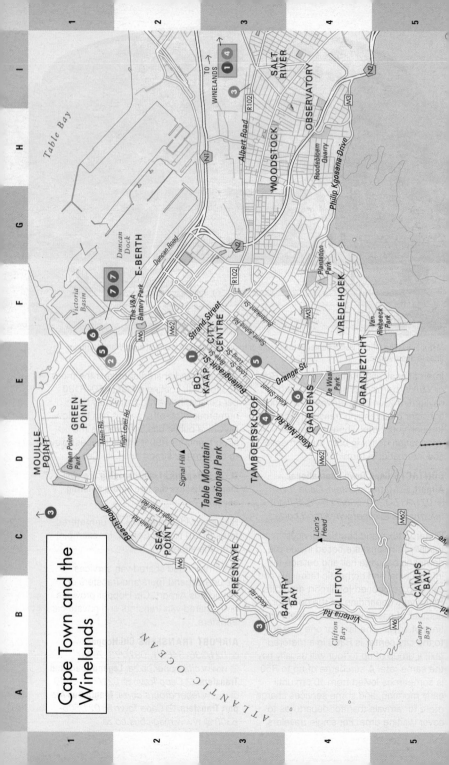

Cape Town and the Winelands

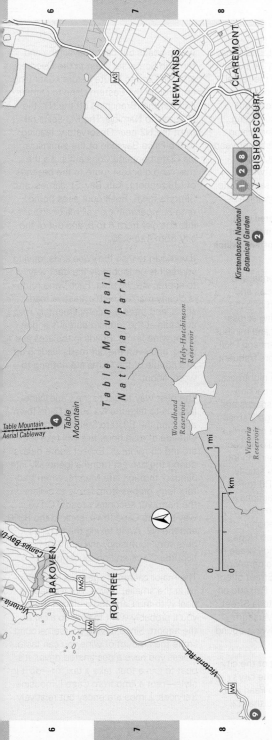

Sights ▶

1 Delaire Graff Estate **I3**
2 Kirstenbosch National
Botanical Garden **G8**
3 Robben Island **C1**
4 Table Mountain **D6**
5 Two Oceans Aquarium **E1**
6 V&A Waterfront **F1**
7 Zeitz Museum of
Contemporary Art Africa ... **F1**

Restaurants ▶

1 La Colombe **H8**
2 Nobu **E1**
3 The Pot Luck Club **I3**
4 Tokara **I3**

Hotels ▶

1 Cape Heritage Hotel **E3**
2 Cellars-Hohenort
Hotel & Spa **H8**
3 Ellerman House **B3**
4 La Grenadine Petit Hotel ... **E3**
5 Long Street
Boutique Hotel **E3**
6 Mount Nelson Hotel **E4**
7 The Silo Hotel **F1**
8 Tintswalo Atlantic **H8**
9 Twelve Apostles
Hotel & Spa **A8**

Although many locals drive, tourists may find public transportation (MyCiti buses) or taxis a better option; save the rental car for when you are getting out of town. Cape Town's roads are excellent, but getting around can be a bit confusing. Signposting is inconsistent, switching between Afrikaans and English, between different names for the same road (especially highways), and between different destinations on the same route. Sometimes the signs simply vanish.

■ TIP→ **Cape Town is also littered with signs indicating "Cape Town" instead of "City Centre," as well as "Kaapstad," which is Afrikaans for Cape Town.**

A good one-page map is essential and available from car-rental agencies and tourism information desks. Among the hazards are pedestrians running across highways, speeding vehicles, and minibus taxis. Roadblocks for document and DWI checks are also becoming more frequent.

Parking in the city center is a nightmare. There are simply not enough parking garages, longer-stay parking spaces are scarce, and most hotels charge a small fortune for parking. There are numerous pay-and-display (i.e., put a ticket in your windshield) and pay-on-exit parking lots around the city, but parking is strictly enforced. Prices range from R6 to R12 per half hour. For central attractions like Greenmarket Square, the Company's Garden, the South African National Gallery, and the Castle of Good Hope, look for a lot around the Grand Parade on Darling Street. The Sanlam Golden Acre Parking Garage on Adderley Street offers covered parking, as does the Parkade on Strand Street, but Queen Victoria Street alongside the South African Museum (and Company's Garden) is always bound to have a few spaces.

The main arteries leading out of the city are the N1, which bypasses the city's Northern Suburbs en route to Paarl and, ultimately, Johannesburg; and the N2,

which heads out past Khayelitsha and through Somerset West to the Overberg and the Garden Route before continuing on through the Eastern Cape to Durban and beyond. Branching off the N1, the N7 goes to Namibia. The M3 splits off from the N2 near Observatory, leading to the False Bay side of the peninsula via Claremont and Constantia; it's the main and quickest route to the beaches of Muizenberg, Kalk Bay, St. James, and Simon's Town. Rush hour sees bumper-to-bumper traffic on all major arteries into the city from 6 to 9, and out of the city from 4 to 6:30.

If you plan to visit the Winelands, driving yourself is undoubtedly the best way to appreciate the area. Each wine route is clearly marked with attractive road signs, and there are complimentary maps available at the tourism bureaus and at most wine farms. Roads in the area are good, and even the dirt roads leading up to a couple of the farms are nothing to worry about.

The best way to get to the Cape Winelands is to take the N2 out of Cape Town and then the R310 to Stellenbosch. Outside of rush hour, this will take you around 45 minutes. Expect some delays during the harvest months (generally late January through late March), when tractors ferry grapes from farms to cellars on the narrower secondary roads. On your way back to Cape Town, stick to the R310 and the N2. Avoid taking the M12, as it gets very confusing, and you'll end up in suburbs that aren't on tourist maps.

The major car-rental agencies have offices in the smaller towns, but it's best to deal with the Cape Town offices. Besides, you'll probably want to pick up a car at the airport. Since driving yourself around limits the amount of wine you can taste, unless you have a designated driver, it's best to join a tour, take a taxi, or—do it in style—rent a limo from Cape Limousine Services. Limos are pricey but relatively cost-effective if you have a group of four or five.

Until the arrival of Uber, Cape Town taxis were expensive and not necessarily easily hailed. This is still the case, so if you are going old-school, don't expect to see the throngs of cabs you find in London or New York. Know that you are unlikely to hail a cab in the street, and taxis rarely have roof lights to indicate availability. If you do flag an occupied cab, the driver may radio another car for you. Your best bet is to summon a taxi by phone or head to one of the major taxi stands, such as those at the V&A Waterfront, Greenmarket Square, or either end of Adderley Street (near the Slave Lodge and outside the train station). Expect to pay R60–R70 for a trip from the city center to the Waterfront (far less if using Uber or Bolt).

In addition to the companies listed here, ask your hotel or guesthouse which company it recommends. Lodging establishments often have a relationship with particular companies and/or drivers, and this way you will be assured of safe, reliable service. If you have the app and a smartphone with data, Uber or Bolt (formerly Taxify) rides are almost always the fastest, cheapest, and best option.

If you're visiting the Winelands, Paarl Radio Taxis and Daksi Cab, based in Stellenbosch, are excellent reliable operators for single travelers or small groups.

CONTACTS Excite Taxis. ✉ *Cape Town* ☏ *021/448–4444* ⊕ *www.excitetaxis. co.za.* **Unicab.** ✉ *Cape Town* ☏ *021/486– 1600* ⊕ *www.unicab.co.za.* **Citi Hopper.** ✉ *Cape Town* ☏ *021/936–3460* ⊕ *www. citihopper.co.za.*

SAFETY
Cape Town is a safe city to enjoy, as long as you make certain adjustments and are careful and knowledgeable about your surroundings.

Women and couples are strongly advised not to walk in isolated places after dark.

If you want to walk somewhere in the evening, make sure you do so in a large group. Keep flashy jewelry and expensive cameras hidden or don't take them with you, much as you would in any unfamiliar city. Street-based people are wrongly blamed for much of the petty crime in the city, but are usually just asking for some change or food. If you are approached for some, please respond humanely.

If you're renting a car, don't leave anything visible on the seats as windows can be smashed to snatch cell phones or bags.

At busy transportation hubs and on trains, mind your belongings and pockets. By rail, it's better to sit in a crowded carriage; if you suddenly find yourself alone, move to another one. Public transportation collapses after dark and is not always safe to use so it's best to use Ubers or metered taxis.

Trendy nightlife areas like Long Street and Kloof Street (which leads on via a dogleg from Long Street), and the predominantly gay nightlife scene around Greenpoint, are frequented by both teens and adults. These areas are safe, but one should always be vigilant at night, i.e., stay in busier areas, don't flash expensive items, and mind your pockets.

Despite thousands of safe visits every year, Lion's Head—the peak below Table Mountain—and the running trails around Newlands Forest have been the sites of some knife-point robberies which occurred around sunrise or sunset. Be sure to hike in a group or on the popular paths during busier times of the day. And even though Table Mountain is in the middle of a major city, a hike to the top should be taken seriously: follow the paths, always bring water, sunscreen, and a warm layer—it's another world up there.

Visiting townships can be an important part of getting to know the real lives of the majority of the people of Cape Town. If you do plan a visit, make sure it's with a resident, or as part of an organized tour.

Known as "The Boomslang," the Centenary Tree Canopy Walkway at the Kirstenbosch National Botanical Garden winds its way through the property.

However, keep in mind that township tours are quite controversial with some residents, as they would not like their lives to be considered tourism. Opt for a small and more intimate tour that supports local residents, their dignity, and their stories.

TOURS

Numerous companies offer guided tours of the city center, the peninsula, the Winelands, and any place else in the Cape (or beyond) that you might wish to visit. They differ in type of transportation used, focus, and size. For comprehensive information on touring companies, head to one of the Cape Town Tourism offices or ask for recommendations at your hotel.

Most tours of the Cape Winelands are operated by companies based in Cape Town; most have half- or full-day tours, but they vary by company and might include a cheese tasting or cellar tour in addition to wine tasting. Expect to pay around R900 for a half day and R1200 for a full day, including all tasting fees.

Though you stop for lunch, it is not included in the cost.

If you're based in Stellenbosch for your Winelands visit, but don't want to drive to the wineries, you can make use of the Vine Hopper, a minibus that follows a fixed route to six wine farms. Tickets cost around R350 for a one-day ticket and R630 for a two-day ticket, and you'll be given a timetable so that you can get on and off as you please.

Wanderlust Audio Walking Tours

WALKING TOURS | These audio tours, based on Ursula Stevens's comprehensive books written on Cape Town, are full of interesting historical information. You can do a self-guided exploration following the VoiceMap audio tours that Ursula created in English and German. These tours are ideal for visitors with less time on their hands and those who wish to be independent of groups. You can purchase a guide on the VoiceMap App. ⊠ Cape Town, Cape Town ⊕ www.wanderlust. co.za ☞ From R40.

City Sightseeing Bus Cape Town

BUS TOURS | FAMILY | This "hop on–hop off" bus tour is a great way to familiarize yourself with Cape Town, especially early on in your trip. It's accessible at various points around the city while hitting all the major landmarks and attractions, including Table Mountain, the V&A Waterfront, Camps Bay, and more. You can choose when to get off and spend some time, skip what you're not interested in, or stay on the bus and see the whole city in a day. Wherever you get off, you'll be able to return back to your starting point. They offer various languages on audio, as well as other tour options that may include walking tours, canal cruises at the waterfront, and trips around the Winelands and peninsula. Tickets are available at the Waterfront outside the aquarium or on the bus. ☎ *021/511–6000* ⊕ *www. citysightseeing.co.za* ✉ *R225, R130 for children.*

Vine Hopper

SELF-GUIDED TOURS | An excellent alternative to a guided tour, the Vine Hopper is a hop-on, hop-off bus tour around the Stellenbosch region. There are three routes to choose from, with up to six wineries on each route. You can opt for a one- or two-day pass. They cover transport only, not wine tasting fees. ✉ *1 Noordwal Wes Rd., Stellenbosch* ☎ *021/882–8112* ⊕ *www.vinehopper.co.za.*

VISITOR INFORMATION

From October to March, the office in City Centre is open weekdays 8–6, Saturday 8:30–2, and Sunday 9–1; from April to September, it's open weekdays 8–5:30, Saturday 8:30–1, and Sunday 9–1. The branch at the Waterfront is open daily 9–7.

CONTACT Cape Town Tourism. ✉ *33 Martin Hammerschlag Way, Cape Town Central* ☎ *021/487–6800* ⊕ *www.capetown. travel.*

Sights

Delaire Graff Estate

WINERY | This has to be one of the most spectacular settings of any winery in the country. Sit on the terrace of the tasting room or restaurant and look past a screen of pin oaks to the valley below and the majestic crags of the Groot Drakenstein and Simonsberg Mountains. It's an ideal place to stop for lunch, and you'll need at least three hours to do your meal and the wines justice. The flagship Delaire Graff Restaurant champions local ingredients, while ultra-high-end Indochine celebrates South Africa's historical links to Southeast Asia through Cape Malay dishes and pan-Asian specialties. Although the Botmaskop Red Blend is the farm's flagship wine, do try the Cabernet Franc Rosé, a lovely take on a varietal that usually gets added to the Bordeaux Blend. The Coastal Cuvée Sauvignon Blanc is exceptional and has won numerous awards. ✉ *Helshoogte Pass Rd., between Stellenbosch and Franschhoek, Stellenbosch* ☎ *021/885–8160* ⊕ *www.delaire.co.za* ✉ *Tastings R125.*

★ Kirstenbosch National Botanical Garden

GARDEN | FAMILY | Spectacular in each season, this renowned botanical garden was established in 1913, and was the first in the world to conserve and showcase a country's indigenous flora. With its magnificent setting extending up the eastern slopes of Table Mountain and overlooking the city and distant Hottentots Holland Mountains, these gardens are truly a national treasure. In addition to thousands of out-of-town visitors, Capetonians flock here on weekends to laze on the grassy lawns, picnicking and reading newspapers while the kids run riot. Walking trails meander through the plantings, which are limited to species indigenous to Southern Africa. Naturally the fynbos biome—the hardy, thin-leaved plants that proliferate in the Cape—is heavily featured, and you will find plenty of proteas, ericas, and restios (reeds). Garden highlights include the Tree Canopy Walkway, a large cycad garden, the Bird Bath (a beautiful stone pool built around a crystal-clear spring), the fragrance garden (which is wheelchair-friendly and has a tapping rail), and the Sculpture Garden. Free 90-minute guided tours take place daily except Sunday. Those who have difficulty walking can enjoy a comprehensive tour lasting one hour (R70, hourly 9–3) in seven-person (excluding the driver) golf carts. Concerts featuring the best of South African entertainment—from classical music to township jazz to indie rock—are held on summer Sundays at 5 (be sure to arrive early to get a spot), and the Galileo Outdoor Cinema screens movies on Wednesdays an hour after sunset. A visitor center by the nursery houses a restaurant, bookstore, and coffee shop. There are also several trails taking you to the top of Table Mountain, from which point you can hike to the cable car station. Unfortunately, muggings have become increasingly more common in the gardens' isolated areas, and women are advised not to walk alone in the upper reaches of the park far from general activity. ⊠ *Rhodes Dr., Newlands* ☎ *021/799–8783* ⊕ *www. sanbi.org* ✉ *R75.*

★ **Robben Island**

ISLAND | Made famous by its most illustrious inhabitant, Nelson Mandela, this island, whose name is Dutch for "seals," has a long and sad history. At various times a prison, leper colony, mental institution, and military base, it is finally filling a positive, enlightening, and empowering role in its latest incarnation as a museum.

Declared a World Heritage site on December 1, 1997, Robben Island has become a symbol of the triumph of the human spirit. In 1997 around 90,000 made the pilgrimage; in 2006 more than 300,000 crossed the water to see where some of the most prominent struggle leaders in South Africa spent decades of their lives. A visit to the island is a sobering experience. The approximately four-hour tour begins at the Nelson Mandela Gateway to Robben Island, an impressive embarkation center that doubles as a conference center. Changing exhibits display historic photos of prisoners and prison life. Next make the 45-minute journey across the water, remembering to watch Table Mountain recede in the distance and imagine what it must have been like to have just received a 20-year jail sentence. Boats leave three or four times a day, depending on season and weather.

Tours are organized by the Robben Island Museum (other operators that advertise Robben Island tours only take visitors on a boat trip *around* the island.) Many of the guides are former political prisoners, and during the two-hour tour, they will take you through the prison where you will see the cells where Mandela and other leaders were imprisoned. The tour also takes you to the lime quarry, Robert Sobukwe's place of confinement, and the leper church. Due to increased demand for tickets during peak season (December and January), make reservations at least three weeks in advance. Take sunglasses and a hat in summer. ▮**TIP**→ **You are advised to tip your guide only if you feel that the tour has been informative.** ⊠ *Nelson Mandela Gateway, V&A Waterfront* ☎ *021/413–4200* ⊕ *www.robben-island. org.za* ✉ *R600.*

★ **Table Mountain**

FOREST | Table Mountain truly is one of Southern Africa's most beautiful and impressive natural wonders. The views from its summit are awe-inspiring. The mountain rises more than 3,500 feet above the city, and its distinctive flat top is visible to sailors 65 km (40 miles) out to sea. Climbing up the step-like Plattekloof Gorge—the most popular route up—will take two to three hours, depending on your fitness level. There is no water along the route; you *must* take at least 2 liters (½ gallon) of water per person.

You can see African penguins, most commonly known as Jackass Penguins, at the beaches in Simon's Town. You can also see African Penguins at Cape Town's Two Oceans Aquarium.

Table Mountain can be dangerous if you're not familiar with the terrain. Many paths that look like good routes down the mountain end in treacherous cliffs. ⚠ **Do not underestimate this mountain: every year local and foreign visitors to the mountain get lost, some falling off ledges, with fatal consequences.**

It may be in the middle of a city, but it is not a genteel town park. Because of occasional muggings near the Rhodes Memorial east of the mountain, it's unwise to walk alone on that side. It's recommended that you travel in a group or, better yet, with a guide. If you want to do the climb on your own, wear sturdy shoes or hiking boots; always take warm clothes, including a windbreaker or fleece; travel with a mobile phone; and let someone know of your plans. Consult the staff at a Cape Town Tourism office for more guidelines. Another (much easier) way to reach the summit is to take the cable car, which affords fantastic views. Cable cars (R135 one way) depart from the Lower Cable Station, which lies on the slope of Table Mountain near its western end; the station is a long way from the city on foot, so save your hiking energy for the mountain, and take a taxi or the MyCiti bus to get here. ✉ *Tafelberg Rd., Table Mountain National Park* ☎ *021/712–0527* ⊕ *www.sanparks.org/ parks/table_mountain.*

★ Two Oceans Aquarium
AQUARIUM | FAMILY | This aquarium is widely considered one of the finest in the world. Stunning displays reveal the regional marine life of the warmer Indian Ocean and the icy Atlantic. It's a hands-on place, with a touch pool for children, opportunities to interact with penguins, and (for certified divers only) to dive in the vast, five-story ocean exhibit with shoals of fish, huge turtles, and stingrays, or the shark exhibit, where you might share the water with large ragged-tooth sharks (*Carcharias taurus*) and enjoy a legal adrenaline rush (for an additional fee, of course). If you don't fancy getting wet, you can still watch daily feedings in either the ocean, penguin, or

South African Wine

When it comes to South African terroir, think sun, sea, and soil. Whereas Northern Hemisphere farmers work hard to get as much sunlight onto their grapes as possible, local viticulturists have to deal with soaring summer temperatures (this is why the cooling influence of the two oceans is so welcome). South Africa also has some of the world's oldest soil, and there's a mineral element to its wines. Although South Africa has a reputation for delivering good quality at the bottom end of the market, more and more ultra-premium wines are emerging. Good-quality wines at varied prices are readily available—even in supermarkets. Currently white wine production outstrips red, but the quality continually improves for both, and they regularly win international awards. Particularly notable is Pinotage, South Africa's own grape variety, a cross between Pinot Noir and Cinsaut (formerly Hermitage). Chenin Blanc is the country's most widely planted variety and is used in everything from blends to Méthode Cap Classique, South Africa's own version of bubbly. You'd be unwise to pass on an offer of Graham Beck Cuvée Clive or Villiera Brut Tradition. Other excellent varietals include Sauvignon Blanc, and Bordeaux-style red blends of Cabernet Sauvignon, Merlot, and Cabernet Franc. Importantly, many wineries are working at Black empowerment. Thokozani, based at Diemersfontein in Wellington, is part-owned by the farm staff. It's one of the earliest and most successful Black empowerment projects in the wine industry. Another farm that has been dedicated to empowerment and transformation is Bosman Family Vineyard, also in Wellington. There is also a growing number of Black-owned wine estates and labels including Aslina (Stellenbosch), Seven Sisters (Stellenbosch), Klein Goederust (Franschhoek), and Tesselaarsdal (Hemel-en-Aarde).

If you're serious about wine, arm yourself with *John Platter's Wine Guide* or visit ⊕ www.winemag. co.za (the new digital form of *Wine* magazine), featuring local wineries. For an in-depth read and fantastic photos, pick up *Wines and Vineyards of South Africa* by Wendy Toerien or *New World of Wine from the Cape of Good Hope: The Definitive Guide to the South African Wine Industry* by Phyllis Hands, David Hughes, and Keith Phillips. *Wines of the New South Africa: Tradition and Revolution* by Tim James is also recommended reading.

shark exhibits. But there's more to the aquarium than just snapping jaws. Look for the fascinating jellyfish display, the endangered Knysna seahorses, and the alien-like spider crabs. ⊠ *Dock Rd., V&A Waterfront* ☎ *021/418–3823* ⊕ *www. aquarium.co.za* ☞ *R210.*

V&A Waterfront

NEIGHBORHOOD | **FAMILY** | The V&A (Victoria & Alfred) Waterfront is the culmination of a long-term project undertaken to breathe new life into the city's historical dockland. Although some Capetonians deem the area too "mallish," the Waterfront remains Cape Town's most popular attraction—probably because of the ease and safety of being a pedestrian here, coupled with favorable currency exchange rates for North American and European visitors, and the ever-increasing number of truly worthwhile attractions and activities on offer. Hundreds of shops, movie theaters, restaurants, and bars share quarters in restored warehouses and dock buildings, all connected by pedestrian plazas and promenades. Newer developments like the excellent Watershed craft market and two fantastic food markets have made the V&A more appealing to locals; it's also home to Two Oceans Aquarium, Zeitz Museum of Contemporary Art—Africa's first such institution, and the Robben Island ferries.

With its crowds of people, security cameras, and guards, this is one of the safest places to shop and hang out in the city. That said, you should still keep an eye on your belongings and be aware of pickpockets. ✉ *V&A Waterfront, Cape Town* 🌐 *www.waterfront.co.za.*

★ Zeitz Museum of Contemporary Art Africa
ART MUSEUM | Opened in September 2017, the Zeitz is the first major museum dedicated to contemporary art from Africa and its diaspora. Inhabiting the massively renovated historic Grain Silo in what is now called the Silo District of the V&A Waterfront, the museum itself is a work of art, reimagined by designer Thomas Heatherwick. Give yourself half a day to go through and look at the provocative and thought-provoking art on the exhibit. ✉ *Silo District, S Arm Rd., V&A Waterfront* ☎ *087/350–4777* 🌐 *www.zeitzmocaa.museum* 🎫 *R230* 🕓 *Closed Mon.*

🍴 Restaurants

Cape Town is the culinary capital of South Africa and quite possibly the continent. It certainly has the best restaurants in southern Africa. Nowhere else in the country is the populace so discerning about food, and nowhere else is there such a wide selection of high-quality restaurants. Western culinary history here dates back to the 17th century—Cape Town was founded specifically to grow food—and that heritage is reflected in the city's cuisine and the fact that a number of restaurants operate in historic townhouses and 18th-century wine estates.

★ La Colombe
$$$$ | **ECLECTIC** | Rightfully known as one of South Africa's most lauded fine-dining establishments and listed in the world's top 100 restaurants, La Colombe's sublime French-Asian inspired tasting menus are served in a delightful minimalist setting overlooking the bucolic green of the Constantia wine valley. The menu changes regularly, but the best option is to order the full eight-course gourmand menu, as there is not a false note to be found. **Known for:** excellent, knowledgeable service; fantastic wine pairings; stellar French-Asian fusion haute cuisine. [$] *Average main: R995* ✉ *Silvermist Wine Estate, Main Rd., Constantia Nek, Constantia* ☎ *021/794–2390* 🌐 *www.lacolombe.co.za.*

Nobu
$$$$ | **JAPANESE FUSION** | If you've always wanted to try Nobuyuki "Nobu" Matsuhisa's famous Japanese cuisine, but were put off by the potential bill in New York or London, Nobu Cape Town offers a chance to sample what may not constitute exactly the same level of cuisine, but will nonetheless make for a highly enjoyable experience. A vast modern space in the Waterfront's One&Only resort provides a fitting backdrop for the splurge of the Omakase multicourse tasting menu, which will likely include dishes such as the signature Alaskan black cod with miso. **Known for:** branch of the famous Nobu chain; glitzy, bold atmosphere. [$] *Average main: R475* ✉ *One&Only Cape Town, Dock Rd., V&A Waterfront* ☎ *021/431–4511* 🌐 *www.oneandonlyresorts.com* 🕓 *No lunch.*

★ The Pot Luck Club

$$$$ | ECLECTIC | A meal at this playful and inventive tapas-style venture from Cape Town star-chef Luke Dale Roberts always promises fabulous fun. With great harbor and mountain views from its position on the sixth floor of a renovated silo, this hip eatery serves an eclectic but clearly Asian-influenced array of fine-dining nibbles. **Known for:** simultaneously hip, elegant, and casual ambience; two seatings for dinner—don't expect to linger if you choose the early one; super-creative and umami-packed dishes with distinct Asian flair. [$] *Average main: R300* ✉ *Old Biscuit Mill, 375 Albert Rd., Silo top fl., Woodstock* ☎ *021/447–0804* 🌐 *www.thepotluckclub.co.za* ⏲ *No dinner Sun.*

★ Tokara

$$$$ | ECLECTIC | At the top of the Helshoogte Pass with absolutely amazing views of the valley and mountains, Tokara is a Winelands must-visit. Chef Carolize Coetzee grew up in small-town South Africa and honors local ingredients and cooking methods in her wide range of dishes. **Known for:** South African specialties; striking local art; upmarket farm-style food. [$] *Average main: R270* ✉ *Helshoogte Pass Rd., Stellenbosch* ☎ *021/885–2550* 🌐 *www.tokara.co.za* ⏲ *Closed Mon. and Tues. No dinner Sun.*

Hotels

Finding lodging in Cape Town can be a nightmare during peak travel season (December–January), as many of the more reasonable accommodations are booked up. It's worth traveling between April and August, if you can, to take advantage of the "secret season" discounts that are sometimes half the high-season rate. Other reduced rates can be scored by booking directly online, checking the "Best Available Rate" at large hotels, or simply asking if any specials or discounts are available.

First-time, short-term, or business visitors will want to locate themselves centrally. The historic city center is a vibrant and pedestrian-friendly place by day, but at night can feel a bit deserted and edgy, depending on where you are. Night owls may prefer to stay amid the nonstop action of Long Street or Kloof Street, or at the V&A Waterfront, with its plethora of pedestrian-friendly shopping and dining options (though be aware that locals don't consider the Waterfront the "real" Cape Town). Boutique hotels and bed-and-breakfasts in Gardens are often within walking distance of attractions and dining but will be quieter and often enjoy lovely views. Options along the Atlantic Seaboard are also close to the action and (mostly) pedestrian-friendly, with the added advantage of sea and sunset views. Staying farther out on the Cape Peninsula, whether the False Bay or Atlantic side, provides the closest thing in Cape Town to a beach-vacation atmosphere despite the cold ocean waters. The Southern Suburbs, especially around Constantia or Tokai, can make a good base from which to explore the area's wine estates as well as the peninsula, but you'll be dependent on a car for everything, and should plan on 25 to 45 minutes to get into town.

When South Africans travel, they often stay in guesthouses or B&Bs. Among them you will find some of the most elegant and professionally run establishments available, offering everything a hotel does but on a smaller, more personal scale. If you prefer a bit more anonymity or want to save money, consider renting a fully furnished apartment, especially if you're staying two or more weeks. Airbnb has listings in Cape Town, and several agencies can help you make bookings.

Cape Heritage Hotel

$$$ | HOTEL | Built as a private home in 1771, this centrally located boutique hotel's spacious rooms are individually decorated, melding the best of South

Africa's dynamic contemporary art scene with its historic architecture, and making the most of the building's teak-beamed ceilings, foot-wide yellowwood floorboards, and numerous other details that recall its gracious past. **Pros:** excellent eateries in adjoining Heritage Square and Bree Street; beautiful old building and quirky style; great location in Cape Town's historic district. **Cons:** parking isn't free; lighting in some rooms is very dark; bordered by one busy road. [$] *Rooms from: R3,135* ✉ *90 Bree St., Cape Town Central* ☎ *021/424–4646* 🌐 *www.capeheritage.co.za* 🛏 *20 rooms* 🍴 *Free Breakfast.*

Cellars-Hohenort Hotel & Spa
$$$$ | HOTEL | With acres of gardens and spectacular views across the Constantia Valley, this idyllic old-school getaway in two historic buildings makes the world beyond disappear. **Pros:** beautiful gardens; two pools (one for children); fantastic breakfast in lovely Conservatory Restaurant. **Cons:** more modern rooms on Cellars side are starting to feel old-fashioned; a lot of stairs to access best rooms; need a car to get around. [$] *Rooms from: R8,706* ✉ *93 Brommersvlei Rd., Constantia* ☎ *021/794–2137* 🌐 *www.collectionmcgrath.com/hotels/the-cellars-hohenort* 🛏 *53 rooms* 🍴 *Free Breakfast.*

★ **Ellerman House**
$$$$ | HOTEL | Built in 1906 for shipping magnate Sir John Ellerman, what may be Cape Town's finest hotel sits high on a hill up from Sea Point in Bantry Bay, graced with stupendous views of the sea and an art collection that puts the National Gallery to shame. **Pros:** fully stocked complimentary guest pantry available 24 hours; amazing sense of intimacy and privacy to enjoy this spectacular environment; lovely treats like canapés and cocktails at sunset. **Cons:** often booked a year in advance; Kloof Road is busy (though noise not audible from hotel). [$] *Rooms from: R14,500* ✉ *180 Kloof Rd., Bantry Bay, Sea Point* ☎ *021/430–3200* 🌐 *www.ellerman.co.za* 🛏 *15 rooms* 🍴 *Free Breakfast.*

★ **La Grenadine Petit Hotel**
$$ | B&B/INN | FAMILY | Built around a verdant courtyard shaded by pomegranate, guava, and avocado trees, the five gorgeous rooms at this well-located and good-value hotel are all Gallic-charm-meets-South-African-vintage-hipster: hand-embroidered bed linens, badminton paddles repurposed as mirrors, and art deco light fittings. **Pros:** great bustling location in walking distance to dozens of restaurants and attractions; excellent Continental breakfast filled with house-made treats; wonderful fusion of French and South African vintage style. **Cons:** limited off-street parking; some rooms have bathrooms that are not fully closed off; no TVs in rooms. [$] *Rooms from: R2,500* ✉ *15 Park Rd., Gardens* ☎ *021/424–1358* 🌐 *www.lagrenadine.co.za* 🛏 *10 rooms* 🍴 *Free Breakfast.*

Long Street Boutique Hotel
$$ | B&B/INN | The upper floors of a beautifully restored Victorian building on trendy Long Street house this incredibly good-value boutique hotel made up of 12 luxurious rooms. **Pros:** surprisingly opulent for the price; free unlimited Wi-Fi and air-conditioning; in the heart of Cape Town's nightlife. **Cons:** not a tranquil neighborhood; must pay for parking (R100 per night); no elevator. [$] *Rooms from: R1,500* ✉ *230 Long St., Cape Town Central* ☎ *021/426–4309* 🌐 *www.longstreethotel.com* 🛏 *12 rooms* 🍴 *No Meals.*

★ **Mount Nelson Hotel**
$$$$ | HOTEL | FAMILY | An icon of Cape Town since it opened its doors in 1899, this superbly located landmark sits on 9 beautifully landscaped acres and retains a charm and gentility unusual even in the world of luxury hotels. **Pros:** decor achieves the perfect balance between colonial elegance and contemporary style; great location in walking distance to Company's Garden and downtown,

or Kloof Street attractions; the "Nellie's" lavish high tea is an institution, and the glam Planet Bar an ideal place for a cocktail. **Cons:** may be booked out during high season as much as a year in advance; spread out across multiple buildings, each with its own style, so you must be sure to state your preferences; breakfast restaurant Oasis lacks the charm of the rest of the hotel. $ *Rooms from: R13,800* ✉ *76 Orange St., Gardens* ☎ *021/483–1000* ⊕ *www.belmond.com/mount-nelson-hotel-cape-town* ⤴ *198 rooms* ▯◉▯ *Free Breakfast.*

The Silo Hotel

$$$$ | HOTEL | Brilliantly melding industrial grit and sumptuous glamour, Cape Town's hottest luxury hotel rises out of the old grain silo in the working harbor section of the Waterfront. **Pros:** surprisingly child-friendly; mind-blowing decor and artwork; incredible views from rooftop bar. **Cons:** starting category rooms are small; extremely pricey; not for the traditionalist. $ *Rooms from: R23,400* ✉ *Silo Square, V&A Waterfront* ☎ *021/670–0500* ⊕ *www.theroyalportfolio.com/the-silo/overview* ⤴ *28 rooms* ▯◉▯ *Free Breakfast.*

★ Tintswalo Atlantic

$$$$ | RESORT | Visitors attracted to the Cape Peninsula for its natural grandeur will think they've died and gone to heaven when arriving at this discreetly luxurious boutique hotel. **Pros:** unique mind-blowing location; attentive service and setup creates a bit of a "safari by the sea" ambience; fantastic breakfast in one of the most beautiful spots imaginable. **Cons:** building requirements in the National Park mean exteriors of buildings have a prefab look; about a 35- to 40-minute drive from Cape Town Central; must drive to all activities and sights. $ *Rooms from: R12,550* ✉ *Chapman's Peak Dr., Km 2, Hout Bay* ☎ *021/201–0025* ⊕ *www.tintswalo.com/atlantic* ⤴ *11 rooms* ▯◉▯ *Free Breakfast.*

★ Twelve Apostles Hotel & Spa

$$$$ | HOTEL | If you fancy taking a helicopter to the airport or lazing in a bubble bath while looking out floor-to-ceiling windows at breathtaking sea and mountain views, then this award-winning, luxurious hotel and spa that is the only such property within Table Mountain National Park may be for you. **Pros:** wonderfully attentive staff; unique location in Table Mountain National Park; great breakfast in Azure restaurant with glorious sea views. **Cons:** nearest off-site restaurant is at least 10 minutes by car; views and room sizes are extremely varied so check when booking; there's a busy road between the hotel and the sea. $ *Rooms from: R9,820* ✉ *Victoria Rd., Camps Bay* ☎ *021/437–9000* ⊕ *www.12apostleshotel.com* ⤴ *70 rooms* ▯◉▯ *Free Breakfast.*

Beach Escapes

Looking for a little R & R after your safari? South Africa's coast provides many opportunities for sun, sand, and smiles. If you're flying in or out of Cape Town, the stunning white sand beaches of the Cape Peninsula are about a 30-minute drive (with no traffic) south of the Mother City. Some of our favorites on the False Bay side (east coast) are Muizenberg, Fish Hoek, Boulders (where you can see penguins), St James, Dalebrook (in Kalk Bay), and Miller's Point. And on the Atlantic side (west coast): Camps Bay, Maiden's Cove (also in Camps Bay), Soetwater (in Kommetjie), and Buffels Bay (in Cape Point nature reserve).

Chapter 6

RWANDA

Updated by
Charlotte Beauvoisin

WELCOME TO RWANDA

TOP REASONS TO GO

★ **Gorilla Trekking:** Navigate your way through emerald foliage, bamboo forests, and gauzelike mists to behold the world's largest living primates on their own turf.

★ **Volcanoes National Park:** Gorilla trekking, stunning views, and rewarding hikes through active volcanoes, lakes, and grasslands.

★ **Kigali:** Arguably East Africa's safest and most future-focused city, Rwanda's capital is a patchwork of palm tree-lined boulevards, artisan coffee shops, international restaurants, and a downtown dotted with new buildings.

★ **Nyungwe Forest National Forest:** Visitors can take a canopy walk, go primate trekking, hike waterfalls, or visit a tea field in this mountainous rainforest.

★ **Akagera National Park:** Night game drives and boat rides in Rwanda's safari park give easy access to diverse wildlife encounters like the Big Five, while the park's diverse landscapes are home to more than 490 bird species.

At 26,338 square km (10,169 square miles), Rwanda encompasses 5 volcanoes, 23 lakes, and a spectacular assortment of wildlife. Biological diversity is concentrated in four national parks:

1 Volcanoes National Park. This slice of the Virunga Mountains may be synonymous with trekking the endangered mountain gorillas and the pioneering work of Dian Fossey, but it also has active volcanoes, stunning lakes, and grasslands worth hiking.

2 Akagera National Park. Just over two hours east of Kigali, the country's capital, Rwanda's safari park is set in the spectacular northern plains. Here you'll find the Big Five.

3 Nyungwe Forest National Park. In Rwanda's southwest, Nyungwe has Africa's largest mountain rain forest that's home to roving families of chimpanzees, habituated colobus monkeys, and hundreds of colorful bird species.

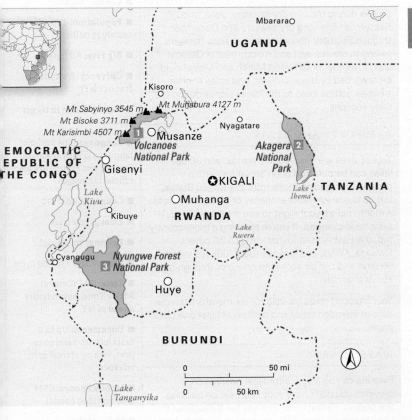

COUNTRY SNAPSHOT

WHEN TO GO

Gorilla trekking occurs year-round, but the optimal time is during the two dry seasons: June through September (the long dry season) and December through February (the short dry season). Travelers willing to brave a wet and muddy hike in October and November or between March and May should be rewarded by fewer crowds, and often shorter treks as gorillas keep to the lower slopes during the rainy seasons.

PASSPORTS AND VISAS

Tourist visas are required in Rwanda, and 30-day visas can be obtained upon arrival for certain passports, including those from the United States, but do check with your embassy or consulate at least a month before your flight to see if rules and regulations have changed. If you're planning a multi-country trip, the East African Tourist Visa (EATV) covers Rwanda, Kenya, and Uganda (US $100). It's valid for 90 days and can be accessed online or through the above channels.

Your passport must be valid for six months from the date of intended travel and contain at least one blank page.

WAYS TO SAVE

Rwanda can be a very affordable destination, provided you don't have your heart set on tracking the gorillas. Permits cost one set fee throughout the year. However, there is far more to the country than just gorillas and, if you want to experience traditional Rwandan culture, enjoy hiking, cycling or birdwatching, the country is an excellent destination to explore. Public transport is very affordable and comparatively safe by African standards. Rwanda has many campsites and homestays, which are arguably more authentic than the glamorous international lodge brands.

AT A GLANCE

- **Capital:** Kigali
- **Population:** approximately 13 million
- **Big Five:** All here
- **Currency:** Rwandan franc (RWF)
- **Money:** ATMs in bigger towns.
- **Language:** The national language is Kinyarwanda. English and French are also official languages.
- **Country Code:** 250
- **Emergencies:** 112
- **Driving:** on the right
- **Electricity:** 230v/50 cycle
- **Time:** CAT (Central Africa Time), seven hours ahead of NY
- **Documents:** Up to 6 months with valid passport, visa on arrival or in advance
- **Mobile Phones:** GSM (900 and 1800 bands)
- **Major Mobile Companies:** MTN, Airtel, Rwandatel, Tigo
- **Rwanda Development Board:** ⊕ www.visitrwanda.com

Rwanda has made massive strides in security and national development in the two decades since the infamous 1994 genocide and is now internationally recognized as one of the safest countries in Africa. A sense of order prevails: violent crime is nearly nonexistent, and police can be spotted at most major intersections. Citizens are required to participate in *umuganda*, a monthly day of community service, and you'll rarely see litter on the streets; plastic bags are banned in Rwanda. You'll find new businesses, homes, and roadways under construction in every corner of the country.

It's worth noting that Rwanda offers more than just gorillas: the primeval forests of Nyungwe Forest National Park are inhabited by more than 75 different mammals, including hundreds of chimpanzees and over 320 bird species. Akagera National Park offers a Big Five savanna safari experience without the usual khaki-clad crowds.

MAJOR REGIONS

You probably won't be able to see all of Rwanda in one trip, so we've broken it down into **Must-See Parks** (Volcanoes National Park, Akagera National Park, and Nyunwe National Forest) and **If You Have Time** areas (Rubavu [Gisenyi] and Lake Kivu, and Gishwati-Mukura National Park) to help you better organize your time. We

suggest, though, that you read about all of them and then choose for yourself. There is also a section on **Gateway Cities,** which for Rwanda is Kilgali.

Planning

Outside the National Parks, travelers may occasionally be confused about Rwandan town names, due to the renaming of some of the country's bigger towns. In some cases, the new name has been adopted; in others, the original name remains more popular.

In this guidebook, where a town has more than one name it is written with the new name (followed by the old name in parentheses).

Getting Here and Around

AIR

Kigali International Airport, sometimes referred to as Kanombe International Airport, is approximately 10 km (6 miles) or a 20-minute drive from central Kigali. It serves as the primary gateway for Rwanda's gorilla safaris. National carrier RwandAir is the only airline that flies direct from the US to Rwanda. Many carriers offer one-stop options: Brussels Airlines and Ethiopian Airlines both depart from Washington, D.C., with a stopover in Brussels and Addis Ababa respectively. Lufthansa flies from Chicago to Kigali via Brussels. Other airlines that serve Kigali include Air France, flydubai, Kenya Airways, KLM, Qatar Airways, and Turkish Airlines. RwandAir operates daily flights to Kamembe International Airport at the southern tip of Lake Kivu and is ideal for visitors tracking chimps in Nyungwe Forest. Akagera Aviation offers chartered plane and helicopter flights. Many high-end lodges have helipads.

TAXI

Uniformed taxi drivers are in abundance around the airport and will zip you downtown for a negotiable fee of around RWF 20,000 (US$20). Pricier hotels like the Kigali Serena Hotel draw higher fare quotes.

AIRPORT Kigali International Airport. (*KGL*) ⊠ *KN5 Rd., Kanombe, Kanombe* ⊕ *www.rac.co.rw.*

Communications

Rwanda is one of Africa's top three countries in terms of internet connectivity. The extensive fiber optic network provides high speed 4G LTE broadband at most restaurants, cafés, and hotels in Kigali and major towns. Networks can be less reliable outside those areas. If you think you will need consistent internet or phone access, bring an unlocked cell phone and buy a local SIM card upon arrival. MTN and Airtel are Rwanda's most reliable providers.

Health and Safety

Visitors to Rwanda are required to present proof of yellow fever vaccination upon arrival at Kigali Airport. Hepatitis A and B vaccinations are recommended. Adventurous eaters and travelers to rural areas should also consider the typhoid vaccine. The biggest health risk is malaria, so consult with your doctor on antimalarial tablet options. At the very least, sleep under a mosquito net at night and wear insect repellent during the day. That said, if you're tracking gorillas, you're unlikely to encounter mosquitoes at altitude. Avoid tap water and opt for filtered or bottled instead. Petty theft and muggings do occur, so don't wander around alone at night, particularly in urban areas.

Hotels and Lodges

The quality of hotels and lodges in Rwanda has improved by leaps and bounds over the past several years. Expect good food; excellent, personalized service; and a few special touches—like a hot water bottle under your sheets—from Rwanda's best. Bring travel necessities, such as toothbrushes and shampoo, but don't be surprised if those items are already awaiting your arrival. Most lodge bedrooms will have mosquito nets, although some properties seal the rooms well enough to do without.

Money Matters

Rwanda's official currency is the Rwandan franc (RWF). At the time of writing, the exchange rate is approximately RWF 1020 to US$1. Larger hotels

Nyungwe Forest National Park's canopy walkway hangs 70 meters (230 feet) above the forest floor providing stunning views of the park.

and tour companies may accept U.S. dollars and credit cards (Visa is more popular than Mastercard) but do check in advance. Expect to pay in francs at local shops and restaurants. You can withdraw local currency at ATMs in Kigali or large towns, or exchange U.S. dollars at the airport, local banks, and forex bureaus. (Banks and forex are closed on Sundays and public holidays). US$50 and US$100 bills will fetch better exchange rates, as will newer notes. Bills printed before 2009 may not be accepted. After cash, mobile money is the most common payment option in Rwanda. To open a mobile money account you will need to show your passport and buy a local SIM card. Western Union is common.

Restaurants

Rwanda's culinary scene is on the rise and local and international restaurants can be found across Kigali. In addition to international offerings, try some of Rwanda's traditional dishes; *brochettes* (grilled meat or fish on a stick), *akabenz* (roasted and marinated pork), and *misuzu* (fried sweet plantains) are delicious and available throughout the country. Tipping is discretionary, though if service is exemplary feel free to leave a few small notes.

■ TIP→ **Restaurant and hotel reviews have been shortened. For full information, visit Fodors.com.**

What It Costs in U.S. Dollars			
$	$$	$$$	$$$$
RESTAURANTS			
under $12	$12–$20	$21–$30	over $30
HOTELS			
under $250	$250–$450	$451–$600	over $600

Tours

Gorilla Highlands

ADVENTURE TOURS | For two decades, Gorilla Highlands has not only promoted but helped develop authentic community tourism experiences and innovative itineraries for all budgets in the mountain gorillas' home range of Rwanda, south-western Uganda, and DR Congo. ⊠ *Cobblestone Rd., Kinigi* ☎ *783/118–421* ⊕ *www.gorillahighlands.com.*

Thousand Hills Expeditions

ADVENTURE TOURS | Named after Rwanda's *milles collines* (thousand hills), this well-established, Rwandan-owned safari operator offers personalized travel in both Rwanda and Uganda, for private and small group safaris. ⊠ *10 KN 46, Kiyovu* ☎ *252/521–000* ⊕ *www.thousandhillsafrica.com.*

Visitor Information

The Rwanda Development Board (RDB) is the government body responsible for overseeing conservation and tourism activities, in partnership with stakeholders such as African Parks.

VisitRwanda.com is Rwanda's official tourism site and provides a helpful overview of destinations and activities, but don't expect a timely response to personal inquiries.

For more candid reviews, your best bet is Living in Kigali, a blog that has restaurant reviews and tips for traveling outside the city. Another useful blog is Diary of a Muzungu, which promotes adventure and conservation in Rwanda and East Africa.

CONTACTS Living in Kigali. ⊕ *www.livinginkigali.com.* **Rwanda Development Board.** ⊠ *KG 220 St, Gishushu* ⊕ *www.visitrwanda.com.* **Diary of a Muzungu.** ⊕ *www.diaryofamuzungu.com.*

Park Ratings

Game: ★★★★★

Park Accessibility: ★★★☆☆

Getting Around: ★★★☆☆

Accommodations: ★★★★★

Scenic Beauty: ★★★★★

Volcanoes National Park

Imagine slashing your way through the undergrowth, sidling around bamboo forests, and peering through eucalyptus leaves to catch a glimpse of the massive and majestic silverback mountain gorilla. He makes eye contact, grunts, then proceeds to pick his nose. Two teenage gorillas, drunk off bamboo sap, roll past in a wrestling match, brushing your leg as they go by. A mother gorilla carts her two-week-old baby around piggyback and throws a cautious glance your way. Visitors describe the hour-long encounter with gorillas in Volcanoes National Park as surreal. Set against the backdrop of the Virunga Mountains, each peak topped by saucer-shape clouds, a visit with mankind's not-so-distant relatives certainly seems to defy reality.

Volcanoes National Park is one of only four places on earth where visitors can commune with the endangered mountain gorillas. The park encompasses a 160-square-km (62-square-mile) slice of the Virunga Mountains, including a string of nine volcanoes that extends into neighboring Uganda and the Democratic Republic of the Congo. The ecologically rich Virunga region is home to more than half of the world's mountain gorillas. In December 2019, it was announced that the world's mountain gorilla population had reached 1,000 individuals for the first time in three decades.

Read and Watch

Dian Fossey's *Gorillas in the Mist* is her personal account of living with gorillas for 13 years. The story was adapted into a film starring Sigourney Weaver in 1988.

Land of a Thousand Hills, My Life in Rwanda is a powerful memoir by American Rosamund Halsey Carr, who moved to Rwanda in the mid-1950s with her then-husband.

Baking Cakes in Kigali by Gaile Parkin is a charming and compassionate novel that gives insights into Rwandan society.

A Sunday at the Pool in Kigali is Gil Courtemanche's debut novel, which centers around a love story set to the tumultuous backdrop of the genocide.

African Bird Club's free identification app, *Birds of Africa*, is available on iOS and Android.

SEE AFRICA BREATHE AFRICA is a weekly podcast set in the Gorilla Highlands. It's hosted by Afro-fusion musician Joe Kahiri and travel consultant and cultural tourism expert Miha Logar.

In 1925 Volcanoes became the first national park in Rwanda. Tourism activities were suspended during the Rwanda Civil War (1990–1994) but resumed in 1999. Now travelers can visit one of 12 habituated gorilla groups by purchasing a permit for US$1,500. A maximum of eight tracking permits are issued per group daily.

Gorillas may be the headline act, but there's plenty more to see and do in the park. Hiking enthusiasts can navigate a network of trails through the Virunga Mountains, including summiting the 3,711-meter (12,175-foot) Mount Bisoke, with its crater lake and rewarding cross-border views of the Democratic Republic of the Congo. History and mammal buffs can visit the grave and research center of prominent primatologist Dian Fossey, whose life and work inspired the movie *Gorillas in the Mist*.

A visit with the park's population of golden monkeys is worth the US$100 permit. These hyper, cherub-cheeked primates swing through the bamboo, occasionally swooping down to the forest floor for a bamboo shoot or two. Volcanoes is also home to forest elephants, buffalo, spotted hyenas, and 200 bird species.

WHEN TO GO

The best time for gorilla trekking is during Rwanda's two dry seasons: from December to early February and from June to September. The drier months make for a more pleasant (and less muddy) hike. The temperate climate can be fickle regardless of when you go, so pack a jacket for cool evenings and a rain jacket.

GETTING HERE AND AROUND

Tour operators can provide transport for the two-hour trip from Kigali to Musanze, the country's bustling gorilla tourism hub. Independent travelers can catch a public bus from Kigali's Nyabugogo bus station to Musanze for less than US$5. Most visitors choose to stay close to the gorilla trekking starting point one night before and one night after their great ape escapade.

All trekkers must arrive at the park's headquarters in the nearby village of Kinigi at 7 am, where they're assigned to a gorilla group. Transportation for the trek is required. Tour operators will generally provide a vehicle, or trekkers can rent a 4x4 and driver in Musanze from US$80.

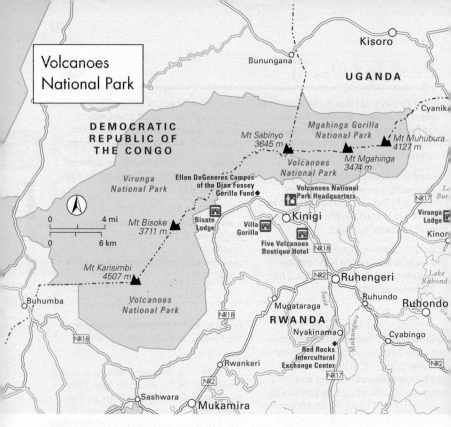

Volcanoes National Park

Kisoro

Bunungana

UGANDA

Cyanik

DEMOCRATIC
REPUBLIC OF
THE CONGO

Mgahinga Gorilla
National Park

Mt Sabinyo
3645 m

Mt Muhubura
4127 m

Volcanoes
National Park

Mt Mgahinga
3474 m

Virunga
National Park

Ellen DeGeneres Campus
of the Dian Fossey
Gorilla Fund

Volcanoes National
Park Headquarters

NR17

Kinigi

Virunga
Lodge

Bisate
Lodge

Villa
Gorilla

Mt Bisoke
3711 m

Five Volcanoes
Boutique Hotel

Kinon

NR18

NR2

Mt Karisimbi
4507 m

Ruhengeri

Lake
Ruhond

Ruhundo

Ruhondo

Buhumba

Volcanoes
National Park

Mugataraga

NR18

RWANDA

Nyakinama

Cyabingo

NR18

Red Rocks
Intercultural
Exchange Center

NR2

Rwankeri

NR17

NR2

Sashwara

Mukamira

👁 Sights

Ellen DeGeneres Campus of the Dian Fossey Gorilla Fund

COLLEGE | FAMILY | The 12-acre Ellen Campus opened in 2022 providing the Dian Fossey Gorilla Fund with a permanent learning and research facility. And while the campus is home to the Sandy and Harold Price Research Center, there are opportunities for the public to learn and explore making this an ideal pre- or post-gorilla tracking activity for young and old. Visitors can see the grounds via the Cleveland Metroparks Zoo Interpretive Trails, which features more than 250,000 native plants, and the Cindy Broder Conservation Gallery which contains an artifact-filled replica of Fossey's mountain cabin as well as a 360-degree immersive theater; allow 1½ hours for the self-guided tour of the exhibit. There's also the Gorilla Café if you need a snack and the gift shop sells unique gorilla nose prints among other things. ☒ *Kinigi ✛ 4.3 km (2.6 miles) north of Kinigi and 3.9 km (2.4 miles) northwest of the Volcanoes National Park Headquarters in Ruhengeri* ⊕ *gorillafund.org/ellencampus/* ☒ *a donation of US$20 is encouraged.*

Red Rocks Intercultural Exchange Center

OTHER ATTRACTION | FAMILY | A 7-km (4-mile) trip from gorilla-tourism hub Musanze, this cultural exchange center offers an eclectic mix of diversions for the post-primate safari crowd and independent travelers alike. Get your cultural fix via an extensive itinerary of activities that includes classes in weaving traditional baskets, dance and drumming, painting with a local artist, brewing banana beer, or cooking local cuisine. Red Rocks can also arrange cultural heritage and wooden-bike tours, or a homestay with a local family. The extensive grounds include a boma fire pit, a gift shop run by a local women's cooperative, a bar, an outdoor dance pavilion, and several campsites. Fifty percent of revenues from Red Rocks' activities are channeled to the communities. The annual Red Rocks Cultural Festival celebrates culture and conservation throughout the week leading up to the Kwita Izina gorilla naming ceremony, which takes place in the first week of September. ✉ *Nyakinama St., Musanze, Nyakinama* ⊕ *19.4 km (12 miles) south of the Volcanoes National Park Headquarters in Ruhengeri* ☎ *789/254–315* 🌐 *www.redrocksrwanda.com* ☞ *Bookings must be made at least 48 hours in advance to ensure availability.*

Hotels

★ Bisate Lodge

$$$$ | HOTEL | Located in the foothills of Mt. Bisoke, this unique eco-lodge combines high-end Rwandan-inspired interiors with sensational views and high environmental credentials. **Pros:** warm and attentive staff; breathtaking views from every large, well-designed suite; excellent food made primarily with local ingredients. **Cons:** road to lodge is only passable in 4x4; 40-minute drive to gorilla trekking; lodge access for elderly and disabled guests is limited. [$] *Rooms from: US$2,200* ✉ *Kinigi* ☎ *27/11–807–1800* 🌐 *www.wilderness-safaris.com/camps/bisate-lodge* 🛏 *6 suites* 🍴 *All-Inclusive.*

Five Volcanoes Boutique Hotel

$$$$ | B&B/INN | FAMILY | This Rwandan-owned boutique hotel is conveniently located on the main tarmac road that leads to the starting point for gorilla tracking. **Pros:** accessible for disabled guests; post-gorilla tracking shoe cleaning service; convenient location. **Cons:** Volcano Manor costs a lip-smacking US$5,500 per night. [$] *Rooms from: US$640* ✉ *Musanze-Kinigi Rd., Kinigi* ☎ *789/924–969* 🌐 *www.fivevolcanoesrwanda.com* 🛏 *14 rooms* 🍴 *All-Inclusive.*

Villa Gorilla

$ | B&B/INN | This Rwandan-owned boutique hotel is a top pick for ape trekkers looking for local flavor without scrimping on comfort. **Pros:** meals included with room; five-minute drive to park headquarters; expert culinary team from New York City. **Cons:** drinks cost extra; noise from the lobby filters into the rooms. [$] *Rooms from: US$212* ✉ *Kinigi* ☎ *646/339–3663 in the US, 788/592–924* 🌐 *www.villagorillarwanda.com* 🛏 *4 rooms, 3 cottages* 🍴 *Free Breakfast.*

Virunga Lodge

$$$$ | HOTEL | FAMILY | Perched on a 2,300-meter (7,500-foot) ridge between Lake Ruhondo and Lake Bulera, this majestic lodge defines Rwandese Afro-chic with breathtaking 360-degree views and your very own personal butler. **Pros:** massive bathrooms with lake-and-mountain views; all-inclusive communal dining table; actively supports community through non-profit Volcanoes Safaris Partnership Trust. **Cons:** 45-minute drive to gorilla trekking; you will wish you had booked an extra night; a few minutes' walk to each room. [$] *Rooms from: US$1,730* ✉ *Mwiko Village* ☎ *788/302–069* 🌐 *www.volcanoessafaris.com* 🛏 *10 rooms* 🍴 *All-Inclusive.*

Akagera National Park

This 1,122-square-km (433-square-mile) park along Rwanda's northeastern border with Tanzania is the safari scene's best-kept secret. You can experience prime safari lands without the Land Rover wagon circles that surround wildlife in Kenya and Tanzania. The borders encompass a labyrinth of lakes and papyrus swamps that are alive with hippos and crocodiles, plus savannas dotted by giraffes, zebras, elephants, and nearly a dozen varieties of antelope. 482 bird

species have been recorded in Akagera, including the rare Shoebill.

Established in 1934, Akagera has weathered a tumultuous history. The park lost half its territory and all of its lions in the wake of the 1994 genocide. Since 2010, however, the country's only protected savanna has experienced a dramatic rebirth thanks to the Rwandan government's partnership with nonprofit African Parks. Animals that had become extinct in Akagera have since been reintroduced to the park: lions are breeding successfully and rhinos are thriving. Akagera National Park is once again home to Africa's Big Five. Park facilities include a thatch-roof reception center, gift shop, and café. Accommodation—in and outside the park's electric-fenced boundary—includes a luxury tented lodge, camping facilities, night game drives, boat cruises, and sports fishing trips on Lake Shakani. African Parks' intervention has raised the bar high: unusual tourism activities include a behind-the-scenes tour of park headquarters and 'Walk the Line', a short inspection of the park's perimeter fence accompanied by community guides.

GETTING HERE AND AROUND

Akagera is 2½ hour drive from Kigali.

The park must be entered at Kiyonza Gate in the south. It takes approximately six hours to drive through the park to Nyungwe Gate in the north, so plan for a long day trip from Kigali.

Visitors who come for gorilla tracking usually opt to hire a driver guide; expect to pay around US$200 a day for the vehicle, guide, and fuel. Park entrance fees are a rather pricey US$100 per day but it does ensure that visitor numbers remain low. Guides can be hired for US$40 a day.

Park Ratings

Game: ★★★★☆

Park Accessibility: ★★★★★

Getting Around: ★★★★☆

Accommodations: ★★★★★

Scenic Beauty: ★★★★★

Hotels

★ **Ruzizi Tented Lodge**

$$ | **HOTEL** | Akagera visitors flock to this solar-powered, tented lodge on the shores of Lake Ihema to commune with nature without foregoing warm showers, three-course meals, and a fully stocked bar. **Pros:** all lodge profits go to conservation activities in the park; beautiful communal deck with lakeside views; excellent showers. **Cons:** hippos and crocs prohibit lake swimming; wildlife may keep you up at night; Wi-Fi may distract from fantastic location. [$] *Rooms from: US$470* ✉ *Akagera National Park* ☎ *787/113300* 🌐 *www.ruzizilodge.com* 🛏 *9 tents* 🍴 *All-Inclusive.*

Nyungwe Forest National Park

Nyungwe Forest National Park may be most famous for chimpanzee trekking, but this stretch of 1,020 square km (394 square miles) in southwestern Rwanda teems with a dazzling array of flora and fauna and an impressive spread of hiking trails. Meander through and you'll feel as though you've wandered onto the set of *Jurassic Park*. You'll spot 100-year-old trees, fern-fringed waterfalls, and oversize driver ants to the accompaniment of a cacophony of bird calls.

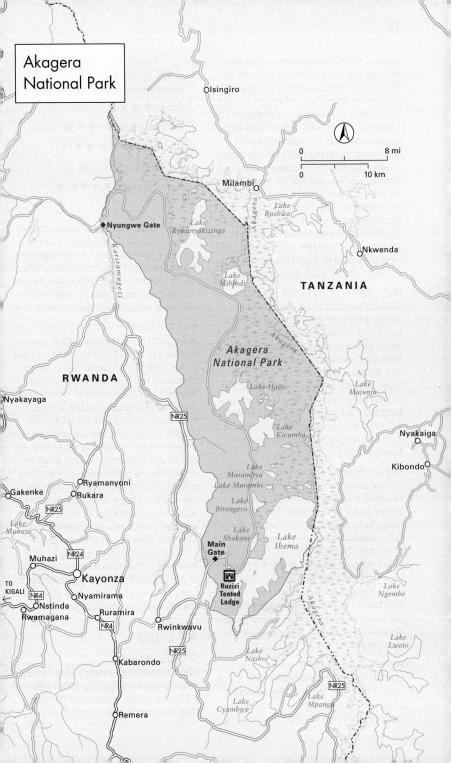

Nestled in the Albertine Rift, a biodiversity-rich area of East Africa, Nyungwe is home to 322 bird species, more than 75 mammal species, 140 orchids, and some 1,000 types of plants. It was recognized as a national park in 2005 and remains Africa's largest protected mountain rain forest. Trails cut through the park's closed-canopy forests, bamboo thickets, and orchid-filled swamps. Be warned that the weather can be wet—it is a rain forest after all—receiving more than 2,000 mm (79 inches) of precipitation annually. In 2006, an exploration team claimed to find the farthest source of the River Nile in Nyungwe—the rains contribute to two of the world's largest rivers: the Nile and the Congo.

Most visitors come to trek the park's 500-some-odd chimpanzees or its "supergroup" of several hundred black-and-white colobus monkeys, whose clever antics and aerial acrobatics will keep your camera clicking. But chimps and giant troupes aren't the only show in town. With 13 species, the park has one of the highest primate diversity concentrations in the world. You'll see L'Hoest's monkeys frolicking around the roads, and if you're really lucky, the reclusive owl-faced monkey.

Primate trekking can be costly (a chimpanzee permit is US$90 for international tourists), but visitors can also opt for guided hikes from US$40. The 15 trails range from the 2 km (1.2 mile) Karamba Trail (excellent for birders), the Source of the Nile Trail at Gisovu (said to be the river's farthest source), and the rigorous Mount Bigugu Trail that leads to the park's highest point. Hardy trekkers can also take in an impressive waterfall on the four-hour Isumo Trail or spend three days camping along the Congo Nile Trail (see Lake Kivu).

WHEN TO GO

Late June through early September is dry season and high season at Nyungwe for good reason: the rain forest receives a reprieve from daily downpours, meaning

Park Ratings

Game: ★ ★ ★ ☆ ☆

Park Accessibility: ★ ★ ★ ☆ ☆

Getting Around: ★ ★ ★ ☆ ☆

Accommodations: ★ ★ ☆ ☆ ☆

Scenic Beauty: ★ ★ ★ ★ ★

you can explore all day. But even during the wet season, from March to May, showers generally arrive in the afternoon, leaving plenty of time for morning hiking and an outdoor lunch. If you want the forest, and the best guides, to yourself, the wet season could be a good time to visit.

GETTING HERE AND AROUND

Nyungwe Forest National Park is approximately 225 km (140 miles), or four to five hours driving, from Kigali. Many visitors choose to hire a car and driver. Budget travelers can choose one of several bus lines from Kigali's central bus station, Nyabugogo, to the park for RWF6,000 (US$6), though quarters are cramped, and drivers can be reckless. Alternatively, you can fly into Kamembe Airport, a half-hour drive from the park's western edge, and arrange for pickup with your lodge. For transport inside the park, your best bet is to hire a car from Kigali or ask for recommended drivers at your accommodation. Most activities depart from the park's Uwinka Reception Center. To get there from nearby Gisakura village, the location of our lodging suggestions, you'll need to use a private car or public bus. Note that chimpanzee trekking requires a 4x4.

◉ Sights

★ Canopy Walkway

OTHER ATTRACTION | FAMILY | East Africa's only Canopy Walkway is a 160-meter (525-foot) bridge suspended 70 meters (230 feet) above the ground. The "hanging trail" affords magnificent views of the treetop canopy and up-close bird encounters. Nyungwe is a little-known birders' paradise, though spotting them typically requires the eyes (and ears) of a trained guide, who can be secured at one of the park's reception centers. The Canopy Walkway trail is a round-trip of approximately two hours on sometimes steep paths. **TIP→ Rain is a frequent occurrence in Nyungwe so a raincoat is essential. Visitors should bring their own raincoats and boots (or comfortable shoes). Walking sticks can be provided on-site.** ☎ *788/625–359* 🌐 *www.africanparks.org/the-parks/nyungwe* 🎫 *US$60.*

Hotels

Nyungwe Top View Hill Hotel
$$ | **HOTEL** | **FAMILY** | Stunning views of mist-veiled mountains, excellent service, and convenient access to Nyungwe Forest National Park, all for US$220, make this hilltop hotel a best-value option. **Pros:** spacious cottages; helpful staff; stunning forest views from every room. **Cons:** rooms show some wear; entrance road is steep and rocky; hotel can be drafty. [$] *Rooms from: US$220* ✉ *Gisakura* ☎ *787/109–335* 🌐 *www.nyungwehotel.com* 🛏 *12 cottages* 🍴 *Free Breakfast.*

★ **One&Only Nyungwe House**
$$$$ | **HOTEL** | You'll forget you're next to a rain forest in this lavish retreat—until you slide back the glass balcony doors to let in forest breezes and birdsong. **Pros:** rooms are practically suites with private balconies; close proximity to the park; good Wi-Fi. **Cons:** no restaurants nearby; short and expensive wine list; eye-wateringly expensive. [$] *Rooms from: US$2,900* ✉ *Gisakura* ☎ *221/011–111* 🌐 *www.oneandonlyresorts.com/nyungwe-house* 🛏 *24 rooms* 🍴 *All-Inclusive.*

If You Have Time

Rubavu (Gisenyi) and Lake Kivu

To the east of Rwanda lies Lake Kivu, a freshwater lake shared with the Democratic Republic of the Congo. Rwanda's largest lake is approximately 90 km (56 miles) long and 50 km (31 miles) at its widest part. It's bordered by tea and coffee plantations and tropical montane forests. Unlike other African Great Lakes, Lake Kivu is free of dangerous wildlife and the bilharzia parasite that frequents many tropical lakes. Swimming and boating are among a growing range of leisure activities.

Rwanda's position in Africa's interior does not prevent it from having sandy beaches and Rubavu is a lively weekend destination for Kigali residents (and even more popular for the Congolese workers who cross into the town from nearby Goma for their working day). This constant flow of traffic gives a cosmopolitan feel to this otherwise small town. Occasionally, distant night skies glow red with the lava from Nyiragongo volcano. (The most active volcano in the Virunga chain last erupted in 2021). Hot springs, Congolese music, and a public beach make Rubavu an appealing base.

Lake Kivu also provides a diverting nocturnal excursion, courtesy of the groups of fishermen who sing traditional songs as they row out from the town of Kibuye at sunset to light their oil lanterns and fish for *sambaza* (sardines). Fishermen sing in the little-used language of Amashi as they wait patiently for fish to be attracted to the lights.

GETTING HERE AND AROUND

The resort town of Rubavu is an hour's drive from Musanze and a short hop from the Congolese town of Goma. Lakeside

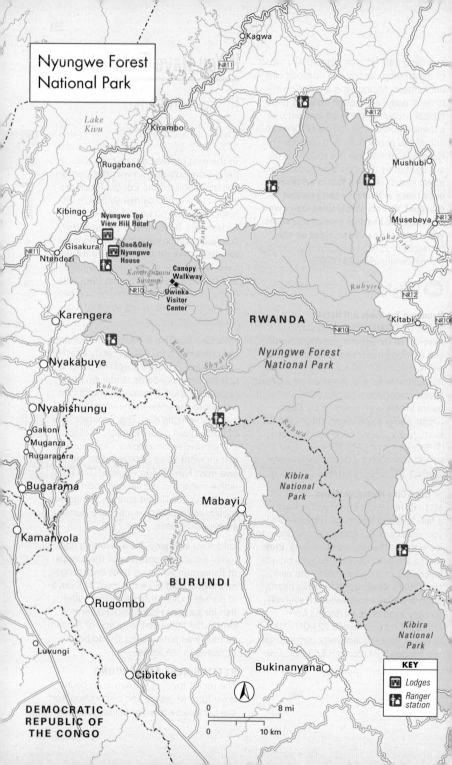

towns include Rusizi (Cyangugu) to the south and Karongi, best known for its island archipelago that can be explored by dugout canoe or kayak. Kibuye is worth visiting if only for the singing fishermen.

Sights

Congo Nile Trail

TRAIL | Rubavu (Gisenyi) is the most common starting point for the 227-km (141-mile) Congo Nile Trail. This clearly marked route skirts the shores of Lake Kivu and the edge of Nyungwe Forest National Park and leads travelers through verdant tea plantations and traditional villages. The full trail takes cyclists 5 days; however, visitors can also walk, boat, or drive the trail, or smaller sections of it. Demarcated overnight stops tend to be simple but accommodation upgrades are available at several (not all) locations. Hiring an experienced guide can boost your experience immeasurably. Not only will they help with logistics, but they can also point you to the trail's must-visit (yet barely documented) community tourism experiences. ✉ *Rubavu* 🌐 *www.gorilla-highlands.com/congo-nile-trail.*

Hotels

★ **Lake Kivu Serena Hotel**

$$ | **HOTEL** | The bird-filled beachfront gardens and suites of this "tropically inspired" four-star hotel have arguably the best views of Lake Kivu. **Pros:** spotless swimming pool overlooks private beach; complimentary weekend entertainment; Rubavu's only beach hotel. **Cons:** a slight detour from customary tourist route; golf course is outside hotel grounds; occasional music from nearby bars. $ *Rooms from: US$325* ✉ *Ave de la Cooperation, Rubavu, Gisenyi* ☎ *252/541–100* 🌐 *www.serenahotels.com/lake-kivu* 🛏 *66 rooms* 🍴 *Free Breakfast.*

Gishwati-Mukura National Park

Opened to the public in 2020, Rwanda's newest protected area brings together Gishwati Forest and the smaller Mukura Forest into one UNESCO Biosphere Reserve. It is part of the Albertine Rift and Congo-Nile Divide, the mountain ridge which separates the Nile and Congo river basins.

Gishwati, Mukura, and Nyungwe Forests once formed a continuous forest (that extended into Burundi as Kibira Forest). Although no longer joined physically, their fate is linked: in time it's hoped that protected land on either side of the Sebeya and Satinsyi rivers will restore the ecological connectivity between the Gishwati and Mukura montane forest fragments.

Once Rwanda's largest indigenous forests, Gishwati and Mukura now cover just 34 km (21 miles) due to resettlement of refugees post-genocide, cattle ranching, and charcoal-making. However, a far-sighted program to restore the landscape has created a visible impact; the creation of alternative economic activities is engendering a renewed appreciation for conservation. The astonishing recovery of Akagera National Park shows that Rwanda's political will—and well-tuned partnerships—can turn almost any degraded environment around, and quickly.

The park's elevation ranges from 2,000–3,000 meters above sea level, the mean annual rainfall is between 1,500–1,600 millimeters and average temperatures range between 20–24°C. This tropical climate nurtures rich biodiversity: 200 species of trees and shrubs, including bamboos and hardwoods; many threatened or endangered species such as Eastern Chimpanzee (their only other Rwandan habitat is Nyungwe), Golden

Monkey, and Mountain (or L'Hoest's) Monkey. Gishwati Forest alone has 232 bird species including Albertine Rift endemics Ruwenzori turaco and Grauer's swamp-warbler.

A Rwandan NGO, the Forest of Hope Association, in partnership with Rwanda Development Board and South African company Wilderness Safaris are monitoring the habituation of chimps for tourism. The great apes numbered just 20 individuals in 2007; forest protection has seen their numbers rise above 30.

GETTING HERE AND AROUND
Gishwati-Mukura is in northwest Rwanda, about a 40-minute drive on good tarmac roads from Rubavu and 1½ hours from Musanze, making it an easy day trip from either location. It's also the closest national park to Kigali; the drive takes 3½ to 4 hours.

Public transport is rarely seen on this excellent (but barely used highway) but moto taxis (ie motorbikes) can be organised from either town; just make sure your driver waits for you while you're in the park as you'll wait a very long time to find passing transport.

The blue roofs of the Rwanda Development Board's state-of-the-art office overlook Pfunda tea plantations and can be easily spotted from the main road from Rubavu.

 Hotels

For now, the only place to stay in Gishwati-Mukura National Park is the Forest of Hope Guesthouse and Camp Site (⊕ *fharwanda.org*) a ten-minute drive from the park's headquarters on an excellent new road. The site has panoramic views of Gishwati Forest from its solitary hilltop location. On a clear day, you can see Karisimbi, Virunga's tallest volcano. Luxury provider Wilderness Safaris is building Gishwati Lodge.

 Activities

Guided nature hikes in search of waterfalls and chameleons, chimpanzee and monkey tracking, and bird-watching in bamboo forests are a few of the park's primary attractions. Community-based tourism is at the heart of Gishwati-Mukura's renaissance: beekeeping, the rich uses of native plants for traditional medicine, dance, basket-weaving, and a tea plantation tour are some of the myriad activities open to visitors.

Gateway City

Kigali's location in the center of Rwanda makes it the logical, and convenient, place to start or finish any Rwandan adventure. It's clean, safe, and home to some great cultural and dining options.

Kigali

Kigali is a fascinating example of a future-focused African city. Rwanda's capital has transformed itself into a model of urban development in the three decades since the genocide. Former exiles have flocked to the city, flush with education, investment dollars, and entrepreneurial ideas. Foreigners have jumped in the mix, opening sushi joints, yoga studios, bakeries, and artisan coffee shops. Co-working spaces for start-ups are thriving. Kigali may not be as exuberant as neighboring Uganda's capital, but nightlife is blossoming, and you'll find dance clubs, sports bars, and live music.

With a population of approximately 1 million people, the city is Rwanda's commercial and governmental hub. Its trash-free boulevards, smooth roads, LED streetlights, and meticulously manicured roadside verges are a closer approximation of Europe than East Africa. It's an image the country is keen to expand. The ultramodern Kigali Convention Centre and slick new hotels have ushered in a wave of international conferences and meetings, as the government's slick masterplan calls for an overhaul of the business district and more urban housing.

Even without its gleaming new buildings, the city is something to behold. The undulating skyline of red-roofed houses, terraced farm plots, and brilliant green foliage is stunning. Kigali is also safe: violent crime is rare, particularly against foreigners, and police do their job, including handing out speeding tickets. You'll rarely find yourself hassled, and negotiating traffic will be your biggest (minor) obstacle. Many expatriates say that they feel safer raising their kids in Kigali than in U.S. cities.

GETTING HERE AND AROUND

Kigali is relatively easy to navigate. Roads are clearly marked but the abundance of hills can mess with your sense of direction. The ubiquitous "motos" (motorbike taxis) are a cheap and convenient mode of transport. Their safety record is questionable but helmets (provided by the driver) are mandatory. Moto fares are best negotiated before your journey or automatically calculated if using the YEGOMOTO app. Ride-hailing apps are relatively new in Rwanda, so you may still be called for directions, which may be problematic if your driver only speaks Kinyarawanda. A moto ride from the airport to the city center costs less than US$3. By comparison, an airport transfer to town in a taxi will cost upward of RWF 20,000 (US$20). Professionally run taxis are marked and metered. Unmarked private taxis are also available, but be prepared to negotiate the fare in advance. If you plan to stay in Kigali for several days, you may want to rent a car. International rental companies charge from US$70 per day. Rwandan companies charge significantly less. The roads are generally in excellent condition but be warned that other drivers, pedestrians, and motos can make driving a stressful experience.

For more information about getting to and from Kigali by air, or traveling around the city by taxi, see the Getting Here and Around section of the chapter planner.

VISITOR INFORMATION

On the last Saturday of every month, Rwandans take part in 'Umuganda' community work in the morning so shops, restaurants, and tourist destinations don't open until mid-morning.

Sights

Kigali Genocide Memorial

HISTORY MUSEUM | Visitors should not miss this well-conceived tribute to victims of the 1994 genocide against the Tutsi, in which an estimated 1 million people were killed in just 100 days. Outside, a terraced series of mass graves entombs some 250,000 victims. Inside, an informative exhibition walks visitors through pre-colonial Rwanda, the historical lead-up to the genocide and the global community's faltering response. A display of skulls and bones alongside personal effects personifies the tragedy. The "Wasted Lives" exhibition explores mankind's capacity for cruelty with a display on genocides from around the world. The exhibition ends with large black-and-white photos of child genocide victims, ranging from 8 months to 17 years. Each picture is accompanied by a placard listing the child's favorite foods and activities and his or her final moments. There is no entrance fee, but donations are encouraged. For $15, visitors can hire a thought-provoking audio guide that allows you to process this solemn experience at your own pace. The *ubumuntu* package includes a rose which you are invited to lay at the burial site. ⊠ *KG 14 Ave., Gisozi* ☏ *784/651–051* ⊕ *www.kgm.rw* ✉ *Free.*

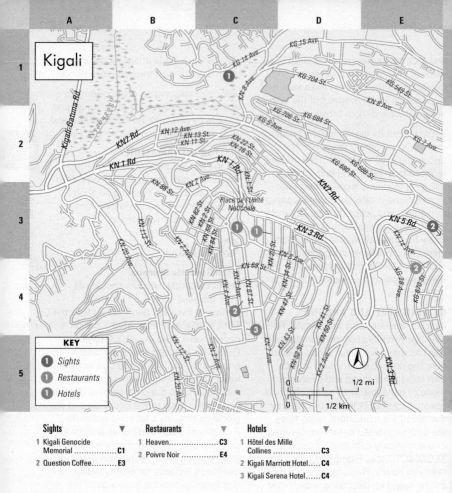

Kigali

★ **Question Coffee**

OTHER ATTRACTION | Social enterprise Question Coffee serves special blends of Rwandan coffee from their Kigali Coffee Center. Despite the fact that there's no tea or food except for the occasional pastry, you'll be lucky to find a vacant seat. Every day starting at 7 am, specialty coffee masterclasses are held. Women-led coffee farm tours run Monday through Friday. ✉ *KG8 #8, Gisozi* ☎ *781/968–027* 🌐 *www.questioncoffee.com.*

Restaurants

Heaven

$$ | **ECLECTIC** | Founded by American couple Alissa and Josh Ruxin, this oasis of gourmet cuisine is a perennial favorite among foreign residents and affluent Rwandans for weekend brunch, evening cocktails, and special-occasion dinners with an international menu that ranges from Chinese stir-fry to pumpkin risotto to goat *brochettes* (a Rwandan staple). The wooden terrace with thatched-roof and recessed lighting affords spectacular hillside views, while art from the adjoining gallery bedecks the brick walls. **Known for:** weekend brunch; terrace view. [$] *Average main: US$15* ✉ *No. 7 KN 29 St., Kiyovu* ☎ *788/486–581* 🌐 *www.heavenrwanda.com.*

★ **Poivre Noir**

$$ | **BELGIAN** | This intimate and quiet setting in Kimihurura, one of the Kigali neighborhoods most known for restaurants and nightlife, is a welcome reprieve. With a French and Belgian focus, Poivre Noir masterfully crafts some of Kigali's best meals. **Known for:** upscale cuisine; intimate setting. [$] *Average main: US$15* ✉ *2 KG 670 St., Kigali* ☎ *735/823–282* 🕒 *Closed Sun.*

Hotels

Hotel des Milles Collines

$ | **HOTEL** | Many international brands have burst onto the Kigali hotel scene in recent years, but this independent, Rwandan-owned hotel still holds its own. **Pros:** central location with great city views on tree-lined street; complimentary evening entertainment; one of Kigali's only independently owned hotels. **Cons:** noisy a/c in some rooms; renovations are protracted; rooms are small compared to those at more modern hotels. [$] *Rooms from: US$160* ✉ *2KN 6th Ave.* ☎ *788/192–000* 🌐 *www.millecollines.rw* 🍴 *Free Breakfast.*

Kigali Marriott Hotel

$$ | **HOTEL** | The Marriott quickly became a see-and-be-seen destination among locals after it opened in 2016. **Pros:** great bar and event offerings; comfortable beds and sophisticated bathrooms; a breakfast that caters for all tastes. **Cons:** majority of guests are business travelers; acoustics of dining area can make conversation difficult; food options can be overpriced. [$] *Rooms from: US$350* ✉ *Kn 3 Ave., Nyarugenge* ☎ *222/111–111 for operator, 788/315–207 for reservations* 🌐 *www.kigalimarriott.com* 🛏 *265 rooms* 🍴 *Free Breakfast.*

★ **Kigali Serena Hotel**

$$ | **HOTEL** | One of the city's only five-star hotels, the Serena draws an elite crowd with its open-air restaurants, heliconia-and-palm-fringed pool, state of the art gym and the exquisite Maisha Mind Body & Spirit Spa. Businesspeople, luxury safari-goers, and diplomats traverse the atrium's marble and carpeted floors. **Pros:** central location; wide array of amenities including ballroom and presidential suites; excellent on-site dining options. **Cons:** on-site hair salon managed by non-Serena staff; air-conditioned rooms feel cold on entering; small standard rooms. $ *Rooms from: US$400* ✉ *KN 3 Ave., Nyarugenge* ☎ *250/788–184–500* 🌐 *www.serenahotels.com* 🛏 *148 rooms* 🍴 *Free Breakfast.*

Nightlife

Pili Pili Bistro Lounge

COCKTAIL LOUNGES | Italian owner Rudy Ghirini cut his teeth on the club scene of Burundi's capital Bujumbura. Pili Pili—meaning "hot" in Kinyarwanda—attracts a cross-section of local and international clientele throughout the week to the DJ nights, live bands, and seven sports TV screens. This huge bar boasts one of Kigali's best views and a wide selection of Champagnes and sparkling wines. The restaurant serves international dishes and local fish specialties such as *njagalas* and *mukeke* from Lake Tanganyika. On Sundays, Kigali residents laze on sun loungers around the bar's open-air swimming pool and 'urban beach.' ☎ *252/601–190* 🌐 *www.instagram.com/pilipilirwanda.*

Chapter 7

UGANDA

Updated by
Charlotte Beauvoisin

WELCOME TO UGANDA

TOP REASONS TO GO

★ **Kampala:** Uganda's capital city is regionally renowned for its dancing-'til-dawn nightlife, bustling markets, and white-knuckle "boda boda" motorbike taxi rides.

★ **Gorilla Trekking:** Climb through a 25,000-year-old rainforest to encounter the world's largest living primates on their own turf. Uganda has the largest mountain gorilla population and is a cheaper option than Rwanda.

★ **Adventure Abounds:** Thrill-seekers can't get enough of Uganda's white-water rafting, kayaking, quad biking, bungee jumping, and volcano climbing.

★ **Bird-Lovers' Paradise:** The Pearl of Africa is home to more than 1,000 bird species, which is half of Africa's total bird population!

★ **Community Tourism:** Gorillas may be the draw but there's so much more to Uganda: learn about the country's 56 tribes; visit a medicinal plant garden; or sip coffee on a community cooperative coffee tour.

Uganda, Rwanda's larger northern neighbor, spans 236,040 square km (146,675 square miles), with Kenya to the east, the Democratic Republic of the Congo to the west, and South Sudan to the north. "The Pearl of Africa" has 10 national parks, more than 1,000 species of birds, and 13 types of primates, including mountain gorillas.

1 Bwindi Impenetrable National Park. Home to over half the world's endangered mountain gorillas, Bwindi's pristine rainforest and rich diversity have earned it UNESCO World Heritage Site status. The forest is resplendent with waterfalls, towering Mahoghany trees, giant ferns, and 347 species of birds, some only found in the Albertine Rift.

2 Kibale National Park. Known as "the primate capital of the world" for its chimps, assorted monkey species, bushbabies, and baboons, Kibale isn't the only place in Uganda

where you can track chimpanzees, but it's the most popular. The region's hilly terrain, glimmering green tea plantations, and dozens of pretty crater lakes make for rewarding biking and hiking. It's also a popular destination for birders, butterfly-lovers, and entomologists.

3 Queen Elizabeth National Park. Uganda's most popular park is the ideal destination for a traditional safari. A boat ride on Mweya's Kazinga Channel Mweya promises hippos cavorting alongside over 600 species of bird. The Ishasha sector to the south is a wilder destination than central Mweya and Kasenyi and is best known for its tree-climbing lions and open savannahs.

4 Murchison Falls National Park. Bisected by the Nile River, MFNP is the largest of Uganda's National Parks, offering abundant wildlife, scenic backdrops, and lots of water-based adventures.

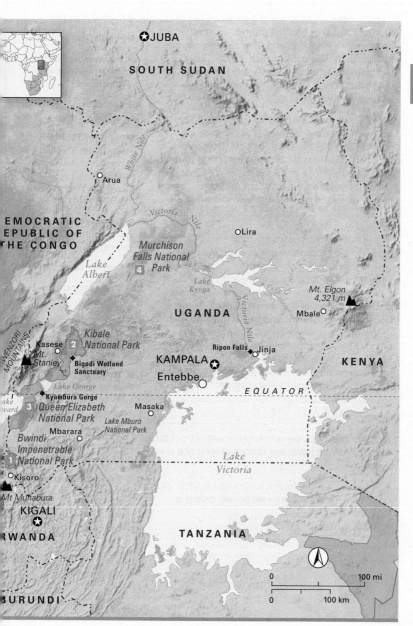

JUBA

SOUTH SUDAN

DEMOCRATIC
REPUBLIC OF
THE CONGO

Arua

White Nile

Victoria Nile

Lira

Murchison
Falls National
Park 4

Lake
Albert

Lake
Kyoga

Mt. Elgon
4,321 m

UGANDA

Mbale

Kibale
National Park 2

RWENZORI MOUNTAINS

Kasese
Mt.
Stanley

Bigodi Wetland
Sanctuary

Ripon Falls   Jinja

KAMPALA

Entebbe

EQUATOR

KENYA

Lake George

Kyambura Gorge

Queen Elizabeth 3
National Park

Masaka

Lake Mburo
National Park

Lake
Edward

Bwindi
Impenetrable 1
National Park

Mbarara

Kisoro

Mt Muhabura

KIGALI

RWANDA

Lake
Victoria

TANZANIA

BURUNDI

0   100 mi

0   100 km

COUNTRY SNAPSHOT

WAYS TO SAVE

If you're determined to see the gorillas, Uganda is probably your best bet. The permits are much cheaper than Rwanda's and Uganda has more gorilla families and lodge choices than the DR Congo (although the latter is the cheapest of the three countries to track gorillas). There are no longer any low-season discounts.

Self-drive holidays are becoming more popular as Uganda's roads (and Google Maps) improve. It's also possible to travel between National Parks by public transport. However, what you save on long-distance routes, you will lose by having to pay for "special hires" for game drives, for example. Buses do not have good safety records and few have seatbelts.

WHEN TO GO

Gorilla trekking occurs year-round, but the optimal time is during the two dry seasons: June through September (the long dry season) and December through February (the short dry season). However, do bear in mind that this is peak season (as are December and January) and permits sell out months in advance. Travelers willing to brave a wet and muddy hike in October and November or between March and May will be rewarded by fewer crowds, and sometimes shorter treks as gorillas keep to the lower slopes during the rainy seasons.

PASSPORTS AND VISAS

Your passport must be valid for six months from the date of intended travel and contain at least one blank page.

A single-entry, three-month tourist visa (US$50, plus US$5 administration fee when buying online) is required as well.

AT A GLANCE

- **Capital:** Kampala

- **Population:** 41 million

- **Big Five:** Big Five plus mountain gorillas and chimpanzees

- **Currency:** Uganda shilling (UGX)

- **Money:** ATMs in big towns (only). Visa and MasterCard accepted in some international hotels. Mobile Money is widely used with local SIM cards.

- **Language:** English; Swahili (although rarely spoken).

- **Country Code:** 256

- **Emergencies:** 999

- **Driving:** on the left

- **Electricity:** 220v/50 Hz; plugs are U.K. standard (square with three pins)

- **Time:** EAT (East African Standard Time), which is eight hours ahead of North American Eastern Standard Time.

- **Major Mobile Companies:** MTN and Airtel

- **Tourism Uganda:** ⊕ exploreuganda.com

Uganda has earned a tourism reputation as the "Pearl of Africa." The country has 10 national parks, numerous reserves, and a dazzling array of landscapes, which range from dry savannas to dense forests and snowcapped mountains. Visitors can observe lions prowling the grasslands one day and go white-water rafting down the Nile the next. Ugandans are also famously friendly, and English is widely spoken.

Uganda is still below the radar for most travelers and if you ask someone if they've heard of the country, you'll often hear grumbles about war or presidents that outstay their mandate. But a country—and its people—is far more than the excesses of its politicians, and Uganda is no different.

This stunningly beautiful country is a wonderful introduction to Africa. Visitors can pack in a multiplicity of extraordinary experiences in a two-week vacation. You may pick up a word or two in several languages, much to the hilarity of local people. You may come to hear that the 1956 classic *African Queen* was filmed on location here; you may even stay at the hotel near where Hemingway crashed his plane. Uganda has something for everyone, and no one leaves without the country making a strong impression on them.

Planning

Getting Here and Around

Most visitors arrive in Uganda via the recently upgraded Entebbe International Airport (EBB). More than a dozen international carriers serve Uganda, including: Brussels Airlines, EgyptAir, Emirates, Ethiopian Airlines, Fly Dubai, Kenya Airways, KLM, Qatar Airways, RwandAir, Turkish Airlines, and Uganda Airlines. There are no direct flights from the U.S. but Emirates and Qatar offer one-stop itineraries from Washington, D.C., to Entebbe via Dubai and Doha, respectively. National carrier Uganda Airlines relaunched in 2020 and is due to start a direct flight from London Heathrow in 2022.

Three operators offer scheduled (and charter) internal air transfers in light aircraft (ferrying max 12 passengers) around Uganda. The Entebbe-based company, Aerolink Uganda, is known for its affordable daily scheduled service plying a circuit that includes many National Parks. For a special treat, ask Aerolink about their scenic charter flights over Kampala or the Source of the Nile at Jinja. Kampala Executive Aviation (KEA) offer private charter plane and helicopter flights in a fleet of various aircraft from their private hub at Kajjansi Airfield (roughly halfway between Kampala and Entebbe). In 2022, Bar Aviation launched daily scheduled flights from Entebbe Airport to the national parks. They also operate charter planes and helicopters from their base in Kajjansi.

CONTACTS AeroLink Uganda. ✉ *Entebbe International Airport, Entebbe* ☎ *317/333–000, 776/882–205* ⊕ *www.aerolinkuganda.com.* **Kampala Executive Aviation (KEA).** ✉ *Kajjansi Airstrip, Kajjansi* ☎ *0772/712–554, 0776/333–114* ⊕ *www.flykea.com.* **Bar Aviation.** ✉ *Kajjansi Airstrip, Kajjansi* ☎ *782/399–388* ⊕ *www.baraviationug.com.*

Communications

Entebbe, Kampala, large towns, and tourist areas are covered by numerous phone networks. Google has installed an 800-km (497-mile) fiber ring around Kampala. Some Wi-Fi is 4G but networks can fluctuate especially in remote areas. Local SIM cards are cheap and international calling bundles make calling home easy. Ideally, have your mobile phone unlocked before you arrive. Phone unlocking is possible in Kampala but may delay your safari. Wi-Fi is provided free in all lodges and hotels listed in this guide, although sometimes just in communal areas.

Health and Safety

Visitors to Uganda are required to present proof of yellow fever vaccination upon arrival at the airport. Note that World Health Organization advises that vaccination is only needed once; over 65's can see healthcare professionals about getting waivers. Vaccination can also be administered at Entebbe Airport for US$40. Hepatitis A and B vaccinations are recommended (but not an entry requirement). Adventurous eaters and travelers to rural areas should also consider the typhoid vaccine. Malaria is a risk in Uganda, so consult with your doctor on antimalarial tablet options. At the very least, sleep under a mosquito net at night and wear insect repellent during the day. Drink bottled or filtered water. Petty theft and muggings do occur, so don't wander around alone at night, particularly in urban areas.

Ugandans are generally tolerant people, but most hold traditional beliefs so public displays of affection (even between a man and a woman) are frowned upon. There is a government-supported anti-homosexuality stance, so LGBTQ+ visitors should travel with caution. Ugandans' welcoming spirit means foreigners are not judged as harshly as Ugandans; however, there is a widespread fear that homosexuality is promoted by foreigners so tread carefully, however well-intentioned your conversations may be.

Hotels and Lodges

Most safari prices refer to an all-inclusive, per person, per night rate and may not include taxes or park or conservancy fees. Make sure to read the terms and conditions of your safari itinerary carefully so you know what's included and what isn't.

Upcountry lodges favored by international tourists generally have a traditional African feel to them but with the modern conveniences of hot water, power (sometimes solar), and Wi-Fi (sometimes slow by Western standards). Many lodges provide massages; some are even complimentary. Upmarket lodges provide turn-down and other housekeeping services as well as daily housekeeping service. Cuisine is international in style and generally offered on a full-board basis; at upmarket lodges, this often includes local beers and spirits.

Restaurant and hotel reviews have been shortened. For full information, visit Fodors.com.

What It Costs In U.S. Dollars			
$	$$	$$$	$$$$
HOTELS			
under $250	$250–$450	$451–$600	over $600
RESTAURANTS			
under $12	$12–$20	$21–$30	over $30

Money Matters

Uganda's shilling (UGX) has an exchange rate of UGX 3,600 to US$1, at the time of writing. Although larger hotels and tour companies may accept U.S. dollars and credit cards, check before you travel. Visa is more popular than Mastercard. Expect to pay in shillings at local shops and restaurants. You can withdraw local currency at ATMs in large towns, or exchange your U.S. dollars at the airport, "forex" foreign exchange bureaus, and local banks. After cash, mobile money is the most common payment option. To open a mobile money account you will need to show your passport and buy a local SIM card. Western Union is common. Travelers checks are no longer accepted in Uganda.

■ TIP→ **US$50 and US$100 bills will fetch better exchange rates, as will newer notes. Bills printed before 2009 may not be accepted.**

Passports and Visas

Your passport must be valid for six months from the date of intended travel and contain at least one blank page.

A single-entry, three-month tourist visa costs US$50 (plus US$5 administration fee when buying online). In theory, visa applications should be made via the Uganda Immigration online system but can also be obtained from the Uganda Embassy in Washington, D.C., or the Uganda Mission to the U.N. in New York City. You'll need to submit a completed application form, two passport-size photos, and the correct visa fee two months before travel. Although not recommended, visas can also be secured at Entebbe International Airport, where you must pay in cash. Accepted currencies are U.S. dollars, pounds sterling, and euros. The East African Tourist Visa (EATV) covers Uganda, Rwanda, and Kenya and costs US$100. It is valid for 90 days and can be accessed online or through the above channels.

Restaurants

Kampala has a thriving restaurant scene offering a diversity of cuisines, from *nyama choma* (roasted meat) and farmed game meats from South Africa, to authentic Indian (best for vegetarians), Italian, Eritrean, Japanese, and Belgian. Ugandan coffee is internationally recognized and excellent cappuccinos are widely available in bigger towns (but request anything other than full fat cow's milk and you will be disappointed). Ugandan-made artisanal chocolate is on the rise.

Ugandans are incredibly sociable every day of the week. Uganda produces excellent beers such as Nile Special and Club. If you like craft beers, look out for Banange in select locations. Triple-distilled Uganda Waragi gin is universally popular.

Ugandans are big eaters and always eat a cooked lunch, sometimes mid-afternoon; traditional African food is heavy on carbs and very light on vegetables. The traditional *luwombo* dish is (usually)

Kyaninga Lodge in Kibale National Park has a breathtaking setting overlooking a crater lake.

meat slow-steamed in smoked banana leaves. Street foods are mainly fried; a trip to Uganda is not complete without the universally popular *rolex*—think "rolled eggs" of an omelette wrapped in a chapati.

International lodges and restaurants cater well to vegetarians.

■ TIP→ If you're visiting in November, keep an eye out for fresh grasshoppers. They are considered a local delicacy.

Tipping is at your discretion in restaurants.

Tours

★ Volcanoes Safaris

ADVENTURE TOURS | For 25 years, Volcanoes Safaris has been at the forefront of developing and promoting primate tourism in Rwanda and Uganda. Their itineraries focus largely on their own four lodges, but they are highly regarded upmarket properties in stunning locations. They are committed to minimizing their environmental footprint and proactively support the community through non-profit Volcanoes Safaris Partnership Trust. They have sales offices in Uganda, Rwanda, and the United Kingdom. ✉ *1 Kololo Hill Drive, Kisementi* ☎ *7753/933–593 UK office, 772/741–720 Uganda office* ✉ *enquiries@volcanoessafaris.com* ⊕ *www.volcanoessafaris.com.*

★ Wild Frontiers

ADVENTURE TOURS | This experienced safari outfitter offers personalized and set departure safaris of Uganda from its base in Entebbe, Uganda. The company operates its own network of upmarket lodges, can set up private mobile camps, and runs an equally tight ship with its well-guided launch cruises and sport fishing operations in Murchison Falls National Park and on Lake Victoria. They also offer day trips to see Shoebill at Mabamba Swamp, Ngamba Island Chimpanzee Sanctuary, and the Uganda Wildlife Education Centre in Entebbe. ✉ *Nakiwogo Rd., Plot 76 B, Entebbe* ☎ *414/321–479, 772/502–155* ⊕ *wildfrontiers.co.ug.*

Read and Watch

• Moses Isegawa's *Abyssinian Chronicles* is a coming-of-age story set in the 1970s about a boy and his country during the reign of former dictator Idi Amin.

• *The Queen of Katwe* by Tim Crothers is a true story about a 10-year-old Ugandan girl who becomes a world chess champion. It was also made into a film starring David Oyelowo and Lupita Nyong'o in 2016.

• For two years, Thor Hanson called Bwindi Impenetrable National Park home. He worked with local guides and trackers to create an ecotourism program for the then newly formed park. *The Impenetrable Forest: My Gorilla Years in Uganda* is the story of Hanson's years in the forest with the gorillas.

• *The Last King of Scotland* is a 2006 historical drama about the brutal rule of former Ugandan dictator Idi Amin, portrayed by Forest Whitaker. James McAvoy plays Scottish doctor Nicholas Garrigan, who became Amin's personal doctor and confidant.

• While most of the classic 1951 film *The African Queen* starring Humphrey Bogart and Katharine Hepburn was filmed in a studio outside of London, many key location shots took place in Uganda including Lake Albert, Murchison Falls, and Port Butiaba.

Visitor Information

The Uganda Tourism Board website has a helpful FAQ and activity suggestions. Most safari operators and high-end lodges provide comprehensive information for guests on their websites and will answer individual concerns.

The Uganda Wildlife Authority (UWA) is in charge of managing Uganda's National Parks and wildlife reserves. UWA issues primate tracking permits but, for the best service, make bookings in advance through a registered tour operator.

Another useful planning resource is Diary of a Muzungu, a travel blog written by British expat (and chapter updater) Charlotte Beauvoisin who has been a Ugandan resident since 2009.

CONTACTS Uganda Tourism Board.
✉ *Lugogo House, Lugogo Bypass (Rotary Avenue), 6th Floor, Block C, Kampala* ⊕ *www.exploreuganda.com.*
Uganda Wildlife Authority. ✉ *Plot 7 Kira Road, Kamwokya* ☎ *0312/355–000,*

0414/355–000 355–000 ⊕ *www. ugandawildlife.org.* **Diary of a Muzungu.**
⊕ *www.muzungubloguganda.com.*

Bwindi Impenetrable National Park

Home to over half the world's remaining population of endangered mountain gorillas, Bwindi is one of only four places in the world where one can spend a magical hour in the company of these gentle giants.

Once part of a much larger forest stretching into Rwanda and beyond, the park is an oasis of 128 square miles of pristine rainforest in southwest Uganda. Designated a UNESCO World Heritage Site, Bwindi is one of the largest African forests encompassing both lowland and montane species. This is reflected in its incredibly rich ecosystem: more diversity of tree and fern species than anywhere else in the region, over 200 species of butterfly, 120 mammal species, and the only forest inhabited by both gorillas and chimpanzees.

Bwindi today is a leading example of ecotourism done well. However, the success of tourism does throw curveballs such as an increase in begging and invitations to take part in orphanage tours (both of which are strongly discouraged).

Gorillas may be the main attraction but keen birders travel to Bwindi for its 347 species and rarities such as African green broadbill and Shelley's Crimsonwing. Forest birdlife is notoriously difficult to see but expert guides are quick to identify myriad species.

WHEN TO GO
Bwindi experiences rainfall year-round (it is a rainforest, after all). The wettest months are March through May and October through November, with comparatively drier weather from June to August and from December to February. Daytime temperatures are fairly constant, hovering around 75°F (24°C), but nights can be chilly, with lows of around 50°F (10°C). Low-season discounts are occasionally available at some lodges. Permit availability can be tricky in peak months of July through September and Christmas and New Year so early booking is essential.

GETTING HERE AND AROUND
Lying about 500 km (300 miles)—a 10-hour drive—from Entebbe International Airport, Bwindi is served by scheduled/charter flights via airstrips around the park. However flying is not cheap, so most people drive to Bwindi, usually as part of a longer safari itinerary. Another option is to fly into Kigali and drive across Rwanda's border into Uganda. This can achieve the best of both worlds: less hours spent driving plus an affordable gorilla tracking permit.

■ TIP→ **Securing your permit in advance from Uganda Wildlife Authority is vital, as this dictates where you track, and therefore**

Park Ratings

Game: ★ ★ ★ ★ ★

Park Accessibility: ★ ★ ★ ☆ ☆

Getting Around: ★ ★ ★ ☆ ☆

Accommodations: ★ ★ ★ ★ ☆

Scenic Beauty: ★ ★ ★ ★ ★

where you stay. And, with Rwanda's high gorilla permit prices, Uganda's permits are in high demand throughout the year, so book as far in advance as you can.

Bwindi has four distinct sectors for tracking: Buhoma (in the north), Ruhija, Rushaga, and Nkuringo (in the south). Some of the best accommodations are at Buhoma and Nkuringo, but don't rule out tracking elsewhere if you plan carefully: Ruhija tracking is viable from Buhoma; Rushaga can be reached from Nkuringo. If driving, you'll need a 4x4 because roads can be difficult, especially in the wettest months. Because of this, and the permit permutations, most people travel with a tour operator.

🛏 Hotels

Buhoma Lodge
$$$ | HOTEL | The cottages at Buhoma Lodge, located within Bwindi Impenetrable National Park, rise up on stilts out of the hillside, ensuring that views from the highest rooms—long, sweeping vistas down the mist-clad valley—are some of the best this side of the forest. **Pros:** two-minute walk from the gorilla tracking briefing point; smiling staff and professional management; in good weather the Wi-Fi reaches bedrooms; in-room USB charging. **Cons:** close to park offices so occasional passing traffic; book your complimentary massage at the spa in advance to avoid disappointment; admirable eco-credentials means hair dryers can

only be used on request. $ *Rooms from: US$440* ✉ *Bwindi Impenetrable National Park, Buhoma* ✛ *400 meters on right after park gate* ☎ *772/721–155* ⊕ *ugandaexclusivecamps.com* ⤳ *10 tented cottages* ❑ *All-Inclusive.*

★ Chameleon Hill

$$ | **ALL-INCLUSIVE** | Set on a tiny promontory of land high above Lake Mutanda, to the south of Bwindi Impenetrable Forest, Chameleon Hill's windmill-like towers and individually color-themed rooms look across to majestic volcanic peaks that wouldn't look amiss in a Disney movie. **Pros:** unique setting with unforgettable view; food is excellent and plentiful; a multitude of innovative adventure activities. **Cons:** 45-minute drive to starting point for gorilla tracking; public transport access can be difficult; remote location. $ *Rooms from: US$350* ✉ *South of Bwindi Impenetrable National Park* ✛ *As you enter Kisoro town look out for "Kindly Petrol Station" where you turn right. From here the lodge is clearly signposted* ☎ *772/721–818* ✉ *welcome@chameleonhill.com* ⊕ *www.chameleonhill.com* ⤳ *10 luxury chalets* ❑ *All-Inclusive.*

Clouds Mountain Gorilla Lodge

$$$$ | **HOTEL** | **FAMILY** | Regarded by many as Bwindi's most exclusive lodge, Clouds also has one of the greatest views in Uganda: high on a ridge in Nkuringo, verdant hills tumble away to a valley below, under distant volcanic peaks. **Pros:** a personal butler/housekeeper at your beck and call; lodge has own helipad on Top of the World; excellent meals full of fresh produce grown on-site. **Cons:** not all cottages have the view, so ask for Safari or Rafiki if this is important to you; Wi-Fi in main building only; rates are pricey. $ *Rooms from: US$1,762* ✉ *Bwindi Impenetrable National Park* ✛ *Entrance on left, opposite UWA ranger post at northern end of Nkuringo village* ☎ *414/251–182, 772/489–497* ⊕ *www.wildplacesafrica.com* ⤳ *8 rooms* ❑ *All-Inclusive.*

Nkuringo Bwindi Gorilla Lodge

$$$ | **HOTEL** | This lodge has graduated from humble beginnings to become an award-winning property offering a range of high-end rooming options from en suite forest suites to garden cottages painstakingly constructed using local materials. **Pros:** choose from garden cottages, family villas, suites, and honeymoon cottage; excellent service; great for walkers and adventurers. **Cons:** the high altitude (7,090 feet/2,161 meters) means it can be chilly at night; lots of concrete steps from main area to most rooms; remote gorilla trekking destination. $ *Rooms from: US$460* ✉ *Bwindi Impenetrable National Park* ✛ *On right-hand side on bend in road, just before Nkuringo village* ☎ *392/176–327* ⊕ *mountaingorillalodge.com* ⤳ *18 rooms* ❑ *All-Inclusive.*

Sanctuary Gorilla Forest Camp

$$$$ | **HOTEL** | A standout property in Buhoma, northern Bwindi, Sanctuary Gorilla Forest Camp delivers impeccable service in a classic forest setting. **Pros:** supersmooth service from award-winning operator; forest location occasionally visited by gorillas; invests in community projects. **Cons:** massages are charged extra; fireplace in dining area (not cottages); closeness of forest to tents obscures views and invites the occasional creepy-crawly. $ *Rooms from: US$880* ✉ *Bwindi Impenetrable National Park, Buhoma* ✛ *500 meters on right after park gate* ☎ *0414/340–290, 0776/340–290* ⊕ *www.sanctuaryretreats.com* ⤳ *10 luxury tents* ❑ *All-Inclusive.*

★ Volcanoes Bwindi Lodge

$$$$ | **HOTEL** | This award-winning ecolodge has the grandest vantage point of Bwindi in its own reserve of secondary forest, creating a 50-acre gorilla-friendly buffer zone. **Pros:** extensive verandah and living area look straight into the forest; friendly, well-trained staff with great attention to detail; innovative food menus, superbly prepared. **Cons:** lots of steps

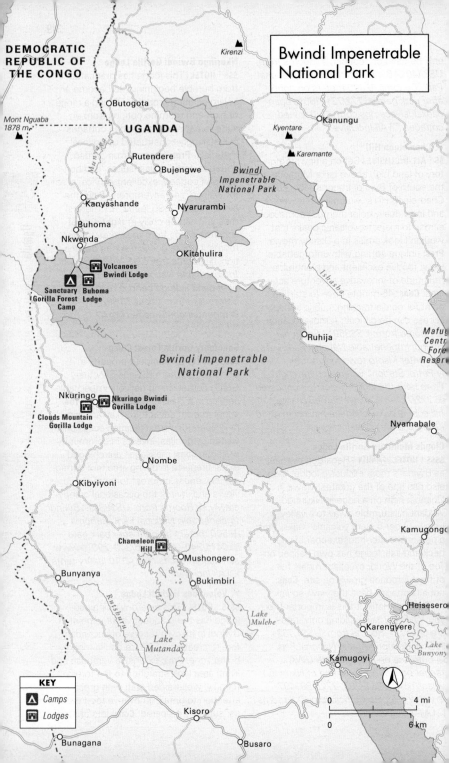

Bwindi Impenetrable National Park is one of only four places in the world where people can spend time with mountain gorillas.

in and out of the lodge; gorilla sightings in lodge grounds can't be guaranteed; Wi-Fi only available in main building. [$] *Rooms from: US$880* ✉ *Buhoma* ⊕ *Look for lodge sign on left as you enter Buhoma village* ☎ *414/346–464, 772/741–720* 🌐 *www.volcanoessafaris.com* 🛏 *10 luxury bandas* 🍴 *All-Inclusive.*

Activities

If visiting Southern Bwindi (Rushaga or Nkuringo sectors), nearby Lake Mutanda beckons for a rather special experience: paddling across its waters in a traditional dug-out canoe. The backdrop is stunning. The island-studded lake is overlooked by distant volcanic peaks and the Virunga Massif that straddles the Uganda/Rwanda border. Canoeing can be combined with a guided hike from nearby Rubuguri to the lakeshore. Canoeing is a peaceful diversion from the hectic pace of safari itineraries, and offers far more insight into the charms and challenges of daily life than driving by in your 4x4 vehicle.

CANOEING

★ Edirisa Canoe Trekking and Batwa Today

CANOEING & ROWING | FAMILY | A social enterprise with a sense of adventure, Edirisa offers its unique blend of hiking, paddling, and community on canoe-trekking expeditions (using wooden dugouts, naturally). This Lake Bunyonyi-based nonprofit's hiking itineraries cover southwestern Uganda and extend into Rwanda, enabling visitors to experience authentic Uganda (and Rwanda and the DRC), while providing employment and promoting local culture. Enthusiastic young guides accompany guests, with assistance from *Bakiga* and *Batwa* tribal elders. Single- or multiday options are available, including the epic week-long Ultimate Hike from Lake Bunyonyi to Mgahinga to Buhoma along one of the Gorilla Highlands Trails. Accommodation can be basic—you camp in tents (upgrade options usually available) but many visitors love the authenticity of the village experience. The popular Batwa Today tour gives access to the Batwa community like no other, and the "Batwa

Bwindi's Gorillas

Since the first group was habituated for tourism nearly three decades ago, a total of 23 gorilla families (out of Bwindi's estimated 459 individuals) are now tracked by visitors. Small groups of tourists set off on bracing hikes every morning for a bucket list encounter with a Silverback and his clan. A maximum of eight visitors can track each gorilla family daily meaning Uganda has a maximum of 184 permits available per day. Permits—$700 per permit through 2024—are strictly controlled to minimize contact between gorillas and the outside world. Human and gorilla DNA differ by less than 2%, making them susceptible to human ailments, so you won't be allowed to track if you're ill. Funds raised from gorilla tracking go toward conservation activities in Bwindi, and all over Uganda. For US$1,500, those who crave a more immersive great ape experience can opt for the habituation experience and spend half a day in the forest with researchers at Rushaga.

When trekking the gorillas (or chimpanzees), it's highly recommended that you hire a porter who will carry your bag (for a fee of US$15 per person) and help you climb muddy slopes. Tips are highly appreciated, at your discretion, of course. Our recommendations are $5–10 for a porter, and $5–15 for ranger guides. Ideally, tips should be paid in local currency.

Gorilla tracking requires a very early start. The day starts at 7 am with registration, a briefing, and a complimentary traditional dance performance prior to the 8 am start. You may track between one and five hours before you reach your gorilla family for the precious hour in their company. Expect a long day (and pack plenty of water to avoid dehydration brought on by altitude).

A percentage of tracking fees supports nearby communities, and many local people now work in tourism: whether as porters on gorilla-tracking expeditions or guiding visitors on forest hikes, community walks, or living history encounters with the Batwa, the ancient forest tribe. For older trackers or those with mobility issues, the "mountain helicopter" or "stretcher" service operated by men from the community can be a real lifesaver. Ideally, this should be booked in advance via a tour operator or Uganda Wildlife Authority (but emergency provision is also there).

Kids" tour is a special program for those under 15. ✉ *Bufuka Village, Lake Bunyonyi, Kabale* ☎ *776/558–123* ⊕ *www.edirisa.org.*

Nkuringo Walking Safaris

CANOEING & ROWING | FAMILY | This pioneering trekking company, with offices in Entebbe and a base at Nkuringo on the south side of Bwindi Impenetrable National Park, offers various guided day and multiday hikes through Bwindi and surrounding farmland, alongside dugout canoe trips on Lake Mutanda. Their professional guides are trained to identify local flora and fauna, and will also share insights into history, culture, local everyday life, and farming practices. Their hiking packages are excellent value and can be combined with your choice of accommodation (so you can scale the comfort factor up or down as required). ✉ *Nkuringo Gorilla Bwindi Lodge, Bwindi Impenetrable National Park*

☎ *0774/805–580, 39/2176–6327* ⊕ *www.*
nkuringowalkingsafaris.com.

HIKING

Various hiking trails exist at Bwindi,
through the forest and its environs.
Shorter hikes of three hours with park
rangers are available: in Buhoma and
Rushaga we recommend the different (but similarly monikered) Waterfall
Trails; birders can head to Ruhija for the
ornithologically rewarding Mubwindi
Swamp hike. Longer forays—arranged
by private outfitters—include the four- to
five-hour Ivy River Trail from Buhoma to
Nkuringo (or vice versa, for a more gentle
gradient). From Nkuringo, the Kashasha
River Trail offers a strenuous seven- to
eight-hour loop, or you can strike out on
the multiday Gorilla Highlands Trail to
scenic Lake Bunyonyi.

Kibale National Park

This 296-square-mile tract of forest is
home to one of the greatest variety and
concentration of primates on the continent, and its population of nearly 1,500
chimpanzees makes it a great place to
track these endangered apes.

Kibale weaves a rich tapestry of rainforest life: 13 primate species; more
than 375 bird species (that have been
identified so far); and nearly 230 species
of tree create a varied canopy, some
towering more than 130 feet (50 meters).
Mammal residents include golden cats,
civets, and bushbuck, and the occasional
forest elephant (smaller than their savanna cousins). Kibale even has an abundant
species of butterflies, moths, and colorful
beetles.

Outside the park, rolling panoramas
of tea plantations and ancient volcanic
craters dominate the landscape between
Kibale and Fort Portal, with plenty of
informal hiking and biking opportunities
offering a pleasant way to pass an afternoon. Ask your lodge or guide for details

Park Ratings

Game: ★★★★★
Park Accessibility: ★★★★☆
Getting Around: ★★★★☆
Accommodations: ★★★★☆
Scenic Beauty: ★★★★★

of local routes; many are self-guided and
offer the chance to witness everyday
rural life in one of the prettiest regions of
Uganda. Runners and competitive types
flock to the annual sporting fundraisers at
Kyaninga Lodge.

WHEN TO GO

Kibale is a rain forest, with the chance
of wet weather year-round. If you avoid
March through May and September
through November you will miss the
worst of it, though dry-season months
can make the chimp tracking more arduous, as the apes travel farther in search
of fruiting trees. Temperatures are fairly
constant, with average daytime highs
around 80°F (27°C) and nights dropping
to about 59°F (15°C). Be sure to secure
chimp tracking or habituation permits
well in advance at any time of year, either
from a tour operator or directly from the
Uganda Wildlife Authority.

GETTING HERE AND AROUND

Located in western Uganda, Kibale lies
about 16 miles (26 km) southeast of
the town of Fort Portal on the excellent
Kamwenge to Lyantonde Road. The park
is about a five-hour drive from Kampala
or Entebbe respectively, and three hours
from northern Queen Elizabeth National
Park. Drive times have improved; take
the road to Lyantonde for Lake Mburo
National Park, an easy three-hour drive.
If you prefer to fly, you can choose from
a small charter to Fort Portal airstrip (its
limited length excludes all but the tiniest

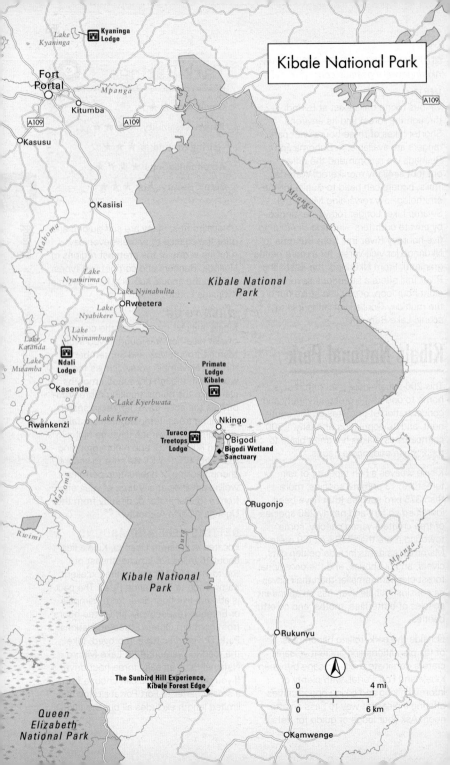

light aircraft), or charter to Kasese, two hours south, in a wider choice of planes.

Sights

Bigodi Wetland Sanctuary

WILDLIFE REFUGE | FAMILY | This community-run conservation project managed by the Kibale Association for Rural and Environmental Development (KAFRED) offers a popular guided nature trail through Magombe Wetland, near Bigodi. Its more open terrain frequently delivers better bird-watching and monkey-spotting than neighboring Kibale Forest. Here, endangered red colobus are common, with the chance of seeing black and white colobus, the Ugandan endemic crested mangabey, and L'Hoest's and red-tailed monkeys. Serious birders will enjoy the knowledgeable guides, who can identify the wetland's 200-odd species with ease. The 5-km (3-mile) trail takes three to four hours, and if you don't have waterproof boots KAFRED can lend you a pair for free. Porters can be booked in advance. Traditional lunches, village walks, and Tinka's Homestay (voted Best Homestay 2016) are also on offer. Created in 1992, KAFRED is the only swamp walk that directly funds the community; its success has birthed multiple copycat swamp walks so be wary of whom you're signing up with. ✉ *KAFRED Office, Fort Portal-Kamwenge Rd., near Kibale National Park, Bigodi* ☎ *0772/468–113* 🌐 *bigoditourism.com* 🎫 *$15.*

★ **The Sunbird Hill Experience, Kibale Forest edge**

WILDLIFE REFUGE | Open exclusively to pre-booked visitors, the immersive Sunbird Hill Experience offers bird and butterfly treks on forest-edge trails in search of more than 250 bird species, insects, reptiles, and hundreds of butterflies and moths. Encounter the reality of human-wildlife conflict as you inspect the elephant trench and beehive fence deterrent with Silver, a reformed poacher and retired wildlife ranger; tour Butterfly Village with expert site guides for a glimpse of the vibrant Red Glider and the curiously named Flying Handkerchief (butterflies). The $30 donation to NGO In the Shadow of Chimpanzees supports grassroots conservation projects and includes refreshments and half-day access to the Birders' Lounge and natural history library. ✉ *Kyabakwerere Village, Bigodi* ✥ *1½ km (1 mile) from tarmac road* ☎ *701/577–784* 🌐 *sunbirdhill.com.*

Restaurants

The Bee Hive Bar & Bistro, Bigodi

$ | INTERNATIONAL | FAMILY | You can't miss Bigodi's only yellow and brown two-story building, perched overlooking Bigodi Wetland Sanctuary. Stop for a coffee or a cold Nile Special beer on the upstairs verandah or for something more substantial, opt for the pepper steak, pumpkin and ginger soup, or Uganda's famous "rolex" (think breakfast wrap). **Known for:** satellite TV and pool table; flush toilet; cold beers and coffee. [$] *Average main: US$10* ✉ *Bigodi Trading Center, On the main Fort Portal–Kamwenge Rd., Bigodi* ✥ *Opposite the turn for KAFRED Office* ☎ *0787/357–717* 💳 *No credit cards.*

Hotels

★ **Kyaninga Lodge**

$$$$ | HOTEL | Overlooking a cobalt-blue crater lake, the design of this fairy-tale property provides serious wow factor: Kyaninga took 130 men, six years, and more than 1,000 hand-carved logs to build this masterpiece. **Pros:** stunning property; friendly, professional staff; much of their tasty food grown on-site. **Cons:** if you struggle with steps ask for Cottage 5 or 6, as they are closest to the lodge; quickly booked up by expats during charity events; farther from Kibale Forest than most. [$] *Rooms from: US$850* ✉ *Fort Portal* ✥ *Lake Kyaninga near Fort Portal* ☎ *0772/999–750*

Chimpanzee Tracking in Kibale

Excursions set out from Kibale National Park's Kanyanchu Tourist Centre (🌐 ugandawildlife.org) twice a day. Accompanied by a forest ranger, guests hike through lush forest in search of these primates; there's no guarantee of a sighting, but the success rate is more than 95%. Once located, the group spends a maximum of one hour with them, watching them feed, groom, play, and sometimes even hunt together.

Those with a real passion for primates (and the stamina to match) can join the daily chimpanzee habituation experience. This unique opportunity to observe chimpanzees from dawn until dusk allows visitors to gather deeper insight into their behavior. Nocturnal primates such as bushbabies may also be seen, with varying degrees of success, on the guided walk that departs Kanyanchu at nightfall (by appointment).

🌐 *kyaningalodge.com* 🛏 *9 cottages* 🍴 *All-Inclusive.*

Ndali Lodge

$$$$ | HOTEL | FAMILY | A Ugandan Downton Abbey, Ndali is a bit of an institution; offering a charming blend of warm hospitality and colonial history (but with the 21st-century convenience of its own unofficial helipad). **Pros:** the home-away-from-home feel; fantastic walking and biking country; massages available; great for kids. **Cons:** if dogs aren't your thing, forget it; alcoholic drinks charged extra; spotty Wi-Fi; hair dryers can only be used on request. [$] *Rooms from: US$890* ✉ *Lake Nyinambuga, Kabata, Bigodi* ☎ *0772/221–309* 🌐 *www.ndalilodge.co.ug* 🛏 *8 cottages* 🍴 *All-Inclusive.*

Primate Lodge Kibale

$$$$ | HOTEL | FAMILY | Right behind the Park Headquarters, Primate Lodge Kibale is convenient for those early mornings when tracking chimps or birding. **Pros:** location next to trailhead; impressive refurbishment and beautiful hardwood interiors; secluded and refurbished honeymoon cottage with bathtub. **Cons:** Wi-Fi available only when generator on; service is too relaxed for some; better value can be found elsewhere. [$] *Rooms from: US$940* ✉ *Kanyanchu, Kibale National Park, Fort Portal* ✣ *behind the Kanyanchu Park headquarters* ☎ *393/267–153* 🌐 *ugandalodges.com* 🛏 *10 cottages* 🍴 *Free Breakfast.*

Turaco Treetops Lodge

$$ | ALL-INCLUSIVE | FAMILY | Turaco Treetops combines nature, good environmental practices, and excellent value for money for the whole family from its jungle site at the edge of Kibale National Park. **Pros:** unusually good value for money; good environmental credentials throughout; spacious cottages are set well apart. **Cons:** slow Wi-Fi that's only available in the main building; books up quickly during peak seasons; easy to get lost on the drive here. [$] *Rooms from: US$230* ✉ *Nkingo, Kibale National Park* ☎ *757/152–323* 🌐 *turacotreetops.com* 🛏 *16 rooms* 🍴 *All-Inclusive.*

Tea plantations dot the landscape between Kibale and Fort Portal.

Queen Elizabeth National Park

Serving up a rich diversity of game and scenery, Queen Elizabeth National Park (QENP) is a rewarding safari stopover between the primate hubs of Kibale and Bwindi.

For the purposes of safari planning, the park is divided into two sectors. The northern sector, Mweya, straddles the equator, the euphorbia-studded valley framed by the Rwenzoris, and the Kichwamba Escarpment to the north and south, with Lakes George and Edward to the east and west.

Despite lower wildlife volumes than the Serengeti in Tanzania, for example, the variety of habitat in QENP provides a wealth of activities. Popular boat cruises ply the bird-lined Kazinga Channel (the park has more than 600 species, more than any other national park in Uganda, Kenya, or Tanzania). The geologically

intriguing Explosion Crater Drive offers panoramic views; guided hikes in Kyambura Gorge—though no substitute for Kibale—provide the chance of spotting chimpanzees; and the Uganda kob breeding grounds of Kasenyi Plains, which attract lions, hyenas, and leopards, offer more traditional wildlife-viewing. At Mweya Visitor Centre, cat-crazed visitors can ask about the Lion Monitoring Experience. This researcher-accompanied activity uses radio technology to get you up close, though availability is weather- (and researcher-) dependent. Tracking mongooses with researchers is another fun reason to get out of your safari vehicle.

To the south, the Ishasha sector is a wilder, more remote destination. Far from the crowds, there are no gimmicks, just plain, old-fashioned wilderness. Rolling plains are home to herds of elephants, kob, and topi, and local lion prides are known for climbing the giant fig trees. These show-stealing cats are usually given top billing for any foray into this sector, but Ishasha's beauty is best savored slowly. Spend time appreciating the full abundance of life on the savanna, and the discovery of telltale feline tails dangling from a tree will not be the only reward.

Nearby, communities have developed several rewarding tourism activities. Visit a working salt mining lake at Katwe or participate in a craft workshop with Kikorongo Community Group near the equator. In Ishasha, take the short but engaging Agartha's Taste of Uganda tour for insight into traditional life. A stone's throw away, climb into the elephant trench on Deo's Homestead Tour to explore the challenges of living with wildlife. These interactions offer a welcome change of pace, the chance to support the community directly, as well as a contrast to this beautiful park's wealth of wildlife.

WHEN TO GO

Located in the Albertine Rift at a lower altitude than most of Uganda, the climate in QENP is warm and constant, with mean annual temperatures of 59°F to 84°F (15°C to 29°C). Biannual wet seasons March through May and August through November are better for photography, with (generally short) storms producing interesting light and clearer skies. Drier periods in January and February and June and July are dusty and hot, with controlled burning by park authorities toward the end of these seasons making wildlife-viewing feel positively post-apocalyptic. As everywhere, climate change has blurred once defined seasons.

GETTING HERE AND AROUND

Around 400 km (250 miles) from Entebbe, Mweya in central QENP is a seven-hour drive on tarmac roads. Ishasha lies two hours (100 km [60 miles]) farther south along a marram road. Kibale is three hours (160 km [100 miles]) north of Mweya, and Ishasha is two hours (60 km [40 miles]) from northern Bwindi.

Park Ratings

Game: ★★★☆☆

Park Accessibility: ★★★★☆

Getting Around: ★★★★☆

Accommodations: ★★★★☆

Scenic Beauty: ★★★★★

Domestic air operators can drop off at Mweya airstrip (conditions apply), and scheduled stops at Kihihi serve Ishasha. Private charters are also available.

To enter the park, pay at Uganda Wildlife Authority (UWA)'s offices at Katunguru or any of the park entry gates using credit cards, online bank transfers, or mobile money. Cash is no longer accepted. If you're traveling with a tour operator, park entry fee and activities are normally paid for in advance in Kampala. UWA's Mweya Visitor Centre (deep in the park at the tip of the peninsula) is a good resource for information and bookings such as UWA's boat cruises, the mongoose experience or lion monitoring (under the Uganda Carnivore Programme). Rangers for game drives on Kasenyi Plains are collected from Kasenyi gate, and in Ishasha from the UWA bandas near the start of the southern circuit.

Sights

★ Explosion Crater Drive

NATURE SIGHT | A stunning three-hour diversion along rocky tracks in northern Queen Elizabeth National Park, the Explosion Crater Drive runs between the Queen's Pavillion (turn off the Kikorongo-Katunguru highway at the Equator Markers) and the Kabatoro Gate (AKA the Main Gate) on the Katwe public road. You don't need a guide but a competent 4x4 driver and vehicle are a must. The drive is known for its scenic vistas rather than wildlife-viewing (though elephants are relatively common, lions are not unheard of, flamingos can be spotted seasonally and the crater environment is great for spotting birds of prey), the drive traverses the Katwe crater field. This area of the park is littered with steep-sided volcanic craters, each containing its own microhabitat, from ancient rainforest to a sulfurous lake. It's enough to make geologists of us all. ✉ *Explosion Crater Dr., Queen Elizabeth National Park* ☎ *782 387–805* ✉ *info@ugandawildlife.org* 🌐 *www.ugandawildlife.org* 🎫 *Included in park entry fee* ✍ *No need to book or take a ranger guide.*

Kyambura Gorge

CANYON | The forested ridges of Kyambura Gorge form a deep cleft in the savanna landscape between Maramagambo Forest and Lake George, creating a natural boundary between Queen Elizabeth National Park and neighboring Kyambura Wildlife Reserve. Offering the chance to spot chimps on guided forest walks, the chimpanzee tracking in Kyambura Gorge is more active than most; you may have to cross the river by fallen log (slippery when wet!) and the steep sides of the gorge can be difficult at best. But it's a mysterious, primeval place (made famous by the BBC's *Chimps of the Lost Gorge*) and worth the 1.6 mile (2.5 km) drive from the Katunguru highway just for the view alone. Chimp permits (USD$50) can be arranged with the UWA locally, but limited availability means it's best to secure them in advance from their HQ in Kampala. Visiting the viewing platform is free, provided one has paid park entry fees. ✉ *Fig Tree Camp, Kyambura Gorge, Queen Elizabeth National Park* ☎ *0414/355–400* 🌐 *www.ugandawildlife.org.*

Hotels

Elephant Plains Lodge

$$$$ | **ALL-INCLUSIVE** | **FAMILY** | A stone's throw from the Equator, high on the western escarpment of the Albertine Rift, sits Elephant Plains, a few minutes' drive from Queen Elizabeth National Park. **Pros:** spacious cottages and communal areas; one of Queen Elizabeth National Park's best vantage points; cottages have showers and bathtubs. **Cons:** community development work at early stages; occasional noise from main road below lodge; little wildlife in immediate vicinity of lodge. [$] *Rooms from: US$940* ✉ *Elephant Plains Lodge, Katunguru, Queen Elizabeth National Park* ✥ *at the Equator crossing take the A109 road toward Bwera. The lodge is on the right after 2.5 km (1.5 miles)* ☎ *393/267–153, 772/426–368* 🌐 *ugandalodges.com* 🛏 *10 rooms* 🍴 *All-Inclusive.*

★ **Ishasha Wilderness Camp**

$$$$ | **HOTEL** | Steeped in classic safari style, this intimate eco-friendly camp will make you feel as if you have stumbled onto the set of *Out of Africa*. **Pros:** remote wilderness location; sundowners and bush breakfasts can be arranged; low season rates available for two nights or more. **Cons:** hot water is on request (bush showers); admirable eco-credentials means hair dryers can only be used upon request; too remote for some tastes. [$] *Rooms from: US$880* ✉ *Ishasha Sector, Queen Elizabeth National Park* ☎ *772/721–155* 🌐 *ugandaexclusivecamps.com* 🛏 *10 rooms* 🍴 *All-Inclusive.*

Mweya Safari Lodge

$$ | **RESORT** | **FAMILY** | Big groups love the location of this "hotel-in-the-bush," situated on the Mweya peninsula overlooking Kazinga Channel (a popular watering hole for big game), in the heart of Queen Elizabeth National Park. **Pros:** located in the park; rooms to suit most budgets/styles; great views in every direction.

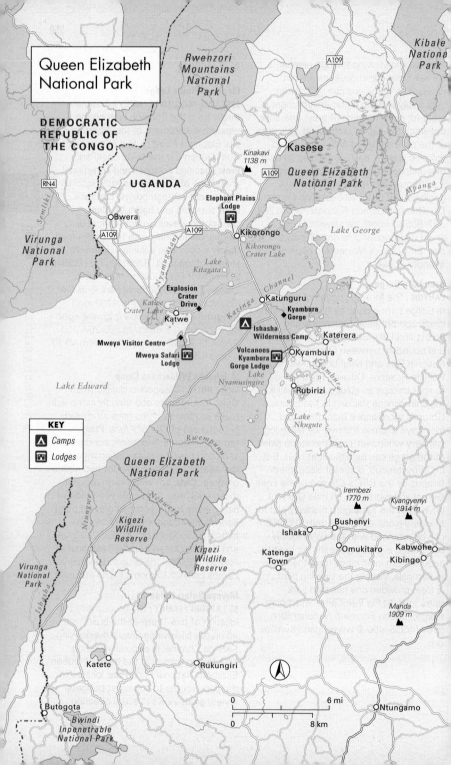

If you're lucky, you may encounter the famous tree-climbing lions in the Ishasha sector of Queen Elizabeth National Park.

Cons: restaurant switches to buffet meals in busy periods; can be very busy during peak seasons; with 46 rooms, 4 tents, and 4 cottages, it can feel big and impersonal. $ *Rooms from: US$430* ✉ *Mweya Peninsula, Queen Elizabeth National Park* ✣ *Gate on left after passing through UWA checkpoint on Mweya peninsula, inside Queen Elizabeth National Park* ☎ *312/260–260* 🌐 *www.mweyalodge.com* 🛏 *54 rooms* 🍴 *All-Inclusive.*

★ **Volcanoes Kyambura Gorge Lodge**

$$$$ | ALL-INCLUSIVE | FAMILY | Expect to be met by your personal butler on arrival at the converted coffee station overlooking Queen Elizabeth National Park. **Pros:** stylish contemporary design; impressive commitment to community and conservation; your own personal butler—staff are eager to please. **Cons:** outside National Park so game drives start very early; a steep walk from lower cottages to dining area; chimp sightings are not guaranteed. $ *Rooms from: US$620* ✉ *Bushenyi* ✣ *Turn off (at lodge sign) at Kyambura trading center on Bushenyi-Katunguru Rd. Continue through village and then turn left at lodge sign* ☎ *414/346–464, 772/741–720* ✉ *enquiries@volcanoessafaris.com* 🌐 *www.volcanoessafaris.com* 🛏 *8 cottages* 🍴 *All-Inclusive.*

Activities

BOATING

In the northern sector of Queen Elizabeth National Park, the Kazinga Channel attracts all manner of game. Herds of elephants and buffalo throng the banks; smaller herbivores such as warthog and kob are also present; pods of hippo and solitary crocs bask in the shallows; and a significant proportion of the park's staggering 600-plus bird species can be seen here. Time it right and you may see seasonal flocks of African Skimmers and two species of flamingo. With such natural bounty, it's no wonder the two-hour boat cruise along its banks is far and away the highlight of this sector of the park. The Uganda Wildlife Authority and Mweya Safari Lodge operate the channel's best-established boat experiences from the jetty below the lodge. These start at US$30 per person and include an expert guide and a lifejacket. If you like a sundowner with your birds, the MV Kazinga sunset cruise sets off at 4:30pm and costs US$70 per person. At the far end of the Kazinga Channel at Katunguru, where the narrow waterway opens into Lake George, lies a hub of community-run boats. Their water-based safaris are essentially the same route but the quality of the experience varies; however, if you're staying outside the National Park, you may appreciate the easier access to the channel's wildlife. Catch a boat from Katunguru and you're not obliged to pay park entry either.

★ **Mweya Safari Lodge Boats**
BOATING | With a variety of comfortable, modern craft, the slick river operations from Mweya Safari Lodge offer several scheduled or private Kazinga Channel cruises a day, leaving at 9 and 11 am and 2 and 4:15 pm, subject to demand. Choose from the 38-seater *Hippo* or 10-seater *Sunbird*. Both are thoughtfully equipped with a cash bar, or book yourself on the luxury 12-seater *Kingfisher* boat, where the price includes drinks and nibbles. ⊠ *Mweya Jetty, Mweya Peninsula, Queen Elizabeth National Park* ☎ *312/260–263, 0752/798–882* ⊕ *www.mweyalodge.com* ✉ *From US$30.*

UWA Mweya Boats
BOATING | The Uganda Wildlife Authority operate their own boat cruises along the Kazinga Channel. Two-hour trips depart daily at 9 and 11 am and 3 and 5 pm from the UWA jetty below Mweya Safari Lodge. There is a relatively large minimum number requirement of 10 passengers; some of their craft are older than the lodge boats but a new 45-seater boat joined the fleet in 2017. The guides certainly know their stuff and departures are often fully booked during peak season. Book ahead at their offices in Kampala, or take your chances locally at the Katunguru HQ and Mweya

Visitor Centre. ⊠ *Plot 7 Kira Rd., Kampala* ☎ *0414/355–400* ⊕ *www.ugandawildlife.org* ✉ *US$30* ⊙ *Kampala reservations office closed Sat. afternoon and Sun. The boats and park offices operate daily.*

Murchison Falls National Park

Historically a highlight of the East African safari circuit, at 1,483 square miles Murchison Falls (referred to as MFNP) is the largest of Uganda's National Parks, offering an abundance of wildlife against a superbly scenic backdrop.

Bisected by the Nile River, many of the activities are centered around the water. Delta cruises offer peaceful contemplation of papyrus-lined channels (and a good chance of spotting Shoebill); half- and full-day sport-fishing trips can be arranged; and the most popular activity is the launch cruise to Murchison Falls. Here, 300 cubic meters of water per second explodes through a narrow gorge, creating the world's most powerful stretch of water. Active adventurers can prearrange to be dropped by boat at the Devil's Cauldron, at the base of the Falls, for a steep hike up to the Top of the Falls where dramatic vistas await. The viewpoints can also be accessed by vehicle, from both banks of the Nile.

North-bank game tracks through Borassus palm savanna promise rewarding wildlife-viewing: herds of elephant, buffalo, and Rothschild's giraffe; smaller herbivores include Uganda kob, Jackson's hartebeest, oribi ,and warthog; elusive predators such as spotted hyena, lion, leopard, and jackal. Murchison's 450 plus bird species include the primitive-looking Abyssinian Ground Hornbill and dazzling carmine bee-eaters. Most activities are centered around Paraa in the heart of the park, but the southerly Budongo Forest provides a worthy diversion for excellent (and affordable) chimpanzee tracking; bird-watching along Budongo's Royal Mile is highly prized.

GETTING HERE AND AROUND

The park lies five to six hours or 320 km (185 miles) northwest of Kampala. Schedule and charter flights fly in from Entebbe International Airport or Kajjansi airfield, landing at Bugungu, Pakuba, or Chobe airstrips as required. Kichumbanyobo gate in the south, just north of Masindi town, is best for access to Budongo Forest. The new road bridge at Paraa has replaced the ferry across the Nile, giving easy access to north bank game drives and lodges. The bridge may have simplified the river crossing but the environmental impact of wide connecting roads (funded by oil companies) and the long-term impact of oil drilling remain to be seen. Uganda's black gold is forecast to flow in 2025.

Alternatively, visitors booked into north bank accommodation can enter MFNP via the Wangkwar and Tangi gates from the main Karuma-Pakwach highway to the east. Although most of Murchison's accommodation has proliferated around Paraa, improved roads make journey times from the east of the park more manageable and lodges are mushrooming within the 10 km (6 miles) radius of Pakwach, towards West Nile. As tempting as it may be to film the turbulent waters at Karuma Bridge, be warned that vigilant police have been known to confiscate cameras at this and other strategic bridges.

Park Ratings

Game: ★★★★☆

Park Accessibility: ★★★★☆

Getting Around: ★★★★☆

Accommodations: ★★★★☆

Scenic Beauty: ★★★★★

Hotels

Baker's Lodge Annex

$$$$ | ALL-INCLUSIVE | Expect privacy, luxury, fabulous food, and professional service at the large, newly built, eco-friendly villa on the boundary of Murchison Falls National Park. **Pros:** outside park boundary so no park fees needed to stay at villa; beautiful riverfront location delivers understated luxury; boat cruises depart five minutes' walk from your room. **Cons:** not part of a resort complex; modern style accommodation; boats, bush breakfast, and game drive require advance booking. [$] *Rooms from: US$800* ✉ *Murchison Falls National Park* ✣ *South bank towards Mubako Gate* ☎ *0772/721–155* 🌐 *www.ugandaexclusivecamps.com* 🛏 *4 rooms* 🍴 *All-Inclusive.*

★ **Murchison River Lodge**

$ | HOTEL | FAMILY | This relaxed mid-range lodge has found its niche; local expats and price-conscious tourists love its laid-back, unpretentious style. **Pros:** warm and welcoming staff; great value for money; boat trips can start from below lodge restaurant. **Cons:** due to environmental considerations the two tents with river views have chemical toilets (the rest have flush); phone reception patchy; Wi-Fi limited to pool lounge. [$] *Rooms from: US$230* ✉ *Paraa* ✣ *Near Murchison Falls National Park* ☎ *0714/000–085, 0782/007–552* 🌐 *murchisonriverlodge.com* 🛏 *17 rooms* 🍴 *All-Inclusive.*

Activities

BOATING

The undisputed highlight of Murchison Falls National Park are the many ways visitors can "mess about on the river": cruises to the Falls, exploring the Nile delta, sundowner trips with chilled drinks onboard, and even sportfishing expeditions for keen anglers. Watching the

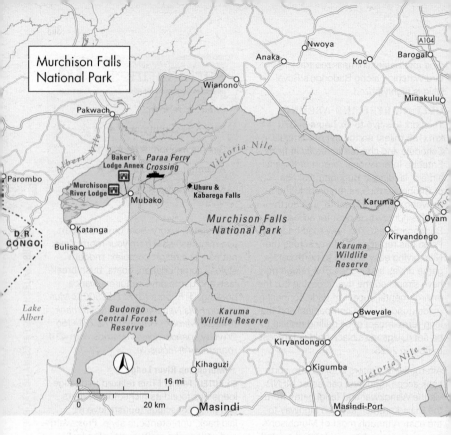

Murchison Falls National Park

sun set (or rise) over this ancient river, to a backing track of hippo snorts and birdcalls, is stirring stuff. Three different outfitters—the park authorities and two private operators with lodges in the area—offer boat cruises from Paraa with varying degrees of choice. Book a scheduled departure for the best value, or ask about private cruising rates for an exclusive experience tailored to your interests.

Paraa Safari Lodge Boats

BOATING | The Paraa Safari Lodge river operations' variously sized watercrafts include the double-decker *African Queen*, the 14-seater *Paraa Voyager*, or the 10-seater *Jewel of the Nile*. Their scheduled trips head upstream to the Falls from their jetty on the north bank, with departures at 9 am and 2 pm, subject to demand. They also offer launch cruises

to the Nile delta area. ⊠ *Paraa, North bank, Murchison Falls National Park* ☎ *200/414–100, 0752/788–880* ⊕ *www. paraalodge.com* ⊠ *From US$32.*

UWA Murchison Boats

BOATING | FAMILY | Operating from their south bank jetty at Paraa, the Uganda Wildlife Authority offers daily cruises upstream to Murchison Falls, departing at 8 am, 11 am, and 2 pm. The various-sized fleet includes a 45-seater boat. A minimum of 10 passengers are required for a cruise to depart, and their seasoned wildlife guides and this remarkable stretch of river ensure the excursion is of excellent value. Cruise seats can be booked at UWA's central reservations office in Kampala, the local park offices at Paraa, or through a registered tour operator. ⊠ *Paraa, South Bank, Murchison Falls National Park* ☎ *0414/355–400,*

Murchison Falls National Park is Uganda's largest national park.

0312/355–000 ⊕ ugandawildlife.org ✉ US$30.

★ **Wild Frontiers Murchison Boats**
BIRD WATCHING | This established safari outfitter, and operator of nearby Baker's Lodge Villa, provides scenic wildlife cruises and sportfishing trips with their fleet of boats stationed at the Paraa jetty. Scheduled and private departures include trips to the Falls and the fabulous Nile delta—the latter providing many a Shoebill sighting.

■**TIP→ When booking your Falls cruise, ask about their Falls & Sundowner option. The later departure time of 3:30 pm generally means better wildlife sightings and a more peaceful river setting.**

They have a variety of comfortable craft; offer the most flexibility for customized trips; and their skippers and guides are well-trained, with a knack for knowing just when to turn off the engines and glide silently past the riverbanks, enjoying the natural sounds of the bush. ✉ South Bank, Murchison Falls National

Park ☎ 772/502–155, 702/152–928 ⊕ wildfrontiers.co.ug ✉ From US$30 per person (short sunset cruise) to over US$1,000 per day for a private group (up to 40 guests).

If You Have Time

Although the must-see parks in Uganda are described in detail above, there are many other places worth exploring if you have time.

Lake Mburo National Park

Roughly halfway between Kampala and Bwindi lies Lake Mburo National Park. Often underrated, its unique variety of game and birdlife, plenty of opportunities to get out of the car, and excellent lodges makes it far more than just a convenient stopover en route to the gorillas. The park's also home to 'near threatened' Rothschild's giraffes, which are breeding well after their 2015 reintroduction from

The prehistoric-looking shoebill can be found nesting in marshy areas like the Mabamba Swamp.

Murchison Falls National Park. Disease and poaching led to giraffes' disappearance from Lake Mburo in the last century; less than three thousand Rothschild's giraffes are believed to be left in Africa's wild places.

This small park (370 square km [143 square miles]) is made up of wetlands, five lakes (Mburo being the biggest), open savanna, and acacia woodland studded with rocky outcrops. Lake Mburo's range of habitats makes it a good park for birders—more than 300 species are found within the park.

For wildlife-lovers, the park delivers a wealth of smaller herbivores: large gatherings of impala not found anywhere else in Uganda mingle with zebra, topi, oribi, and bushbuck; herds of eland, the largest living antelope, take up seasonal residence; and dainty klipspringers hide out on rocky *koppies* (a small hill in an otherwise flat area). Hippos thrive in Lake Mburo, best seen on the Uganda Wildlife Authority's boat cruise. Leopard sightings are common and hyena are heard regularly; plenty of smaller predators, such as genet and white-tailed mongoose, make for interesting nocturnal viewing, as the park is one of the few places that allow night drives. Other novel activities include horseriding and walking safaris that offer a different perspective on wildlife-viewing and allow you to appreciate the peaceful serenity of the bush.

GETTING HERE AND AROUND

City traffic allowing, Lake Mburo is less than a four-hour drive (230 km [140 miles]) from Kampala, with resurfaced highways making the journey relatively pleasant. A handy café/crafts pit stop can be made at the equator, 75 km (47 miles) south of Kampala. The Nshara park gate is reached by turning off the Masaka-Mbarara highway about 20 km (12 miles) past Lyantonde; turn off for the more westerly Sanga gate 37 km (23 miles) shy of Mbarara, at the town of the same name. No public transport exists beyond the main highway, and a 4x4 is recommended for navigating the park and approach roads. If you prefer to fly in, charters to nearby Mbarara airstrip are available, just more than an hour from the park.

Hotels

★ **Mihingo Lodge**

$$$ | **HOTEL** | **FAMILY** | High up on a *kopje* (rocky outcrop), the cottages at this superb boutique lodge blend seamlessly into the landscape. **Pros:** a true eco-lodge; delicious buffet meals from 100% organic garden; vast array of activities to satisfy young and old. **Cons:** limited Wi-Fi; holiday weekends can see it filled with expats; often overlooked as off the mainstream safari trail. [$] *Rooms from: US$480* ✉ *Lake Mburo National Park* ☎ *0752/410–509* 🌐 *mihingolodge.com* 🛏 *12 rooms* 🍴 *All-Inclusive.*

★ **Rwakobo Rock**

$$ | **HOTEL** | **FAMILY** | A gem of a budget eco-lodge, Rwakobo Rock is deservedly popular with the adventure crowd. **Pros:** relaxed, informal style offering great value; climbers will love bouldering on the rock; pay no park fees by taking a walking safari outside the park. **Cons:** watch your step—occasionally herds of cattle come through the lodge, with slippery consequences; small swimming pool; poorly lit paths to the rooms. [$] *Rooms from: US$260* ✉ *Near Nshara Gate, Lake Mburo National Park* ✣ *lodge is 1½ km (1 mile) from Nshara Gate* ☎ *0755/211–771* 🌐 *www.rwakoborock.com* 🛏 *16 rooms* 🍴 *All-Inclusive.*

Jinja and the River Nile

The age-old quest to locate the source of the Nile finally ended at Jinja, now the self-appointed adventure capital of East Africa where today's modern explorers avail themselves of a veritable smorgasbord of white-knuckle activities.

Back in 1862, John Hanning Speke declared Ripon Falls to be the source of the Nile. Today, the laid-back town of Jinja overlooks this mighty river as it flows out of Lake Victoria, at the start of its 6,800-km (4,200-mile) journey to the Mediterranean. Thanks to a 1950s hydropower dam, Ripon Falls are now completely submerged; visitors can still view the official "source" in a 30-minute boat trip, but all that remains is a suggestive ripple on the water's surface, so it can be rather an anticlimax.

The river remains the reason behind why people come, but for a cluster of adventure activities rather than a history lesson. An industry fueled by sheer adrenaline has sprung up around the Nile's greatest asset: a series of dramatically churning white-water rapids that mark its course. White-water rafting is the main attraction, but visitors can choose from a mind-boggling variety of other thrills (and possible spills): kayaking, bungee jumping, quad bike safaris, horseback riding, mountain biking, and the latest craze: tubing. For fans of more serene outdoor pursuits, the "lake" of flat water at Bujagali, created by the second hydropower dam, offers stand-up paddleboarding, sit-on kayak trips, birding, and sunset cruises. Golf, sports fishing, and sailing on Lake Victoria are all on offer, too.

Jinja is the gateway to northeastern Uganda where up and coming adventure tourism activities include abseiling at Sipi Falls and high altitude running in Kapchorwa in the foothills of Mount Elgon (home of Olympic marathon champion Stephen Kiprotich).

Venture farther north and cheetahs are frequently spotted in Pian Upe Wildlife Reserve and Kidepo Valley National Park (the only Ugandan protected areas where you can see them). Another big lure to this corner of the country are deeply traditional cultures of the Karamojong, Tepeth and Ik. The annual multi-day Tour of Karamoja cycling and hiking event ends in Kidepo Valley National Park, bordered by Kenya and South Sudan. Although less visited to date, improved infrastructure suggests this region's time is yet to come.

GETTING HERE AND AROUND

A two- to three-hour drive (80 km/50 miles) east of Kampala, Jinja can be reached by the direct (but juggernaut-choked) Jinja Road through Mabira Forest, or the longer but more peaceful Gayaza Road and Mukono-Njeru Roads to the north and south respectively. The final approach to Jinja for both routes involves crossing the Nile over the Owen Falls Dam. Enjoy the views but don't take any pictures—cameras can be confiscated at this strategic government installation. Bujagali, with its community of adventure companies and budget camps, lies 12 km (7 miles) north of Jinja on the east bank. A smaller but growing adventure hub is based at Kalagala on the north side of the river. Flights can be chartered to nearby Jinja Airstrip.

Hotels

Adrift River Camp

$ | **HOTEL** | Opened in 2022, this lodge is ideal for adventurers who want to upgrade their creature comforts. **Pros:** 450 yards from jaw-dropping Kalagala Waterfall Viewpoint; main power grid hookup and backup generator adds to the comfort levels; all rooms have bathrooms and balconies. **Cons:** riverfront views partially obscured by trees; new facility but investors have high standards; natural tones of decor too austere for some. [$] *Rooms from: US$235* ✉ *Kalagala Falls, River Nile, Jinja* ☎ *755/225–587* 🌐 *adrift.ug* 🛏 *16 rooms* 🍴 *All-Inclusive.*

★ **Lemala Wildwaters Lodge**

$$$$ | **HOTEL** | If this world-class lodge, part of the respected Lemala group, does not enchant you with its magical location, it will captivate you with its winning service, spa, and superb cuisine. **Pros:** one of the best lodges in Uganda, Wildwaters is a destination in itself; an excellent spot to wind down after a safari; a great base for adrenaline adventures. **Cons:** some people find the roar of the rapids too noisy; occasional tsetse flies can be annoying; not on the main safari trail. [$] *Rooms from: US$940* ✉ *Kalagala Falls, River Nile, Jinja* ☎ *039/277–6669, 0772/237–400* 🌐 *www.lemalacamps.com* 🛏 *10 suites* 🍴 *All-Inclusive.*

Activities

WHITE-WATER RAFTING

None of Jinja's activities is more popular than rafting the Nile. Trips tackle a sequence of white-water rapids, graded between 3 and 5, with names such as Vengeance and the ominous-sounding Bad Place. At local beauty spot Itanda Falls, a Class VI rapid necessitates a portage via surrounding rocks that fall within a nature reserve. A number of companies offer similarly priced half- and one-day packages, including transport from Kampala if required, lunch on the river, and beers afterward to toast the excitements of the day. Two-day or longer expeditions are also available. Packages generally include photography and video of your flips and grins!

★ **Adrift East Africa**

WHITE-WATER RAFTING | **FAMILY** | Established in 1981, Adrift has pioneered rafting on the Nile in Uganda and on the Zambezi in Zimbabwe. Their client list includes royals, actors, and TV celebrities. In September 2022 they relaunched their Nile High Bungee from the Adrift Riverbase Activity Centre on the north bank of the Nile, a stone's throw from their sister business, the acclaimed Lemala Wildwaters Lodge. Expect full-moon jumps, tandem jumps, and water touches. ✉ *Lemala Wildwaters Lodge, Kangulumira, Jinja* ☎ *0755/225–587* 🌐 *adrift.ug* 🎫 *Full-day rafting package, US$140 per person (includes pick up and*

The self-appointed adventure capital of East Africa, the Nile River near Jinja is a hot spot for white-water rafting.

drop off, breakfast, lunch, and photos); bungee jump US$115 per person.

Nalubale Rafting

WHITE-WATER RAFTING | FAMILY | The folks at Nalubale Rafting are a friendly and enthusiastic bunch. Groups of volunteers, students, and independent travelers paddle, riverboard, and tandem kayak confidently under supervision from Nalubale's professional river guides; families are well catered to on family floats. The all-inclusive rafting package includes accommodation at the cheap and cheerful Nile River Camp at Bujagali. ⊠ *Nile River Camp, Bujagali, Eastern Region, Jinja* ☎ *782/638–938* ⊕ *nalubalerafting. com* ✉ *Rafting from US$125 per person.*

★ Nile River Explorers

WHITE-WATER RAFTING | The NRE camp at Bujagali, high above the Nile, is a chill hangout for backpackers and a good base for Jinja's adventure tourism activities: rafting, tubing, mountain biking, and bungee. Their famous river boat cruises embark daily from their Bujagali camp; the 2-hour sunset cruise with drinks and

nibbles is sensational. Guests at Nile Explorers Camp get free access to the 20-meter water slide into the Nile. ⊠ *Bujagali, Eastern Region, Jinja* ☎ *772/422– 373* ⊕ *www.raftafrica.com* ✉ *Full-day rafting US$140 (includes breakfast, snacks and drinking water, post-rafting sodas/beers and sandwiches, photos).*

Gateway Cities

Entebbe

Entebbe is a peaceful, sleepy town, situated at the tip of a peninsula extending south of Kampala into Lake Victoria. Just a couple of miles from the country's only international airport, overnighting here is convenient for anyone with early or late flight arrival/departure times. Entebbe's proximity to the airport, and Kajjansi Airfield a few miles up the road, also makes it handy for the domestic air services to the national parks. Charming, boutique guesthouses or mediocre business hotels typify the accommodations here. If these are not your style they become significantly more appealing when you realize that the 40-km (25-mile) journey between Kampala and Entebbe can sometimes take more than 90 minutes to complete.

GETTING HERE AND AROUND

Entebbe International Airport (EBB) is 5 km (3 miles) from the town of Entebbe. Regional services from RwandAir, Air Tanzania, Kenya Airways, Jambojet, AirKenya Express, and Uganda Airlines serve destinations in Rwanda, Tanzania, and Kenya respectively. From Entebbe, licensed airport taxis are available at all hours from the stand just outside arrivals, though it's less stressful to prebook a hotel or tour company driver to meet your flight since most Entebbe properties include this in their rates. Uber, Bolt (⊕ *bolt.eu*), and SafeCar can be booked using the airport's free Wi-Fi (but don't be surprised if the drivers refuse credit card payment and want cash). Uganda's capital Kampala lies 40 km (25 miles) to the east.

Sights

★ Ngamba Island Chimpanzee Sanctuary

WILDLIFE REFUGE | FAMILY | Delivering a different experience to tracking chimps in the wild, this sanctuary occupies its own island in Lake Victoria. Here visitors can observe the rescued and orphaned chimps during any of the three outdoor feedings; for an extra fee, get an up-close view during the 6 pm indoor feeding. Lying 23 km (14 miles) southeast of Entebbe, the sanctuary was established in 1998 and is run by the Chimpanzee Trust whose mission is to conserve the chimpanzees' natural habitat as well as provide care to rescued animals that can't survive in the wild. A portion of the sanctuary is fenced off for day-trippers to observe feeding sessions from a raised viewing platform—an excellent photographic opportunity in itself. The real appeal, however, lies in getting to spend a night or even volunteer: overnight visitors (the island has an eco-lodge overseeing the lake with a fresh breeze) can opt for the volunteering experience. Be prepared for extensive medical requirements, but the chance to care for our closest relatives will melt your heart. ⊠ *Chimpanzee Trust, Plot 1, Bank Close, Entebbe* ☏ *0414/320–662, 0758/221–880* ⊕ *ngambaisland.org* ⊠ *A half-day visit US$88 per person; Volunteer Experience US$550 per person.*

Uganda Wildlife Education Centre

COLLEGE | FAMILY | On the lakeshore in Entebbe, the Uganda Wildlife Education Centre plays a multifaceted role: it's an animal rescue center, veterinary institution, and tourist attraction all rolled into one—but perhaps its most significant role is as an education facility for the country's schoolchildren, who roll up in busloads daily. UWEC (pronounced *Ooh-Eck*), is home to an array of Ugandan species. Facilities for the animals may feel a little cramped, but the team places great importance on putting conservation first, making it a pleasant place to while away a spare morning or afternoon in Entebbe. Kids love the camel and donkey rides, the children's play center, and beach games. For maximum interaction, UWEC offers a Keeper for the Day program ($150); for those who like sleeping to the sounds of the wild, traditional banda (cottages) are for rent in UWEC's grounds. Visitors can also book the Behind-the-Scenes tour ($70) for a chance to enter some of the enclosures and meet the animals, or the Chimpanzee Close-up ($260) for a grooming session courtesy of one of UWEC's orphaned chimpanzees. ⊠ *Plot 56/57, Lugard Ave., Entebbe* ☏ *0414/320–520, 0706/505–722* ⊕ *uwec.ug* ⊠ *US$15.*

🍽 Restaurants

★ Faze 3

$ | ECLECTIC | A lively choice for Entebbe nights out, and handy for diners en route to the airport for late-night flights, Faze 3 boasts a mind-boggling menu that encompasses a wide range of cuisines: from starters and snacks, light salads, pita pockets, and sandwiches to Continental classics, authentic curries, and meaty feasts served sizzlingly hot on cast-iron skillets. Well-trained staff provide snappy service. **Known for:** meaty feasts served sizzlingly hot on cast-iron skillets; authentic curries. $ *Average main: US$10* ⊠ *106 Circular Rd., Entebbe* ✛ *Last turn on the left before the airport* ☎ *0778/609–595, 0393/671–345.*

★ Goretti's Beachside Pizzeria and Grill

$ | PIZZA | FAMILY | A cold beer, crisp pizza, and curling your toes in the sand are a few of life's simple pleasures. Enjoy all three simultaneously at Goretti's Beachside Pizzeria, a popular haunt for tourists and locals alike. **Known for:** crisp, wood-fired pizza; grilled fish and meat. $ *Average main: US$10* ⊠ *Anderita Beach, Nambi Rd., Entebbe* ☎ *0772/308–887* ▭ *No credit cards* ☞ *Pay in Uganda shillings or you risk extortionate dollar exchange rates.*

★ Gorilla Conservation Cafe

$ | CAFÉ | FAMILY | Set on the main road in mature gardens, this clever café concept directly supports mountain gorilla conservation. The extensive international-style menu includes coffee, milkshakes, salads, sandwiches, pasta, and burgers. **Known for:** friendly baristas who know as much about gorillas as they know about coffee; ethically sourced coffee that directly supports mountain gorilla conservation; excellent coffee in laid-back setting. $ *Average main: US$10* ⊠ *Plot 13 Portal Rd., Entebbe* ☎ *752/330–139* ⊕ *gorillaconservationcoffee.org.*

🛏 Hotels

★ The Boma Entebbe

$ | B&B/INN | This popular boutique hotel with a reputation for great service is tucked away on a leafy residential street in Entebbe, a few minutes' drive from the airport. **Pros:** superb service; professional service at an affordable price; rate includes airport transfers if required. **Cons:** incoming/outgoing guests can make it noisy at night; can get booked up quickly. $ *Rooms from: US$170* ⊠ *Plot 20A, Gowers Rd., Entebbe* ✛ *Turn off airport road at AAR Victoria Medical Centre (and Boma sign)* ☎ *0772/467–929* ⊕ *www.boma.co.ug* ⇱ *16 rooms* ❂ *Free Breakfast.*

★ Hotel No. 5

$$ | HOTEL | Entebbe's only luxury boutique hotel provides consistently high service levels in an intimate setting. **Pros:** their Cinque restaurant serves authentic Italian pizzas; ideal stopover between flights to Uganda's National Parks; highly trained staff. **Cons:** in a class of its own, thus early booking essential; gym is small. $ *Rooms from: US$390* ⊠ *5 Edna Rd., Entebbe* ☎ *757/401–299* ⊕ *hotelnumber5.com* ⇱ *15 rooms* ❂ *Free Breakfast.*

Karibu Guesthouse

$ | B&B/INN | An unpretentious guesthouse in a peaceful area of Entebbe, Karibu lives up to its name (*"you're welcome"* in Swahili) with friendly, well-trained staff. **Pros:** free 24-hour airport taxi service; lovers of French cuisine will appreciate the food; natural swimming pool and spa. **Cons:** rooms aren't modern but they are clean; some airport/guest noise at night. $ *Rooms from: US$186* ⊠ *84 Nsamizi Rd., Entebbe* ☎ *0777/044–984, 0788/714–587* ⊕ *karibuguesthouse.com* ⇱ *8 ensuite rooms* ❂ *Free Breakfast.*

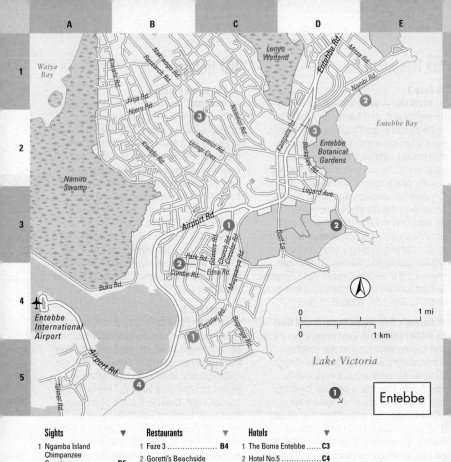

Sights ▼

1 Ngamba Island
  Chimpanzee
  Sanctuary.................. **D5**
2 Uganda Wildlife
  Education Centre **D3**

Restaurants ▼

1 Faze 3 .... **B4**
2 Goretti's Beachside
  Pizzeria and Grill **D1**
3 Gorilla Conservation
  Cafe **D2**

Hotels ▼

1 The Boma Entebbe **C3**
2 Hotel No.5 .... **C4**
3 Karibu Guesthouse **B1**
4 Protea Hotel
  Entebbe **B5**

Protea Hotel Entebbe

$$ | **HOTEL** | Part of the established Marriott network of business hotels, the Protea Entebbe is just off the main approach road to the airport, offering a practical base to stay. **Pros:** super-convenient for the airport; beautiful beach location; international brand. **Cons:** spa needs renovating; food gets mixed reviews; service can be slow. $ *Rooms from: US$346* ✉ *36-40 Sebugwawo Dr., Entebbe* ☎ *0414/323–132* ⊕ *marriott.com* ⇆ *70 rooms* ⧉ *Free Breakfast.*

Kampala

If the bright lights of Kampala beckon—and if time is not a precious commodity—then Uganda's dynamic capital offers an impressive roll call of positive qualities: a far wider range of fashionable eateries dot the city, it delivers a better standard of high-end hotels, the nightlife is buzzing, the city is host to a growing arts and festival scene, and shopping mavens will love the craft markets. Buildings of historical interest include sub-Saharan Africa's only Baha'i Temple, the dated (but still worth a visit) Uganda Museum, the Uganda National Mosque (East Africa's biggest mosque, a gift from Muammar Gaddafi of Libya, and a great vantage point to survey the city), and the Uganda Martyrs Shrines in Namugongo. Sadly the magnificent Kasubi Tombs—a burial ground for members of the Buganda royal family, are still under reconstruction more than a decade after a fire. For many visitors, however, Kampala's own brand of vibrant urban chaos has an appeal all of its own. The historic city of 7 hills has mushroomed to three times that number but the city pulses with energy. This really is a tale of two cities.

GETTING HERE AND AROUND

Uganda's capital Kampala lies 40 km (25 miles) to the east of Entebbe. Licensed airport taxis are available at all hours; some hotels include airport pick-ups in their rates, although Kampala hotels are more likely to charge a premium rate. If you're coming to Uganda on safari, your driver should meet you at the airport (but do check). Most hotels and restaurants have Wi-Fi, and English is the country's *official language*, so booking an Uber, Bolt, or SafeCar should be fairly easy. Confusingly, all public transport is actually privately owned but it's cheap and there's plenty of it. However, private cars are always a safer option. *Matatu* minibus taxis ply main routes in and out of Kampala city, buses connect cities and towns, *boda boda* motorbike taxis connect the dots. If you're feeling brave, download the Safe-Boda app but insist on wearing a helmet.

🍴 Restaurants

Kampala's social scene is diverse and constantly evolving. New restaurants pop up quickly. The country's middle-class has embraced coffee culture, pizzas, and smoothies. Cocktails, mocktails, all-you-can-eat brunches, mussels nights, and tapas bars flourish. Kampala's messy traffic means you shouldn't stray too far from where you're staying (if you have limited time in the city). Wherever you end up, you're likely to dine outside almost every day of the year. Most restaurants and bars sell alcohol (unless you're eating at one of the highly popular Somali-owned CJ's (Cafe Java's). It's illegal to smoke in public in Uganda so expect restrictions (even outdoors). International restaurants are well priced compared to many other countries but expect substantial single course meals rather than entrées and desserts. Wine is becoming more popular but frequently overpriced with limited options (unless you're a fan of sweet South African wines).

★ The Bistro

$$ | **ECLECTIC** | This stylish, modern restaurant in the heart of buzzing Kisementi delivers accomplished fusion cuisine with considerable flair, transforming effortlessly from convivial café by day to

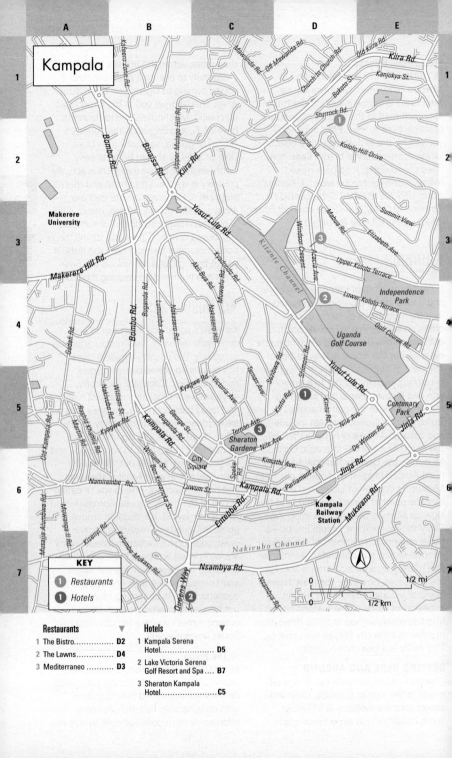

Kampala

Makerere University

Kiitante Channel

Independence Park

Uganda Golf Course

Centenary Park

Sheraton Gardens

City Square

Kampala Railway Station

Nakivubo Channel

| 0 | | 1/2 mi |
| 0 | | 1/2 km |

KEY

1 *Restaurants*

1 **Hotels**

Restaurants ▼

1 The Bistro................ **D2**
2 The Lawns................ **D4**
3 Mediterraneo **D3**

Hotels ▼

1 Kampala Serena
Hotel..................... **D5**
2 Lake Victoria Serena
Golf Resort and Spa **B7**
3 Sheraton Kampala
Hotel...................... **C5**

When in Kampala...The Lawns is the only restaurant in town with a license to serve game. Ostrich burgers, anyone?

happening eatery by night. Customers love the laid-back atmosphere of the Bistro's shaded terrace. **Known for:** Happy Hour every day between 3 and 6 pm; live music Friday night; café by day, eatery by night. $ *Average main: US$15* ⊠ *15 Cooper Rd., Kisementi* ☎ *0757/247–876* ⊕ *facebook.com/thebistrokampala.*

The Lawns

$$ | FUSION | The only restaurant in Kampala with a license to serve game—the meat is sourced legally from registered South African game ranches—the Lawns unashamedly celebrates the wildest cuts of meat, with dishes like ostrich burgers, smoked kudu steak, or whole crocodile tail (preorder 2–3 hours). Manicured gardens and a beautiful wooden deck overlooking the perennially verdant golf course adds to the charm and ambience of this large eatery in central Kampala. **Known for:** legally sourced game meat; diverse and original menu for all tastes; excellent service. $ *Average main: US$20* ⊠ *Plot 3A, Lower Kololo Terr., Kololo* ✢ *On Acacia Avenue, next to Golf Course* ☎ *751/895–653 WhatsApp* ⊕ *www.thelawns.co.ug.*

★ Mediterraneo

$$ | ITALIAN | Kampala's Mediterraneo serves up world-class Italian food to a fashionable crowd. Tiered hardwood decks encircle a leafy courtyard, creating intimate spaces decorated with vintage bric-a-brac. **Known for:** romantic atmosphere; excellent desserts; genuine Italian cooking. $ *Average main: US$20* ⊠ *Villa Kololo, 42 Windsor Crescent, Kololo* ☎ *0701/098–732.*

Hotels

★ Kampala Serena Hotel

$$ | HOTEL | Towering above sculpted water features and landscaped gardens like a modern-day Moorish palace, the 5-star Kampala Serena sets *the* standard for hotel service in Uganda. **Pros:** international standards with African style; central location; extremely professional. **Cons:** long lines at security when president visits; the building has a macabre history—before it was extensively renovated by the Serena chain the property was the infamous Nile Hotel, associated with state-sanctioned torture that took place under the bloody regimes of Obote and Amin; too large and impersonal for some tastes. $ *Rooms from: US$325* ✉ *Kintu Rd., Kampala* ☎ *0312/309–000* ⊕ *serenahotels.com/serenakampala* 🛏 *122 rooms* ⦿| *Free Breakfast.*

Lake Victoria Serena Golf Resort and Spa

$$ | RESORT | FAMILY | Thanks to the new ExpressWay road, this resort has come of age, and visitors to this pastel-hue citadel on Lake Victoria happily trade off the remote position for the plush comfort of this 5-star hotel's rooms and extensive facilities. **Pros:** well-appointed rooms with lake views; play 18 holes of golf next to Lake Victoria; a comfortable spot to wind down post-safari. **Cons:** massage charged extra; guests complain of poor Wi-Fi in some rooms; popular wedding venue may be busy at weekends. $ *Rooms from: US$322* ✉ *Lweza-Kigo Rd., off Entebbe Rd., Kampala* ☎ *0417/121–000, 0313/221–000* ⊕ *www.serenahotels. com/lake-victoria* 🛏 *124 rooms* ⦿| *Free Breakfast.*

Sheraton Kampala Hotel

$ | HOTEL | Located in the city's Central Business District, among mature palm-tree-filled gardens, the world has been meeting at this hotel since 1967. **Pros:** central Kampala location; global brand with international service standards; themed evenings guaranteed to keep you entertained. **Cons:** security lines at main entrance gate; gym can get very busy; caters largely to a business clientele. $ *Rooms from: US$236* ✉ *Ternan Ave., Kampala* ☎ *0312/322–499* ⊕ *sheratonkampala.com* 🛏 *236 rooms* ⦿| *Free Breakfast.*

 Activities

Lake Victoria Serena Golf Resort

GOLF | Uganda has a sprinkling of small golf courses across the country but this is East Africa's first 9-hole island green (playing as 18 holes). Constructed to full USGA specifications, Serena Hotels' championship golf course pans across reclaimed wetlands on the shores of Africa's largest lake. The clubhouse has locker rooms with showers and a steam room, two restaurants, a bar, and pro shop. Golf equipment can be rented on-site and individual and group golf lessons are available with the resident pro. Caddies are on hand, too. ✉ *Lweza-Kigo Rd., off Entebbe Rd., Kajjansi* ☎ *313/221–000, 417/121–000* ⊕ *www.serenahotels. com/lake-victoria* 🏌 *Serena Hotel guests: US$15 for 9 holes, US$25 for 18 holes* 🏌 *18 holes, par 70.*

Chapter 8

BOTSWANA

Updated by
James Gifford

WELCOME TO BOTSWANA

TOP REASONS TO GO

★ **The Okavango Delta:** Whether you're drifting dreamily in a *mokoro* (canoe) through crystal clear, papyrus-fringed channels or walking among ancient trees on one of the many islands, your everyday world is guaranteed to fade from your consciousness.

★ **Big Game:** You won't find huge herds as in the Serengeti, but you'll come face-to-face with more critters than you ever knew existed. And there won't be hordes of other visitors blocking your view or diluting the experience.

★ **Birding:** Marvel at more than 900 species—many endemic—that crowd the game reserves. A sighting of a Pel's fishing owl, one of the world's rarest birds, will have Audubon twitching in his grave.

★ **Walking with the Bushmen:** Far from being lifeless, deserts are miracles of plenty, you just have to be in the right company—that of the Kalahari Bushmen. Listen to their dissonant music and watch them dance a dance as old as time.

Botswana is roughly the size of France, and nearly 30% is protected for conservation and tourism.

1 The Okavango Delta. Originating in the Angolan highlands, the Okavango River takes several months to complete its journey southwards before fanning out over northwestern Botswana, forming the Okavango Delta. The magical scenery of this UNESCO World Heritage Site is particularly impressive from the air.

2 Moremi Game Reserve. In the southeastern sector of the Okavango lies this spectacular reserve where the life-giving waters of the Okavango meet the vast Kalahari.

3 Chobe National Park. Huge herds of elephants roam this 11,700-squarekm (4,500-square-mile) park that borders the Chobe River in northeast Botswana.

4 Kwando, Selinda, and Linyanti Reserves. These three neighboring, gamerich private concessions lie on Botswana's northern border tracking the Kwando River, which becomes the Linyanti and finally the Chobe River.

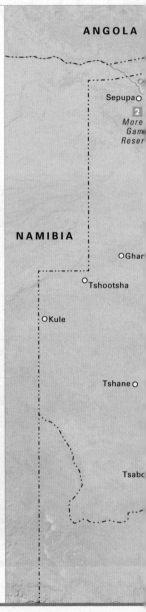

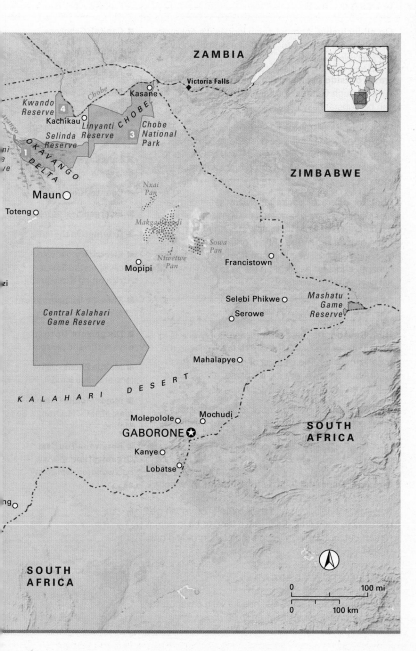

COUNTRY SNAPSHOT

WAYS TO SAVE

Go all-inclusive. At most safari lodges it's not even an option, it's a requisite. But rest assured, you will eat and drink well.

Travel outside peak season. Prices are highest June through October, but outside peak season rates can be substantially lower.

Pack light. Bush planes are the main way to travel across Botswana. If you go over the maximum baggage allowance of 44 pounds, you may have to leave stuff behind or pay extra for a bag to be brought to you on a separate flight the next day.

Look for operator packages. Many safari companies offer deals on room rates or flights if you do a circuit with the same company, staying at two or more of their properties. All accommodation bookings will include room and transport, which is cheaper and a lot easier than trying to book the internal charter flights yourself.

WHEN TO GO

High Season: The best time to visit Botswana is in the dry season (May–October), though it's also the most expensive. The Delta is brimming with fresh water, but since vegetation is sparse, it's easier to see game.

Low Season: From December to March, expect great economy deals offered by most of the lodges. You may encounter rain, but the bush is lush and populated with lots of baby animals and migrant birds.

Shoulder Seasons: Temps start dropping in March and April, but rates are not yet at their peak; however, the tall grass and thick vegetation mean it's not easy to see game. Prices also tend to be lower in November, but expect the odd thunderstorm and hot temps.

PASSPORTS AND VISAS

All visitors, including infants, need a valid passport to enter Botswana for visits of up to 90 days.

AT A GLANCE

- **Capital:** Gaborone
- **Population:** 2,449,200
- **Big Five:** All here
- **Currency:** pula
- **Money:** ATMs in bigger towns; cash far more common than credit.
- **Language:** English, Setswana
- **Country Code:** 267
- **Emergencies:** 997/911
- **Driving:** On the left
- **Electricity:** 230v/50 cycle; plugs are South Africa round three-prong
- **Time:** Seven hours ahead of NY
- **Documents:** Up to 90 days with valid passport
- **Mobile Phones:** GSM (900 and 1800 bands)
- **Major Mobile Companies:** MASCOM, Orange, Be Mobile
- **Botswana Tourism Organization:** ⊕ www. botswanatourism.co.bw

More than half a century ago Botswana was a Cinderella among nations. Then the Fairy Godmother visited and bestowed upon her the gift of diamonds. The resulting economic boom transformed Botswana into one of Africa's richest countries (as measured by per capita income). In 1966 the British Protectorate of Bechuanaland was granted independence and renamed Botswana, and the first democratic president, the internationally respected Sir Seretse Khama, guided his country into a peaceful future.

Where other nations' celebrations quickly turned sour, Botswana's independence brought an enduring tide of optimism. The country sidestepped the scourge of tribalism and factional fighting that cursed much of the continent and is considered one of Africa's most stable democracies. The infrastructure is excellent, and the country is extremely safe. Another big bonus is that nearly everybody speaks English—a legacy from when Botswana was a British protectorate.

Although cities such as Gaborone (pro-nounced "ha-bo-ronee"), the capital, have been modernized, Botswana has little in the way of urban excitement. But outside the cities it's a land of amazing variety: the Kalahari Desert lies in stark contrast to the lush beauty of the Okavango Delta, one of Botswana's most magnifi-cent and best-known regions. Botswana is passionate about conservation, and its legendary big game goes hand-in-hand with its admirable conservation record.

Botswana's policy of low-impact, high-cost tourism ensures the wilderness remains pristine and exclusive. The great rivers—the Chobe, the Linyanti, and the Kwando—are teeming with herds of elephants and packs of wild dogs, otherwise known as the elusive "painted wolves" of Africa. The Savuti Channel, which flowed for a brief period from 2010 to 2015, may now have been reduced to a river of sand but the nearby hills and golden grass of the Savuti plains are still home to prowling leopards and huge prides of lions that hunt under skies pulsing with brilliant stars. Then there are the vast white pie-crust surfaces of the Makgadikgadi Pans (the nearest thing on earth to the surface of the moon), once a mega inland lake where flamingos still flock to breed and strange prehistoric islands of rock rise dramatically from the flaky, arid surface.

If you'd like to meet some of the most fascinating people in existence, the stark wilderness of the Central Kalahari Game Reserve is the ancestral home for one of the fastest disappearing indigenous populations on earth, the Kalahari San Bushmen, as well as majestic black-maned lions.

MAJOR REGIONS

This chapter has been broken down by **Must-See Parks** (Okavango Delta, Moremi Game Reserve, Chobe National Park, Kwando Reserve, and Linyanti Reserve) and **If You Have Time Parks** (Selinda Reserve, Central Kalahari Game Reserve, Makgadikgadi Pans, and Mashatu Game Reserve in the Tuli Block region) to help you better organize your time. There is also a section on **Gateway Cities**, which for Botswana is Maun.

Planning

Getting Here and Around

AIR

In this huge, often inaccessible country, air travel is the easiest way to get around. Most tourists' port of entry is the busy Maun International Airport (MUB), the gateway to the Okavango Delta, which is 1 km (½ mile) from the town center of this northern safari hub. Sir Seretse Khama International Airport (GBE) is in Botswana's capital, Gaborone, 15 km (9½ miles) from the city center. Kasane International Airport (BBK) is 3 km (2 miles) from the entrance to Chobe National Park. All three are relatively

small and it's easy to find your way around.

FLIGHTS

Air Botswana has scheduled flights from Johannesburg to Gaborone and Maun on a daily basis. The airline also flies Johannesburg to Kasane and from Cape Town to Gaborone three times a week. Note their schedule changes frequently. SA Airlink also has daily flights from Johannesburg to Gaborone, Maun, and Kasane and from Cape Town to Maun.

Mack Air, Wilderness Air, and Delta Air fly directly between Johannesburg's Lanseria airport and Maun on private charters. Air charter companies operate small planes from Kasane and Maun to all the camps. Flown by some of the youngest-looking pilots in the world, these flights, which your travel agent will arrange, are convenient, reliable, and average between 25 and 50 minutes. Maximum total baggage allowance is 20 kilograms (44 pounds) in a duffel bag or similar (no hard cases allowed), including hand luggage and camera equipment. Since most flights are in the middle of the day when thermal air currents are at their strongest, flights can sometimes be very bumpy. Take air-sickness pills if you're susceptible to motion sickness; then sit back and enjoy the fabulous bird's-eye views. You're sure to spot elephants and hippos from the air.

AIRLINES Air Botswana. ✉ *Dalale House, Queens Rd., Main Mall, Gaborone* ✛ *Behind South African Embassy* ☎ *310–5476, 368–0900* ⊕ *www.airbotswana.co.bw.* **SA Airlink.** ✉ *Sir Seretse Khama International Airport, Gaborone city* ✛ *Inside Airport* ☎ *11/451–7300 in South Africa, 395–1820* ⊕ *www.flyairlink.com.*

AIRPORTS Kasane International Airport. (*BBK*) ✉ *Upper Rd., Kasane* ☎ *625–5000.* **Maun International Airport.** (*MUB*) ✉ *Mathiba I St., Maun* ☎ *681–7800.* **Sir Seretse Khama International Airport.** (*GBE*)

✉ *Airport Rd., Phakalane, Gaborone* ☎ *369–2504.*

CHARTER FLIGHTS Delta Air. ✉ *Mathiba I St., Maun* ✛ *Inside airport, opposite terminal* ☎ **686–0044. Mack Air.** ✉ *Airport Road, Maun* ✛ *next to Dusty Donkey* ☎ *686–0675* ⊕ *www.mackair.co.bw.* **Wilderness Air.** ✉ *Mathiba I St., Maun* ☎ *686–0778* ⊕ *www.wilderness-air.com.*

CAR

All the main access roads from neighboring countries are paved, and cross-border formalities are user-friendly. Maun is easy to reach from South Africa, Namibia, and Zimbabwe, but the distances are very long and not particularly scenic. Gaborone is 360 km (225 miles) from Johannesburg via Rustenburg, Zeerust, and the Tlokweng border post. Driving in Botswana is on the left-hand side of the road. The "Shell Tourist Map of Botswana" is the best available map. Find it at Botswana airports or in airport bookstores.

Forget about a car in the Okavango Delta unless it's amphibious. Only the western and eastern sides of the Delta panhandle and the Moremi Game Reserve are accessible by car; but you will need a 4x4 vehicle. The road from Maun to Moremi North Gate is paved for the first 47 km (29 miles) up to Shorobe, where it becomes gravel for 11 km (7 miles) and then a dirt road.

A 4x4 vehicle is also essential in Chobe National Park, Central Kalahari Game Reserve, and the Makgadikgadi Pans National Park. The roads are sandy and/or very muddy, depending on the season.

Health and Safety

There are high standards of hygiene in all the private lodges, and most hotels are usually up to international health standards. But malaria is present, so don't forget to take those antimalarials. Botswana has one of the highest AIDS rates

in Africa, but it also has one of Africa's most progressive and comprehensive programs for dealing with the disease. All the private lodges and camps have excellent staff medical programs; you're in no danger of contracting the disease unless you have sex with a stranger. As in most cities, crime is prevalent in Gaborone, but simple safety precautions such as locking up your documents and valuables and not walking alone at night will keep you safe. On safari, there's always potential danger from wild animals, but your ranger will brief you thoroughly on the dos and don'ts of encountering big game.

The American embassy is in Gaborone, the country's capital city.

Most safari companies include emergency medical evacuation insurance for public liability to the nearest hospital, but you must have your own travel and medical insurance as well. There are two 24-hour emergency rescue companies: Medical Rescue International, which will require confirmation with your insurance company before evacuation, and Okavango Air Rescue, which will liaise with your insurance after your safe evacuation.

EMBASSIES U.S. Embassy. ✉ *Embassy Dr., Government Enclave, Gaborone* ☎ *373–2322, 395–3982 after hours* ⊕ *bw. usembassy.gov.*

EMERGENCIES Ambulance. ☎ *997.* **Police.** ☎ *999.*

EMERGENCY SERVICES Medical Rescue International. ☎ *390–1601, 992 Emergency toll-free.* **Okavango Air Rescue.** ☎ *686–1506, 995 emergency toll-free.*

Hotels and Lodges

Most camps accommodate 12 to 24 people, so the only traffic you'll encounter among the Delta's waterways and roads in the private concessions is that of dozing hippos and lumbering elephants. In the national parks and particularly in the northern part of Chobe, which attracts the greatest number of tourists, the roads and river are noticeably busier but it's still significantly quieter than most of the East African parks. Many lodges now have family units although most have a minimum age requirement of six or above; some even provide an extra staff member and specialist bush-related activities to keep youngsters occupied. A luxury arms race among operators in recent years has led to a leap in extravagance at the premium end of the spectrum. Many mid-range camps now offer some form of Wi-Fi, helicopter flights and even spa treatments (the latter two at a surcharge). The most expensive ones boast apartment-sized suites complete with mini-bars, nespresso machines and cooling systems. Room prices are highest June through October.

A word about terminology: "Land camps" are in game reserves or concessions and offer morning and evening game drives. If you're not in a national park, you'll be able to go off-road and on night drives with a powerful spotlight to pick out nocturnal animals. "Water camps" are deep in the Okavango Delta and are often only accessible by air or water. Many camps offer both a land and a water experience, but their water activities tend to be seasonal and are only possible during the flood months (May-October).

There's limited local cuisine in Botswana, so the food, which is all house-made and of good quality, is designed to appeal to an international palate. Most camps bake their own delicious bread, muffins, and cakes while dinners are hearty three-course affairs, washed down with a selection of South African wines and beers. A handful of the premium camps now offer à la carte menus. Don't expect TVs, even at very expensive camps (with the exception of Xigera).

For information on converters and electricity while on Safari, see Electricity, in the Planning Your Safari chapter.

MOBILE SAFARIS

Often incorrectly viewed only as a cost-cutting measure, the range of mobile safari options in Botswana is staggering. At the top end, your large walk-in en suite tent will have Persian rugs, antique furniture and flush toilets; at the other extreme, you will help with the cooking and even setting up camp. The most popular option lies somewhere in the middle—a non-participatory safari with en suite tents, hot-water bucket showers, and a talented chef who can create delicious three-course meals that would rival many lodges, all on an open fire. As well as feeling closer to nature (lions can easily walk through your camp at night), mobile safari guides tend to be the most knowledgeable in the country, and spending 10 days with the same guide as you move through different habitats gives you a greater depth of understanding. It also gives the guide the opportunity to tailor the focus of game drives to your specific interests, helped by the inherently flexible nature of mobiles. The one downside is that although you will have your own private campsite, you will probably be in the national parks so will see other vehicles during the day.

DINING AND LODGING PRICES

Most lodging prices are quoted in U.S. dollars, and you can use dollars, euros, or South African rand as tips wherever you stay. The price per person per night at private lodges can range from US$500 to US$5,000. The all-inclusive rates include accommodations, all game activities, all meals, local beers, non-premium spirits, and good South African wine. Camps arrange transfers from the nearest airport or airstrip. It's important to note that there are few budget lodging options available in Botswana, and most of the camps we write about fall into the "luxury" category.

Restaurant and hotel reviews have been shortened. For full information, visit Fodors.com.

GOING GREEN

In such a pristine, finely balanced environment, it's vital to limit the impact on the flora and fauna, and many safari companies have installed ecologically sound practices. Gone are the days of camps accruing mountains of empty, plastic water bottles—almost all lodges (and some mobile operators) will give you metal water bottles to fill and reuse with filtered drinking water from their reverse osmosis plants. Solar power has also largely taken over from noisy, diesel-guzzling generators. In addition, the major companies run a range of community initiatives aimed at ensuring the local Batswana population see the benefits from the unique habitat and its wildlife, creating a framework for long-term sustainable tourism.

Money Matters

The pula and the thebe constitute the country's currency; one pula equals 100 thebe. This is the only legally accepted currency in local restaurants and shops (you can draw Pula from ATMs or change money at banks) but almost all establishments accept credit cards. Lodge prices are quoted in U.S. dollars, which are also mostly used for tips.

There are no restrictions on foreign currency notes brought into the country as long as they're declared. Travelers can carry up to P10,000 (about US$1,000), or the equivalent in foreign currency, out of the country without declaring it. Banking hours are weekdays 9–3:30, Saturday 8:30–12:30. Hours at Barclays Bank at Sir Seretse Khama International Airport are Monday–Saturday 6 am–10 pm.

■ TIP➡ **Though the national currency is the pula, you can use U.S. dollars or euros as tips. Your information folder at each lodge will give helpful suggestions on whom and what to tip.**

Passports and Visas

All visitors, including infants, need a valid passport to enter Botswana for visits of up to 90 days.

When to Go

The best time to visit Botswana is in the autumn and winter months (April–September), the dry season; however, it's also the most expensive time. In the Delta during the winter months the water comes in from the Angolan highlands, and the floodplains, channels, lakes, and inland waterways are literally brimming with sparkling, fresh water. Elsewhere, because it's the dry season, the grass and vegetation are sparse, and it's much easier to see game, which often have no choice but to drink at available waterholes or rivers. But be warned: it can be bitterly cold, particularly early in the morning and at night. Dress in layers, which you can discard or add to as the sun goes up or down.

During the green season (November–February), aptly named since it's when the bush is at its most lush and is populated with lots of baby animals, you'll find great economy deals offered by most of the lodges, but it can be very hot, especially in October and early November when temperatures can reach up to 35°C (95°F) or more. The rains tend to arrive

The Bayei people live along the tributaries of the Okavango and Chobe Rivers.

from November onwards and can continue until late March or early April, which helps to cool things down but can impact your activities. If you're a birder (Botswana has more than 400 species of birds), this is the best time to visit because all the migratory birds have returned; the green vegetation also provides an attractive backdrop for keen photographers. Generally speaking, though, unless you can stand great heat, don't mind getting wet, or are a devoted bird-watcher, stick with fall and winter.

FESTIVALS AND EVENTS

April: Enjoy music, dance, and theatrical performance across the capital during the Maitisong Festival.

May: Expect few tourists but incredible fun at the Tjilenje Cultural Festival in the country's northeast.

July: Presidents Day is a four-day celebration across the country. The Makgadikgadi Epic is an adrenaline-fueled festival featuring skydiving, quad bikes, helicopter flights, and horse rides.

September: Celebrate independence in a big way on Botswana Day.

Visitor Information

Visit Botswana Tourism's website for tour operator and travel agency information. To be listed on the website, these organizations must satisfy and adhere to the high standards demanded by Botswana Tourism

Botswana phone numbers begin with the 267 country code, which you don't dial within the country. (There are no internal area codes in Botswana.)

CONTACTS Botswana Tourism Organization. ✉ *Plot 50676, Fairgrounds Office Park, Blocks B & D, Gaborone city* ⊕ *www. botswanatourism.co.bw.*

Read and Watch

The No. 1 Ladies' Detective Agency by Alexander McCall Smith follows Motswana Mma Precious Ramostwe, Botswana's first female private detective. The wildly popular book series was made into a popular TV series for BBC and HBO in 2009.

Cry of the Kalahari is the best-selling autobiography by Mark and Delia Owens about their life and love for animals in the Kalahari Desert.

Whatever You Do, Don't Run: True Tales of a Botswana Safari Guide by Peter

Allison includes funny accounts from the field by a Botswana safari guide.

In *The Gods Must be Crazy* (1980), a Coke bottle falls from the sky, perplexing a group of bushmen.

Set in the heart of the Okavango Delta, *The Flood* (2018) tells an enchanting story of life in a wild paradise like no other on earth.

Filmed entirely in Botswana *Savage Kingdom* (2016–2020) is an immensely popular wildlife documentary series, narrated in the style of *Game of Thrones*.

Plan Your Time

HASSLE FACTOR
Medium. There are no direct flights from the U.S. to Botswana, but it is easily reached via South Africa. Once in country, bush planes connect remote reaches.

3 DAYS
Fly into Maun and head directly to the Okavango Delta. Stay at either a land-based or land and water safari camp. Soak up the scenery, the mokoro rides and marvel at the wildlife and sheer wilderness.

1 WEEK
Fly into Maun and split four to five nights between a land-based and a water-based safari camp, making the most of the Okavango Delta's variety of landscape and activities. Then round out the trip by heading on a traditional safari in Chobe National Park.

2 WEEKS
After exploring the Okavango Delta and Chobe National Park, head south to the Central Kalahari Game Reserve. Try a cross-cultural tour with local bushmen,

then revel in the unique scenery and wildlife of the Makgadikgadi Pans. Finish off the trip at Mashatu before flying directly to Johannesburg for your onward flight.

The Okavango Delta

There's no place on earth like the Okavango. The world's largest inland delta is the culmination of the Okavango River, which floods down from the Angolan highlands once a year and fans out into northwestern Botswana in a meandering complex network of papyrus-lined channels, deep, still pools (where crocodiles and hippos lurk), secret waterways (where reeds and grass almost meet over your head), palm-fringed islands, and natural lagoons.

The flood arrives just as rain-filled pans are drying, creating a watery network covering an area of more than 15,000 square km (5,791 square miles). This vast area is sometimes referred to as the Swamps, but there are no murky mangroves or sinister everglades here. It's just open, crystal clear waters linking myriad islands in one of the world's last great wilderness areas. Often, the only way to get around this network of waterways is by boat.

The *mokoro*, a canoelike boat synonymous with the Okavango, was introduced to the Delta in the mid-18th century by the Bayei people who moved down from the Zambezi. Invented as a controllable craft that could be maneuvered up- or downstream, these boats were traditionally made from the trunks of the great jackalberry, marula, and sausage trees. Today, the need to conserve the trees means you will likely find yourself in a fiberglass version. Either way, a skilled poler (think gondolier) will stand or sit at the rear of the narrow craft guiding you through the Delta's waterways—he'll be on full alert for the ubiquitous and unpredictable hippos but may be a bit more laid-back when it comes to the mighty crocs that lie in the sun. (Powerboats are an option in deeper waters.) Bird-watching from these boats is a special thrill: dazzling Malachite kingfishers zoom between the reeds at lightning speed while African darters emerge from underwater hunting expeditions and perch like statues with wings outstretched to dry themselves.

TIP→ Don't miss the chance to go on a guided walk on one of the many islands.

Although many camps are now both land- and water-based to some degree, in a true water camp—usually an island surrounded by water—you'll almost certainly see elephants, hippos, crocs, and red *lechwes* (beautiful semi-aquatic antelope), and you may catch a glimpse of the rare, aquatic sitatunga antelope. You'll probably hear lions but are unlikely to spot them; if you're very lucky, you may see a pride swimming between islands. On the other hand, if you're in a land-only or land-and-water camp, you should see lots of wildlife on game drives, from lions and leopards to elephants, zebra and tons of other herbivores.

Park Ratings

Game: ★★★★★

Park Accessibility: ★★★☆☆

Getting Around: ★★★★☆

Accommodations: ★★★★★

Scenic Beauty: ★★★★★

GETTING HERE AND AROUND

You'll fly into Maun and then be transferred by your tour operator to a small plane that'll bring you to an airstrip in the Delta. Distance from the airstrip to camps varies, but normally won't be much longer than 20–25 minutes, and this is often an exciting game drive through the bush. Roads are bumpy—but you're in a game viewer.

Hotels

Abu Camp

$$$$ | **RESORT** | Although Abu's resident elephant herd has now been reintroduced back into the wild, this bespoke-service camp still holds plenty of appeal, from excellent elephant, buffalo, and predator sightings (particularly leopards) to the intimate luxury of the camp itself. **Pros:** good leopard sightings; intimate atmosphere; great food. **Cons:** one of the most expensive camps; separate dining tables results in less safari camaraderie; water activities are seasonal. [$] *Rooms from: US$3,632* ✉ *Okavango Delta* ☎ *11/257–5000 in South Africa* 🌐 *www.wilderness-safaris.com* 🛏 *6 tents* 🍴 *All-Inclusive.*

&Beyond Nxabega Okavango Safari Camp

$$$$ | **RESORT** | **FAMILY** | Renowned for its beauty, Nxabega (pronounced *na*-becka) is in the very heart of the Delta and offers both a land and a water experience. **Pros:** land and water camp; children's program; chance to see Pel's fishing

owl. **Cons:** game can be less spectacular than elsewhere; no private plunge pools; no sweeping views of the Delta. $ *Rooms from: US$2,115* ✉ *Okavango Delta* ☎ *11/809–4300 in South Africa* ⊕ *www.andbeyond.com* 🛏 *9 tents* ❤ *All-Inclusive.*

&Beyond Sandibe Okavango Safari Lodge

$$$$ | **RESORT** | **FAMILY** | Sandibe clings to the edge of a pristine channel of the Santantadibe River and has the reputation for being &Beyond's best camp for wildlife viewing in the Delta. **Pros:** stylish accommodation; great game; good food. **Cons:** no water activities; universal child policy may not suit everyone; might be too modern for some. $ *Rooms from: US$3,465* ✉ *Okavango Delta* ☎ *11/809–4300 in South Africa* ⊕ *www.andbeyond.com* 🛏 *12 suites* ❤ *All-Inclusive.*

&Beyond Xaranna Okavango Delta Camp

$$$$ | **RESORT** | Inspired by the colors of the myriad waterlilies which fill the surrounding waterways in high flood, Xaranna's bright palette has mellowed with age, its pointed canvas roofs and rose, sage, and white decor blending into and complementing the natural beauty of its surroundings. **Pros:** luxurious rooms; great food; private concession. **Cons:** water activities are seasonal; not cheap; not renowned for big game. $ *Rooms from: US$2,115* ✉ *Okavango Delta* ☎ *11/809–4300 in South Africa* ⊕ *www.andbeyond.com* 🛏 *9 tents* ❤ *All-Inclusive.*

Camp Okavango

$$$ | **RESORT** | Unrecognizable from its former, humbler self, this solar-powered camp was rebuilt in 2016 on a grand scale comprising multi-layered decks and curved walkways that link the thatched dining, library, and lounge areas set among a forest of palm, knobthorn, and jackalberry trees. **Pros:** a truly authentic water camp; great views; eco-friendly. **Cons:** unlikely to see much big game other than elephants and hippos; lots of long walkways; no game-viewing by road. $ *Rooms from: US$1,104* ✉ *Shinde Concession* ☎ *680–1494* ⊕ *www.desert-delta.com* ✇ *Closed Feb.* 🛏 *12 rooms* ❤ *All-Inclusive.*

Chitabe Camp and Chitabe Lediba

$$$$ | **RESORT** | **FAMILY** | Be sure to have your camera at the ready in this predator-rich concession that borders the Moremi Wildlife Reserve; you'll want to take pictures of everything. **Pros:** Lediba is great for families; excellent reputation for predators; unpretentious. **Cons:** not ultraluxurious; multiple vehicles can make game-drives busier than elsewhere; no water activities. $ *Rooms from: US$2,625* ✉ *Chitabe Concession* ☎ *11/257–5000 in South Africa* ⊕ *www.wilderness-safaris.com* 🛏 *13 tents* ❤ *All-Inclusive.*

Delta Camp

$$ | **RESORT** | **FAMILY** | One of the first tourism properties to open in the Okavango Delta, the focus of this enchanting camp, set on a remote island, is on experiencing the tranquility of the environment. **Pros:** splendid isolation; no noise from boats or vehicles; accepts children of all ages. **Cons:** no power in rooms; no game drives, mokoro is seasonal; less likely to see big game. $ *Rooms from: US$850* ✉ *Okavango Delta* ☎ *61/419–5064 in South Africa* ⊕ *www.footsteps-in-africa.com* 🛏 *8 chalets* ❤ *All-Inclusive.*

Duba Plains

$$$$ | **RESORT** | Completely rebuilt in 2017, this new Relais & Chateaux member has been propelled from the ranks of simple comfort into the echelons of luxury with five giant, safari-style suites bursting with character. **Pros:** real opportunity to see hunting lions, potentially in water; luxurious rooms; can boat as well as drive. **Cons:** no wild dogs; leopards and cheetahs seen less frequently; very pricey. $ *Rooms from: US$3,445* ✉ *Okavango Delta* ☎ *87/354–6591 in South Africa* ⊕ *greatplainsconservation.com* 🛏 *5 suites, 1 villa* ❤ *All-Inclusive.*

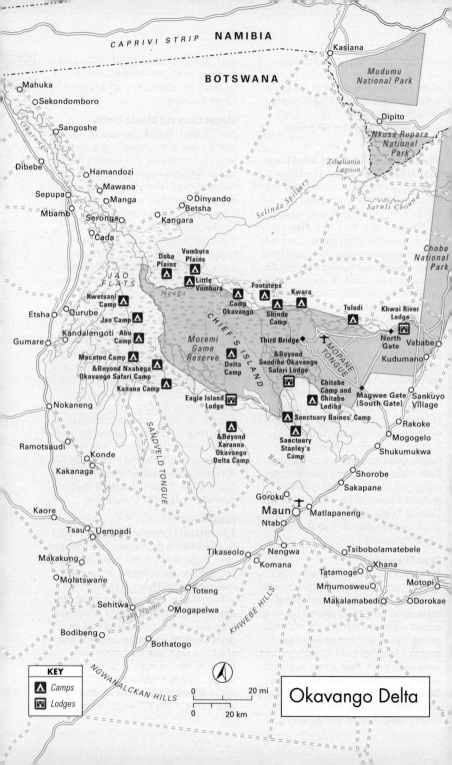

Okavango Delta

Eagle Island Lodge

$$$$ | RESORT | Surrounded by pristine waterways, tall palm trees, and vast floodplains, this predominantly solar-powered camp was imaginatively designed to mimic its surroundings. **Pros:** gorgeous views of the Delta; genuine Delta water experience most of the year; air-conditioned rooms. **Cons:** no game drives in peak flood; water activities seasonal; less chance of seeing predators. $ *Rooms from: US$2,460* ✉ *Okavango Delta* ☎ *21/483–1600 in South Africa* ⊕ *www.belmond.com* 🛏 *12 tents* ❍ *All-Inclusive.*

Footsteps

$$ | RESORT | FAMILY | This is the ultimate back-to-nature experience but you'll be more than rewarded for the lack of luxury by a safari adventure that will live long in your memory. **Pros:** this is the real thing, a genuine close-to-nature experience; best children's program in the Delta; families can have the entire camp to themselves. **Cons:** wilderness experience may not suit all; no WiFi; rustic. $ *Rooms from: US$913* ✉ *Shinde Concession* ☎ *686–1282* ⊕ *www.kerdowneybotswana.com* 🛏 *3 tents* ❍ *All-Inclusive.*

Jao Camp

$$$$ | RESORT | FAMILY | Aptly rhyming with 'wow', this opulent, inventive camp, which was completely rebuilt in 2021, is a cocktail of innovative modern design and sustainability, with a squeeze of African flavor. **Pros:** African fantasy deluxe; superb food and service; gorgeous views. **Cons:** game not always on tap; expensive; might be too decadent for some. $ *Rooms from: US$3,307* ✉ *Jao Concession* ☎ *11/257–5000 in South Africa* ⊕ *www.wilderness-safaris.com* 🛏 *7 suites* ❍ *All-Inclusive.*

Kanana Camp

$$$ | RESORT | The simple, natural charm of solar-powered Kanana makes you feel part of the Delta, not cocooned away from it. **Pros:** superb birding in the nearby heronry; private sleep-out deck; authentic safari atmosphere. **Cons:** boating is

A Hazardous Herbivore

They may look cute and harmless, but hippos are allegedly responsible for more human fatalities than any other large animal in Africa. Though they're not threatening creatures by nature and quickly retreat to water at any sign of danger, the trouble occurs when people get between a hippo and its watery refuge.

seasonal; no spa; no wooden walkway between rooms. $ *Rooms from: US$1,221* ✉ *Kanana Private Concession* ☎ *686–1282* ⊕ *www.kerdowneybotswana.com* 🛏 *8 tents* ❍ *All-Inclusive.*

Khwai River Lodge

$$$ | RESORT | It's easy to forget the outside world exists as you savor brunch on the wooden deck jutting out over the narrow Khwai river at this camp renowned for its personal attention and friendly service. **Pros:** romantic bar with fabulous sunset views; great game especially in dry season; a/c in rooms. **Cons:** the publicly accessible concession can get busy in peak season; not as eco-friendly as some other camps; no water activities. $ *Rooms from: US$1,430* ✉ *Moremi Game Reserve* ☎ *21/483–1600 in South Africa* ⊕ *www.belmond.com* 🛏 *15 rooms* ❍ *All-Inclusive.*

Kwara

$$$ | RESORT | Spun from the same cloth as the properties in the Kwando concession, this 100% solar camp is a rare year-round land and water camp, located in a prolific wildlife area. **Pros:** year-round land and water camp; old-fashioned safari ambience; spectacular predator-viewing and heronry. **Cons:** no Wi-Fi; menu is not à la carte; no children. $ *Rooms from: US$1,720* ✉ *Okavango Delta* ☎ *686-1449*

The elephants at Vumbura camp can be quite friendly and curious.

🌐 *www.kwando.co.bw* ⛺ *9 rooms* 🍴 *All-Inclusive.*

Kwetsani Camp

$$$$ | RESORT | Perched on high wooden stilts amid a forest canopy on a small island surrounded by enormous open plains, this intimate, unpretentious camp exudes an authentic safari atmosphere. **Pros:** treehouse feel; small and intimate; authentic, all-round safari experience. **Cons:** water activities can be seasonal; no family rooms; predators may be less common in the wet season. [$] *Rooms from: US$2,123* ✉ *Jao Concession, Jao Concession* ☎ *11/257–5000 in South Africa* 🌐 *www.kwetsani.com* ⛺ *5 tents* 🍴 *All-Inclusive.*

★ **Little Vumbura**

$$$$ | RESORT | Situated on its own tiny, private island, Little Vumbura has a genuine water-camp feel, yet just a short boat drive away lies the predator-packed Vumbura concession. **Pros:** best of both land and water activities; unpretentious; tranquil, relaxed ambience. **Cons:** room decks could be larger; can get booked up a long way in advance; rooms not as cavernous as some of the premier camps. [$] *Rooms from: US$2,459* ✉ *Vumbura Concession* ☎ *11/257–5000 in South Africa* 🌐 *www.wilderness-safaris.com* ⛺ *6 tents* 🍴 *All-Inclusive.*

Macatoo Camp

$$$ | RESORT | Be prepared to get wet as you gallop through knee-deep, crystal clear floodwaters among herds of giraffe on your chosen steed at this specialist horseback safari camp. **Pros:** an alternative safari perspective; stable of 50 horses ensures a match for your riding style; can cater for non-riders. **Cons:** no Wi-Fi; rooms are comfortable rather than luxurious; riders must be experienced. [$] *Rooms from: US$1,070* ✉ *Okavango Delta* ☎ *686–1523* 🌐 *www.africanhorseback.com* ⛺ *8 tents* 🍴 *All-Inclusive.*

Sanctuary Baines' Camp

$$$$ | RESORT | Named after the 19th-century explorer Thomas Baines, whose imposing portraits adorn the dining area walls, the focus of this intimate and innovative camp is more on experiential luxuries such as candle-lit private dinners and à la carte meals served with a selection of artisan breads. **Pros:** intimate and relaxed atmosphere; water views in high flood; eco-conscious construction methods. **Cons:** rooms less luxurious than at some other camps; no spa; water activities are seasonal. $ *Rooms from: US$2,045* ✉ *Okavango Delta* ☎ *11/438–4650 in South Africa* ⊕ *www.sanctuaryretreats.com* ⇆ *6 rooms* ❑❙ *All-Inclusive.*

Sanctuary Stanley's Camp

$$$ | **RESORT** | Named after the famous adventurer who uttered the immortal lines, "Dr Livingstone, I presume", Sanctuary Baines' Camp's friendly sister camp is built in a traditional East African style on an island of jackalberry, fever berry, and sausage trees. **Pros:** friendly, unpretentious ambience; traditional safari decor; excellent service. **Cons:** boating has to be done from Baines; no outdoor shower; water activities are seasonal. $ *Rooms from: US$1,490* ✉ *Okavango Delta* ☎ *11/438–4650 in South Africa* ⊕ *www.sanctuaryretreats.com* ⇆ *10 tents* ❑❙ *All-Inclusive.*

★ Shinde Camp

$$$ | **RESORT** | Ker & Downey's oldest camp, and possibly its loveliest, boasts enticing views over a carpet of emerald papyrus and golden reeds, bordering an expansive shimmering lagoon. **Pros:** true land and water camp; great predators and birdlife; fabulous bush dinners. **Cons:** no spa; no children under 10 in main lodge; no wooden walkway between rooms. $ *Rooms from: US$1,342* ✉ *Shinde Concession* ☎ *686–1282* ⊕ *www.kerdowneybotswana.com* ⇆ *8 tents* ❑❙ *All-Inclusive.*

★ Tuludi

$$$$ | **RESORT** | **FAMILY** | Rain trees sprout through the main deck of this delightfully intimate Khwai Private Reserve camp, which serves up a winning combination of classic safari luxury and authentic, unpretentious charm. **Pros:** great service; luxurious yet unpretentious; Sky suite comes with private fire deck. **Cons:** water activities are seasonal; no small boats; no lounge area in rooms. $ *Rooms from: US$2,760* ✉ *Okavango Delta* ☎ *21/001–1574 in South Africa* ⊕ *www.naturalselection.travel* ⇆ *7 rooms* ❑❙ *All-Inclusive.*

Vumbura Plains

$$$$ | **RESORT** | If it's old-style African safari ambience you're looking for, then this camp, which was renovated in 2022, is not for you as these modern-style buildings are all about space, shape, light, and texture on a grand scale. **Pros:** uniquely modern design; awesome game; hot air balloon rides. **Cons:** many steps and long up-and-down boardwalks between the widely spaced rooms; pretty pricey; concession can get busy on game drives. $ *Rooms from: US$3,546* ✉ *Vumbura Concession* ☎ *11/257–5000 in South Africa* ⊕ *www.wilderness-safaris.com* ⇆ *14 rooms* ❑❙ *All-Inclusive.*

Moremi Game Reserve

Prolific wildlife and an astonishing variety of birdlife characterize this reserve, which was the first in southern Africa to be proclaimed by the local people (the Batswana) themselves. As there are no fences, the big game—and there's lots of it—can migrate to and from the rest of the country.

Water levels are highest when the floods arrive in the middle of the year, which is paradoxically in the dry season, but game-viewing is good throughout the year. Be prepared to check off on your game list lions, cheetahs, leopards, hyenas, wild dogs, buffalo, hippos, dozens of different antelopes, zebras, giraffes, monkeys, baboons, and more than 400 kinds of birds.

WHEN TO GO

The dry season (May–October) is generally the best time for game-viewing, the vegetation becoming sparser towards the end of the season making it easier to spot wildlife. Also, as the flood waters recede from August onwards, animals are forced to congregate close to the steadily shrinking sources of permanent water creating some dramatic inter-species interaction. Be warned though, in October and November, it can get very dusty and temperatures can soar to 100°F and higher. In contrast to this peak period, during the rainy season from December to March—also known as the green season—you'll often get fantastic offers with greatly reduced lodge rates. If you're a birder these wetter summer months, when migrants flock here in the thousands, are fantastic. The return of the Carmine bee-eaters and Woodland kingfishers is a dazzling sight, and they are joined by hosts of raptors, water birds, and dozens of other species. During the South African school vacations (July and December) there are more vehicles than during the rest of the year but traffic is rarely a problem, and the extensive game-drive network means you might feasibly be the only ones at a sighting.

GETTING HERE AND AROUND

Self-driving is possible in Moremi, but a 4x4 is essential because road conditions are poor (sometimes impassable in the rainy season) and distances from cities are long. Unless you have lots of time, are a really experienced 4x4 driver and camper, and are prepared for only limited camping facilities, it's recommended that you stick to an all-inclusive fly-in package.

Hotels

National-park amenities are better than in the old days, with new ablution blocks at the campsites. But remember, you have to bring all your own equipment, supplies, and drinking water, and roads can get very bad, especially in the wet season. The campsites aren't fenced and lions, hyenas, and all sorts of game frequent them. Unless you are an adventurous, old African hand, we suggest you stick to the private lodges. They might be pricey, but they're worth every penny.

Park Ratings

Game: ★★★★★

Park Accessibility: ★★★☆☆

Getting Around: ★★★★☆

Accommodations: ★★★★★

Scenic Beauty: ★★★★☆

Camp Moremi
$$$ | **RESORT** | **FAMILY** | Rebuilt in 2018 to match the style and specification of its sister Camp Okavango with spacious rooms and an expansive multi-level main area, this cleverly designed camp blends seamlessly into the woodland on the banks of Xakanaxa lagoon. **Pros:** excellent location in good game area; great value-for-money accommodation; boating all year round. **Cons:** located inside a national park, so no exclusivity; game-viewing can be less predictable in the wet season; no mokoros or walks. [$] *Rooms from: US$1,104* ✉ *Moremi Game Reserve* ☎ *680–1494* 🌐 *www.desertdelta.com* 🕑 *Closed in Feb.* 🛏 *12 tents* 🍴 *All-Inclusive.*

★ **Camp Xakanaxa**
$$$ | **RESORT** | From the moment you walk through the rustic reception area of this old-fashioned camp (pronounced ka- *kan*-ah-ka), a feeling of unpretentious warmth and relaxation envelops you, though you shouldn't expect unnecessary frills—this is a genuine bush-camp experience. **Pros:** authentic, unpretentious, out-of-Africa experience; heaps of return guests; generally good game. **Cons:** not in a private concession; no guided walks; it's not drop-dead luxury. [$] *Rooms from: US$1,104* ✉ *Moremi Game Reserve* ☎ *680–1494* 🌐 *www.desertdelta.com* 🕑 *Closed Feb.* 🛏 *12 tents* 🍴 *All-Inclusive.*

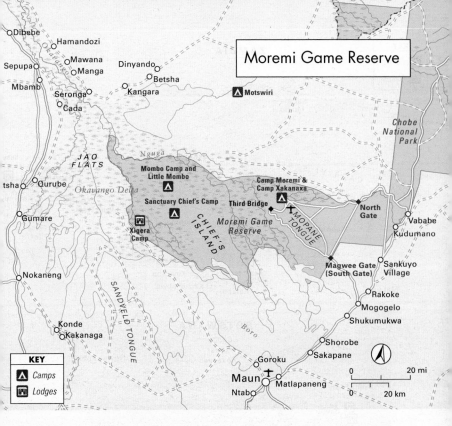

Moremi Game Reserve

KEY

🔺 Camps
🏠 Lodges

⭐ Mombo Camp and Little Mombo

$$$$ | RESORT | This legendary camp, set on a private corner of Chief's Island, is nick-named 'the place of plenty' after its spectacular wildlife—both BBC and National Geographic have filmed here—but its moniker is equally applicable to the camp itself. **Pros:** spectacular game-viewing; one of the best safari lodges in Botswana; tailor-made luxury experiences. **Cons:** no cooling system in rooms; no water activities; very, very pricey. $ *Rooms from: US$4,487* ✉ *Chief's Island, Moremi Game Reserve* ☎ *11/257–5000 in South Africa* ⊕ *www.wilderness-safaris.com* ⤴ *12 suites* ❤️ *All-Inclusive.*

Sanctuary Chief's Camp

$$$$ | RESORT | Ultra-luxurious Chief's Camp is set on its eponymous island, with some of the greatest predator and wildlife viewing on the continent. **Pros:** extensive spa treatments; uber-luxurious rooms; fantastic game. **Cons:** might feel too formal for some; very pricey; have to book a long way in advance. $ *Rooms from: US$3,650* ✉ *Chief's Island, Moremi Game Reserve* ☎ *11/438–4650 in South Africa* ⊕ *www.sanctuaryretreats.com* ⤴ *11 pavilions* ❤️ *All-Inclusive.*

⭐ Xigera Camp

$$$$ | RESORT | Under new ownership and completely rebuilt in 2020, this spectacular camp, pronounced *kee*-jer-ah, sets a new precedent for luxury and service. **Pros:** impeccable service; exceptional food; incredibly luxurious. **Cons:** no night drives; might be too fancy for some tastes; very expensive. $ *Rooms from: US$4,794* ✉ *Moremi Game Reserve* ☎ *833/846–9510 in US* ⊕ *www. redcarnationhotels.com* ⤴ *12 suites* ❤️ *All-Inclusive.*

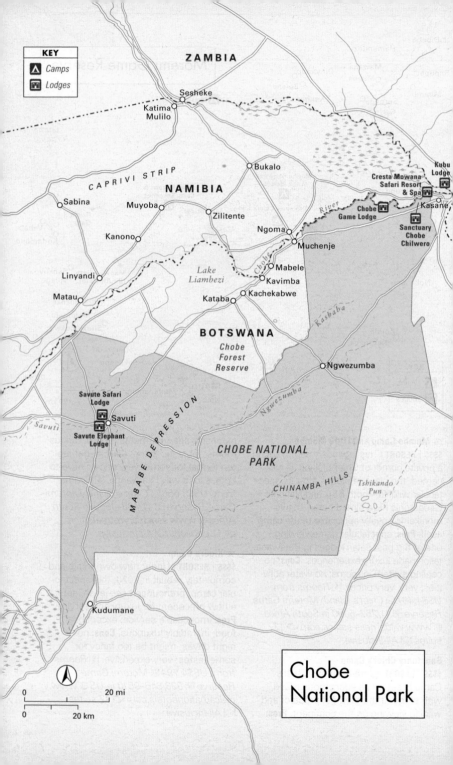

Chobe National Park

This 12,000-square-km (4,500-square-mile) reserve is the second largest national park in Botswana, and contains four very different ecosystems: Chobe riverfront in the extreme northeast with fertile plains and thick forests; Savuti in the west, where the ephemeral Savuti channel dried up in 2015; the Linyanti Swamps in the northwest; and the arid hinterland in between.

The whole area, however, is home to a shifting migratory population of more than 15,000 elephants. In addition to spotting Chobe's pachyderm herds, you might see lions, leopards, hyenas, wild dogs, impalas, waterbucks, kudus, zebras, wildebeests (gnus), giraffes, and warthogs. Watch closely at the water-holes when prey species come down to drink and are most vulnerable—they are so palpably nervous that you'll feel jumpy, too. Lions in this area are often specialized killers; one pride might target giraffes, while others target zebras, buffalo, or even young elephants. But lions are also opportunistic, and you could see them pounce on anything from a porcupine to a lowly scrub hare. Bird life along the river is awesome and the major must-sees are the slaty egrets, rock pratincoles, pink-throated longclaws, and lesser gallinules.

The northern section of the park comprises riverine bush devastated by the hordes of elephants coming down to the perennial Chobe River to drink in winter. Fortunately, the wide sweep of the Zambezi Region's floodplains and river islands, where hundreds of buffalo and elephants graze silhouetted against almost psychedelic sunsets, softens this harsh, featureless landscape where it faces neighboring Namibia. Among the smorgasbord of herbivores, which entice all the major predators, are several endemic species such as the Chobe bushbuck. This is also the only place in the country where you can see puku antelope.

Park Ratings

Game: ★★★★☆

Park Accessibility: ★★★★☆

Getting Around: ★★★★☆

Accommodations: ★★★★★

Scenic Beauty: ★★★★☆

Unlike the rest of Botswana, the Chobe riverfront can get crowded, particularly in the dry season, because there are simply too many vehicles on too few roads. Most vehicles return to Kasane in the late morning, so the western side of the riverfront tends to be much quieter.

In the southwestern part of the park lies the fabled Savuti area, famous for its predators. Large swaths of savanna woodland are punctuated by seven rocky outcrops guarding an open plain that periodically morphs into a lush marsh, courtesy of the occasionally flowing Savuti Channel. Rows of starkly beautiful dead trees line the edges of the marsh beyond which miles of tall golden grass melt into an infinite horizon. The juxtaposition of contrasting habitats has enabled a melting pot of species to thrive, especially when the river is flowing. Even though it has been dry since 2015, your chances of seeing wild dogs, lions, and leopards are good. Like the rest of the park, Savuti is famed for its elephants, but breeding herds are only present for a two- to three-month period before the first rains. The rest of the year, Savuti is the domain of the bull elephants: old grandfathers, middle-aged males, and feisty young teenagers. The old ones gaze at you with imperturbable dignity, but it's the youngsters who'll get your adrenaline pumping when they kick up the dust and bellow belligerently as they mock

Mombo Camp is one of the best safari lodges in Botswana.

charge towards you. After the first rains, thousands of migrating zebra arrive along with the summer avian visitors including Carmine bee-eaters, pratincoles, eagles, and kestrels.

In the northwest of the park are the Linyanti Swamps, where wildlife flocks to the permanent water in the dry season. In addition to the ubiquitous elephants, all manner of plains game can be found here, from impala and tsessebe to wildebeest and zebra. There are predators here too, but the limited road network can make spotting them difficult.

Early morning and late afternoon are the best game-spotting times.

WHEN TO GO

In the rainy season, roughly November through April, much of the game moves away from the permanent water provided by the rivers so if you are visiting the riverfront, then you should come from May through September to find out why this place is unique. In Savuti the wildlife-viewing is good throughout the year—the dry season is better to see predators, but the zebra herds and bird migrants are only present in the rainy season.

GETTING HERE AND AROUND

You can fly straight to Kasane from Johannesburg where your lodge will meet and transfer you. Most lodges are 10 minutes from the airport. Like the other parks, don't consider self-driving unless you have a 4x4 vehicle and lots of off-road experience.

 Hotels

Chobe Game Lodge

$$$ | **RESORT** | **FAMILY** | The only permanent lodge in the northeastern section of Chobe National Park, this grand old dame—Liz Taylor and Richard Burton got married for the second time here in the '70s—is a cut above the larger Kasane hotels and still maintains a lodge feel despite its size. **Pros:** Botswana's first electric game-viewers and boats; excellent boardwalk and viewing decks;

its location means you are ahead of the crowds. **Cons:** concrete rooms mean you are segregated from nature; Chobe National Park can get busy; bigger than most lodges. $ *Rooms from: US$1,340* ⊠ *Chobe National Park* ☎ *680–1494* ⊕ *www.chobegamelodge.com* ⌁ *44 rooms* ¶◎¶ *All-Inclusive.*

Cresta Mowana Safari Resort & Spa

$ | **RESORT** | **FAMILY** | Built around an 800-year-old baobab tree situated among lovely private gardens on the banks of the Chobe River, you'll find this lodge just 8 km (5 miles) from the entrance to Chobe National Park. **Pros:** great location; relatively cheap; golf course. **Cons:** lacks the flexibility of smaller operators; more like a hotel than a lodge; big and bustling. $ *Rooms from: US$270* ⊠ *President Ave., Kasane* ☎ *625–0300* ⊕ *www. crestahotels.com* ⌁ *106 rooms* ¶◎¶ *Free Breakfast.*

Kubu Lodge

$ | **RESORT** | **FAMILY** | If you want to escape the real world for a while, then this small, quiet, attractive lodge on the banks of the Chobe, which prides itself on its seclusion, is right for you; it has no phones, radios, or TV in its rooms. **Pros:** very affordable; located outside Kasane; comfortable rooms. **Cons:** activities are additional costs; not as luxurious as other lodges; 14 km (9 miles) from Chobe National Park. $ *Rooms from: US$365* ⊠ *Kubu Rd., Kazungula, Kasane* ☎ *625– 0312* ⊕ *www.kubulodge.net* ☾ *Closed Feb.* ⌁ *11 chalets* ¶◎¶ *Free Breakfast* ☞ *Rates are per room based on 2 people sharing.*

Sanctuary Chobe Chilwero

$$$ | **RESORT** | **FAMILY** | Smaller and more intimate than most of the accommodation options around Kasane, this peaceful luxury lodge, perched on a small hill on the border of Chobe National Park, is probably the closest fit to the small camps prevalent around the rest of the country. **Pros:** lovely views; intimate atmosphere; great spa. **Cons:** Chobe

National Park can get busy; manicured gardens might feel too tame for some; situated near the town, which means you are not in the bush. $ *Rooms from: US$1,200* ⊠ *Kasane* ☎ *11/438–4650 in South Africa* ⊕ *www.sanctuaryretreats. com* ⌁ *15 cottages* ¶◎¶ *All-Inclusive.*

Savute Elephant Lodge

$$$ | **RESORT** | Situated in the thriving Savuti region famed for its elephants, this lodge, the most luxurious in the area, is 100% solar-powered, offers à la carte meals and features a ground-level hide to gawp at drinking pachyderms. **Pros:** great location; good predators all year round; dedicated spa. **Cons:** no water activities; no exclusivity as not in a private concession; no night drives. $ *Rooms from: US$1,660* ⊠ *Chobe National Park* ☎ *21/483–1600 in South Africa* ⊕ *www.belmond.com* ⌁ *12 rooms* ¶◎¶ *All-Inclusive.*

Savute Safari Lodge

$$$ | **RESORT** | You will lose count of the number of elephants you spot from your room in this friendly lodge, nestled on the banks of the now-dry Savuti Channel. **Pros:** elephants galore; great predator sightings; spacious rooms. **Cons:** inside a national park, so no exclusivity; no night drives or walks; if you have an elephant phobia stay away. $ *Rooms from: US$1,104* ⊠ *Savuti, Chobe National Park* ☎ *680–1494* ⊕ *www.desertdel- ta.com* ☾ *Closed Feb.* ⌁ *12 rooms* ¶◎¶ *All-Inclusive.*

Kwando Reserve

The Kwando Reserve is a 2,300-square-km (900-square-mile) private concession that has more than 80 km (50 miles) of river frontage and stretches south from the banks of the Kwando River, through open plains and mopane forests to the Okavango Delta.

The concession is crisscrossed by thousands of ancient game trails traversed

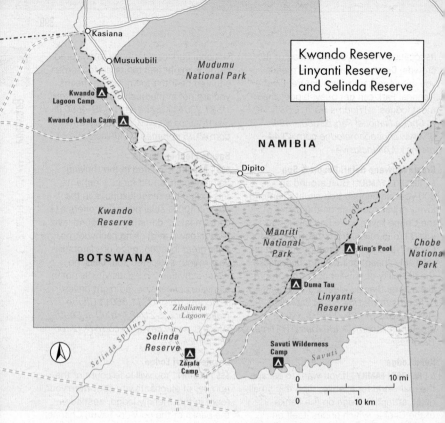

by wildlife that move freely between the Okavango Delta, Chobe, and the open Namibian wilderness to the north. As you fly in to the reserve, you'll see this web of thousands of interlacing natural game trails—from hippo highways to the tiny paths of smaller animals. This should clue you in to Kwando's diverse animal life: elephants, buffalo, zebras, antelope of all kinds, wild dogs, lions, leopards, and wildebeests. Predators are a particular specialty and the trackers perched on the front of the vehicle are experts at interpreting the breadcrumb trail that the big cats and dogs leave behind.

Kwando is also well suited for families with children older than six years (for under-12s, you will need to book a private vehicle). Kids learn to track, even sitting

Park Ratings

Game: ★ ★ ★ ★ ★

Park Accessibility: ★ ★ ★ ☆ ☆

Getting Around: ★ ★ ★ ★ ☆

Accommodations: ★ ★ ★ ☆ ☆

Scenic Beauty: ★ ★ ★ ☆ ☆

up in the tracker's seat, take plaster casts of spoor, cook marshmallows over the fire, and make bush jewelry. Children can eat on their own or with you, and if you want an afternoon snooze, they'll be supervised in a fun activity. The program is available at both Kwando camps.

At dawn, an African bush elephant crosses the Chobe River.

WHEN TO GO

May through September is the peak season for game-viewing. You'll see loads of wildlife, especially predators, with fewer than 40 other guests in the whole reserve. October and November are also good for sightings but it can get very hot. The influx of migrants in the rainy season (December through April), when the vegetation is lush, makes it best for birders.

GETTING HERE AND AROUND

Guests fly directly into Kwando Reserve from Maun; the flight takes about 35–40 minutes. Transfer to lodges will take between 10 and 30 minutes.

VISITOR INFO

CONTACTS Kwando Safaris. ✉ *Airport road, Maun* ✣ *Cnr Sir Seretse Khama Rd. and Airport Rd.* ☎ *686–1449* 🌐 *www.kwando.co.bw.*

Hotels

★ Kwando Lagoon Camp

$$$ | RESORT | FAMILY | Perched on the banks of a tributary of the fast-flowing Kwando River, this delightful camp boasts water views from every angle. **Pros:** private concession; water views; good chance to see predators especiallly wild dogs. **Cons:** no spa; no a/c; no mokoros. [$] *Rooms from: US$1,560* ✉ *Kwando Reserve* ☎ *686–1449* 🌐 *www.kwando.co.bw* 🛏 *9 tents* 🍴 *All-Inclusive.*

Kwando Lebala Camp

$$$ | RESORT | FAMILY | Looking out over the endless floodplains of the Kwando river, Lebala (the sister camp to Kwando Lagoon Camp) is aptly named (it means wide, open spaces) and benefits from the same fantastic wildlife arena. **Pros:** superb predator viewing; private concession means you can go off-road; night drives. **Cons:** no Wi-Fi; no spa; no water activites. [$] *Rooms from: US$1,560*

✉ *Kwando Reserve* ☎ *686–1449* 🌐 *www.kwando.co.bw* 🛏 *9 tents* 🍴 *All-Inclusive.*

Linyanti Reserve

Sandwiched between Chobe National Park on its eastern side and the Kwando and Selinda private concessions to the west, Linyanti is, like its western neighbors, a spectacular wildlife area comprising the Linyanti marshes, open floodplains, rolling savanna, and the Savuti Channel. As in all the government-leased private concessions, you can drive off-road and at night.

Your choices for viewing wildlife include game drives (including thrilling night drives with spotlights), boat trips, and walks with friendly and knowledgeable Batswana guides. Even in peak season, there's only a minimal number of vehicles, so you can see Africa as the early hunters and explorers might have first seen it. The Savuti Channel is a 100 km (62 miles) long seasonal river that has appeared in several *National Geographic* documentaries and occasionally flows all the way into the Savuti area of Chobe National park. Take lots of pictures, and for once you won't bore your friends with the results: hundreds of elephants drinking from pools at sunset, hippos and hyenas nonchalantly strolling past a pride of lions preparing to hunt under moonlight, and thousands of water and land birds everywhere.

WHEN TO GO

Like its western neighbors, game viewing is best in the dry season from May–October, when the wildlife throngs around the permanent water of the Linyanti river, though October can get very hot. After the rains, the emerald landscape is more photogenic but much of the wildlife disperses making sightings less reliable.

Park Ratings

Game: ★★★★☆

Park Accessibility: ★★★☆☆

Getting Around: ★★★★☆

Accommodations: ★★★★★

Scenic Beauty: ★★★☆☆

GETTING HERE AND AROUND

Flights from Maun take about 40 minutes (air is the only option); don't be shocked when you land on a dirt airstrip in the middle of the bush. Your transportation to and from the lodge and on all game drives will be in an open-sided vehicle.

Hotels

Duma Tau

$$$$ | RESORT | Completely rebuilt in 2021 when it was catapulted into the premier ranks of Wilderness Safaris's properties, this lavish, solar-powered camp boasts a spectacular location on the banks of the broad Linyanti river. **Pros:** small groups can book Little Duma Tau all to themselves; great predator viewing; fantastic river views. **Cons:** no mokoros; expensive; no bathtubs. [$] *Rooms from: US$3,751* ✉ *Linyanti Reserve* ☎ *11/257–5000 in South Africa* 🌐 *www.wilderness-safaris.com* 🛏 *12 suites* 🍴 *All-Inclusive.*

King's Pool

$$$$ | RESORT | Despite its traditional thatched roof and African artifact adornments, a handful of modern design elements distinguish this regal camp, overlooking the Linyanti River. **Pros:** classy, comfortable; 100% solar-powered; private concession. **Cons:** game less reliable in the wet season; no mokoros; very grand—you may prefer something simpler. [$] *Rooms from: US$3,410* ✉ *Linyanti Reserve* ☎ *11/257–5000 in South*

A baby baboon takes a rest under the watchful eye of mommy baboon.

Africa 🌐 *www.wilderness-safaris.com* 🛏 *9 chalets* 🍴 *All-Inclusive.*

Savuti Wilderness Camp

$$$ | RESORT | This intimate friendly camp has only six thatched chalets, which are raised on stilts above the seasonal Savuti Channel. **Pros:** good animal variety; opportunity to sleep under the stars; photographic hides. **Cons:** no boating; no a/c; very dry and hot in summer. [$] *Rooms from: US$1,941* ✉ *Linyanti Reserve* ☎ *11/257–5000 in South Africa* 🌐 *www.wilderness-safaris.com* 🛏 *6 tents* 🍴 *All-Inclusive.*

If You Have Time

By all means, do your Big Five, big-park thing, but if you can make the time, the following parks will really open your eyes to the landscape diversity and sheer wilderness of Botswana.

Selinda Reserve

Sandwiched between the Kwando and Linyanti concessions, this 1,300-square-km (500-square-mile) reserve trades the river frontage of its neighbors for the Zibadianja Lagoon, a sprawling, permanent body of water fed by the Kwando River and presided over by towering African mangosteen and jackalberry trees. It is also the location for the seasonal and intriguing Selinda Spillway. After a multidecade arid period, the spillway sprang to life in 2009 as water from the Kwando River flooded the Linyanti Swamps, filling this narrow, west-flowing channel until it eventually joined up with the Okavango River. The Okavango, which tends to flood a couple of months before the Linyanti Swamps, flows in the opposite direction, leading to the remarkable phenomenon that the Selinda Spillway can flow in both directions at the same time.

Game viewing is as good as in the Kwando and Linyanti reserves: lions, leopards, and wild dogs are all sighted regularly in the dry season, along with elephants, hippos, and the usual plains game. The permanent water also means there is a tremendous variety of birdlife. Activities are equally diverse: search for prowling predators on an early morning game drive, marvel at fishing herons on a sunset boat cruise, or learn how your expert guide interprets the maze of tracks in the sand on a fascinating bush walk.

WHEN TO GO

Like elsewhere in this region, the dry season (May–October) has the best game viewing, but be aware October can get very hot. Bird migrants arrive in the wetter summer months.

GETTING HERE AND AROUND

The only way for tourists to reach the concession is by air; flights from Maun take about 45 minutes. The transfer time to the lodges varies depending on the camp.

Hotels

★ Zarafa Camp

$$$$ | RESORT | There is a welcome air of authenticity surrounding this intimate, luxury, Relais & Chateaux camp set on the banks of Zibadianja Lagoon. **Pros:** understated luxury; flexible timetables; reliable game. **Cons:** very pricey; no mokoros; rooms can be a bit hot in summer. $ *Rooms from: US$3,445* ✉ *Selinda Reserve* ☎ *87/354–6591 in South Africa* ⊕ *www.greatplainsconservation.com* ⇲ *4 suites, 1 villa* ⦿ *All-Inclusive.*

The Central Kalahari Game Reserve

The second largest national park in Africa has its own unique beauty that's only enhanced by its vastness, emptiness, grandeur, and desolation. You won't see the prolific game of Chobe or Moremi, but there's unusual wildlife, such as the elusive brown hyena, stately gemsbok, pronking springbok, bat-eared foxes, African wild cats, cheetahs, leopards, and porcupines. And if you're lucky, you may spot the huge, black-maned Kalahari lions, which dwarf their bush counterparts. Deception Valley—named after a shimmering dry pan which appears to hold water when viewed from afar—is located in the north of the park and is the primary game-viewing area.

WHEN TO GO

Summer days are very hot while winter nights and early mornings can get bitterly cold. Temperatures are most comfortable in the shoulder seasons (April and September). Game viewing is best during and just after the rains (December through April) when large herds of gemsbok and springbok converge on the pans followed by large lion prides and cheetah families.

GETTING HERE AND AROUND

Although self-drives are possible here, it's not advised. Instead, fly in from Maun. Your lodge can and will arrange all your transportation to and from the airstrip for you in an open-sided game vehicle.

Hotels

★ Deception Valley Lodge

$$ | RESORT | Situated on private land bordering the Central Kalahari Game Reserve, this striking wood-and-thatch lodge was the first to be built in the Central Kalahari and is arguably still the best. **Pros:** great value; amazing tracking skills; fantastic bushman experience. **Cons:** landscape not as scenic as inside the park; can get very dry and hot in summer; no water activities. $ *Rooms from: US$780* ✉ *Central Kalahari Game Reserve* ☎ *61/419–5064 in South Africa* ⊕ *www.deceptionvalleylodge.co.bw* ⇲ *10 chalets* ⦿ *All-Inclusive.*

Continued on page 409

(top) Uganda woman weaving baskets. (bottom) Botswana basket.

AFRICAN ARTS & CULTURE

African art is as diverse as its peoples. If you're a collector, an artist, or just an admirer, you'll find everything from masks and carvings to world famous rock art, hand-painted batiks, and hand-woven cloths.

African art is centered on meaning. Its sculptures, carvings, and masks symbolize the powerful spirit world that underpins most African societies. Christianity and the Westernization of many African communities has stifled much of the traditional craftsmanship by imposing new themes and, in the past, denigrating traditional religions. Fortunately, wooden masks—some genuine, some not, some beautiful, some seriously scary—wire and bead tribal necklaces, beadwork, woven baskets, and much, much more continue to be big sellers all over Southern and East Africa.

If you're looking for something a little funky or unique, check out the handmade bead-and-wire animals, birds, cars, and mobiles for sale along South Africa's roads and in Tanzania's markets.

TYPES OF CRAFTS AND ART

High-quality crafts abound, from handwoven cloths in East Africa, to stunning soapstone and wood carvings at Victoria Falls, handwoven baskets in Botswana and Zululand, leatherwork, pottery and embroidery in Namibia, and jewelry just about everywhere.

BOTSWANA BASKETS

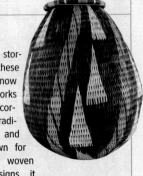

Once used for storage purposes, these baskets are now sought-after works of art that incorporate many traditional designs and patterns. Known for the intricately woven geometric designs, it can take up to six weeks to make a basket. Zulu baskets, from South Africa's KwaZulu province, can be made of brightly colored wire or grass and palm coils. For either type, expect to pay anywhere from US$20 to US$300.

MASKS

Masks were often worn by tribal elders in rites of passage (birth, initiation, weddings, and funerals) and can range from frightening depictions of devils and evil spirits, to more gentle and benign expressions. A few dollars will buy you a readily available tourist mask; an authentic piece could run you hundreds, sometimes thousands of U.S. dollars.

BEADWORK

Each color and pattern has meaning. Green is for grass or a baby, red is for blood or young women, and white is for purity. By looking at a woman's beadwork you can tell how many children she has (and what sex), how old she is or how long she's been married. Beading is used in headdresses, necklaces, rings, earrings, wedding aprons, barrettes, and baskets. Expect to pay US$10 for a Zulu bracelet or US$200 for a Masai wedding necklace.

WEAVING

The striking red handmade robes of East Africa's Masai people are a fine example of a centuries-old African weaving tradition. Fabrics, like kekois and Masai cloaks, are usually made of cotton. Handpainted or batik cloths are more expensive than factory printed ones. A cotton kekoi will cost you US$15, a red Masai cloth US$20, a batik US$30.

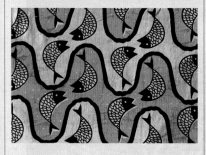

WIRECRAFT FIGURES

Wire-and-bead animals and all kinds of previously unimagined subjects are now contemporary works of art. First made and sold in South Africa, you can now buy them just about anywhere. A palm-sized critter usually sells for US$10, but a nearly-life-sized animal can cost up to US$450; you'd pay three times more in a European or U.S. gallery. Tip: Beaded key rings (US$5) make great easy-to-pack gifts.

ROCK ART

Engravings (made by scratching into a rock's surface), paintings, and finger paintings are found all over sub-Saharan Africa, particularly in South Africa. The rock paintings in the Drakensburg Mountains in Kwa-Zulu Natal, are regarded as the world's finest. Central Namibia has the world's largest open-air art gallery at Twyfelfontein, where thousands of paintings and engravings line the sides of the rocks and mountain. Materials came from the immediate environment: ocher (red iron-oxide clay) for red, charcoal for black, and white clay for white. Many images illustrate the activities and experiences of the African shamans. The shamans believed that when an image was drawn, power was transferred to the people and the land.

PAINTING

Painting in acrylics is a fairly recent medium in Africa. Keep an eye out for Tinga Tinga paintings (above) at curio shops or stalls in Kenya and Tanzania. Prices range from $10 to $50; you can expect to pay upwards of $100 online. The semi-impressionistic wildlife paintings of Keith Joubert are particularly sought-after. Consult his website (⊕ www.keith-joubert.com) for locations of his exhibitions.

SMART SHOPPING TIPS

So where should you buy all of this amazing handiwork? And what do you do when you've found that piece you want to take home? Read on for helpful tips and locations across our Safari coverage.

■ Local markets, roadside stalls, and cooperatives often offer the cheapest, most authentic crafts.

■ Safari lodge shops can be pricey, but stock really classy souvenirs (often from all over Africa) and cool safari gear.

■ A universal rule for bargaining is to divide the seller's first price by half, then up it a bit.

■ If possible, carry your purchases with you. Try to get breakables bubble-wrapped and pack securely in the middle of your main suitcase. Pack smaller purchases in your carry-on.

■ Mail your dirty clothes home or donate them to a local charity so you'll have more room for purchases.

■ Only ship home if you've bought something very big, very fragile, or very expensive.

AFRICAN BEADS

Small discs, dating from 10,000 B.C., made from ostrich eggshells are the earliest known African beads. The introduction of glass beads came with the trade from around 200 B.C. Subsequently, European and Arab traders bartered beads for ivory, gold, and slaves. In many African societies, beads are still highly prized for both everyday and ceremonial ornamentation.

Kalahari Plains Camp

$$$ | **RESORT** | **FAMILY** | Situated in the desolate northern part of the Central Kalahari Game Reserve—one of the largest game reserves in the world and bigger than Switzerland—this solar-powered camp overlooks a huge pan, with eight en suite, innovatively insulated canvas tents designed to keep you cool in summer and warm in winter. **Pros:** stunning desert scenery all year round; abundant game in season; interpretive walks with the local San Bushmen. **Cons:** water can be salty; game not as varied as in the Delta; tents get very hot in summer, even with the insulation. $ *Rooms from: US$1,222* ✉ *Central Kalahari Game Reserve* ☎ *11/257–5000 in South Africa* ⊕ *www. wilderness-safaris.com* ⇝ *8 tents* ⦿ *All-Inclusive.*

★ The Lodge

$$$ | **RESORT** | **FAMILY** | From the moment you arrive at this remote, independently owned, Kalahari oasis it's clear that The Lodge represents a welcome break from the safari mold. **Pros:** refreshingly different ambience; extensive range of activities; great place to relax at the end of a safari. **Cons:** no water activities; style may not suit traditionalists; not a place for big game. $ *Rooms from: US$1,700* ☎ *686–5756* ⊕ *www.felinefields.com* ⇝ *7 suites* ⦿ *All-Inclusive.*

The Makgadikgadi Pans

These immense salt pans in the eastern Kalahari—once the bed of an African superlake—provide some of Botswana's most dramatic scenery. Two of these pans, Ntwetwe and Sowa, the largest of their kind in the world, have a flaky, pastry-like surface that might be the nearest thing on earth to the surface of the moon. In winter (May–September) these huge bone-dry surfaces, punctuated by islands of grass and lines of fantastic palm trees, dazzle and shimmer into hundreds of dancing mirages under the midday sun. In summer months (October–April) the last great migration in Southern Africa takes place here: more than 20,000 zebras and wildebeests with predators on their heels come seeking the fresh young grass of the rainwater-flooded pans. Waterbirds also flock here from all over the continent; the flamingos are particularly spectacular. The introduction of pumped waterholes in the vicinity has now allowed some of the animals to stay year-round, adding another dimension to dry season activities.

You can see stars as never before, and if you're lucky, as the San Bushmen say, even hear them sing. Grab the opportunity to ride 4x4 bikes into an always-vanishing horizon; close your eyes and listen as an ancient San Bushman hunter tells tales of how the world began in his unique language (which uses a series of clicks) or just wander in wonder over the pristine piecrust surface of the pans.

WHEN TO GO

During May through September you will experience the surreal, dry winter landscapes, but, although some zebras, wildebeests, and the occasional lion may be present, the focus is on the desert species, such as meerkats and brown hyenas. November through March are the months of the migration when thousands of zebras, wildebeests, and predators join the desert residents, but after the first rains it is impossible to access the pans themselves.

GETTING HERE AND AROUND

Just like in the Central Kalahari Game Reserve, self-drives are possible here but not advised. Instead, have your lodge arrange your transportation. Flights from Maun take about 40 minutes, and don't be shocked when you land on a dirt airstrip in the middle of the bush. Your transportation to and from the lodge and on all game drives will be in an open-sided vehicle.

Hotels

Camp Kalahari

$$$ | RESORT | FAMILY | Offering all the Makgadikgadi activities, Camp Kalahari represents a more down-to-earth and affordable option in this area and is ideally suited to families. **Pros:** 100% solar; accepts children of all ages; great range of activities. **Cons:** no plug sockets in rooms; can be hot and dusty in summer; not fancy. $ *Rooms from: US$1,095* ✉ *Makgadikgadi Pans* ☎ *21/001–1574 in South Africa* ⊕ *www.naturalselection. travel* ⇆ *10 tents* ¶⊙¶ *All-Inclusive.*

Jack's Camp

$$$$ | RESORT | Rebuilt in 2020 on a grand scale, the new Jack's Camp represents a significant luxury upgrade while still maintaining its classic 1940s East African safari style and whimsical sense of adventure. **Pros:** exclusivity and isolation; unique, alternative safari experience; good chance to see meerkats. **Cons:** the desert locale can be dusty; not renowned for big game; no Wi-Fi. $ *Rooms from: US$2,950* ✉ *Makgadikgadi Pans* ☎ *21/001–1574 in South Africa* ⊕ *www.naturalselection.travel* ⇆ *9 tents* ¶⊙¶ *All-Inclusive.*

★ San Camp

$$$$ | RESORT | It's all about the view from this collection of snow-white tents looking out over the surreal, stark landscape of Botswana's Makgadikgadi salt pans. **Pros:** friendly, knowledgeable staff; more intimate than its neighbors; stunningly surreal setting. **Cons:** game not as prolific as elsewhere in the country; can get very hot and dusty in October; no fans in rooms. $ *Rooms from: US$2,110* ✉ *Makgadikgadi Pans* ☎ *21/001–1574 in South Africa* ⊕ *www.naturalselection.travel* ⊙ *Closed during rainy season (mid-Oct.– Mar.)* ⇆ *7 tents* ¶⊙¶ *All-Inclusive.*

Mashatu Game Reserve

Part of the privately owned Northern Tuli Game Reserve and still relatively unknown to foreign travelers, this ruggedly beautiful corner of northeastern Botswana is easily accessible from South Africa though flights are more expensive from northern Botswana. Huge, striking red-rock formations and rolling hills morph into acacia forests, riverine woodlands, and grassy plains, forming a landscape unlike anywhere else in the country. Be sure to visit the Motloutse ruins, where ancient baobabs stand sentinel over Stone Age ruins that have existed here for more than 30,000 years, while majestic black eagles soar overhead.

Named after the magnificent Mashatu or nyala trees, the 31,000-hectare reserve is known as the "land of the giants" both for its arboreal behemoths and its huge elephant herds. Other specialties include *eland*—Africa's largest antelope—aardwolf and bat-eared fox as well as zebra, wildebeest, lion, leopard, and cheetah, not to mention over 350 species of birds. Not everything is super-sized: try to catch a glimpse of the elusive and diminutive klipspringer, a rock-dwelling antelope that often appears to be walking on tiptoes.

The diverse range of activities includes game drives, walks, ground-level photographic hides, horseback, and even cycle safaris. If the Limpopo River is full, you'll be winched into Botswana over the river in a small cage—a unique way of getting from one country to another. If not, it's just a simple drive across the dry riverbed.

GETTING HERE AND AROUND

Mashatu is an easy six- to seven-hour drive from Johannesburg and Gaborone. You'll be met at Pont Drift, the South African–Botswana border post, where you leave your car under huge jackalberry trees at the South African police station before crossing the Limpopo River by

4x4 vehicle or cable car—depending on whether the river is flooded.

If you'd rather fly, South African Airlink flies daily from OR Tambo International Airport, Johannesburg, to Polokwane, where you can either rent a self-drive vehicle or book an air or road transfer to Pont Drift (around two hours by car). You can also fly by direct charter from Mala Mala in South Africa, or from Maun (to link to the Okavango Delta), although the latter can be quite expensive.

AIRLINES South African Airlink. ☎ *11/451–7300* 🌐 *www.flyairlink.com.*

CAR RENTALS Budget. ✉ *Natlee Centre, Mathiba Rd., Maun Airport, Maun* ☎ *686–0039* 🌐 *www.budget.co.za.*

Hotels

★ Mashatu Lodge

$$ | RESORT | FAMILY | A sister camp to South Africa's world-famous Mala Mala Camp, Mashatu's game-viewing lives up to its billing with a deserved reputation for prolific predators. **Pros:** game galore, particularly lions and leopards; superb service and guiding; amazing photographic opportunities from low-level hides. **Cons:** no wild dogs; lacks some of the charm of the camps in the north; atmosphere feels more like South Africa than Botswana. [$] *Rooms from: US$730* ✉ *Mashatu Game Reserve* ☎ *31/761–3440 in South Africa* 🌐 *www.mashatu.com* 🛏 *14 suites* 🍴 *All-Inclusive* ☞ *Alcohol not included.*

Mashatu Tent Camp

$$ | RESORT | This small and intimate camp offers the same excellent service as Mashatu Lodge and its location, deep in the wilderness, will make you feel part of the heartbeat of Africa as you lie in your tent and listen to a lion's roar, a hyena's whoop, or a leopard's cough. **Pros:** true wilderness experience; splendid isolation; great game, especially predators. **Cons:** no a/c; not uber-luxurious; very close to nature. [$] *Rooms from: US$540* ✉ *Mashatu Game Reserve* ☎ *31/761–3440 in South Africa* 🌐 *www.mashatu.com* 🛏 *8 tents* 🍴 *All-Inclusive* ☞ *Alcohol not included.*

Gateway City

Many visitors to Botswana will find themselves with a layover in Johannesburg before or after their safari. It's a massive metropolitan area—more than 1,300 square km (800 square miles)—that epitomizes South Africa's paradoxical makeup: it's rich, poor, innovative, and historical all rolled into one. Most of the sights and many of the city's good hotels and major malls are in the northern suburbs (Greenside, Parkhurst, Sandton, and Rosebank, among many others). Some notable destinations for food include Melrose Arch, Parkhurst, Sandton, the South (for its Portuguese cuisine), Melville, and Chinatown in the CBD (Central Business District).

For some ideas and suggestions to help determine where you should stay, eat, and, if you have time, sightsee, see Johannesburg (Chapter 5 South Africa).

In Botswana, the little town of Maun serves as the gateway to the Okavango Delta and Moremi Game Reserve. Although several new attractions have sprung up in the last few years, the town is not really an established tourist destination in itself—at best you'd probably stay a night or two before setting off farther afield.

Maun

Despite the city's rapid development in the last decade, Maun has kept the feel of a pioneer border town. The name comes from the San word *maung*, which means the "place of short reeds," and Maun became the capital of the Tawana people in 1915; it's now Botswana's

Also known as "painted dogs," African Wild Dogs are an endangered species found only in Zimbabwe, Tanzania, Botswana, and South Africa.

fifth-largest town. Although there are now shopping centers and a paved road to Botswana's capital, Gaborone, cement block houses and mud huts still give Maun a rural feel, especially since goats and donkeys roam the roads.

The town spreads along the banks of the seasonal Thamalakane River, and it's possible to take mokoro trips into the Delta directly from Maun. It's also a good base from which to explore the Tsolido hills and the Makgadikgadi Pans by road.

The bustling airport has new runways and planes of all sizes taking off and landing at all hours of the day, delivering tourists to and from the camps in the Delta and Moremi. There are a handful of supermarkets, so you can stock up on supplies if you're setting off on a road trip, but in general, most camps are accessible only by air, so you'll probably only see the airport.

GETTING HERE AND AROUND
If you don't fly to Gaborone, your first entry into Botswana will probably be by air into Maun, the gateway to the Delta. At most, you'd spend only one or two nights here, though most visitors are picked up at Maun airport immediately on arrival by their respective tour operators and whisked away to their lodges by charter planes.

If you are here overnight, local taxis are your best bet for getting around, as there's no public transportation. Taxis are usually available outside Maun airport. It's possible to hire a fully equipped 4x4 for camping, but generally speaking, you're better off and safer (the roads in the parks range from bad to impassable) to fly between Maun and the tourist camps. Make sure your tour package includes all local flights.

SAFETY AND PRECAUTIONS
Although Maun is still safe by global standards, petty crime can be a problem, so take good care of your belongings and utilize your hotel's safe. Don't walk alone

What to Eat

Amarula: liqueur made from Botswana's marula fruit

Seswaa: boiled meat, salted, then mashed or shredded and served with cornmeal

Mopane worm: edible, protein-rich caterpillars often simply dried or stir-fried with tomatoes and onions

Samp and Beans: a hot mix of crushed corn kernels and sugar beans

Magwinya: deep-fried dough balls, with either sweet or savory stuffings

Lerotse: the daintier cousin of the watermelon

at night. If you want to leave the hotel, have the concierge or front desk call a taxi for you.

BANKS ABSA Bank. ⊠ *Old Mall, Tshe-ko-Tsheko Rd., Maun* ☎ *686–0210.* **First National Bank.** ⊠ *1-2 Ngami Centre, Koro St., Maun* ☎ *686–0919.* **Stanbic Bank.** ⊠ *Natlee Centre, Mathiba I Rd., Maun* ☎ *686-2132.*

MEDICAL ASSISTANCE Doctors Inn. ⊠ *Moeti Rd., Maun* ☎ *686–5115, 7123–3329 emergency* ⊕ *www.doctorsinn. co.bw.* **General Emergency Number.** ☎ *911.*

TIMING

Most people will be here just a few hours or a night or two at most. Use the time to relax or book up an excursion through your hotel. If you are self-driving you can stock up on supplies at one of the local grocery stores.

TOURS
Maun Experience
CULTURAL TOURS | Learn about local customs and traditions on this immersive 3-hour tour around Maun, on which you can also sample local cuisine and meet Batswana artisans. Tours start from The Duck (see Maun restaurants) and you can either book online or through your hotel. ⊠ *Maun* ⊕ *www.yourbotswanaex-perience.com* 💳 *US$110 per person (min 2 passengers)* 🕙 *Closed Sat. afternoon and Sun.*

Sights

Nhabe Museum
ART MUSEUM | Housed in a former British military building, Nhabe Museum has a few permanent displays of Ngamiland's history and artifacts, including musical instruments and hunting tools. More interesting are the rotating exhibitions featuring the work of local Botswana painters, photographers, sculptors, woodworkers, and weavers. There is also a very good café serving lunches, snacks, juices, and coffees on-site. ⊠ *Sir Seretse Kharma Rd., Town Center, Maun* ☎ *686–1346* 💳 *Free* 🕙 *Closed weekends except for special exhibitions.*

★ Okavango Craft Brewery
BREWERY | Winner of several international awards, Maun's first craft brewery ingeniously uses locally grown millet and water from the Okavango Delta in its secret recipe. Tours should be booked in advance, or you can drop by unannounced to sample their wares in the brewpub, which also serves excellent pizzas and burgers. A playground in the beer garden is ideal for families. ⊠ *Sir Seretse Khama St., Maun* ☎ *686–0069* ⊕ *www.okavangocraftbrewery.com* 💳 *Rates depend upon size of group* 🕙 *Closed Mon.*

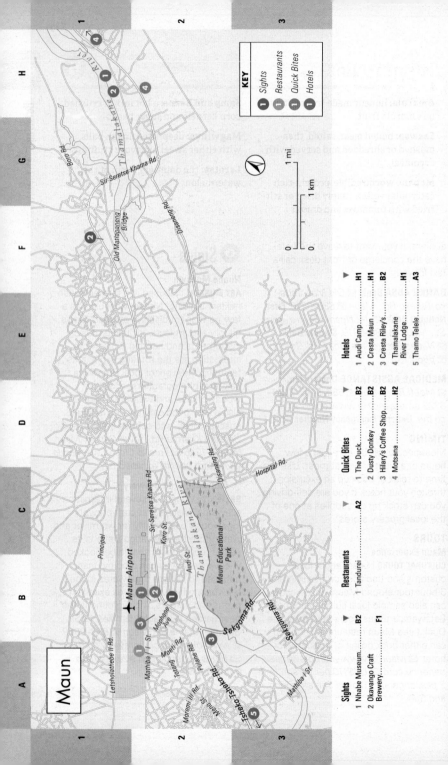

Maun

KEY

- Sights
- Restaurants
- Quick Bites
- Hotels

Sights ▶

1 Nhabe Museum.................**B2**
2 Okavango Craft
Brewery........................**F1**

Restaurants ▶

1 Tandurei **A2**

Quick Bites ▶

1 The Duck.........................**B2**
2 Dusty Donkey.................**B2**
3 Hilary's Coffee Shop......**B2**
4 Motsana........................**H2**

Hotels ▶

1 Audi Camp......................**H1**
2 Cresta Maun...................**B2**
3 Cresta Riley's.................**B2**
4 Thamalakane
River Lodge...................**H1**
5 Thamo Telele..................**A3**

Restaurants

Tandurei

$ | **INDIAN** | Serving up a wide range of classic curries and tandoori dishes as well as some Chinese staples, this is the most reliable of Maun's selection of Indian restaurants. The alfresco ambience—a thatched roof provides cover for inclement weather—is relaxed and the service is consistently good. **Known for:** good service; reliable food. $ *Average main: P80* ✉ *Moeti Rd., Maun* ☎ *680–0227.*

Coffee and Quick Bites

★ The Duck

$ | **INTERNATIONAL** | Maun's newest eatery, ideally situated just outside the airport, serves up the best coffee in town together with fresh juices and a varied and original brunch and lunch menu that caters to all palates, ranging from salads and burgers to Asian specialties. **Known for:** centrally located near airport; best coffee in town; efficient service. $ *Average main: P85* ✉ *Mathiba I St., Maun* ⚓ *opposite Maun International Airport* ☎ *77/012–978* ⊕ *www.facebook.com/theduckmaun* ☉ *No dinner.*

Dusty Donkey

$ | **CAFÉ** | Located just a short walk from the airport, this reliable, friendly café offers a variety of wraps, salads, sandwiches, and a handful of daily specials all washed down with great coffee, milkshakes, smoothies, or a glass of locally brewed craft beer. If you still have space, there's also a great selection of house-made cakes and pastries. **Known for:** close to Maun International Airport; house-made sourdough bread; tantalizing cakes. $ *Average main: P80* ✉ *Airport Rd., Maun* ☎ *76/157–105* ⊕ *www.facebook.com/dustydonkeycafe* ☉ *No dinner.*

Hilary's Coffee Shop

$ | **CAFÉ** | If you've time for a cup of coffee and a quick snack between flights or before you set out on safari, leave the airport and turn right. You'll find this coffee shop behind the offices of Okavango Wilderness Safaris. **Known for:** reliable service; great house-made lemonade. $ *Average main: US$8* ✉ *The Studio Complex, Mathiba Rd., next to the Studio gym, Maun* ☎ *686–1610* ⊕ *www.hilaryscoffeeshop.wordpress.com* ☉ *Closed Sun. No lunch Sat. No dinner.*

Motsana

$ | **CAFÉ** | **FAMILY** | The café at the Gothic-looking Motsana Center serves tasty sandwiches, American pancakes, lip-smacking milkshakes, and a handful of simple main courses. Wander around the curio shops while you wait for your food or make use of the free Wi-Fi. **Known for:** good coffee; good brunch options; tasty milkshakes. $ *Average main: P90* ✉ *Shorobe Rd., Maun* ☎ *684–0405* ⊕ *www.facebook.com/MotsanaCentre* ☉ *No dinner.*

Hotels

Audi Camp

$ | **RESORT** | **FAMILY** | This lively tented camp offers a budget option for the Okavango Delta with comfortable no-frills en suite tents either in the campsite or (for a small premium) on raised wooden stilts overlooking the river. **Pros:** affordable lodging; excellent service and staff; good value excursions. **Cons:** tents can be cold in winter; all activities extra; only 4 tents have river views. $ *Rooms from: US$85* ✉ *Shorobe Rd., Maun* ⚓ *12 km (7½ miles) from Maun* ☎ *686–0599* ⊕ *www.audisafaris.com* ⇥ *14 tents, 1 self-catered house* ⼝ *Free Breakfast.*

Cresta Maun

$ | **HOTEL** | Situated on the banks of the Thamalakane River, Cresta Maun is one of Maun's largest and most modern hotels. **Pros:** river view from the terrace; good location; all mod-cons. **Cons:** service can be hit-and-miss; pool is a bit small; lacks intimacy and safari ambience. $ *Rooms from: US$130* ✉ *Maun*

✈ *Situated off the Shorobe road to Moremi, 100 meters from Audi Camp* ☎ *686–3455* 🌐 *www.crestahotels.com* 🛏 *83 rooms* 🍴 *Free Breakfast.*

Cresta Riley's

$ | **HOTEL** | A Maun institution, this comfortable modern hotel, now under Cresta ownership and situated on the banks of the Thamalakane River, is a far cry from the seven dusty rooms built by the legendary Harry Riley in the 1930s. **Pros:** central location; clean and comfortable; attractive gardens and pool. **Cons:** inside restaurant lacks character; in the busy center of town; bland hotel-like rooms. [$] *Rooms from: US$140* ✉ *Tsheko Tsheko Rd., Maun* ☎ *686–0204* 🌐 *www.crestahotels.com* 🛏 *51 rooms* 🍴 *Free Breakfast.*

Thamalakane River Lodge

$ | **RESORT** | **FAMILY** | Situated en route to Moremi Game Reserve, this lovely lodge sits on the bank of the Thamalakane River with 32 very comfortable stone-and-thatch en suite chalets that overlook the river. **Pros:** lodge feel; closest accommodation in Maun to Moremi Game Reserve; good atmosphere and service. **Cons:** dinner may not be à la carte; there are cheaper options; if you're not en route to Moremi it's a bit out of the way. [$] *Rooms from: US$295* ✉ *Shorobe Rd., Maun* ☎ *76/315–207* 🌐 *www.trlmaun.com* 🛏 *34 chalets* 🍴 *Free Breakfast.*

Thamo Telele

$$ | **RESORT** | Recently rebuilt, renovated, and renamed, this giraffe-themed camp (formerly Royal Tree Lodge) is the closest you will get to a safari camp in Maun. **Pros:** horse riding available; only Maun accommodation with wildlife; chance to get up close to giraffes. **Cons:** more expensive than most alternative options; no desk in tents; 30 minutes' drive from airport. [$] *Rooms from: US$600* ✉ *Maun* ☎ *21/001–1574 in South Africa* 🌐 *www.naturalselection.travel* 🛏 *11 rooms* 🍴 *All-Inclusive* ☞ *Rate includes walks, 1 horse ride, and 1 massage.*

Beach Escapes

Looking for a little R & R after your safari? Botswana may not be a coastal country, but its close proximity to South Africa's coast provides many opportunities for sun, sand, and smiles.

Just (762 km) 474 miles southeast from Botswana's capital Gaborone, Durban's accessible, beautiful, and safe beaches make it a great escape for this landlocked country (as well as for South Africa). Plus, there are daily flights between Gaborone and Durban (though you'll probably have to do a stopover in Johannesburg), making it a quick escape as well.

If you're passing through Cape Town, the Cape Peninsula's stunning white beaches are about a 30-minute drive (with no traffic) south of the Mother City (some are farther south). On the West, you have the Atlantic Ocean with colder water but longer hours of sunshine and protection from the "Cape Doctor" (the strong southeasterly wind), which means better conditions for sunbathing, beach picnics, and sunset walks. Some of our favorite towns include Camps Bay, Maiden's Cove (also in Camps Bay), Soetwater (in Kommetjie), and Buffels Bay (in Cape Point nature reserve). On the east coast, you have False Bay and the warmer Indian Ocean which is better for swimming, surfing, and diving. Towns like Muizenberg, Fish Hoek, Boulders (where you can see penguins), St James, Dalebrook (in Kalk Bay), and Miller's Point are good bets.

Chapter 9

NAMIBIA

Updated by
Iga Motylska

WELCOME TO NAMIBIA

TOP REASONS TO GO

★ **The world's oldest living desert:** Marvel at The Namib from the air during a scenic flight or up close as you ascend the world's highest sand dune.

★ **A memorable drive:** The road from Walvis Bay to Aus (along the C14 and C13) is one of the world's most beautiful and unusual routes. Keep a look out for the wild horses between Aus and Luderitz.

★ **The desert-adapted elephants of Damaraland:** Arm yourself with binoculars, a camera, and patience as you embark on a safari in search of Damaraland's desert-adapted elephants.

★ **Africa's first International Dark Sky Reserve:** Do a star-gazing safari, look through a telescope at a private observatory, or sleep under the stars at the privately owned NamibRand, the continent's first and only International Dark Sky Reserve (IDSR).

★ **Kolmanskop:** Outside of Luderitz, which is famed for its oysters, this ghost town reminisces about the region's diamond-mining heydays.

Four times as large as the U.K. and bigger than Texas, Namibia's bordered by the Atlantic on the west, the Kalahari Desert on the east, the Kunene River to the north, and the Orange River to the south. Its vast road network means the entire country is fairly easily accessed with a 4x4, but most of these roads are unpaved.

1 Namib-Naukluft Park. This park, which harbors the world's oldest desert, is also one of Africa's largest national parks. Expect classic desert scenery alongside windswept gravel plains, rocky outcrops, and some of the earth's strangest living things.

2 Damaraland. Situated in northwest Namibia, this is a different desert from the Namib. This barren and inhospitable landscape has life and plenty of it, including *Welwitschia mirabilis*, the world's longest-living plant, and numerous desert-adapted species.

3 Etosha National Park. Regarded as one of Africa's great national parks, Etosha is dominated by Etosha Pan: a landscape of white, salty plains. The numerous waterholes make this park ideal for game viewing.

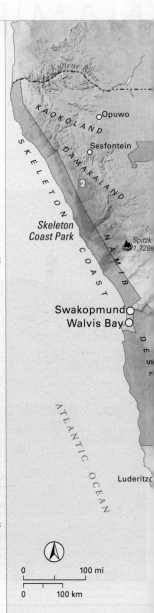

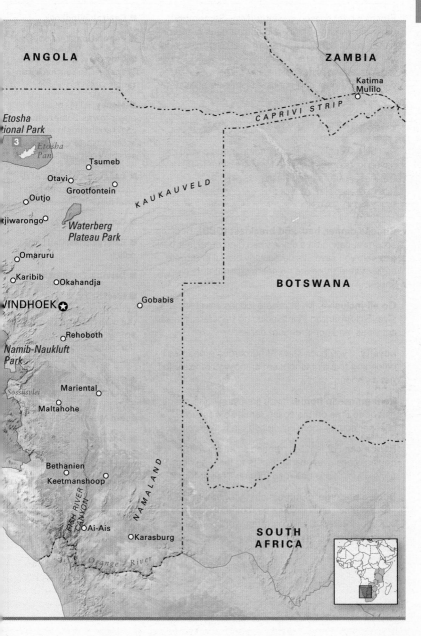

ANGOLA

ZAMBIA

Katima Mulilo

CAPRIVI STRIP

Etosha
ional Park

3   *Etosha Pan*

Tsumeb

Otavi
Grootfontein

KAUKAUVELD

Outjo

tjiwarongo

Waterberg Plateau Park

Omaruru

Karibib   Okahandja

BOTSWANA

VINDHOEK ✪

Gobabis

Rehoboth

Namib-Naukluft Park

Sossusvlei

Mariental

Maltahohe

NAMALAND

Bethanien

Keetmanshoop

FISH RIVER CANYON

Ai-Ais

Karasburg

SOUTH AFRICA

Orange River

COUNTRY SNAPSHOT

WHEN TO GO

Etosha's best season is winter (May–September) when the weather is dry and cool. It rains predominantly in the northeast (the Zambezi Region) during the Namibian summer (October–April), which makes for spectacular water safaris and game viewing. October and April are Namibia's shoulder season.

PASSPORTS AND VISAS

All non-nationals, including infants, need a valid passport to enter Namibia for visits of up to 90 days. Business visitors need visas.

WAYS TO SAVE

Choose dinner, bed, and breakfast (DBB). Booking accommodation on a dinner, bed, and breakfast basis can help you save; it's particularly useful in remote areas where there are no nearby restaurants or shops.

Go all-inclusive. Most private lodges are all-inclusive (Full American Plan), including transfers, meals, activities, and non-premium drinks.

Loyalty. If you book stays at numerous properties belonging to a single tourism brand, you're likely to get a discount.

Rent an ocean home. If you are planning to spend extended time on the coast, rental homes are cheaper and far more spacious than hotel rooms.

Rent a car. For families, renting a car is a tremendous savings over charter flights to far-flung destinations. Plus, this is one road trip you'll never forget!

Book a package. Outfitters string together itineraries that touch on Namibia's best offerings as well as suit your interests, and can often work out better deals over longer stays.

AT A GLANCE

- **Capital:** Windhoek

- **Population:** 2,541,000

- **Currency:** Namibian dollar; pegged to South African rand

- **Money:** ATMs in all major towns. Some remote gas stations might only accept cash. Most hotels accept credit cards.

- **Language:** English, Afrikaans, German, numerous local dialects

- **Country Code:** 264

- **Emergencies:** Call local police

- **Driving:** On the left

- **Electricity:** 220v/50 cycles; plugs are South African with three, thick round prongs, and two-prong Europlug. Rooms in high-end hotels have USB ports.

- **Time:** Six hours ahead of New York during daylight saving time; seven hours ahead otherwise.

- **Documents:** Up to 90 days with valid passport; must have 6 blank pages.

- **Mobile Phones:** GSM (900 and 1800 bands)

- **Major Mobile Companies:** MTC, TN Mobile

- **Namibia Tourism Board:** ⊕ www.visitnamibia.com.na

Many countries in Africa boast teeming wildlife and gorgeous scenery, but few, if any, can claim such limitless horizons; untamed wilderness; a pleasant climate; so few people (fewer than two per square mile); the oldest desert in the world; a wild, beautiful coastline; one of Africa's greatest game parks; plus—and this is a big bonus—a well-developed infrastructure and tourist facilities that are among the best in Africa. Welcome to Namibia.

Humans have lived here for thousands of years; the San (Bushmen) are the earliest known residents, although their hunter-gatherer way of life is now almost extinct. Often called the "Land God Made in Anger" because of its stark landscapes, untamed wilderness, harsh environment, and rare beauty, Namibia was carved out by the forces of nature. The same continuous geological movements produced not only spectacular beauty but also considerable mineral wealth: uranium, gold, lead, zinc, silver, copper, tungsten, and tin—still the cornerstone of Namibia's economy. In addition, it also has a significant resource of alluvial diamonds (from South Africa via the Orange River), as well as semi-precious stones (tourmaline, citrine, amethyst, topaz, and aquamarine) and mineral specimens for buyers and collectors.

A former German colony, South West Africa, as it was then known, was a pawn in the power games of European politics.

Although the Portuguese navigators were the first Europeans to arrive, in 1485, they quickly abandoned the desolate and dangerous Atlantic shores of the "Coast of Death," as they called it. By the late 1700s British, French, and American whalers were using the deep-water ports of Lüderitz and Walvis (Whalefish) Bay, which the Dutch, now settled in the Cape, then claimed as their own. A few years later, after France invaded The Netherlands, England seized the opportunity to claim the territory, together with the Cape Colony. Then it became Germany's turn to throw its hat into the ring. In the wake of its early missionaries and traders, Germany claimed the entire country as a colony in 1884, only to surrender it to the South African forces fighting on the Allied side during World War I. South Africa was given a League of Nations mandate to administer the territory after the war, and despite a 1978 UN resolution to revoke that mandate,

South Africa held on to Namibia for 10 years. A bitter and bloody bush war with SWAPO (South West African People's Organization) freedom fighters raged until Namibia finally won its independence on March 21, 1990, after 106 years of foreign rule. Although most of the earlier colonial influences have now vanished, everywhere you go in Namibia today you'll find traces of the German past—forts and castles, place names, cuisine, and even German efficiency.

Namibia prides itself on its conservation policies and vision. In many conservation areas, local communities, the wildlife, and the environment have been successfully integrated. Wilderness Safaris and its seven Namibian camps, for example, are an internationally acclaimed role model in linking tourism with community development projects.

Meanwhile, hunting, a controversial issue for many people, is carefully controlled so that the impact on the environment is minimal and the revenue earned is substantial and can often be ploughed back into sustainable conservation. Today, most Namibians work in agriculture, from subsistence farms to huge cattle ranches and game farms, as well as in the tourism industry.

MAJOR REGIONS

We've broken down this chapter by **Must-See Parks** (Namib-Naukluft Park, Damaraland, and Etosha National Park) and **If You Have Time Parks** (the Skeleton Coast, Zambezi Region [Caprivi Strip], and Waterberg Plateau Park) to help you organize your time. There is also a section on **Gateway Cities,** which for Namibia is Windhoek, and **Beach Escapes** (Swakopmund and Walvis Bay).

Planning

Getting Here and Around

AIR

Namibia has eight public airports and countless privately-owned and managed airstrips. The main point of entry is Hosea Kutako International Airport (WDH), near Windhoek, which services regional and international flights. FlyNamibia has direct flights from Cape Town to Windhoek daily, except on Saturdays.

The smaller Eros Airport (ERS) handles local flights and charters. Once in the country, you can make use of scheduled or charter flights that service all domestic destinations.

Walvis Bay International Airport (WVB)—the nearest airport for the Namib-Naukluft and the Skeleton Coast—is a small international airport with flights to and from Windhoek, Johannesburg, and Cape Town.

CONTACTS FlyNamibia. ⊠ *Eros Airport, 3 Aviation Rd, Windhoek* ☎ *83/339–0011* ⊕ *www.flynamibia.com.na.* **Westair Aviation.** ⊠ *Eros Airport, 3 Aviation Rd, Windhoek* ☎ *83/937–8247* ⊕ *www.westair.com.na.* **Sossusfly.** ☎ *81/250–7171* ⊕ *www.sossusfly.com.*

CHARTER FLIGHTS

All camps in Etosha National Park, as well as high-end lodges, have private landing strips. Have your tour operator arrange charters or fly-in safaris if you're short on time and budget allows. FlyNamibia, Scenic Air, and Desert Air are recommended for private charters and fly-in safaris.

FlyNamibia has daily 'Safari Circuit' flights between Windhoek and Sossusvlei and Etosha, with onwards flights from Sossusvlei to Swakopmund. It also operates flights to Ondangwa, Rundu, Katima Mulilo and Oranjemund a number of times a week.

CAR

Namibia's vast road network reaches all of the country's major tourist attractions and regions of interest, but distances are vast and most roads are unpaved and only occasionally leveled. Always check the state of the roads with the nearest tourist office before you set off. The 'DriveNam' Facebook Group is an invaluable online resource and community.

Don't drive at night since roads are unlit and run through wildlife corridors. If you hit an animal, even a small one, it could be the end of your vehicle, not to mention the critter. Don't speed on gravel roads as it's very easy to skid or roll your vehicle. Don't drive off marked roads: Namibia's "empty" landscapes are incredibly fragile habitats that cars can scar for hundreds of years. Make sure you have plenty of water and *padkos,* Afrikaans for "road food." Try out the ubiquitous *biltong,* Namibia's version of seasoned, dried game meat. Finally, keep in mind that gas stations sometimes only accept cash and can be few and far between, so fill up whenever you can and take extra jerry cans of fuel.

There are many reputable 4x4 car rental companies. It's advisable to have brand new spare tires, tire repair kits, plenty of drinking water, and an extra supply of fuel as remote gas stations may run out of fuel during peak season. Air conditioning is also a must at any time of the year.

Rental cars can be picked up at the town nearest whichever park you're visiting or at Etosha, but it's better to book them before you leave home. For driving on the main roads, a two-wheel-drive vehicle is fine. In some areas, though, including parts of the Namib-Naukluft Park and Damaraland, four-wheel drive is essential. In Etosha, a two-wheel-drive car is fine; don't exceed the speed limit of 60 kph (37 mph).

FROM SOUTH AFRICA

Driving to Namibia from South Africa is possible, and there's an excellent road network for all in-country tourist attractions, but be warned that the trip is tiring and time-consuming because of the huge distances involved. The Trans-Kalahari Highway links Johannesburg to Windhoek and Gaborone. From Johannesburg to Windhoek on this road it's 1,426 km (884 miles). To allow free access to game, there are no fences in the Kalahari, so don't speed, and look out for antelope as well as donkeys and cows on the road. You can also drive from Johannesburg to Windhoek (1,791 km [1,110 miles]) via Upington, going through the Narochas (Nakop) border post. This is a good route if you want to visit the Augrabies Falls and Kgalagadi Transfrontier Park in South Africa first. You can also drive from Cape Town to Namibia along the N7, an excellent road that becomes the B1 as you cross into Namibia at the Noordoewer border post. It's 763 km (473 miles) from Cape Town to Noordoewer, 795 km (493 miles) from Noordoewer to Windhoek. Border posts are efficient and friendly. Make sure you have all your paperwork to hand over—you'll need a current international driver's license and proof of car ownership or registration.

FROM BOTSWANA

Coming from Botswana, Namibia is entered at the Buitepos on the Trans-Kalahari Highway if coming from Gabarone, or through Ngoma on the Zambezi Region (Caprivi Strip) if coming from the Okavango Delta. Border posts aren't open 24 hours, and opening times should be confirmed before traveling. Cross-border charges (CBCs) must be paid by all foreign-registered vehicles entering Namibia, and cost about N$340 per vehicle (more for buses and motor homes). Tourists driving a rental car must also pay the CBC and will receive a CBC certificate for every entry into Namibia. If you're traveling onwards to Botswana, it's advisable to have Pula (Botswana's currency) or a working credit card for these charges.

TO ETOSHA NATIONAL PARK

You can drive from Windhoek, via Otjiwarongo and Tsumeb, and arrive at the park on its eastern side by the Von Lindequist Gate, 106 km (66 miles) from Tsumeb and 550 km (341 miles) north of Windhoek. Alternatively, you can drive from Windhoek via Otjiwarongo and Outjo and come in the Anderson Gate, south of Okaukuejo, 120 km (74½ miles) from Outjo, 450 km (279 miles) north of Windhoek. The latter is the more popular route. The newest option is to drive through Kamanjab to access the park's recently opened western side through the Galton Gate, 476 km (296 miles) north of Windhoek. All three drives are long, hot, and dusty, so you might want to fly to your camp's landing strip if you're short on time. Travel time will depend on your driving and choice of vehicle, so check with your car-rental company.

CONTACTS Automobile Association of Namibia (AAN). ✉ *Windhoek* ☎ *085/255–5500, 61/224–201, 081/218–4552 Emergency towing* ⊕ *www.aa-namibia.com.*

Communications

The country code for Namibia is 264. When dialing from abroad, drop the initial 0 from local area codes.

CALLING WITHIN NAMIBIA

Namibian telephone numbers vary and are constantly changing; many have six digits (not including the area and country code), but some have fewer or more digits.

MOBILE PHONES

There's cellphone reception in all major towns, though it is very unpredictable in far-out-of-town areas, and understandably so. Instead of enabling international roaming, rather buy a local SIM card when you arrive (as this is a much more

affordable option, and is very easy to do). The two major cellphone networks are MTC, and the newer (government-owned) TN Mobile. The former has better cellphone coverage and offers a 4G/LTE service, which is of utmost importance in Namibia. A SIM card will cost around N$10–N$20, and you can choose between prepaid bundles that include local talking minutes, SMSs, data, and social media data (which are valid for a week); international voice bundles; data bundles (which are valid for two months); or recharge vouchers–it goes without saying that the first option offers the best value for money overall. Top-up vouchers are available at cellphone providers' offices countrywide, and in most supermarkets and convenience stores.

Health and Safety

There is a negligible risk of malaria in Windhoek, central and southern Namibia, as well as along the Skeleton Coast in the west. Malaria is endemic in the east, north, and northeast, particularly between June and November, so antimalarials are recommended when traveling there. However, you should have peace of mind that all reputable establishments in these regions will have mosquito nets, and in-room mosquito repellent and insect spray.

Take lots of ice water, a sun hat, sunglasses, a high SPF sunblock, and wear longer sleeves and trousers made of natural fabric when venturing out into the desert, especially in the summer months.

Tap water often comes from deep boreholes and is always purified at lodges, hotels, and accommodations. It is perfectly safe to drink, unless specified in very rare cases. There is no need for bottled water and by traveling with a reusable water bottle and refiling it at the water station at your establishment of choice (which is very common), you can

Located in Namib-Naukluft National Park, the salt and clay pans of Sossusvlei are surrounded by Namibia's famous dunes.

truly help to alleviate single-use plastic to keep this natural environment pristine.

As elsewhere in Africa, AIDS is problematic, with an estimated 8.3% of the population affected in 2020; unprotected sex with a stranger puts you at higher risk.

Though Namibia is a relatively safe country, even for solo and female travelers, in towns it is not advisable to walk alone at night. Be sure to lock your valuables, documents, and cash in the hotel or in-room safety box no matter where in the country you're staying.

In game reserves and national parks, don't walk after dark unless accompanied by a guide, as you might have an unexpected encounter of the wild kind.

Because there's comparatively little traffic and very long distances, self-driving visitors are often tempted to speed. However, gravel roads can be tricky to navigate, especially at high speeds if you need to avoid an obstruction, passing animal, or sharp stones.

Be sure to have comprehensive medical insurance before you leave home. There's a high standard of private medical care in Namibia. If you get sick, go to a private clinic rather than a government-run one. Windhoek and Otjiwarongo have excellent private clinics. Both cities have a Medi-Clinic, and Windhoek has the Roman Catholic Hospital. Consult your hotel for medical practitioners.

EMBASSIES U.S. Embassy. ⊠ *14 Lossen St., Windhoek* ☎ *61/295–8500* ⊕ *na. usembassy.gov.*

EMERGENCY SERVICES International SOS. ☎ *112 from mobile phone, 61/289–0999 in Windhoek* ⊕ *www.namibweb.com/ emergency-numbers-namibia.htm.*

HOSPITALS Mediclinics. ⊠ *Heliodoor St. and Eros St., Eros Park* ☎ *61/433–1000.* **Roman Catholic Hospital.** ⊠ *92 Werner List St., Windhoek* ☎ *61/270–2004.*

Hotels and Lodges

Namibia's private camps, luxurious lodges, and high-end hotels (four- and five-star) are up to very high international standards. Other accommodations are often very clean, comfortable, and well-run. Tented camps have en-suite bathrooms and private verandahs, but don't expect TVs—besides there are much better things to see and do. Most private lodges are all-inclusive (Full American Plan), including transfers, meals, activities, and in-house alcoholic drinks and beverages. Camps usually offer at least two activities a day. Remote lodges, those that are far away from towns and restaurants, also offer the option to make a DBB booking, which includes dinner, bed, and breakfast. When this is the case, we noted it in the miscellaneous field of the review.

The government-run Namibia Wildlife Resorts (NWR) offers information on accommodations in the national parks, which you can also book through them. At the national park camps, self-catering (with cooking facilities) accommodations are basic, clean, comfortable, and much cheaper than private lodges outside the park. In Etosha each camp has a restaurant with adequate food, a shop selling basic foodstuffs and curios, a post office, a gas station, and a pool. Most rooms have private toilets, baths or showers, air-conditioning, a refrigerator, and a *braai*. Linens and towels are provided. Some bigger bungalows have a full kitchen.

In Windhoek and Swakopmund, a large array of lodgings, from large upmarket hotels to intimate boutique hotels and family-run bed-and-breakfasts, are yours to choose from. All urban lodging rates include breakfast, but rarely any other meals.

Restaurant and hotel reviews have been shortened. For full information, visit Fodors.com.

CONTACTS Namibia Wildlife Resorts. (*NWR*) ✉ *Independence Ave., 181 Gathemann Bldg., Windhoek* ☎ *61/285–7200* ⊕ *www.nwr.com.na.*

What It Costs in U.S. Dollars			
$	$$	$$$	$$$$
RESTAURANTS			
under $12	$12–$20	$21–$30	over $30
HOTELS			
under $250	$250–$450	$451–$600	over $600

Money Matters

Namibia's currency—the Namibian dollar (N$)—is pegged to the South African rand, though it cannot be used in South Africa, except unofficially at border posts and towns; South African rands are accepted throughout Namibia though. At the time of writing, the Namibian dollar was trading at around N$15–17 to US$1. Bureau de change offices at the airports often stay open until late.

There are main branches of major banks near or in the city center of Windhoek, Swakopmund, and Walvis Bay, plus several easy-to-find ATMs. Ask at your accommodation for more information. Major credit cards are accepted everywhere but at street markets, with Visa being the preferred card. In more rural or remote areas, carry Namibian dollars or South African rands. Note that some gas stations only take cash.

TIPPING
Tipping is tricky and at your own discretion. It depends on where you're staying and what services you've received. Your in-room lodge-information package often makes tipping suggestions. Tips can be

given in U.S. or Namibian dollars or South African rands. Most luxurious (four- and five-star) lodges suggest US$10 per person per day for your guide and US$5 per person per day for your tracker, as well as a tip for the general staff, though this is purely up to you and not a requirement.

Passports and Visas

All non-nationals, including infants, need a valid passport to enter Namibia for visits of up to 90 days. Business visitors need visas.

Plan Your Time

HASSLE FACTOR

Medium. There are no direct flights from the U.S. to Namibia, but it is easily reached via South Africa and neighboring countries. Once there, FlyNamibia offers daily and weekly flights to various towns and most luxury lodges have private airstrips for private charters.

3 DAYS

Head directly north toward Etosha National Park and plant yourself at a lodge adjacent to or within the park. This startlingly beautiful park with its diverse flora and fauna will blow you away.

1 WEEK

Split your time between the world's oldest living desert and Etosha National Park. In the Namib Desert, gawk over the shadows cast by the enormous sand dunes and search for wildlife that has adapted to these harsh conditions around Namib-Naukluft Park.

2 WEEKS

After hitting the world's oldest living desert, take a coastal road trip between Walvis Bay and Swakopmund. See the seals at Cape Cross. Head up to the Skeleton Coast and north to Kunene to observe indigenous tribes. Experience the ultimate safari in Etosha National Park before returning to Windhoek.

Restaurants

You won't find much truly Namibian food (although local venison, *biltong*, Kalahari truffles, seafood, and Namibian oysters are superb); the cuisine is mainly European, often German, though international variety and standards can easily be found in the larger towns. Lodges usually serve good home-style cooking—pies, pastries, bakes, fresh vegetables and salads, lots of red meat, mouthwatering desserts, and the traditional *braai* (barbecue). Because of its past as a German colony, Namibia is known for its lager beer. South African wine, which is excellent, is readily available across the country. Filtered tap water (which comes from deep boreholes) is perfectly safe for drinking and there is no need for bottled water.

Visitor Information

The Namibia Tourism Board (NTB) can provide a free map and a free copy of *Welcome to Namibia—Official Visitors' Guide,* which gives useful information plus accommodation lists, but doesn't provide detailed personalized advice. It's open weekdays 8–5. For more hands-on assistance, check out the tourist information centers (all run by different agencies, from the City of Windhoek to private companies) located in Windhoek and Swakopmund. However, it might be more useful, and worth your time, to consult online resources instead.

CONTACTS City of Windhoek Tourism Office. ⊠ *80 Independence Ave., Windhoek* ☎ *61/290–3777* ⊕ *www.windhoekcc.org. na.* **Namibia Tourism Board.** (*NTB*) ⊠ *Haddy St. and Sam Nujoma Dr., Windhoek* ☎ *61/290–6000* ⊕ *visitnamibia.com.na.*

When to Go

Namibia has a subtropical desert climate with nonstop sunshine throughout the year. It's classified as arid to non-arid, and, generally speaking, it gets wet only in the northeast and then only during the rainy period (October–April), which is the hottest season. The south is warm and dry, although temperatures can vary dramatically between night and day, particularly in the desert, where the air is sparkling, and pollution practically unheard of. Days are crystal clear and perfect for traveling. Elsewhere the weather is clear, dry, crisp, and nearly perfect, averaging 25°C (77°F) during the day. In the desert areas, temperatures can drop to freezing at night, especially in winter, so bring warm clothes for after the sun goes down.

The climate can be breathtakingly varied along the Skeleton Coast because of the Atlantic Ocean and its cold Benguela current, which makes the night cool and damp and brings thick morning coastal fog. Days are usually bright and sunny, and in summer, extremely hot, so dress in layers.

Etosha's best season is winter (May–September), when the weather is cooler, the grass shorter, and game easier to see. But if you can stand the heat, consider a summer visit to see the return of thousands of waterbirds, as well as tens of thousands of animals, to the lush feeding grounds around Okuakuejo.

FESTIVALS AND EVENTS

March: Independence Day on March 21 is a big party across Namibia.

May: Cassinga Day is commemorated on May 4. Many take extended leave between the public holiday on May 1 (Workers' Day) and May 4.

August: On Herero Day in the small city of Okahandja, the Herero people pay

Desert Art

In 2019, German conceptual artist Max Siedentopf, who grew up in Namibia, created an installation in the Namib Desert constructed of six plinths holding speakers and a solar-powered mp3 music player loaded with one song intended to play on an endless loop: Toto's 1982 hit, "Africa." He created *Toto Forever* both as what he calls "the ultimate homage" and to satirize stereotypical notions of African culture. Fans of his work are in for a challenge, however; the artist hasn't disclosed its exact location, so exercise caution if you embark on an art safari.

homage to their beloved chieftains who fought against German colonialism.

September: Celebrate Mfawe tribal culture during the Lusata Festival in Chinchimani village, near Katima Mulilo.

October: Namibia celebrates its German heritage during Oktoberfest, especially in Windhoek.

Namib-Naukluft Park

Namib-Naukluft Park, south of Walvis Bay, is the world's fourth-largest national park. It's renowned for its beauty, isolation, tranquility, romantic desert landscapes, and rare desert-adapted plants and creatures. Part of the Namib Desert, the world's most ancient desert, is found within the park.

Covering an area of 12.2 million acres, Namib-Naukluft Park stretches 400 km (248 miles) long and 150 km (93 miles) wide, along the southern part of Namibia's coastline from Walvis Bay to Lüderitz, and accounts for a tenth of Namibia's surface area. To examine the park properly, it's best to think of it as

Namib-Naukluft National Park's stark white Dead Vlei is dotted with dead, black camel thorn trees, thought to be almost 900 years old.

five distinct areas: the northern section—between the Kuiseb and Swakops rivers—synonymous with rocky stone surfaces, *inselbergs* (granite islands), and dry riverbeds; the middle section, the 80-million-year-old heart of the desert and home of Sesriem Canyon and Sossusvlei, as well as the highest sand dunes in the world; Naukluft (meaning "narrow gorge"), some 120 km (74½ miles) northwest of Sesriem, this mountain range has wall-to-wall game and birds and is the home of the Kuiseb Canyon; the western section, with its lichen-covered plains, prehistoric plants, and the natural bird sanctuaries of Walvis Bay and Sandwich Harbour; and the southern section, where, if you're traveling up from South Africa by road, it's worth having a look at Duwisib Castle, 72 km (45 miles) southwest of Maltahöhe beside the D286—an anachronistic stone castle built in 1909 by a German army officer who was later killed at the Somme. The park's southern border ends at the charming little town of Lüderitz, which is a good base for exploring Kolmanskop, a deserted mining town.

The kind of wildlife you'll encounter will depend on which area of the park you visit. In the north look out for the staggeringly beautiful *gemsbok* (oryx), the quintessential desert antelope, believed by some to be the animal behind the unicorn myth. Well-adapted for the desert, they obtain moisture from roots, tubers, and wild melons when water is scarce, and adapt their body temperatures and brains through specialized nasal blood vessels. Also found in the park are more than 50 species of mammals, including springboks, Hartmann's mountain zebras, leopards, caracals, Cape and bat-eared foxes, aardwolves, and klipspringers, as well as cheetahs, spotted hyenas, black-backed jackals, and the awesome lappet-face vultures, the biggest in Africa.

There are almost 200 species of birds, from the startlingly beautiful crimson-breasted shrike to soaring falcons and buzzards. You'll notice huge haystacks weighing down tall camel thorn trees and telephone poles. These are the condominiums of the sociable weavers, so-called because they nest communally, sometimes with thousands of fellow weavers.

You'll be able to observe some of the earth's strangest creatures in the sand dunes: the dune beetle, which collects condensed fog on its back into a single droplet that it then rolls down its back into its mouth; the blind golden mole (thought until recently to be extinct), which "swims" beneath the sand, ambushing beetles and grubs on the surface; the side-winding adder; and the shovel-snouted lizard (also known as the Namib sand-diver) that raises one foot at a time above the hot sand in a strange stationary dance.

Don't overlook the amazing desert-adapted plants including the nara melon, still harvested and eaten by the locals, the baffling geophytes, plants that disguise themselves as stones, and the mind-boggling *Welwitschia mirabilis,* the Namib's most famous, and the world's oldest, living plant.

WHEN TO GO

Temperatures can be extremely variable, with days generally hot (sometimes exceeding 104°F [40°C]) and nights that can descend to freezing. Given these extremes, the dunes are best visited early in the morning, especially in the summer (September–March). The park is open throughout the year, and in winter you can visit the dunes during the day, though note that it can still get warm, especially when you're climbing the dunes.

GETTING HERE AND AROUND

At its closest, the Namib-Naukluft is approximately 200 km (124 miles) from Windhoek and can be accessed by many roads, both major and minor. Entry permits for the park, including Sossusvlei and Sandwich Harbour, are required, and can be obtained from the Ministry of Environment Tourism offices in Windhoek, Swakopmund, or Sesriem. The

Park Ratings

Game: ★ ★ ☆ ☆ ☆

Park Accessibility: ★ ★ ★ ★ ☆

Getting Around: ★ ★ ★ ★ ☆

Accommodations: ★ ★ ★ ★ ★

Scenic Beauty: ★ ★ ★ ★ ★

park is split into four sections: Sesriem and Sossusvlei; Namib; Naukluft; and Sandwich Harbour. Entrance is between sunrise and sunset only. The distance between Sesriem and Sossusvlei is 65 km (40 miles), the last 5 km (3 miles) of which require a 4x4. The dunes are easily accessible by foot from the sedan car park. Sandwich Harbour is accessible only with a 4x4, and an experienced guide is highly recommended.

SAFETY AND PRECAUTIONS

Stay on existing roads and tracks, and always have plenty of water available (at least a liter per person in case the car breaks down and it takes time for help to arrive) as well as sunblock, a hat, and sunglasses, regardless of the season. If traveling in an open vehicle, bring a thick jacket (i.e., a windbreaker) as the wind while driving can be freezing (even in summer in the early morning before sunrise).

At Sesriem Canyon and at numerous stops near the most famous dunes, there are ablution blocks (think public bathrooms) with potable water. There are picnic tables, positioned in the shade of trees, near Sossusvlei, which make for perfect rest stops. Campsites, which are mostly concentrated in the northern section of the park, have limited facilities. Always take your trash with you if you can.

The lichen and gravel plains are extremely fragile and tire tracks can last for hundreds of years, which is why it's

In the early 20th Century, Kolmanskop was the heart of diamond mining, but by the 1950s it was a ghost town.

forbidden to go off-roading. Avoid disturbing nesting raptors if mountain climbing.

TIMING

Those only intending to visit the Sossusvlei section of the park should stay in the area for at least two full days, so as to have an entire day to climb Big Daddy Dune, visit Dead Vlei at its base, the eponymous Sossusvlei (a salt and clay pan), and also stop at all the other dunes along the way. Climbing the dunes should be done very early in the morning to avoid the heat. Since you're already here, it's really well worth doing a scenic sunset flight over the dunes to see their vastness from a different vantage point and marvel at the sun's shadows in their creases and crevices. There are four flight routes to choose from depending on your budget, and the more passengers there are, the more affordable the flights become. A flight might very well be the highlight of your entire trip. If you're planning to hike the Namib-Naukluft Trail as well, five days total should suffice.

Sights

Even if you're not a romantic, the Sossusvlei's huge, star-shape desert dunes, which rise dramatically 1,000 feet above the surrounding plains and sprawl like massive pieces of abstract sculpture, are guaranteed to stir your soul and imagination. The landscape has continuously shifting colors—from yellow-gold and ocher to rose, purple, and deep red—that grow paler or darker according to the time of day. The dunes have their own distinctive features, ranging from the crescent-shape barchan dunes—which migrate up to 2 or 3 yards a year, covering and uncovering whatever crosses their path—to the spectacular, stationary star-shape dunes, formed by the multidirectional winds that tease and tumble the sands back and forth. Park gates open an hour before sunrise, so if you can, try to be among the dunes as the sun comes up—it's a spectacular sight.

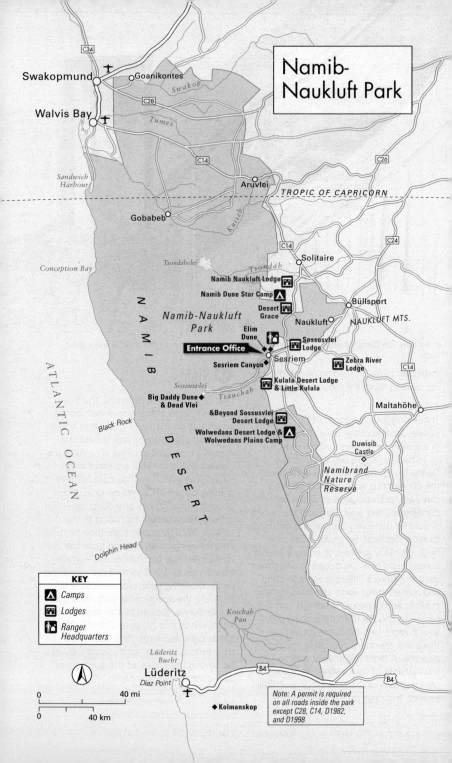

Namib-Naukluft Park

Swakopmund

Goanikontes

Swakop

C34

C28

Tumes

Walvis Bay

C14

Sandwich Harbour

Aruvlei

TROPIC OF CAPRICORN

Gobabeb

Kuiseb

Conception Bay

Tsondabvlei

Tsondab

C14

Solitaire

C26

C24

Namib Naukluft Lodge

Namib Dune Star Camp

Büllsport

Desert Grace

Naukluft

NAUKLUFT MTS.

Namib-Naukluft Park

N
A
M
I
B

Elim Dune

Entrance Office

Sossusvlei Lodge

Sesriem

Sesriem Canyon

Zebra River Lodge

C14

Sossusvlei

Big Daddy Dune & Dead Vlei

Tsauchab

Kulala Desert Lodge & Little Kulala

Maltahöhe

Black Rock

&Beyond Sossusvlei Desert Lodge

Wolwedans Desert Lodge & Wolwedans Plains Camp

D
E
S
E
R
T

Duwisib Castle

Namibrand Nature Reserve

Dolphin Head

A
T
L
A
N
T
I
C

O
C
E
A
N

KEY

▲ Camps

🏠 Lodges

🧍 Ranger Headquarters

Koichab Pan

Lüderitz Bucht

Lüderitz

Diaz Point

B4

B4

0 — 40 mi

0 — 40 km

◆ Kolmanskop

Note: A permit is required on all roads inside the park except C28, C14, D1982, and D1998

Big Daddy Dune

NATURE SIGHT | If you're in good shape, you can hike to the top of Big Daddy, the highest sand dune in the world at around 360 meters (1,181 feet). But it's tough going: more than an hour of very hot trudging and wading through ankle- and sometimes knee-deep sand to climb along the ridge that overlooks the famous Dead Vlei (where ghostly skeletons of ancient camel thorn trees jut up from a flat, sandy, dried-up lake). If you don't feel up to any physical exertion at all, then sit in the shade of camel thorn trees at the bottom of the dunes and watch the birdlife, or focus your binoculars on the distant climbers. ⊠ *Namib Naukluft Park* ✛ *70 km (43 miles) from the Sesriem gate.*

Dead Vlei

NATURE SIGHT | If you're not up to trudging up the steep edges of sand dunes, head in the direction of Sossusvlei and take a shorter, gradual walk from the parking lot to the much-photographed Dead Vlei. This stark white dried pan is dotted with dead, black camel thorn trees, thought to be almost 900 years old, and surrounded by red sand dunes. The image of Dead Vlei is almost synonymous with Namibia and is as picturesque as it is remarkable.

If you're not traveling by 4x4 you can park at the 2x4 parking and pay to take the NWR shuttle (it runs all day long) that covers the 5 km (3 miles) to Sossusvlei. ⊠ *Namib Naukluft Park* ✛ *1 km (0.6 mile) from Sossusvlei 4x4 parking.*

Elim Dune

NATURE SIGHT | If you're fairly fit, it's well worth climbing the towering Elim Dune, the nearest sand dune to Sesriem, about 5 km (3 miles) away; it will take you more than an hour, but the superb views of the surrounding desert and gravel plains are infinitely rewarding. Be warned: dune climbing is exhausting, so make discretion the better part of valor. This is an excellent place to photograph the early morning or late afternoon light as it's a lot closer to the park's entrance gate. ⊠ *Namib Naukluft Park* ✛ *5 km (3 miles) from Sesriem.*

Sesriem Canyon

CANYON | About 4 km (2½ miles) from Sesriem Gate, your entry point to Sossusvlei, is Sesriem Canyon, named after the six *rieme* (thongs) that were tied to the buckets of the early Dutch settlers when they drew up water from the canyon. A narrow gorge of about 1 km in length, the Sesriem Canyon is the product of centuries of erosion. Plunging down 30–40 meters (98–131 feet) at its end are a series of pools that fill with water during the rains, which might only happen during the rainy season (October to March) though not very often, especially if there is a drought. If you are lucky you will get to cool off in the pools, otherwise climbing down into the canyon offers you a wonderful escape from the desert heat as you wander along in the deep shade. ⊠ *Near entry to Sossusvlei, Namib Naukluft Park.*

Hotels

★ &Beyond Sossusvlei Desert Lodge

$$$$ | **ALL-INCLUSIVE** | This gorgeous glass and natural stone lodge has a spectacular setting on the border of the NamibRand Nature Reserve–Africa's first International Dark Sky Reserve. **Pros:** lodge looks out onto a waterhole that attracts scores of animals; everything has been thought of at this lodge; explore the area on an eco-friendly quad bike, guided nature walk or drive, or hot air balloon ride. **Cons:** spa facilities and certain activities at additional cost; distance from Sossusvlei makes visiting the dunes a whole day trip; the dressing room/area is in the hallway of the suites. $ *Rooms from: US$2,120* ⊠ *Namib Naukluft Park* ☎ *1111/809–4300 in South Africa* ⊕ *www.andbeyond.com* ⌺ *12 villas* ⦿*| All-Inclusive.*

Kolmanskop: Namibia's Ghost Town

This dilapidated ghost town found in the very south of the Namib Desert, near the little coastal town of Luderitz, was once home to hundreds of miners during the diamond boom over 100 years ago. It's now a collection of once-glorious homes filled to the windowsills with the desert sand, a famous spot for capturing emotive photographs of the peeling walls and the soft dunes that fill the rooms and doorways.

A permit (N$85) is required to enter Kolmanskop. The pass allows entrance between 9 am to 1 pm (closing time) and includes a guided tour (Monday–Saturday, 9:30 am or 11 am and Sunday, 10 am). You can book a private tour after 1 pm, and there's a restaurant and museum (Monday–Saturday, 9 am–1 pm) on the premises. Find more information visit 🌐 www.kolmanskuppe.com.

★ Desert Grace

$$$ | HOTEL | When you see the sunset reflecting off the Namib-Naukluft Mountains from this elegant hotel, you'll understand why this safari shabby chic establishment is done up in accents of dusty pink. **Pros:** decor gets 10/10 for originality and photo opportunities; private plunge pool on room verandahs overlook grassy dunes; excellent selection and quality of buffet meals and a la carte food. **Cons:** each room is very close to the next, yet still has privacy; come for the location and landscapes, not so much for game viewing; an hour away from Sossusvlei. *[$] Rooms from: US$470 ✉ Namib Naukluft Park ☎ 61/427–200 landline 🌐 www.gondwana-collection.com 🛏 24 rooms 🍴 Free Breakfast.*

Kulala Desert Lodge

$$$$ | HOTEL | FAMILY | In the heart of the Namib, set on a private wilderness reserve that borders the Namib-Naukluft Park with an exclusive-use entrance gate, this is the closest you could possibly stay to the famous red dunes of Sossusvlei (along with Wilderness Safaris's adjoining property on the same reserve). **Pros:** private Namib-Naukluft Park entrance saves time and waiting in long queues; exceptional staff with genuine warm-heartedness will make you feel at home; activities include morning and evening game drives, trips to Sossusvlei, birding, guided walks, fat biking. **Cons:** no mosquito nets on the star bed experience; not all activities are included in the half-board option, but can be booked at an additional cost; guests can't do self game drives through the private concession area. *[$] Rooms from: US$720 ✉ Namib Naukluft Park ☎ 11711/257–5000 in South Africa 🌐 www.wilderness-safaris.com 🛏 23 chalets 🍴 All-Inclusive.*

★ Little Kulala

$$$$ | HOTEL | This intimate and luxurious lodge in the 66,718-acre private Kulala Wilderness Reserve faces the mesmerizing red dunes of Namib-Naukluft Park with the ever-shifting sands and a waterhole that attracts all manner of game and birdlife. **Pros:** staff go out of their way to ensure that your stay is impeccable in every way; magical dining experience under the desert night sky; has a very strong social responsibility and ecotourism model. **Cons:** remotely located (but that could equally be one of it key selling points); if not on an all-inclusive package, some activities are at an extra cost; you'll be doing yourself and the lodge a disservice if you come for less than two

Continued on page 440

The Sossusvlei salt pans.

THE NAMIBIA DUNES

Be prepared for sand like you've never seen it before: in dunes that roar, rumble, and ramble. We guarantee the sight will stir your soul and imagination.

Namibia's dunes, which rise dramatically more than 1,000 meters (3,281 feet) above the surrounding plains, are said to be the world's highest. But don't think that if you've seen one sandy ridge you've seen them all. Expect great variety here. There are crescent-shaped dunes that migrate up to 2 or 3 meters (7 to 10 feet) a year, covering and uncovering whatever's in their path. There are also fossil dunes made of ancient sand that solidified millions of years ago, and star-shaped dunes formed by multidirectional winds teasing and tumbling the sand.

Amid this unique landscape live some of the world's strangest, most well-adapted creatures. The golden mole, for instance, spends its life "swimming" under the sand, popping up to the surface to grab unwary insects. Certain types of beetles collect condensed droplets of water on their backs and then roll the liquid down to their mouths; still other beetles dig trenches to collect moisture. As its name suggests, the side-winding adder moves itself from side to side over the sand, while, contrary to its name, the sand-diving lizard stands motionless, one foot raised, as if in some ancient ritual dance. And then there's the quintessential desert antelope: the beautiful gemsbok (oryx), which is believed by some to be the animal behind the unicorn myth.

WHERE DID THE DUNES COME FROM?

The formation and structure of sand dunes is extremely complex, but basically there are three prerequisites for dunes: plenty of loose sand, plenty of wind, and a flat surface with no obstacles like trees or mountains to prevent dunes building up. Namibia has these three things in abundance.

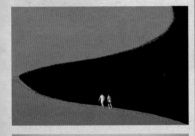

EXPLORING THE DUNES

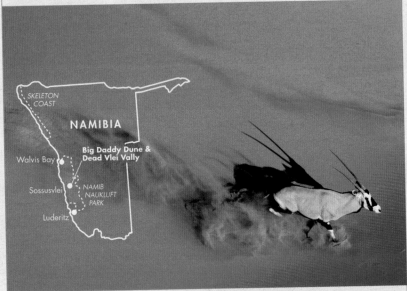

Gemsbok in the desert dunes of Namib-Naukluft Park.

WHERE ARE THE DUNES?

Enormous Namib-Naukluft Park—renowned for its isolated, romantic desert scapes—stretches 400 km (250 miles) along the southern part of Namibia's coastline, from Walvis Bay to Lüderitz, and accounts for a tenth of the country's surface area. Sossusvlei, the 80-million-year-old heart of the desert, is in the middle section of the park. It's a great entry point from which you can start your adventures. This desert is thought to be the oldest desert in the world. Although its geological base area is relatively stable, the dunes themselves are continuously sculpted by the desert winds.

DUNE EXPLORER

Sure, you could explore the dunes on your own, but you really can't beat the know-how of an experienced guide; ask your lodge to arrange this. Look to climb "Big Daddy," a dune that's as tall as a seven-story building, or Dune 7 (about 1,256 feet) or Dune 45 (557 feet). You could also just climb to the halfway point of Big Daddy or simply sit in the shade at the bottom of a dune and watch the distant climbers exert themselves.

WHEN TO GO

Sunset and sunrise are the best times to visit (be at the gates of Sesriem when it opens at sunrise or camp in the park), because the colors of the dunes change in spectacular fashion from yellow-gold and ocher to rose, purple, and deep red. Keep in mind that midday temperatures can peak at over 40°C (104°F) in summer.

THE SLOW PACE

Sip sundowners as the sun sinks, go hot-air ballooning at dawn, or simply marvel at the life that is found in this harsh environment. You won't see big game, but you will see a wealth of unique birds, insects, plants, and geological formations. Whatever you do, make sure you take a moment to appreciate the soul-searing and soul-searching silence.

ADRENALINE JUNKIES WELCOME

(top) Preparing to sandboard. (bottom) Sandboarding.

Looking for some excitement? Adrenaline junkies can try their hand (or feet) at skydiving, dune-buggying, paragliding, sandboarding, or dune-boarding (for the more advanced). The less adventurous (but romantic) can take day, moonlight, sunrise, or sunset horseback or camel rides through the riverbeds and up into the moonlike landscape.

If you have time for just one thing, make it sandboarding because it will certainly get your heart pumping. Once you climb up the dunes armed with your sandboard (it works the same on sand as it does on snow) or a flat piece of hardboard known as the "Kalahari Ferrari," there's only one way down. It's also a good idea to wear long pants, long sleeves, and any provided safety equipment to avoid a sandburn. Beginners should head to the smaller dunes to practice sliding down on their stomachs to get the feel of it. As you get better and more adventurous, head to the top of a high dune, but be advised,

you can reach speeds of up to 80 kph (50 mph). Once you get the hang of it, try standing up on your sandboard.

If you get really advanced, there's always dune-boarding. You use all the same gear as sandboarding, except your board is similar to a regular surfboard on which you stand up and "surf" down the dunes.

If you want to be one of the first ones into Namib-Naukluft National Park in the morning, Sossusvlei Lodge is located by the park's Sesriem entrance.

days. $ *Rooms from: US$1,436* ✉ *Namib Naukluft Park* ☎ *111/257–5000 in South Africa* ⊕ *www.wilderness-safaris.com* ⇨ *11 suites* ⦿ *All-Inclusive.*

Namib Dune Star Camp

$$ | HOTEL | FAMILY | These eco-friendly, solar-powered chalets with spacious wood decks balance atop grassy sand dunes that show off stunning sunset vistas. **Pros:** each clean, comfortable cabin sleeps three; meals at the communal table are great for meeting other travelers; personalized and attentive service at this intimate camp. **Cons:** no power outlets in the rooms, only at restaurant; can only do a self-drive to reception, so don't leave anything in your car when you pack a small overnight bag; no Wi-Fi and poor cellphone reception at the camp. $ *Rooms from: US$355* ✉ *Namib Naukluft Park* ☎ *061/427–200 landline* ⊕ *www.gondwana-collection.com* ⇨ *9 cabins* ⦿ *Free Breakfast.*

Namib Naukluft Lodge

$ | B&B/INN | Resembling children's building blocks set down by a giant hand in the middle of nowhere, this earth-toned lodge sits in the midst of a wide plain of desert, backed by gorgeous granite hills. **Pros:** shuttle available from Windhoek and Swakopmund to the lodge at additional cost; friendly service; stunning location. **Cons:** no-frills accommodations; some expected activities are at extra cost; 45-minute drive to Sesriem (the entrance to Sossusvlei). $ *Rooms from: US$122* ✉ *Namib Naukluft Park* ☎ *061/372–100* ⊕ *www.namib-naukluft-lodge.com* ⇨ *15 rooms* ⦿ *Free Breakfast.*

Sossusvlei Lodge

$$ | HOTEL | If you want to be on the spot when the park gates open at first light, this hotel (right at the Sesriem entrance) is the right choice for you. **Pros:** very convenient location for early-morning drives; many rooms have a good view of the waterhole; excellent buffet. **Cons:** service can be hit or miss; lacks the personal touch of a smaller, more intimate lodge; Wi-Fi is inconsistent and only available in the bar and reception. $ *Rooms from: US$275* ✉ *Namib Naukluft Park* ☎ *63/293–636 lodge, 63/930–4564 reservations* ⊕ *www.sossusvleilodge.com* ⇥ *51 rooms* ❍ *Free Breakfast* ⚲ *can also be booked on a DBB basis.*

Wolwedans Desert Lodge

$$$$ | ALL-INCLUSIVE | For seclusion and green, conscience-free travel in a ridiculously pretty setting, book Wolwedans Desert Lodge (previously Dune Camp), which is set against an 820-foot-high sand dune that faces a mountain that turns different shades of pink in the setting sun. **Pros:** an all-inclusive stay includes a variety of activities; this is the brands' hospitality training facility, which forms part of the Wolwedans Desert Academy; a clean conscience thanks to Wolwedans's in-depth green efforts. **Cons:** distance from Sossusvlei makes it a full day trip; minimum two-night stay, sustainability levy of US$65 per person per night; fixed arrivals on Monday, Wednesday and Friday, closed on Sunday. $ *Rooms from: US$875* ✉ *Namib Naukluft Park* ☎ *21/876–2153 in South Africa* ⊕ *www.wolwedans.com* ◷ *Closed Sun.* ⇥ *10 tented suites* ❍ *All-Inclusive.*

Wolwedans Plains Camp

$$$$ | ALL-INCLUSIVE | FAMILY | This exclusive-use private villa, in the serene and secluded NamibRand Nature Reserve—which is Africa's first Dark Sky Reserve—gives its guests up-close access to the surrounding desert habitat. **Pros:** beautiful, private, and intimate location with outdoor salas and decks to enjoy the views; comes with private chef and guide; guided activities include drives, sundowners, e-biking, various walks and tours. **Cons:** minimum two-night stay; some activities and compulsory sustainability fee are at an extra charge; you won't meet any other guests. $ *Rooms from: US$2,775* ✉ *Namib Naukluft Park* ☎ *21/876–2153 in South*

Africa ⊕ *www.wolwedans.com* ⇥ *1 villa* ❍ *All-Inclusive.*

Damaraland

Stretching 600 km (370 miles) from just south of Etosha to Usakos in the south and 200 km (125 miles) from east to west, this stark, mountainous area is inland from Skeleton Coast National Park.

You can drive into Damaraland from the park via the Springbokwater Gate or drive from Swakopmund to Uis, where you can visit the Daureb Craft Centre and watch the craftspeople at work, or make it part of your customized safari. A good base for touring southern Damaraland is the little town of Khorixas. From here you can watch the rising or setting sun bathe the slopes of Burnt Mountain (Brandberg Mountain) in fiery splendor. You'll find yourself surrounded by a dramatic landscape of steep valleys; rugged cliffs of red, gray, black, and brown; and towering mountains, including Spitzkoppe (Namibia's Matterhorn, which towers nearly 610 meters [2,000 feet] above the plains). Spend at least three to four hours exploring Spitzkoppe's Golden Snake and the Bridge—an interesting arch-like rock formation—and the San paintings at Bushman's Paradise, which must be visited with a guide for an additional charge (entrance fee $N80 per adult and vehicle).

There are more spectacular rock paintings at Brandberg Mountain, especially the famous White Lady of Brandberg at Tsisab Gorge, whose depiction and origin have teased the minds of scholars for decades. (Is she of Mediterranean origin? Is "she" really a "he" covered in white initiation paint?). The entrance fee (N$100 per adult) includes a guide and it's best to go as early in the morning as you can, as the 60- to 90-minute walk can get scorching hot, even in the cooler months and despite being fairly flat.

Read and Watch

The Purple Violet of Oshaantu by Namibian writer Neshani Andreas examines the plight of African women in rural Namibia.

A young girl looks to elephants for guidance in saving her family's game reserve in *The Elephant's Tale* by Lauren St. John.

Daniel by Henning Mankell follows the journey of a Swedish entomologist who visits Namibia and brings a young boy home.

The documentary *Milking the Rhino* examines the relationship between the Ovahimba people of Namibia, wildlife, and conservation.

Based on the novel by the same name, the 2019 drama *Hairareb* is set in Namibia's desolate and harsh landscape as the lead characters struggle to survive a drought and everything else in between.

Katutura (2015) movie delves into the everyday struggles of what it's like to live in one of Windhoek's informal settlements.

A love story set in the early 1960s, *The White Line* (2019) shows how apartheid spilled into then South West Africa before it gained independence from South Africa.

The fourth installment of the Mad Max franchise, *Mad Max: Fury Road* (2015) was filmed in the Namibian desert and starred Charlize Theron and Tom Hardy.

Many scenes of the prehistoric adventure fantasy blockbuster *10,000 BC* (2018) were filmed in Namibia.

The first UNESCO World Heritage Site in Namibia, Twyfelfontein, 90 km (56 miles) west of Khorixas, is also the biggest outdoor art gallery in the world, where thousands of rock paintings and ancient rock engravings are open to the sky. It's extremely rare for this many paintings and engravings to be found at the same site. As you approach, you'll see scattered boulders everywhere. The entrance fee (N$250 per international adult) includes a knowledgeable guide who narrates the timeline of the landscape and the people who lived here. Start early (it's hard to make out some of the art in full sunshine), bring binoculars, wear sturdy shoes, and bring lots of water (at least a liter) and a hat.

Though the Organ Pipes, a small-ish site of hundreds of angular rock formations, are very close by, the entrance for international travelers (N$250) is really not worth it and can be somewhat underwhelming, unless you are a very avid geology-lover. Other stops of interest are the Petrified Forest, 42 km (25 miles) west of Khorixas, where the corpses of dead trees lie forever frozen in a bed of sandstone, but this site, too, should only be a secondary consideration unless you have lots of time to spare.

Northern Damaraland consists of concession areas that have been set aside for tourism, with many tourist operators working hand-in-hand with the local communities. This is a desert of a different kind from the classic sand dunes of the Namib. It's a landscape of almost unsurpassed rugged beauty formed by millions of years of unending geological movement. Vivid brick-red sediments complement gray lava slopes punctuated by black fingers of "frozen" basaltic rock creeping down from the jagged rocky horizons. Millions of stones, interspersed with clumps of silvery-gray shrubs and pioneer grass, litter the unending slopes, hillsides, and mountain faces. There seem to be as many rocks, huge and small, as there are grains of sand on the beaches of the windswept, treacherous Skeleton Coast, some 90 km (56 miles) to the west. But there's life, and plenty of it, in this seemingly inhospitable landscape, including dozens of *Welwitschia mirabilis*—plants that can live for up to 1,000 years.

The landscape is also dotted with colorful lichen fields, dark-green umbrella-shape camel thorn trees, candelabra euphorbias raising their prickly fleshy arms to the cloudless sky, saltbushes, and the ubiquitous shepherd's tree. Also here is the *moringa* tree—the "enchanted" tree, so-called because according to San legend, the god of thunder, not wanting moringa trees in heaven, pulled up all of them and threw them out. They fell upside down into the earth, looking like miniature baobab trees. In the middle of this rocky desert rubble is Slangpost, a small, verdant oasis in the middle of what seems to be nowhere (not even the mountains have a name in this part of the world; they're referred to simply as the "no-name mountains").

Look out for traces of the desert-adapted elephants in these parts, with their huge footprints trodden over by the healthy herds of goats and sheep belonging to the local Damara farmers. Your best chance of seeing these elephant herds is along the surprisingly green and fertile dry Huab River bed, where they browse on the large seedpods of the Ana tree and whatever else they find. Many lodges in the region offer sunrise or half-day game drives in search of them with a high likelihood of getting lucky. The great gray shapes silhouetted against the dry river's sandy mounds ringed by mountains and sand dunes are an incredible sight.

The Kaokoveld, north of Damaraland, although enticing because it's pristine

Park Ratings

Game: ★ ★ ★ ☆ ☆
Park Accessibility: ★ ☆ ☆ ☆ ☆
Getting Around: ★ ★ ☆ ☆ ☆
Accommodations: ★ ★ ☆ ☆ ☆
Scenic Beauty: ★ ★ ★ ★ ★

9

Namibia DAMARALAND

and rarely visited, is also inhospitably rugged. Self-drives are for the really intrepid, do-it-yourself explorer.

WHEN TO GO
The area can be visited throughout the year. However, during the rainy season (January–April), roads and tracks may be difficult to negotiate, or not accessible at all due to flooding. Come May the area has a special splendor with waves of green grass growing on the plains and hills. From May to September the days will be cooler and more bearable, but nights can be very cold, especially for the camper. From October to December nights can be cool and days very hot.

GETTING HERE AND AROUND
One can access Damaraland from the coast (Swakopmund and Walvis Bay) by traveling via Henties Bay and Uis on the C35, or farther up the coast, accessing the park from Springbokwater on the C39. Coming from Windhoek, drive via Omaruru (C33) and Uis (C36) to Damaraland. From the north, travel via Kamanjab (C35) and Outjo (C39) to Khorixas. Good gravel roads can be traveled between attractions. The area is extremely fragile, and vehicles must always stay on existing roads and tracks. It's not advised to travel on to smaller tracks without the company of an experienced Namibian guide, as tourists frequently lose their way in these parts.

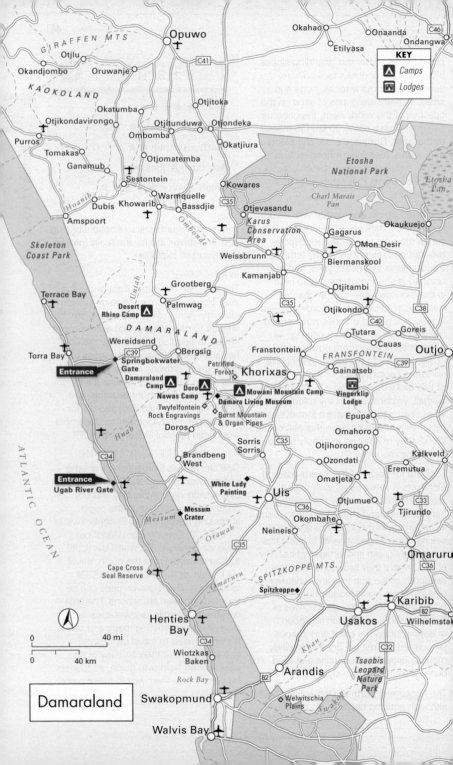

In Damaraland, there are numerous stone arches and rock formations near Spitzkoppe (Namibia's Matterhorn).

SAFETY AND PRECAUTIONS

Don't travel faster than 80 kph (50 mph) on gravel roads. Always fill up your tank when a gas station is available (e.g., Kamanjab, Outjo, Khorixas, and Uis). Smaller towns such as Palmwag and Sesfontein may not have gas available, so it's also advisable to take an additional filled gas can if you plan to travel long stretches between places where gas isn't available. Always bring sufficient water.

TIMING

Four days is the suggested minimum, especially if you plan to visit Spitzkoppe on the first day; Brandberg (Burnt Mountain) on the second; Twyfelfontein and the Damara Living Museum (for insights into how the hunter-gatherer bushman once lived) on the third. The Organ Pipes and Petrified Forest are a good idea only if you have more time to spare, as you may be left feeling underwhelmed, especially considering the entrance fee. Rather spend your final day (or two) in search of the the desert-adapted elephant and other wildlife in the Huab River. Additionally, a day trip to the Welwitschia plains and Messum Crater is worthwhile.

Sights

Damara Living Museum

MUSEUM VILLAGE | The Damara are one of Namibia's oldest nations. This living history museum provides insight into how the hunter-gatherer bushman once lived with a reconstructed village. ✉ *Damaraland* ✛ *About 10 km (6 miles) north of Twyfelfontein* ⊕ *www.lcfn.info/damara* ✉ *village N$90, bushwalk N$70, combo N$150.*

Spitzkoppe

MOUNTAIN | What could be described as Namibia's Matterhorn, Spitzkoppe towers nearly 610 meters (2,000 feet) above the plains. Plan to spend at least three to four hours exploring Spitzkoppe's Golden Snake—a gigantic rock formation popular with rock climbers—and the Bridge—an interesting arch-like rock formation. The San paintings at Bushman's Paradise are also worth a look though they must be visited with a guide for an additional charge. ✉ *Spitzkoppe, Damaraland* 🎫 *entrance fee $N80 per adult and $N80 vehicle.*

Hotels

★ Damaraland Camp

$$$$ | **HOTEL** | This exceptional camp on the Huab River in central Damaraland is the ideal starting point for searching for desert-adapted elephants, with guides who are astute in accommodating photographers' need to get the perfect shot. **Pros:** one of Namibia's most pristine wilderness areas and the perfect place to see the desert-adapted elephants; sustainability is at its core from solar power and environmentally-friendly amenities to eco-building techniques; the country's most impressive community-based responsible tourism model. **Cons:** chances of seeing the desert-adapted elephants are very high, but never guaranteed; 2x4 vehicles will be left in a parking area 45 minutes away; game drives are additional on a half-board basis. [$] *Rooms from: US$850* ✉ *Damaraland* ☎ *21/257–5000 in South Africa* 🌐 *www.wilderness-safaris.com* 🛏 *10 tents* 🍴 *All-Inclusive.*

Desert Rhino Camp

$$$$ | **ALL-INCLUSIVE** | If it's rhinos you're after, especially the rare black rhino, then this very remote tented camp in the heart of the private 1-million-acre Palmwag Reserve is a must. **Pros:** a plunge pool to cool off in the main lodge on hot days; amazing educational experience on black rhinos and their ecology; evening meals taken together by the fire pit allow guests to mingle. **Cons:** the roads are very bumpy, especially after a few hours; the drive to camp from the parking takes 2.5 hours, as self-drives to the camp are not permitted, but allows for game viewing; some visitors could find this experience overly rustic and remote. [$] *Rooms from: US$832* ✉ *Damaraland* ☎ *21/257–5000 in South Africa* 🌐 *www.wilderness-safaris.com* 🛏 *8 tents* 🍴 *All-Inclusive.*

Doro Nawas Camp

$$$$ | **HOTEL** | Blending into the backdrop and set amid stony slopes, rugged boulders, the distant Entendeka Mountains, and the pink and russet sandstone cliffs of Twyfelfontein to the south (where you can visit some of the most famous San rock paintings and engravings in the world), this is classic Damaraland. **Pros:** the king-size beds can be rolled out onto your private porch to sleep under the stars; great community-based responsible tourism model; the staff seem genuinely thrilled to meet you, which carries through to their service. **Cons:** no a/c, only ceiling and pedestal fans in tents; Wi-Fi only in the main camp area; half-board clients must pay for guided trips to see the elephants. [$] *Rooms from: US$718* ✉ *Damaraland* ☎ *11/257–5000 in South Africa* 🌐 *www.wilderness-safaris.com* 🛏 *32 chalets* 🍴 *All-Inclusive.*

★ Mowani Mountain Camp

$$ | **ALL-INCLUSIVE** | The picturesque Mowani Mountain Camp lies atop a scattered pile of giant ochre-colored boulders in sight of the impressive Brandberg Mountain. **Pros:** stunning sundowner rock, complete with an alfresco bar and rustic seating; conveniently located near all of Damaraland's major attractions; unsurpassable service always comes with a genuine smile. **Cons:** not all rooms have a/c and the large fans can be noisy; activities are extra if you're not on fully inclusive plan; Wi-Fi is limited due to remote location. [$] *Rooms from: US$318* ✉ *Damaraland* ☎ *61/232–009* 🌐 *www.mowani.com* 🛏 *15 rooms* 🍴 *All-Inclusive.*

Vingerklip Lodge

$ | **HOTEL** | **FAMILY** | In a dramatic locale in Damaraland's Valley of the Ugab Terraces, this lodge is set against the backdrop of a mighty stone finger pointing toward the sky. **Pros:** desert elephants often visit the lodge's dam in November and December;

Vingerklip Lodge has a dramatic location in Damaraland's Valley of the Ugab Terraces.

underwent renovations during the pandemic; fully off-grid and solar-powered since renovations. **Cons:** limited seating at Eagles Nest restaurant atop the plateau, booking is essential; Damaraland's key attractions are an hour away; rooms are not large, but there are 11 family rooms with lofts for kids. $ *Rooms from: US$240* ✉ *Damaraland* ☎ *61/255–344 reservations, 67/290–319 lodge* 🌐 *www.vingerklip.com.na* 🛏 *23 bungalows* 🍴 *All-Inclusive.*

Etosha National Park

This photogenic, startlingly beautiful park takes its name—meaning Great White Place—from a vast flat depression that was a deep inland lake 12 million years ago. The white clay pan, also known as the Place of Mirages, covers nearly 25% of the park's surface.

Although it's usually dry, in a good rainy season (like in early 2022) it floods and becomes home to many waterbirds, including tens of thousands of flamingos that feed on the blue-green algae of the pan. Although the park is never crowded with visitors like some of the East African game parks, the scenery here is no less spectacular: huge herds that dot the plains and gather at the many and varied waterholes. The dust devils, mirages, and terrain that changes from densely wooded thickets to wide-open spaces, and from white salt-encrusted pans to blond grasslands, will keep you captivated for hours.

The game's all here—the Big Five—large and small, fierce and gentle, beautiful and ugly. But one of Etosha's main attractions isn't the numbers of animals that you can see (more than 114 species), but how easily you can see them. The game depend on the natural springs that are found all along the edges of the pan, and as the animals have grown used to drinking at these waterholes for decades, they're not put off by vehicles or game-seeking visitors. On the road from the Von Lindequist Gate, the eastern entrance to Etosha, look out for the smallest of all African antelope, the Damara dik-dik. If you see a diminutive "Bambi" sheltering under a roadside bush, that's it. The Namutoni area and the two Okevi waterholes—Klein Namutoni and Kalkheuwel—probably provide the best chances to see leopards. Don't miss the blackface impala, native to Etosha, and one of the rarest of antelope and an endangered species. Bigger and more boldly marked than its smaller cousin, the impala, you'll find it drinking in small herds at waterholes all over the park.

The real secret of game-watching in the park is to settle in at one of the many waterholes, most of which are on the southern edges of the pan, and wait. And wait. Each waterhole has its own unique personality and characteristics. Even if the hole is small and deep, like Ombika, on the western side, you'll be amazed at what may arrive. You should be up at dawn for the best sightings, though you can see marvelous game at all times of the day. The plains, where you'll likely spot cheetahs, are also home to huge herds of zebras and wildebeests, and you may see the silhouettes of giraffes as they cross the skyline in stately procession. Watch out for herds of springbok "pronking"—an activity wherein these lovely little antelope bounce and bound high into the air as they run. Zoologists argue over the reason for this behavior. Some say it's to avoid predators, others that it's to demonstrate agility, strength, and stamina; most visitors like to believe that pronking is just for fun. Salvadora, a constant spring on the fringe of Etosha Pan near Halali, is a favorite watering point for some of these big herds. Also watch out for the stately eland, Africa's largest antelope. As big as a cow, although more streamlined and elegant, this antelope can jump higher than any other African antelope—amazing when you consider its huge size. And where there's water, there's always game.

Predators, especially lions, lurk around most of the waterholes looking for a meal.

Plan to spend at least half a night sitting on a bench at the floodlit Okaukuejo waterhole where you really are within spitting distance of the game. Bring a book, write in your journal, or just sit while you wait. You may be amazed at the variety of animals that come down to drink: black and white rhinos, lions, jackals, and even the occasional leopard. This is a particularly good place to look out for black rhinos, which trot purposefully up to drink and in so doing scare all but the bravest of game away. Groot Okevi waterhole, close to Namutoni, is also good for black rhinos.

Don't overlook the more than 340 dazzling varieties of bird—the crimson-breasted shrike is particularly gorgeous—and watch for ostriches running over the plains or raptors hunting silently overhead. There are many endemics, including the black-faced and bare-cheeked babblers, violet wood-hoopoe (look for them in Halali camp), Rüppell's parrot, Bradfield's swift, and the white-tailed shrike.

Be aware of the trees, shrubs, and plants as well. Just east of Okaukuejo is the legendary Haunted or Ghost Forest, where moringa trees have morphed into twisted, strange, and grotesque shapes: you may feel as if you're in Snow White's forest or deep in Middle Earth.

WHEN TO GO

The best time to visit is from April to September, when the temperatures are cooler, and the increasingly thirsty animals gather at waterholes, making it easier to see them (the driest time of year when this will be the case is August to September). May to August is the coolest time of year, and nights can be downright freezing—be sure to bring adequate warm clothes for night drives. Bird-watchers will want to visit in the

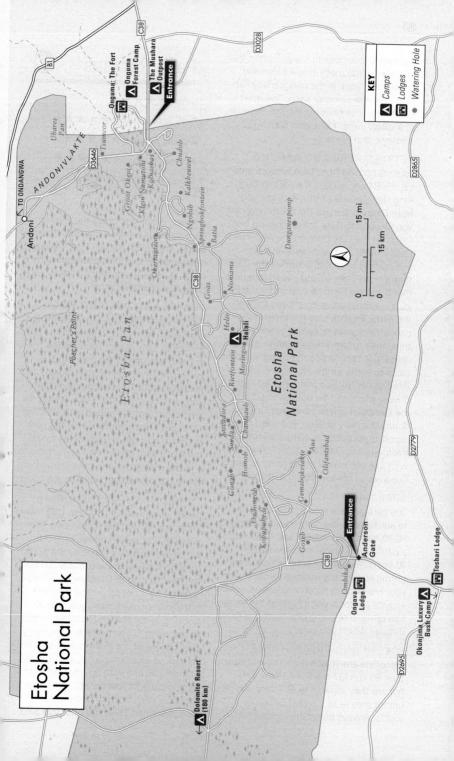

summer (November to March) when the migratory birds (both intra-African and Palaearctic) flock in the park's many habitats after the summer rains. The main Etosha Pan can become a huge expanse of shallow water filled with flamingos, wildfowl, and waders.

GETTING HERE AND AROUND

Tourists coming from the Oshakati area via the B1 can access the park through King Nehale Gate (northeast); coming from Tsumeb also via the B1 through the Von Lindequist Gate (east); coming from Outjo via the C38 through the Anderson Gate (south) from sunrise to sunset; and coming from Kamanjab via the C35 through the Galton Gate (west) (but note that if you are heading east to Okaukuejo, it is almost a five-hour drive through the park). Tourists may not drive in the park after sunset or before sunrise, and thus need to allow time to arrive at their respective rest camps if moving around close to these times. Namibia Wildlife Resorts (NWR) also offers guided night drives, which can be booked directly at the camps. If you're staying at Onkoshi during the rainy season, you need to report to reception at Namutoni to be transferred to Onkoshi, as only guests with 4x4 vehicles are able to travel along this section of road during that time.

ADMISSION

The park gates are open from sunrise to sunset, and the daily entrance fee is N$80 for foreign visitors and N$10 for a passenger vehicle with fewer than 10 seats. You pay for your vehicle entry permit and for any balance remaining on your pre-booked accommodations (which include personal entry fees) at the reception of the rest camp closest to the gate through which you enter.

SAFETY AND PRECAUTIONS

Motorists aren't allowed to travel faster than 60 kph (37 mph) inside the park, nor are they allowed to exit their vehicles unless they're at the rest camps or toilets. Always be on the lookout for animals, which can cross the road at random, and often are concealed by bushes before emerging. Refrain from making noise and getting too close to any animals, especially elephants, as they could panic and charge your car.

TIMING AND TOURING TIPS

Two to three days will allow you to visit the eastern and central parts of the park, as well as Okaukuejo. Taking in the "newer" western part of the park properly will require at least two days due to its relative isolation from the rest of the park—it's only 180 km (112 miles) to the next camp, but the speed limit is 60 kph (37 mph). Throughout most of the park there are numerous waterholes to visit, but that's best done in the early morning and late afternoon when the animals are more active and temperatures are cooler.

The park is huge—22,270 square km (8,598 square miles), 300 km (186 miles) wide, and 110 km (68 miles) long. The western part, which makes up a third of the overall park, is open to the public through the Galton Gate, but if you plan to drive through to Okaukuejo you need to arrive by 1 pm otherwise they will not allow access (unless you have a booking at the NWR's Dolomite Camp in the west). If you prefer to visit the park on one of the many safaris offered by various tour companies, make sure you choose one with an open vehicle or pop-top with few passengers—you probably don't want to find yourself in an air-conditioned 75-seater bus. That said,

Park Ratings

Game: ★ ★ ★ ★ ★

Park Accessibility: ★ ★ ★ ★ ★

Getting Around: ★ ★ ★ ★ ★

Accommodations: ★ ★ ★ ★ ★

Scenic Beauty: ★ ★ ★ ★ ★

Namibia's Herero women are known for their colorful gowns and wide-brimmed hats.

the best way to see the park is to drive yourself so you can stop at your leisure. A two-wheel-drive car is fine, as the roads are good, but the higher up you sit, the better your view, so opt for the more expensive *combis* (vans) or 4x4s if possible. In addition to patience, you'll need drinks, snacks, field guides to the animals and birds, binoculars, and your camera. There are more than 40 water-holes, with Rietfontein, Okaukuejo, Goas, Halali, Klein Namutoni, and Chudob regarded as the best for game-watching and taking pictures, but nothing is certain in the bush. Keep your eyes and ears open, and you may come across game at any time, in any place. Arm yourself with the MET map of Etosha (available in the camps), which shows the names and locations of the waterholes and indicates which roads are open.

Hotels

If you wish to stay inside Etosha itself you can lodge at one of the NWR rest camps (book months in advance, especially for the peak periods of July to September and around Christmas and Easter, though you may want to avoid the crowds at these times). The rest camps of Halali, Onkoshi, Dolomite, Namutoni, and Okaukuejo have pools, grocery-cu-rio-liquor stores, gas stations, and restaurants serving breakfast, lunch, and dinner. There are also numerous full-ser-vice private lodges and guest farms near the park.

Dolomite Resort
$$ | HOTEL | Set among the Dolomite hills in the previously off-limits western section of the park, this camp is for those looking for something unique and far from the madding crowd with its sports bar, sunset deck, and infinity pool perfect for scoping out the scorched plains and

hills while cooling off. Tented deluxe chalets with mesmerizing views are elegantly appointed and some have plunge pools. Having been untouched by tourists for almost 50 years, this section of the park has allowed animals like black rhino and black-faced impala to breed successfully. You may also be lucky enough to see roan antelope, Moneiro's hornbill, and Hartmann's zebra—species specific to the area. **Pros:** no crowds; more personal service than other Namibia Wildlife Resorts camp; a newer, better-designed camp than the other NWR offerings. **Cons:** far from the rest of the park and the Etosha Pan; not all units have plunge pools; long uneven pathways from chalets to lodge. [$] *Rooms from: US$295* ✉ *Etosha National Park* ☎ *61/285–7200* 🌐 *www.nwr.com.na* 🛏 *20 chalets* 🍴 *Free Breakfast.*

★ The Mushara Outpost

$$$$ | HOTEL | If you're a fan of old-fashioned luxury, warm service, and accommodations that combine the authenticity of the bush with a stylish and comfortable interior, then this is an excellent option. **Pros:** rooms are bright and comfortable; indoor and outdoor showers; excellent service. **Cons:** no longer offer guided bush walks; no children under 12; laundry services are an additional charge. [$] *Rooms from: US$736* ✉ *Etosha National Park* ☎ *81/148–4357 mobile, 67/229–106 lodge* 🌐 *www.musharalodge.com* 🛏 *8 tents* 🍴 *All-Inclusive.*

Okonjima Luxury Bush Camp

$$$$ | ALL-INCLUSIVE | This family-run, private lodge, with numerous accommodation options to suit various budgets, is located in the Okonjima Nature Reserve about halfway between Windhoek and Etosha making it an excellent stopover point on your way to the park. **Pros:** numerous activities including rhino, pangolin and leopard tracking, guided walking trails and bird watching; in a malaria-free area; kitchen facilities are available. **Cons:** no longer a release site for rehabilitated cheetahs; too far from Etosha to make it a base for exploration; can seem rather busy during peak season. [$] *Rooms from: US$1,300* ✉ *Otjiwarongo* ☎ *67/314–000 reservations* 🌐 *www.okonjima.com* 🛏 *9 rooms* 🍴 *All-Inclusive.*

Ongava Lodge

$$$$ | ALL-INCLUSIVE | Located in the Onguma Game Reserve on the southern boundary of Etosha close to the Anderson Gate, each thatched unit at this lodge features its own plunge pool, sala (a covered open-air pavilion), outdoor shower and bath with magnificent views, and wooden decks that cling to the side of a steep, rocky outcrop. **Pros:** large luxurious rooms; great wildlife viewing from the lodge waterhole; guided walks include white rhino tracking. **Cons:** private vehicles can be booked at an extra cost; there are many stairs to the lodge; pool on the small side. [$] *Rooms from: US$1,312* ✉ *Etosha National Park* ☎ *83/330–3920 reservations* 🌐 *www.ongava.com* 🛏 *14 rooms* 🍴 *All-Inclusive.*

Onguma Forest Camp

$ | HOTEL | This small, ultra-friendly thatched camp is set in a beautiful natural forest within a nature reserve 10 km (6 miles) east of the Von Lindequist Gate—about a 30-minute drive from the park. **Pros:** the recently enlarged waterhole attracts more animals and birds; the lodge can arrange guided trips into Etosha; has an extensive wine cellar. **Cons:** no children under 7, but has 3 family rooms; camp is unfenced; rooms on the small side, despite a recent refurb to the main lodge. [$] *Rooms from: US$248* ✉ *Etosha National Park* ☎ *61/237–055 bookings, 67/229–100 lodge* 🌐 *www.onguma.com* 🛏 *11 bungalows* 🍴 *Free Breakfast.*

★ Onguma: The Fort

$$$$ | ALL-INCLUSIVE | This flagship lodge in the Onguma Game Reserve on the eastern border of Etosha National Park's Fischer Pan is the epitome of luxury and style blending unique Moroccan-style fort architecture with subtle hints of color and raw African textures. **Pros:** recent refurbishments to the property; stunning swimming pool and sundowner area; extensive wine cellar and first-class food. **Cons:** the rhino levy is a small additional cost (per person per night) that subsidizes the anti-poaching unit; can be rather costly, but they offer more affordable options at the Bush Camp, Tented Camp and Treetop Camp; no children under 7 years. $ *Rooms from: US$1,354* ✉ *Etosha National Park* ☎ *61/237–055 reservations, 67/229–135 lodge* ⊕ *www.onguma.com* ⤴ *13 suites* ⦿ *All-Inclusive.*

Toshari Lodge

$ | **HOTEL** | **FAMILY** | This pleasant and affordable lodge about 25 km (15½ miles) south of Etosha's Anderson Gate makes a great base for exploring the park. **Pros:** convenient location; clean, comfortable rooms with a/c; great service. **Cons:** difficult to contact directly; due to proximity to the main road, some traffic noise can be heard in the campsites (though not the rooms); not a luxury lodge. $ *Rooms from: US$138* ✉ *Etosha National Park* ☎ *64/405–045 reservations, 67/333–440 lodge* ⊕ *www.toshari.com* ⤴ *38 rooms* ⦿ *Free Breakfast.*

If You Have Time

Although the must-see parks in Namibia are described in great detail above, there are still other places worth exploring if you have time.

The Skeleton Coast

This wildly beautiful shore, which makes up a third of Namibia's coastline, stretches from the Ugab River in the south to the Kunene River, at the border with Angola, in the north. The Portuguese seafarers who explored this area in the 15th century called this coast, with its cold Benguela current and deadly crosscurrents, the "Coast of Death." Its newer, no-less-sinister name, the Skeleton Coast, testifies to innumerable shipwrecks, lives lost, whale bones, and the insignificant, transient nature of humans in the face of the raw power of nature. Still comparatively unknown to tourists, this region has a stark beauty and an awesomely diverse landscape—gray gravel plains, rugged wilderness, rusting shipwrecks, desert wastes, meandering barchan dunes, distant mountains, towering walls of sand and granite, and crashing seas. You'll rarely see more than a handful of visitors in this inaccessible and rugged coastal area. This isn't an easy ride, as distances are vast, amenities scarce or non-existent, and the roads demanding. Don't exceed 80 kph (50 mph) on the gravel roads, and never drive off the road onto the ecologically vulnerable salt pans and lichen fields: the scars left by vehicles can last for hundreds of years and do irreparable damage.

Skeleton Coast National Park extends along this rugged Atlantic coast and about 40 km (25 miles) inland. The 200-km (125-mile) stretch of coast from Swakopmund to the Ugab River is the National West Coast Tourist Recreational Area. You can drive along a coastal road from Swakopmund up to Terrace Bay, and for the first 250 km (155 miles) of this journey you'll find not sand dunes but glinting gravel plains and scattered rocks. Stop and sift a handful of gravel: you may well find garnets and crystals among the tiny stones. In other places the plains are carpeted with lichens— yellow, red, orange, and many shades of green. In the early morning these lichen fields look lushly attractive, but during the heat of midday they seem dried up and insignificant. But don't whiz by. Stop and pour a drop of water on the lichens and watch a small miracle as they unfurl and seemingly come alive. If you're a birder, the salt pans on the way from Swakopmund to Henties Bay are worth a visit; you might spot a rare migrant wader

Seeing the dramatic meeting of the Namib Desert and the Atlantic Ocean along the Skeleton Coast is breathtaking.

there. The famous Namibian oysters are farmed here in sea ponds—don't leave Namibia without tasting these. The surreal little seaside holiday town of Henties Bay seems almost entirely deserted in winter, but is full of holidaying Namibian fisherfolk from Swakopmund, Windhoek, and Tsumeb in the summer.

You'll surely smell the hundreds of thousands of Cape fur seals (*Arctocephalus pusillus pusillus*) at the Cape Cross seal colony, north of Henties Bay, long before you get there, but stifle your gags and go goggle at the seething mass on land and in the water. If you visit in late November or early December, you can "ooh" and "aah" at the furry baby seal pups, as well as the marauding jackals looking for a fast-food snack. Farther north the dunes begin, ending in the north at the Kunene River. This northern stretch of coast from the Ugab River to the Kunene River is managed by the government as a wilderness area. But if it's lush green vegetation and an abundance of game you want, then this raw, and

uncompromising landscape isn't for you. You'll find dramatically different sceneries—big skies and unending horizons—an absence of tourists ("crowds" around here means one or two vehicles), and some wildlife: brown hyenas, springbok, oryx, jackals, and, if you're really lucky, a cheetah or rhino. The sight of a majestic oryx silhouetted against towering sand dunes or a scavenging jackal is extremely rewarding. The best activity, however, is simply concentrating on the strange solitude of the area.

WHEN TO GO

The northern Skeleton Coast experiences the same weather year-round: moderate temperatures with mist, wind, and hardly any rain. For anglers, the best time to visit is November to March. For the inland Kaokoveld, the dry winter season from May to August is best. The rainy summer months of January to March can bring extremely high temperatures and flash floods.

From Portugal to the Skeleton Coast

More than 500 years ago, a daring little band of Portuguese sailors, inspired by the vision of their charismatic leader, Prince Henry the Navigator—who, contrary to what you might expect from his name, never left his native land—set sail from the School of Navigation at Sagres, the farthest western point of Europe, to find fame, fortune, and new lands for the Crown. Facing unknown dangers and terra incognita—the maps of the time were little more than fanciful sketchbooks filled with dragons and warnings that "here be monsters"—the intrepid sailors pushed back the edges of the known world nautical mile by nautical mile until they entered the waters of the southwest coastline of Africa on tiny, frail caravels. In 1485, Captain Diego Cão and his battered crew finally dropped anchor off a desolate beach thousands of miles from home and safety. There, on the lonely windswept sands, they erected a cross both in honor of their heavenly king, whom they credited with protecting and directing them during their arduous journey, as well as to King John I, their earthly monarch. North of Swakopmund, as you marvel at thousands upon thousands of the Cape fur seals at Cape Cross, you can see a replica of that cross (the original is in the Berlin Oceanographic Museum). Sadly, the courageous Captain Cão never made it home: he's buried nearby on a rocky outcrop.

GETTING HERE AND AROUND

You can drive (a 4x4 gives you more flexibility) from Swakopmund north through Henties Bay via the Ugab Gate, with its eerie painted skulls and crossbones on the gates, or from the more northerly Springbokwater Gate. You must reach your gate of entry before 3 pm. Always stick to the marked roads and avoid driving on the salt pans. Look out for an abandoned 1960s oil rig lying next to the road between the Ugab River and Terrace Bay.

The Uniab River valley, between Torra Bay and Terrace Bay, is your best chance of spotting big game such as rhinos and occasionally elephants. Terrace Bay, 287 km (178 miles) north of Henties Bay, is the last outpost. If you want to explore further, like onwards to Wilderness Safaris' Hoanib Skeleton Coast Camp or Serra Cafema, then a fly-in safari is your only option.

Many parts of the Skeleton Coast can be visited only with a dedicated operator, and the lengths of tours vary. If you only intend to spend time in Torra Bay or Terrace Bay, two to three days will suffice. Bear in mind that this coastline doesn't conform to the usual "beach holiday" image: Namibia's beaches are wild and desolate, offering a welcome respite from the hot inland areas during summer months and a wonderful destination for fishermen.

The C34 road runs parallel to the coast, and then a rough track continues up past Torra Bay to the ranger station (Ministry of Environment and Tourism). Driving the C34 is straightforward, although fog can make the surface slick and the road is mostly gravel, so keep speeds below 80 kph (50 mph). You can purchase your entry permit either at the Ugab or Springbokwasser gates. There are several short detours to points of interest, but off-road driving is strictly prohibited.

Hotels

Hoanib Skeleton Coast Camp

$$$$ | ALL-INCLUSIVE | This luxurious and completely solar-powered, low-impact camp is located in the remote, broad valley of the Hoanib River; with one foot in the dramatic Namibian Kaokoveld and the other in the Skeleton Coast National Park, the unique and exquisitely appointed tented rooms look out over scenery that's hard to find adjectives to describe. **Pros:** absolute luxury in a totally remote setting; game drives and guides that are some of the best in the country; guests can learn about the research conducted at the research center from on-site researchers. **Cons:** no a/c, only ceiling and pedestal fans, but tents are designed to allow for natural air flow; the camp is not fenced so you have to be escorted to your tent at night; only accessible by fly-in. $ *Rooms from: US$1,904* ✉ *Hoanib Skeleton Coast Camp* ☎ *2111/257–5000 in South Africa* ⊕ *www.wilderness-safaris.com* ⇌ *8 tents* ⬦ *All-Inclusive.*

★ Serra Cafema

$$$$ | ALL-INCLUSIVE | This astonishingly different and dramatically sited camp in the extreme northwest of Namibia on the Angolan border is the most remote camp in southern Africa and you are guaranteed to gasp with awe when you first catch sight of the camp from a high sand dune. **Pros:** surreal remote wilderness area (malaria-free zone); a wealth of activities beyond game drives (in-tent massage treatments can be booked at an additional cost); outstanding service. **Cons:** you may find yourself torn between activities and relaxing in your lovely tent; not a lot of wildlife, except Nile crocodiles and birdlife; arduous travel to get here. $ *Rooms from: US$1,589* ☎ *21/257–5000 in South Africa* ⊕ *www.wilderness-safaris.com* ⇌ *8 tents* ⬦ *All-Inclusive.*

Zambezi Region (Caprivi Strip)

This lovely unspoiled area—one of Namibia's best-kept secrets—lies in northeast Namibia (and is sometimes simply referred to as "northeast Namibia") even though it was renamed the Zambezi Region in 2013. It's situated at the confluence of the Zambezi and Chobe rivers, and serves as a gateway to Zimbabwe's Victoria Falls and Botswana's Chobe National Park. Because it has been relatively less visited in comparison to other parts of the country—it's at least 1,000 km (621 miles) from Windhoek depending on where in the region you visit—you'll get the feeling that you're mostly alone with nature.

Think of the Zambezi Region as a long finger of land at the top of the country pointing eastward for 450 km (280 miles) toward Zimbabwe and Zambia; in many ways, because of its rivers, wetlands, marshes, and forests, the area is much more like those countries than the rest of Namibia. This part of Namibia is the closest thing to Botswana's Okavango Delta, and it shelters much of the same game: elephants, giraffes, the aquatic lechwe and the rare sitatunga antelope, the uncommon roan and sable antelope, and, hardly ever seen in Namibia, big buffalo herds, but you'll rarely see predators.

This corridor of land became strategically important when Germany annexed South West Africa (now Namibia) in 1884. The British, concerned about further German colonial expansion up into Africa, struck a deal with Khama, a local Bechuana king, and formed the British Protectorate of Bechuanaland (now Botswana); the Caprivi Strip was part of the deal. It was then shuttled back and forth between Britain and Germany until it finally passed into the hands of South Africa at the end of World War II. However, its troubles were far from over, and during the

Namibian struggle for independence, the area became the scene of bitter fighting between Sam Nujoma's freedom fighters (Sam Nujoma became the first president of Namibia in 1990) and the South African Defence Force (SADF). Today, the game that was scared away has returned, and the area is once again peaceful. If you've seen your Big Five, had your classic desert experience, and are looking for somewhere lusciously verdant and offbeat, this is the destination.

You've got to be fairly determined to get here because the journey can be long if you drive, which is why it's a good idea to combine it with a trip to Etosha. You can fly in to Katima Mulilo on FlyNamiba's weekly return flights. The vibey little main town is closer to Gaborone, Botswana, or Lusaka, Zambia, than it is to Windhoek. From here, you can rent a vehicle or get an air-conditioned airport transfer across the entire region. However you get here, the destination is well worth every last mile for a remote, water-wilderness experience. Your best bet is to choose a lodge and then let it make all your travel arrangements for you.

Neither of the region's Mudumu National Park or Mahango National Park is easily accessible—particularly in the wet season—but if you're a do-it-yourself adventure type, you might enjoy a visit to either park. You'll see plenty of game, including hippos, elephants, buffalo, roan and sable antelope, kudu, zebras, and maybe even wild dogs. Mahango is great for bird-watching, with more species than any other Namibian park.

GETTING HERE AND AROUND
The Wenela/Sesheke border between Katima Mulilo (Namibia) and Sesheke (Zambia) is open from 6 am to 6 pm.

The Ngoma Border between Katima Mulilo (Namibia) and Kasane (Botswana) is open between 7 am to 6 pm.

There is a border at Kasane Immigration to enter the Namibian side of the Chobe

River, which is open from 7:30 am to 4:30 pm, or back via Impalila Immigration, which is open from 7am to 5 pm.

The Kazungula border between Botswana and Zambia, via the Kazungula Bridge, is open between 6 am and 6 pm.

The Kazungula Border between Botswana and Zimbabwe, via Kazungula Border Post (Zimbabwe), is open between 6 am and 8 pm.

Air: FlyNamibia operates a weekly return flight from Windhoek to Katima Mulilo.

Car: The B8 tarred road (or Trans-Caprivi Highway) connects the borders of Sesheke/Wenela to Zambia; Ngoma Bridge in Botswana to Katima Mulilo; and the Kwando area of Kongola as well as the Kavango area of Divundu, onwards to Rundu. The B8 also connects to Windhoek, Swakopmund, Walvis Bay and Etosha National Park.

Just outside of Katima Mulilo there is a newly tarred road (C49) that takes you to the three National Parks of the Zambezi Region, namely Nkasa Rupara National Park, Mudumu National Park and Bwabwata National Park. This makes it easy to take a day- or multi-day trip to and within these parks.

■ TIP→ **A 4x4 vehicle is required for some of the parks. One can travel on the main roads by sedan car.**

TIMING
To explore the Zambezi Region from east to west and to enjoy its peace and quiet, at least a week should be set aside.

TOURS AND TRANSFERS
Caprivi Adventures
ADVENTURE TOURS | No matter where you need to go within the Zambezi Region, Caprivi Adventures can get you there with their fleet of big and small transfer vehicles and friendly drivers, who become your guide to this north-eastern section of Namibia. The transfer company comes highly recommended by

the travel industry in the area because it also does intra-African transfers between the Zambezi Region and Victoria Falls (Zimbabwe and Zambia side); Botswana; and Angola. It also rents cars for use in and around the region.

Caprivi Adventures also specializes in tailor-making itineraries depending on personal interests, available time and budget. They also offer day trips, such as tiger fishing, birdwatching, water safaris, and more. ✉ *539 Trans Caprivi Hwy.* ☎ *81/206–1514* 🌐 *www.capriviadventures.com.*

WHEN TO GO

For bird-watchers the best time to visit is summer (December–February), but be forewarned that the heat and humidity can be unbearable. Toward the end of summer, the Zambezi, Chobe, and Linyanti rivers usually flood, making access to Lake Liambezi and Nkasa Rupara National Park (formerly Mamili) difficult. Access will be by 4x4, and will require negotiating completely submerged roads. Otherwise, the Caprivi can be visited for most of the year, but inquire at the lodge you're interested in how negotiable their roads are during the rainy season (November–April/May). The winter months of April to October are great for game-viewing, and far more pleasant what with the cooler temperatures and lack of rainfall.

Coffee and Quick Bites

Green Basket Cafe

$ | CAFÉ | If you're looking for something traditionally Namibian/South African to eat, try the vetkoek with savory mince or the mielie pap and stew, as well as the peppermint crisp tart at this café on the main road through Katima Mulilo. Wash it down with a smoothie, shake, or gourmet coffee, as you watch indigenous birds frolicking in the luscious garden. **Known for:** doubles up as an unofficial tourism information center; sells handmade souvenirs made by locals; you can rent a car or book a transfer, tour, or accommodation here. [$] *Average main: N$5* ✉ *539 Mpacha Rd., Katima Mulilo* ☎ *66/252–739* 🌐 *www.capriviadventures.com* 🕓 *No dinner.*

Hotels

Lianshulu Lodge

$$$$ | ALL-INCLUSIVE | You might be lucky enough to encounter wildlife in and around this unfenced, thatched lodge that's located under huge jackalberry and mangosteen trees in a private concession within Mudumu National Park. **Pros:** exclusive use of the river (the nearest lodge is over 20 km (12 miles) away); by far some of the best food you'll find in the region, with some hints of German influence; spectacular riverside location, superb for bird and game watching. **Cons:** expensive, paid-for Wi-Fi (mobile reception is patchy); unable to charge electronics in rooms; generator noise may be audible from some rooms. [$] *Rooms from: US$857* ✉ *Mudumu National Park* ☎ *66/686–073 landline, 81/377–7621 mobile (reservations)* 🌐 *www.caprivicollection.com* 🛏 *10 chalets, 1 family unit* 🍴 *All-Inclusive.*

Nambwa Tented Camp

$$$ | HOTEL | Situated in a tall shady forest, this lodge stands on its tiptoes high up off the ground overlooking the lush floodplain below. **Pros:** the treetop setting is especially unusual and exciting; location allows for close encounters with game such as elephants; warm personal service. **Cons:** tents can get very hot in the summer months; Wi-Fi only available in the main area; access road only passable by 4x4, transfers to/from park gates are not included. [$] *Rooms from: US$544* ☎ *61/400–510* 🌐 *www.africanmonarchlodges.com* 🛏 *10 tents* 🍴 *All-Inclusive.*

Nkasa Lupala Tented Lodge

$$ | ALL-INCLUSIVE | FAMILY | On the edge of Nkasa Rupara National Park, this intimate, unfenced tented camp—which is part of the award-winning, joint-venture Wuparo conservancy program—offers the best of both worlds, namely river cruises and game drives through wetlands, woodlands, and grass plains. **Pros:** peaceful and remote with a very relaxed atmosphere; free, reliable Wi-Fi (in the main lodge only); sustainability plays a key role in their operations. **Cons:** tents are simple and rustic rather than luxury; the staff come across as unenthusiastic at times; big game is somewhat elusive (come in the dry season for elephants). $ *Rooms from: US$338* ☎ *66/686–101 landline* ⊕ *www.nkasalupalalodge.com* ⮑ *10 tents* ⦿l *All-Inclusive* ☞ *can also be booked on a DBB basis.*

Serondela Lodge

$$$ | ALL-INCLUSIVE | The best time of year to visit Serondela Lodge, on the flood plains of the Chobe River, is just after the rainy season (October – March), when the Zambezi Region erupts in bursts of green and swells with an abundance of wildlife. **Pros:** community partnership is key: it's part of the WWF and IRDNC joint-venture program; communal dinners offer a chance to mingle with other guests; plunge pool offers reprieve in the summer months. **Cons:** rooms only have a dividing wall to the bathroom; despite being simple, the menu prioritizes sustainability and seasonality; the lodge is only accessible by boat after the rains (but this is part of the fun of getting there). $ *Rooms from: US$579* ☎ *61/224–712 landline* ⊕ *www.serondelalodge.com* ⮑ *8 rooms* ⦿l *All-Inclusive.*

Waterberg Plateau Park

This lovely game reserve, established in 1972 when several rare and endangered species were introduced from other areas of Namibia and South Africa, is one of the most peaceful and relatively unknown wilderness areas in Namibia. About 91 km (56 miles) east of Otjiwarongo, it's also an ideal stopover on the way from Windhoek to Etosha. The plateau is a huge, flat-top massif rising abruptly from the surrounding plain and offering superb views of the park, the outstanding rock formations, and the magnitude of the plateau itself. Edged with steep-sided, rugged, reddish-brown cliffs, the plateau is covered with red Kalahari sand that supports a range of dry woodland vegetation, from the red syringa trees and Kalahari apple leaf to the kudu bush. You're not allowed to drive yourself, but game-viewing tours operate every morning and evening from the beautifully landscaped Waterberg Camp (book in advance through the NWR; you can join a tour even if you're not a guest of the camp). Although you won't see the big numbers of game that you'll find in Etosha, you could spot the rare roan and sable antelope, Cape buffalo, white and black rhinos, giraffes, hyenas, leopards, and cheetahs. But game-spotting isn't an exact science, so there are no guarantees; however, it is often frequented by birders. The park is a wonderful place to hike, whether on the much-sought-after, three-day, accompanied Waterberg Wilderness Trail (book through the NWR at the Waterberg Camp [formerly the Bernabé de la Bat Rest Camp] in advance) or on a short 3-km (2-mile) walk around camp.

WHEN TO GO

The park can be visited throughout the year. During the rainy season (December–April) the last stretch of road (which is gravel) must be negotiated very carefully as the surface can be slippery when wet.

GETTING HERE AND AROUND

The park is located about 300 km (186 miles) northeast of Windhoek. Visitors can't drive up onto the plateau in their

The Waterberg Plateau Park is one of Namibia's most peaceful and relatively unknown wilderness areas.

own vehicles but can explore by foot on self-guided wilderness trails. Daily guided game drives (about four hours) include visits to fantastic hides on the plateau that offer excellent views of waterhole life. Daily game drives can be booked at the Waterberg Camp.

SAFETY AND PRECAUTIONS

Don't feed the animals, and keep your belongings safely away from inquisitive baboons. Lock your bungalow when leaving, as baboons may try to enter an unlocked room. Bring warm clothing for winter weather: game drives in the early morning or late afternoon can be very chilly—even in summer, and especially when it's rained.

TIMING

There are hikes of differing lengths, so inquire how much time you'll need for your chosen route from NWR. If not hiking, then a minimum stay of two nights is recommended so you'll have one whole day to climb the mountain, go on a game drive, relax at the pool, and explore the walking trails around the camp.

Hotels

Waterberg Plateau Lodge

$ | **HOTEL** | Located on the magnificent rock terrace of the geological phenomenon known as the Waterberg Plateau, the chalets of this lodge are hidden from one another by bush and red sandstone boulders. **Pros:** nature conservation efforts are funded by their hospitality arm; genuine warm and friendly staff; opportunity to see rhinos on the game drive is almost guaranteed. **Cons:** free Wi-Fi only in the restaurant; sometimes the baboons can be a little pesky trying to enter the rooms; not as luxurious as other lodges but they make up for it with the views. [$] *Rooms from: US$215* ✉ *Waterberg Plateau Park* ☎ *61/217-110 reservations, 67/687–018 reception* 🌐 *www.waterberg-wilderness.com* 🛏 *8 chalets* 🍴 *All-Inclusive* ☞ *can also be booked on a DBB basis.*

Gateway City

If you're going on safari in Namibia, it's very likely that you'll have to take a connecting flight through Windhoek en route to your safari destination, so you'll likely spend at least one overnight here.

Windhoek

The pleasant if provincial little capital city of Windhoek lies almost exactly in the center of the country and is surrounded by the Khomas Highland and the Auas and Eros mountains. With its colonial architecture, sidewalk cafés, shopping centers, and shady parks, it's by no means a hardship to spend a day or two here.

Settled by the Germans in the 1890s, it's an easy town to explore on foot (though summers are blisteringly hot). Main sights, which are clustered around the downtown area, include the National Gallery (where you can often purchase works in the temporary exhibits), the remarkably good craft center, and some old German architecture. The city has a population of about 460,000 and growing. If you have a few free hours, a visit to Katutura makes an interesting half-day expedition that gives visitors an idea of how the majority of urban Namibians live. Windhoek is also home to the country's brewing industry—a holdover from its days as a German colony—and a guided visit to the brewery is possible.

GETTING HERE AND AROUND

Namibia's main point of entry is Hosea Kutako International Airport. It's a small, bustling, modern airport that's a scenic 45-km (28-mile) drive from Windhoek. The smaller Eros Airport handles commercial flights and private charters to destinations around the country.

Licensed shuttle companies (look for a sticker that shows they're registered with the NTB) offer service from

Eat This

Biltong: Namibia's upgraded version of jerky

Braai: traditional barbecue with meats and fixins'

Namibian oysters: freshly shucked from Walvis Bay

Mahangu: pearl millet, prepared in a variety of ways

Kalahari truffles: truffles from the desert

Ostrich stir-fry: steak-like ostrich meat stir-fried with vegetables

Hosea Kutako International Airport to Windhoek's city center; the pickup and drop-off point is at the taxi stand on Independence Avenue, next to the Tourist Information Center. Expect to pay N$300 each way. Many larger hotels run a courtesy shuttle service to and from the airport. "Radio taxis" (taxis with radio contact to the dispatch) are available, but negotiate the price before you get in and write it down on a piece of paper to show them as a confirmation of the agreed upon rate, so that there's never a misunderstanding. Check on current fares at the airport information counter.

If you're only in Windhoek for 24 hours or so, you won't need a car. It's a small city that's easy enough to walk around, and taxis are available everywhere.

Intercape Mainliner runs buses between Windhoek and Swakopmund, as do other smaller and reliable shuttle services. Information on these is available at the Tourist Information Center in both cities.

If you plan to drive across the country, pre-book and rent a car from here. Gas is sold in all towns, but if you're planning a long journey between towns, fill up in

Windhoek and it never hurts to have a spare (filled) gas can.

HEALTH AND SAFETY

If you need medical attention in Windhoek, consider the Medi-Clinic, an excellent private clinic, or the Roman Catholic Hospital. Ask at your accommodation for the nearest pharmacy.

Pickpockets work the city center, particularly the markets and the Post Street Mall. Lock your valuables away in the hotel safe, and carry only what you need. Never travel with expensive jewelry. Don't walk alone at night, and stick to well-lit areas.

VISITOR INFORMATION

The very helpful Tourist Information Bureau (run by the City of Windhoek) in the FNB Building on Independence Avenue, is open weekdays 7:30–1 and 2–4:30. It also operates a kiosk on Independence Avenue next to the main taxi stand and opposite the Avani Windhoek Hotel and Casino. Here you can book accommodations and car rentals, and get advice about travel throughout the country.

The Namibia Tourism Board (NTB) has general information on Windhoek as well as the rest of Namibia, but isn't tailored to individual consultation. It's open weekdays 8–5.

The head office of the Namibia Wildlife Resorts (NWR) is also on Independence Avenue. Here you can get information on NWR lodging in all the parks and make bookings.

ESSENTIALS

AIRPORTS Eros Airport. (*ERS*) ✉ *Windhoek ✈ 5 km (3 miles) from Windhoek's city center* ☎ *61/295–5501* ⊕ *www. airports.com.na.* **Hosea Kutako International Airport.** (*WDH*) ✉ *Hosea Kutako International Airport, Windhoek ✈ 45 km (28 miles) east of Windhoek* ☎ *61/295–5600* ⊕ *www.airports.com.na.*

BUS LINE Intercape Mainliner. ☎ *61/227–847* ⊕ *www.intercape.co.za.*

CAR RENTALS Avis. ☎ *61/233–166* ⊕ *www.avis.co.za/namibia.* **Budget.** ✉ *Hosea Kutako International Airport* ☎ *62/540–271* ⊕ *www.budget.co.na.* **Hertz.** ✉ *Hosea Kutako International Airport, Windhoek* ☎ *61/540–116* ⊕ *www. hertz.co.za.* **Namibia2Go.** ✉ *2 Bassingthwaighte St., Klein Windhoek* ☎ *81/145–8202 mobile* ⊕ *www.namibia2go.com.*

DESTINATION MANAGEMENT COMPANIES African Extravaganza. ☎ *61/372–100* ⊕ *www.african-extravaganza.com.* **Out and About Travel.** ☎ *72/954–3776 in South Africa* ⊕ *www.oatravel.co.za.*

VISITOR INFORMATION Namibia Tourism Board. (*NTB*) ✉ *Haddy and Sam Nujoma Dr., Windhoek* ☎ *61/290–6000* ⊕ *www. visitnamibia.com.na.* **Namibia Wildlife Resorts.** (*NWR*) ✉ *189 Independence Ave., Windhoek* ☎ *61/285–7200* ⊕ *www. nwr.com.na.*

Sights

Bushman Art Gallery

STORE/MALL | This souvenir and curio shop on bustling Independence Avenue distinguishes itself from the rest with its fairly sizable collection of cultural objects (religious, ceremonial, drums, etc.) and domestic utensils of local bushman and Himba tribes (not for sale). A large assortment of other carvings and antiques from around Africa adorn the walls and display cases. ✉ *187 Independence Ave., Windhoek* ☎ *61/228–828* ⊕ *www.bushmanart-gallery.com.*

Christuskirche

CHURCH | The Lutheran Christ Church is a good representation of German colonial architecture—a mixture of art nouveau and neo-Gothic dating from 1896. Although the church is sometimes locked, you can obtain a key from the nearby church office at 12 Fidel Castro Street (down the hill from the church).

■TIP→ **You must book in advance to be able to go inside.** ⊠ *Robert Mugabe Ave., Windhoek* ☎ *61/236–002* ⊙ *Closed Sat. and Sun.*

Katutura

NEIGHBORHOOD | Created in the early 1960s for the forced evictions of blacks from the town center under Apartheid, Windhoek's vast informal settlement (Katutura) translates to 'The place where people do not want to live' in the Otjiherero language. It now houses more than half of the capital city's population and makes for an insightful guided tour. You will learn about the Old Location Uprising and the reason why Namibia commemorates Human Rights Day on 10 December each year. Be sure to visit the Oshetu Market ("our market"), where northern Namibian fare like mopane worms and dried patties of a type of local spinach are sold, and whose bustling meat market includes a barbeque area where the adventurous can try succulent slices of all types of roasted meat, dipped in a mixture of salt and chili. You can also have the chance to engage with community members and small business owners, while visiting various NGO projects in the informal settlement.

■TIP→ **Be sure to go with a guide, who can navigate the dirt roads and provide commentary; Katu Tours and Safaris (a Black, female-owned company) does this via bicycle (12km, 3.5 hours, two daily departures) and it's one of the best ways to experience it.** ⊠ *SL10 Soweto Market, Independence Ave., Kautura, Windhoek* ☎ *81/303–2856* ✉ *katutours@gmail.com* 🖃 *Tours N$750 per person.*

Namibia Craft Centre

MARKET | On Tal Street in the old breweries building behind the Avani Windhoek Hotel and Casino, the Namibia Crafts Centre offers beautiful and unique pieces of work. Dozens of stalls showcase the work of more than 1,500 rural craftspeople, and include items such as fine woven baskets, original beadwork, distinct Caprivian pots, handmade contemporary jewelry, eye-catching prints, and much more. ⊠ *40 Tal St., Windhoek* ☎ *61/242–2222.*

National Gallery

ART MUSEUM | **FAMILY** | This small but lovely museum features contemporary Namibian art. The somewhat ho-hum permanent exhibit downstairs features German-Namibian painters from the 20th century. Head upstairs, where cool contemporary lithographs by young Namibian artists line the walls, and regularly changing temporary exhibits feature very good work by Namibian and other African artists, most of which is for sale. A small café and shop adjoin. ⊠ *John Meinart St. at Robert Mugabe Ave., Windhoek* ☎ *61/231–160* ⊕ *www.nagn. org.na* 🖃 *Suggested donation N$20.*

Post Street Mall

MARKET | At this open-air market known for its colorful sidewalk displays of curios, crafts, and carvings of all kinds, international tourists and businesspeople rub shoulders with Herero women in full traditional Victorian dress. Keep an eye out for the meteorites mounted on slender steel columns. These meteorites hit the earth during the Gibeon meteorite shower, which rained down some 600 million years ago, the heaviest such shower known on earth.

■TIP→ **There are some curios and beadwork on sale here but be sure to check out the sidewalk curio market farther down on Independence Avenue.** ⊠ *Post St., Windhoek.*

Tintenpalast

GARDEN | The handsome circa-1912 Palace of Ink is fronted by beautiful formal gardens. Formerly the administration offices of the German colonial government, the two-story building now houses the National Assembly. Nearby is the Office of the Prime Minister, decorated in mosaics, indigenous woods, and murals. You can take gorgeous photos from the

464

Windhoek

KEY

1 Sights
1 Restaurants
1 Hotels

outside. ✉ *Robert Mugabe Ave., Windhoek* ☎ *61/288–9111* 🎫 *Free* ⏲ *Closed daily noon–1 pm.*

🍴 Restaurants

★ Joe's Beerhouse

$$ | GERMAN | FAMILY | If you only have a single night to spend in the capital city, make sure you swing by Joe's Beerhouse, whether it's to sample a large selection of local craft beers, savor their generous portions of German and Namibian food, or to marvel at the thousands of pieces of eclectic memorabilia and knick-knacks on display, from stuffed animals and road signs to antiques and wire art. This quirky Windhoek institution will make for very memorable photos no matter whether you choose to sit indoors or out. **Known for:** extensive menu with a variety of choices— try Joe's Jägerschnitzel; their own branded merchandise; lively atmosphere which makes it easy to meet other travelers. [$] *Average main: US$15* ✉ *160 Nelson Mandela Ave., Windhoek* ☎ *61/232–457 landline, 81/123–2457 mobile* 🌐 *www.joesbeerhouse.com.*

★ Leo's at the Castle

$$ | EUROPEAN | Arguably Windhoek's only true fine-dining establishment—with a price tag to match—Leo's is literally in a castle on a hill. The small chandelier-dazzled dining room has fabulous views of the city and the haute cuisine is both gorgeously prepared and presented. **Known for:** excellent wine selection; the outside seating is delightful; outstanding service. [$] *Average main: US$17* ✉ *Hotel Heinitzburg, 22 Heinitzburg St., Windhoek* ☎ *61/249–597* 🌐 *www.heinitzburg.com.*

The Stellenbosch Wine Bar and Bistro

$$ | STEAKHOUSE | A favorite restaurant among locals, this bistro-style steak house champions perfectly prepared Namibian meat and first-rate South African wine. The fairly large menu can be overwhelming, but only because it's all so delicious. **Known for:** matchless wine selection at good range of prices; prompt and professional service; selection of grass-fed beef classic steaks. [$] *Average main: US$15* ✉ *320 Sam Nujoma Dr., BougainVillas, Windhoek* ☎ *61/309–141* 🌐 *www.thestellenboschwinebar.com* ⏲ *Closed Sun.*

🛏 Hotels

Avani Windhoek Hotel and Casino

$ | HOTEL | This comfortable and elegant hotel has all the conveniences of a large, smooth-running operation, with staff on hand at every corner to assist and pleasant rooms that characterize the property. **Pros:** underwent a recent renovation; most of downtown Windhoek is within walking distance; impressive breakfast buffet. **Cons:** doesn't have as much character as smaller, boutique hotels; the surrounding area is popular with vagrants; navigating the entrance and parking area (if self-driving) can be confusing. [$] *Rooms from: US$113* ✉ *Gustav Voigts Centre, 129 Independence Ave., Windhoek* ☎ *61/280–0664 central reservations* 🌐 *www.avanihotels.com/en/windhoek* 🛏 *173 rooms* 🍴 *Free Breakfast.*

Droombos

$ | HOTEL | With its vibrant sprawling gardens, this new, family-owned establishment will make you do a double take when you realize it's within the capital city. **Pros:** just 10 minutes from downtown Windhoek; try their gourmet garden picnic set up; the restaurant serves herbs and greens from their vegetable garden. **Cons:** the dim sound of the main road can be heard at night; weekends can be rather busy with locals dining at the restaurant; regularly hosts weddings and conferences. [$] *Rooms from: US$169* ✉ *Windhoek* ✣ *Travel on the B6 towards Hosea Kutako airport, past the entrance to Avis Dam and the old Red Train Bridge. Turn right toward Rivercrossing and*

Vineyard, keep left towards Vineyard. ☎ *81/872–2613 mobile, 61/250–238 landline* 🌐 *www.droombos.com.na* 🛏 *30 suites* 🍴 *Free Breakfast.*

GocheGanas

$$ | HOTEL | Just on the outskirts of Windhoek, this well-appointed lodge has all the safari charm and sophistication of a luxury lodge. **Pros:** close to Windhoek but far enough away to feel like a safari lodge; wellness village, spa, and indoor pool; excellent service. **Cons:** all activities at an additional cost; restaurant feels a little sparse and hollow; limited wine selection. [$] *Rooms from: US$383* ✉ *Windhoek* ✣ *20 km (12 miles) along D1463 to South of Windhoek* ☎ *61/224–909* 🌐 *www.gocheganas.com* 🛏 *16 suites* 🍴 *All-Inclusive* ☞ *can also be booked on a DDB basis.*

★ **Habitas Namibia**

$$$$ | ALL-INCLUSIVE | Constructed from natural materials in a low-impact manner (including being completely solar powered), this luxe tented camp seamlessly blends into its surroundings atop a rocky outcrop that's reminiscent of the Masai Mara all while offering guests every creature comfort. **Pros:** unsurpassable service—the staff clearly love what they do; spectacular sunsets and panoramic views of the savannah; delectable food that incorporates Namibia flavors and culinary heritage. **Cons:** no Wi-Fi in the luxe tents (but we argue that's a good thing); an hour from Windhoek or 30 minutes from the airport, but most certainly worth the drive; a safari from the entrance gate to the lodge is part of the journey. [$] *Rooms from: US$758* ✉ *Farm Coas 501, Windhoek* ☎ *81/470–1035 mobile* 🌐 *www.ourhabitas.com/namibia* 🛏 *12 tented suites* 🍴 *All-Inclusive.*

Hotel Heinitzburg

$$ | HOTEL | This is your chance to stay in a turn-of-the-20th-century castle, a white fort with battlements set high on a hill and commissioned by a German count for his fiancée in 1914. **Pros:** lavishly decadent interior styling; great personalized service; five-minute drive from city center. **Cons:** can be difficult to contact directly; only a small number of rooms, so it books up fast; rooms don't have tons of natural light (it's a castle, after all). [$] *Rooms from: US$260* ✉ *22 Heinitzburg St., Windhoek* ☎ *61/249–597* 🌐 *www.heinitzburg.com* 🛏 *16 rooms* 🍴 *Free Breakfast.*

★ **Olive Exclusive Boutique Hotel**

$$$ | HOTEL | Windhoek's premier boutique hotel, the Olive Exclusive, with its six large suites each decorated thematically according to each of Namibia's regions, is an upmarket treat either before or after your safari. **Pros:** in-house spa therapist; excellent restaurant; wonderful staff and management. **Cons:** very challenging to reach the property over the phone; the view onto the hills of Windhoek and the olive grove could seem spoiled by shabby housing on one side; you need a car to get around. [$] *Rooms from: US$505* ✉ *22 Promenaden St., Klein Windhoek* ☎ *61/383–890* 🌐 *www.theolive-namibia.com* 🛏 *7 suites* 🍴 *Free Breakfast.*

Zannier Hotels Omaanda

$$$$ | ALL-INCLUSIVE | The concept of conservation and the genuine rehabilitation of the resident flora and fauna is at the forefront for Zannier Hotels, as is property design as evidenced by these airy and spacious thatched villas built to reflect Owambo architecture fused with five-star flare. **Pros:** the French-inspired meals are scrumptious; you'll be torn between relaxing in your villa or the stunning lodge; immaculate lodge and villas with understated elegance. **Cons:** it's a conservancy so wildlife is somewhat sparse; 30 minutes outside of Windhoek; staff is a bit green. [$] *Rooms from: US$1,600* ✉ *Windhoek* ☎ *81/145–5261 mobile* 🌐 *www.zannierhotels.com* 🍴 *All-Inclusive* ☞ *Also available on a DBB basis.*

Beach Escapes

You don't come to Namibia for beaches, but if you do fancy a dip in the freezing Atlantic waters, Swakopmund, the country's only real beach resort, is your best bet.

Swakopmund

Although the desert continues to sweep its remorseless way toward the mighty Atlantic and its infamous Skeleton Coast, humans have somehow managed to hang on to this patch of coastline, where Swakopmund clings to the edge of the continent. The first 40 German settlers, complete with household goods and breeding cattle, arrived here with 120 German colonial troops on the *Marie Woermann* in the late 19th century.

Today, instead of the primitive shelters that the early settlers built on the beach to protect themselves from sand and sea, stands Swakopmund, or "Swakops," as the resort town is affectionately known. There's something surreal about Swakops. On the one hand, it's like a tiny European transplant, with its seaside promenade, sidewalk cafés, fine German colonial buildings, trendy bistros, friendly and neat-as-a-pin pensions, and immaculate boarding houses and hotels. On the other hand, this little town is squashed between the relentless Atlantic and the harsh desert, in one of the wildest and most untamed parts of the African continent—something you might understandably forget while nibbling a chocolate torte or sipping a good German beer under a striped umbrella.

Swakops makes for a different, unique beach escape because of its history and surreal surroundings. It's one of the top adventure centers in Africa, second only to Victoria Falls in Zimbabwe. Adrenaline junkies can try their hand (or feet) at skydiving, sandboarding, kayaking, dune-buggying, paragliding, or wave-skipping in a light aircraft. The less adventurous (but romantic) can take day, moonlight, sunrise, or sunset horseback or camel rides through the riverbeds and up into the moonlike landscape. The curious can partake in one of the fabulous "little five" living-desert tours through the dunes that represent the northern extent of the Namib-Naukluft. There are also lots of curio shops and commercial art galleries, making Swakops great for shopping, and the dining options are improving all the time.

WHEN TO GO

Keep in mind that the town is packed with vacationing Namibians and South Africans at Christmas, New Year's, and Easter, so avoid these times if you can. The sea keeps temperatures relatively comfortable year-round, and positively chilly outside of summer.

GETTING HERE AND AROUND

The closest airport, handling domestic and international flights, is about a 45-minute drive from Swakopmund at Walvis Bay.

Intercape Mainliner runs buses between Windhoek and Swakopmund.

The Town Hoppers shuttle service runs a daily return shuttle from Windhoek to Walvis Bay and Swakopmund, with en route pick ups and drop offs in Arandis, Usakos, Karibib, Wilhelmstal, and Okahandja, for N$300 one way. For an additional fee, they'll provide door-to-door pickup and/or drop-off, and can also offer private transportation and airport transfers from Walvis Bay. There are no reliable bus services within Swakopmund for visitors.

If you have the time, it's worth renting a car to drive from Windhoek to Swakopmund. It's a very scenic and easy four-hour drive, about 368 km (228 miles) on the B1, a good paved road. Once in Swakopmund, it's easy to find your way around. With a car, you'll also be able to

The tiny resort town of Swakopmund has a seaside promenade, sidewalk cafés, trendy bistros, and immaculate hotels.

visit the Cape Cross seal colony and drive farther north toward the Skeleton Coast, or drive 30 km (19 miles) south to Walvis Bay, where numerous outdoor activities start.

A two-wheel-drive vehicle is fine, but if you intend to visit Sandwich Harbour or Sossusvlei in Namib-Naukluft Park, then four-wheel drive will give you more access and better viewing (and is essential for Sandwich Harbour).

If you arrange to rent a car in advance at any of the reliable agencies, you'll be met at Walvis Bay Airport. The car-rental agencies also have offices in Swakopmund.

SAFETY AND PRECAUTIONS
Swakopmund is a very safe little town, but you should always be aware of potential pickpockets. Lock your valuables away in the hotel safe, and carry only what you need. Never travel with expensive jewelry. Don't walk alone at night, and stick to well-lit areas.

Mediclinic Swakopmund is a private clinic. Ask at your accommodation about the nearest pharmacy.

TIMING
Swakopmund is both a pleasant place in itself and offers a surprising array of activities and good shopping, as well as some culinary variety if you've been on safari for a while. Visitors generally stay two nights, but three to four nights is better if you really want to partake in a few of the outdoor activities for which this area is famous (several of which happen in Walvis Bay, a 40-minute drive south), as well as relax and stroll around town.

VISITOR INFORMATION
Namib-I, the tourist information center (on the corner of Hendrik Witbooi Street and Dr Sam Nujoma Avenue), provides excellent national and local information, maps, and more.

CONTACTS

AIRPORT Walvis Bay Airport. *(WVB)*
☎ *64/271–102* ⊕ *www.airports.com.na.*

SCENIC FLIGHTS AND CHARTERS Scenic Air (Swakopmund office). ☎ *81/127–0534 Mobile, 64/403–575 Landline* ⊕ *www. scenic-air.com.*

BUS LINE Intercape Mainliner. ☎ *61/227– 847* ⊕ *www.intercape.co.za.*

CAR RENTALS Avis. ⊠ *Swakopmund Hotel and Entertainment Centre, 2 Theo-Ben Gurirab Ave., Swakopmund* ☎ *64/402–527* ⊕ *www.avis.co.za/ namibia.* **Crossroads 4x4 Hire.** ⊠ *3 Moses Garoëb St., Swakopmund* ☎ *81/127–2560 mobile/WhatsApp (24/7), 64/403–777* ⊕ *www.crossroadscarhire.com.* **Hertz.** ⊠ *Walvis Bay Airport, Walvis Bay* ☎ *64/200–853* ⊕ *www.hertz.co.za.* **Town Hoppers Shuttle.** ⊠ *23 Marconi Rd, Walvis Bay* ☎ *81/210–3062 mobile, 64/221–713 landline* ⊕ *www.namibiashuttle.com.*

EMERGENCY CONTACTS Ambulance. ☎ *96960 toll free from a local number, 81/147–3387 WhatsApp* ⊕ *www.namib-iaambulance.com.* **Police.** ☎ *62/10111.*

HOSPITAL Mediclinic Swakopmund. ⊠ *Franziska van Neel St., Swakopmund* ☎ *64/412–200, 064/412–205 Emergency Department* ⊕ *www.mediclinic.co.za.*

VISITOR INFORMATION Namib-I Tourist Information. ⊠ *28 Sam Nujoma Ave., at Hendrik Witbooi St., Swakopmund* ☎ *64/404–827.*

 Sights

Kristall Galerie

OTHER MUSEUM | FAMILY | This sizable gallery (which underwent a major renovation in early 2022) houses the largest known quartz-crystal cluster in the world—an awesome natural wonder more than 520 million years old and weighing 14,000 kilograms. Numerous smaller but no less beautiful chunks of Namibian minerals and gems, including a wide variety of quartz crystals, rainbow tourmalines, and other semiprecious stones, are also on display. Some great souvenirs can be had in the adjoining large gift shop and high-end jewelry boutique to allow you to take home a unique piece of Namibia. ⊠ *Tobias Hainyeko at Theo-Ben Gurirab Ave., Swakopmund* ☎ *64/406–080* ⊕ *www. namibiangemstones.com* ⊠ *N$30* ⊗ *Closed Sun.*

National Marine Aquarium

AQUARIUM | FAMILY | This small aquarium showcases great displays of marine life, including a huge main tank that can be viewed from different angles. A great feature is the walk-through tunnel. It's a worthwhile attraction if you are traveling with young kids and is a great way to spend half an hour to 45 minutes.

■ **TIP →** **The bigger fish, especially the sharks, are fed around 3 pm so try to time your visit for then.** ⊠ *South Strand St. (at the southern end), Swakopmund* ☎ *64/410–1214* ⊠ *N$30* ⊗ *Closed Mon.*

Old Station Building

HOTEL | Probably Swakops's most notable landmark, the gorgeous, historic Old Station Building was built in 1901. Declared a national monument in 1972, this magnificent example of German colonial architecture came to life again in the early 1990s, when it was restored and renovated in a style evoking the charm and nostalgia of the old railway days. Don't miss the huge bustling lobby—a remnant of the building's former life as a railway station. Today, the building houses the Swakopmund Hotel and Entertainment Centre, which includes a movie theater, casino, spa, and two restaurants. ⊠ *2 Theo-Ben Gurirab Ave., Swakopmund* ☎ *64/410–5200* ⊕ *www.legacyhotels. co.za* ⊠ *Free.*

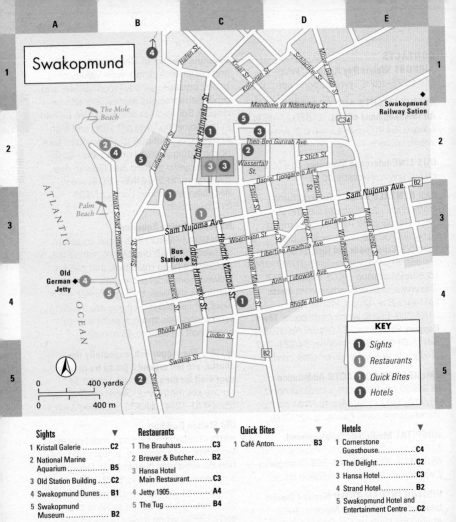

Swakopmund

The Mole Beach

ATLANTIC

Palm Beach

Old German Jetty

OCEAN

Hafen St.

Kraai St.

Kolonien St.

Schlachter St.

Moses Garoeb St.

Mandume ya Ndemufayo St.

Swakopmund Railway Sation

C34

Theo-Ben Guirirab Ave.

Wasserfall St.

F Stich St.

Daniel Tjongarero Ave.

Francois St.

Sam Nujoma Ave.

B2

Ludwig Koch St.

Tobias Hainyeko St.

Estorff St.

Olavi St.

Luderitz St.

Leutwein St.

Windhoeker St.

Moses Garoeb St.

Sam Nujoma Ave.

Woermann St.

Nathaniel Maxuilili St.

Libertina Amathila Ave.

Strand St.

Arnold Schad Promenade

Bus Station ♦

Hendrik Witbooi St.

Anton Lubowski Ave.

Bismarck St.

Rhode Allee

Linden St.

Swakop St.

B2

Strand St.

0   400 yards
0   400 m

KEY

1 Sights

1 Restaurants

1 Quick Bites

1 Hotels

Sights ▼

1 Kristall Galerie **C2**

2 National Marine Aquarium **B5**

3 Old Station Building **C2**

4 Swakopmund Dunes ...**B1**

5 Swakopmund Museum **B2**

Restaurants ▼

1 The Brauhaus **C3**

2 Brewer & Butcher **B2**

3 Hansa Hotel Main Restaurant **C3**

4 Jetty 1905 ....**A4**

5 The Tug **B4**

Quick Bites ▼

1 Café Anton **B3**

Hotels ▼

1 Cornerstone Guesthouse **C4**

2 The Delight **C2**

3 Hansa Hotel **C3**

4 Strand Hotel **B2**

5 Swakopmund Hotel and Entertainment Centre ...**C2**

★ **Swakopmund Dunes**

NATURE SIGHT | **FAMILY** | Though you may have already visited higher or more visually stunning dunes, the Swakop dune belt has the unique distinction of being the subject of a truly fascinating tour that introduces visitors to the numerous—and normally invisible—creatures thriving in this surreal ecosystem of the Namib Desert. The passionate and well-informed guides leap out of 4x4s to catch the desert's perfectly camouflaged lizards, geckos, and snakes. A visit here is a unique, educational, and often humorous experience. ⊠ *Swakopmund* ☏ *81/128– 1038 mobile or WhatsApp* ⊕ *www. livingdeserttours.com.na* ⊟ *N$ 850, incl. transfers, snacks, and refreshments.*

Swakopmund Museum

HISTORY MUSEUM | **FAMILY** | The largest private museum in Namibia, this historical building down by the lighthouse was built in 1951 and houses a surprisingly large and varied collection of items. Displays on everything from natural history, archaeology, and ethnology to the German colonial period are informative and worth a look, especially if traveling with kids. ⊠ *Strand St., just below the lighthouse, Swakopmund* ☏ *64/402–046* ⊕ *www.scientificsocietyswakopmund. com* ⊟ *N$30* ⌕ *No credit card facilities.*

⊕ Beaches

Though Namibia is hardly a beach destination, if you really want some sand and sun time, head to the Mole and adjacent Palm Beach, Swakops's most popular beaches (in front of the lighthouse). Keep in mind that this isn't Mauritius or the Caribbean: the sea can be treacherous, and the temperature usually runs in the lower 50s. Both of these beaches are a short walk from the center of town, and there are numerous cafés and restaurants along here to stop for a quick drink or bite to eat. The beach is sheltered by a breakwater, so its calm waters attract crowds, especially on the weekends; if

you do swim out, beware of the strong currents just off the breakwater. There's a paved promenade that heads north along the beach if you need to stretch your legs. You can also head to the jetty at the southern end of the beach for a stroll.

The Mole Beach

BEACH | **FAMILY** | The designated swimming beach at Swakopmund, The Mole, is actually a failed engineering project. In 1899 the South Africans controlled the closest harbor at Walvis Bay, so attempts were made to build a harbor at Swakopmund. The engineer, FW Ortloff, failed to take into account the force of the Benguela current flowing down the length of Namibia and dumping desert sands on the shore. The result is the promontory you see today with The Mole now forming a secluded swimming beach. A short walk from the center of town, the beach is serviced by a number of restaurants and small cafés. The Atlantic Ocean is generally cold and rough, so if you're set on swimming, you'll have to brave it. Lifeguards are on duty during the summer. **Amenities:** lifeguards (in summer), toilets. **Best for:** sunsets, sundowners, swimming. ⊠ *A. Schad Promenade, Swakopmund* ⊟ *Free.*

Palm Beach

BEACH | **FAMILY** | At a manageable 500 meters (1,640 feet), Palm Beach, which stretches along the western side of Swakopmund and effectively forms the western border, is the recommended beach for gentle walking. Swimming isn't encouraged due to rough waters and strong currents (and the icy Atlantic waters). Instead stroll from the north, starting at The Mole beach, and watch the sun go down in the west. Enjoy a sundowner on Swakopmund's famous Jetty 1905 restaurant and if you're hungry try the festive scene at the famous Tug restaurant. The palms the beach is named after are set back against the access road offering limited shade. Busy in summer, but quiet in winter, Palm

Beach is also often in fog due to the cold air of the Atlantic hitting the heat of the desert. **Amenities:** food and drink, parking, toilets. **Best for:** sunsets, walking. ✉ *A. Schad Promenade, Swakopmund* 🎫 *Free.*

🍴 Restaurants

The Brauhaus

$ | **GERMAN** | A Swakopmund institution, the Brauhaus is a typical German restaurant where the beer flows and the big wooden tables invite long sit-downs over hearty lunches and dinners. The German fare—schnitzel, bratwurst, and rosti (similar to a potato pancake)—is excellent, but if goulash and sauerkraut don't do it for you, there is a large selection of steaks and game meat, as well as seafood and even a few pasta and vegetarian options. **Known for:** good selection of beers; great vibe especially on Saturday; hearty German fare, especially the eisbein. [$] *Average main: US$10* ✉ *The Arcade 22, Sam Nujoma Ave., Swakopmund* ☎ *64/402–214* 🌐 *swakopmundbrauhaus.com/* ⏲ *Closed Sun.*

Brewer & Butcher

$$ | **STEAKHOUSE** | One of the in-house restaurants at the Strand Hotel, this genuine steak house has an inviting and lively atmosphere that will set you at ease at once. The steaks are A+ and the four craft beers from the in-house microbrewery pair well with a succulent piece of grilled game loin or a grilled Namibian Kapana experience, where the meat is grilled on an open fire, sliced, and sprinkled with traditional kapana spice. **Known for:** a gourmet twist on traditional foods; in-house craft beer and microbrewery on-site; many options for meat-lovers. [$] *Average main: US$15* ✉ *Strand Hotel, Molen Rd., Swakopmund* ☎ *64/411–4512* 🌐 *www.strandhotelswakopmund.com.*

Hansa Hotel Main Restaurant

$$ | **EUROPEAN** | Full of old-world charm, the restaurant in this perfectly restored 1905 German colonial building looks out onto the manicured garden. This is the perfect place for that special-occasion dinner because the service is impeccable, the wine list excellent, and the menu is a broad selection of good, rich food such as venison steak and Namibian seafood delicacies. **Known for:** generous portions; first-class service; come here for something unique. [$] *Average main: US$17* ✉ *3 Hendrik Witbooi St., Swakopmund* ☎ *64/414–200* 🌐 *www.hansahotel.com.na.*

Jetty 1905

$$ | **SEAFOOD** | This restaurant, situated right at the end of Swakopmund's famous Jetty 1905, is a cocoon of warmth where patrons can sip wine and eat oysters while watching the Atlantic Ocean heave around them. Seafood is the recommended food choice—try the crumbed Camembert starter or the finger-licking-good grilled prawns—but there are meat options as well. **Known for:** fresh oysters and well-prepared sushi; a bustling yet romantic option; great location. [$] *Average main: US$16* ✉ *The Jetty 1905, Molen Rd., on the Pier, Swakopmund* ☎ *81/380–3595 mobile* 🌐 *www.lighthousegroup.com.na* ⏲ *No lunch Mon.–Thurs.*

The Tug

$$ | **SEAFOOD** | It's all about location at the Tug, which, as its name suggests, is actually an old tugboat that has been raised up and moored next to the jetty. The restaurant is known for its fresh, locally sourced seafood—especially the local Walvis Bay oysters—which are some of the best in the world, but there are creative seafood alternatives like venison (oryx, springbok, kudu and zebra), though not many vegetarian meals. **Known for:** fresh, locally sourced

seafood; incredible location and views; lively atmosphere. $ *Average main: US$16* ✉ *The Strand, Swakopmund* ☎ *64/402–356* ⊕ *www.the-tug.com* ◷ *No lunch Mon.–Fri.*

 ## Coffee and Quick Bites

Café Anton

$ | **CAFÉ** | The palm-shaded terrace at this classic little café is a good place to take a break after perusing the curio market around the lighthouse. Watch the world go by while you savor scrumptious home-baked cakes and pastries, or enjoy a late afternoon tea with hazelnut triangles, custard-filled danishes, or croissants. **Known for:** Black Forest cake; apple strudel; chocolate Florentiner cookies. $ *Average main: US$5* ✉ *Schweizer-haus Hotel, 1 Bismarck St., overlooking the Mole, Swakopmund* ☎ *64/400–331* ⊕ *www.schweizerhaus.net.*

🛏 Hotels

Several of the lodging establishments listed don't have air-conditioning, but because of the cool climate this is actually standard practice in the smaller guesthouses. They all have fans for use in summer, and it's rarely so hot that the average person would consider air-conditioning necessary. For much of the year, having a heater indoors is more of an issue.

Cornerstone Guesthouse

$ | **B&B/INN** | **FAMILY** | Walking into Cornerstone one is struck by the lovely manicured garden and the pleasantly homey ambience. **Pros:** same day laundry service; international wall sockets; secure off-street parking. **Cons:** often fully booked; rooms are not huge; one family room looks onto parking area instead of garden. $ *Rooms from: US$145* ✉ *40 Hendrik Witbooi St., Swakopmund* ☎ *64/462–468* ⊕ *www.cornerstoneg-uesthouse.com* ↘ *7 rooms* ⦿ *Free Breakfast.*

★ The Delight

$ | **HOTEL** | **FAMILY** | As its name suggests, The Delight ticks all the boxes for a wonderful stay: modern decor, the best buffet breakfast in town, cheerful rooms, a funky bar, and a welcoming lounge. **Pros:** safe, off-street parking; exceptional breakfast and colorful bar area; family-friendly and centrally located establishment. **Cons:** can seem quite bright for more conservative travelers; does not serve dinner. $ *Rooms from: US$210* ✉ *Theo Ben Gurirab Ave. and Nathanael Maxuilie Str., Windhoek* ☎ *61/427–200* ⊕ *www.gondwana-collection.com* ↘ *54 rooms* ⦿ *Free Breakfast.*

Hansa Hotel

$ | **HOTEL** | **FAMILY** | This old-world grand dame, which was established in 1905 a few years after the town was founded, gives guests a Belle Epoque-era feeling with its hushed solicitude, gleaming brass and manicured garden. **Pros:** seating in the small yet stunning garden; gorgeous old bar with a fireplace, order their signature hot drink; fast and unlimited internet. **Cons:** overflow parking is on the roadside, but there are security guards; there are no sea views and the interior is rather dark; could be a bit stuffy for younger travelers. $ *Rooms from: US$141* ✉ *3 Hendrik Witbooi St., Swakopmund* ☎ *64/414–200* ⊕ *www. hansahotel.com.na* ↘ *58 rooms* ⦿ *Free Breakfast.*

Strand Hotel

$$ | **HOTEL** | This large beachfront property is built on Mole Beach overlooking the Atlantic Ocean. **Pros:** all the amenities you could want or need; has a full-service spa and gym; excellent in-house restaurants; recently underwent a renovation. **Cons:** can seem too big and busy for

travelers who prefer more peace; the standard rooms don't have step-out balconies or sea views; restaurants are often fully booked. [$] *Rooms from: US$325* ⊠ *An der Mole, A. Schad Promenade, Swakopmund* ☎ *64/411–4308 reservations* ⊕ *www.strandhotels-wakopmund.com* ↩ *125 rooms* ⏲ *Free Breakfast.*

★ Swakopmund Hotel and Entertainment Centre

$ | HOTEL | FAMILY | At this family-friendly hotel within the 1901 Old Station Building, the huge, bustling lobby is a reminder of the building's previous incarnation as a railway station. **Pros:** for a romantic evening at the nearby 'moon landscape', book the desert dinner experience; conveniences of a large hotel with numerous facilities; lovely lobby architecture and history. **Cons:** often used as a business or conference center; bath showers; lacks character or intimacy of smaller boutique hotels. [$] *Rooms from: US$189* ⊠ *2 Theo-Ben Gurirab Ave., Swakopmund* ☎ *64/410–5200* ⊕ *www.legacyhotels.co.za* ↩ *90 rooms* ⏲ *Free Breakfast.*

Activities

As Namibia's adventure-activity capital, Swakopmund is the departure point for all manner of tours that showcase its surreal location between the dunes and the sea. No matter how you prefer to experience it there's lots to do, from sky diving (Swakopmund Skydiving Club) and sandboarding (Khoisan Tours And Safaris) to fat biking on an electric bike along the dunes (Swakopmund Fat Biking Tours) and doing a 4x4 day trip to Sandwich Harbour which is offered by various tour operators, this is the place for adrenaline junkies to get their fix. There's also a number of more relaxing activities that'll allow you to take in the gorgeous natural environment, from a sunrise hot air balloon excursion over the moon landscape followed by a sparkling wine breakfast (Hot Air Ballooning Namibia), to horseback rides throughout the day (Okakambe Trails), and The Living Desert Tour (Tommy's Tours and Safaris) to encounter the so-called 'Little Five' amid the sea of sand dunes. Most of sea-based tours depart from Walvis Bay, a 30-minute drive away (see Walvis Bay for more details) – here you can kayak with Cape Fur seals, spot whales during whale on a catamaran trip or do a sundowner cruise. Finally, Namib Tracks & Trails can organize all manner of trips, including day trips a bit farther afield to sights like the amazing rock formations and bush paintings at Spitzkoppe.

TOUR OPERATORS

Desert Explorers

ADVENTURE TOURS | FAMILY | ⊠ *Nathaniel Maxuilili St., Swakopmund* ☎ *644/406–096 landline* ⊕ *www.namibiadesertexplorers.com.*

Hot Air Ballooning Namibia

AIR EXCURSIONS | FAMILY | ⊠ *Hendrik Witbooi Ave., Swakopmund* ☎ *81/835–0827 mobile, 81/808–6743 mobile* ⊕ *www.ballooning-namibia.com* 🎫 *N$4,850* ☞ *Includes drop off, pick up, and sparkling wine breakfast.*

Khoisan Tours And Safaris

ADVENTURE TOURS | FAMILY | ⊠ *The Courtyard, Tobias Hainyeko St., Swakopmund* ☎ *81/273–4936 mobile/WhatsApp* ⊕ *www.khoisantours.com* ☞ *Includes drop off and pick up.*

Living Desert Tour

ADVENTURE TOURS | FAMILY | ⊠ *Swakopmund* ☎ *64/405–070 landline, 81/127–5070 mobile* ⊕ *www.livingdesertnamibia.com.*

Namibia Tracks & Trails
HIKING & WALKING | ✉ *13 Hidipo Hamuten-ya St., Swakopmund* ☎ *81/269–7271 mobile, 64/416–820 landline* ⊕ *www.namibia-tracks-and-trails.com.*

Okakambe Trails
HORSEBACK RIDING | FAMILY | ✉ *Erf 378 Swakopmund river plots, Swakopmund* ⚓ *11 km (7 miles) east of Swakopmund on the B2 to Windhoek, next to the camel farm* ☎ *64/402–799* ⊕ *www.okakambe.iway.na.*

★ Swakopmund Fat Bike Tours
BICYCLE TOURS | FAMILY | ✉ *6 Hendrik Witbooi St., Swakopmund* ☎ *81/395–5813 mobile* ⊕ *www.swakopfatbiketours.com* ☞ *e-bikes also available.*

Swakopmund Skydiving Club
SKYDIVING | ✉ *Hanger 13B, Swakopmund* ⚓ *5 km (3 miles) east of Swakopmund on B2, near airport turn-off* ☎ *64/405–671* ⊕ *www.skydiveswakopmund.com.*

★ Tommy's Tours and Safaris
ADVENTURE TOURS | FAMILY | ✉ *Swakopmund* ☎ *81/128–1038 mobile/WhatsApp* ⊕ *www.livingdeserttours.com.na* ☞ *Includes drop off and pick up.*

Shopping

African Art Jewellers
JEWELRY & WATCHES | A cut above the rest, the original and African-inspired designs and materials used by this fine jeweler are worth checking out. ✉ *1 Hendrik Witbooi St., Swakopmund* ☎ *64/405–566* ⊗ *Closed Sun.*

Art Africa
CRAFTS | A lovely emporium of high-quality crafts and curios from all over Namibia, as well as other parts of Africa. Items include rural art, contemporary jewelry, ceramics, leather products, masks, baskets, and funky whimsical crafts. They ship worldwide. ✉ *Shop 6, The Arcade, Sam Nujome St., Swakopmund* ☎ *81/127–0931, 64/404–024* ✎ *tribal@artafrica.com.na.*

Die Muschel
BOOKS | This beautiful book and coffee shop in the center of Swakopmund, specializes in gorgeous coffee-table books of African landscapes, people, and animals, as well as a great selection of field guides, maps, and other books about Namibia and Southern Africa. It's a perfect spot to buy postcards and find a new book to read for the rest of your trip. ✉ *Brauhaus Arcade, Tobias Hainyeko St., Swakopmund* ☎ *64/402–874.*

Peter's Antiques
ANTIQUES & COLLECTIBLES | This store has been described as an antique store, a curio shop, and a museum. Whether you're looking for something to buy or not, it's worth a visit to meet and chat with the proprietor, who is very amiable and full of information about Namibia. ✉ *24 Tobias Hainyeko St., Swakopmund* ☎ *64/405–624* ⊕ *www.facebook.com/PetersAntiquesNamibia* ⊗ *Closed Sun.*

Walvis Bay

One of southern Africa's most important harbor towns, the once-industrial Walvis Bay has recently developed into a seaside holiday destination with a number of pleasant lagoon-front guesthouses and several good restaurants—including one of Namibia's best, Lyon des Sables. The majority of water activities advertised in Swakopmund actually depart from Walvis's small waterfront area, and there's an amazing flamingo colony residing in the Bay's 3,000-year-old lagoon.

WHEN TO GO
Like Swakopmund, Walvis Bay enjoys a mild climate. Although most of the local Christmas and Easter holidaymakers head to Swakops, the overflow can spill out here, so it can get crowded during these times.

GETTING HERE AND AROUND

About 15 km (9 miles) east of town, the Walvis Airport serves the region (including Swakopmund) and has direct flights to South Africa. The major car-rental companies are located at the airport. Thirty kilometers (18 miles) from Swakopmund, the drive takes about 40 minutes on the B2. The town itself lacks attractions, and most visitors will head straight to the Walvis Bay lagoon. Here you'll find the majority of accommodations; the waterfront, from where almost all activities (both sea- and land-based) depart; and a handful of restaurants. Most everything in the lagoon area is within walking distance.

SAFETY AND PRECAUTIONS

Be sure to turn your lights on when driving between Walvis and Swakopmund, even in the daytime. Locals say that the way light reflects between the dunes and the sea impairs depth perception.

TIMING

Most of Walvis's activities, including bird-watching, boat tours, and 4x4 day trips to Sandwich Harbour, depart relatively early. As such, spending the night before such an activity is certainly worthwhile. Given the new accommodations and restaurants in town, if time allows and you plan on participating in more than one activity, two nights wouldn't be wasted.

 Restaurants

Anchors @ The Jetty

$ | SEAFOOD | This popular quintessential seaside restaurant is under new management as of late 2021 and has received a facelift, plus a distinct Portuguese flavor to its new menu – worry not as their world-famous grilled or fried calamari is still available. This is the place to satisfy your appetite for seafood, with a decent selection of meat options, as well as a superb view. **Known for:** unrivaled grilled and fried calamari; postcard-type sunsets over the Atlantic Ocean; prompt and friendly service. $ *Average main: US$11* ✉ *Waterfront, Atlantic St., Walvis Bay* ☎ *81/269–8108 mobile, 64/205–762 landline* ⊕ *www.anchors-the-jetty-restaurant. business.site/* ✆ *Also accept US dollars and euros as a form of payment.*

★ Flamingo Villa Restaurant

$$$ | MEDITERRANEAN | The in-house restaurant at the Flamingo Villa Boutique Hotel, with a stunning view of the lagoon, is the best fine-dining establishment in Walvis Bay. With exceptional attention to detail and service, the menu combines flavors of Europe and the Mediterranean with Namibian ingredients. **Known for:** cocktails at sunset; local cuisine; seafood platter. $ *Average main: US$30* ✉ *30 Kavambo Nujoma Dr., Meersig, Walvis Bay* ☎ *64/205–631* ⊕ *www. flamingovillana.com.*

The Raft

$$ | SEAFOOD | The Raft enjoys a spectacular view from its perch out over beautiful Walvis Bay Lagoon. Divided into two parts—bar to the right, restaurant to the left—this warm and friendly establishment seems to be a favorite with locals. **Known for:** wooden, stilted restaurant with views over the lagoon; a good place to watch sports; melt-in-your mouth fresh linefish and fresh west coast oysters. $ *Average main: US$12* ✉ *The Esplanade, on the lagoon, Walvis Bay* ☎ *64/204–877* ⊕ *www.facebook.com/ theraftrestaurant.*

 Hotels

Flamingo Bay Boutique Hotel

$ | HOTEL | FAMILY | This hotel has one of the most spectacular views of the Walvis Bay Lagoon with its peaceful flamingos and idyllic sunsets. **Pros:** friendly service and personal attention all around; close proximity to the palm-lined promenade; offers an airport shuttle service. **Cons:** some of the decor is garish; breakfast could do with some more daily variety; doesn't feel authentically African. [$] *Rooms from: US$195* ✉ *30 Kovambo Nujoma Dr., Walvis Bay* ☎ *64/205–631* 🌐 *www.flamingovillana.com* 🛏 *27 suites* 🍴 *Free Breakfast.*

★ **Pelican Point Lodge**

$$ | **HOTEL** | Built from the old Lighthouse and Port Authority building, this completely unique lodge is as beautiful as it is stark. **Pros:** the dolphin cruise back to Walvis Bay is a highlight; incredible 360-degree view of the ocean; personal service. **Cons:** poor telephone reception, email instead; long and very bumpy ride to get out there (it is remote, after all); no electricity after 10 pm. [$] *Rooms from: US$360* ✉ *Pelican Point, Walvis Bay* ☎ *64/221–282, 81/800–9301 mobile* 🌐 *www.pelicanpointlodge.com* 🛏 *10 suites* 🍴 *Free Breakfast.*

Protea Hotel by Marriott Pelican Bay

$ | **HOTEL** | **FAMILY** | This centrally located establishment is right on the water's edge and along the palm-lined promenade, which means you can look out onto the Walvis Bay Lagoon from all of the rooms (but the junior suite) and the restaurant. **Pros:** prime location with lagoon-facing rooms that have wooden decks; family-friendly, with connecting rooms; safe and secure, complimentary parking. **Cons:** restaurant and bar are outside the main hotel building; might be busy with conferencing at times; rooms and bathrooms could do with a soft refurb. [$] *Rooms from: US$113* ✉ *Esplanade Park, Walvis Bay* ☎ *64/214–000 hotel, 61/209–0300 central reservations* 🌐 *www.protea.marriott.com* 🛏 *50 rooms* 🍴 *Free Breakfast.*

Activities

The most popular activities here are the seal and dolphin tours, fishing, kayaking, and day trips to Sandwich Harbour.

Catamaran Charters

BOAT TOURS | **FAMILY** | Catamaran Charters runs a seal and dolphin cruise on a 45-, 55- or 60-foot catamaran. The three-and-a half-hour cruise, which sets sail at 8:45 am, visits Pelican Point and the lighthouse, with guaranteed seal sightings along the way, and the chance to see Southern Right and Humpback whales (June to November), as you indulge in lunch onboard. Their selection of cruises can also cater for people with disabilities with prior notice. ✉ *Atlantic St., Unit A, Walvis Bay* ☎ *64/200–598, 81/129–5393 mobile* 🌐 *www.namibiancharters.com* 🎟 *US$62, includes lunch.*

Eco-Marine Kayak Tours

KAYAKING | **FAMILY** | If you want to peacefully paddle the calm waters of the Walvis Bay lagoon from Pelican Point, while enjoying the scenery and up-close encounters with marine and bird life, try Eco-Marine Kayak Tours. Their daily four-and-a-half-hour return trips depart at 7:45 and allow you to kayak for up to an hour and a half as you visit the permanent Cape Fur Seal colony. No previous experience is needed and this tour can also be combined with a Sandwich Harbour tour. ✉ *Walvis Bay Waterfront, Atlantic St., Walvis Bay* ✥ *just before the entrance to the Yacht Club* ☎ *81/293–144 mobile* 🌐 *www.ecomarinekayak.com* 🎟 *US$56.*

Sandwich Harbour 4x4

FOUR-WHEELING | **FAMILY** | Sandwich Harbour 4x4 runs an excellent half- or full-day trip to the dunes that includes a hearty lunch (snacks, oysters, drinks and sparkling wine). Expect to drive over the dunes as if they were a series of roller coasters. They also run bird-watching trips, shipwreck tours, and a diamond tour in a concession area in Luderitz, as well as combination trips (a boat trip and the dunes, or kayaking and the dunes). ⊠ *Waterfront, Atlantic St., Unit B, Walvis Bay* ☎ *81/147–3933* ⊕ *www. sandwich-harbour.com* ⊠ *half-day tours from US$123.*

Sun Sail Catamarans

WILDLIFE-WATCHING | FAMILY | Sun Sail Catamarans has daily departures at 8:15 am to Pelican Point. Sunset cruises can also be booked. During the three-hour cruise you'll likely see seals, dolphins, numerous marine birds (pelicans, flamingos, cormorants), and Humpback whales (in season: June to November) as well as mola mola (sun fish), particularly on sunny days. If you're really lucky you might also see penguins and turtles. Fresh oysters, sparkling wine, and snacks are served on board. Ask about their half- and full-day 4x4 tours of Sandwich Harbour. ⊠ *Walvis Bay Waterfront, Atlantic Street, Walvis Bay* ☎ *81/788–6800* ⊕ *www. sunsailnamibia.com* ⊠ *US$56.*

VICTORIA FALLS

Updated by
Christopher Clark

WELCOME TO VICTORIA FALLS

TOP REASONS TO GO

★ **World-Class Phenomenon:** Not only can you experience Victoria Falls and the Batoka Gorge from every angle—the sheer size of this wonder fosters the delightful illusion of exclusivity.

★ **The Adrenaline Rush:** Looking for an adventure to get your heart pounding? From bungee jumping to white-water rafting and skydiving, Victoria Falls truly has it all.

★ **Perfectly Indulgent Relaxation:** Massages are offered on the banks of the Zambezi River, sumptuous food is served wherever you turn, and there are few sights on earth that rival watching the spray of the Falls fade from rainbow to starlight while enjoying cocktails at the end of the day.

★ **Intact Africa:** The warm, rich heart of Africa is proudly showcased in a region governed by people who have lived here for centuries, adeptly utilizing the very latest in ecotourism and benefiting from environmentally conscious development.

Victoria Falls is in southern Africa and physically provides a natural border between Zambia and Zimbabwe. Each country has a national park that surrounds the Falls (Mosi-oa-Tunya National Park in Zambia and Victoria Falls National Park in Zimbabwe), as well as a town (Livingstone in Zambia and Victoria Falls in Zimbabwe) that serves as the respective tourist center for each country. The fissure currently framing the Falls stretches over a mile, roughly from northwest to southeast. Livingstone lies to the north and the town of Victoria Falls is immediately to the south of the Falls. The official border between the countries is within walking distance of the compact town of Victoria Falls but around 10 km (6 miles) from Livingstone. The stretch between the Falls border and town center on the Livingstone side should not be attempted on foot because of the dangers of wandering elephants, the African sun, and the occasional opportunistic thief.

1 **Livingstone, Zambia.** Named after the famous Dr. David Livingstone, the town, just 10 km (6 miles) north of the Falls, was established in 1900 and was once Zambia's capital city. Its main street, Mosi-oa-Tunya Road, still boasts examples of classic colonial (albeit occasionally ramshackle) buildings. In past years, the much-publicized political unrest in Zimbabwe has often caused tourists to choose Livingstone rather than the quieter town of Victoria Falls on the Zimbabwean side as a base for exploration of the area.

2 **Victoria Falls, Zimbabwe.** The town of Victoria Falls hugs the Zimbabwean side of the Falls on the Zambezi's southwestern bank. The view of the Falls and the gorge is spectacular from Zimbabwe. At one time, the town was the principal tourist destination for the area. It continues to be perfectly safe, more relaxed than Livingstone, and cheaper, and the general atmosphere has greatly improved in recent years despite the political and economic travails that continue to afflict much of the rest of the country.

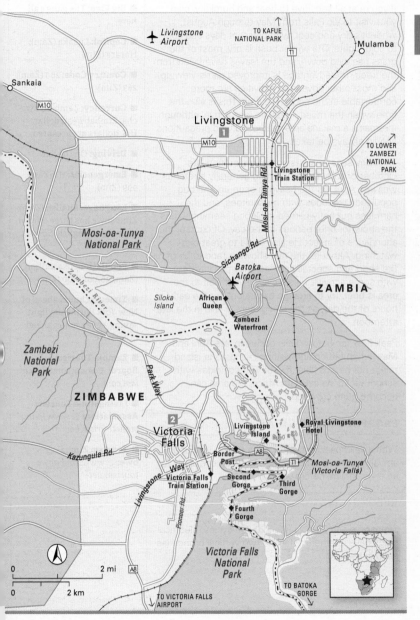

COUNTRY SNAPSHOT

WHEN TO GO

If you're at all sensitive to heat and humidity, plan your visit to Vic Falls from May through August, when it's dry and cool, with pleasant days and cool to cold nights. The winter bush is dry, most of the grass has died down, and the leaves have fallen from the trees. The advantage is improved game-viewing, and most other adventure activities are more comfortable in the cooler weather. This is also the time when the mosquitoes are less active, although it remains a malaria area year-round, and precautions should always be taken.

The rainy season starts sometime around late October or early November and generally stretches well into April. As the heavens open up, the bug population explodes with mosquitoes, and the harmless but aptly named stink bug seemingly runs the show for brief periods of the day. Of course, the abundance of insect life also leads to great bird-watching. Although the rain showers tend to be of the short and spectacular kind, they can interfere with some activities, especially if your visit to the area is brief. Try to arrange excursions for the early hours of the day, as the rain generally falls in the late afternoon.

Peak flow for Victoria Falls occurs in late April and May, when rafting and visiting Livingstone Island might not be possible. If your visit coincides with school vacations in South Africa, the area can become quite crowded.

PASSPORTS AND VISAS

With a valid passport, you'll get a 90-day visa upon arrival to Zambia and Zimbabwe, or you can apply for an e-visa online before you travel.

ELECTRICITY

Zimbabwe and Zambia use 220v/50 cycles; electrical plugs have one horizontal and two vertical prongs (as used in the UK).

AT A GLANCE

■ **Big Five:** The gang's all here.

■ **Capital:** Lusaka (Zam); Harare (Zim)

■ **Country Code:** 260 (Zam); 263 (Zim)

■ **Currency:** Zambian kwacha; Zimbabwean dollar. U.S. dollars are accepted.

■ **Driving:** On the left

■ **Emergencies:** 112 (Zam); 999 (Zim)

■ **Language:** English (Zam); Zimbabwe has three official languages: English, Shona, and Ndebele.

■ **Population:** 18.4 million (Zam); 15.1 million (Zim)

■ **Time:** Six hours ahead of New York during daylight saving, seven hours ahead otherwise.

■ **Zambia Tourism Board:** ⊕ www.zambiatourism.com

■ **Livingstone Tourism Association:** ⊕ www.livingstonetourism.com

■ **Tourism Zimbabwe:** ⊕ www.zimbabwetourism.net

Roughly 1,207 km (750 miles) from its humble origins as an insignificant spring in northern Zambia, the Zambezi River grows to more than a mile wide. Without much warning the river bends south, the current speeds up, and the entire mass of water disappears into a single fissure. More than 1 million gallons of water rush over a vertical, 328-foot-high drop in the time it takes an average reader to reach the end of this paragraph. The resulting spray is astounding, the brute force forming a cloud of mist visible 64 km (40 miles) away on a clear day.

The settlements of Livingstone in Zambia and Victoria Falls in Zimbabwe both owe their existence to the Zambezi and the Falls. Though they're located in different countries and intriguingly diverse in character, they function almost like two sides of one town. Crossing the border is a formality that generally happens with minimum fuss. Zambia spoils guests with an overabundance of top-class safari lodges along the Zambezi, and this strong competition has resulted in an emphasis on personalized service, which enables you to tailor your visit. Livingstone is determined to remain the favored destination.

On the Zimbabwean side, the town of Victoria Falls has generally escaped the worst of the bouts of political turmoil that continue to afflict the rest of the country, but not entirely the reputational damage. However, the relative absence of large numbers of travelers is a luxury in itself, and this area currently provides good value for money. It also remains perfectly safe for tourists, though it's still always advisable to check the security situation before you travel, particularly around elections.

The region as a whole deserves its reputation as an adventure center and offers adrenaline-inducing activities by the bucketful. The backdrop for any of these is stunning, and the safety record nothing less than spectacular.

Livingstone, Zambia

This marvelous old town, once the government capital of Northern Rhodesia (now Zambia), boasts a wealth of natural beauty and a surplus of activities. After decades of neglect, it's more recently recast itself as Zambia's tourism and adventure capital.

There's a tangible whiff of the past here: historic buildings outnumber new ones, and many local inhabitants live a life not that dissimilar to the one they would have experienced 50 years ago. Livingstone handles the surge of tourists with equal parts grace, confidence, banter, and annoyance.

Many visitors to this side of the Falls opt to stay in one of the secluded safari-style lodges on the Zambezi River. The Zambian experience sprawls out along the many bends of the large river and time ticks by in a very deliberate African manner.

GETTING HERE AND AROUND

If you plan to add the popular Kafue and Lower Zambezi camps to your trip, you should book your transfers together with your accommodations through a travel agent or with your camp reservations, as air-transfer companies change hands and/or minds quite often in Zambia. A travel agent or camp will also assure that connection times work to your best advantage if they're responsible for the transfers.

AIR

Lusaka is Zambia's main entry point for international arrivals. Flights from a handful of African destinations land at Harry Mwanga Nkumbula International Airport (LVI), which is 5 km (3 miles) out of Livingstone. The airport is small and friendly, with helpful staff to speed you on your way.

Airlink regularly flies from Johannesburg. The flight is a comfortable hop, less than two hours in duration.

■ TIP → **If at all possible, don't check your luggage in Johannesburg and always lock suitcases securely, as luggage theft in South Africa is an everyday occurrence.**

AIRLINES South African Airways.
☎ *0213/323–031* ⊕ *www.flysaa.com.* **Proflight Zambia.** ☎ *0977/335–563* ⊕ *www.proflight-zambia.com.* **Airlink.** ☎ *11/451–7300* ⊕ *www.flyairlink.com.*

AIRPORTS Harry Mwanga Nkumbula International Airport. (*LVI*) ✉ *Livingstone* ⊕ *www.zacl.co.zm/airport-section/ airports/hmnia.*

BUS

Zambia is well connected by bus, and there are nine Lusaka-to-Livingstone routes that leave every half hour from 6 am.

CAR

There's a perfectly reasonable traffic code in Zambia. Unfortunately, not many people have ever heard of it. Unless you're an experienced self-drive safari-goer, you would do well to leave the driving to your local guides or negotiate an all-inclusive rate with a taxi driver recommended by your hotel or lodge for the duration of your stay. Note that taxis are generally not allowed to cross the border, so if you want to visit Zimbabwe, you'll have to book a tour that includes transfers. Once at the border, it's feasible to walk into and around Victoria Falls town or rent a bicycle.

If you insist on renting a car, you should know that some of the roads have more potholes than tar. You don't necessarily need a 4x4, but it's not a bad idea, especially if you want to go off-road at all. Voyagers has two offices in Livingstone: Mosi-oa-Tunya Road (opposite Ngolide Lodge) and Livingstone Airport. Hemingway's rents out Toyota Hilux Double Cabs (similar to the Toyota Tacoma), fully equipped with tents and other camping equipment—you can even hire a driver! Costs start from about US$220 per day for a fully equipped vehicle.

CAR RENTALS Hemingway's. ☎ *0213/323–097, 0977/866–492* ⊕ *www.hemingwayszambia.com.* **Voyagers.** ☎ *0213/32–3259* ⊕ *www.voyagerszambia.com.*

TRAIN
Zambia Railways operates slow but reliable services between Livingstone and Lusaka. There's also a train service that runs from Kapiri Mposh, North of Lusaka, to Dar es Salaam in Tanzania.

CONTACTS Zambia Railways. ☎ *215/227–000* ⊕ *zrl.com.zm.*

COMMUNICATIONS
Telephone rates in Zambia are much cheaper and more stable than those in Zimbabwe. Check numbers very carefully, as some are Zimbabwean mobile phones. Zambian towns and cities generally have good cell coverage, but some of the remote lodges may not. If you have any trouble dialing a number, check with a hotel or restaurant owner, who should be able to advise you of the best and cheapest alternative. International roaming on your standard mobile phone is also an option, as coverage is quite extensive. Alternatively, you could purchase a local SIM card with pay-as-you-go fill-ups and data bundles—this is probably your cheapest option. Pay phones aren't an option, and the costs of all telephone calls out of the country can be exorbitant.

The country code for Zambia is 260. When dialing from abroad, drop the initial 0 from local area codes and cell-phone numbers. Note that all telephone numbers are listed as they're dialed from the country that they're in. Although the number for operator assistance is 100, you'll be much better off asking your local lodge or restaurant manager for help.

Most of the major lodges, hotels and backpacker places in and around Livingstone have reasonably fast free Wi-Fi. There are also a few cheap internet cafes in town. But as with cell service, Wi-Fi is less consistently available, or can be much slower when it is, in more remote lodges and camps.

HEALTH AND SAFETY
For minor injuries, a test for malaria, or the treatment of non-life-threatening ailments, you can go to the Rainbow Trust's Mwenda Medical Centre, Southern Medical Centre, or Dr. Shafik Hospital. For serious emergencies, contact SES (Specialty Emergency Services). There are a number of pharmacies in town including Health and Glow Pharmacy, Link Pharmacy, and HK Pharmacy. Pharmacies are generally open weekdays 8–8, Saturday 8–6, and Sunday 8–1.

Wild animals abound throughout this area (even in the center of town from time to time) and must be given a lot of physical space and respect. You must also remember that Zambia is relatively poor. There are tourism police, but opportunistic thieving still happens occasionally. Although crime in this area is generally nonviolent, losing your money, belongings, or passport will result in spending the remainder of your trip with various officials in stuffy, badly decorated offices instead of sitting back on the deck of your sunset cruise with drink in hand.

As for the water, it's always advisable to drink bottled water, although the tap water in Zambia is generally considered safe. Should you develop any stomach upset, be sure to contact a physician, especially if you're running a fever, in order to rule out malaria or a communicable disease. Do remember to mention your visit to a malaria area to your doctor in the event of illness within a year of leaving Africa.

Both sides of Victoria Falls are an epicenter of extreme adventures like white-water rafting on rapids rated between Class I and Class V.

EMBASSIES U.S. Embassy. ✉ *Ibex Hill. (eastern end of Kabulonga Rd.), Lusaka* ☎ *0211/357-000* ⊕ *www.zm.usembassy. gov.*

EMERGENCIES Fire. ☎ *993.* **General emergencies.** ☎ *999, 112 from mobile phones.* **Police.** ☎ *991.* **SES Emergency Medical Assistance.** ☎ *737 in Zambia* ⊕ *www. ses-zambia.com.*

HOSPITALS Rainbow Trust Mwenda Medical Centre. ✉ *Lusaka Rd., about 1 mile from center of Livingstone, Livingstone* ☎ *0213/323–519.* **Dr. Shafik Hospital.** ✉ *Katete Rd., Livingstone* ☎ *0213/321–130.* **Southern Medical Centre.** ✉ *House 9, 1967 Mokambo Rd., Livingstone* ☎ *0213/323–547.*

HOTELS
It's advisable to make both flight and lodge reservations ahead of time. Lodges tend to have all-inclusive packages; hotels generally include breakfast only.

All hotels and lodges quote in U.S. dollars but accept payment in other major currencies at unfriendly exchange rates. It might be best to take an all-inclusive package tour because meals can be exorbitantly expensive. A 10% service charge is either included or added to the bill (as is the value-added tax) in both countries, which frees you to include an extra tip only for exceptional service. Although air-conditioning can be expected in the hotels, lodges tend to have fans.

■ **TIP→ Travel with a sarong (locally available as a chitenge), which you can wet and wrap around your body, guaranteeing a cooler siesta.**

Restaurant and hotel reviews have been shortened. For full information, visit Fodors.com.

What It Costs in U.S. Dollars

	$	$$	$$$	$$$$
RESTAURANTS				
	under $12	$12–$20	$21–$30	over $30
HOTELS				
	under $250	$250–$450	$451–$600	over $600

RESTAURANTS

Game meat is something of a delicacy in Zambia, but superior free-range beef and chicken are available everywhere. The local bream, filleted or whole, is excellent, and the staple starch, a thick porridge similar to polenta—*nshima*—is worth a try; use your fingers to eat it (you'll be given a bowl for washing afterward). Adventurous? Try *macimbi* or *vinkuvala* (sun-dried mopane worms) or *inswa* (flash-fried flying ants) during the flood season.

Meals are taken at regular hours, but during the week, restaurants close around 10. Dress is generally casual, but this part of Africa easily lends itself to a little bling, so you'll never be out of place in something more glamorous.

MONEY

In recent years, the Zambian government has tried to curb the use of U.S. dollars. By law, all payments made within the country are now supposed to be made in Zambian *kwacha (ZMW)*, although many larger establishments will still accept dollars. The kwacha comes in denominations of ZMW2, ZMW5, ZMW10, ZMW20, ZMW50, and ZMW100 bills. Coins start at 5 *ngwee* (the local equivalent of cents) and work up to ZMW1. At the time of this writing, the conversion rate was about ZMW17 to US$1.

Tipping is less common in Zambia because service charges are included, but it's appreciated. Small notes or 10% is appropriate. Gas-station attendants can be tipped, but tip a taxi driver only on the last day if you've used the same driver for a number of days.

Zambia has a 17.5% V.A.T. and a 10% service charge, which is included in the cost or itemized on your bill. International banks along Mosi-oa-Tunya Road in Livingstone have ATMs and exchange services. Banking hours are generally weekdays 8–2 (although some do open the last Saturday of the month). Many bank ATMs accept only Visa. It's also worth noting that queues for ATMs can get very long during working hours.

■ TIP→ **You may be invited to do a little informal foreign exchange by persuasive street financiers. Resist the temptation—it's not worth the risk of being ripped off or arrested.**

There are many reputable exchange bureaus throughout town, though they're sometimes flooded with dollars and low on kwacha, generally toward the end of the month. MasterCard and Visa are preferred by business owners and banks to American Express or Diners Club. Business owners always prefer cash to credit cards, and some smaller hotels levy fees up to 10% to use a credit card.

PASSPORTS AND VISAS

You'll need a valid passport and visa to enter Zambia. Nationals of any country not on the Zambian Immigration Referred Visa list can simply purchase a visa on entering the country or apply for an e-visa online before travelling. At this writing, a standard U.S. single-entry visa costs US$50. A transit visa costs the same, as does the so-called KAZA visa for those planning to do both the Zambian and Zimbabwean sides of the Falls. Day-trip visas cost US$20 (often included in the cost of pre-booked activities, so check with your booking agent). If you plan to return to Zambia in the near future, you'll need a multiple-entry visa, or you'll have to buy another visa on your return. Multiple-entry visas and visas for nationals from countries on the referred visa list can be purchased only at Zambian Missions abroad and not on arrival.

VISITOR INFORMATION

Although the Zambia National Tourist Board (next to the museum; open weekdays 8–1 and 2–5, Saturday 8–noon) is very helpful and friendly, you might be better off visiting Jollyboys (behind the Livingstone Museum; open daily 7 am–10 pm) for comprehensive and unbiased advice.

CONTACTS

VISITOR INFORMATION Jollyboys. ✉ 34 Kanyanta Rd., Livingstone ☎ 0213/324–229 ⊕ www.backpackzambia.com. **Zambia National Tourist Board.** ✉ Tourist Centre, Mosi-Oa-Tunya Rd., Livingstone ☎ 0213/321–404 ⊕ www.zambiatourism.com.

WHEN TO GO

High Season: If you're at all sensitive to heat and humidity, visit from May through August, when it is dry and cool, with pleasant days and cool to cold nights. Although the bush can resemble a wasteland, with short brown stubble and bare trees, it does improve game-viewing, and most other adventure activities are more comfortable in the cooler weather.

Low Season: Known locally as the Emerald Season, Zambia's off-season runs from November to March. This is the rainiest time of year, and when the bush is at its lushest. That said, heavy rains often result in road closures, and many safari camps close down for the season.

Value Season: Camps start to open in April, and while there may still be some rain, it's nowhere nearly as heavy as during the summer months. It's usually pretty dry by the end of April and this is a great time to visit if you want to beat the crowds. At the tail end of the tourist season, September offers beautiful, dry days.

Chobe: A Great Day Trip 👁

If it's serious game-viewing you desire, join a one-day excursion to Chobe National Park in Botswana. A trip will cost you about US$200 and usually includes transfers from Livingstone, a morning boat cruise, lunch with a drink, and an afternoon game drive. Reservations must be in writing and prepaid for both.

To make reservations, see Bushtracks, in Activities, for more information.

FESTIVALS AND EVENTS

July: Dance, music, and ritual mark the Mutomboko, an annual ceremony in honor of the victories of Mwata Kazembe, chief of the Luba-Lunda people.

August: Every year, the Bwile people of Lake Mweru host swimming, fishing, and paddling competitions to mark Ubuilile, a celebration of human resilience.

September–October: Live music and films from across Africa are the focus of the eight-day Lusaka International Film and Music Festival. ⊕ www.lifmf.com

September–November: Every spring, the Ba-ila people give thanks and usher in the new year during the three-day Shimunenga Ceremony.

WAYS TO SAVE

Eat like a local. Instead of dining in restaurants aimed at tourists, try out the staple diet of nshima and relish (usually meat, fish, or vegetables).

Stay in B&Bs. Bed-and-breakfasts are an affordable alternative to luxury lodges and offer a more immersive cultural experience.

The thundering roar of Victoria Falls and its many rainbows leave many visitors speechless.

Take local buses. The cheapest way to get around the country is by local bus. The trade-off is that the ride is generally not that comfortable.

Make your own safaris. Some national parks allow self-driving tours, and if you go without a guide you can save a fair bit of cash.

PLAN YOUR TIME
HASSLE FACTOR
High. Getting to Zambia can take upwards of 40 hours, and many routes from North America require multiple stopovers in Europe and Africa.

3 DAYS
With three days in Zambia, it's best to stick to Livingstone, the gateway to Victoria Falls, perhaps devoting one of your days to a side trip to Chobe National Park in neighboring Botswana or the Zimbabwean side of the Falls.

1 WEEK
A week is about enough time to visit Victoria Falls and spend a few days on safari in Kafue National Park or Lower Zambezi National Park.

2 WEEKS
With two weeks in Zambia, you can visit Victoria Falls, spend some time in Lusaka experiencing the capital's culture, and still have time left over for a safari in Kafue National Park or Lower Zambezi National Park.

Sights

Batoka Gorge
NATURE SIGHT | FAMILY | Just below the Falls, the gorge forms an abyss between the countries with edges that drop away from the cliffs of both Zambia and Zimbabwe. Each successive sandstone gorge is numbered in sequence starting from the youngest (First Gorge to the Fifth Gorge), followed by Songwe Gorge and finally the official Batoka Gorge; it is common for all these gorges to be referred

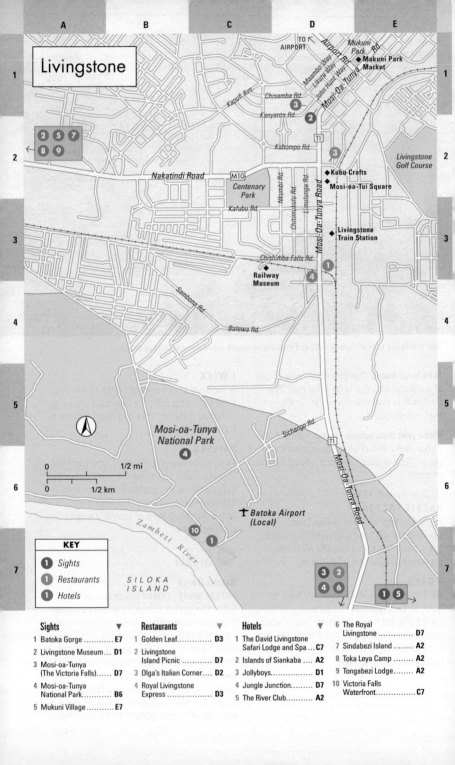

Livingstone

Sights ▼

1 Batoka Gorge **E7**
2 Livingstone Museum ... **D1**
3 Mosi-oa-Tunya
  (The Victoria Falls) ... **D7**
4 Mosi-oa-Tunya
  National Park **B6**
5 Mukuni Village **E7**

Restaurants ▼

1 Golden Leaf **D3**
2 Livingstone
  Island Picnic **D7**
3 Olga's Italian Corner **D2**
4 Royal Livingstone
  Express **D3**

Hotels ▼

1 The David Livingstone
  Safari Lodge and Spa ... **C7**
2 Islands of Siankaba **A2**
3 Jollyboys **D1**
4 Jungle Junction **D7**
5 The River Club **A2**
6 The Royal
  Livingstone **D7**
7 Sindabezi Island **A2**
8 Toka Leya Camp **A2**
9 Tongabezi Lodge **A2**
10 Victoria Falls
  Waterfront **C7**

KEY

- ❶ Sights
- ❶ Restaurants
- ❶ Hotels

to collectively as The Gorge or Batoka Gorge. Batoka Gorge is more than 120 km (75 miles) long with vertical walls that are an average of 400 feet high (the Zambezi river water levels fluctuates up to 65 feet between the wet and dry season). On the Zambian side, the gorge is surrounded by the Mosi-oa-Tunya National Park, which contains a tropical rain forest that thrives on the eternal rainfall from the Falls. Victoria Falls National Park in Zimbabwe surrounds the other side of the gorge. Operators from both countries offer excursions to what is reputed to be the world's best one-day white-water rafting, with rapids rated between Class I and Class VI (amateurs can do only Class V and down commercially) that have been given evocative nicknames like "The Ugly Sisters" and "Oblivion." If you're "lucky" enough to experience what locals call a "long swim" (falling out of the raft at the start of a rapid and body surfing through), your definition of the word *scary* will surely be redefined. The walk in and out of the gorge is quite strenuous on the Zimbabwe side, but as long as you are reasonably fit and looking for adventure, you need no experience. On the Zambian side, travelers can walk down into the Boiling Pot (the first bend of the river after the Falls) in the First Gorge. It's an easy walk down and slightly more challenging walk out of the gorge (lots of steps), but even young children enjoy it—be sure to carry extra sun protection and water. ✉ *Livingstone.*

Livingstone Museum

HISTORY MUSEUM | FAMILY | The country's oldest and largest museum contains history, ethnography, natural history, archaeology sections, and materials ranging from newspaper clippings to photographs of Queen Elizabeth II dancing with Kenneth Kaunda (Zambia's first president) to historical information dating back to 1500. Among the priceless David Livingstone memorabilia is a model of the mangled arm bone used to identify his body and various journals and maps

from the period when he explored the area and claimed the Falls for the English queen. ✉ *Mosi-oa-Tunya Rd., between civic center and post office, Livingstone* ☎ *0213/324–429* ✉ *USD$5.*

★ Mosi-oa-Tunya (The Victoria Falls)

NATURE SIGHT | FAMILY | Literally translated as "the Smoke that Thunders," the Falls more than lives up to its reputation as one of the world's greatest natural wonders. Words can never do these incredible Falls justice, and it's a difficult attraction to fully appreciate in a single visit, as it's constantly changing. The Zimbabwean side offers famously panoramic views, while the Zambian side of the Falls features the Knife Edge bridge, which allows guests to stand virtually suspended over the Boiling Pot (the first bend of the river after the Falls), with the deafening water crashing everywhere around you. From around May through August the Falls are a multi-sensory experience, and there may be too much spray to see the bottom of the gorge. In high season the entire experience can be summed up in two words: power shower! Prepare to get soaked. If you stand with your back to the sun, you'll be surrounded by a symphony of rainbows. A network of paths leads to the main viewing points; some are not well protected, so watch your step and wear sensible shoes, especially at high water. You will have dramatic views of the full 1½ km (1 mile) of the ironstone face of the Falls, the Boiling Pot directly below, the railway bridge, and Batoka Gorge. During low water levels, it's possible to take a guided walk to Livingstone Island and swim in the Devil's Pool, a natural pond right on the lip of the abyss. ✉ *Mosi-oa-Tunya Rd., just before border post, Livingstone* ☎ ✉ *USD$10.*

Mosi-oa-Tunya National Park

NATIONAL PARK | FAMILY | This park is a quick and easy option for viewing plains game. In fact, you are almost guaranteed to spy white rhinos. You can also visit the

At the edge of Victoria Falls, the naturally formed Devils Pool promises an amazing experience (and awesome photos) for thrill seekers.

Old Drift graveyard, as the park marks the location of the original settlement of Livingstone. The park's guides are very knowledgeable, and while you're free to explore on your own, the roads do get seriously muddy in the rainy season, and a guide who knows where to drive becomes a near-necessity. ■TIP→ It's best to find out about park entry details from your accommodations or a local tour operator, as park management can be less than helpful. ☒ Sichanga Rd., off Mosi-oa-Tunya Rd., 3½ km (2 miles) from Livingstone, Livingstone ☒ US$10 per person per day and US$15 per vehicle per day.

Mukuni Village

OTHER ATTRACTION | FAMILY | Fascinated by the history, customs, and traditions of the area? Local guides can escort you on an intimate visit inside a house and explain the customs of the village. This is not a stage set but a very real village, so your tour will be different depending on the time of day. It is customary to sign in the visitors' book and to pay a small fee

to your guide. Many of the lodges and camps outside of town also offer a similar experience in conjunction with other local villages. ☒ Livingstone.

🍴 Restaurants

Golden Leaf

$$ | INDIAN | The Moghuls themselves might declare a meal here a feast. Spicy but not hot, the curries are lovingly prepared from ingredients imported from India. **Known for:** good variety of curries; great service; authentic ambience and food. $ Average main: $18 ☒ 110 Mosi-oa-Tunya Rd., Livingstone ✢ Opposite Ravine Lodge ☎ 0213/321–266 ⏰ No dinner Mon.

★ Livingstone Island Picnic

$$$$ | ECLECTIC | FAMILY | Available throughout the year whenever the water levels are low enough, this is a spectacular dining option. Livingstone Island is perched right on the edge of the void, where you'll dine at a table dressed with linen

Continued on page 497

The first European to set eyes on the Falls was the explorer and missionary Dr. David Livingstone in the mid-1850s. Overcome by the experience he named them after the English queen, Victoria.

VICTORIA FALLS

Expect to be humbled by the sheer power and majesty. Expect to be deafened by the thunderous noise, drenched by spray, and overwhelmed at the sight. Expect the mighty swath of roaring, foaming Victoria Falls—spanning the entire 1-mile width of the Zambezi River—to leave you speechless.

On a clear day the spray generated by the Falls is visible from 31 miles (50 km) away—the swirling mist rising above the woodland savanna looks like smoke from a bush fire inspiring their local name, Mosi-Oa-Tunya, or the "Smoke that Thunders." The rim of the Falls is broken into separate smaller falls with names like the Devil's Cataract, Rainbow Falls, Horseshoe Falls, and Armchair Falls.

The Falls, which are more than 300 feet high, are one of the world's seven natural wonders and were named a UNESCO World Heritage Site in 1989. Upon seeing Victoria Falls for the first time Dr. David Livingstone proclaimed, "Scenes so lovely must have been gazed upon by angels in their flight." Truer words were never spoken.

FALLS FACTS

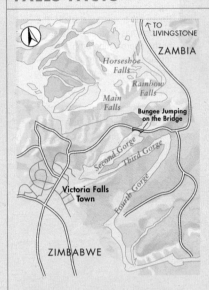

Map labels:
TO LIVINGSTONE
ZAMBIA
Horseshoe Falls
Rainbow Falls
Main Falls
Bungee Jumping on the Bridge
Second Gorge
Third Gorge
Fourth Gorge
Victoria Falls Town
ZIMBABWE

FORMATION OF THE FALLS

A basaltic plateau once stood where the Falls are today. The whole area was once completely submerged, but fast-forward to the Jurassic Age and the water eventually dried up. Only the Zambezi River remained flowing down into the gaping 1-mile-long continuous gorge that was formed by the uneven cracking of the drying plateau. The river charges through the ancient gorges creating some of the world's best commercial white water rapids.

WHEN TO GO

The Falls are spectacular at any time, but if you want to see them full, visit during the high water season (April–June) when more than 2 million gallons hurtle over the edge every second. The resulting spray is so dense that, at times, the view can be obscured. Don't worry though, the frequent gusts of wind will soon come to your aid and your view will be restored. If you're lucky to be there during a full moon, you might be able to catch a moonbow or lunar rainbow (a nighttime version of a rainbow) in the spray. The rest of the year offers its own charms with dry season–only activities like visiting Livingstone's Island, swimming in the Devil's Pool, and walking along the bottom of the Falls.

TO ZIM OR TO ZAM

Honestly? *Both* sides are great, but if you have to choose one, take the following into consideration: The Zambian side has more than four times the physical Falls frontage of Zimbabwe, but you're mostly looking across the gorge which means that Zimbabwe offers four times the visual display. Zimbabwe definitely has the most spray, the most rainbows, the best flat stone pathways for easy access, and the only views of the incredible Devil's Cataract. Rain forests with exotic flowers can be enjoyed on the Zimbabwe side year round and on the Zambian side during high water. Adventure seekers will love the Zam side's steep steps, the trail into the Boiling Pot, the slick Knife Edge bridge, and, during low water season visits to Livingstone Island, swimming in the Devil's Pool.

CROSSING THE FALLS

Built in 1905, Victoria Falls Bridge is one of the few useful remnants of the Colonial era. An important link in former South African Prime Minister Cecil John Rhodes's dream of creating the Cape-to-Cairo railway—it was never finished—the bridge continues to provide a convenient link between Zimbabwe and Zambia. It also offers a knockout view of the Falls and the Zambezi River raging through the Gorge, plus the added bonus of watching adrenaline junkies taking the 364-foot bungee plunge.

and gleaming silver on a delicious organic lunch (with salads) served by attentive waiters. **Known for:** unique, spectacular location; delectable sweets; unparalleled proximity to the Falls. $ *Average main: $155* ⊠ *Livingstone Island, Livingstone* ☎ *0979/312–766* ⊕ *www.livingstoneisland.com* ⊗ *Closed a couple of months around Feb.–June, depending on water levels. No dinner.*

Olga's Italian Corner

$ | **ITALIAN** | **FAMILY** | This restaurant delivers a double whammy. Not only does it serve genuine house-made Italian food prepared from fresh local ingredients, it's also part of an NGO project that trains and benefits the local youth. **Known for:** probably the best pizza in Zambia; good value for money; its strong social conscience. $ *Average main: $10* ⊠ *20 Mokambo Rd., Livingstone* ☎ *0213/324–160* ⊕ *www.olgasproject.com* ▭ *No credit cards.*

★ Royal Livingstone Express

$$$$ | **SOUTH AFRICAN** | Walking the stretch of red carpet alongside Locomotive 156 while it blows steam and rumbles in preparation for its journey is an ultimately exciting and romantic Vic Falls experience with a beautifully presented and meticulously prepared gourmet dinner. Dinner guests are seated in either the Wembley or Chesterfield dining carriage (both exquisitely restored). **Known for:** stellar romantic sunsets; delectable menu; unashamedly decadent decor. $ *Average main: $199* ⊠ *Km 0 of the Mulobezi line on Mosi-oa-Tunya Rd., Livingstone* ☎ *213/323–232* ⊕ *www.bushtracksafrica. com/signature-royal-livingstone-express* ⊗ *Closed Mon. and Tues.* 🏚 *Smart casual. No shorts allowed.*

 Hotels

The David Livingstone Safari Lodge and Spa

$$ | **RESORT** | Rooms at this luxury waterfront lodge, which is set within Mosi-oa-Tunya National Park, have their own

---

What to Eat

Nshima: a type of thick cornmeal porridge and the region's staple starch

Ifisashi: peanut stew with greens and cabbage

Munkoyo: a fermented beverage made of munkoyo root and cornmeal

Finkubala: a type of caterpillar, eaten as a meat relish with nshima

Kapenta: dried fish stewed in tomato sauce

Binch Akara: fritters made from black-eyed peas

---

private views of the Zambezi and feature a tasteful blend of teak furnishings, big four-poster beds, and ornate standalone bathtubs. **Pros:** an excellent Afro-Arabian fusion food menu; very easy access to the Zambian side of the Falls; extensive spa offerings. **Cons:** with 77 rooms, it doesn't have the exclusivity factor of some other lodges; it's child-friendly, so not always the quietest spot; this section of the river can become quite congested with boats at sunset. $ *Rooms from: $360* ⊠ *Riverside Dr., off Sichango Rd., Livingstone* ☎ *021/332–4601* ⊕ *www. aha.co.za/david-livingstone* ⤶ *77 rooms* ❑ *Free Breakfast.*

Islands of Siankaba

$$$$ | **RESORT** | The lodge, located on two beautiful forested islands in the Zambezi River about 48 km (30 miles) upstream from Victoria Falls, was awarded the Environmental Certificate by the Environmental Council of Zambia in 2002. **Pros:** beautifully secluded location; unique activity options; easy access to Chobe National Park just across the border into Botswana. **Cons:** not for those on a tight budget; bugs galore in

Overlooking the Zambezi River, the Tongabezi Lodge is a classic safari experience.

the rainier months; 40-minute transfer from Livingstone. $ *Rooms from: $1,360* ✉ *Livingstone* ✥ *40 km (25 miles) from Livingstone along Nakatindi Rd. on the Zambezi* ☎ *0213/327–490* ⊕ *www.siankaba.net* ⤳ *7 suites* ⦿ *All-Inclusive.*

Jollyboys
$ | **B&B/INN** | The entire design of this small establishment is user-friendly, inviting, and certainly aimed at both private relaxation and easy interaction with other travelers. **Pros:** very central location; free daily transfers to the Falls; social atmosphere. **Cons:** not for those looking for tranquil accommodations surrounded by nature; can get a bit rowdy; the lodge and camp are for backpackers, so are pretty basic. $ *Rooms from: $50* ✉ *34 Kanyanta Rd., Livingstone* ☎ *0213/324–229* ⊕ *www.backpackzambia.com* ⊟ *No credit cards* ⤳ *32 rooms* ⦿ *No Meals.*

Jungle Junction
$ | **B&B/INN** | **FAMILY** | The vibe of California and Marrakesh in the '60s and '70s is alive and well at this collection of thatch huts and campsites along the banks of

the Zambezi, 52 km (32 miles) upstream of the Falls. **Pros:** good value for money; a great way to combine an educational canoe trip with a basic overnight camp; the perfect balance between comfort and a real commune with nature. **Cons:** meals, fishing, and transfers are charged separately; guests have to bring their own towels; this might be too basic for travelers who like their little luxuries. $ *Rooms from: $50* ✉ *Livingstone* ✥ *52 km (32 miles) upstream from Victoria Falls, on Zambezi River* ☎ *097/872–5282* ⊕ *www.junglejunction.info* ⊟ *No credit cards* ⤳ *8 huts* ⦿ *No Meals.*

The River Club
$$$$ | **HOTEL** | With split-level rooms that cling to the edge of the great Zambezi, The River Club puts a modern spin on a Victorian house party. **Pros:** beautiful location with stunning views of the Zambezi; a/c and enclosed rooms are pluses for those who don't want to give up too many modern conveniences; excellent service. **Cons:** 20-minute drive from town for any activities that are not

Naming the Falls

Dr. David Livingstone, a Scottish medical doctor and missionary, visited Victoria Falls in 1855 and is widely credited with being the first European to document the existence of this natural wonder. He named it Victoria Falls in honor of his queen, although the Makololo name, Mosi-oa-Tunya (literally, "the Smoke that Thunders"), remains popular. Livingstone fell madly in love with the Falls, describing them in poignant prose. Other explorers had slightly different opinions. E. Holub could not contain his excitement and spoke effusively of "a thrilling throb of nature," A. A. de Serpa Pinto called them "sublimely horrible" in 1881, and L. Decle (1898) declared ominously that he expected "to see some repulsive monster rising in anger" at any moment. The modern traveler has the luxury of exploring every one (or all) of these perspectives. There's so much to do around the Falls that the only limitations will be your budget and sense of adventure or lack thereof.

run in-house; food not quite up to the standard of some other top lodges in the area; colonial decor may not be Zambian enough for some travelers. ⓢ *Rooms from: $1,070* ✉ *Livingstone* ✛ *About 18 km (11 miles) upstream from Victoria Falls town, on Zambezi River, down same road as Tongabezi* ☎ *0211/391-051* ⊕ *www.theriverclubafrica.com* ⇱ *11 rooms* ⎢⊙⎢ *Free Breakfast.*

The Royal Livingstone

$$$ | **HOTEL** | This high-volume, high-end hotel has an incredibly gorgeous sundowner deck, arguably on the best spot on the river, just upstream from the Falls. **Pros:** location, location, location; the level of service here is definitely that of a five-star international hotel; there is direct access to the Falls via a resort gate that opens onto the eastern cataract. **Cons:** it can feel a little impersonal; stay clear if colonial nostalgia isn't your thing; volume of people can lead to occasional problems, omissions, and errors. ⓢ *Rooms from: $600* ✉ *Livingstone Way, Livingstone* ☎ *0213/321-122* ⊕ *www.anantara.com/en/royal-livingstone* ⇱ *173 rooms* ⎢⊙⎢ *Free Breakfast.*

★ Sindabezi Island

$$$$ | **RESORT** | This is the most environmentally friendly property on the Zambezi. **Pros:** lovely views of the national park on the Zimbabwean side from parts of the island; if you're lucky, elephants might swim across the Zambezi and graze a few meters from your bed; service is top-notch. **Cons:** there's no pool; it's difficult to get to; it's very open, so if you are a bit nervous in the African bush, this might not suit you. ⓢ *Rooms from: $1,190* ✉ *Livingstone* ✛ *About 19 km (12 miles) upstream from Victoria Falls, on Zambezi River* ☎ *0979/312-766* ⊕ *www.greensafaris.com/sindabezi* ⇱ *5 suites* ⎢⊙⎢ *All-Inclusive.*

★ Toka Leya Camp

$$$$ | **RESORT** | Spread out along the banks of the Zambezi River, the tents are set up on stilts, surrounded by a wooden deck that you can sit on and watch the world and the Zambezi River go by. **Pros:** the camp is close to Livingstone and all of the activities offered in the area; there's a small spa on the banks of the river; almost all your activities are included in the rates. **Cons:** prices will be prohibitive to many; not the most remote of the

Read and Watch

Want some inspiration before your trip? Here are a few suggestions to read and watch.

- *The Garden of Burning Sand* by Corban Addison is a crime thriller centered on an American human rights lawyer working in Lusaka.
- *Bitterness* by Zambian poet Malama Katulwende is a novel that deals with themes relating to life in modern Africa.
- Mark Burke's *Glimmers of Hope: A Memoir of Zambia* tells of a British teacher's years spent volunteering in Zambia.
- *Killing Heat* (1981) is a Swedish film about European farmers in colonial Rhodesia (now Zimbabwe), shot in Zambia.
- *The Hippo*, an episode from season 4 (2012) of the BBC series *Inside Nature's Giants* focused on the hippos of Zambia's Luangwa Valley.
- *When China Met Africa* (2010) is a documentary on Chinese-led development in Zambia.

riverfront camps; the decor makes it feel a bit like a hotel as opposed to a bush camp. [$] *Rooms from: $1,540* ✉ *Livingstone* ✥ *On the Zambezi River, 12 km (7½ miles) upstream from Victoria Falls* ☎ *011/807–1800* 🌐 *www.wilderness-safaris.com* 🛏 *12 rooms* 🍴 *All-Inclusive.*

★ Tongabezi Lodge

$$$$ | **RESORT** | If you're looking for a truly idyllic African experience, this is it. **Pros:** the original open-fronted Zambezi lodge; excellent service and lots of thoughtful touches; management is environmentally focused and community aware. **Cons:** interaction with others is limited—though some might count this as a pro; a bit of a distance from town and most activities; no longer owner-run. [$] *Rooms from: $1,480* ✉ *Livingstone* ✥ *About 19 km (12 miles) upstream from Victoria Falls, on Zambezi River* ☎ *0979/312–766* 🌐 *www.greensafaris.com/tongabezi* 🛏 *11 suites* 🍴 *All-Inclusive.*

Victoria Falls Waterfront

$ | **RESORT** | There's a hive of happy activity and gorgeous sunsets to be found at this well-located and refreshingly unpretentious accommodation. **Pros:** great location right on the river with beautiful sunsets; many of the adventure activities in the area are managed from the Waterfront; very social atmosphere at the bar. **Cons:** food can still be a little inconsistent; a bit outside of town, so transfers are required to the Falls and most activities; can be very noisy as it caters to campers and backpackers. [$] *Rooms from: $225* ✉ *Sichango Rd., just off Mosi-oa-Tunya Rd., Livingstone* ☎ *0213/320–606* 🌐 *www.thevictoriafallswaterfront.com* 🛏 *47 rooms* 🍴 *Free Breakfast.*

Activities

Livingstone can compete with the best as far as indulging the wildest fantasies of adrenaline junkies and outdoor enthusiasts goes. You can reserve activities directly with the operators, let your hotel or lodge handle it, or book through a central booking agent.

BOATING

African Queen

BOATING | Truly the monarch of the river, the *African Queen*—no relation to the movie—is an elegant colonial-style riverboat. Their sunset cruises offer the maximum style and splendor. ✉ *Livingstone* ☎ *0978/770–175*

*⊕ www.livingstonesadventure.com/
african-queen/* ✉ *2-hr sunset cruise with
open bar and snacks from US$75.*

CANOEING

A gentle canoeing trip on the upper
Zambezi is a great opportunity to see
birds and a variety of game. Many of
the lodges upriver have canoeing as an
inclusive activity, but trips are also run
by a number of companies, which are all
reputable.

Bundu Adventures

CANOEING & ROWING | Bundu Adven-
tures offers custom-made canoe and
white-water rafting trips that range from
half-day outings to multi-day excursions.
✉ *Livingstone's Adventure, Sichango Rd.,
Livingstone* ☎ *0213/323–587* ⊕ *www.
bunduadventures.com* ✉ *From US$120
for a half-day cruise.*

FLYING

Batoka Sky

SKYDIVING | Batoka Sky offers weight-shift
Aerotrike twin-axis microlighting (flying
jargon for what resembles a motorized
hang glider) and helicopter flights over
the Falls and through the gorges. There's
a minimum of two passengers for
helicopters. You are issued a flight suit
(padded in winter) and a helmet with a
headset before you board the microlight,
but you may not bring a camera for safety
reasons. Batoka Sky has been operating
since 1992, and has a 100% microlighting safety record. Flights are booked for
early morning and late afternoon and are
dependent on the weather. Transfer and
a day visa, if you are coming from Victoria
Falls, are included. The Helicopter Gorge
picnic includes lunch and drinks for a
minimum of six people. ✉ *Livingstone's
Adventure, Just off Sichango Rd., Livingstone* ⊹ *Near the Chrismar Hotel Livingstone* ☎ *0213/323–589* ⊕ *www.living-
stonesadventure.com* ✉ *From US$185
depending on length of flight and aircraft;
Helicopter gorge picnic $440.*

HORSEBACK RIDING

Chundukwa River Lodge

HORSEBACK RIDING | You can take a placid
horseback ride through the bush along
the banks of the Zambezi from Chunduk-
wa River Lodge's horse ranch. If you are
comfortable enough to keep your cool
while riding through the African hinterland, you may want to book a horseback
bush trail. Half-day trips include lunch and
refreshments. Fully inclusive overnight
or even multi-night horseback camping
safari options are also available. ✉ *Chun-
dukwa River Lodge, 25 km (15 mi) from
Livingstone along Nakatindi Rd., Livingstone* ☎ *0969/641-797* ⊕ *www.chunduk-
wariverlodge.com* ✉ *From US$75.*

RAPPELLING AND SWINGING

Zambezi Eco Adventures

ZIP LINING | For something completely
different, Zambezi Eco Adventures has
taken some specially designed heavy-du-
ty steel cables, combined them with various pulleys and rigs, one dry gorge, and a
100% safety record to entertain both the
fainthearted and the daring. Keep in mind
that you will have to climb out after the
gorge swing and the rappel.

Work up an appetite for more daring
drops by starting on the zip line (or flying
fox). You run off a ramp while attached
to the line, and the sensation is pure
freedom and surprisingly unscary, as you
are not moving up or down. Next rappel
down into the 175-foot gorge, and, after
you climb out, try it again facing forward.
It's called a rap run. You're literally walking down the cliff face. End the day with
the king of adrenaline activities, a whop-
ping 175-foot, 3½-second vertical free-fall
swing into the gorge. ✉ *Batoka Gorge,
Livingstone* ☎ *0950/070–954* ⊕ *www.
zambeziecoadventures.com* ✉ *From $80.*

TOURS

Bushtracks

ADVENTURE TOURS | This operator runs
one-day excursions to Botswana's Chobe
National Park. The trip includes transfers
from Livingstone, a morning boat cruise,

lunch with a drink, and an afternoon game drive. Bushtracks also handles bookings for the Royal Livingstone Express, operates its own river cruises on the Zimbabwean side of the Falls, and is your best bet for a visit to Mukuni Village. Reservations must be prepaid for all of the above. ✉ *Livingstone* ☎ *0213/323–232, 011/469–9300 in South Africa* ⊕ *www.bushtracksafrica.com* ⊠ *Chobe National Park, US$200; Mukuni Village, US$50.*

Livingstone Rhino Walking Safaris

WALKING TOURS | Many park guides are well informed, but the ultimate Mosi-oa-Tunya National Park experience is this three-hour guided walking safari. Not only can you see the endangered white rhino and other plains game, but your professional guide and park scout will impart detailed information on birding, flora, and the modern use of plants by local people. Walks are conducted early in the morning and late in the afternoon and cost US$85, including transfers within Livingstone, park fees, and refreshments. ✉ *Livingstone* ☎ *0213/322–267* ⊕ *www.livingstonerhinosafaris.com* ⊠ *$80.*

Safari Par Excellence

ADVENTURE TOURS | Half- and full-day rafting excursions to Batoka Gorge are available through Safari Par Excellence. A cable car transports rafters out of the gorge, so you only have to climb down—secure shoes, dry clothes, a baseball cap to wear under your helmet, and plenty of sunscreen are essential. River-boarding (hop off the raft onto a body board and surf suitable rapids) excursions, game drives, river cruises and canoeing are also available, as are trip combinations such as a helicopter-and-rafting trip. Combo trips are a good option if your time is limited or you just want to go wild. ✉ *Riverside Dr., off Sichango Rd., Livingstone* ⊹ *Near the Waterfront Lodge* ☎ *0213/320–606* ⊕ *www.safpar.net* ⊠ *Rafting US$140 half-day; river safari $100 half day.*

Shopping

Kubu Crafts

CRAFTS | This stylish home-decor shop features locally made furniture in hardwood and wrought iron. There's also a selection of West African masks and weavings and the work of numerous local artists. Local curios are attractively displayed and screened for quality. Kubu Crafts also provides both fair employment and training opportunities for the community. ✉ *Mosi-O-Tunya Sq., 133 Mosi-Oa-Tunya Rd., Livingstone* ☎ *0213/320–230* ⊕ *www.kubucrafts.com.*

Mukuni Park Market

MARKET | Although the park at the entrance to the Falls has stalls where you can find stone and wood carvings and simple bead and semiprecious-stone jewelry, the real gem of an African bazaar lies in the center of town, at Mukuni Park Market—it's the place to try your hand at bargaining. You'll be quoted top dollar initially, but shop around. Look out for individual and unusual pieces, as it is occasionally possible to find valuable antiques. The market is open daily approximately 7–6. ✉ *Mosi-oa-Tunya Rd. at Libala Dr., Livingstone.*

Zambian Safari Circuit

If you are eager to see more of Zambia than just Livingstone and the Victoria Falls area, Lower Zambezi National Park and Kafue National Park (one of the biggest parks in Africa) are spectacular destinations teeming with big game and first-class luxury lodges. Both are within easy striking distance of Lusaka, while the southern part of Kafue is also just a four-hour drive due north from Livingstone. Most lodges and hotels in and around the town can arrange transfers either by road or by air.

Zambia's oldest and largest national park, Kafue is home to incredible game including lions, elephants, and leopards.

Sights

Kafue National Park

NATIONAL PARK | Kafue is Zambia's oldest and largest national park, covering a massive 2,240,000 hectares (about the size of Wales in the United Kingdom), which also makes it one of the largest parks in Africa and, for that matter, the world. Thanks to its size, variety of ecosystems, and the beautiful Kafue River, this park is absolutely teeming with game, from crowd-pleasers like lions, elephants, and leopards to one of Africa's largest wild dog populations—right through to rare species such as lechwe and yellow-backed duiker and more than 400 types of bird. The park is an easy few hours' drive from Livingstone and Lusaka. Despite all its highlights, it remains largely wild and unexplored, particularly the northern reaches. But this may be its number one draw. There are a handful of first-rate campsites and luxury lodges dotted in and around the edges of the park, almost all of which offer typically Zambian attention to detail in terms of service and providing the real bush experience. ⊠ *Livingstone* ✢ *About 200 km (125 miles) from Livingstone via the T1* ☎ *0213/321–404* ⊕ *www.zambiatourism.com.*

Lower Zambezi National Park

NATIONAL PARK | Lower Zambezi National Park may not be Zambia's biggest or best-known national park, but these are two of the main reasons it's so worth a visit. The whole park retains a unique feeling of untouched African wilderness, and you certainly wouldn't think you were just a few hours from the urban hub of Lusaka. When on game drives or guided bush walks through the park, you can go for miles without seeing another car, but the density of big game is astonishing. The vegetation and landscapes are spectacularly diverse, too, ranging from rugged, forested mountain escarpments to wide-open plains punctuated only by the occasional lonely baobab or palm tree. The park's handful of luxury and secluded camps are all situated along the lush banks of the mighty Zambezi River, which serves as the natural southern border to the park as well as between Zambia and Zimbabwe's Mana Pools on the other side. Lower Zambezi is a particularly special place for canoeing safaris and boat cruises, and is also a favorite with fishing aficionados. The quickest and easiest way to get there is to fly from Livingstone to Lusaka and then take a short chartered flight to Jeki Airstrip within the park. If you leave Livingstone in the late morning, you'll arrive at your accommodation in time for high tea. ⊠ *Lusaka* ☎ *0213/321–404* ⊕ *www.zambiatourism.com.*

 ## Hotels

KaingU Safari Lodge

$$$$ | **RESORT** | **FAMILY** | KaingU Safari Lodge is a small camp comprised of a family house with two bedrooms and six classic en suite safari tents. **Pros:** Africa untouched in all its glory; the owners have a true commitment to environmental and community development; very friendly service. **Cons:** the area has less big game than some other areas of the park; food is a little unspectacular for a top-end lodge; road transfers from Lusaka take 5–6 hours. $ *Rooms from: $900* ⊠ *Livingstone* ⊹ *South Kafue, 400 km (250 miles) north of Victoria Falls* ☎ *097/784–1653* ⊕ *www.kaingu-lodge.com* ⊟ *No credit cards* ⬚ *9 suites* ⫣ *All-Inclusive.*

★ Old Mondoro Camp

$$$$ | **ALL-INCLUSIVE** | The legend of a great white-maned lion that used to call this area its home lives on in the name of this camp, which is Shona for the "king of cats." If you're looking for an African adventure of the original epic variety, then you need to stay at Old Mondoro. **Pros:** great game drives led by top-notch wildlife guides; one of the best places to see leopards; best walking area in the Lower Zambezi. **Cons:** difficult to get to for those wanting to self-drive; not for those who need modern conveniences;

the open rooms have only canvas flaps to ward off the wild at night, and this might be too daring for some. $ *Rooms from: $2,680* ⊠ *Lower Zambezi National Park* ⊹ *Jeki Airstrip is a 30-minute game-drive away from Old Mondoro and can be reached via 2-hr flight from Livingstone and then a 40-minute flight from Lusaka* ☎ *0211/261–588* ⊕ *www.chiawa.com/old-mondoro* ◷ *Closed Nov.–May 1* ⬚ *5 tents* ⫣ *All-Inclusive.*

Sausage Tree Camp

$$$$ | **RESORT** | There is no formal dress code, but this camp offers the perfect backdrop for throwing practicality to the wind and dressing up for dinner. **Pros:** elephants are regular visitors; stunning riverside location; gorgeous food. **Cons:** no fences to keep wildlife at bay, so not for the faint of heart; not open all year-round; the remote location and expensive rates will be prohibitive for some. $ *Rooms from: $2,800* ⊠ *Lower Zambezi National Park, Livingstone* ⊹ *140 km (85 miles) from Lusaka* ☎ *76/586–1927 in South Africa* ⊕ *www.sausagetreecamp.com* ◷ *Closed Nov. 20–Apr.* ⬚ *8 rooms* ⫣ *All-Inclusive* ⌕ *The rate includes all meals, activities, and domestic flights to and from the camp.*

Victoria Falls, Zimbabwe

Victoria Falls started with a little curio shop and slowly expanded until the 1970s, when it became the mecca around which the tourist phenomenon of Victoria Falls pivoted. The political problems following independence have been well documented in the press worldwide and have certainly taken their toll, as has poaching in Zambezi National Park to the northwest. (If you really want to have the African game experience, take a day trip to Chobe National Park, only 70 km/44 miles away in Botswana.)

However, the country has regained some semblance of political stability and the town of Victoria Falls enjoys the happy coincidence of being a curio shopper's paradise inside a national park. This means you can literally buy an elephant carving while watching the real McCoy march past the shop window. The town has an easygoing feel and is extremely compact. Almost all the hotels are within walking distance, and the Falls are only 10 minutes away on foot. The main road that runs through town and goes to the Falls in one direction and to the airport in the other is called Livingstone Way. Park Way is perpendicular. Most of the shops, banks, and booking agents can be found on these two streets, and this part of town is also where most of the hawkers operate.

■ TIP➜ **Give these vendors a clear berth, as their wares are cheap for a reason (the boat cruise is substandard, it's illegal to change money, etc.).**

GETTING HERE AND AROUND
AIR
Tourists have gradually returned to Victoria Falls, and as a result, there is also an increasing number of flights available.

Zimbabwe's largest airport is Robert Gabriel Mugabe International Airport (HRE) in Harare, the capital city, followed by the international airports in Victoria Falls (VFA) and Joshua Mqabuko Nkomo International Airport (BUQ) in Bulawayo.

Fastjet runs a regular route from Johannesburg. Otherwise, Ethiopian Airlines is a good option via Addis Ababa. If you choose to fly in and out of Victoria Falls Airport, most hotels will provide a free shuttle service; book in advance. Hotels can also summon reputable taxis quickly and advise you on the cost. Tipping isn't mandatory, but change is always appreciated.

AIRLINES Fastjet. ☎ *086/7700–6060* ⊕ *www.fastjet.com.* **Ethiopian Airlines.** ☎ *0242/795–215* ⊕ *www.ethiopianairlines.com.*

AIRPORTS Victoria Falls Airport. (*VFA*) ✉ *Livingstone Way, Victoria Falls* ☎ *013/4–4428.* **Robert Gabriel Mugabe International Airport.** (*HRE*) ⊕ *www.harare-airport.com/.* **Joshua Mqabuko Nkomo International Airport.** (*BUQ*) ✛ *25 km (15 miles) outside Bulawayo.*

CAR
Foreign tourists driving in Zimbabwe is not unheard of, but avoid driving at night. Road conditions vary quite a bit and you're better off with a 4x4 if you plan to drive on backstreets and in national parks.

COMMUNICATIONS
The country code for Zimbabwe is 263. When dialing from abroad, drop the initial 0 from local area codes. Ask a hotel or restaurant manager for exact telephone numbers and costs, should you wish to make any telephone calls from within Zimbabwe.

As with Livingstone, most of the major lodges, hotels, and backpackers in and around Victoria Falls have reasonably fast free Wi-Fi. There are also a couple of cheap internet cafes in town. But Wi-Fi and cell service are less consistently available, and sometimes very slow in the case of the former, in more remote lodges and camps.

HEALTH AND SAFETY
The political situation in Zimbabwe is currently relatively calm compared to the upheavals of past decades, but the damage from the lengthy dictatorship and persisting internal strife is still very apparent. Prices have mostly stabilized and basic goods have reappeared on the shelves, but the tourist capital of Victoria Falls has not yet regained its status as a prime international destination. All the activities, shopping, and dining options on offer on the Zimbabwean side can also be enjoyed across the border in Zambia—without any of the uncertainty and potential for sudden political and economic upheavals that could result in cancellations or threats to visitors' safety.

■TIP→ **The Victoria Falls town and tourism industry has managed to build itself up in a remarkably short time. The political situation is still not 100% resolved, but for now, Zimbabwean lodges offer good value and service.**

MARS (Medical Air Rescue Services) is on standby for all emergencies. Dr. Nyoni is a trauma specialist and operates a hospital opposite the Shoestring Lodge. Go to Victoria Falls Pharmacy for prescriptions.

Male homosexuality is illegal in Zimbabwe—female homosexuality isn't mentioned in law—and same-sex relationships receive no recognition. Attitudes are slowly improving, but it's advisable to be extremely circumspect.

It's always a good idea to leave ample space in your luggage for common sense when traveling to Victoria Falls. Wild animals abound throughout this area (even in the center of town) and must be given a lot of physical space and respect.

As for the water, it's always advisable to drink bottled water. Should you develop an upset stomach, be sure to contact a physician, especially if you're running a fever, in order to rule out malaria or a communicable disease. Do remember to mention your visit to a malaria area to your doctor in the event of illness within a year of leaving Africa.

CONTACTS Medical Air Rescue Services. ⊠ *Flat No. 1, Stanley House, 3rd St., opposite Shoestring, Victoria Falls* ☎ *024/277–1221.* **U.S. Embassy.** ⊠ *172 Herbert Chitepo Ave., Box 4010, Harare* ☎ *04/250–593* ⊕ *www.zw.usembassy. gov.*

HOTELS

It's advisable to make both flight and lodge reservations ahead of time. Most of the luxury safari camps and lodges offer all-inclusive packages; hotels generally include breakfast only. All hotels and lodges quote in U.S. dollars; while some will accept payment in other major international currencies, this is not a suggested option due to the unfavorable exchange rates. Having said that, accommodation on this side of the border is generally much more affordable than in Zambia. A 10% service charge is either included or added to the bill (as is the V.A.T.) in both countries, which frees you to include an extra tip only for exceptional service.

Restaurant and hotel reviews have been shortened. For full information, visit Fodors.com.

What It Costs in U.S. Dollars			
$	$$	$$$	$$$$
RESTAURANTS			
under $12	$12–$20	$21–$30	over $30
HOTELS			
under $250	$250–$450	$451–$600	over $600

MONEY

Zimbabwe's official currency is the Zimbabwe dollar, but given its consistent volatility, foreign currency is generally the best and often the only acceptable method of payment. Carry U.S. dollars in small denominations and stick to U.S. dollars for all activity payments to Zimbabwe-based operators (all activities are quoted in U.S. dollars). Credit card facilities aren't always readily available. (You'll also find Western Union banks in Victoria Falls and Livingstone, should you need to do cash transfers.)

PASSPORTS AND VISAS

It's possible to buy point-of-entry visas for Zimbabwe for US$55 for a single entry. If you leave Zimbabwe for more than 24 hours, you'll need to buy another to reenter (unless you bought a double-entry visa for US$70). Visas can be purchased from a Zimbabwean embassy before departure (application for multiple-entry visas can only be lodged here), but it'll almost certainly be more trouble and generally cost more than buying them at the border or point of entry.

RESTAURANTS

In Zimbabwe, excellent game meat such as warthog, crocodile, and various antelope species are a commonly found specialty in the lodges, hotels, and touristy restaurants; at the more local joints in town, hearty chicken and beef stews are more common. The local bream, filleted or whole, is always a good bet, and the staple starch, a stiff porridge similar to polenta—known as *sadza* this side of the border—is worth a try; use your fingers to eat it. Adventurous? Try *macimbi* or *vinkuvala* (sun-dried mopane worms), which are a favored Zimbabwean delicacy. Excellent high teas are a regular feature at hotels and camps, one of the few more favorable legacies of British colonialism.

Meals are taken at regular hours, but during the week restaurants close around 10. Dress is generally pretty casual, like most things in Victoria Falls.

VISITOR INFORMATION

While there isn't an official tourism office in town, there are a number of well-established local operators with centrally-located premises where you can seek advice on activities, accommodation, tours and more. These include Wild Horizons, Shearwater, and Love for Africa.

WAYS TO SAVE

Eat at buffets. If you're a big eater, or like to have a large lunch, you'll find plenty of restaurants offering all-you-can-eat buffets that are generally good value.

Stay in backpackers. Known as hostels in the northern hemisphere, backpackers are a good option if you want cheap accommodations and don't mind sharing a room.

Take the slow route. Non-express buses and trains take a long time to get from point to point, but they're a cheap way to travel and a great way to meet locals.

Find travel buddies. If you can round up other people interested in safaris or other activities you may be able to negotiate a group discount and split the savings.

WHEN TO GO

High Season: May–September is the high and dry season in Zimbabwe, and this is when the parks are at their busiest and the mosquitos are few. It's also the best time for safaris, as wildlife tends to group around water sources much more at this time of year.

Low Season: November–March is the low season in Zimbabwe, as this is when the country gets most of its rains. It's usually pretty quiet at the parks, but if your visit coincides with school vacations in South Africa (mid-December through mid-January), the area around Victoria Falls can be quite crowded.

Value Season: April and October are the shoulder months between Zimbabwe's high and low seasons. April can still have some residual rain showers in the afternoons, but usually nothing that stops people from camping or going on safaris. October doesn't usually get much rainfall, but it's also the hottest month of the year, a deterrent for those sensitive to heat.

FESTIVALS AND EVENTS

April: Zimbabwe's Independence Day is celebrated every year with the Zimbabwean Independence Trophy, a national soccer knockout tournament.

April–May: Music and culture are celebrated through six days of performance and workshops at the Harare International Festival of the Arts.

September–October: African films are screened in eight different locations around Harare during the Zimbabwe International Film Festival. ⊕ www.zimfilmfest.co.zw

December: Animation screenings, workshops, talks, and interdisciplinary collaboration are at the core of the Zimbabwe Festival of African Inspired Animation.

PLAN YOUR TIME
HASSLE FACTOR

High. Getting to Zimbabwe is time-consuming, and usually requires at least two stopovers. If you're coming from the West Coast it can take you more than two full days to reach Harare.

3 DAYS

With three days, you can spend a couple of days exploring Victoria Falls and enjoying some of the wide range of activities and also take a day trip to Chobe National Park in Botswana.

1 WEEK

A week is enough time to thoroughly explore Victoria Falls and its myriad attractions with a day or two left over to get a taste of Harare too.

2 WEEKS

With two weeks in Zimbabwe you'll have time for Victoria Falls and Harare as well as a safari in Hwange National Park and a trip to the 11th-century ruins of Great Zimbabwe.

 Sights

Victoria Falls Bridge

NOTABLE BUILDING | FAMILY | A veritable monument to Cecil Rhodes's dream of completing a Cape-to-Cairo rail line, this graceful structure spans the gorge formed by the Zambezi River. It would have been far easier and less expensive to build the bridge upstream from the Falls, but Rhodes was captivated by the romance of a railway bridge passing over this natural wonder. A net was stretched across the gorge under the construction site, which curiously prompted the construction workers to go on strike for a couple of days. They resumed work only when it was explained that they would not be expected to leap into it at the end

of every workday. Although the workers did not share the current adrenaline-fueled obsession with jumping into the abyss, the net probably had a lot to do with the miraculous fact that only two people were killed during construction. The bridge was completed in only 14 months, and the last two cross-girders were joined on April 1, 1905.

To get onto the bridge, you first have to pass through Zimbabwean immigration and customs controls, so bring your passport. Unless you decide to cross into Zambia, no visa is necessary, though you will need a gate pass.

Depending on crowds, the simple procedure can take from five minutes to a half hour. The border posts are open daily from 6 am to 10 pm, after which the bridge is closed to all traffic. From the bridge you are treated to a fabulous view of the river raging through Batoka Gorge, as well as a section of the Falls on the Zambian side. An added bonus is watching the bungee jumpers disappear over the edge. ⊠ *Livingstone Way, Victoria Falls.*

★ Victoria Falls National Park

NATIONAL PARK | FAMILY | Plan to spend at least two hours soaking in the splendors of this park. Avoid the crowds and the heat by getting there as early as possible. Bring snacks and water, and supervise children extremely well, as the barriers are by no means safe. Babies and toddlers can be pushed in a stroller. If you visit the Falls during the high-water peak, between April and June, you'd do well to carry a raincoat or umbrella (you can rent them at the entrance) and to bring along a waterproof, disposable camera because you *will* be drenched in the spray from the Falls, which creates a permanent downpour. Be prepared for limited photo opportunities due to the mist.

■ TIP→ **Leave expensive cameras, cell phones, and wristwatches in your hotel or lodge safe.**

The constant drizzle has created a small rain forest that extends in a narrow band along the edge of the Falls. A trail running through this dripping green world is overgrown with African ebony, Cape fig, Natal mahogany, wild date palms, ferns, and deep-red flame lilies. A fence has been erected to keep non-fee-paying visitors at bay. Clearly signposted side trails lead to viewpoints overlooking the Falls. The most spectacular is Danger Point, a perilous rock outcropping that overlooks the narrow gorge through which the Zambezi River funnels out of the Boiling Pot, but be careful, as this viewpoint is hazardously wet and precarious. In low-water months (September–November) most of the water goes over the Falls through the Devil's Cataract, a narrow and mesmerizingly powerful section of the Falls visible from Livingstone's statue. Around the full moon, the park stays open late so you can see the lunar rainbow formed by the spray—a hauntingly beautiful sight. Early morning and late afternoon are the best times to see the daylight rainbows most vividly. A booklet explaining the formation and layout of the Falls is available from the Victoria Falls Publicity Association for a small fee. ✉ *Off Livingstone Way, Victoria Falls* ☎ *013/42–294* 💲 *US$30.*

🍴 Restaurants

At the peak of Zimbabwe's political problems, shortages of even the most basic foods, like vegetables, were an everyday occurrence. But in the years since, in large part thanks to the widespread adoption of the US dollar as the primary currency, hotels and restaurants have been able to restore some sanity and reestablish their unique flair for first-rate hospitality while maintaining a healthy dose of local flavor.

The Cassia Restaurant
$$ | AFRICAN | With tables flowing out onto the deep veranda of Ilala Lodge, the Cassia has old-world grandeur with delicious modern cuisine. The lunch menu mixes light Mediterranean-style dishes with popular pub favorites such as burgers and fish-and-chips. **Known for:** stellar service; decent cocktails at the poolside bar; great location. 💲 *Average main: $20* ✉ *Ilala Lodge, 411 Livingstone Way, Victoria Falls* ☎ *0213/284–4737* 🌐 *www.ilalalodge.com* ☞ *Reservations aren't necessary, but advisable for dinner.*

Lookout Cafe
$$ | AFRICAN | Perched on the edge of Batoka Gorge, the popular open-air Lookout Cafe offers spectacular sweeping views of the rapids below and the iconic Victoria Falls Bridge. Open for breakfast, lunch and monthly full moon dinners, it serves up an eclectic and innovative menu with a strong emphasis on fresh local ingredients. **Known for:** incredible views; a decent cocktail menu to be enjoyed on the sundowner deck; unusual game meat options. 💲 *Average main: $15* ✉ *Batoka Gorge, Victoria Falls* ☎ *078/274–5112* 🌐 *www.thelookoutcafe.com.*

MaKuwa Kuwa
$$ | AFRICAN | Perched above a game-rich waterhole at the Victoria Falls Safari Lodge, a spectacular view awaits diners at this memorable dining spot. On offer at breakfast is a combination of both cold and hot dishes; lunch ranges from great salads to huge gourmet burgers; dinnertime guests are treated to local a cappella performers. **Known for:** expansive views; decent cocktails; unique dining/game-viewing combo. 💲 *Average main: $20* ✉ *Victoria Falls Safari Lodge, 471 Squire Cummings Rd., Victoria Falls* ☎ *013/432–1120* 🌐 *www.victoria-falls-safari-lodge.com* 🧥 *Jacket required.*

Mama Africa Eating House
$$ | AFRICAN | This is a good local food experience as the menu offers typical Zimbabwean dishes along with other African food and the atmosphere is colorful and celebratory. Tuesday and Friday nights are "Africa Nights" with a buffet dinner and live music from the local jazz band; it's best to make a reservation for

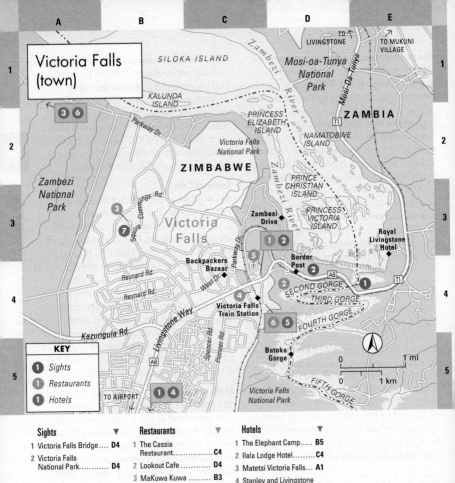

Victoria Falls (town)

SILOKA ISLAND

KALUNDA ISLAND

Zambezi River

TO LIVINGSTONE

TO MUKUNI VILLAGE

Mosi-oa-Tunya National Park

Z A M B I A

Mosi-Oa-Tunya

Victoria Falls National Park

PRINCESS ELIZABETH ISLAND

NAMATOBWE ISLAND

Z I M B A B W E

Zambezi National Park

Squire Cummings Rd.

PRINCE CHRISTIAN ISLAND

PRINCESS VICTORIA ISLAND

Royal Livingstone Hotel

Victoria Falls

Zambesi Drive

Border Post

Backpackers Bazaar

Reynard Rd.

Reynard Rd.

West Dr.

SECOND GORGE

THIRD GORGE

Victoria Falls Train Station

FOURTH GORGE

Kazungula Rd.

Livingstone Way

Spence Rd.

Pioneer Rd.

Batoka Gorge

FIFTH GORGE

Victoria Falls National Park

TO AIRPORT

0   1 mi

0   1 km

KEY

- 1 Sights
- 1 Restaurants
- 1 Hotels

Sights ▼

1 Victoria Falls Bridge.... **D4**
2 Victoria Falls
   National Park............ **D4**

Restaurants ▼

1 The Cassia
   Restaurant.............. **C4**
2 Lookout Cafe **D4**
3 MaKuwa Kuwa **B3**
4 Mama Africa
   Eating House **C4**
5 The River
   Brewing Company....... **C4**
6 Stanley's Terrace **C4**

Hotels ▼

1 The Elephant Camp..... **B5**
2 Ilala Lodge Hotel......... **C4**
3 Matetsi Victoria Falls... **A1**
4 Stanley and Livingstone
   at Victoria Falls.......... **B5**
5 Victoria Falls Hotel....... **C4**
6 Victoria Falls
   River Lodge.............. **A1**
7 Victoria Falls
   Safari Lodge............. **B3**

Read and Watch

Before you embark on your travels to Zimbabwe, here are a few suggestions to read and watch.

• *We Need New Names* by NoViolet Bulawayo is a semiautobiographical novel about growing up first in Zimbabwe and then in the U.S.

• *African Laughter: Four Visits to Zimbabwe* by Nobel Prize-winning author Doris Lessing is an account of four trips she made to her Zimbabwean homeland after many years abroad.

• *When a Crocodile Eats the Sun: A Memoir of Africa* by Peter Godwin is a memoir of a white journalist's 1996 return to Zimbabwe under Mugabe.

• *Neria* (1991) is a Zimbabwean drama about a widow in a rural part of the country.

• The Oscar-winning short documentary *Music by Prudence* is about Zimbabwean singer Prudence Mabhena, who was born disabled.

• *Rhodes of Africa* (1936) is a biographical film about Cecil Rhodes, the controversial imperialist who gave Zimbabwe its former name (Rhodesia).

---

these nights. **Known for:** unpretentious atmosphere; traditional dishes including game meats, mopane worms, and peanuts (plan accordingly if you have allergies); local flavor. $ *Average main: $15* ⊠ *Landela Complex, Matcalfe Rd., Victoria Falls* ☎ *083/284–1725* ⊕ *www. facebook.com/MamaAfricaEatingHouse/.*

The River Brewing Company

$ | **AFRICAN** | Since its inception in 2018, this artisanal brewery, the first of its kind in town, has become a veritable Victoria Falls institution. The brewery's laid-back bar-restaurant is characterized by vaulted ceilings, long wooden tables, exposed brick walls, and a range of craft beers brewed from pure Zambezi water and the finest German hops, as well as a hearty pub-style food menu. **Known for:** a good spot to mingle with the locals; Zimbabwe's best craft beers; very reasonably-priced food. $ *Average main: $10* ⊠ *270 Adam Stander Drive, Victoria Falls* ✛ *Near Elephant's Walk shopping centre* ☎ *077/216–3512* ⊕ *www.riverbrewco. com* ⋔ *Casual.*

★ **Stanley's Terrace**

$$$ | **BRITISH** | A trip to Victoria Falls isn't complete without high tea (3 pm–6 pm) on the Victoria Falls Hotel's terrace—Don't have a big lunch beforehand. A multilayered cake stand filled with an array of delicious treats, including cakes, tarts, and sandwiches, is served with a pot of tea or coffee. The hotel is very grand, and although some of the furnishings are a little tired, the view out over the gorge and onto the bridge and falls is unforgettable. **Known for:** colonial decadence; the occasional warthog running across the lawn; unforgettable vistas. $ *Average main: $30* ⊠ *The Victoria Falls Hotel, 2 Mallet Dr., Victoria Falls* ☎ *083/284–4751* ⊕ *www. victoriafallshotel.com.*

 Hotels

Booking an all-inclusive package tour in advance is a good bet in this area to try to minimize the need for carrying bundles of cash or falling prey to unfavorable in-country exchange rates. Hotels and lodges will always quote in US dollars. Electricity and voltage are the same in Zimbabwe and South Africa.

★ The Elephant Camp

$$$$ | RESORT | From the deck of your luxurious tented suite within Victoria Falls National Park, you gaze out across the bush and down to the Batoka Gorge and the "smoke" rising up from the Falls, just 10 km (6 miles) away. **Pros:** every suite has a plunge pool that's most welcoming in the summer months; peaceful location; spectacular views. **Cons:** the kind of elephant encounters on offer here remain controversial; expensive for this side of the Falls; even though it's in the middle of a national game park, you'll be disappointed if you're there to see a variety of game. [$] *Rooms from: $1276* ✉ *Victoria Falls* ✥ *10 km (6 miles) outside of Victoria Falls, on Livingstone Way (road to the airport)* ☎ *213/284-4571* 🌐 *www.theelephantcamp.com* 🛏 *12 suites* 🍴 *All-Inclusive.*

Ilala Lodge Hotel

$$$ | HOTEL | FAMILY | The lodge's elegant interior design is tempered with thatch roofs, giving it a graceful African look. **Pros:** great central location; family-friendly; only 10 minutes from the Falls by foot. **Cons:** the noise from passing helicopters can be disturbing; the size of the place may deter those seeking a more exclusive experience; the location in town can ruin expectations if you are keen on the peace of the African bush. [$] *Rooms from: $470* ✉ *411 Livingstone Way, Victoria Falls* ☎ *083/284–4737* 🌐 *www.ilalalodge.com* 🛏 *73 rooms* 🍴 *Free Breakfast.*

★ Matetsi Victoria Falls

$$$$ | ALL-INCLUSIVE | FAMILY | About 40 km (25 miles) upstream from Victoria Falls lies Matetsi Victoria Falls, which is at the center of Matetsi Game Reserve, one of the largest private game reserves in Zimbabwe. **Pros:** superb personal butler service; 13 km (8 miles) of exclusive Zambezi waterfront that's bordered on both sides by unfenced national parks; interpretative wildlife experience with extensive information on fauna, flora, and history available for the telling by all the guides. **Cons:** most of the adrenaline activities have to be sought elsewhere; the lodge is child-friendly, which might put off those looking to escape their own kids; About 40 minutes from town and the Falls. [$] *Rooms from: $1700* ✉ *Victoria Falls* ✥ *On southern banks of Zambezi River, 40 km (25 miles) upstream from Victoria Falls* ☎ *0867/004–779* 🌐 *www.matetsivictoriafalls.com* 🛏 *18 suites* 🍴 *All-Inclusive.*

What to Eat 🍴

Mutakura: a mash of corn, peanuts, and different legumes

Sadza: a thick porridge made with mealie-meal, a coarse variety of cornmeal

Mukaka wakakora: curdled milk, also known as lacto

Mazhanje: a small, sweet fruit also known as a sugar plum

Boerewors: a spiced sausage of South African origin that's popular in Zimbabwe

Biltong: cured meat, similar to jerky

★ Stanley and Livingstone at Victoria Falls

$$$ | B&B/INN | It's almost surreal to step from the surrounding bushveld into the meticulously composed rooms of this small hotel, which is set on a 6,000-acre private game reserve. **Pros:** rooms have a/c; 10 minutes outside town; unbelievably over-the-top and decadently indulgent decor. **Cons:** you might find yourself wanting to use words like "mahvelous" a lot!; service can be impersonal at times; the design of this lodge owes very little to Africa. [$] *Rooms from: $600* ✉ *Victoria Falls* ✥ *Off Ursula Rd., 13 km (8 miles) south of Victoria Falls town* ☎ *8677/000–457* 🌐 *www.more.co.za/contact-us/* 🛏 *16 suites* 🍴 *Free Breakfast.*

Suspended over the Zambezi River, Knife Edge Bridge offers incredible views of the eastern cataract of Victoria Falls and the main gorge. Be prepared to get soaking wet and spot a rainbow.

Victoria Falls Hotel

$$$ | **HOTEL** | Hotels come and go, but this landmark built in 1904 has retained its former glory as a distant, stylish outpost in empire days, while pandering to today's modern tastes, needs, and wants. **Pros:** one of the very best views of the Falls—it does not come closer than this!; world-famous high teas; easy access to town and all its amenities. **Cons:** it's big and busy, so can feel impersonal; service is sometimes patchy; hotel is slightly run-down in parts. [$] *Rooms from: $520* ✉ *2 Mallet Dr., Victoria Falls* ☎ *083/284–4751* 🌐 *www.victoriafallshotel.com* 🛏 *161 rooms* 🍴 *Free Breakfast.*

Victoria Falls River Lodge

$$$$ | **RESORT** | This exclusive tented lodge is a relative newcomer to the area, having opened its doors in late 2012, but it has established itself as one of the most reputed luxury accommodations on this side of the river. **Pros:** exceptional cuisine; every suite has a private plunge pool; spectacular location. **Cons:** service is occasionally spotty; bugs galore in the wetter months; a bit of a schlep from town and many of the activities. [$] *Rooms from: $1514* ✉ *Zambezi National Park, Victoria Falls* ✣ *14 km (8.7 miles) from Vic Falls* ☎ *87/0210–737 in South Africa* 🌐 *www.victoriafallsriverlodge.com* 🛏 *19 suites* 🍴 *All-Inclusive.*

★ **Victoria Falls Safari Lodge**

$$$ | **HOTEL** | **FAMILY** | The lodge's location is atop a natural plateau that perfectly frames the African sunset against a private waterhole frequented by various game throughout the entire year. **Pros:** fabulous architecture; beautiful location; great African sunsets are guaranteed. **Cons:** service can be a tad slow; a little bit of a distance from the town's amenities; can get quite busy. [$] *Rooms from: $490* ✉ *471 Squire Cummings Rd., Victoria Falls* ☎ *083/284–3202* 🌐 *www.victoria-falls-safari-lodge.com* 🛏 *72 rooms* 🍴 *Free Breakfast.*

Activities

The town of Victoria Falls was the epicenter of extreme adventures for many years. But at the peak of Zimbabwe's civil unrest, many of the adventure operators either closed down or moved to the Zambian side. Livingstone took over as the gateway to the Victoria Falls, the Zambezi River, and all the activities associated with them. Over the last few years, however, the Zimbabwean side has made a remarkable comeback, with companies such as Adventure Zone, Wild Horizons, and the original Shearwater offering all manner of thrills.

ADVENTURE TOURS

Adventure Zone

ADVENTURE TOURS | This is a one-stop booking agent for bungee jumping, upper Zambezi River canoeing, white-water rafting, Victoria Falls Bridge tours, transfers, and many other activities Victoria Falls has to offer. ✉ *Shop No. 4, Phumula Centre, Victoria Falls* ☎ *0712/205–306* ⊕ *www.adventurezonevicfalls.com.*

Backpackers Bazaar

ADVENTURE TOURS | Backpackers Bazaar offers rafting, riverboarding, kayaking, canoeing, wine drift (you don't do any work except empty the cooler box on the canoe!), flight of the angels (a helicopter or microlight ride over Victoria Falls), sunset cruises, bungee jumping, horseback safaris, game drives on the Zimbabwe side of the Falls, and day trips to Chobe. If your time is limited or you just want to go wild, request prices for activity combinations. ✉ *Shop 5, Old Bata Bldg., Vic Falls Centre Pkwy., Victoria Falls* ☎ *0772/225–488* ⊕ *www.zimtravelagent.com.*

Shearwater

ADVENTURE TOURS | One of the oldest operating companies in Victoria Falls (thrill-seeking since 1982) and unique in that it owns and operates many of the activities available in Victoria Falls, including the bridge bungee jump. Shearwater can also put you in a helicopter or raft, or on an elephant or boat cruise. ✉ *Park Way Ave. at Fox Rd., Victoria Falls* ☎ *083/284–4471* ⊕ *www.shearwatervictoriafalls.com.*

Wild Horizons

ADVENTURE TOURS | Need to get around? Wild Horizons runs transfers in and around Victoria Falls, Livingstone, and Chobe, including airport pickups and drop-offs as well as multiday tours and cross-border transfers between Zambia, Zimbabwe, and Botswana. They also operate a range of adrenaline activities in and around the Falls, as well as running the Lookout Cafe and Elephant Camp. ✉ *310 Park Way Ave., Victoria Falls* ☎ *083/284–2279* ⊕ *www.wildhorizons.co.za.*

Index

Photo Credits

Front Cover: Steady Images / Alamy Stock Photo **[Description:** Lions under stormy sky with rainbow, Masai Mara Kenya]. **Back cover, from left to right:** Volodymyr Burdiak/ Shutterstock. Delbars /iStockphoto. Anna_Om/iStockphoto. **Spine:** Etienne Outram/ iStockphoto. **Interior, from left to right:** Paul Hampton/Shutterstock (1). Villiers Steyn/ Shutterstock (2-3). Ericsch/Dreamstime (5). **Chapter 1: Experience an African Safari:** Calinat/Dreamstime (6-7). Feiflyfly/Shutterstock (8-9). Onyx9/Shutterstock (9). Victor717 /Dreamstime (9). Ingus Kruklitis/Shutterstock (10). Rich T Photo/Shutterstock (10). Ivansabo/ Dreamstime (10). Jonmilnes/Dreamstime (10). Machaba Safaris (11). South African Tourism (11). Tonyzhao120/Shutterstock (12). Simon Dannhauer/Shutterstock (12). Sergey Novikov/ Shutterstock (12). South African Tourism (12). Mauriehill/Dreamstime (13). South African Tourism (13). Bbingzhu/Dreamstime (14). More Family Collection (14). Schusterbauer.com/ Shutterstock (14). Nick Fox/Shutterstock (15). Phillip Allaway/Shutterstock (16). Owen Ruck/Shutterstock (16). Nantonov/ iStockphoto (16). Mya2019/Shutterstock (16). Gerhardus Kotze/Shutterstock (17). AndreyGudkov/iStockphoto (17). EcoPrint/Shutterstock (21). Singita Lebombo Lodge/African Elephant (22-23). Martin Harvey/World Wildlife Fund WWF (24-25). Mzedig/Dreamstime (26-27). Ecophoto/ Dreamstime (28-29). Ondrej Prosicky/Shutterstock (30). Fiona Miller/istockphoto (30). Chris Burt/Shutterstock (31). Creative Nature (31). Ariadne Van Zandbergen/Alamy (31). Possent Macrography (31). Gerrit_de_Vries/Shutterstock (31). Grobler du Preez/ iStockphoto (32). Yuliia Lakeienko/iStockphoto (32). USO/iStockphoto (32). Jayaprasanna T.L/Shutterstock (32). Volodymyr Burdiak/Shutterstock (32). Vaclav Sebek/ Shutterstock (33). Lajos Endredi/ iStockphoto (33). PaulaFrench/iStockphoto (33). Dennis Stogsdill/iStockphoto (33). USO/iStockphoto (33). Gudvok Andrey/Shutterstock (34). Davehavelcz/Dreamstime (34). Photography74/Dreamstime (34). South African Tourism (34). Katobrood/ Dreamstime (34). Chedko/Shutterstock (35). Tswalu Kalahari Reserve (35). Delbars/Shutterstock (35). Foto Mous/Shutterstock (35). PhotocechCZ/Shutterstock (35). Utopianepa/Dreamstime (35). Ecophoto/Dreamstime (36). Justin Bartels/iStockphoto (36). Sekarb/Dreamstime (36). Ondrej_Novotny_92/Shutterstock (36). Steve Adams/iStockphoto (37). Zoomwiz/Dreamstime (37). Michael Potter11/Shutterstock (37). Victor Soares/Shutterstock (37). Madele/Shutterstock (37). DarthArt/iStockphoto (38). Patrice Correia/Dreamstime (38). Anka Agency International / Alamy Stock Photo (38). Ecophoto/Dreamstime (38). Katae.Olaree/Shutterstock (38). HordynskiPhotography/Shutterstock (39). Perambulator/ Dreamstime (39). Photography74/ Dreamstime (39). Arlette Lopez/Shutterstock (39). Radek Borovka/Shutterstock (39). **Chapter 3: Kenya:** RealityImages/Shutterstock (85). HordynskiPhotography/Shutterstock (92). Marta Drozdziel/Shutterstock (95). Jeff Stamer/ Shutterstock (98). Courtesy of Angama Mara (101). The Swain Family, Fodors.com member (102). Heinz Peter Schwerin (107). Liz1940, Fodors.com member (109). JohnHickeyFry/Flickr (111). Kyslynskahal/Shutterstock (113). Loisaba (116). Natalie Merlini Gaul, Fodors.com member (121). Terry Wall / Alamy (128). Huang Jenhung/Shutterstock (131). Bob Pool/Shutterstock (134). Malajscy/Dreamstime (143). Erichon/ Shutterstock (148). Jen Watson/Shutterstock (151). **Chapter 4: Tanzania:** Blickwinkel / Alamy (123). Steve Bloom Images / Alamy (124-125). Blaircostelloe/ Dreamstime (127). Juergen_Wallstabe/ Shutterstock (155). Victor Lapaev/Shutterstock (163). Travel Stock/Shutterstock (171). Serengeti National Park (174). HaJo Schatz/Flickr (177). Hyserb/Shutterstock (184). St.Perrier (187). Andrew Marinkovich (194). Nicki Geiger, Fodors. com member (200). Alfredlind, Fodors.com member (208). Brytta/iStockphoto (217). Sun_Shine/Shutterstock (219). **Chapter 5: South Africa:** Bennymarty/iStockphoto (231). Mdluli Safari Lodge (240) Lawrence Lew, OP/Flickr (247). Linda R. Hansen, Fodors.com member (250). EcoPrint/Shutterstock (254). Adkinsek, Fodors.com member (257). BernardDUPONT/Flickr (263). Wlbox, Fodors.com member (271). Daniel Harwardt/Shutterstock (275). Pedro Ferreira do Amaral (277). Great Stock/Shutterstock (282). Johannes M Vos / Alamy Stock Photo (299). Roger de la Harpe/Shutterstock (304). Flatscreen/Dreamstime (307). Andreawillmore/Dreamstime (310-311). **Chapter 6: Rwanda:** Kjersti Joergensen/Shutterstock (315). Tetyana Dotsenko/Shutterstock (321). Sbedaux / Shutterstock.com (326-327). **Chapter 7: Uganda:** Dmitrii Pichugin/Dreamstime (339). VentureUgandaTravel_Photo01 (346). GUDKOV ANDREY/Shutterstock (351). Ryan M Bolton/Shutterstock (357). Betti Matteo/Shutterstock (361). Lennjo/Shutterstock (365). Piu_Piu/Shutterstock (366). Anil Varma/Shutterstock (369). Stock_und_hut/Shutterstock (375). **Chapter 8: Botswana:** Vadim Petrakov/Shutterstock (377). Des Curley / Alamy (386). Kim Freedman, Fodors.com member (392). Wilderness Safaris (398). Jen Watson/Shutterstock (401). GlenRidgeDoug, Fodors.com member (403). Ron Giling / Alamy Stock Photo (405). Meredith Lamb/Shutterstock (405). Meredith Lamb/Shutterstock (406). Bill Bachmann/Alamy (406). Tom Grundy/Stockfresh (406). YAY Media AS / Alamy Stock Photo (407). J Marshall - Tribaleye Images/Alamy (407). Ulrich Doering/Alamy (407). Kobuspeche/ Dreamstime (407). Neil Moultrie/South African Tourism (408). DAleffi, Fodors.com member (412). Evenfh/iStockphoto (435). Images of African Photobank/ Alamy (436-437). Namibia Tourism Board/African Desert (436). Dave Humphreys/Namibia Tourism Board (436). Namibia Tourism Board/ Desert Trees (436). 2630ben Mcrae/iStockphoto (438). Dean Brian (438). Charles Sturge/Alamy (439). Richard Wareham Fotografie/Swakopmund Nambia (439). **Chapter 9: Namibia:** Krilt/Dreamstime (417). Yury Birukov/Shutterstock (425). Efimova Anna/Shutterstock (429). Demerzel21/Dreamstime (431). HeribertBechen (440). BlueOrange Studio/Shutterstock (445). jbdodane (447). Oleg Znamenskiy/ Shutterstock (451). Smelov/Shutterstock (454). Fotografie-Kuhlmann/Shutterstock (466). Ado van de Filmchens/Shutterstock (468). **Chapter 10: Victoria Falls:** Anton_Ivanov/ Shutterstock (479). Cordelia Bua/Shutterstock (486). Pam Record, Fodors.com member (489). StanislavBeloglazov/ Shutterstock (492). Patrick Ward/Popperfoto/Victoria Falls Zimbabwe (493). Ericsch/Dreamstime (494-495). Peter Hessels (498). Paulo Pina/ Dreamstime (503). Sean Heatley/Shutterstock (513). **About Our Writers:** All photos are courtesy of the writers except for the following: Lizzie Williams Courtesy of Shane P White. Linda Markovina Courtesy of Linda Markovina. Iga Motylska Courtesy of Nicola Lavin.

*Every effort has been made to trace the copyright holders, and we apologize in advance for any accidental errors. We would be happy to apply the corrections in the following edition of this publication.

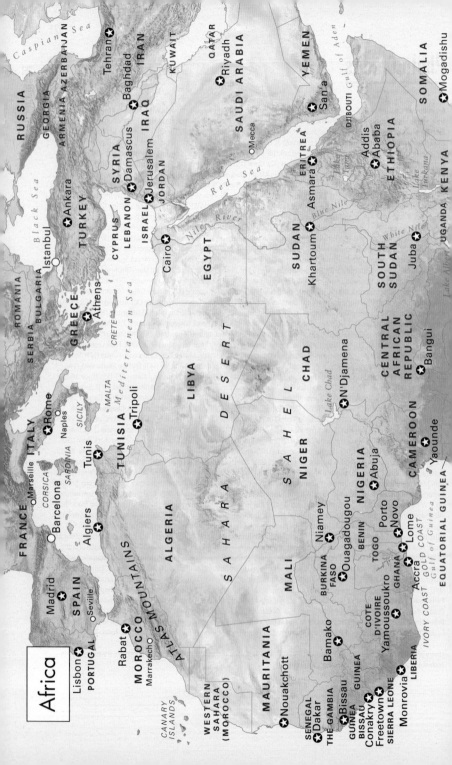

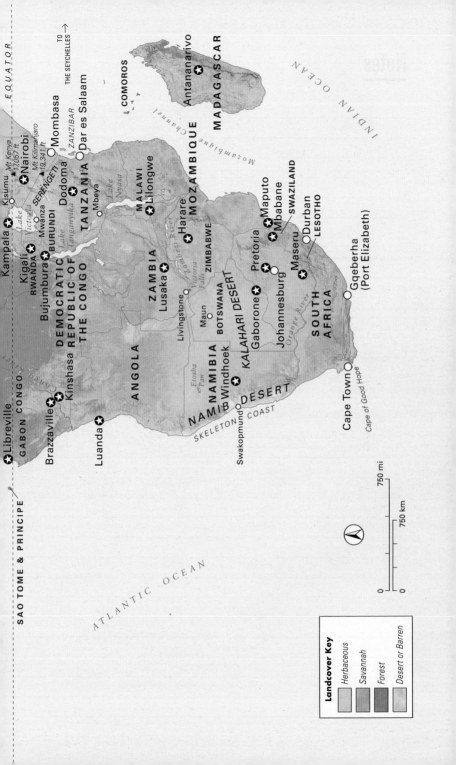

Notes

Notes

Fodor's COMPLETE GUIDE TO AFRICAN SAFARIS

Publisher: Stephen Horowitz, *General Manager*

Editorial: Douglas Stallings, *Editorial Director;* Jill Fergus, Amanda Sadlowski, *Senior Editors;* Kayla Becker, Brian Eschrich, Alexis Kelly, *Editors;* Angelique Kennedy-Chavannes, *Assistant Editor*

Design: Tina Malaney, *Director of Design and Production;* Jessica Gonzalez, *Senior Designer;* Erin Caceres, *Graphic Design Associate*

Production: Jennifer DePrima, *Editorial Production Manager;* Elyse Rozelle, *Senior Production Editor;* Monica White, *Production Editor*

Maps: Rebecca Baer, *Senior Map Editor;* Mark Stroud (Moon Street Cartography), *Cartographer*

Photography: Viviane Teles, *Senior Photo Editor;* Namrata Aggarwal, Neha Gupta, Payal Gupta, Ashok Kumar, *Photo Editors;* Eddie Aldrete, *Photo Production Intern;* Kadeem McPherson, *Photo Production Associate Intern*

Business and Operations: Chuck Hoover, *Chief Marketing Officer;* Robert Ames, *Group General Manager*

Public Relations and Marketing: Joe Ewaskiw, *Senior Director of Communications and Public Relations*

Fodors.com: Jeremy Tarr, *Editorial Director;* Rachael Levitt, *Managing Editor*

Technology: Jon Atkinson, *Director of Technology;* Rudresh Teotia, *Associate Director Of Technology;* Alison Lieu, *Project Manager*

Writers: Charlotte Beauvoisin, Christopher Clark, James Gifford, Linda Markovina, Iga Motylska, Kate Turkington, Wendy Watta, Lizzie Williams

Editor: Alexis Kelly

Production Editor: Jennifer DePrima

6th Edition

ISBN 978-1-64097-507-1

ISSN 1941-0336

All details in this book are based on information supplied to us at press time. Always confirm information when it matters, especially if you're making a detour to visit a specific place. Fodor's expressly disclaims any liability, loss, or risk, personal or otherwise, that is incurred as a consequence of the use of any of the contents of this book.

SPECIAL SALES

This book is available at special discounts for bulk purchases for sales promotions or premiums. For more information, e-mail SpecialMarkets@fodors.com.

PRINTED IN CHINA

10 9 8 7 6 5 4 3 2 1

About Our Writers

Charlotte Beauvoisin first touched down in Uganda as a volunteer with the Uganda Conservation Foundation. Her award-winning blog Diary of a Muzungu chronicles almost 15 years of travels across East Africa. She contributes to the *Ng'aali Uganda Airlines Magazine*, *Horizon Guides* and *Wanderlust* from her wooden house at Sunbird Hill on the edge of Kibale National Park, a forest famous for chimps, elephants and the endangered African Grey Parrot. You can follow her adventures at her website⊕ www.diaryofamuzungu.com, on Facebook @diaryofamuzungu, or on Instagram @diary_of_a_muzungu. She updated the Rwanda and Uganda chapters for this guide.

Christopher Clark is an itinerant freelance multimedia journalist, documentary filmmaker, and author mostly based between South Africa and France. His varied work from across 16 different African countries has been commissioned by leading outlets including *The Atlantic, CNN, the Guardian, Harper's*, and the *Washington Post*. With more than a decade's intimate experience of traveling in Africa, he's also worked on a number of Fodor's guidebooks and updated the Victoria Falls chapter of this guide.

James Gifford is a multiple award-winning photographer, writer, and videographer based in Botswana, whose work has been published in numerousmagazines and books. When not guiding photographic safaris or creating marketing content for safari companies, he can most often be found in the bush, creating images that can influence the way we think about the world. You can follow his adventures at his website⊕ www.jamesgifford.co.uk; Instagram: @jamesgiff; and Facebook @ James Gifford Photography. He updated the Botswana chapter.

Linda Markovina is a freelance photography and travel journalist with a home base in South Africa. She and her husband have lived and traveled extensively through East and West Africa for the past 13 years, including driving up both coastlines. She has written for various local and international publications garnering awards in the process as one of the directors of the expedition team of Moving Sushi, a nonprofit company that unlocks scientific data on ocean systems in Africa. Her focus is on conservation, travel, the natural world around us and how we as people interact with it... as long as it has nothing to do with snakes. Snakes give her the willies. You can follow her @ moving_sushi on Twitter. She updated the Tanzania chapter of this guide.

Johannesburg-based journalist and photographer **Iga Motylska** has collected passport stamps from over 40 countries in search of World Heritage Sites, culinary delights, and cultural experiences. Her adventures have seen her travel India by rail, hunt (and eat) scorpions in Laos, trace dinosaur tracks in Bolivia, scuba dive with turtles in Reunion, and write about it all for over 50 publications. At the end of the day, it's always good to return home to Mzansi. You can follow her adventures at her website ⊕ www.eagerjourneys. com, on Instagram @igamotylska, and on TikTok @eagerjourneys. She updated the Namibia chapter.

About Our Writers

Kate Turkington is one of South Africa's best-known broadcasters and travel writers. Like Shakespeare's Puck, she has girdled the world but her heart remains in Africa. She's been there, done that in African countries from Ghana to Lesotho, from Uganda to Morocco, from Burkino Faso to Ethiopia. But South Africa is home where she shares her travels with her four children, nine grandchildren, and assorted rescue dogs. Visit her website ⊕ www.kateturkington.com to follow along. She updated the South Africa chapter for this edition.

Wendy Watta, a freelance travel writer based in Nairobi, Kenya, covers everything from adventure and hotels to food and conservation, primarily across Africa. Whether cooling off in a natural pool in the middle of a salt desert in Ethiopia, rhino tracking on foot through a muddy plain in Zambia or taking blurry selfies at a vineyard in Cape Town, she's always ready to pack for the next trip, to be shared on magazines or social media. You can check out her work on Instagram @wattaonthego, Youtube @c/wendywatta, and on Twitter @WendyWatta22. She updated the book's Kenya chapter.

Originally from London, **Lizzie Williams** has been exploring Africa for two decades—first as a tour leader and now as a prolific guidebook author and travel writer. She's visited 20 African countries and more than 100 parks and reserves, and as well as being a safari specialist, is an expert at negotiating African border crossings. When not on the road, Lizzie lives in beautiful Cape Town. You can learn more about her at her website ⊕ www.write-travel.com. For this guide, she updated the Experience and Planning chapters.